INTELLECTUAL PROPERTY OVERLAPS

Intellectual property rights, conventionally seen as quite distinct, are increasingly overlapping with one another. There are several reasons for this: the expansion of IPRs beyond their traditional borders, the creation of new IPRs especially at EU level, the exploitation of gaps in the law by shrewd lawyers, and the use of unfair competition as an alternative when IPRs are either not available at all or expired. The convergence of several IPRs on the same subject-matter poses problems. As they are normally envisaged as water-tight categories, there are very few rules which cater for the sort of regime clash that any overlap of IPRs necessarily entails. This book's aim is to find appropriate rules to regulate overlaps and thereby avoid regime conflicts and undue unstructured expansion of IPRs. The book studies the practical consequences of each overlap at the international, European and national levels (where the laws of France, the UK and Germany are reviewed). It then analyses the reasons for the prohibition or authorisation of overlaps. This analysis enables the determination of criteria and principles that can be used to (re) map the overlaps to achieve appropriateness and legitimacy.

Intellectual Property Overlaps

A European Perspective

Estelle Derclaye

and

Matthias Leistner

·HART·
PUBLISHING

OXFORD AND PORTLAND, OREGON

2011

Published in the United Kingdom by Hart Publishing Ltd
16C Worcester Place, Oxford, OX1 2JW
Telephone: +44 (0)1865 517530
Fax: +44 (0)1865 510710
E-mail: mail@hartpub.co.uk
Website: http://www.hartpub.co.uk

Published in North America (US and Canada) by
Hart Publishing
c/o International Specialized Book Services
920 NE 58th Avenue, Suite 300
Portland, OR 97213-3786
USA
Tel: +1 503 287 3093 or toll-free: (1) 800 944 6190
Fax: +1 503 280 8832
E-mail: orders@isbs.com
Website: http://www.isbs.com

British Library Cataloguing in Publication Data
Data Available

ISBN: 978-1-84113-950-0

Typeset by Hope Services, Abingdon
Printed and bound in Great Britain by
Lightning Source UK Ltd

Preface

The area of intellectual property overlaps has in recent years been discussed by a growing number of contributors, but as we came to realise when thinking about writing a book on this topic, remarkably, there is no comprehensive study on the issue, particularly so from a comparative angle. This came as even more of a surprise to us given that the topic comprises very interesting theoretical questions which also have great practical relevance. We have therefore attempted to conceive this book for an audience of both academics and practitioners. To that end, it includes concise descriptions of the positive law but also in-depth normative analyses and proposals to solve the twin problems caused by the cumulation of intellectual property rights in the same subject matter or product, namely regime clashes and overprotection.

As is the case with most books, we have benefitted from kind and precious help along the way. We would like to thank the publishers, especially Richard Hart and Rachel Turner for their valuable recommendations; two anonymous referees for their insightful comments on our proposal; Simon Baker, Phillip Elam, Dr Marcella Favale, Manuel Kleinemenke, Dr Felix Stang and Pierre-Yves Thoumsin for research assistance; Brendan Barnes for reviewing the English language in parts of the book; Professor Lisa Ramsey for her comments on the international chapter; and finally each other.

We have attempted to set out the law as it stands at 31 May 2010, but where possible we have taken into account important developments up to proof stage.

ESTELLE DERCLAYE AND MATTHIAS LEISTNER
Nottingham and Bonn, September 2010

Abbreviations

AC	Law Reports Appeal Cases
All ER	All England Law Reports
Ann Ind Prop	*Annales de la Propriété Industrielle, Littéraire et Artistique*
CA	Court of Appeal
Cass	Court of Cassation (France)
Cass Civ	Court of Cassation (France), civil chamber
Cass Com	Court of Cassation (France), commercial chamber
CDPA	Copyright, Designs and Patents Act 1988
CFI	Court of First Instance
Ch	Chancery Division
Ch Com	Chambre commerciale
CPR	Canadian Patent Reporter
CPVR	Community plant variety right
CRDR	Community registered design right
CTM	Community trademark
CTMR	Community Trademark Regulation
CUDR	Community unregistered design right
ECJ	European Court of Justice
ECDR	European Copyright & Design Reports
ECR	European Court Reports
ECT	European Community Treaty
EDV	essentially derived variety
EMLR	Entertainment and Media Law Reports
EPC	European Patent Convention
EPO	European Patent Office
EPOR	*European Patent Office Reports*
ER	English Reports
EU	European Union
EWCA	Court of Appeal, Civil Division (England & Wales)
FSR	*Fleet Street Reports*
GRUR Int	*Gewerblicher Rechtsschutz und Urheberrecht Internationaler Teil*
GRUR-Prax	*Gewerblicher Rechtsschutz und Urheberrecht Praxis im Immaterialgüter- und Wettbewerbsrecht*
GRUR-RR	*Gewerblicher Rechtsschutz und Urheberrecht Rechtsprechungs-Report*
IPC	Intellectual Property Code (France)
IPR	intellectual property right
IPRs	intellectual property rights
JCP E	*Juris-Classeur Périodique édition Entreprise*
JCP G	*Juris-Classeur Périodique édition Générale*
MCAD	Misleading and Comparative Advertising Directive

OHIM	Office for the Harmonisation of the Internal Market
OJ	Official Journal
PC	Privy Council
PIBD	*Propriété Intellectuelle Bulletin Documentaire*
PVRA	Plant Variety Rights Act 1997
RDA	Registered Designs Act 1949
RPC	Report of Patent Cases
TFEU	Treaty on the Functioning of the European Union
TGI	Tribunal de Grande Instance (France)
TMA	Trademark Act 1994
TPM	technological protection measure
Trib Com	Tribunal de commerce (France)
TRIPs	Agreement on Trade-Related Aspects of Intellectual Property Rights
UCPD	Unfair Commercial Practices Directive
UDR	unregistered design right
UKHL	UK House of Lords
UK UDR	UK unregistered design right
UK PVR	British plant variety right
UPOV	International Union for the Protection of New Varieties of Plants
WCT	WIPO Copyright Treaty
WLR	Weekly Law Reports
WPPT	WIPO Performances and Phonograms Treaty

Contents

Table of Cases

In alphabetical order within each jurisdiction, except for France and the EPO, which are presented in chronological order owing to the wide variety of citation styles.

EUROPEAN UNION

Court of Justice

CFI/General Court

EPO

OHIM

Plant Variety Office

NATIONAL

Canada

France

Germany

Netherlands

United Kingdon

Table of Legislation

EUROPE

COUNCIL OF EUROPE

EUROPEAN UNION

INTERNATIONAL

NATIONAL

Australia

France

Germany

India

Italy

Thailand

United Kingdom

1

Introduction

I. DEFINITION OF THE PROBLEM

IN THE EIGHTEENTH and nineteenth centuries and for the greater part of the twentieth century, the landscape of intellectual property rights (IPRs) resembled a small, well-ordered, simple walled garden. Only copyright, trademarks and patents[1] existed and with very few exceptions, these three rights were meant to be water-tight. In other words, they were not meant to overlap with one another. Since the latter part of the twentieth century, the existing species have increasingly grown outside their boundaries and numerous other species have been added to the garden, which in turn have grown over the other species and the walls have begun to crumble. The issue of overlaps (the cumulation of several IPRs on the same subject matter or object) has started to emerge, or has become more acute in the few cases where overlaps were traditionally envisaged (mainly copyright and designs).

There are five main reasons for this state of affairs. First, IPRs have proliferated, principally because of European Union (EU) harmonisation initiatives. More rights have been created both at national level (plant variety rights, *sui generis* right on topographies of semi-conductor chips, database *sui generis* right) and at EU level (Community registered and unregistered design, Community trademark and Community plant variety right). Secondly, legislation and/or case law have expanded some IPRs internally, thereby making them go beyond their historical borders. This has happened in two main ways: through the extension of some IPRs' traditional subject matter[2] and through the lowering of protection thresholds;[3] for instance, copyright originally only protected books.[4] Over the centuries, the list has increased considerably. Trademark law traditionally protected only

[1] Designs were really optional (and they still are, see TRIPs Agreement, Arts 25–26) as they could be solely protected by copyright.

[2] G Dinwoodie, 'Copyright, Trade Marks and Trade Dress: The Overlap (and Conflict?) in Intellectual Property Regimes Concerning Designs and Visual Images, General Report' in J Ginsburg and J Besek (eds), *Adjuncts and Alternatives to Copyright, Proceedings of the ALAI Congress, June 13–17, 2001, New York USA* (New York, Columbia University School of Law, 2002) 497, 499; V Moffatt, 'Mutant Copyrights and Backdoor Patents: The Problem of Overlapping Intellectual Property Protection' (2004) *Berkeley Technology Law Journal* 1473, 1496; A Quaedvlieg, 'Concurrence and Convergence in Industrial Design: Three-Dimensional Shapes Excluded by Trade Mark Law' in W Grosheide and J Brinkhof (eds), *Intellectual Property Law: Articles on Crossing Borders between Traditional and Actual* (Antwerpen, Intersentia, 2004) 23, 25, noting specifically for trademarks, designs and copyright that 'the aesthetic and functional domain and the features identifying the origin of the goods are no longer separated'. Unless otherwise stated in the book, footnotes in citations are omitted.

[3] A Kur, 'Exceptions to Protection Where Copyright and Trade Mark Overlap: Parody, News Reporting and Other "Speech" Use of Trade Marks", General Report' in J Ginsburg and J Besek (eds), *Adjuncts and Alternatives to Copyright, Proceedings of the ALAI Congress, June 13–17, 2001, New York USA* (New York, Columbia University School of Law, 2002) 593, 594.

[4] The first copyright Act, the Statute of Anne, only protected books. The text of the statute is available at www.copyrighthistory.org/cgi-bin/kleioc/0010/exec/ausgabe/%22uk_1710%22.

two-dimensional representations (words and images) but now it protects shapes and sounds too.[5] Design laws initially only protected features appealing to the eye but now they also protect purely functional designs.[6] All this has not been done in a systematic and orderly way but rather is a product of piecemeal changes, often themselves the result of specific interests.[7] As we will see throughout the book, therefore, rules have rarely been designed to regulate the overlaps, leaving some regime clashes and specific situations of overprotection without solutions. Thirdly, and in the same vein, the purposes of some of the rights are changing. For instance, the justification for protecting trademarks was originally only to safeguard the origin of goods/services, but now trademark law also protects the advertising function and, therefore, can also protect the investment in a trademark and consequently the interests of the seller/producer and no longer only those of the consumer/user.[8] This historical change in the purposes of IPRs towards simple protection of investment is in fact a sign of convergence, be it for better or worse. Fourthly, apart from the now typical reason for stronger rights in general – namely lobbying – the issue of overlaps has also grown because of lawyers' tactics to obtain maximum protection by exploiting the loopholes of the law.[9] When right-holders failed to win their case in respect of one of their IPRs, their counsel advised them to use another right to 'fill the gaps' left by the first right (eg use of copyright to prevent parallel imports of trademarked products, as famously illustrated in *Dior v Evora*[10]). Finally, as unfair competition laws on slavish imitation are still not harmonised in the European Union, claimants also exploit the possibility that the national laws give them of using unfair competition as an alternative when the IPR is either not available at all or has expired. The result of all this is that the boundaries between IPRs have begun to blur and overlap questions have started to spring up.[11]

[5] Quaedvlieg, 'Concurrence and Convergence in Industrial Design' (n 2) 23, 24, noting that the subject matter of copyright and trademark laws has become vaguer.

[6] Dinwoodie, 'Copyright, Trade Marks and Trade Dress' (n 2) 497, 499–501. On the other hand, copyright subject matter has not expanded much if at all into the realm of subject matter that can be protected by trademark law. Kur, 'Exceptions to Protection Where Copyright and Trade Mark Overlap' (n 3) 593, 596. Similarly, Dinwoodie (n 2) 497, 506: 'Viewed merely in terms of recent developments (rather than over the entire history of intellectual property law), the increased overlap of distinct intellectual property rights is heavily dependent upon the expansion in trademark and design law, rather than copyright law . . . Rather, copyright law continues in many countries to insist on limiting protection from designs and visual images in ways that invite trademark and design law to fill gaps in copyright protection'. However, Dinwoodie (n 2) 497, 499 also notes that '[c]opyright has been invoked with respect to an increased range of works that would often in the past have been regarded as too banal to warrant protection, including labels on shampoo and perfume bottles and emblems'.

[7] Moffatt, 'Mutant Copyrights and Backdoor Patents' (n 2) 1473, 1496, noting that 'overlapping protection has arisen mostly by accretion, as a result of the expansion of intellectual property rights, rather than by design'.

[8] Kur, 'Exceptions to Protection Where Copyright and Trade Mark Overlap' (n 3) 593, 594; Dinwoodie, 'Copyright, Trade Marks and Trade Dress' (n 2) 497, 503–4.

[9] Moffatt, 'Mutant Copyrights and Backdoor Patents' (n 2) 1473, 1499; A Kur, 'Exceptions to Protection Where Copyright and Trade Mark Overlap' (n 3) 593, 594; W Grosheide, 'Crossing Borders: Convergence in the Field of IPRs', paper delivered to Ninth Annual Fordham Conference on International Intellectual Property Law and Policy, April 2001; Quaedvlieg, 'Concurrence and Convergence in Industrial Design' (n 2) 23, 24, noting that '[f]rom the 1980s in particular, the market has been attempting to see how far IP rights can be stretched, frequently pushing the limits far beyond the traditional borderline'.

[10] Case C-337/95 *Parfums Christian Dior v Evora* [1997] ECR I-6013.

[11] Quaedvlieg, 'Concurrence and Convergence in Industrial Design' (n 2) 23, 24–25; Moffatt, 'Mutant Copyrights and Backdoor Patents' (n 2) 1473, 1499.

II. METHODOLOGY

Before anything else, we need to be clear on what we mean exactly by overlap and on the terminology that will be used in the book. As was briefly stated above, by overlap, (ac)cumulation or piling up,[12] we mean the situation where two or more IPRs apply to the same physical object, where they have partially or fully the same legal subject matter.[13] This coexistence can occur at the same point in time (simultaneously) or after one of the IPRs has expired (*a posteriori*). Additionally, there can be what we call a negative overlap, ie one IPR can subsist while the scope or conditions of another make it impossible for it to subsist. Therefore, this definition of overlap excludes other overlap situations such as that between an IPR and another type of right, for example a tangible property right (eg between the image of goods and copyright).[14]

Whatever the level examined in this book (international, European or national), rules organising IPR overlaps (are overlaps excluded or allowed, and if so how is their coexistence organised?) are rare, thereby leaving the law uncertain. The quest(ion) is to determine which overlaps pose problems, and which do not, and to find ways to resolve the identified problems. Most overlaps potentially pose two main challenges. The first is a reduction of the public domain by the concurrent application of two or more rights. In this case, the question is then which IPR has priority over the other when one 'intends to grant an exclusive right on certain works or uses and another . . . expressly intends to keep those works or uses free'.[15] The second issue is regime clashes or conflicts.[16] The terms 'conflict' or 'regime clash' will be used to describe a specific problem that happens when there is a simultaneous overlap, namely when the rules applying in the two or more different IPRs provide different outcomes which cannot be reconciled. In addition to these two main problems, overlaps create unnecessary costs on intellectual property owners, such as administrative and enforcement costs, but also on competitors, users and more generally the public.[17] To these costs are added complexity and legal uncertainty,[18] which are all further reasons to resolve the problematic overlaps.

[12] *Cumulare* in Latin means 'to pile up'.

[13] We adopt with a small difference the definition given by JC Galloux, *Des possibles cumuls de protection par les droits de propriété intellectuelle* (Paris, Litec, Coll IRPI 2003), vol 23, 84.

[14] Ibid.

[15] A Quaedvlieg, 'Overlap/Relationships between Copyright and Other Intellectual Property Rights' in E Derclaye (ed), *Research Handbook on the Future of EU Copyright* (Cheltenham, Edward Elgar Publishing, 2009) 479, 480.

[16] Ibid.

[17] Moffatt, 'Mutant Copyrights and Backdoor Patents' (n 2) 1473, 1512, 1515; D Vaver, 'Taking Stock' (1999) *European Intellectual Property Review* 339.

[18] Moffatt, 'Mutant Copyrights and Backdoor Patents' (n 2) 1473, 1512; Vaver, 'Taking Stock' (n 17); S Dusollier, 'Introduction' in S Dusollier and A Cruquenaire (eds), *Le cumul des droits intellectuels* (Brussels, Larcier, 2009), 5, 19. In relation to designs, W Cornish, 'Informal Rights in Industrial Designs: Why Impose Community Constraints?' in J Kabel and G Mom, *Intellectual Property and Information Law: Essays in Honour of Herman Cohen Jeroham* (The Hague, Kluwer Law International, 1998) 253, 259 ('The Community UDR is likely to achieve very little other than a new layer of complication and uncertainty'). See also U Suthersanen, *Design Law in Europe* (London, Sweet & Maxwell, 2000) 80 ('Ironically, the proposed "harmonised" Community design regime will lead to a more bewildering array of potential modes of protection', namely Community registered design right, Community unregistered design right, national registered design right, copyright, UK unregistered design right, Community trademark, national trademark, unfair competition and proposed utility model Directive).

The book's aim is to find appropriate principles regulating overlaps where necessary to avoid regime conflicts and undue unstructured expansion of IPRs. We will also use specific terminology to describe specific types of overlap apart from the three main ones, namely simultaneous,[19] negative and *a posteriori*.[20] Subjective cumulation means that two or more IPRs protect one subject matter, but the rights belong to different persons (different 'subjects').[21] Objective cumulation simply refers to the same subject matter being protected by two different IPRs.[22] Another term we will use is 'convergence'. This means that two IPRs converge to provide the same rules. There are different types of convergence. Asymmetric convergence occurs when part of the rights (eg subject matter, protection requirements, rights) converge, if not totally in their intention, at least in their result, but other parts do not (eg the two or more rights have different exceptions). Conversely, symmetric convergence means that the IPRs in question tend not only to have the same subject matter, protection requirements and rights but also comparable rules on exceptions.[23] This has also been called positive convergence.[24] Negative convergence, on the other hand, is not the opposite of positive convergence. It means that different intellectual property regimes 'converge in excluding an achievement from their respective protection'.[25] An example would be ideas, which can be protected neither by copyright nor by (registered or unregistered) design right. It can also mean that 'one IP regime is assigned to exclusively govern the whole situation, and that all others refrain from protecting that achievement, as is – almost – the case with the protection of technical subject matter by patent law'.[26] 'Negative convergence can take the absolute form of "exclusionary convergence", meaning that all potentially concurring IP regimes converge in excluding an achievement from protection: it stays in the free domain.'[27] An example would be scientific discoveries.

Some other terminological clarifications: by European law, we mean EU primary and secondary law and the European Patent Convention. Finally, we will use the term 'copyright' throughout the book to include both the common law notion (copyright *sensu stricto*) and the civil law notion, namely 'author's right'. Unless otherwise stated, the word 'copyright' will therefore encompass neighbouring rights. As far as the EU courts are concerned, the terms Court of Justice and General Court will be used for decisions dating from after 1 December 2009 while European Court of Justice (ECJ) and Court of First Instance (CFI) will be used for decisions prior to this date.

We will examine the overlap issue at the international and EU levels along with the laws of some Member States. The laws of France, United Kingdom and Germany have been chosen as they provide both different and similar rules on overlaps, and there is already a significant body of case law, which makes the comparison relevant and interesting.

[19] The term 'concurrent' will also be used for simultaneous overlap.

[20] The terms 'subsequent', 'sequential' or 'consecutive' will also be used to describe *a posteriori* overlap.

[21] D Feer Verkade, 'The Cumulative Effect of Copyright Law and Trademark Law: Which Takes Precedence?' in J Kabel and G Mom, *Intellectual Property and Information Law: Essays in Honour of Herman Cohen Jeroham* (The Hague, Kluwer Law International, 1998) 69, 70.

[22] Ibid.

[23] The two terms are used by Kur. A Kur, 'Cumulation of IP Rights Pertaining to Product Shapes: An "Illegitimate Offspring" of IP Law?' in G Ghidini and M Genovesi (eds), *Intellectual Property and Market Power, ATRIP Papers 2006–2007* (Buenos Aires, Eudeba, 2008) 613, 615–16.

[24] Quaedvlieg, 'Concurrence and Convergence in Industrial Design' (n 2) 23, 26.

[25] Ibid 26.

[26] Ibid 27 mentioning, re the 'almost', that computer programs can be protected both by patent and copyright law.

[27] Ibid 27.

We will not examine the *sui generis* right created to protect topographies of semi-conductor chips because of its totally negligible relevance in practice.[28] For reasons of space we also leave out the potential overprotection and clashes concerning procedural aspects (including remedies, limitation periods to bring an action, jurisdictional issues), important questions, however, which may well deserve to be explored in separate scholarship. Geographical indications and appellations of origin have also been left out because they do not present an overlap issue but rather conflicts between two IPRs. Finally, we do not discuss 'inner overlaps', ie those existing inside a particular IPR. These overlaps mainly occur in copyright and related rights law (eg between the database *sui generis* right and copyright). Overlaps between copyright and other types of protection apart from unfair competition, namely contracts, technological protection measures (TPMs) or digital rights management (DRM) are also not touched upon as they have been comprehensively dealt with elsewhere.[29]

The several types of overlap which can occur will be identified separately in each chapter. As will become clear, the same main overlaps generally occur at all levels (international, European and national) as the legal instruments generally allow them. There are eight, namely, copyright/design; copyright/trademark; trademark/design; trademark/patent; copyright/patent; patent/design; patent/plant variety right; IPR/unfair competition law.

III. STRUCTURE OF THE BOOK

We have purposely adopted a country by country, or level by level, approach rather than an overlap by overlap approach. This has enabled us to draw conclusions at each level in order to highlight any specific characteristics or rules peculiar to each legal system. The last chapter then brings together the results from the previous chapters and compares the overlaps one by one. Cross-references further help the reader to make links across the book between the same overlaps at different levels.

To achieve our goal (ie find principles and rules to avoid irreconcilable regime clashes or undue expansion of IPRs), chapters two to six will in turn study the practical consequences of each overlap at the international, European and national levels. Each chapter will first set out the legal framework. Each 'subject matter overlap' (eg copyright/design, patent/plant variety right, etc) is then scrutinised at the three levels, namely simultaneous, negative and *a posteriori* overlaps, to discover if the law implicitly or explicitly envisages the overlap and, if so, if it lays down any rules to regulate it. The chapters will answer, among others, the following questions: What happens if the parody exception is allowed in copyright law but not in trademark law and the subject matter parodied is

[28] See G Karnell, 'Protection of Layout Designs (Topographies) of Integrated Circuits: RIP?' (2001) 32(6) *International Review of Intellectual Property and Competition Law* 648. According to P Torremans, '[i]t was never used much, as the legislation is based on an outdated business and technology model. It is still in use though, but most developed countries with a chip industry see three to four registrations per year only. Litigation is in these circumstances very rare' (email on file with the authors, 22 August 2009).

[29] L Guibault, *Copyright Limitations and Contracts: An Analysis of the Contractual Overridability of Limitations on Copyright* (The Hague, Kluwer Law International, 2002); E Derclaye, *The Legal Protection of Databases: A Comparative Analysis* (Cheltenham, Edward Elgar Publishing, 2008); S Dusollier, *Droit d'auteur et protection des oeuvres dans l'univers numérique, droits et exceptions à la lumière des dispositifs de verrouillage des œuvres* (Brussels, Larcier, 2005); M Favale, *Access to Copyright Works: Fine-Tuning DRM to Balance the Rights of Owners and Users* (PhD Thesis, University of Nottingham, 2007).

protected by both rights? Can the decompilation exception in copyright law be exercised on a computer program which is also patented? Can an expired copyright or design be resuscitated or kept alive by a trademark? What about the uncoordinated exceptions of patent law, on the one hand, and plant variety protection, on the other, where both areas of law overlap with respect to protection of 'green' biotechnology? At the end of each of these chapters, the relevant approaches to the overlap problems in the respective international, European and national practice will be summarised, and inconsistencies will be identified and criticised. This will allow the inductive development of certain general principles concerning overlaps in the final chapter (chapter seven). The latter will first critically compare the differences and similarities between the rules relating to overlaps in the chosen legal systems. Next, it will analyse the reasons for the prohibition or authorisation of overlaps. This analysis will enable the determination of a number of criteria that will be used to (re)map the overlaps to achieve appropriateness and legitimacy. Solutions to the problems caused by overlaps and answers to remaining open questions will then be developed according to these criteria.

2

International Law

I. THE LEGAL FRAMEWORK

THE INTERNATIONAL LEGAL instruments in the field of IPRs which deal with substantive law, with various degrees of depth, are as follows.[1] Two conventions deal with all or most IPRs (so-called multi-regime conventions or treaties): the Paris Convention for the Protection of Industrial Property of 1883 (1967 revision with 1979 amendments) and the TRIPs Agreement of 1994. The relevant conventions in the field of copyright and related rights are the Berne Convention for the Protection of Literary and Artistic Works of 1886 (1971 revision with 1979 amendments[2]), the Rome Convention for the Protection of Performers, Producers of Phonograms and Broadcasting Organisations of 1961, and the WIPO Copyright and WIPO Performances and Phonograms Treaties both of 1996 (WCT and WPPT). In the field of trademarks and patents, there is no binding international instrument dealing with substantive law apart from the two above-mentioned multi-regime treaties. Concerning plant variety rights, the UPOV Convention for the protection of new varieties of plants of 1961 (in force in 1968, as last revised in 1991) is the governing document.[3] The European Union is a party to the TRIPs Agreement and the WIPO Internet Treaties.

II. COPYRIGHT AND DESIGNS

A Simultaneous Overlap

(i) Subject Matter

The relevant provisions of the Berne Convention, Paris Convention, WCT and TRIPs Agreement show that a simultaneous overlap between copyright and designs is possible.

First let us see what the copyright conventions cover. The Berne Convention protects 'literary and artistic works'. Article 2(1) further provides that:

[1] Note that we are only discussing the multilateral treaties not the bilateral or regional treaties. The only regional treaties we will look at are those binding the European Union, as only the European Union is the topic of this book in this respect.

[2] The EU Member States are party to the 1971 revision.

[3] Although some member states are not party to the 1991 act of the UPOV Convention, their laws comply with it as a result of the Community Plant Variety Right Regulation (EC) 2100/94. See chapter 3, section VIII.

> the expression 'literary and artistic works' shall include *every production* in the literary, scientific and artistic domain, whatever may be the mode or form of its expression, such as . . . (emphasis added)

A long list of examples follows. The expression 'literary and artistic works' is thus wide[4] and it is not disputed that the list is illustrative and not exhaustive so that the Berne Convention protects any work, so long as it can be broadly said to be literary or artistic.[5] The coverage is also wide because fixation is not required by the Convention but left for members to decide. Likewise, members have the choice to protect official texts and their translations, political speeches and speeches delivered in the course of legal proceedings. Although the extent of works protected is broad, some uncertainty remains. It is clear, however, that news of the day and facts of press information are excluded from protection (Article 2(8)).[6] Let us now look at what the Berne Convention says about specific categories of work where an overlap could possibly occur with designs. First of all, the Convention does not define most categories of works. It is unlikely, although not completely impossible, for there to be an overlap with regard to 'writings'. Even though the term 'writings' is broad (it encompasses anything in written form[7]), an overlap between copyright and designs will be rare because designs generally reside only in the appearance of the words used, and the amount of words used may not be sufficient to qualify the literary work as original.

Drawings, paintings, architectural works, sculptures, engravings and lithographies are not defined, either.[8] However, Article 2(1)'s 'opening general definition still presupposes that a wide interpretation will be adopted'.[9] Therefore, works of architecture include 'all kinds of structure which are fixed to the ground, for example, monuments, arches, fountains, steps and so on'.[10] Photographs are also not defined. There is little guidance from the *travaux préparatoires* on the meaning of illustrations, maps, plans, sketches and plastic works relative to geography, topography, architecture or science.[11] What is clear is that the plans, sketches and plastic works must be relative to geography, topography, architecture or science. Other plans, etc which do not pertain to those are protected by the previous category of drawing, etc. The Convention therefore makes a distinction between artistic and non artistic two- and three-dimensional works. In relation to works of applied art, Berne Article 2(7) reads:

> Subject to the provisions of article 7(4) of this convention, it shall be a matter for legislation in the countries of the Union to determine the extent of the application of their laws to works of applied art and industrial designs and models, as well as the conditions under which such works, designs and models shall be protected. Works protected in the country of origin solely as designs and models shall be entitled in another country of the Union only to such special protection as is granted in that country to designs and models; however, if no such special protection is granted in that country, such works shall be protected as artistic works.

[4] S Ricketson and J Ginsburg, *International Copyright and Neighbouring Rights: The Berne Convention and Beyond*, 2nd edn (Oxford, Oxford University Press, 2006) 407; S Von Lewinski, International Copyright Law and Policy (Oxford, Oxford University Press, 2008) 121.

[5] It has even been argued that artistic works could possibly include perfumes and culinary creations. See Von Lewinski, *International Copyright Law and Policy* (n 4) 122.

[6] Ricketson and Ginsburg, *International Copyright and Neighbouring Rights* (n 4) 412.

[7] Ibid 413.

[8] Ibid 436–37.

[9] Ibid 437.

[10] Ibid 442.

[11] Ibid 470–71.

This rule means that countries are allowed to choose between copyright and designs law to protect works of applied art. They have three choices: copyright law only, design law only or both.[12] It is clear, however, that cumulative protection is generally the norm throughout the world and this is not likely to change, at least in the near future.[13] Finally, the TRIPs Agreement and WCT have extended the coverage of copyright to computer programs and databases but it is unlikely there could be an overlap with designs in this respect.

According to the Paris Convention, designs must be protected (Article 5*quinquies*[14]) but the Convention does not prescribe a specific type of protection. Consequently, the Convention is silent on the possibility of cumulation. Therefore, member states are free to protect designs as they wish, for instance by copyright or unfair competition law,[15] or both. As we saw above, the Berne Convention specifically states that works of applied art can be protected by copyright law.

Finally, whilst the TRIPs Agreement does not define the term design,[16] it explicitly leaves the choice of a copyright or design right protection, at least for textile designs (Article 25(2)).[17] It does not even prescribe a registered system for designs.[18]

(ii) Protection Requirements

Experts on the Berne Convention agree that it requires works to be creative.[19] However, some note further that whilst the 'word "production" implies the presence of some element of creativity . . ., it is not clear whether the required creative elements should be of any particular standard or level'.[20] In summary, the Berne Convention leaves it to member states to adopt the definition of the minimum of intellectual creation required for works listed in Article 2(1).[21] Therefore, the amount of overlap is slightly reduced as there can only be overlap if the design is also creative. This is theoretical, of course, as most common law systems are still known to protect copyright works at a level below creativity and this practice has not been challenged over the years.[22] TRIPs Article 25(1) requires

[12] Von Lewinski, *International Copyright Law and Policy* (n 4) 114, paras 5.46–5.47.

[13] Ricketson and Ginsburg (n 4) 469. However, Italy is a striking example of a country which has chosen a 'design only' system and this has led to considerable frictions in the internal market (see most recently the Court of Justice's *Peek and Cloppenburg* decision (Case C-456/06 *Peek and Cloppenburg v Cassina* [2008] ECR I-2731) which effectively results from the fact that copyright protection for designs is excluded in Italy).

[14] Article 5quinquies simply states: 'Industrial designs shall be protected in all the countries of the Union'.

[15] C Correa, *Trade Related Aspects of Intellectual Property Rights: A Commentary of the TRIPs Agreement* (Oxford, Oxford University Press, 2007) 259; D Gervais, *The TRIPs Agreement: Drafting History and Analysis*, 2nd edn (London, Sweet & Maxwell, 2003) 212.

[16] At least one delegation had provided one but it did not end up in the final text. See preparatory material of the TRIPs Agreement available at www.wto.org/english/tratop_e/trips_e/trips_e.htm#NegHist.

[17] For the definition of 'textile', 'one should refer to specialised WTO agreements in this field'. See Gervais, *The TRIPs Agreement* (n 15) 214.

[18] Correa, *Trade Related Aspects of Intellectual Property Rights* (n 15) 261.

[19] von Lewinski, *International Copyright Law and Policy* (n 4) 122–23 also citing other sources; Ricketson and Ginsburg (n 4) 402–5; D Gervais 'The Compatibility of the "Skill and Labour" Originality Standard with the Berne Convention and the TRIPS Agreement' (2004) *European Intellectual Property Review* 75.

[20] Ricketson and Ginsburg (n 4) 402–5.

[21] Ibid 405.

[22] See, however, Case C-5/08 *Infopaq International AS v Dankse Dagblades Forening* [2009] ECR I-6569. On this, see chapter 3, s IIB(i).

designs to be original or new. There is no definition of what is required by the term 'original'.[23]

(iii) Excluded Subject Matter

The Berne Convention only excludes news of the day and facts of press information from protection but this is not relevant to the possible overlap with designs. TRIPs Article 25(1) leaves the option to member states to exclude designs dictated essentially by technical or functional considerations.

In conclusion, cumulative protection is possible between copyright and design, but also implicitly between an unregistered and a registered design right.[24] Now, do the international instruments deal with possible regime clashes?

(iv) Ownership

Neither the Berne Convention, WCT, Paris Convention nor the TRIPs Agreement has anything to say about ownership. The overlap is therefore a purely regional and/or national issue.

(v) Rights and Infringement

The Berne Convention requires a reproduction or communication to the public (Articles 9, 11 and 11*bis*). The TRIPs Agreement also requires a copy for design infringement (Article 26). Neither the Berne Convention nor TRIPs Agreement refers to the likelihood of confusion. However, the TRIPs Agreement only sanctions copies which are made for commercial purposes.

(vi) Exceptions Including Exhaustion Principle

Berne Articles 9(2), 10 and 10*bis* provide for exceptions. Article 9(2) embodies the original three-step test but only for the right of reproduction.[25] WCT Article 10 and TRIPs Article 13 have broadened this test so that it now applies to all economic rights. In addition, the Berne Convention provides for specific exceptions. Article 10 allows:

> quotations from a work which has already been lawfully made available to the public, provided that their making is compatible with fair practice, and their extent does not exceed that justified by the purpose, including quotations from newspaper articles and periodicals in the form of press summaries.

[23] Gervais, *The TRIPs Agreement* (n 15) 213, para 2.244, however, notes that the optional requirement excluding designs essentially dictated by their technical or functional considerations may be linked to the definition of originality, 'which seems to refer to choices made by the designer other than those dictated by such considerations'.

[24] N Pires de Carvalho, *The TRIPs Regime of Trademarks and Designs* (The Hague, Kluwer Law International, 2006) 405; Correa, *Trade Related Aspects of Intellectual Property Rights* (n 15) 261.

[25] 'It shall be a matter for legislation in the countries of the Union to permit the reproduction of such [literary and artistic] works in certain special cases, provided that such reproduction does not conflict with a normal exploitation of the work and does not unreasonably prejudice the legitimate interests of the author.'

Paragraph 3 of the same article requires that the source be mentioned, including the name of the author if it appears on the work. Articles 10(2) and 10*bis* allow members to enact exceptions for the purposes of teaching and reporting current events and provide conditions that they must respect if they do so. As to designs, TRIPs Article 26(2) also provides a three-step test, albeit with some slightly different words and an additional step:

> Members may provide *limited exceptions* to the protection of industrial designs, provided that such exceptions do not unreasonably conflict with the normal exploitation of protected industrial designs and do not unreasonably prejudice the legitimate interests of the owner of the protected design, *taking account of the legitimate interests of third parties*. (emphasis added)

This test only applies to commercial acts, as non-commercial acts are not within the scope of protection.[26] The difference is that TRIPs Article 26(2) refers to 'limited exceptions' whereas Berne Article 9(2) and TRIPs Article 13 refer to 'special cases', which is arguably a narrower concept.[27] Finally, compulsory licences are permitted under the TRIPs Agreement for both copyright and designs through Article 8, which 'permits measures that limit IPRs for the sake of the public interest and the prevention of abusive and anti-competitive practices, provided they are consistent with the provisions of the agreement'.[28]

Only the TRIPs Agreement refers to international exhaustion, but it leaves it untouched (Article 6). The matter is therefore for member states to regulate.

B Negative Overlap

The international instruments are silent on this issue.

(i) Copyright Protection Unavailable

Because of the breadth of its coverage, protection under the Berne Convention will rarely be unavailable. Of course, Article 2(7) allows members to exclude works of applied art and industrial designs and models from copyright protection but this is a regional/national issue not an international issue, as the Convention does not regulate it as such but leaves it to member countries to do so. One minor possibility might arise if the criterion of originality is ever determined by a WTO panel differently for designs and copyright, when negative overlap would be possible, one way or the other (ie should copyright protection become unavailable, or conversely design protection).

[26] Correa, (n 15) 267.

[27] Ibid.

[28] Pires de Carvalho, *The TRIPs Regime of Trademarks and Designs* (n 24) 421 ('because there are no provisions to the contrary, compulsory licenses of industrial designs are consistent with article 8'). 'In view of the unequivocal language of article 2(7) of the Berne Convention according to which countries may determine "the conditions under which . . . designs and models shall be protected", copyright industrial designs may also be subject to compulsory licensing on the same grounds and conditions as those covered by industrial property.' Ibid 423.

(ii) Design Protection Unavailable

If a country chooses novelty as a requirement, and it does not coincide with originality for the specific design in question, then copyright will be able to fill the gap.

C *A Posteriori* Overlap

The international instruments are not explicit on this but the rules clearly do not preclude a continued application of copyright law once design protection has expired, and vice versa.

III. COPYRIGHT AND TRADEMARKS

A Simultaneous Overlap

(i) Subject Matter

The scope of literary and artistic works has been discussed in section II and we refer the reader to it. A few additional comments are in order. Although Berne Article 2 does not mention titles, slogans and other insubstantial works, as it stands, so long as short works are creative and of a literary or artistic nature, there is nothing in the Convention that would prevent them from being protected. The details are left to national legislatures.[29] However, TRIPs Article 9(2) may stand in the way of the overlap for single words because it may be argued that single words, even if original, are just ideas and TRIPs Article 9(2) prevents the protection of ideas by copyright. The Convention does not define the terms 'musical compositions with or without words'. The definition is once again left to national law.[30]

The Paris Convention does not define trademarks. Thus, potentially anything can be a trademark. However, according to Paris Article 7, trademarks only apply to goods. The TRIPs Agreement adds more detail. First of all, the TRIPs Agreement extends the protection of trademarks in relation to services and not only to goods (Article 15(4)).[31] By contrast with the Paris Convention, TRIPs Article 15(1) gives a comprehensive definition of a trademark. It states:

> Any sign, or any combination of signs, capable of distinguishing the goods or services of one undertaking from those of other undertakings, shall be capable of constituting a trademark. Such signs, *in particular* words including personal names, letters, numerals, figurative elements and combinations of colours as well as any combination of such signs, shall be eligible for registration as trademarks. . . Members may require, as a condition of registration, that signs be visually perceptible. (emphasis added)

As a result, there is no limit as to what can be a trademark, as the TRIPs definition is not exhaustive (it uses the term 'in particular'). As the list in Article 15 is illustrative,

[29] Ricketson and Ginsburg (n 4) 510–11.

[30] Ibid 426. As will be seen in chapter five (UK law), a definition of music has recently been attempted by the Court of Appeal of England and Wales.

[31] Correa, *Trade Related Aspects of Intellectual Property Rights* (n 15) 182; Pires de Carvalho, *The TRIPs Regime of Trademarks and Designs* (n 24) para 15.23.

shapes, single colours and single letters could be trademarks.[32] However, the TRIPs Agreement allows members to require that signs be visually perceptible. This means that they can exclude from protection audible and olfactory signs.[33]

(ii) Protection Requirements

The protection requirement in international copyright law has been explained above at IIA(ii). It must now be verified under which condition(s) a trademark is protectable to see the extent of the overlap and whether the international instruments regulate it. The Paris Convention requires that marks have distinctive character but does not define the requirement. However, the TRIPs Agreement elaborates on the requirement of distinctiveness. It can be direct (immediate) or acquired through use. Only signs that *are not inherently capable of distinguishing* can acquire distinctiveness through use, not signs that *are inherently incapable of distinguishing*.[34] In addition, Article 19 requires that trademarks be used, so if they are not used for an uninterrupted period of at least three years without valid reason, the right lapses.[35] As long as the conditions of both rights are fulfilled, an original work can also be a distinctive trademark and vice versa.

(iii) Excluded Subject Matter

In the Berne Convention, excluded subject matter is not relevant. Apart from the requirements set out above for trademarks, there is no specific excluded subject matter. Therefore, there can be a simultaneous overlap between trademarks and some copyright works, namely literary and artistic (both two- and three-dimensional), and possibly also musical. Neither the copyright conventions nor the TRIPs Agreement is explicit on the issue of the overlap between copyright and trademarks, but the TRIPs definition of a trademark itself implies the possibility of an overlap. Thus, both trademark and copyright laws can protect subject matter if it is both creative and distinctive and is used on goods or services.

(iv) Ownership

Neither the copyright nor the multi-regime international instruments refer to ownership.[36]

[32] Correa (n 15) 177. Gervais, (n 15) 167, paras 2.157–2.196. *Contra*: Pires de Carvalho, *The TRIPs Regime of Trademarks and Designs* (n 24) 224–25. 'The fact that article 15.1 refers to combinations of colours means that WTO members are not obliged to make registration available for individual, isolated colours. Para 1 is worded in a manner that implies that the exclusion of individual colours from this elicited listing was intended, because the word "combination" in that listing is used twice: the first time it is used in connection with colours, and a second time it is used generally in connection with "such signs". It is clear that the TRIPs agreement wished to refer specifically to "combinations of colours" as opposed to "colours" or "isolated or individual colours". Otherwise, the presence of the expression "combination of colours" which is singled out because it refers to a sign that is not individually listed, would make no sense. However, WTO members may make registration of isolated colours available if they have acquired distinctiveness through use.'

[33] Correa, (n 15) 176; Gervais, (n 15) 167, paras 2.157–2.196; Pires de Carvalho, *The TRIPs Regime of Trademarks and Designs* (n 24) 228.

[34] Pires de Carvalho, *The TRIPs Regime of Trademarks and Designs* (n 24) 235. Article 15(1) provides in relevant part: 'Where signs are not inherently capable of distinguishing the relevant goods or services, Members may make registrability depend on distinctiveness acquired through use'.

[35] See also a similar but less detailed requirement in Paris Art 5C.

[36] TRIPs Art 21, however, requires that 'the owner of a registered trademark shall have the right to assign the trademark with or without the transfer of the business to which the trademark belongs'. Contrast with Paris Art 6*quater* which states in relevant part: '(1) When, in accordance with the law of a country of the Union, the assignment of a mark is valid only if it takes place at the same time as the transfer of the business or goodwill

(v) Rights and Infringement

In copyright law, a reproduction or communication to the public is necessary (Berne Articles 9, 11 and 11*bis*), both of which imply a prior access to the work. In trademark law, copying is not required, only likelihood of confusion.[37] In addition, the goods or services must be identical or similar (Paris Article 6*bis* and TRIPs Article 16), except if the mark is well known (TRIPs Article 16(3)). Thus, except where a mark is well known, an overlap will only occur if there is copying and likelihood of confusion at least between similar goods or services, which further reduces the occurrences of overlap.

(vi) Exceptions Including Exhaustion Principle

TRIPs Article 17 allows members to:

> provide limited exceptions to the rights conferred by a trademark, such as fair use of descriptive terms, provided that such exceptions take account of the legitimate interests of the owner of the trademark and of third parties.

In contrast to the situation of the overlap between copyright and designs, TRIPs Article 21 clearly prohibits the compulsory licensing of trademarks. Further exceptions are therefore not possible.

On exhaustion, we refer the reader to IIA above.

B Negative Overlap

As for the copyright/design overlap, the international instruments are silent on this issue.

(i) Copyright Protection Unavailable

Copyright protection will not be available for unoriginal works but the latter may be protected as trademarks if they are distinctive of goods or services. (Think of APPLE (a single word) for computers.)

(ii) Trademark Protection Unavailable

Even if a trademark is not distinctive, it can still be original, although this may not be very frequent.

to which the mark belongs, it shall suffice for the recognition of such validity that the portion of the business or goodwill located in that country be transferred to the assignee, together with the exclusive right to manufacture in the said country, or to sell therein, the goods bearing the mark assigned'.

[37] 'Based on the textual analysis of the Paris convention and the TRIPs agreement, the [WTO Appellate Body] concluded that "the use of the trademark should result in the 'likelihood of confusion'. This requirement, which breaks new ground in international trademark law, implies that the mere possibility of confusion is not sufficient for legitimising the exercise of the exclusive rights"'. Correa, (n 15) 186.

C *A Posteriori* Overlap

An *a posteriori* overlap is not prohibited so is possible in either form: protecting by trademark law a copyright work whose protection has expired is something the international instruments do not prevent. Likewise, copyright protection for an expired trademark is also possible; this could happen if the trademark is no longer distinctive or has expired because it is no longer used.

IV. TRADEMARKS AND DESIGNS

As has become clear from the above discussion in sections II and III, although the international instruments are silent on the issue, they also leave a possibility of overlaps between trademarks and designs.

Simultaneous overlap will occur if the subject matter is not only distinctive but also original or new, and (depending on the country) is not dictated essentially by technical or functional considerations. At the level of infringement, the result is very similar to that of the overlap between trademark and copyright since, as under copyright law, copying is necessary to infringe a design. As for the two previous overlaps, the regime clashes as regards the exceptions will depend on the national law involved. As to negative overlap, again similarly to the overlap between copyright and trademark, single words or colours may be protected by trademark but not by design, and designs which are not new or original may still be distinctive. Conversely, it may be (although probably more rarely) that a sign is not distinctive but is original or new. Finally, with respect to the *a posteriori* overlap, similarly to the overlap between trademark and copyright, trademarks can prolong the normal life of a registered or unregistered design. A design right can prolong a trademark right if the trademark has not been used or has lost distinctive character. Once more, no rules regulate these overlaps.

V. TRADEMARKS AND PATENTS

There is nothing in the Paris Convention on this potential overlap. There is nothing explicit in the TRIPs Agreement but implicitly it seems the overlap is allowed. As will be seen below, TRIPs Article 27(1) provides that patents must be granted for all inventions, be they products or processes, in all fields of technology, provided that they are new, involve an inventive step and are capable of industrial application. Surprisingly perhaps, the definition of trademarks does not exclude shapes essentially dictated by their function. Therefore, functional shapes which are distinctive, new, inventive and capable of industrial application could benefit from the double protection of trademark and patent laws. This is not an academic issue, as will be made clear in the discussion of the EU *Philips v Remington* case (see chapter three, section IV). Negative overlaps are also possible. If a shape is not patentable then it could be registered as a trademark, as long as it is distinctive. If a shape is not registrable as a trademark because it is not distinctive, it may be patentable as long as it fulfils the patentability requirements. The overlap could also happen *a posteriori*. A trademark could be sought for an invention whose patent has expired, even if the trademark is sought for a functional shape. But the converse is not true: if a trademark has been granted for a functional shape, by definition the shape is no longer new and a patent is not available.

VI. PATENTS AND DESIGNS

Likewise, overlaps between patents and designs can occur. Again this is implicit. Indeed, unless countries preclude the protection of designs dictated essentially by technical or functional considerations, as allowed by TRIPs Article 25(1), a simultaneous overlap is possible between design and patent. Negative overlap can also occur both ways. The *a posteriori* overlap can present itself when the patent has expired, the condition under national law is originality rather than novelty and the protection is longer than 20 years. The converse *a posteriori* overlap cannot happen as the subject matter will no longer be new when the design protection ends.

Similarly, there could be an overlap between plant variety rights and designs, and plant variety rights and trademarks. Indeed, if a member state opts for a *sui generis* right for plant varieties and does not exclude essentially functional plant varieties, since all types of shapes can be protected by trademarks and designs, the shape of the new plant variety could be protected also by trademark and/or design rights. Indeed, arguably, a new plant variety (say a new type of flower) has a shape which could also be distinctive or original. We can already note that this overlap will not be possible at EU or national level. The reasons are that design rights are only accepted for products and plants are not considered products,[38] and trademark law excludes from registration shapes which result from the nature of the goods themselves (Trademark Directive, article 3(1)(e)(i)).

VII. COPYRIGHT AND PATENTS

Even if the idea/expression dichotomy is enshrined in both the TRIPs Agreement (Article 9(2)) and the WCT (Article 2) and aims to avoid the overlap between patent and copyright law,[39] these international texts implicitly allow the simultaneous overlap between patent and copyright for computer programs, although they have no specific rule organising this overlap. WCT Article 4 and TRIPs Article 10(1) expressly state that computer programs, whatever their form of expression, are to be treated as literary works under the Berne Convention.[40] On the other hand, the patent provisions of the TRIPs Agreement also implicitly cover computer programs as patents must be granted to inventions in all fields of technology (Article 27(1)).[41] However, one commentator thinks that when TRIPs

[38] See presentation on the Community design system by H Salmi, Examination Co-ordinator, OHIM's Designs Department, at Queen Mary University of London, 15 December 2004, on file with the authors.

[39] The Articles provide that '[c]opyright protection [shall] extend to expressions and not to ideas, procedures, methods of operation or mathematical concepts as such'.

[40] 'In stating that if they must be protected as *literary* works, the provision basically prohibits the qualification of computer programs as works of "applied art" or an equivalent thereof, which would have allowed a limitation of the term and other conditions of protection.' Gervais, (n 15) 135, para 2.106. In addition, 'the WCT modifies the TRIPs wording in two aspects. First, the words "shall be protected" (TRIPs) are replaced by "are protected". This means that computer programs have already been protected as literary works and that this provision is of a declaratory nature'. Von Lewinski, *International Copyright Law and Policy* (n 4) 467, para 17.104.

[41] Pires de Carvalho, *The TRIPs Regime of Trademarks and Designs* (n 24) 395.

Articles 9(2) and 10(1) are read together, they seem to mean that computer programs are as a matter of law expressions and not ideas, with the consequence that they cannot be inventions.

> In other words, articles 9(2) and 10(1) seem to exclude computer software from patentability per se, thus preventing WTO members from applying article 1(1) and resort to the national practices so as to identify computer programs as protectable inventions.[42]

We believe, however, that the distinction can be made between ideas and expressions in computer programs and therefore that this argument does not hold good. An overlap easily occurs since a computer program, which is new, inventive and industrially applicable, will generally be at the same time original. But the simultaneous overlap will be reduced because the patent will protect only the ideas whereas copyright will protect only the expressions. A program which would not be patentable could, however, quite easily be copyrightable. The converse is possible but will be rarer. Of course, a program the copyright protection of which has expired cannot be patented for lack of novelty. But the converse *a posteriori* overlap will often occur. When the patent has expired, the copyright can still subsist.

Normally, the idea/expression dichotomy should ensure that apart from this specific overlap, no other copyright creation could also be protected by a patent, and vice versa, so that there should not be any overlaps, be they simultaneous, negative or *a posteriori.*

VIII. PATENTS AND PLANT VARIETY RIGHTS

A Simultaneous Overlap

There are two instruments regulating this area: the International Convention for the Protection of New Varieties of Plants (UPOV, acts of 1961, 1978 and 1991) and the TRIPs Agreement. The focus will be on the UPOV Convention's 1991 act because most EU Member States have adhered to it and those which have not have in any case 'amended their law to come into line with the Community plant variety right, which is based on the 1991 Convention'.[43] UPOV Article 2, which existed in the previous act, was not included in the 1991 act. This article stipulated that member countries had the choice to protect plant variety rights through patents or a *sui generis* system based on the Convention, but if an applicant did, s/he had to choose between the two and could not cumulate them.[44] With the deletion of this article, the 1991 act implicitly allows the overlap but does not regulate any conflicts which may arise. This is left to national law.[45] There is no chapter

[42] N Pires de Carvalho, *The TRIPs Regime of Patent Rights* (The Hague, Kluwer Law International, 2002) 149.

[43] G Tritton, R Davis, M Edenborough, J Graham, S Malinicz and A Roughton, *Intellectual Property in Europe* (London, Sweet & Maxwell, 2008) 599, 614 (there are still a number of European countries who have not adhered to the 1991 act of UPOV).

[44] J Straus, 'The Relationship between Plant Variety Protection and Plant Protection from an International Viewpoint' (1987) *International Review of Intellectual Property and Competition Law* 724. 'The architects of the international system for the protection of plant breeding, conceived at the end of the 1950s and in the early 1960s, believed at that stage in the possibility of a permanent, precise and clear distinction between the two protective systems, without any overlapping and without conflict.'

[45] B Greengrass, 'The 1991 Act of the UPOV Convention' (1991) *European Intellectual Property Review* 466, 467.

or even a section on plant variety rights in the TRIPs Agreement. However, TRIPs Article 27(3)(b) provides that:

> Members shall provide for the protection of plant varieties either by patents or by an effective *sui generis* system or by *any combination thereof.* (emphasis added)

It goes on to state that the conditions of this subparagraph will be reviewed four years after entry into force of the WTO Agreement.[46] As can readily be seen, the TRIPs Agreement expressly allows the overlap between patents and plant variety rights:[47]

> As a result of the practice of implementing TRIPs obligations, both texts of UPOV can be deemed as effective protection for the purposes of article 27(3)(b) . . . but nothing would stand in the way of members designing different standards of protection – provided they are likewise effective.[48]

The Thai Plant Variety Protection Act 1999 and the Indian Protection of Plant Varieties and Farmers Rights' Act 2001 can be cited as examples of this (although their effectiveness can be disputed).[49] 'Since the patent system allows for stronger (though not longer) protection, the possibility of overlap has resulted in increased attempts to obtain patent protection for plant related products.'[50]

(i) Subject Matter

In order to benefit from the protection of both rights, a plant variety will need to be patentable or a patentable invention will also have to be a plant variety. As case law has shown in Europe, this is often the case.[51]

(ii) Protection Requirements

There will be an overlap if the variety fulfils the conditions of both the UPOV Convention (novelty, distinctness, uniformity and stability), or another *sui generis* right chosen by a member state, and patent law (novelty, inventive step and industrial application). The overlap may be possible in many cases. This is because, although the plant variety right does not allow application in respect of a single gene, it allows the holder to control the internal genetic components of a plant, such as a gene which could be patented, even if 'these elements may not be subject of a plant variety application'.[52] Conversely, 'in patent

[46] This review has happened but does not treat much of plant variety rights. In any case the text of the Agreement has not been amended. See Note by the Secretariat, IP/C/W/370/Rev.1, 9 March 2006, available at http://docsonline.wto.org/GEN_highLightParent.asp?qu=&doc=D%3A%2FDDFDOCUMENTS%2FT%2FIP%2FC%2FW370R1.DOC.HTM&curdoc=3&popTitle=IP%2FC%2FW%2F370%2FRev.1.

[47] Pires de Carvalho, *The TRIPs Regime of Patent Rights* (n 42) 185. However, some doubt this. See M Llewelyn and M Adcock, *European Plant Intellectual Property* (Oxford, Hart Publishing, 2006) 121. 'In addition, notwithstanding that art 27.3.b provides member states with a measure of choice as to the form of protection they adopt over plant varieties, there is a question over the extent to which their choice is real in practice.'

[48] See Pires de Carvalho, *The TRIPs Regime of Patent Rights* (n 42) 184–85 on Art 27, the breeders' exemption, writing further (in 2000) that 'so far, no such different standards have been developed outside the UPOV or the patent system'.

[49] Llewelyn and Adcock, *European Plant Intellectual Property* (n 47) 125.

[50] L Bently and B Sherman, *Intellectual Property Law*, 3rd edn (Oxford, Oxford University Press, 2009) 601.

[51] See chapter 3, section VIII.B.

[52] Llewelyn and Adcock, *European Plant Intellectual Property* (n 47) 124.

law, a plant application may not include a claim to a plant variety but it may claim plant genetic materials which could be used to affect the characteristics or traits of a variety'.[53] Therefore, although the two protections can be seen as totally separate at first sight, in effect, the separation between the two is not as water-tight as it first appears and overlaps can easily occur.[54]

(iii) Excluded Subject Matter

TRIPs Article 27(2) gives the option to member states to exclude some inventions if their commercial exploitation affects *ordre public* or morality:

> including to protect human, animal or plant life or health or to avoid serious prejudice to the environment, provided that such exclusion is not made merely because the exploitation is prohibited by their law.

A similar exception does not exist in the UPOV Convention. The probable reason is that, as plant variety rights are concerned with biological (in other words 'natural') processes, questions of morality or public policy do not occur. Thus, if an invention also covers a plant variety but a patent is not available in a member state because of this exclusion, this may indirectly affect the plant variety. However, if a choice is left between patent and plant variety right, since the morality exclusion does not exist in the UPOV Convention, the inventor, who is barred from obtaining a patent, can then try and obtain a plant variety right instead. This possibility of choosing between patent and plant variety right will depend on the national laws.

(iv) Ownership

Neither the UPOV Convention (1991 act) nor the TRIPs Agreement have provisions regarding ownership of plant variety rights. While UPOV Article 1(iv) simply says that the right-holder is the employer or commissioner if that is what the applicable national law provides, the TRIPs Agreement only states that patent holders will have the right to assign their patents and conclude licensing contracts (Article 28(2)).

(v) Rights and Infringement

The TRIPs Agreement and UPOV Convention rights are in the main identical but differ in two respects. TRIPs Article 28(1) gives the patent owner the following rights: making, using, offering for sale, selling, and importing; so it also gives the right against simple use of the patented invention. This does not appear in the UPOV Convention, Article 14 of which lists the following rights: (i) production or reproduction (multiplication); (ii) conditioning for the purpose of propagation; (iii) offering for sale; (iv) selling or other marketing; (v) exporting; (vi) importing; and (vii) stocking for any of the purposes mentioned in (i) to (vi). On the other hand, the UPOV Convention gives the right to prevent export of the plant variety, which does not appear in the TRIPs Agreement. One could say that making or using includes exporting. However, nothing appears from the

[53] Ibid.
[54] Ibid.

travaux préparatoires of the TRIPs Agreement on this, and probably exporting is excluded as the provision comes from many national laws which do not include the term.[55] What is clear is that the patentee's TRIPs rights do not include stocking.[56] UPOV Article 14(5) also gives to the breeder the same rights as stated in (i) to (iv) against essentially derived varieties. Whether the same could be said of TRIPs Article 28 depends on national or regional law, which may or may not have a doctrine of equivalents.

(vi) Exceptions Including Exhaustion Principle

Similarly to the TRIPs provisions on trademark and copyright, TRIPs Article 30 also has a general test, and like that in trademark law, it includes a fourth step:

> Members may provide limited exceptions to the exclusive rights conferred by a patent, provided that such exceptions do not unreasonably conflict with a normal exploitation of the patent and do not unreasonably prejudice the legitimate interests of the patent owner, taking account of the legitimate interests of third parties.

As to plant variety rights, the breeder's exemption (UPOV Article 15) allows breeders to use protected material for research purposes, even if commercial. 'When the research leads to a new variety then the breeder of that new variety can claim rights over it without having to obtain permission from the first breeder.'[57] The UPOV Convention also has an exception for farmers to save seeds over the years (ie without having to pay a royalty). These exceptions do not appear as such in the TRIPs Agreement, but if they respect the four-step test then no conflicts occur. Indeed, it is generally agreed that TRIPs Article 30 allows the research and farm saved seed exemptions.[58] Neither the UPOV Convention nor the TRIPs Agreement refers to a potential conflict as to exceptions. TRIPs Article 31 gives options to members to include compulsory licences in their national laws. The conditions member states must respect if they do so are set out in considerable detail in Article 31. UPOV Article 17 is more general. It states:

> Except where expressly provided in this Convention, no Contracting Party may restrict the free exercise of a breeder's right for reasons other than of public interest.

It goes on to add in the following paragraph that in these cases, an equitable remuneration needs to be paid to the breeder. In addition:

> there is no suggestion in the essential derivation provision that the breeder of an essentially derived variety should be able to force the breeder of the initial variety to grant a licence through some compulsory licence procedure. This possibility was considered and rejected in the course of the revision process.[59]

Conflicts may occur at regional/national level if member states' laws do not match their further exceptions in both areas.

[55] Gervais, *The TRIPs Agreement* (n 15) 236, para 2.282. *Contra*: Correa, *Trade Related Aspects of Intellectual Property Rights* (n 15) 296, referring to the Doha Declaration which states that a compulsory licence is required in order to export a patented medicine.

[56] Gervais (n 15) 236, para 2.282.

[57] Llewelyn and Adcock, *European Plant Intellectual Property* (n 47) 178.

[58] Ibid 109.

[59] Greengrass, 'The 1991 Act of the UPOV Convention' (n 45) 466, 471.

The UPOV Convention has a detailed provision on exhaustion (Article 16). Since the TRIPs Agreement does not, possible conflicts on this issue do not arise at international level, but can do so at regional or national level.

B Negative Overlap

Negative overlap is clearly possible, as the TRIPs Agreement specifically allows it. It will depend on the regional and national laws in question.

C *A Posteriori* Overlap

The duration of a patent is 20 years (TRIPs Article 33) and for most plant varieties as well (UPOV Article 19). However, the duration of the plant variety right for trees and vines is no less than 25 years.[60] So a patent could be 'prolonged' by a plant variety right. In addition, the requirement of novelty is not as strict as that in patent law. Therefore, it may be possible to apply for a plant variety right after having applied for a patent as long as the invention was not commercialised (UPOV Article 6), again allowing an overlap *a posteriori*. Moreover, durations in both the TRIPs Agreement and the UPOV Convention are minima, so *a posteriori* overlaps could occur at national or regional level if member states decide to grant longer protections to either plant variety rights or to patents.

Finally, it must be briefly noted that there cannot be an overlap between trademark and the denomination that must be given to a plant variety because the UPOV Convention specifically forbids it (Article 20).

IX. INTELLECTUAL PROPERTY RIGHTS AND UNFAIR COMPETITION

A Intellectual Property Rights and Trade Secrets (Confidential Information)

The two relevant legal instruments in the field of unfair competition law are the Paris Convention and the TRIPs Agreement. The Paris Convention does not include confidential information as part of industrial property and does not deal with it, although it might be argued that, implicitly, it could be covered by Article 10*bis*. TRIPs Article 39(1) provides that:

> In the course of ensuring effective protection against unfair competition as provided in article 10bis of the Paris Convention (1967), Members shall protect undisclosed information in accordance with paragraph 2 and data submitted to governments or governmental agencies in accordance with paragraph 3.

Thus, the TRIPs Agreement includes the protection of undisclosed information within the prohibition of unfair competition and does not consider it as an exclusive IPR.[61] Therefore, member countries are not obliged 'to confer exclusive rights on undisclosed

[60] Tritton *et al*, *Intellectual Property in Europe* (n 43) 599 ('This [difference in duration] was justified on the grounds that the protection that was thereby conferred could be tailored to suit the specific biological and commercial requirements of the different plant varieties').

[61] Correa (n 15) 367–68.

information, but just protect it against unfair commercial practices'.[62] In other words, Article 39(2) makes clear that members are not obliged to go beyond the requirements of the Paris Convention.[63] Of course, 'what is protected is not really undisclosed information (since, if no one has disclosed it to anyone, it could not be used at all), but rather information disclosed selectively and under precise conditions'.[64] The information does not have to be inventive or creative[65] but it can be.

The TRIPs Agreement does not expressly envisage any overlap concerning confidential information. Normally, as patent specifications must disclose the invention there should not be an overlap, but sometimes there could be one. For instance, in the case of software, the code does not always need to be disclosed; as long as the invention can be made by a person skilled in the art without him or her needing to know the source code, the patent is valid. Therefore, the source code of the invention often remains secret, creating an overlap which is anti-competitive because competitors need interoperability in order to compete in the same or a secondary market.[66] The overlap could be simultaneous, negative and *a posteriori*. Under Article 39(3), there could be an overlap between any copyright in the data compiled and protection of it as confidential information. The overlap could be simultaneous, negative and *a posteriori*.

B Intellectual Property Rights and Other Acts of Unfair Competition

It is not clear whether the TRIPs Agreement includes the repression of unfair competition as a whole. According to the most commonly accepted interpretation, the TRIPs Agreement does not require that member states give protection against unfair competition, apart from undisclosed information and geographical indications (TRIPs Article 22(2)(b) states that, for geographical indications only, Article 10bis of the Paris Convention must be respected).[67] Apart from the provisions on the protection of trade secrets and geographical indications, no other provision exists that directly relates to unfair competition law.[68] The TRIPs Agreement thus only provides protection against unfair competition in a few specific cases.[69] But according to some, and on the face of the text of the agreement, TRIPs Article 2(1) requires member states to comply with Paris Article 10*bis* on unfair competition.[70] A ruling of the Court of Justice also seems to favour this opinion. In 2000, the Court held that:

[62] Ibid 368.
[63] Ibid.
[64] Gervais (n 15) 74, para 2.355 et seq.
[65] Correa (n 15) 373.
[66] G Ghidini and E Arezzo, 'One, None or a Hundred Thousand: How Many Layers of Protection for Software Innovations?' in J Drexl (ed), *Research Handbook on Intellectual Property and Competition Law* (Cheltenham, Edward Elgar Publishing, 2008) 363.
[67] R de Vrey, *Towards a European Unfair Competition Law: A Clash between Legal Families* (Leiden, Martinus Nijhoff, 2006) 18, 24; F Henning Bodewig, *Unfair Competition Law: European Union and Member States* (The Hague, Kluwer Law International, 2006) 22.
[68] De Vrey, *Towards a European Unfair Competition Law* (n 67) 18; Henning Bodewig, *Unfair Competition Law: European Union and Member States* (n 67) 22.
[69] De Vrey (n 67) 17.
[70] Correa, *Trade Related Aspects of Intellectual Property Rights* (n 15) 38. See also T Cottier and A Jevtic, 'The Protection against Unfair Competition in WTO Law: Status, Potential and Prospects' in J Drexl (ed), *Technology and Competition: Contributions in honour of Hanns Ullrich (Technologie et concurrence, Mélanges en l'honneur de Hanns Ullrich)* (Brussels, Larcier, 2009) 670, 677.

> Article 50 of TRIPs leaves to the Contracting Parties, within the framework of their own legal systems, the task of specifying whether the right to sue under general provisions of national law concerning wrongful acts, in particular unlawful competition, in order to protect an industrial design against copying is to be classified as an 'intellectual property right' within the meaning of Article 50(1) of TRIPs.[71]

The 'final answer as to the precise scope of article 10*bis* as part of TRIPs law'[72] is in the hands of one of the WTO panels or the Appellate Body. If the first interpretation is correct, there can only potentially be an implicit overlap between the protection against unfair competition and geographical indications. If the second interpretation is correct, the possible overlaps are more numerous.

Paris Article 1(2) states that the repression of unfair competition is part of industrial property. Since the 1911 Washington revision of the Convention, Article 10*bis* provides protection against unfair competition.[73] It states:

> (1) The countries of the Union are bound to assure to nationals of such countries effective protection against unfair competition.
> (2) Any act of competition contrary to honest practices in industrial or commercial matters constitutes an act of unfair competition.
> (3) The following in particular shall be prohibited:
>   1. all acts of such a nature as to create confusion by any means whatever with the establishment, the goods, or the industrial or commercial activities, of a competitor;
>   2. false allegations in the course of trade of such a nature as to discredit the establishment, the goods, or the industrial or commercial activities, of a competitor;
>   3. indications or allegations the use of which in the course of trade is liable to mislead the public as to the nature, the manufacturing process, the characteristics, the suitability for their purpose, or the quantity, of the goods.

Paris Article 10*bis* therefore does not require members to provide that the parties have to compete against each other.[74] However, because of the words an 'act of competition' in Article 10*bis*(2), 'the allegedly unfair act should be trade related and be liable to distort free competition'.[75] Thus, as long as the act can distort competition, all three possible overlaps (simultaneous, negative and *a posteriori*) can occur with potentially all IPRs protected by the international instruments reviewed above. The text of Paris Article 10*bis*(3)(1) suggests an implicit overlap between unfair competition law and trademark law which requires likelihood of confusion for there to be trademark infringement.[76] As Article 10*bis*(2) is very general,[77] if a country's unfair competition prohibits slavish imitation or parasitism without requiring a risk of confusion, there could be overlaps with all IPRs whose infringement provisions require copying (eg copyright, unregistered design). But

[71] Cases C-300/98 and C-392/98 *Parfums Christian Dior* [2000] ECR I-1307. See also Correa (n 15) 39.

[72] Cottier and Jevtic, 'The Protection against Unfair Competition in WTO Law' (n 70) 670, 677.

[73] De Vrey, (n 67) 12. Henning Bodewig (n 67) 19 also notes that there is little literature on the Paris Convention.

[74] De Vrey, (n 67) 12.

[75] Ibid 13 n 11.

[76] See also Correa (n 15) 258; de Vrey (n 67) 14. For well-known marks (Paris Art 6*bis* and TRIPs Art 16(3)), confusion is not necessary but the overlap between unfair competition and trademark laws can then occur by using Paris Art 10bis(2).

[77] There is unanimous agreement that those acts which do not fall into Paris Art 10*bis*(3) can nevertheless be acts of unfair competition because of the generality of Art 10bis(2). Henning Bodewig (n 67) 20. Ibid 19–20 also notes that the distinction between Paris Art 10*bis* and IPR is not clarified.

this latter overlap will be a regional or national issue. According to some, TRIPs Article 25(2) 'seems to rule out the application of other systems, such as unfair competition'.[78] However, such a construction would bluntly contradict the Paris Convention, which TRIPs member states must respect. Article 25(2) most likely just *requires* copyright or design right for designs but does not rule out additional layers of protection.

X. CONCLUSION: IDENTIFICATION OF PRINCIPLES GOVERNING OVERLAPS IN THE INTERNATIONAL AGREEMENTS AND REMAINING OPEN QUESTIONS

As can now be seen, generally, international instruments are silent on possible overlaps. However, most of the time, their broad language implicitly allows an overlap. More rarely is an overlap clearly allowed (works of applied art and designs in the Berne Convention, and patents and plant variety rights in the TRIPs Agreement). However, whether they allow overlaps explicitly or implicitly, the instruments do not provide any rule to organise the overlap. Any principles governing overlaps in the international instruments must necessarily be found in their general rules of interpretation. These are found in their Preambles and sometimes in the provisions of the instruments themselves.

By far the greatest number (and the most elaborated) of the rules which can help in interpreting any overlaps are to be found in the TRIPs Agreement. Whilst the Preamble to the TRIPs Agreement obviously first insists on the protection of IPRs, one of its paragraphs, located right in the middle, also states:

> Recognizing the underlying public policy objectives of national systems for the protection of intellectual property, including developmental and technological objectives . . .

This is echoed in TRIPs Article 7, which is entitled 'Objectives':

> The protection and enforcement of intellectual property rights should contribute to the promotion of technological innovation and to the transfer and dissemination of technology, to the mutual advantage of producers and users of technological knowledge and in a manner conducive to social and economic welfare, and to a balance of rights and obligations.

TRIPs Article 8, entitled 'Principles', in paragraph (2), can also help in interpreting the overlaps. It provides:

> Appropriate measures, provided that they are consistent with the provisions of this Agreement, may be needed to prevent the abuse of intellectual property rights by right holders or the resort to practices which unreasonably restrain trade or adversely affect the international transfer of technology.

First, the express recognition in the Preamble of other interests or objectives than those of IPR holders is an important aspect to note. The fact that it is reiterated in Article 7 makes that article an important interpretative tool for the whole agreement. Even though nothing in Articles 7 and 8 of the TRIPs Agreement really concerns the issue of overlaps, principles or rules to regulate the overlaps can usefully be derived from their interpretation. In the following, the meaning of Article 7 will first be set out, and secondly, its effect will be considered. Article 8 will then be scrutinised and finally, the other international instruments.

[78] Correa, (n 15) 265.

A TRIPs Articles 7 and 8

(i) Meaning of TRIPs Article 7

TRIPs Article 7 can be broken down into several aspects. Article 7 is in essence a compromise between the 'prevailing justification for the granting of IPRs in the technology-related fields, as a tool for the promotion of innovation, but also the developing countries' concerns about transfer and dissemination of technology'.[79] So, most importantly, IPRs should not only promote the development of new technologies but also further their dissemination. A second aspect is that this should happen 'in a manner conducive to social and economic welfare'. 'This means that the recognition and enforcement of intellectual property rights are subject to higher social values (as further developed in article 8.1 of the agreement)'[80] and it has been argued that this includes human rights. The third and final aspect in fact goes back to the first essential element, that of balance between the promotion of innovation and access to it. The TRIPs Agreement's requirement that IPRs should lead to a 'balance of rights and obligations' confirms that 'IPRs can be seen neither as an end in themselves nor as absolute rights, but subject to appropriate balances'.[81] Some commentators have added that this 'shows that the balance of rights and obligations should be assessed using well-established principles of intellectual property law. Indeed, the reference to the "promotion of technological innovation and to transfer and dissemination of technology, to the mutual advantage of producers and users of technological knowledge" is a summary of the most important such principles'.[82] Intellectual property policy is thus considered at international level as a balance between rewarding creators and taking the interests of the public into account. Thus, according to Gervais, 'on the policy level, this translates into a need to grant investors rights that are necessary to recoup the investment without stifling competition for an *unduly long period of time*'[83] (emphasis added).

Finally, it must be stated that not only should the previous drafts of the TRIPs Agreement help us understand the actual text of the Agreement, they may also have legal value.[84] 'Under traditional GATT law and practice, drafting history is often referred to as a guide' in trying 'to interpret the meaning and scope of a provision'.[85] In this connection, it is interesting to note that a previous draft of the TRIPs Agreement (23 July 1990, W/76) said in relevant part that 'parties agree that this balance of rights and obligations inherent in all systems of intellectual property rights should be observed', which is much

[79] Ibid 91–92.

[80] Ibid 99–101. See eg the High Commissioner's Report to the 52nd session of the Commission on Human Rights, Sub-Commission on the Promotion and Protection of Human Rights, *The Impact on the Agreement on Trade-Related Aspects of Intellectual Property Rights on Human Rights*, E/CN.4/sub.2/2001/13, June 2001, para 28: 'the TRIPs agreement offers significant operational flexibility and the High Commissioner urges Member States of the WTO to use this operational flexibility in ways that would be fully compatible with the promotion and protection of human rights. In this regard, it is important to note that out of 141 members of the WTO 111 have ratified the ICESCR'.

[81] Correa (n 15) 101. See also UNCTAD-ICTSD, *Resource Book on TRIPs and Development* (Cambridge, Cambridge University Press, 2005) 125–26.

[82] Gervais (n 15) 117, para 2.76, citing M McGrath, 'The Patent Provisions in TRIPs: Protecting Reasonable Remuneration for Services Rendered – or the Latest Development in Western Colonialism' (1996) 7 *European Intellectual Property Review* 398.

[83] Gervais (n 15) 117, para 2.76.

[84] Ibid 74, para 2.02.

[85] Ibid.

stronger language than the current text. The same draft of Article 8 was also much more open:

> each party will take measures it deems appropriate with a view to preventing the abuse of intellectual property rights or the resort to practices which unreasonably restrain trade or adversely affect the international transfer of technology. Parties undertake to consult each other and to co-operate in this regard.

(ii) Effect of TRIPs Article 7

Even though TRIPs Article 7 states the objectives of only some IPRs, namely those which involve technological innovation (ie patents, some categories of trade secrets, topographies of semi-conductor chips and designs), it does not mean that Article 7's narrow scope has no relevance for other IPRs.[86] The overall general objectives of the TRIPs Agreement are set out in the Agreement's Preamble in paragraphs 1 to 4.[87] Although the term 'balance' does not appear in the Preamble, the WTO system's main goal is an adequate balance of rights and obligations,[88] therefore notwithstanding the limited number of IPRs named in Article 7, the same principle arguably applies to all IPRs covered by TRIPs.

In sum, Article 7 is an important tool in interpreting and implementing the rights and obligations throughout the agreement.[89] This assertion is also found in article 3(5) of the WTO Dispute Settlement Understanding (DSU) and has been confirmed many times by panels.[90] In addition, and of note, in paragraph 19 of the Doha Declaration on the TRIPs Agreement and Public Health, the Ministerial Conference also highlighted the importance of Articles 7 and 8 as guides for implementing the Agreement,[91] stating, for instance, that the articles could be used to 'legitimis[e] exceptions to exclusive rights, such as for fair use in the copyright field, and research and humanitarian access to drugs in the context of patent rights'.[92] The Declaration also 'confirmed the interpretative value of article 7 *for each provision* of the agreement'[93] (emphasis added). According to the Declaration, all articles of the TRIPs Agreement must be read in the light of its object and purpose, in particular, its objectives and principles.[94] Customary rules of interpretation of public international law provide that supplementary means of interpretation (ie the *travaux préparatoires* and the circumstances of the conclusion of the treaty in question) may be used to confirm, but only to confirm, the interpretation arrived at by the application of the primary rules of interpretation.[95] Even if the Doha Declaration attached great importance to Articles 7 and 8, it will probably have no effect on their legal status.[96] However, a panel

[86] Pires de Carvalho, *The TRIPs Regime of Patent Rights* (n 42) 111; Correa (n 15) 92; P Yu, 'The Objectives and Principles of the TRIPs Agreement' (2009) 46(4) *Houston Law Review* 979, 1000.

[87] Pires de Carvalho, *The TRIPs Regime of Patent Rights* (n 42) 110.

[88] Correa (n 15) 92.

[89] Ibid 91–92.

[90] Pires de Carvalho, *The TRIPs Regime of Patent Rights* (n 42) 111.

[91] Correa, (n 15) 103; Gervais (n 15) 120, para 2.80; Llewelyn and Adcock, *European Plant Intellectual Property* (n 47) 103, however, noting that 'the use of these articles and plant related inventions remains unclear'.

[92] Correa (n 15) 103.

[93] Ibid.

[94] Ibid.

[95] Ricketson and Ginsburg, *International Copyright and Neighbouring Rights* (n 4) 198.

[96] Gervais (n 4) 120, para 2.80. See also Yu, 'The Objectives and Principles of the TRIPs Agreement' (n 86) 1004.

may be inclined to 'take a longer look at how these provisions should be interpreted in the context of the agreement as a whole, especially with respect to the need for "balance"'.[97]

Not only is Article 7 an important interpretative tool because of its content, but also because of its place in the Agreement. As it is within the text of the Agreement itself rather than simply in its Preamble, this heightens and thus strengthens its legal status.[98] This also means that panels and the WTO Appellate Body must take Article 7 into consideration when interpreting the whole agreement, as the panel in *Canada – Patent Protection for Pharmaceutical Products* clearly did.[99] It held: '[b]oth the goals and the limitations stated in articles 7 and 8.1 must obviously be borne in mind when doing so as well as those of other provisions of the TRIPs agreement which indicate its subject and purposes'.[100] Thus, according to some commentators, the TRIPs Agreement must both induce innovation *and* access to the results thereof.[101] In other words, as has been said, 'the objectives of the patent system would not be fulfilled if it only served to induce innovations to the benefit of those who control them'.[102] As the TRIPs Agreement is part of the WTO legal system as a whole and that system's overriding objective is a proper balance of rights and obligations, TRIPs Articles 7 and 8 must be interpreted in accordance with such appropriate balance.[103]

What can be drawn from these reflections in respect of the issue of overlaps? It would seem that according to TRIPs Article 7, if any overlap occurs in national law as a result of the explicit or implicit permission of the TRIPs Agreement, a balance must be maintained between rights-holders and the public interest, and competition should not be stifled for an unduly long period of time. Human rights will be relevant public interests here. In other words, if a particular combination of rights overprotects the rights-holders in the sense that competition is stifled for too long, then the right(s) should be curtailed or trimmed or else made to converge. If necessary, the overlap may have to be prohibited. For example, if the combined effect of two rights is to restrict the exceptions so that users can benefit from fewer of them than if only one type of IPR was applicable, this could be said in some cases to stifle competition 'for too long', especially if the right in question has a long duration, such as copyright law. This would be a powerful statement; first, this 'rule' will by definition apply in all countries who adhere to the TRIPs Agreement and can be enforced by the WTO panels; and secondly, it applies to all IPRs (at least all those included in the TRIPs Agreement which, for instance, does not include

97 Ibid 999–1000 argues that the Doha Declaration could itself constitute a subsequent agreement regarding the interpretation of the TRIPs Agreement, which panels and the WTO Appellate Body should take into consideration when interpreting the TRIPs Agreement and thus Arts 7 and 8, according to Art 31(1) of the Vienna Convention.

98 Correa (n 15) 93; Gervais (n 15) 116, para 2. 75.

99 Correa (n 15) 93.

100 Ibid 93–94, quoting from the panel. However, as P Yu notes, 'neither the Appellate Body nor the WTO panels have made any definitive interpretation and application of Articles 7 and 8 of the TRIPs agreement'. Yu, 'The Objectives and Principles of the TRIPs Agreement' (n 86) 994.

101 Correa (n 15) 94. It is interesting to note that '[th]e use of "should" in article 7 seems to indicate that IPRs do not necessarily promote innovation and dissemination and transfer of technology, but that they should do so in order to satisfy the overall objectives of the TRIPs agreement, as stated in the first provision of the preamble. That wording suggests that members must implement their obligations under the agreement in a way that effectively contributes to the objectives of promoting innovation and the transfer *and* dissemination of technology'. Ibid 97.

102 Ibid 94.

103 UNCTAD-ICTSD, *Resource Book on TRIPs and Development* (Cambridge, Cambridge University Press, 2005) 130.

the database right and arguably a big chunk of unfair competition law), and thus to all overlaps.

It could be said that Article 8 elaborates on Article 7. If an IPR is abused, it stifles competition and thus undermines the public interest, likewise if an IPR holder resorts 'to practices which unreasonably restrain trade or adversely affect the international transfer of technology'. So as a preliminary example, it could be said that if an IPR holder attempts to prolong its copyright protection through a trademark and that unreasonably restrains trade, this overlap could be contrary to Articles 7 and 8. These arguments may seem to some a bit general and thus can appear far-fetched or far-reaching, but they seem less so when they are envisaged as applicable on a case by case basis. It is difficult to see a general application of Articles 7 and 8 to the issue of overlaps. If stretched to the maximum, their application might even overrule all overlaps. Surely that cannot be so. But a concrete application of these articles to specific cases may be more likely. Any rule organising the overlaps at regional and national level will thus have to take TRIPs Articles 7 and 8 into account.

B Other International Instruments

The WCT and WPPT strike the same chord as the TRIPs Agreement, not surprisingly perhaps as they built on it and were drafted around the same time. Whilst their Preambles both start by emphasising the importance of copyright and related rights, the Preambles' last clauses state:

> Recognizing the need to maintain a balance between the rights of authors [and in the WPPT: between the rights of performers and producers of phonograms] and the larger public interest, *particularly* education, research and access to information [and the WCT adds: as reflected in the Berne Convention]. (emphasis added)[104]

Under the accepted rule, Preambles serve to interpret the treaty, as prescribed by the Vienna Convention.[105] In addition, a 'preamble is not just an element of the content but an integral part of the treaty concerned, and its status is the same as that of the provisions of the treaty'.[106] Accordingly, the Preambles' objectives will be helpful in interpreting the treaties.[107] Apart from its status and its similar content to that of TRIPs Article 7, what is striking in the WCT Preamble is the fact that the parties acknowledge that this balance already existed in the Berne Convention.[108] Accordingly, the Berne Convention also has to be interpreted according to this principle. Similar conclusions could thus be drawn for the Berne Convention as those for the TRIPs Agreement. As in the TRIPs

[104] As well noted by M Ficsor, *The Law of Copyright and the Internet* (Oxford, Oxford University Press, 2002) 415–16, 'the paragraph speaks about "the *rights* of authors and larger *public interests*" (emphasis added). Since, obviously, interests may only be duly balanced with other interests, this phrase may be regarded as a shorthand version of what it actually seems to mean; namely balancing between the interests of authors – along with the underlying larger public interest in granting "protection of authors in their literary and artistic works in a manner as effective . . . as possible" to providing by this "an incentive for literary and artistic creation" – on the one hand, and on the other hand, the "larger public interests", that is all the other relevant interests of the public.'

[105] Ibid 411.

[106] Ibid.

[107] Ricketson and Ginsburg (n 4) 1234, para 19.36.

[108] Ficsor, *The Law of Copyright and the Internet* (n 104) 415.

Agreement, copyright should also promote dissemination of knowledge. And this is achieved through a balance of rights and obligations. However, the idea of competition is intrinsically not inherent to this balance. Perhaps this is so because copyright has traditionally been seen as less likely than patents to lead to monopolies. Finally, the social and economic welfare aspect is strictly speaking also absent in the WCT, but it can perhaps be partially if not completely achieved by the balance of rights and obligations. This shows that the three components of Article 7's principle are all interlinked, facets of the same thing.

Nevertheless, Berne Article 19 may be seen as an obstacle to this balance of rights and obligations so that, in the end, it is difficult to extract any cogent rule of interpretation about overlaps in the Berne Convention, especially if combined with the express overlap between copyright and designs stated in Article 2(7). Berne Article 19 provides that:

> The provisions of this Convention shall not preclude the making of a claim to the benefit of any greater protection which may be granted by legislation in a country of the Union.

This seems to imply that a copyright work could be protected by another type of protection, be it an IPR or by some other law (unfair competition law comes to mind as an example).[109] In any case, this problem is irrelevant, as the TRIPs Agreement absorbs this article (in view of its incorporation of the Berne Convention and its application of Articles 7 and 8). While TRIPs Article 1 allows member states to grant TRIPs-plus protection, this must not contravene the TRIPs Agreement's provisions, and therefore Articles 7 and 8. This example of potential incompatibility between the Berne Convention and the TRIPs Agreement is not the only one. As Ricketson and Ginsburg explain well, the TRIPs Agreement and the Berne Convention do not have exactly the same goal:

> The TRIPs agreement is clearly an instrumentalist agreement that views intellectual property rights, including copyright, as means for promoting certain trade, economic and social purposes: the rights of authors here are only one aspect of the matrix of interests involved . . . The different objects and purposes of the above agreements therefore create potential difficulties when seeking to interpret and harmonise their provisions *inter se*, notably with respect to those provisions of Berne that are incorporated in the later agreements, such as the WCT and the TRIPs agreement. This is particularly so in the case of TRIPs which incorporates the substantive provisions of Berne (arts 1–21 and the appendix), suggesting that there may ultimately be an irreconcilable area of difference between the two instruments.[110]

However, this reasoning is without consideration to the balance of rights and obligations referred to in WCT and WPPT, which supposedly the Berne Convention should already abide by.

Finally, it is worth mentioning that the 1991 act of the UPOV Convention is silent in terms of interpretation principles. All that can be said is that there is no explicit reference to the public interest in the Convention (except in Article 17), and that the 1991 act has increased the rights of the breeder. Thus, one could think that:

> the primary objective of the convention is now to provide 'effective protection', the benefit to society coming through the provision of protection rather than through any overarching notions

[109] Although Ricketson and Ginsburg (n 4) 351–53 do not seem to interpret the article this way. For them, Arts 19 and 20 must be read together. If Art 19 is read alone, it seems like a most favoured nation (MFN) clause.

[110] Ricketson and Ginsburg (n 4) 197, para 5.27.

> of limiting the rights granted. However, it is also possible to read into the reference to the provision of an effective system which encourages the development of plant varieties for the benefit of society a clear public interest element, not least as it is unlikely that anything which prevented the development of new varieties (for example, through an overly protectionist approach to the provision of protection) would be regarded as benefiting society.[111]

The addition of the broadened breeder's exemption in Article 15(1)(iii) may also confirm this statement.

In conclusion, as the TRIPs Agreement encompasses most IPRs, its principles will apply despite the non-existence or lack of coherence of interpretation rules directly or indirectly relating to overlaps. However, uncertainty remains in respect of part of unfair competition law, as it is unclear whether the TRIPs Agreement only encompasses confidential information and geographical indications in this respect. It is problematic if the TRIPs Agreement only applies to those two subsets of unfair competition law, because unfair competition law can (re)create an IPR by the back door, and TRIPs Articles 7 and 8 cannot apply as the TRIPs Agreement does not govern this part of unfair competition law. It is to be hoped that if ever the issue comes before a WTO panel, and even before the EU and national courts, common sense will dictate a similar approach to that of TRIPs Articles 7 and 8 in these cases, as it would add essential coherence to the framework.

[111] Llewelyn and Adcock, *European Plant Intellectual Property* (n 47) 159.

3

European Law

I. THE LEGAL FRAMEWORK

VIRTUALLY ALL INTELLECTUAL property rights are harmonised at EU level, although the breadth and depth of this harmonisation is different for each IPR.[1] Let us start the presentation of the European legal framework with trademarks and designs, which are the most harmonised so far. The Trademark Directive and Design Directive[2] regulate virtually all substantive aspects of trademarks and designs. Procedural aspects are not harmonised. The Community Trademark Regulation (EC) 207/2009 (CTMR) and Community Design Regulation (EC) 6/2002 create a unitary trademark and design system and thus harmonise procedural and substantive law. Both the Community trademark (CTM) and the Community design are registered at a single office, the Office for the Harmonisation of the Internal Market (OHIM) in Alicante. Patents are not harmonised at EU level but at European level through the European Patent Convention (EPC).[3] All EU Member States are party to that Convention. Only certain aspects of patent law are harmonised in the EPC, in sum patentability requirements, procedural aspects and infringement. The rest remains regulated by national law. In addition, there is one Directive, the so-called Biotech Directive,[4] which harmonises certain aspects of patentability for biotechnological inventions and some aspects of the interface between plant variety rights and patents. Plant variety rights also have their Regulation and thus there is a unitary plant variety right;[5] however, there is no Directive harmonising national laws in that respect. Copyright is still the least harmonised IPR in the European Union with seven Directives all harmonising only parts of copyright.[6] Only

[1] As previously stated in the introduction to the book, this chapter will not deal with the *sui generis* right for topographies of semi-conductor products, as this IPR is hardly used in practice. However, it must be noted that Council Directive 87/54/EEC of 16 December 1986 on the legal protection of topographies of semiconductor products [1987] OJ L24/36 has harmonised this right.

[2] Directive 2008/95/EC of the European Parliament and of the Council of 22 October 2008 to approximate the laws of the Member States relating to trade marks (codified version) [2008] OJ L299/25; Directive 98/71/EC of 13 October 1998 on the legal protection of designs [1998] OJ L289/28.

[3] Convention on the Grant of European Patents of 5 October 1973 as amended by the act revising EPC Art 63 of 17 December 1991, by decisions of the Administrative Council of the European Patent Organisation of 21 December 1978, 13 December 1994, 20 October 1995, 5 December 1996, 10 December 1998 and 27 October 2005 and EPC Revision Act of 29 November 2000.

[4] Directive 98/44/EC of the European Parliament and of the Council of 6 July 1998 on the legal protection of biotechnological inventions [1998] OJ L213/13.

[5] Council Regulation (EC) 2100/94 of 27 July 1994 on Community plant variety rights [1994] OJ L227/1.

[6] Directive 2009/24/EC of 23 April 2009 on the legal protection of computer programs (codified version) [2009] OJ L111/16 ('Software Directive'); Directive 2006/115/EC of the European Parliament and of the Council of 12 December 2006 on rental right and lending right and on certain rights related to copyright in the field of intellectual property [2006] OJ L376/28; Directive 2006/116/EC of the European Parliament and of the Council

the Software Directive 2009/24/EC and the Infosoc Directive 2001/29/EC will be discussed as they are the only ones relevant for the issue of overlaps. Finally, unfair competition is even less harmonised than copyright. The only instruments are the Unfair Commercial Practices Directive (UCPD) and the Misleading and Comparative Advertising Directive (MCAD).[7] All these instruments are, of course, accompanied by recitals, Explanatory Memoranda and Green Papers which assist in interpreting the legislative texts and will also be discussed in the course of the chapter.

II. COPYRIGHT AND DESIGNS

A The Legal Framework

Before starting the description of the statutory law for this overlap, it is important to note that two types of overlaps occur with regard to EU law. As for any overlap, there is of course an overlap as to the content of the laws, but there is also an overlap as to the level of the laws. Thus, there can be an overlap between different levels for the same right: for instance between national registered design and Community registered design. Finally, there can also be a 'mixed' overlap, ie one between the content and the level, eg copyright and the Community registered design right (CRDR). Content and level overlaps will be explored further below whilst mixed overlaps will be explored in the chapters on national law.

The two Directives in the field of copyright which may concern possible overlaps with designs are the Software Directive and the Infosoc Directive. Software Directive, article 9 leaves it open to Member States to protect software by other rights. Whilst it does not list designs, the clause uses the term 'such as', clearly indicating that the list is not exhaustive. The overlap between copyright and design rights is, on the other hand, clearly allowed by Infosoc Directive, recital 60 and article 9. Article 9 states in relevant part:

> Continued application of other legal provisions. This Directive shall be without prejudice to provisions concerning in particular . . . design rights.[8]

of 12 December 2006 on the term of protection of copyright and certain related rights [2006] OJ L372/12; Directive 2001/84/EC of the European Parliament and of the Council of 27 September 2001 on the resale right for the benefit of the author of an original work of art [2001] OJ L272/32; Directive 2001/29/EC of the European Parliament and of the Council of 22 May 2001 on the harmonisation of certain aspects of copyright and related rights in the information society [2001] OJ L16/107 ('Infosoc Directive'); Directive 96/9/EC of the European Parliament and of the Council of 11 March 1996 on the legal protection of databases [1996] OJ L77/20; Council Directive 93/83/EEC of 27 September 1993 on the coordination of certain rules concerning copyright and rights related to copyright applicable to satellite broadcasting and cable retransmission [1993] OJ L248/15.

[7] Directive 2005/29/EC of the European Parliament and of the Council of 11 May 2005 concerning unfair business-to-consumer commercial practices in the internal market and amending Council Directive 84/450/EEC, Directives 97/7/EC, 98/27/EC and 2002/65/EC of the European Parliament and of the Council and Regulation (EC) 2006/2004 of the European Parliament and of the Council ('Unfair Commercial Practices Directive') [2005] OJ L149/22 and Directive 2006/114/EC of the European Parliament and of the Council of 12 December 2006 concerning misleading and comparative advertising (codified version) [2006] OJ L376/21.

[8] Recital 60 reads: 'The protection provided under this Directive should be without prejudice to national or Community legal provisions in other areas, such as industrial property, data protection, conditional access, access to public documents, and the rule of media exploitation chronology, which may affect the protection of copyright or related rights'.

It must be noted that recital 20 specifically avoids any conflicts that could emerge from the new general rules laid down in the Infosoc Directive and the previous rules laid down in the prior copyright Directives. Recital 20 reads:

> This Directive is based on principles and rules already laid down in the Directives currently in force in this area, in particular Directives 91/250/EEC, 92/100/EEC, 93/83/EEC, 93/98/EEC and 96/9/EC, and it develops those principles and rules and places them in the context of the information society. The provisions of this Directive should be without prejudice to the provisions of those Directives, unless otherwise provided in this Directive.

The same is restated in Infosoc Directive, article 1(2):

> Except in the cases referred to in Article 11, this Directive shall leave intact and shall in no way affect existing Community provisions relating to: (a) the legal protection of computer programs; (b) rental right, lending right and certain rights related to copyright in the field of intellectual property; (c) copyright and related rights applicable to broadcasting of programmes by satellite and cable retransmission; (d) the term of protection of copyright and certain related rights; (e) the legal protection of databases.

Whilst the overlap between copyright and design right is allowed, there are no rules in either Directive to organise any conflicts that may result from it. There is not much either in the amended proposal for a Directive on the legal protection of computer programs,[9] the Green Paper on copyright and the challenge of technology,[10] its follow-up,[11] nor the Green Paper on copyright and related rights in the information society.[12] However, the latter Green Paper has a section entitled 'The danger that the internal market may relapse into fragmentation', which appears in a section reviewing all the then current and proposed Directives in the field of copyright,[13] and which interestingly states that:

> The Commission must keep a close eye on the nature and consequences of any regulations introduced, in order to ensure that the overall framework will be coherent in the future . . . The Commission must make a special effort to ensure that the desire to regulate is reasonable, and that regulation does not simply respond to isolated requests for action on a one-off basis. All rulemaking must be subject to rigorous evaluation in the light of the objectives of the internal market and the principle of proportionality. One major concern must be to prevent any new fragmentation of the internal market, which might be the result if national rules were to diverge from those of other Member States, or were incompatible with the requirements of the internal market and hampered the free movement of services in the European Union.[14]

This puts an onus on the Commission to monitor the coherence of its now extensive legislation in the field of intellectual property, and it certainly applies to the area of overlaps. But not much is to be gleaned on how exactly the Commission is to do this. All that seems to underlie this promise is the internal market objectives, including, of course, the free movement of services, and we imagine that of goods as well. Thus, an overarching principle that could be used if overlaps between IPRs were to happen within the European

[9] COM(90)509 final (Brussels, 18 October 1990).
[10] COM(88)172 final (Brussels, 7 June 1988).
[11] COM(90)584 final (Brussels, 17 January 1991).
[12] COM(95)382 final (Brussels, 19 July 1995).
[13] Ibid 32. Note that there is a new Green Paper on Copyright in the Knowledge Economy, COM(2008)466/3, available at http://ec.europa.eu/internal_market/copyright/docs/copyright-infso/greenpaper_en.pdf, and already a Follow-up Paper, although no Directive proposals have yet been issued.
[14] COM(95)382 final, 32–33.

legislation is the free movement of goods and services. If an overlap unjustifiably hampers it, a solution must be found to allow this free movement. As will be seen, this is a *leitmotiv* which is constantly repeated in the case law of the EU courts in the field of copyright/trademark/designs overlaps.[15]

In contrast with the legal instruments in the field of copyright, the Green Paper on the Legal Protection of Industrial Design[16] abounds in rules regulating overlaps and the Design Directive 98/71/EC and Design Regulation (EC) 6/2002 which came out of it reflect some of them. They can be classified in different categories and will be examined in turn: (1) general rules concerning overlaps (importance of keeping competition effective, general allowance of overlaps); (2) rules for overlaps between different types of rights in terms of their content (designs, patents and copyright); and (3) rules regarding overlaps between different levels of rights (national and Community rights).

(i) General Rules

The Green Paper starts by prudently stating that '[t]he creation of the Community design right will probably have an impact on design activities which can hardly be foreseen today'.[17] It goes on to say that '[t]his will therefore, in all likelihood, require, also in the future, a dynamic legislative activity by the Community, to remove or smooth out unwanted effects and to proceed towards a more intimately unified system of protection'.[18] In short, the rules relating to the overlaps laid down in the Green Paper are not set in stone and the Commission is ready to review them as things develop, especially if they create some problems. So far the Commission has not acted upon this but initiatives such as this book will provide some suggestions. The next section of the Green Paper ('3.11. Establishing a balance between the rights of the design owner and the interests of third parties and of the public at large') addresses the important issue of competition. The Green Paper states:

> The grant of exclusive rights to design owners must be carefully weighed against other considerations in order to avoid unduly restrictive effects on legitimate competition. This problem *particularly* arises with functional designs in which case a technological innovation is very often involved. It is important that due regard be paid to the interests of third parties and of the public at large in defining the rules which should govern exclusive rights under a Community solution. (emphasis added)[19]

This passage emphasises the importance the Commission places on free competition, which the EU courts and other legislative instruments have also insisted on in the past (see eg Software Directive, recital 27; Database Directive, recital 47). The Green Paper

[15] See a recent case in this respect, Case C-456/06 *Peek and Cloppenburg v Cassina* [2008] ECR I-2731, and the Advocate-General's Opinion, discussed by M Leistner, 'Copyright Law in the EC: Status Quo, Recent Case Law and Policy Perspectives' (2009) 46 *Common Market Law Review* 847, 860–65. In this case, chairs were exposed in a shop in Germany where their design was protected by copyright but had been imported from Italy where it was not. The question was whether the right of distribution was exhausted by the first transfer of ownership (here sale) of these chairs in a country (here Italy) where copyright was not available for their design.

[16] III/F/5131/91-EN (Brussels, June 1991).

[17] See European Commission, Green Paper on the Legal Protection of Industrial Design, Working Doc. 111/F/5131/91–EN (June 1991) 40, under the heading '3.10. Relationship of a Community-wide design with other forms of protection'.

[18] Ibid.

[19] See Green Paper on the Legal Protection of Industrial Design (n 17) 40.

addresses the issue later on when discussing functional designs. These three sentences could provide one of the rules to govern the overlaps. If a particular cumulation between designs and another IPR, or even another type of right (seemingly only unfair competition or civil liability if it is not considered as part of intellectual property, see Design Directive, article 16 and Design Regulation, article 96(1)) unduly restricts legitimate competition, then a solution may have to be found to restore effective competition.

The Green Paper specifically allows overlaps in general. Its general approach is that there should be no interference with the other IPRs, at least when the Directive and Regulation were first introduced into EU legislation.[20] This is reflected in Design Directive, recital 7 and article 16[21] and Design Regulation, recital 31 and article 96(1).[22] However, the Green Paper then goes on to add that '[t]he position should be reconsidered in the context of the further harmonisation of the laws of copyright of the Member States'.[23] Again, this is an explicit invitation to review any problem that may arise, for instance from any overlaps created by the new design legislation. Interestingly though, and by contrast with Infosoc Directive, article 9, neither the Design Directive in article 16 nor the Design Regulation in article 96(1) allow for the same overlaps. Of relevance to designs, neither topographies of semiconductor products nor contract law, for instance, are cited. Since the term 'in particular' is also omitted, it seems that the overlap between designs and topographies and between designs and contract law are not allowed. Although this book does not deal with the relationship between IPRs and contract law, nor that of IPRs and topographies of semiconductor products, it is worth stating that a combined reading of Design Directive, recital 7 and article 16 and Design Regulation, recital 31 and article 96(1) (possibly) does not allow the holder of a design right to override the right's limits by contract.

We can now elaborate on the extent and consequences of the several overlaps identified above. As seen in the introduction to the book, there are three types of overlaps: simultaneous, negative and *a posteriori*. Simultaneous overlaps happen when it is possible for a subject matter to be protected at the same time by one right and by another, or several others, and lasts until the expiration of one of the rights. Negative overlaps occur when it is not possible to obtain the protection of one right but another right is able to fill this gap. *A posteriori* overlaps occur when it is (still) possible to obtain the protection of one right when another has expired.

[20] Ibid ch 11 'Community design and other legal instruments of protection: the general approach to problem', 141–42.

[21] Recital 7: '(7) Whereas this Directive does not exclude the application to designs of national or Community legislation providing for protection other than that conferred by registration or publication as design, such as legislation relating to unregistered design rights, trademarks, patents and utility models, unfair competition or civil liability'.

Article 16: 'Relationship to other forms of protection. The provisions of this Directive shall be without prejudice to any provisions of Community law or of the law of the Member State concerned relating to unregistered design rights, trademarks or other distinctive signs, patents and utility models, typefaces, civil liability or unfair competition'.

[22] Recital 31: '(31) This Regulation does not preclude the application to designs protected by Community designs of the industrial property laws or other relevant laws of the Member States, such as those relating to design protection acquired by registration or those relating to unregistered designs, trademarks, patents and utility models, unfair competition or civil liability'. (This is almost identical to the Design Directive's corresponding recital.)

Article 96: 'Relationship to other forms of protection under national law. 1. The provisions of this Regulation shall be without prejudice to any provisions of Community law or of the law of the Member States concerned relating to unregistered designs, trademarks or other distinctive signs, patents and utility models, typefaces, civil liability and unfair competition'. (Identical to the Design Directive's corresponding article.)

[23] Green Paper on the Legal Protection of Industrial Design (n 17) 142.

B 'Content Overlap'

This section discusses the content overlap between copyright and design without distinguishing between Community registered design right (CRDR), Community unregistered design right (CUDR) and national registered design right (RDR), as the provisions of these three rights are virtually identical.

(i) Simultaneous Overlap

(a) Subject Matter

The Green Paper imposes the cumulation of copyright with both national and Community registered designs.[24] This is reflected in Design Directive, recital 8 and article 17[25] and Design Regulation, recital 32 and article 96(2).[26] At the level of the subject matter, there can be an overlap between copyright and design, as any two- or three-dimensional artistic work (depending how they are protected in each Member State as this copyright subject matter has not yet been harmonised at EU level[27]) can also be a design in view of the very broad definition of design in the Design Directive and Regulation. Neither the Software Directive, the Design Directive nor the Design Regulation regulates the possibility of an overlap between design law and copyright law for preparatory design work. While this overlap is most certainly only academic (as one can hardly imagine that a company would register a flowchart as a design), nevertheless, the CRDR is automatic, so cumulation between copyright and CRDR for flowcharts is possible and can bring advantages. It is extremely unlikely that there would be an overlap

[24] Ibid 143.

[25] Recital 8: '(8) Whereas, in the absence of harmonisation of copyright law, it is important to establish the principle of cumulation of protection under specific registered design protection law and under copyright law, whilst leaving Member States free to establish the extent of copyright protection and the conditions under which such protection is conferred'.

Article 17: 'Relationship to copyright. A design protected by a design right registered in or in respect of a Member State in accordance with this Directive shall also be eligible for protection under the law of copyright of that State as from the date on which the design was created or fixed in any form. The extent to which, and the conditions under which, such a protection is conferred, including the level of originality required, shall be determined by each Member State'.

[26] Recital 32: '(32) In the absence of the complete harmonisation of copyright law, it is important to establish the principle of cumulation of protection under the Community design and under copyright law, whilst leaving Member States free to establish the extent of copyright protection and the conditions under which such protection is conferred'.

Article 96(2): 'A design protected by a Community design shall also be eligible for protection under the law of copyright of Member States as from the date on which the design was created or fixed in any form. The extent to which, and the conditions under which, such a protection is conferred, including the level of originality required, shall be determined by each Member State'.

[27] It has been submitted that the European *acquis* on the topic of copyright subject matter is of virtually no help in determining any overlaps. A Quaedvlieg, 'Overlap/Relationships between Copyright and Other Intellectual Property Rights' in E Derclaye (ed), *Research Handbook on the Future of EU Copyright* (Cheltenham, Edward Elgar, 2009) 479, 484–85. It is true that, strictly speaking, photographs, computer programs and databases are the only subject matter to have been the subject of EU copyright legislation. (The only provision which indirectly touches upon subject matter is Infosoc Directive, art 2, which provides that not only authors, but also performers, producers of the first fixations of films and phonograms, and broadcasting organisations benefit from a right of reproduction. Whilst this means that all these actors benefit from copyright, it is silent as regards rules governing any overlap this could generate.) In fact, when the European Union legislated on those specific subject matters, it was mainly aiming at ensuring protection in Member States where the level of originality was too high so that it precluded protection.

with copyright in a literary work (eg slogans) and a design right. This is because the design right will protect the appearance of the words depicted (ie the colours, font, etc) not the meaning of the words. It is clear that there cannot be an overlap between design and copyright in respect of computer programs as computer programs are expressly excluded in Design Directive, article 1(b) and the corresponding article of the Design Regulation.[28] Indeed, an additional limit in respect of the subject matter is that, under design law, the design is associated with a product, unlike in copyright law. 'Product' is defined rather broadly to include both mass-produced and handicraft items (Design Directive, article 1(b)) which implicitly means that the definition does not include animals, plants or human beings. Therefore, as human beings are excluded, even if they have become icons or are used in publicity campaigns, they or their likeness cannot be protected under design law in addition to the possible protection under copyright or trademark law.[29] In conclusion, the overlap at this level is not total and will mainly concern artistic works in two or three dimensions, and audiovisual works.[30]

(b) Protection Requirements

If an original copyright work, which is a design according to the Design Directive or Regulation, also fulfils the conditions of novelty and individual character, and of visibility if the work is a component part of a complex product, then the overlap is complete. This may occur quite frequently. This is because individual character in practice encompasses the notion of novelty[31] and is close to the notion of originality now harmonised for all works by the Court of Justice,[32] namely the author's own intellectual creation. However, the *Infopaq* ruling should not have changed the provisions of Design Directive, article 17 and Design Regulation, article 96(2), which specifically leave Member States free to decide the level of originality for copyright works which can also be designs. Therefore, if a Member State decides that the level of originality should be higher for designs, the overlap could be less frequent.

The converse situation is even more frequent: a design will often be original if it is novel and has individual character.[33] This is because novelty is often a higher threshold to meet than originality. It will not always be the case, however, namely with works which in some Member States (such as Germany and the United Kingdom) need to meet a higher threshold of originality.

[28] Please note that when the provisions of the Directive and the Regulations are identical, only reference to the Directive will be made throughout.

[29] P Torremans, 'Three Dimensional Trade Marks and Designs for Packaging' in G Ghidini and M Genovesi (eds), *Intellectual Property and Market Power, ATRIP Papers 2006–2007* (Buenos Aires, Eudeba, 2008) 745, 762.

[30] As regards audiovisual works, as per OHIM practice. Presentation at Queen Mary University of London on the Community design system by H Salmi, Examination Co-ordinator, OHIM's Designs Department, 15 December 2004, on file with the authors.

[31] CH Massa and A Strowel, 'Community Design: Cinderella Revamped' (2003) *European Intellectual Property Review* 68, 73.

[32] See Case C-5/08 *Infopaq International AS v Danske Dagblades Forening* [2009] ECR I-6569 and E Derclaye, 'Wonderful or Worrisome? The Impact of the ECJ Ruling in *Infopaq* on UK Copyright Law' (2010) *European Intellectual Property Review* 247.

[33] See CH Massa and A Strowel, 'Le cumul du dessin ou modèle et du droit d'auteur: orbites parallèles et forces d'attraction entre deux planètes indépendantes mais jumelles' in S Dusollier and A Cruquenaire (eds), *Le cumul des droits intellectuels* (Brussels, Larcier, 2009) 21, 80. The objective novelty of a work will often suggest its subjective originality so that there is a presumption of (factual) originality.

(c) Excluded Subject Matter

While the rule in Design Directive, article 7 helps to separate the subject matter of designs and of patents, it also corresponds to the idea/expression dichotomy in copyright law.[34] The Green Paper further explains the meaning of the rule: '[w]hat is meant is in reality that if there is no choice when designing a product with a given effect, there is no personal creativity displayed and consequently nothing to protect – at least under copyright or design law'.[35] Accordingly, Design Directive, article 7 and Design Regulation, article 8 both provide in exactly the same terms that national or Community design right:

> shall not subsist in features of appearance of a product which are solely dictated by its technical function [and] shall not subsist in features of appearance of a product which must necessarily be reproduced in their exact form and dimensions in order to permit the product in which the design is incorporated or to which it is applied to be mechanically connected to or placed in, around or against another product so that either product may perform its function.

However, in their respective final paragraphs, both instruments make an exception to article 7(2) for 'design[s] serving the purpose of allowing multiple assembly or connection of mutually interchangeable products within a modular system'.

Some authors think that there is no reason to assume that the 'must-fit' exclusion (Design Directive, article 7(2)) would not also apply in copyright law.[36] On the other hand, the Design Directive has not harmonised the so-called 'must-match' exception. The latter is not by definition encompassed within the technical exclusion and therefore whether spare parts should be copyrightable or not is a matter of policy.[37] But this 'does not mean that other reasons of economic policy could lead to certain restrictions in protection'.[38] Therefore, convergence arguably exists on excluded subject matter but is not perfect because the must-match exception is not harmonised. This problem arises at the level of exceptions, as is discussed below.

(d) Ownership

If the overlap exists, conflicts can occur at several different levels: ownership, rights and exceptions. At the level of ownership, the rules may be different as to who – the creator, the employer or commissioner of the creator – owns the rights. Whilst the Design Regulation has a clear ownership rule (article 14),[39] copyright and national design laws vary in this respect, as again this area is not harmonised at EU level. The Green Paper on designs envisaged 'the possibility that the rights to the Community design could belong to a person other than the one who is entitled to copyright protection under the relevant national law',[40] but the Commission did not think that there were any reported problems

[34] Green Paper on the Legal Protection of Industrial Design (n 17) 60.

[35] Ibid.

[36] Quaedvlieg, 'Overlap/Relationships between Copyright and Other Intellectual Property Rights' (n 27) 500.

[37] Ibid 501.

[38] Ibid 501.

[39] Recently further clarified by the Court of Justice on reference by a Spanish court. See Case C-32/08 *Fundación Española para la Innovación de la Artesanía (FEIA) v Cul de Sac Espacio Creativo, SL and Acierta Product and Position, SA* [2009] ECR I-5611. The Court held that the term 'employment' did not include 'commission'. This strict interpretation may help reduce uncertainty in cases of 'level overlaps'.

[40] Green Paper on the Legal Protection of Industrial Design (n 17) 152.

associated with this issue (including the possibility that the author invokes his or her moral rights). Therefore, it did not include a specific rule in the Design Directive or Regulation. It noted that, as far as it was aware, the risk seemed to have been avoided because interested parties indicate in their contracts that both the economic rights under copyright and the design right belong to the employer or commissioner. The discussion of potential conflicts at the level of ownership is thus left for the national chapters.

EU law provides for a conflict rule when someone tries to register a design the copyright in which belongs to someone else and whose use has not been licensed. Under Design Regulation, article 25(1)(f) and Design Directive, article 11(2)(b),[41] a (Community) design may be declared invalid if 'the design constitutes an unauthorised use of a work protected under the copyright law of a Member State'. This rule will help to resolve some of the conflicts that could arise due to the diversity of ownership rules in national laws. For instance, if a design is commissioned and the contract does not envisage ownership issues, in the United Kingdom, the author will own the copyright (Copyright, Designs and Patents Act (CDPA) 1988, section 11(1)) but the commissioner will own the registered design right (Registered Designs Act (RDA) 1949, section 2(1A)). However, Design Directive, article 11(2)(b) as implemented in UK law (RDA 1949, section 11ZA(4)) will prevent the commissioner from registering the design unless s/he has a copyright licence or even a simple authorisation from the author. However, the case law on implied licences would often lead to a solution that granted the ownership of the copyright to the commissioner because of the circumstances in which the commission took place.[42]

(e) Rights and Infringement

The main difference between copyright and registered design right is that the latter provides a monopoly right whilst the former only provides an anti-copying right. If the two protections are available, the owner has the advantage of not having to prove copying. The list of rights in Design Directive, article 12 is so broad ('use . . . in particular . . .') that it easily encompasses those granted by the Infosoc Directive and national laws. As regards the CUDR, the same rights as for a national or Community registered design right are granted but, as in copyright law, copying must be proved (Design Regulation, article 19(2)). Community or national design rights at this level therefore totally absorb copyright. In other words, it does not matter if the owner of a registered design has a copyright or not, as it would not give him or her more rights. However, as the test of infringement and the remedies may be different in the two bodies of law, and also if the sums granted as a remedy can be cumulated, then the combination of copyright and design right at that level is very advantageous for the right-holder.

(f) Exceptions Including Exhaustion Principle

The exceptions in design and copyright law differ greatly. Both Community and national registered design law have four exceptions: private use, use for teaching and citation purposes, experimental use and use to facilitate international travel. As is known, copyright exceptions are hardly harmonised at EU level. All the Infosoc Directive does is to set an

[41] Design Directive, article 11(2)(b) provides that it is an option for the Member States.
[42] See chapter 5, section II.A.

exhaustive list from which Member States can pick and choose. Therefore, whilst the wording of the exceptions chosen by each Member State must comply with that of the Directive's list, the number of exceptions effectively existing in each Member State varies greatly.

Therefore, at the level of exceptions, the combination of the two protections restricts the uses that can be made of protected subject matter if the particular Member State's copyright law has none or few of the corresponding exceptions in design law. Convergence is helped somewhat if a particular Member State has implemented in its copyright law the exceptions for private, teaching/citation purposes and/or use in connection with the demonstration or repair of equipment (Infosoc Directive, article 5(3)(l)). This situation is of course problematic, as it restricts the amount of exceptions users can benefit from. In addition, if, in the future, the spare parts (must-match features) exception is harmonised and thus made mandatory at EU level, the effect of the total cumulation imposed by the Design Directive may not be achieved, as many of these parts could probably be protected in many Member States by copyright,[43] as an equivalent exception does not necessarily exist in every national copyright law (it is in the list in Infosoc Directive, article 5(3)(l) but as stated above, it is not mandatory).[44] However, two rules of primary EU law would resolve the overlap in a situation involving spare parts crossing borders. Using copyright law to block the importation of such spare parts legally manufactured in another Member State would probably fall foul of Article 36 of the Treaty on the Functioning of the European Union (TFEU) (ex-Article 30 of the European Community Treaty (ECT)) and if not, may be an abuse under TFEU article 102 (ex-ECT Article 82).[45] This solution is arguable because copyright law is still national and registered design law has been harmonised and therefore should take precedence over national law.[46] In any case, until must-match parts have been harmonised within EU designs law, these arguments are not applicable, though they will be useful when the EU decides to harmonise must-match parts.[47] The reasoning of *Dior v Evora* would, however, be applicable.[48] As will be restated in the conclusion to this book, although the free movement of goods and services is a useful rule in many situations, it is not useful at purely national and international levels so that other rules need to be used to counteract the negative effects of the overlap. Of course, the best solution would be to harmonise the exceptions to copyright and design. For Massa and Strowel, who propose this solution, divergences of goals between design right and copyright do not justify asymmetrical obstacles between them.[49]

[43] A Kur, 'Cumulation of IP Rights Pertaining to Product Shapes: An "Illegitimate Offspring" of IP Law?' in G Ghidini and M Genovesi (eds), *Intellectual Property and Market Power, ATRIP Papers 2006–2007* (Buenos Aires, Eudeba, 2008) 613, 630, mentioning France as an example.

[44] See also subsection on excluded subject-matter above, section II.B(i)(a)(c).

[45] Kur, 'Cumulation of IP Rights Pertaining to Product Shapes' (n 43) 630–31; A Kur, 'Cumulation of Rights with Regard to Three-Dimensional Shapes: Two Exemplary Case Studies' in S Dusollier and A Cruquenaire (eds), *Le cumul des droits intellectuels* (Brussels, Larcier, 2009) 155, 172.

[46] Kur, 'Cumulation of Rights with Regard to Three-Dimensional Shapes' (n 45) 172–73 ('The question to be posed would be whether and under which circumstances national copyright protection might take precedence over the decision by the European lawmaker to liberalise the market in spare parts, and thereby preserving impediments for the free movement of goods that were intended to be removed by the legal action taken on the Community level . . . There is no pertinent reason why copyright should be able to set aside a solution applying within design law throughout the EU').

[47] Ibid 172–73.

[48] Kur, 'Cumulation of IP Rights Pertaining to Product Shapes' (n 43) 632.

[49] Massa and Strowel, 'Le cumul du dessin ou modèle et du droit d'auteur' (n 33) 85.

On the issue of free movement of goods, the Design Regulation, Design Directive and Infosoc Directive all include the principle of exhaustion:

> Article 21 Exhaustion of rights
>
> The rights conferred by a Community design shall not extend to acts relating to a product in which a design included within the scope of protection of the Community design is incorporated or to which it is applied, when the product has been put on the market in the Community by the holder of the Community design or with his consent.
>
> Article 15 Exhaustion of rights
>
> The rights conferred by a design right upon registration shall not extend to acts relating to a product in which a design included within the scope of protection of the design right is incorporated or to which it is applied, when the product has been put on the market in the Community by the holder of the design right or with his consent.
>
> Article 4 Distribution right
>
> . . .
>
> 2. The distribution right shall not be exhausted within the Community in respect of the original or copies of the work, except where the first sale or other transfer of ownership in the Community of that object is made by the right-holder or with his consent.

The meaning is identical in the three articles even if the wording is slightly different. Any putting on the EU market (gratuitous or not) will do. There is therefore total convergence between copyright and design law on this aspect.

In conclusion, simultaneous overlaps will be rather frequent and may create conflicts if the ownership is split. In addition, exceptions will generally be more restricted in case of an overlap.

(ii) Negative Overlap

When copyright protection is not available, the question is whether design right can fill the gap and vice versa.

(a) Copyright Protection Unavailable

Copyright protection would be unavailable if the design did not fit the copyrightable subject matter. As the breadth of copyright works is very large, it is hard to think of something which cannot be protected by copyright but can be protected by design right. The idea/expression dichotomy applies to both copyright and design law (Design Directive, article 7(1)). The design would also need to be unoriginal. Whether something is not original but has individual character will depend on national law (because in Germany and the United Kingdom, originality differs depending on the work in question).[50]

[50] For details, see chapter 5, section II.B and chapter 6, sections II.B and II.C.

(b) Design Protection Unavailable

For design protection to be unavailable, the subject matter must not be a design according to the definition in the Design Directive and Regulation. The definition is so broad that it is difficult to find an example (apart from computer programs).

It would also be necessary for the design not to be novel and to have individual character. This can often be the case. Under copyright law originality suffices, novelty is irrelevant. An important area where design right would not be available is that of purely functional designs, ie those whose *entire* shapes are dictated solely by their function, situations which, although rare, can still occur.[51] If a design's aspect is solely functional, it will be excluded from design protection but it will be a matter of national copyright law whether it can still benefit from copyright protection. Normally, the idea/expression dichotomy should prevent such protection so that there should be absolutely no overlap for pure functions, which are the domain of patent law and not of design or copyright law, as reflected in the Green Paper. However, paradoxically such 'hyperfunctional' designs are generally also intrinsically highly aesthetic.[52] This situation presents a dilemma as, even though such designs are primarily aesthetic, because they are entirely dictated by function, in addition to being excluded from design protection, they should not be protectable by copyright law either. Only patent law can protect such designs. However, as noted by Suthersanen:

> not all Member States' laws have the appropriate exclusionary device to prohibit copyright protection for such designs. There will be an ever-present temptation to resort to copyright law in an attempt to by-pass the functionality, interconnection and spare part provisions under European and national design laws.[53]

Negative overlaps are therefore possible. This may pose a problem when design protection is not available and the creator relies on copyright law in Member States which do not apply the idea/expression dichotomy properly, as it will allow for by-passing the exclusions in design law. However, if copyright law is applied properly, the problem can be solved at the level of protection requirements.

(iii) A Posteriori *Overlap*

It is unclear whether EU legislation allows an *a posteriori* overlap. The literature is divided. At first sight, it appears that the normal copyright term (70 years after the death of the creator) is not and cannot be curtailed for works of applied art/designs. But other commentators think that because the words 'irrespective of the number of products in which such design is intended to be incorporated or to which it is intended to be applied' and 'irrespective of whether the design can be dissociated from the products in which such design is intended to be incorporated or to which it is intended to be applied' (which were

[51] Quaedvlieg, 'Overlap/Relationships between Copyright and Other Intellectual Property Rights' (n 27) 493. 'According to the Advocate General Ruiz-Jarabo Colomer in no. 34 of his opinion in *Philips/Remington,* a functional design may be eligible for protection if it can be shown that the same technical function could be achieved by another different form'.

[52] Ibid 494.

[53] U Suthersanen, *Design Law in Europe* (London, Sweet & Maxwell, 2000) 80. See also Quaedvlieg, 'Overlap/Relationships between Copyright and Other Intellectual Property Rights' (n 27) 502 who notes that some courts have allowed copyright protection in such cases because they consider them 'as exquisite design'.

included in article 14(1) of the originally proposed Directive, now article 17) were in the end deleted, Member States seem to be allowed to limit the term of copyright for works of applied art.[54] Others argue that the term 'eligible for protection' in Design Directive, article 17 can be interpreted narrowly so as to allow some states such as the United Kingdom to curtail the duration of copyright or the owner's right to pursue a copyright action.[55] Indeed, the United Kingdom did so before the Directive was adopted and still does so (CDPA 1988, section 52 provides that when a work is applied industrially, its term will be of 25 years from that moment).[56] In the same vein, section 44 of Italian Act of 10 February 2005, no. 30, provided a term of a maximum of 25 years after the death of the author for works of applied art.[57] The Italian legislature shortened the copyright duration because it thought that owners of copyright in designs are more likely to have a monopoly, which would be anti-competitive. It has been argued that this rule was not only unconstitutional but also in contradiction with the Term Directive and therefore arguably contrary to EU law.[58] Indeed, the rule was changed back to the normal copyright duration of 70 years after the death of the creator[59] following an infringement action by the European Union against Italy.[60] The case was withdrawn and thus never tried as Italy complied with the Commission's request. (Strangely, the Commission did not take action against the United Kingdom over CDPA 1988, section 52.) There is also the possibility, if the spare parts exception is in future harmonised at EU level, that the effect of copyright, at the expiry of design right, will be to reactivate protection in the spare parts.

In conclusion, apart from the Green Paper's statement of intent to respect the objectives of the internal market and the rule regarding the prohibition on registering a copyright work as a design without authorisation, no rule at EU level deals with any of the three overlaps. All that EU law provides is that the overlap between copyright and design right is allowed.

C 'Level Overlap'

The level overlap happens when an overlap occurs between the same type of right which exists at two different levels. In the case of designs, it concerns the overlap between

[54] D Musker, *Community Design Law: Principles and Practice* (London, Sweet and Maxwell, 2002) 80–81.

[55] Suthersanen, *Design Law in Europe* (n 53) 76.

[56] On CDPA 1988, s 52, see chapter 5, section II.C.

[57] M Venturello, 'Recent Constructions of Italian Law on Designs and Models in Case Law, Comment under CFI Turin, 17 December 2004, Casa Damiani v Re Carlo' (2005) *Italian Intellectual Property* 201, 210; S Guizzardi, *La Tutela d'autore del Disegno Industriale: Incentivi all'Innovazione e Regime Circolatorio* (Milan, Giuffrè, 2005) 106–10.

[58] Directive 2006/116/EC of the European Parliament and of the Council of 12 December 2006 on the term of protection of copyright and certain related rights (codified version) [2006] OJ L372/12. See Guizzardi, *La Tutela d'autore del Disegno Industriale* (n 57) 106–10, also saying that the term chosen does not address the anti-competitive concerns, because contrary to UK law, it depends on the author's death which is not foreseeable and therefore not an objective factor. See also P Marchetti and L Ubertazzi, *Commentario Breve alle Leggi su Proprietà Intellettuale e Concorrenza*, 4th edn (Padova, CEDAM, 2007) 378–79.

[59] See art 4(4) of the Act of 15 February 2007, no 10.

[60] Infringement procedure no. 2005/4088, C (2005) 2900 for violation of art 1 of Directive 98/38. For more details, see Marchetti and Ubertazzi, *Commentario Breve alle Leggi su Proprietà Intellettuale e Concorrenza* (n 58) 378–79. See Annex, Commission Staff Working Document SEC(2007)976 (Brussels, 17 July 2007) to the 24th Annual Report from the Commission on Monitoring the Application of Community Law (2006), COM(2007)398 final, SEC(2007)975. The 25th Annual Report from the Commission indicated that the case is now closed.

national and Community designs, be they registered or unregistered. This type of overlap can only occur when there are parallel national and Community rights, and will therefore be the case solely for overlaps involving trademarks or designs.

The Green Paper on the Legal Protection of Industrial Design sets out rules concerning overlaps between different levels of design rights. Some rules clearly prohibit some overlaps whilst other rules clearly allow other overlaps. First of all, the Green Paper clearly allows the overlap between the Community design rights and national design protection systems.[61] This is further detailed. The Green Paper expressly allows the overlap between the CUDR and national registered designs:

> There appears to be no reason why a national registered design which presents a greater legal certainty and which is easier to base oneself upon in legal proceedings than an unregistered Community design should be affected in its existence for the sole reason that the right holder could also rely upon an unregistered Community design.[62]

Cumulation between the (still only existing) national unregistered design right, namely the UK unregistered design right (UK UDR), and both the CRDR and CUDR is also expressly allowed.[63] The Commission states that it does not foresee any problems arising from the overlap between the CUDR and UK UDR. It adds that '[t]o introduce a prohibition of "cumulation" would be tantamount to making the UK specific protection completely ineffective'.[64] As to the cumulation between the UK UDR and the CRDR, perhaps naively,[65] the Commission has declared that '[t]he greater legal certainty of the Community design makes it unlikely that a UK unregistered design would often be invoked in parallel'. On the other hand, an overlap between the CUDR and a newly created national unregistered design right (UDR) is expressly prohibited. Very judiciously, the Commission says that 'the Community unregistered design renders in the future the introduction of similar national rights superfluous', adding that 'it could even be counter-productive as regards the functioning of the internal market if such rights were to be introduced'.[66] This is not reflected in a specific provision as it does not spring from Design Directive, article 16 and Design regulation, article 96(1), rendering this prohibition a little uncertain, as the Green Paper describes it.

However, the Green Paper expressly forbade a cumulation between the CRDR and national registered designs. The (totally legitimate) reason was:

> That the legal force in the state concerned of a registered national design and of any registered Community design would be the same is therefore no reason for multiplying the number of identical protections in the hand of the same right holder in the same territory.[67]

The idea was that it would be possible to file a CRDR and a national right at the same time, or file first at national level and then at EU level, claiming the national priority. Once that has been done, the national RDR would become ineffective and give place to the Community one.[68] This was expressed in article 96 of the Draft Regulation. However,

[61] Green Paper on the Legal Protection of Industrial Design (n 17) 134.
[62] Ibid 138.
[63] Ibid 137, 139.
[64] Ibid 139.
[65] As will be seen in the chapter on UK law, there have been cases where both rights have been successfully used: *Landor & Hawa International v Azure Designs* [2007] FSR 9. See below chapter 5, section II.A.
[66] Green Paper on the Legal Protection of Industrial Design (n 17) 137.
[67] Ibid 138.
[68] Ibid 139.

this article was deleted and an overlap between CRDR and national RDR has in the end (albeit implicitly, through this deletion) been allowed. This overlap contrasts with the ban on an overlap between the Community and the national plant variety right, which will be analysed below.

(i) Overlap Between National and Community Registered Design Rights and Infringement

As the rules are the same for national and Community registered design rights (except perhaps for Design Regulation, article 14 concerning ownership where a designer is employed) there will be no clashes. However, since the procedural rules may differ at the national and Community levels, discrepancies and conflicts could arise; for instance, for procedural reasons, a CRDR could not be registered but a national right could, and vice versa. This allows for a negative overlap. Also, at the level of registrability and infringement, a national right could be refused protection, declared invalid or held to be infringed, whilst the equivalent CRDR could not. This creates a discrepancy because the rights are the same in content but not in territorial effect. The CRDR will be refused, valid or infringed throughout the European Union, whilst the national right will obviously only be so within the country or countries concerned. This discrepancy can be advantageously exploited by shrewd applicants, when they have a doubt as to the validity of their design, or even simply to protect themselves against a pan-European declaration of non-infringement or invalidity. This protection *cum* forum-shopping is evidently not ideal if the internal market objectives are to be fulfilled.

In this latter respect, a rule organising the potential conflicts between national and Community RDR was included in the Design Regulation. Article 95 organises the way judges must act when parallel actions are launched on the basis of Community designs and national design rights. In short, it provides that once a court has been seized with the same cause of action between the same parties in an action for infringement or for threatened infringement, the second court must decline jurisdiction. This second court is allowed simply to stay its proceedings where the jurisdiction of the other court is contested. Similarly, if a Community design court has been seized with an action for infringement or threatened infringement of a Community design but a national court has already given a judgment on the merits in the same action (concerning the parallel design) between the same parties, it must reject the action and vice versa (a national court should do the same if a judgment on the merits was already handed down by a Community design court). However, these provisions do not apply in respect of provisional measures, including protective measures.

(ii) Overlap Between National Registered and/or Unregistered and Community Unregistered Design Rights

First of all, it must be noted that, as the CUDR does not differ (apart from the starting point and length of its term and the fact that it is an anti-copying right) from the CRDR and national RDR, the overlap should not be problematic. Secondly, the possibility of an overlap between CUDR and CRDR is by definition impossible, since after 12 months during which a CUDR has been in use and not yet registered, there is a ban on registration as the design will no longer be considered novel (Design Regulation, article 7(2)(b)).

On the other hand, during this 'grace' period of 12 months after first 'publication' of the CUDR, the creator can transform it into a CRDR.

Some problems may occur between a CUDR and a national RDR, even though the provisions are virtually identical. These problems will be similar to those for the overlap between national and Community registered design rights examined above. The problems will be more acute when a CUDR overlaps with a national UDR, which will be the case only in the United Kingdom (as it is the only country in the European Union to have a national UDR). There will not only be clashes and conflicts but potentially overprotection. These issues will be examined in the national chapters.

D Conclusion

As can now readily be seen, whereas certain overlaps are clearly allowed or prohibited, there are virtually no rules regulating any clashes or conflicts that can result from them. The only three provisions which do so are Design Directive, articles 7 and 11(excluding purely functional shapes from design law and prohibiting the unauthorised registration of a copyright work), and Design Regulation, article 95, which provides rules to avoid clashing judicial decisions between national RDR and Community design rights. Notwithstanding this dearth of rules regulating cumulation of rights, the Green Paper nevertheless specifically refers to the principle of free competition and the internal market objectives, in particular free movement of goods and services, as regulators of conflicts or overprotection that could be caused, inter alia, by overlaps.

It must also be highlighted that the imposed cumulation between copyright and design (Design Directive, article 17) is in reality without much substance. Whilst in effect it incorporates the French theory of the unity of art (*l'unité de l'art*) or 'cumulation of rights' into EU law,[69] what it requires from the Member States is only 'to avoid attempts to exclude (registered) designs per se from copyright protection'.[70] As the provision leaves Member States free to decide the conditions of protection under copyright law for designs, including most importantly the level of originality,[71] if a country (as is the case in Italy and Germany, and in the United Kingdom to a lesser extent[72]) requires a high level of originality for works of applied art, most such works will in effect be deprived of copyright protection in any event and be left with design protection only. The practical effect of such provisions is almost the same as prohibiting the cumulation in the first place. This was in effect meant to be that way, as the Green Paper on the Legal Protection of Industrial Design specifically states that the harmonisation of designs should not interfere with other types of IPRs or be a pretext to harmonise copyright laws.[73] There

[69] Musker, *Community Design Law* (n 54) 79.

[70] Ibid and also 80 ('This provision does not force any state to deem designs per se, or particular classes of designs, to be protectable subject matter of copyright. All that is required is the avoidance of specific exclusions of protection for registered designs').

[71] See Suthersanen, *Design Law in Europe* (n 53) 76; A Quaedvlieg, 'Three Times a Hybrid between Copyright and Industrial Property' in J Kabel and G Mom, *Intellectual Property and Information Law: Essays in Honour of Herman Cohen Jeroham* (The Hague, Kluwer Law International, 1998) 47, 52 n 17; Musker, *Community Design Law* (n 54) 80 ('Requiring copyright protection, yet not harmonising it is a curious strategy').

[72] See E Derclaye, 'Are Fashion Designers Better Protected in Continental Europe than in the United Kingdom? A Comparative Analysis of the Recent Case Law in France, Italy and the United Kingdom' (2010) *Journal of World Intellectual Property* 315.

[73] Green Paper on the Legal Protection of Industrial Design (n 17) 148–50.

are, however, good policy reasons for prohibiting the overlap, mainly to prevent the prolongation by copyright law of the registered design right upon its expiry, and to encourage registration.

There is surprisingly little academic commentary on the concrete problems the overlap between copyright and design can engender, although they are potentially not insignificant. The scholarship of the few commentators who have addressed the issue has been discussed above. Certain rules will, therefore, have to be developed to settle the conflicts or cut down any resulting overprotection which the overlaps between copyright and design (content overlap), and national and Community designs (level overlap) create.

III. COPYRIGHT AND TRADEMARKS

A The Legal Framework

Infosoc Directive, recital 60 and mirroring article 9, allow cumulation between copyright and a number of rights, including trademarks. The Trademark Directive also has a similar provision. Recital 6 states:

> Whereas this Directive does not exclude the application to trademarks of provisions of law of the Member States other than trademark law, *such as* the provisions relating to unfair competition, civil liability or consumer protection. (emphasis added)

CTMR, article 14(2) provides in similar terms that:

> This Regulation shall not prevent actions concerning a Community trademark being brought under the law of Member States relating *in particular* to civil liability and unfair competition. (emphasis added)

Neither the Trademark Directive nor the CTMR excludes the application of copyright law since they use the terms 'such as' and 'in particular'. Apart from recital 6,[74] in terms of the relationship between copyright and design, the Trademark Directive is silent.[75] The only other relevant provisions are the (perfect twin) articles Trademark Directive, article 3(1)(e) and CTMR, article 7(1)(e) on the exclusion of certain shapes. In contrast with the Green Paper on the Legal Protection of Industrial Designs, the Explanatory Memorandum of the Proposal for a Trademark Directive and Trademark Regulation is laconic on the reasons for this exclusion, perhaps because it is a much older document,[76] published at a time where intellectual property issues had not yet matured at EU level. The document states (at 57): 'Also, the shape of goods will not be refused registration unless the fact of registration would make it possible for an undertaking to monopolise that shape to the detriment of its competitors and of consumers'. Like the Design Regulation, the CTMR

[74] Recital 5 of the codified Trademark Directive.

[75] G Dinwoodie, 'Copyright, Trade Marks and Trade Dress: The Overlap (and Conflict?) in Intellectual Property Regimes concerning Designs and Visual Images, General Report' in J Ginsburg and J Besek (eds), *Adjuncts and Alternatives to Copyright, Proceedings of the ALAI Congress, June 13–17, 2001, New York USA* (New York, Columbia University School of Law, 2002) 497, 510 reports that few countries (the national reports also included countries outside the European Union) have 'rules that categorically exclude copyright protection based upon the parallel existence or non-existence of trademark protection, and vice versa'.

[76] COM(80)635 final (19 November 1980).

also organises the potential conflicts that would result from different decisions involving the same mark registered both at national and EU level (article 105).[77] Notwithstanding its almost non-existent rationales for the Trademark Directive and CTMR's provisions, the document still sets out a clear underlying theme. As the proposals date from 1980, follow the Court of Justice's case law on free movement of goods and trademarks, and also predate the achievement of the internal market in 1992 (with the 'four freedoms' as its goal), it is not surprising that the Explanatory Memorandum insists that the CTM will (in the long term) eliminate barriers to trade and promote free competition. So the themes of the harmonisation underlying the Trademark Directive and Regulation are very clear: free movement of goods and services and undistorted competition. One can justifiably speculate that the document was inspired by the early ECJ case law on industrial property and the free movement of goods/exhaustion principle, such as the several *Centrafarm* cases and the *Hag I* case from the 1970s.[78]

B 'Content Overlap'

(i) Simultaneous Overlap

(a) Subject Matter

A first potential overlap between copyright and trademark can occur if a word mark is long enough to be considered a literary work. This will be the case only in Member States which protect titles, such as France. Following the *Infopaq* decision, presumably, all Member States must now grant protection to short works as long as they reflect the author's own intellectual creation. This was not the case in the United Kingdom prior to the ruling, as titles could very exceptionally obtain copyright protection (they needed to be highly original and relate to an underlying work). The argument that titles are per se descriptive and thus non-registrable is flawed. 'Harry Potter' is not descriptive as it does not serve to identify the product (book or film) being the story of Harry Potter but the story of a young wizard.[79] Of course, some titles will be purely descriptive such as 'Intellectual Property Law' for a book on intellectual property law.

Slogans can also be protected by both copyright and trademark laws. Although slogans are not per se non-registrable[80] or subject to a higher criterion of distinctiveness,[81] they can rarely function as trademarks as they do not generally indicate the origin of a product. Instead, either they are descriptive[82] or they promote the product or service in

[77] For the similar provision in design law, see section II above.

[78] COM(80)635 final, 53–55.

[79] P Reeskamp, 'Dr No in Trade Mark Country: A Dutch Point of View' (2010) *Journal of Intellectual Property Law and Practice* 29, 30.

[80] See Case T-130/01 *Sykes Enterprises v OHIM* [2002] ECR II-5179, para 19. 'Registration of a trademark which consists of signs or indications that are also used as advertising slogans, indications of quality or incitements to purchase the goods or services covered by that mark is not excluded as such by virtue of such use (see, by way of analogy, the judgment in Case C-517/99 *Merz and Krell* [2001] ECR I-6959, para 40)'.

[81] Case C-64/02 P *Erpo Möbelwerk* [2004] ECR I-10031, para 36. See also A Folliard-Monguiral and D Rogers, 'Significant Case Law from 2004 on the Community Trademark from the Court of First Instance, the European Court of Justice and OHIM' (2005) *European Intellectual Property Review* 134.

[82] See eg Case T-88/06 *Dorel Juvenile Group* (2008, nyr) available at www.europa.curia.eu, concerning the words 'SAFETY 1ST' for bicycles, car seats and children's play equipment which was rejected 'on the basis that

question so that the consumer does not immediately perceive the slogan as a trademark but simply as a promotional message.[83] Nonetheless, there are slogans or sentences which are trademarks and could attract copyright protection in some Member States. The following examples spring to mind: 'And so to bed', 'I can't believe it's not butter!' and 'Das Prinzip der Bequemlichkeit'[84] which are all registered and valid trademarks.[85] The idea is to use the slogan, teach the public to consider it as a trademark, and then register it on the basis of the proviso when it has acquired distinctiveness.[86] As trademarks can also be figurative, a second overlap can occur with graphic works, drawings and paintings, and even photographs, as well as possibly also audiovisual works.[87] One can think of the famous MGM lion whose roar is a trademark[88] but whose appearance (as an audiovisual mark) could also very well be. A third overlap can occur with three-dimensional artistic works, as trademarks can also consist of shapes. Finally, a fourth overlap can occur with musical works and sound recordings.

(b) Protection Requirements

Often, besides being distinctive, a mark will also be original; and vice versa, an original work can be distinctive of the goods or services in question. This will be even more frequent than with the overlap between design and copyright, as distinctiveness does not require novelty. However, it is clearly not sufficient that a sign be original or even novel for it to be distinctive as well. As to shapes, they 'must differ substantially from the basic shapes of the goods in question, commonly used in the trade, and not look like a mere variant of those shapes'.[89] In addition, Trademark Directive, article 3(1)(e)(iii) excludes from the protection of trademark law 'signs which consist exclusively of the shape which gives substantial value to the goods'.[90] As to colours, they cannot be registered in the abstract. There must be 'a systematic arrangement associating the colours concerned in a predetermined and uniform way'.[91] The combination must give a shape of contours to

this would be perceived as a general slogan that safety is a priority, not as an indication of origin'. L Bently and B Sherman, *Intellectual Property Law*, 3rd edn (Oxford, Oxford University Press, 2009) 831–32.

[83] See Case T-130/01 *Sykes Enterprises v OHIM* [2002] ECR II-5179, paras 20 and 29 ('Real People Real Solutions' for inter alia technical support, software and hardware).

[84] This mark was the object of the *Erpo* case (n 81).

[85] Recently, the Court of Justice confirmed that slogans can be distinctive notwithstanding their laudatory connotation. See Case C-398/08 *Audi AG v OHIM* (2010, nyr) para 45, available at www.europa.curia.eu (concerning Audi's slogan 'Vorsprung Durch Technik').

[86] J Phillips, *Trade Mark Law: A Practical Anatomy* (Oxford, Oxford University Press, 2003) 141.

[87] Registration of an audiovisual mark seems to have been done by several companies by filing a series of photographs. See eg CTM 008668949 owned by O2 (bubbles bursting behind blue background) published in March 2010 and CTM 008884447 owned by Procter & Gamble (a man taking his jacket off and throwing it in the air), which is currently still being examined. Other examples include CTM 008679748 (animal's tail swinging), CTM 08840894 and CTM 008833394. See CTM database www.oami.europa.eu.

[88] It is registered as a CTM. See the CTM database www.oami.europa.eu.

[89] *Wim De Waele*, Board of Appeal, confirmed by Case T-15/05 *Wim De Waele v OHIM* [2006] ECR II-1511, para 38 (shape of sausage (twisted)), citing Joined Cases T-324/01 and T-110/02 *Axions and Belce v OHIM* [2003] ECR II-1897, para 44 (brown cigar shape and gold ingot shape).

[90] For an in-depth discussion of the exclusions of Trademark Directive, art 3(1)(e), see sections IV.B(i) and IV.C(i).

[91] Case C-49/02 *Heidelberger Bauchemie* [2004] ECR I-6129, para 42 (undertaking sought to register colours blue and yellow 'as such'). 'Such representations would allow numerous different combinations, which would not permit the consumer to perceive and recall a particular combination, thereby enabling him to repeat with certainty the experience of a purchase, any more than they would allow the competent authorities and economic operators to know the scope of the protection afforded to the proprietor of the trademark' (para 35).

the colours.[92] The Court of Justice also restated the public interest 'in not unduly restricting the availability of colours for other traders who market goods or services of the same type as those in respect of which registration is sought'.[93] It could be said that this ruling coincides with the idea/expression dichotomy in copyright law which does not allow the protection of concepts. The registration of two colours as such is comparable to an author decreeing s/he has copyright in two colours. Sometimes even putting the two colours in the simplest form will be deemed an idea, even if it is expressed, or if it is considered an expression, it will be deemed unoriginal.

(c) Excluded Subject Matter

The exclusions in trademark law which are relevant to copyright works are those set out in Trademark Directive, article 3(1)(e),[94] mainly signs which consist exclusively of (i) the shape which results from the nature of the goods themselves; and (iii) the shape which gives substantial value to the goods. Although not elaborated upon in the Explanatory Memorandum to the Trademark Directive and Regulation,[95] these (in addition to indent (ii) which relates to the exclusion of technical forms) are meant to reflect the trademark/patent, trademark/design and trademark/copyright interfaces. Particularly, the exception concerning signs which consist exclusively of the shape which gives substantial value to the goods, which is inspired from the former Benelux trademark law,[96] 'expresses trademark law's natural reflex that the trademark cannot coincide with the essential properties of the good'.[97] According to the Benelux Common Governmental Comment, its purpose was 'to create, to a certain extent, a limit on the possible concurrence of trademark protection and the protection which results from copyright law or the law on models and designs'.[98] It is also not possible to register emblems, badges and the like without the consent of the relevant authorities (Trademark Directive, article 3(1)(h)). The overlap is therefore virtually complete for musical works and for two-dimensional works (both literary and artistic) but not for all three-dimensional ones. Article 3(1)(e) is discussed in more detail in the next section.

(d) Ownership

The CTMR makes provision for the situation when a trademark applicant wishes to register a copyright work or any other industrial property right without authorisation of the copyright holder, similar to the rule that exists in the Design Regulation (see above at B(i)). The copyright or other industrial property right-holder can oppose the registration and/or use of such trademark (CTMR, article 53(2)(c) and (d)). Also, apart from the

[92] Ibid para 34.

[93] Ibid paras 41 and 42, citing Case C-104/01 *Libertel Groep BV v Benelux-Merkenbureau* [2003] ECR I-3793, paras 52–56.

[94] As in the previous section, when the provisions of the Directive and Regulations are identical, only references to the Directive will be given.

[95] See the laconic comment at 57 of the document, cited below in section IV.A.

[96] Which in turn was based on an American doctrine. See Quaedvlieg, 'Overlap/Relationships between Copyright and Other Intellectual Property Rights' (n 27) 507.

[97] Ibid. That exclusion is also justified because such shapes cannot be indicating origin. See also Trademark Directive, art 3(1)(c).

[98] Quaedvlieg, 'Overlap/Relationships between Copyright and Other Intellectual Property Rights' (n 27) 507.

situation described above and similarly to the situation under the copyright/design interface, there will be other conflicts if the trademark and copyright holders are different persons. Indeed, there will also be cases where the ownership is split after registration of the trademark or design. This may occur, for instance, as a result of the transfer of the trademark to subsequent companies. This is a national issue which will be examined in the subsequent chapters.

(e) Rights and Infringement

By contrast with copyright law, there is no need to copy a sign, be it identical or similar to a trademark, in order to infringe the trademark holder's rights: use is sufficient. However, the use must be in the course of trade and as a trademark[99] and in relation to identical or similar products or services, or if the mark has acquired reputation, dissimilar products or services are included as well. Also, likelihood of confusion is required if there is no identity between the defendant's sign and trademark and the goods or services in question when the mark has no reputation. Therefore, the instances of overlap at the level of rights can arise but are far less frequent than under the copyright/design interface. For instance, private use of a trademark and more generally use for non-commercial (eg most educational) purposes does not fall within the scope of the trademark owner's rights. In this respect, there is negative convergence between copyright and trademark law.

(f) Exceptions Including Exhaustion Principle

Apart from the exceptions stated in Trademark Directive, article 6 and CTMR, article 12, which are not relevant as regards overlaps,[100] there are no exceptions to the rights in trademark law. However, there are some free uses, namely when the mark is used outside the course of trade, for dissimilar goods or services if the mark is not famous, or for similar goods or services as long as there is no confusion. The question therefore arises as to whether an exception under copyright law can trump trademark infringement.

There are some cases where the overlap between copyright and trademark will pose problems because there is no convergence between copyright and trademark exceptions. Because the EU courts have interpreted the term 'use as a mark' broadly, it seems that all references to a trademark in commercial publications will be considered as use as a mark.[101] If such publications involve identical goods, proof of likelihood of confusion is not necessary and therefore trademark infringement is straightforward. Thus, news reporting, which is generally exempted under copyright law, is for commercial purposes

[99] See also Dinwoodie, 'Copyright, Trade Marks and Trade Dress' (n 75) 517, adding that 'On the other hand, trademark law classically protects only against use of the mark in commerce and as a trademark (private, non-commercial copying can less easily be treated as trademark infringement). Courts have, however, interpreted the trademark requirements of use in commerce and use as a trademark very broadly, such that this may be a relatively insignificant limitation'.

[100] CTMR, art 6(1)(c) (the repair clause) could, however, be useful if a trademark is also a copyright work (such as a logo).

[101] A Kur, 'Exceptions to Protection Where Copyright and Trade Mark Overlap: Parody, News Reporting and Other "Speech" Use of Trade Marks", General Report' in J Ginsburg and J Besek (eds), *Adjuncts and Alternatives to Copyright, Proceedings of the ALAI Congress, June 13–17, 2001, New York USA* (New York, Columbia University School of Law, 2002) 593, 603. *Contra*: Reeskamp, 'Dr No in Trade Mark Country' (n 79) 34.

and therefore will often constitute trademark infringement.[102] The same may occur with parodies, which are often exempted under copyright law, although some conditions are generally attached (eg respecting the author's moral rights). Simply because parodies may be done for commercial purposes and because use as a mark covers so many uses, a clash between the two regimes can happen more often than one might think.[103] Nevertheless, in the cases where the goods or services are not identical, likelihood of confusion will need to be proved and this may be more difficult, so that the two systems will converge.[104] The defence of due cause, which includes freedom of speech, could also help the parodist.[105] In the cases where the parodied mark has a reputation, the two regimes might also often converge. This is because copyright laws will generally examine the motives behind the parody and the reputation of the mark may be taken into account in this assessment. In trademark law, the more famous a mark is, the more likely the courts will tend to consider the parody as a pretext for the user to profit from the attention raised in order to promote his own business.[106]

Both copyright and trademark laws have an exhaustion principle.[107] Although the wording of the clauses is not identical, their meaning and effect are. There is a major difference though, in that there is no equivalent to Trademark Directive, article 7(2) in copyright law. Finally, a problem can occur when, as in the *Dior v Evora* case,[108] there is a reproduction forbidden by copyright law of a work 'attached' to a trademark good or service (ie commercialised as such by the trademark owner) but no trademark infringement. In such a situation, copyright law then could trump the free movement of goods or services which would have prevailed if trademark law had been exclusively applicable. The *Dior v Evora* decision set out a rule that in this situation, at least when advertising is necessary, copyright law must yield before the Community principle of free movement of goods or services. This rule is thus not intrinsic to any of the IPR regimes but is a higher

[102] Kur, 'Exceptions to Protection Where Copyright and Trade Mark Overlap' (n 101) 602–3.

[103] Ibid 604, also noting at n 30 that 'as far as can be seen, there is no national law incorporating an express exemption shown from trademark protection in favour of parodies'. See also V Moffatt, 'Mutant Copyrights and Backdoor Patents: The Problem of Overlapping Intellectual Property Protection' (2004) *Berkeley Technology Law Journal* 1473, 1516, also noting this in relation to US law.

[104] Kur, 'Exceptions to Protection Where Copyright and Trade Mark Overlap' (n 101) 607. Reeskamp, 'Dr No in Trade Mark Country' (n 79) 34, noting that in most cases, the trademark holder will not be able to do anything against the application of the copyright limitations because the essential function of the trademark, ie guaranteeing the origin of the product, is not affected; citing EU case law including Case C-2/00 *Michael Hölterhoff v Ulrich Freiesleben* [2002] ECR I-4187; Case C-206/01 *Arsenal Football Club v Matthew Reed* [2002] ECR I-10273; Case C-48/05 *Adam Opel v Autec* [2007] ECR I-1017 and Case C-533/06 *O2 Holdings and O2 (UK) v Hutchison 3G UK* [2008] ECR I-4231. This case law may now, however, be outdated because of the additional trademark functions recognised by the Court of Justice in Case C-487/07 *L'Oréal SA, Lancôme Parfums et Beauté & Cie SNC and Laboratoire Garnier & Cie v Bellure NV, Malaika Investments Ltd and Starion International Ltd* [2009] ECR I-5185.

[105] Reeskamp, 'Dr No in Trade Mark Country' (n 79) 34, citing Dutch literature and Trademark Directive, arts 5(2) and 6(1).

[106] Kur, 'Exceptions to Protection Where Copyright and Trade Mark Overlap' (n 101) 607; Reeskamp, 'Dr No in Trade Mark Country' (n 79) 34–35.

[107] Trademark Directive, art 7. 'Exhaustion of the rights conferred by a trademark. 1. The trademark shall not entitle the proprietor to prohibit its use in relation to goods which have been put on the market in the Community under that trademark by the proprietor or with his consent. 2. Paragraph 1 shall not apply where there exist legitimate reasons for the proprietor to oppose further commercialisation of the goods, especially where the condition of the goods is changed or impaired after they have been put on the market.'

Infosoc Directive, art 4. 'Distribution right. . . . 2. The distribution right shall not be exhausted within the Community in respect of the original or copies of the work, except where the first sale or other transfer of ownership in the Community of that object is made by the right holder or with his consent.'

[108] Case C-337/95 *Parfums Christian Dior v Evora* [1997] ECR I-6013.

rule stemming from the TFEU.[109] However, the *Dior* ruling does come with an exception. The trademark owner can still prevent the use of the work if it is established that, having regard to the specific circumstances of the case, the use of respectively those goods or this trademark, as it may be, for the purpose of bringing to the public's attention the further commercialisation of those goods seriously damages the reputation, or respectively the goods or the trademark.[110]

(ii) Negative Overlap

(a) Copyright Protection Unavailable

There is certainly some subject matter which is not copyrightable but can be registered as a trademark. All *de minimis* works, be they literary, musical or artistic, provided that they are distinctive, can be trademarks. In most Member States, they would not be able to obtain copyright protection because they would not be works, or would be mere ideas or simply not original. However, there might more often be works which copyright law cannot protect because they do not reach the level of originality required (be it the normal level or a higher level for most or all works of applied art in some countries such as the United Kingdom and Germany), but which are distinctive of the goods or services for which they are registered or have acquired distinctiveness through use. In addition, trademark law can also fill the gap by sometimes protecting ideas that can never be protected in copyright law.[111] Indeed, if such ideas are 'super-distinctive' then under trademark law, they are even more worthy of protection.

(b) Trademark Protection Unavailable

The definition of a trademark is so broad that it is difficult to think of subject matter which could not be a trademark (apart from the excluded shapes). However, since the trademark must be represented graphically and smells such as perfumes (at this stage of human development at least) cannot be represented graphically according to the case law,[112] the gap can be filled by copyright law, if the country in question admits such protection (at the moment the Netherlands does so,[113] but no longer France [114] nor the United Kingdom or Germany). This issue is not really an issue of a gap in trademark law which is filled by copyright law, but rather whether copyright law should protect perfumes in the first place (not smells occurring in nature as they are not human creations). Also, a

[109] A Quaedvlieg, 'Concurrence and Convergence in Industrial Design: Three-Dimensional Shapes Excluded by Trade Mark Law' in W Grosheide and J Brinkhof (eds), *Intellectual Property Law: Articles on Crossing Borders between Traditional and Actual* (Antwerpen, Intersentia, 2004) 23, 29 concerning *Dior*. 'This offers a clear example of negative convergence. At first glance, it might seem as if the court wanted to curtail copyright *by* trademark law and to keep it within the boundaries set by the regime. However, the judgment as a whole makes it clear that the limits of *both* rights are subjected to the *overriding* interest of the free movement of goods within the internal market and the purpose of the exhaustion rule.'

[110] Case C-337/95 *Parfums Christian Dior v Evora* [1997] ECR I-6013, paras 48 and 59.

[111] However, there is a limit, see Case C-49/02 *Heidelberger Bauchemie* [2004] ECR I-6129 and the *Libertel* decision (n 93) (not possible to register single or simple combination of colours). See also Case C-321/03 *Dyson v Registrar of Trademarks* [2007] ECR I-687, discussed below section VI.B(i).

[112] See Case C-273/00 *Sieckmann (Ralf) v Deutsches Patent- und Markenamt* [2002] ECR I-11737.

[113] *Kecofa v Lancôme* [2006] ECDR 26.

[114] *Bsiri-Barbir v Haarmann and Reimer* [2006] ECDR 28.

trademark cannot be registered if it is devoid of distinctive character or describes the qualities, characteristics, etc of the goods or services for which it is proposed to register it. If the unregistrable trademark is also a copyright work, it can therefore obtain that protection.

(iii) A Posteriori *Overlap*

The trademark/copyright interface obviously presents an issue of overlap *a posteriori* as trademarks are indefinitely renewable and remain valid if they continue to be used and remain distinctive.[115] Conversely, if a trademark ceases to be used for five continuous years (Trademark Directive, article 10) or is no longer distinctive, the right expires, but if the copyright is still in force at that time, the work subject matter of the trademark will still be protected. There is no rule regulating the *a posteriori* overlap in the EU legislative instruments or the EU courts' case law.[116] In fact, the rationales of copyright and trademark law are difficult to reconcile on this point. On the one hand:

> it is clear that the [sign], which is also protected by copyright, should continue to be protected by trademark law even after expiry of the copyright term. On the other hand, works of art must fall into the public domain one day.[117]

C 'Level Overlap'

The issue is similar to that arising between the Community and national design rights, namely a possible overlap between national and Community trademarks. We thus refer the reader to section II.C above for the potential problems associated with this type of overlap. However, contrary to the level overlap concerning designs, no rules exist to regulate it to some extent. The only reference to the overlap between Community and national marks is in CTMR, recital 6, which provides:

> The Community law relating to trademarks nevertheless does not replace the laws of the Member States on trademarks. It would not in fact appear to be justified to require undertakings to apply for registration of their trademarks as Community trademarks. National trademarks continue to be necessary for those undertakings which do not want protection of their trademarks at Community level.

In conclusion, apart from the legislative and judicial rules regulating the simultaneous overlap (exclusion from trademark protection of natural, functional and ornamental shapes; invalidity of a trademark that seeks to register a copyright work; *Dior v Evora* and the procedural rules similar to those existing under the Design Regulation), there is no further rule regulating any of the other types of overlaps between copyright and trademark law.[118]

[115] See also Dinwoodie, 'Copyright, Trade Marks and Trade Dress' (n 75) 517.

[116] See also Quaedvlieg, 'Overlap/Relationships between Copyright and Other Intellectual Property Rights' (n 27) 511–12, noting that '[a]lthough the Term Directive has not shown particular attention for the public interest in *ending* protection, it should not be ruled out that the ECJ will be called one day to rule whether such an interest exists and whether it could produce a reflex on trademark law'.

[117] Ibid 511.

[118] See also Kur, 'Exceptions to Protection Where Copyright and Trade Mark Overlap' (n 101) 597; Kur, 'Cumulation of Rights with Regard to Three-Dimensional Shapes' (n 45) 157.

D Literature

As an initial comment, it is worth reporting that many commentators believe that problems created by the copyright/trademark overlap will occur rarely because their requirements and purposes still differ quite a bit.[119] Nevertheless, as can be seen from the discussion above, because the scope of trademark law has expanded over the years and may carry on expanding, overlaps between the two rights cannot be discounted. Indeed, although the simultaneous overlap of copyright/trademark will occur less often, as the need to have a trademark in addition to a copyright during the copyright term is not urgent, sometimes it is useful, for instance if only the title of a book is used but the story is different.[120] In addition, it is useful to have trademark rights because title is easier to prove ((official) registration as opposed to (private) statement as to date of creation; distinctiveness as opposed to originality).[121]

The views of the literature as to how the overlaps should be regulated are classified by type of overlap (simultaneous, negative and *a posteriori*).

(i) Simultaneous Overlap

Some authors have suggested general rules that should apply when there is 'pure objective cumulation' (ie without simultaneous subjective cumulation) and when there is both objective and subjective cumulation (ie when there is only one owner for both IPRs, here copyright and trademark). Feer Verkade proposes that in these cases, both right-holders must respect each other's rights.[122] He gives several reasons for this:

> abuse of a right; exercise incompatible with the principles of reasonableness and fairness; exercise incompatible with freedom of information under article 10 of the ECHR; nullity of a relevant legal relationship under article 85 of the EC treaty [now TFEU article 101]; precedence for the free movement of goods (including advertising the goods offered) under articles 30–36 of the EC Treaty [now TFEU articles 34–36], where the relationship between the copyright holder and the trademark holder is an obstacle to action by the copyright holder.[123]

Many of these rules could also serve more generally for most of the overlaps identified in this book, in addition to simultaneous overlaps between copyright and trademark law. The pertinence of these rules to organising overlaps in general will be revisited later in the last chapter. Feer Verkade's proposed rule when there is both objective and subjective cumulation is that 'one law should not be able to cut across the object of another'.[124] Otherwise, the owner of both rights could enjoy the best of both worlds,

[119] Ibid; Kur, 'Exceptions to Protection Where Copyright and Trade Mark Overlap' (n 101) 597 (requirements); Reeskamp, 'Dr No in Trade Mark Country' (n 79) 33–35 (purposes).

[120] See Reeskamp, 'Dr No in Trade Mark Country' (n 79) 34. '[T]he name "Harry Potter" as such lacks sufficient originality in order to qualify as a work under copyright protection, but it is sufficiently distinctive as an indication for the exciting adventures of a student wizard.' And ibid 35 for the simultaneous overlap; it is really a question of how trademark can cumulate with/add to copyright rather than the other way round, 'ie, the question whether owners of a copyright can prohibit any acts allowed under trademark law, is less interesting'.

[121] Reeskamp, 'Dr No in Trade Mark Country' (n 79) 34.

[122] D Feer Verkade, 'The Cumulative Effect of Copyright Law and Trademark Law: Which Takes Precedence?' in J Kabel and G Mom, *Intellectual Property and Information Law: Essays in Honour of Herman Cohen Jerobam* (The Hague, Kluwer Law International, 1998) 69, 70–71. He also cites a decision from the Court of Appeal of the Netherlands Antilles and Aruba applying this principle.

[123] Ibid n 16.

[124] Ibid 72.

where it is obviously not the aim of the copyright and trademark laws taken separately.[125] In practice, in each case, an enquiry has to be made as to whether it is trademark law or copyright law which takes precedence. Thus, there is no general rule but decisions will have to be made on a case-by-case basis and in his view it will generally not be difficult to decide which one prevails.[126] Finally, he does not think that in cases where the TFEU rules are not affected, the solution could be left to national courts, as this would risk destroying uniformity.[127]

Reeskamp thinks that when there is concurrence, whether subjective or objective, it is not really a problem since copyright and trademark laws have different purposes, so the overlap should be allowed.[128] However, he recalls a decision of the Dutch Supreme Court which set limitations to concurrence if 'the tenor of one of these regulations expressly constitutes the opposite'.[129] This is similar to Feer Verkade's general rule that 'one law should not be able to cut across the object of another'.

Other authors have suggested specific rules for each aspect of the simultaneous overlap. No comments or rules could be found in the literature specifically for the issue of protected subject matter, so that we start here with excluded subject matter.

(a) Excluded Subject Matter

Some signs which cannot be registered are those signs which consist exclusively of the shape which gives substantial value to the goods. However, as a result of the importance given to the design of goods (as perceived also by the purchasing public), many goods nowadays have shapes which give them substantial value, which has led some to say that the exclusion will apply to the vast majority of goods.[130] This contradicts the intention of the EU legislature when it adopted the Trademark Directive and Regulation to open up the registration of shapes. Some commentators have therefore suggested abolishing the exclusion[131] and others have even suggested disregarding it in the meantime.[132]

[125] Ibid.

[126] Ibid 73.

[127] Feer Verkade, 'The Cumulative Effect of Copyright Law and Trademark Law' (n 122) 75. He cites a comparable case where there was a conflict between domestic law and Benelux law, and the Benelux Court of Justice gave precedence to the need for uniformity (*Kim*, BCJ, 19 November 1988, NJ 1989, 299).

[128] Reeskamp, 'Dr No in Trade Mark Country' (n 79) 33. 'Copyright law protects an original work against unauthorised publication and duplication while trademark law protects the distinctive feature of a brand against the likelihood of confusion, and if it is a known brand, also against the likelihood of dilution.'

[129] *Bigott/Doucal*, Dutch Supreme Court, 16 April 1999 [1999] *Nederlandse Jurisprudentie* 697, comment Hugenholtz.

[130] Quaedvlieg, 'Overlap/Relationships between Copyright and Other Intellectual Property Rights' (n 27) 509; P Torremans, *Holyoak and Torremans Intellectual Property Law*, 5th edn (Oxford, Oxford University Press, 2008) 388.

[131] U Koschtial, 'Die Freihaltebedürftigkeit wegen besonderer Form im Europäischen und Deutschen Markenrecht' (2004) *GRUR Int* 106, 110, and further references cited by Quaedvlieg, 'Overlap/Relationships between Copyright and Other Intellectual Property Rights' (n 27) 509.

[132] See A Kur, 'Harmonization of the Trademark Laws in Europe: An Overview' (1997) 28 *International Review of Intellectual Property and Competition Law* 1, v 17 n 106, also noting that 'the provision is probably not in accordance with art 15(2) of the TRIPs Agreement'; Kur, 'Formalschutz Dreidimensionaler Marken – Neue Aufgaben für die Markenabteilung des Deutschen Patentamts' in DPA (ed), *100 Jahre Marken-Amt* (Munich, Wila Verlag, 1994) 175, 192–93, cited by Quaedvlieg, 'Overlap/Relationships between Copyright and Other Intellectual Property Rights' (n 27) 509.

(b) Ownership

As to the issue of different owners, Quaedvlieg refers to a solution given by the Dutch Supreme Court in a case where a trademark right in a logo had been assigned to another party but the copyright in the same had not, although the parties clearly intended assignment of all rights in the logo.[133] The Court held that the party who had transferred the trademark right had waived its copyright. This solution results in 'convergence as to the determination of the right holder':[134]

> The nature of the work as a logo obviously must have played a role, for it seems very unlikely that the transfer of the trademark rights in, for example, a normal painting would have entailed a waiver of copyright to the same extent.[135]

This situation is an easy one when the intention of the parties is clear, but things are more complicated when the parties' intention is unclear and no literature exists on how to resolve this more complex issue.

(c) Exceptions

For the cases where there is no convergence, the question remains whether an exception for parodic uses should be included in EU and national trademark law. As Kur notes, it is certainly a good idea, although not one requiring urgent action as, in most cases, the systems converge on this point.[136] However, she recommends that trademark law be amended to increase the number of its exceptions in view of the recent trend that sees trademarks being used more and more as a tool to control commercial communication.[137] Maniatis and Gredley share the same opinion, at least as regards the parody exception.[138] A parody exception does not even exist in UK copyright law. They recommend enacting one in both UK copyright and trademark law because it would offer more certainty to the parodist. The limitation would, of course, be that such exception would not be available if the parodist free-rides on the reputation of the trademark. They also justify the enactment on the basis of the right to free speech. Like Kur, they believe that '[t]oo great an extension of trademark rights may lead to a situation in which trademark law can be used to curtail freedom of expression in a way that copyright law has hitherto resisted'.[139] This recommendation is all the more valid now after the *Intel* and *L'Oréal* cases,[140] which have further expanded the scope of protection for famous marks.

[133] Quaedvlieg, 'Overlap/Relationships between Copyright and Other Intellectual Property Rights' (n 27) 515, referring to *Laser Vloerplan*, Dutch Supreme Court, 20 March 1992, *BIE* 1993, 39. See also Quaedvlieg, 'Concurrence and Convergence in Industrial Design' (n 109) 38.

[134] Quaedvlieg, 'Concurrence and Convergence in Industrial Design' (n 109) 38.

[135] Ibid.

[136] Kur, 'Exceptions to Protection Where Copyright and Trade Mark Overlap' (n 101) 608, also noting that obviously the exception should also be made mandatory in all national copyright laws (it is included in the list in Infosoc Directive, art 5(3) but as is well-known, none of the exceptions is mandatory).

[137] Ibid.

[138] S Maniatis and E Gredley, 'Parody: A Fatal Attraction' (1997) *European Intellectual Property Review* 339, 420.

[139] Ibid.

[140] Case C-487/07 *L'Oréal SA, Lancôme Parfums et Beauté & Cie SNC and Laboratoire Garnier & Cie v Bellure NV, Malaika Investments Ltd and Starion International Ltd* [2009] ECR I-5185; Case C-252/07 *Intel Corporation v CPM United Kingdom* [2008] ECR I-8823.

As we saw, another limit on the scope of both copyright and trademark rights is the principle of exhaustion. Although it is unlikely that the *Dior* ruling will be reversed or modified, it would be better if it were to be integrated in the Trademark Directive and Regulation or in the Infosoc Directive. For instance, a rule like that introduced in section 44(c)(1) of the Australian Copyright Act 1968 as amended could be used:

> The copyright in a work a copy of which is on, or embodied in, the non-infringing accessory to an article is not infringed by importing the accessory with the article.[141]

Perhaps it would also make sense to provide for such principle independently from the nexus with the free movement of goods or services, to make it even stronger in purely national cases. For example, one could expand the wording of Infosoc Directive, article 5(3)(j), and make the exception mandatory.[142] It has even been suggested that in Member States currently providing for such exception in their national laws, despite the fact that it applies only for the selling of 'original works of art' (ie paintings, sculptures, etc), courts could take the *Dior* decision into account when interpreting it.[143]

(ii) Negative Overlap

There is almost no literature on the negative overlap. Quaedvlieg has criticised it, saying that when trademark law allows the protection of ideas, which should by definition always remain free for all, it gives the impression 'that the cause of cultural innovation will not suffer great harm if they [ie ideas] were to be protected. Copyright and trademark logic . . . here really clash'.[144] However, as we have seen above, this comment is less dramatic than it seems, as trademarks will very rarely protect ideas.

(iii) A Posteriori *Overlap*

The literature is divided on the issue whether trademark law should be able to prolong a copyright.[145] All seem to agree that there is nothing as such in the written law that prevents a trademark from extending the length of protection of a work whose copyright has expired. Some think that in fact very few problems will occur in practice, in the sense that the occurrences will be rare and therefore the free domain of copyright will generally be left intact.[146] This is because trademark law requires distinctiveness. Therefore, many famous artistic and musical works will not be registrable unless they can establish acquired distinctiveness or secondary meaning.[147] Nevertheless, the once copyrighted

[141] Cited by Kur, 'Exceptions to Protection Where Copyright and Trade Mark Overlap' (n 101) 609 n 48.

[142] Ibid 611. The article states 'Member States may provide for exceptions or limitations to the rights provided for in Articles 2 and 3 in the following cases: . . . use for the purpose of advertising the public exhibition or sale of artistic works, to the extent necessary to promote the event, excluding any other commercial use'.

[143] Ibid.

[144] A Quaedvlieg, 'Protection of Three-Dimensional Models as a Trade Mark, in Adjuncts and Alternatives to copyright' in J Ginsburg and J Besek (eds), *Adjuncts and Alternatives to Copyright, Proceedings of the ALAI Congress, June 13–17, 2001, New York USA* (New York, Columbia University School of Law, 2002) 576, 581.

[145] Reeskamp, 'Dr No in Trade Mark Country' (n 79) 34–35, noting that the majority of Dutch literature (Visser, Cohen Jeroham, Spoor, Verkade) is against the prolongation, following the ruling of the Dutch Supreme Court in the *Bigott/Doucal* case (n 129).

[146] Kur, 'Exceptions to Protection Where Copyright and Trade Mark Overlap' (n 101) 600; Quaedvlieg, 'Protection of Three-Dimensional Models as a Trade Mark' (n 144) 578.

[147] Kur, 'Exceptions to Protection Where Copyright and Trade Mark Overlap' (n 101) 600–1.

expression can in the end acquire distinctiveness. Therefore, in those cases (maybe not so rare, think of Mickey Mouse or Peter Rabbit[148]), 'the paradoxical situation is created that where the anti-monopoly concern is most urgent, namely in the case of shapes which after a century still fascinate the public and are "wanted" by it, nothing will stop trademark protection'.[149] Whereas these positions are not extreme, they still clash. More extreme positions are also found in the literature. On the one hand, there are those who think that since there is no 'written rule' prohibiting the overlap, it must be that the existence of the overlap is legitimate, even though they admit that in some cases the extension of the protection can have undesirable effects.[150] On the other hand, others find that such overlap after the term of copyright has expired should be prohibited as a matter of principle, in other words that it is against the public order so that such trademark registrations should be cancelled.[151] A more moderate view is that of Quaedvlieg. For him, the expiry of copyright protection is not per se a public interest, there needs to be special circumstances for copyright law to trump trademark law.[152] He suggests that:

> [t]he more a work falls under the core competence of copyright and the less it has to do with the commercial world of the trademark, the sooner other regimes could have a reason to negatively converge with the expiry of the copyright term.[153]

Thus, for him, trademark should not protect 'works of art of which only one single copy has been made' nor 'literary characters, titles, and cartoon characters (insofar as they are used in connection with the authentic works they are a part of)' after the expiry of the copyright term. On the other hand, logos which are still used 'as signs distinguishing the origin of goods or services . . . fall as much, if not more, under the core competence of trademark law'.[154]

He has the same opinion on the issue regarding shapes:

> As for the shapes of goods, the problem is somewhat complex. A first approach would consist of saying that if, 70 years after the death of the author, the shape is still used by a particular undertaking in order to distinguish those goods as to their origin, and if the relevant public identifies the origin of these good on the basis of their shape, there is no reason to suddenly terminate trademark protection. The reason for this is that if the sign has in fact acquired distinctiveness

[148] Moffatt, 'Mutant Copyrights and Backdoor Patents' (n 103) 1509 and 1516, mentioning several US cases.

[149] Quaedvlieg, 'Protection of Three-Dimensional Models as a Trade Mark' (n 144) 583. Reeskamp, 'Dr No in Trade Mark Country' (n 79) 36, but not seeing this as a problem since the copyright holders have during the lifespan of the copyright been able to make the literary or artistic work known as a trademark for the form of entertainment in question and thus seeing no reason for trademark law to apply. Reeskamp, however, only sees the negative effect of the release into the public domain of famous works (registration as a trademark by anyone being first to do so, so for profit purposes) not the beneficial effects (free use for non-commercial purposes by anyone). His argument that not allowing the registration of titles of films or characters (eg James Bond) will confuse the public if the same title is used by other competitors for the same goods (films), is however convincing. In short, he holds 'that the undesirability of the artificial extension of protection under copyright does in fact constitute an argument for restricting the protective scope under trademark law, but is not an argument for dismissing title and character trademarks altogether'.

[150] C van Woensel, *Merk, God en verbod. Oneigenlijk Gebruik en Monopolisering van Tekens met een Grote Symbolische Waarde* (Amsterdam, DeLex, 2007) 327, 354, cited by Quaedvlieg, 'Overlap/Relationships between Copyright and Other Intellectual Property Rights' (n 27) 512; Wichers Hoeth cited by Feer Verkade, 'The Cumulative Effect of Copyright Law and Trademark Law' (n 122) 70 and 72.

[151] H Cohen Jeroham cited by Feer Verkade, 'The Cumulative Effect of Copyright Law and Trademark Law' (n 122) and also Feer Verkade himself it seems (at 72).

[152] Quaedvlieg, 'Concurrence and Convergence in Industrial Design' (n 109) 53.

[153] Ibid 54.

[154] Ibid.

> and is actively used as a distinctive sign – and would perhaps have been so for generations – it seems rather drastic to change that status quo, unless there would be very strong reasons to the contrary . . . If, however, at any moment after the expiry of the copyright term, such shapes have been without trademark protection, a new registration should not be allowed. Trademark law should respect the status quo of what has been absorbed by the free domain, just as the free domain should respect the status quo of what is still protected, used and perceived as an identification of origin.[155]

This elaborated suggestion seems in effect close to Feer Verkade's statement of principle that 'one law should not be able to cut across the object of another'. It also converges with commentators' suggestions to abolish the exclusion for shapes which give substantial value to goods.

These proposals, along with other 'overarching' rules or principles, will be discussed in chapter seven as possible criteria to organise the overlaps.

IV. TRADEMARKS AND DESIGNS

A The Legal Framework

Nothing prevents a design which fulfils the conditions of protection under copyright, design and trademark laws from receiving protection under all three intellectual property rights.[156] In fact, more bluntly and as stated in the previous section, cumulation of rights is clearly allowed by the provisions of the Trademark and Design Directives and the Trademark and Design Regulations (Design Directive, article 16; Design Regulation, article 96(1); Trademark Directive, recital 6; CTMR, article 14(2)). While these provisions do not force Member States to cumulate rights, including trademark and design rights,[157] some have gone as far as suggesting that cumulation is 'recommended'.[158] Nothing in the Directives and their *travaux préparatoires* seems to favour such an extended reading, however. Apart from these provisions, the only relevant articles for the possible overlap are Trademark Directive, article 3(1)(e), CTMR, article 7(1)(e), Design Directive, article 7 and Design Regulation, article 8. Whilst the Design Directive is remarkably liberal and also provides in detail for overlap and cumulation of rights,[159] the Trademark Directive is timid on those same issues.[160] The Green Paper on the Legal

[155] Ibid.

[156] U Suthersanen, 'Breaking Down the Intellectual Property Barriers' (1998) *Intellectual Property Quarterly* 267, 273. A Carboni, 'The Overlap between Registered Community Designs and Community Trade Marks' (2006) 1(4) *Journal of Intellectual Property Law and Practice* 256, 258, adds that neither the Trademark Directive nor the Design Regulation 'expressly prohibits registration of a sign or a design under one system where the other might also apply, or (ii) its registration under both systems . . . [In fact,] OHIM's CTM and CD databases reveal numerous interesting examples of "designs" registered as CTMs and "trademarks" registered as CDs'.

[157] With only the exception of designs and copyright (Design Directive, art 17 and Design Regulation, art 96(2)).

[158] Musker, *Community Design Law* (n 54) 75.

[159] A Firth, 'Signs, Surfaces, Shapes and Structures: The Protection of Product Design under Trade Mark Law' in G Dinwoodie and M Janis (eds), *Trade Mark Law and Theory: A Handbook of Contemporary Research* (Cheltenham, Edward Elgar, 2008) 498, 502, adding that the Design Directive was very liberal about cumulation of rights.

[160] A Firth, E Gredley and S Maniatis, 'Shapes as Trade Marks: Public Policy, Functional Considerations and Consumer Perception' (2001) *European Intellectual Property Review* 86, 88. Indeed, it only has one small recital referring to it (recital 5 of the codified Trademark Directive).

Protection of Industrial Design refers only briefly to these provisions as it finds the relationship between design and trademark protection more satisfactory than that with copyright.[161] However, as will be seen below, it is only superficially so, as the vast amount of literature on the topic proves.

B 'Content Overlap'

(i) Simultaneous Overlap

(a) Subject Matter

Since a design is the appearance of a product and can be in two or three dimensions, there can be overlap with two and three dimensional trademarks;[162] for instance, packaging, get-up and graphic symbols, which the Design Directive cites as examples of possible products in which design right can subsist, as well as logos, can also be signs that can be registered as trademarks.[163] We are therefore in the realm of combinations of colours, graphic design (drawings, etc) and shapes. It has been noted that '[u]nlike in the U.S., architectural design has enjoyed scant trademark recognition in the UK and Europe'.[164] So, although the overlap technically also exists at this level of 'shape', it has so far not been used very often.

(b) Protection Requirements

It is possible that a design may also be distinctive in addition to being novel and having individual character. Vice versa, a trademark can also be novel and have individual character, although this may happen less often than designs being distinctive.[165] However, as will be seen below, shapes will generally have to have a high degree of distinctiveness in order for them to be protected by trademark law so that they may more often also meet the criteria of novelty and individual character. Nevertheless, sometimes it will be easier to obtain design protection (as novelty is relative) than trademark protection, eg for packaging. Thus, design right can be acquired first and then trademark applied for later when the public has been educated to recognise the packaging as a trademark, ie consumers only see it as indicating the origin of the goods as coming from a single company.[166]

[161] Green Paper on the Legal Protection of Industrial Design (n 17) 153.

[162] Musker, *Community Design Law* (n 54) 78, noting that '[t]here is no obstacle to dual protection for two-dimensional logos as both designs and trademarks'.

[163] Carboni, 'The Overlap between Registered Community Designs and Community Trade Marks' (n 156); Torremans, 'Three Dimensional Trade Marks and Designs for Packaging' (n 29) 762.

[164] Firth, 'Signs, Surfaces, Shapes and Structures' (n 159) 502.

[165] See also Torremans, 'Three Dimensional Trade Marks and Designs for Packaging' (n 29) 763, noting that '[t]he novelty requirement is clearly more restrictive than what is required in relation to trademark registration. Shapes and packaging that are not new will not pass the test even if they may still be a distinctive sign for the purposes of trademark law, but the really valuable packaging shapes will be the new ones and for them the dual protection will remain possible'. Ibid 764: 'this requirement [individual character] is clearly tougher than its trademark equivalent of distinctiveness. It will therefore filter out some trademarks and deny them dual protection. They will not be registered designs'.

[166] Kur, 'Cumulation of IP Rights Pertaining to Product Shapes' (n 43) 617; Bently and Sherman, *Intellectual Property Law* (n 82) 830, further noting the paradox of trying to get a trademark for packaging. 'If this has

It is worth summarising the EU courts' case law concerning the protection requirement of distinctiveness as, although it is technically exactly the same for all signs, some peculiarities make it more difficult to obtain trademark protection for shapes. As a result, the overlap with designs is at this stage already somewhat curtailed. These peculiarities may also exist because the distinctiveness requirement arguably reflects the European Union's tenets of market freedom and undistorted competition.[167] This has made commentators say that 'it is likely that trademark jurisprudence in Europe generally will be influenced by that of shape marks'.[168] The starting point is that shape marks are not subject to a more stringent test of distinctiveness.[169] For goods which have no shape, the packaging can be said to be their shape.[170] However, it is already difficult at this stage for packaging to act as a trademark. This is because consumers do not generally perceive it as an indication of origin. This is mainly because words and figurative marks are independent of the appearance of the products they are attached to.[171] As:

> average consumers are not in the habit of making assumptions about the origin of goods based on the shape of their packaging, in the absence of any graphic or word element, . . . it could therefore prove more difficult to establish distinctive character in the case of such a three-dimensional trademark than in the case of a word or figurative mark.[172]

The same goes for shapes in general (consumers do not see them as trademarks, especially if used in conjunction with eg words or figurative marks[173]), so that very few trademark applications for shapes are successful. This is not the end of the story. Not only is it already difficult for a shape to be distinctive, there are absolute grounds of refusal, especially for shapes.

been achieved, then whether particular packaging is devoid of distinctive character is likely to turn on whether the get-up is sufficiently noticeable in the circumstances to catch the attention of consumers. If this is not the case, as where a compact disc of a sound recording is suddenly sold in an unusual packaging, the position is problematic. On the one hand, the packaging will be memorable. On the other, it is unlikely to be perceived as an indication of origin.'

[167] Firth, 'Signs, Surfaces, Shapes and Structures' (n 159) 514, quoting U Suthersanen, 'The European Court of Justice in *Philips v Remington*: Trade Marks and Market Freedom' (2003) *Intellectual Property Quarterly* 257.

[168] Firth, 'Signs, Surfaces, Shapes and Structures' (n 159) 514, noting however that 'a "keep free" competitive aspect did not conclusively militate against registration in the "stand-up pouches" case'.

[169] Case C-299/99 *Koninklijke Philips Electronics v Remington Consumer Products* [2002] ECR I-5475, para 48. As this case will be discussed at length in the sections below, its facts are important to summarise. Philips developed a new type of three-headed rotary electric shaver in 1966, the shape of which it registered as a trademark in the United Kingdom in 1985. In 1996, Remington started to commercialise a shaver similar to that of Philips. Thus, Philips sued for infringement and Remington sought to invalidate Philips' trademark. See also Joined Cases C-53/01–C-55/01 *Linde, Winward Industries and Rado Uhren* [2003] ECR I-3161, para 42; Case T-88/00 *Mag Instrument v OHIM* [2002] ECR II-467, para 32 (torch shape); Case C-305/02 *Nestlé Waters France v OHIM* [2003] ECR II-5207, para 35.

[170] Case C-218/01 *Henkel KGaA* [2004] ECR I-1725, para 37; Case C-173/04 *Deutsche SiSi Werke v OHIM* [2006] ECR I-551, para 33.

[171] Case C-218/01 *Henkel KGaA* [2004] ECR I-1725, para 52.

[172] See ibid. See also Carboni, 'The Overlap between Registered Community Designs and Community Trade Marks' (n 156) 258.

[173] See Phillips, *Trade Mark Law* (n 86) 143–44. See also Suthersanen, 'The European Court of Justice in *Philips v Remington*' (n 167) 275, noting that '[t]he hostility to shapes as evidenced by the extra hurdles placed is akin to that traditionally shown under copyright law where three-dimensional works have always had extra barriers placed on them. Both trademark and copyright laws appear to be more at ease in granting protection to works comprising of "writings" and "drawings" as opposed to three-dimensional shapes'.

(c) Excluded Subject Matter

The same exclusions which are relevant for the overlap between trademarks and copyright are relevant for that of trademarks and designs, namely Trademark Directive, article 3(1)(e) and CTMR, article 7(1)(e) concerning natural, functional and ornamental shapes.[174] Trademark Directive, article 3(1)(e)'s second indent (technical function) is also reflected in Design Directive, article 7. We refer the reader to section III.B(i) above (simultaneous overlap between copyright and trademarks). Just as for the overlap between trademarks and copyright, the overlap between trademarks and designs is therefore complete for two-dimensional but not for three-dimensional subject matter. However, in addition to article 3(1)(e), Trademark Directive, article 3(1)(b) and (c) also curtail the scope of the overlap for both two and three-dimensional signs. Indeed, a copyright work or design whose holder would also like to register it as a trademark may be original or novel but devoid of any distinctive character (article 3(1)(b)) or under article 3(1)(c):

> consist exclusively of signs or indications which may serve, in trade, to designate the kind, quality, quantity, intended purpose, value, geographical origin, or the time of production of the goods or of rendering of the service, or other characteristics of the goods or services.

In fact, Trademark Directive, article 3(1) contains more exclusions, which are also more demanding than under the Design Directive.[175] Therefore, the overlap of trademark/design is already quite curtailed. In order to determine the boundaries of the overlap, it is useful to examine the EU courts' case law on article 3(1)(b)–(e). First of all, each of the grounds for refusal listed in article 3(1) is independent of the others and calls for separate examination.[176] Thus, all signs must pass all the hurdles set out in article 3(1)(a)–(h). Article 3(3) (allowing signs which have acquired distinctive character over time to be registered) cannot override any of the indents in article 3(1)(e).[177] In addition, the EU courts have constantly held that the various grounds for refusing registration set out in article 3 must be interpreted in the light of the public interest underlying each of them.[178] The public interests behind indents (b), (c) and (e) are similar if not identical. The general public interest behind article 3(1)(b)–(e) is that it would be wrong to grant exclusive (trademark) rights to a single operator as it could hinder competition on the market for the goods or services concerned.[179] It is already clear from the case law on article 3(1)(b) that it will be more difficult for shapes to be trademarks. Whilst, on the one hand, it is sufficient for this

[174] So nicknamed by the Advocate-General in his Opinion in *Philips*, para 16.

[175] See Carboni, 'The Overlap between Registered Community Designs and Community Trade Marks' (n 156) table 2.

[176] Joined Cases C-53/01–C-55/01 *Linde, Winward Industries and Rado Uhren* [2003] ECR I-3161, para 67.

[177] See Case C-299/99 *Koninklijke Philips Electronics v Remington Consumer Products* [2002] ECR I-5475, paras 57 and 75 (extremely clear on this); Case C-371/06 *Benetton Group v G-Star International* [2007] ECR I-7709, para 26 (decision only in relation to the third indent). See also a confirmation of this in the United Kingdom in *Julius Sämaan v Tetrosyl* [2006] EWHC 529 (Ch D) per Kitchin J (the prohibition is equally mandatory across all limbs), cited by Firth, 'Signs, Surfaces, Shapes and Structures' (n 159) 509.

[178] See Joined Cases C-108/97 and C-109/97 *Windsurfing Chiemsee* [1999] ECR I-2779, paras 25–27; Case C-299/99 *Koninklijke Philips Electronics v Remington Consumer Products* [2002] ECR I-5475, para 77; Joined Cases C-53/01–C-55/01 *Linde, Winward Industries and Rado Uhren* [2003] ECR I-3161, para 71.

[179] Joined Cases C-108/97 and C-109/97 *Windsurfing Chiemsee* [1999] ECR I-2779, para 25; Joined Cases C-468/01 P–C-472/01 P *Procter & Gamble v OHIM* [2004] ECR I-5141, para 73 (tablets for washing machines or dishwashers not distinctive).

ground to be dismissed if there is a minimal degree of distinctiveness,[180] on the other, in order to be distinctive, a mark (any mark not only shapes) must significantly depart from the norm or customs of the sector.[181] The courts have subsequently added, in cases involving shapes, that it is not sufficient that the shape is a variant of a common shape of that type of product.[182] Furthermore, the shape's high quality design does not mean automatic distinctiveness.[183] It appears from the case law that more shapes have been invalidated or refused registration for lack of distinctive character (ie on grounds of Trademark Directive, article 3 or Design Directive, article 7(1)(b) alone) than not.[184]

To go back to the public interest underlying indents (b) to (e) of article 3(1), it appears from the case law that it is in broad terms identical: namely to make sure that various alternatives are kept available for competitors; in other words (in relation to article 3(1)(c)), that 'descriptive signs or indications relating to the characteristics of goods or services in respect of which registration is applied for may be freely used by all'.[185] This is unsurprising as it corresponds to two major aims of the European Union, namely a (1) competitive (2) single market, ie without national barriers.[186] For article 3(1)(b) and (c), which are subject to the proviso (article 3(3)), it needs to be added that these alternatives are available only to the extent to which the sign is not capable of distinctiveness a priori

[180] Case C-305/02 *Nestlé Waters France v OHIM* [2003] ECR II-5207, para 42 (water bottle shape); Case T-128/01 *Daimler Chrysler* [2003] ECR II-701, para 49 (Jeep grille); Case T-393/02 *Henkel KGaA v OHIM* [2004] ECR II-4115, para 42 (shape of transparent bottle in the form of a crystal).

[181] Case C-218/01 *Henkel KGaA* [2004] ECR I-1725, para 49. In the same vein, see *Wim de Waele* (n 89) para 40 (twisted appearance of the mark applied for is *only slightly* more marked than that of other charcuterie); see also Joined Cases C-456/01 P–C-457/01 P *Henkel v OHIM* [2004] ECR I-5089, para 10. Compare with Case T-460/05 *Bang & Olufsen v OHIM* [2007] ECR II-4207, para 42 ('the mark applied for departs significantly from the customs of the sector').

[182] Case C-136/02 P *Mag Instrument Inc v OHIM* [2004] ECR I-9165, para 32.

[183] Ibid para 68.

[184] Cases where the mark was found distinctive include: *Daimler Chrysler* (n 180) 6 March 2003 (picture (2D) of a shape (grille) for a motor vehicle (jeep); grilles no longer have a purely technical function and they help differentiate between models and motor vehicles manufacturers; at the time of registration it was distinctive for motor vehicles); Case C-305/02 *Nestlé Waters France v OHIM* [2003] ECR II-5207 (water bottle shape); Case T-393/02 *Henkel KGaA v OHIM* [2004] ECR II-4115 (shape of transparent bottle in the form of crystal). Cases where the marks were found devoid of distinctive character include: Case C-286/04 P *Eurocermex v OHIM* [2005] ECR I-5797 (shape of Corona bottle with piece of lemon inside at the top); Case C-445/02 P *Glaverbel v OHIM* [2004] ECR I-6267 (patterned glass); Case C-24/05 P *Stork v OHIM* [2006] ECR I-5677 (three-dimensional shape of a light-brown sweet); Case T-449/07 *Rotter v OHIM* (nyr), available at www.curia.europa.eu (sausage in the form of pretzel); *Deutsche SiSi Werke* (n 170) (shape of stand-up pouches for juice drinks). It may be useful to remember that under Trademark Directive, art 3(1)(b), the criterion to judge distinctiveness is that of the average consumer, i.e. someone who is reasonably well informed and reasonably observant and circumspect, and does not conduct an analytical examination or pay particular attention (Case C-136/02 P *Mag Instrument Inc v OHIM* [2004] ECR I-9165, para 32); but for some goods, it is 'the average consumer who exhibits a particularly high level of attention when he prepares and makes his choice between different goods in the category concerned' (see Case C-361/04 P *Ruiz-Picasso and others v OHIM* [2006] ECR I-643, paras 40 and 41; Case T-460/05 *Bang & Olufsen v OHIM* [2007] ECR II-4207, para 35).

[185] See Case C-299/99 *Philips v Remington* [2002] ECR I-5475, para 80, more specifically indent (ii): 'Article 3(1)(e) of the Directive pursues an aim which is in the public interest, namely that a shape whose *essential characteristics perform a technical function* and were chosen to fulfil that function may be freely used by all' (emphasis added) citing *Windsurfing Chiemsee* (n 178) para 25; Joined Cases C-53/01–C-55/01 *Linde, Winward Industries and Rado Uhren* [2003] ECR I-3161, paras 73–74; Case C-173/04 *Deutsche SiSi Werke v OHIM* [2006] ECR I-551, para 62, citing Case C-191/01 P *OHIM v Wrigley* [2003] ECR I-12447, para 31; Case C-326/01 P *Telefon und Buch v OHIM* [2004] ECR I-1371, para 27; Case C150/02 P *Streamserve v OHIM* [2004] ECR I-1461, para 25). See also later Joined Cases C-468/01 P–C-472/01 P *Procter & Gamble v OHIM* [2004] ECR I-5141 and *Lego Juris AS v OHIM*, GBA, para 34, confirmed by Case T-270/06 *Lego Juris AS v OHIM* [2008] ECR II-3117.

[186] Firth, Gredley and Maniatis, 'Shapes as Trade Marks' (n 160) 89.

and irrespective of the use made of it within the meaning of article 3(3).[187] The case law on article 3(1)(e) repeats this *leitmotiv*[188] and adds more specifically that the public interest is 'to prevent trademark protection from granting its proprietor a monopoly on technical solutions or functional characteristics of a product which a user is likely to seek in the products of competitors'.[189] Advocate-General Ruiz-Jarabo Colomer in *Philips v Remington* had further elaborated this principle by stating that it is 'clear that the legislature wanted to delimit the scope of protection of a trademark from that of an industrial patent', adding that the same goal appears in Design Directive, article 7(1).[190] The Court of Justice then added that indent (ii) 'reflects the *legitimate aim* of not allowing individuals to use registration of a mark in order to *acquire or perpetuate* exclusive rights relating to technical solutions' (emphasis added).[191] The Advocate-General had specifically mentioned designs and patents and the public interest in having the subject matter free for all 'once the time-limit expires'.[192] The Court thus ruled that:

> Article 3(1)(e), second indent, of Directive 89/104 must be interpreted to mean that a sign consisting exclusively of the shape of a product is unregistrable by virtue thereof if it is established that the essential functional features of that shape are attributable only to the technical result. Moreover, the ground for refusal or invalidity of registration imposed by that provision cannot be overcome by establishing that there are other shapes which allow the same technical result to be obtained.[193]

It needs to be emphasised that *Philips* only precludes the registration of shapes 'whose *essential characteristics* perform a technical function' (emphasis added).[194] After the *Philips* case, the EU courts held that adding an arbitrary element from a functional point of view (eg the colour red to a Lego brick) will not make the shape escape the prohibition.[195] Further, 'the essential characteristics of a shape must be determined objectively

[187] Joined Cases C-468/01 P–C-472/01 P *Procter & Gamble v OHIM* [2004] ECR I-5141, para 73 (tablets for washing machines or dishwashers); Joined Cases C-53/01–C-55/01 *Linde, Winward Industries and Rado Uhren* [2003] ECR I-3161, para 74; Case C-173/04 *Deutsche SiSi Werke v OHIM* [2006] ECR I-551, para 61, adding that 'the public interest underlying Article 7(1)(b) of that regulation is, manifestly, indissociable from the essential function of a trademark', citing Case C-329/02 P *SAT.1 v OHIM* [2004] ECR I-8317, para 27, and Case C-37/03 P *BioID v OHIM* [2005] ECR I-7975, para 60.

[188] In Case C-299/99 *Koninklijke Philips Electronics v Remington Consumer Products* [2002] ECR I-5475, the term 'free' or 'freedom' is even repeated three times. See paras 78, 79 and 80. See again later the confirmation in *Lego Juris AS v Mega Brands Inc*, OHIM First Board of Appeal's decision of 9 February 2005, available at http://oami.europa.eu/LegalDocs/BoA/2004/en/R0856_2004-1.pdf, and see Opinion of Advocate-General Mengozzi, C-48/09, 26 January 2010, available at www.curia.europa.eu.

[189] Case C-299/99 *Koninklijke Philips Electronics v Remington Consumer Products* [2002] ECR I-5475, para 78.

[190] See Advocate-General's Opinion, 23 January 2001, para 32.

[191] Case C-299/99 *Koninklijke Philips Electronics v Remington Consumer Products* [2002] ECR I-5475, para 82.

[192] See paras 30 and 31. Some commentators have suggested that it applies to all rights limited in time, ie patent, design or copyright laws. See Firth, Gredley and Maniatis, 'Shapes as Trade Marks' (n 160) 88; Firth, 'Signs, Surfaces, Shapes and Structures' (n 159) 508, citing A Folliard-Monguiral and D Rogers, 'The Protection of Shapes by the Community Trademark' (2003) *European Intellectual Property Review* 169.

[193] Case C-299/99 *Koninklijke Philips Electronics v Remington Consumer Products* [2002] ECR I-0475, para 84. This is similar to what the Advocate-General recommended in his Opinion at paras 35 and 54 and to what both the High Court and Court of Appeal also held. See Suthersanen, 'The European Court of Justice in *Philips v Remington*' (n 167) 261.

[194] See paras 79 and 84.

[195] This idea comes from Advocate-General Colomer's Opinion in Case C-299/99 *Koninklijke Philips Electronics v Remington Consumer Products* [2002] ECR I-5475, which he again restated in his Opinion in Case C-104/00 P *DKV v OHIM* [2002] ECR I-7561, para 53. Although the case dealt with a word mark, the

for the purposes of applying article 7(1)(e)(ii) of Regulation No. 40/94, on the basis of its graphic representation and any descriptions filed at the time of the application for the trademark'.[196] As a result, it will be extremely difficult to register a shape which performs a technical function.[197] In *Lego Juris v Mega Brands* in 2007, the Grand Board of Appeal at OHIM dismissed Lego's appeal against cancellation of its registration of a Lego brick, noting that 'a prior patent is practically irrefutable evidence that features therein disclosed or claimed are functional'.[198] Article 3(1)(e) is therefore relevant to the trademark/design overlap but also the trademark/copyright and trademark/patent overlaps. The *Lego* case will therefore be further discussed under the latter overlap (section VI.B(i)).

(d) Ownership

As regards the two previous overlaps (copyright/design and copyright/trademark), there will be problems in the case of objective cumulation without subjective cumulation. Two rules can sometimes avoid this problem. CTMR, article 52(2)(d) lists in its relative grounds for invalidity the case where the mark conflicts with an earlier industrial property right. A similar rule exists in the Design Regulation.[199] Its article 25(1)(e) states that a design may be declared invalid 'if a distinctive sign is used in a subsequent design'.[200]

(e) Rights and Infringement

Depending whether the right-holder asserts a (national or Community) registered or Community unregistered design, there will be more or less convergence at the level of rights. If it is a registered design, no copying will need to be proved, as in trademark law. Conversely, if it is a Community unregistered design, copying will need to be proved, unlike in trademark law but as under the trademark/copyright overlap. For the rest, in both situations (registered or unregistered designs), design rights are more comprehensive than the trademark holder's rights as there is no need to prove that the use is made 'as a design'. There is also no need to prove likelihood of confusion if the goods on which

Advocate-General refers to Trademark Directive, art 3(1)(e)(ii) to say that "a shape that simply incorporates an arbitrary element that is *negligible* from a functional point of view cannot escape the prohibition" (emphasis in the original). Even earlier, Jacob J in the *Philips v Remington* first instance case [1998] RPC 283, 308, had also said that he did not believe that 'shapes with trivial embellishments or variants are outside the exclusion from registrability'. In *Lego*, the CFI confirmed the Grand Board of Appeal of OHIM's decision. The Grand Board of Appeal had held that 'a shape does not escape that prohibition if it contains a minor arbitrary element such as a colour' (para 36) and '[i]t is apparent from that expression that the addition of non-essential characteristics having no technical function does not prevent a shape from being caught by that absolute ground of refusal if all the essential characteristics of that shape perform such a function. Accordingly, the Grand Board of Appeal was right to analyse the functionality of the shape at issue by reference to the characteristics which it considered to be essential' (para 38).

[196] Case T-270/06 *Lego Juris AS v OHIM* [2008] ECR II-3117, para 70.

[197] See eg Case C-107/03 P *P&G v OHIM* (2004), available at www.curia.europa.eu (bone shaped soap), the Court of Justice confirmed the CFI's judgment which had confirmed that of OHIM (no distinctiveness as a result of the application of Trademark Directive, art 3(1)(e)(i) and (ii)).

[198] See para 40. The case has been confirmed by the General Court and also by the Court of Justice, Case C-48/09 P (14 September 2010, nyr), available at www.curia.europa.eu.

[199] See above section II.B(i).

[200] The article has recently been interpreted by the General Court in Case T-148/08 *Beifa Group v OHIM* (2010), available at www.curia.eu.europa. The provision applies to declarations of invalidity of designs which are not only identical but also similar to the distinctive sign (paras 55 and 59).

the (non-famous) design is applied are simply similar rather than identical.[201] There is also convergence as both trademark and design laws allow private use/use for non-commercial purposes. However, a trademark will generally be more easily infringed than a design. This is because the test of informed user is stricter than the test of average consumer. In addition, current national courts' divergences in the interpretation of the text of infringement for registered design right also make it easier for a trademark to be infringed than a design.[202]

(f) Exceptions Including Exhaustion Principle

There are three additional exceptions under design law that do not exist under trademark law. The three exceptions are: acts done for experimental purposes; acts of reproduction for the purposes of making citations or of teaching; and transit of aircrafts and ships' equipment embodying design infringements, including importation of equipment for repairs and execution of such repairs on the equipment of such aircrafts and ships in transit. Apart from teaching and research, which generally are not done in the course of trade, in case of an overlap, the other two exceptions will clash with the trademark holder's rights and therefore trademark law will prevail over the design right exceptions.

The two rights, however, enshrine the exhaustion principle (Trademark Directive, article 7 and Design Directive, article 15).[203] As with copyright, there is no equivalent to Trademark Directive, article 7(2) in the Design Directive. The very same situation as occurred in the *Dior v Evora* case can happen if instead or in addition to copyright, there is a registered or unregistered design right on the product, be it two- or three-dimensional. In all likelihood, the *Dior* ruling would also apply by analogy.

(ii) Negative Overlap

(a) Design Protection Unavailable

Single letters or numbers and simple combinations of colours can be protected by trademark which would not be protected by design right because they would not be designs, or if they were they would not be novel or have individual character. The law is so crafted that there is no gap as regards shapes which are dictated by their technical function (Trademark Directive, article 3(1)(e)(ii) and Design Directive, article 7(1)). A design which cannot obtain protection as a result of Design Directive, article 7(1) cannot a fortiori obtain protection as a trademark. So trademark law cannot fill this gap. This should also apply to the cases covered by Design Directive, article 7(2). Some think that Design Directive, article 7(1) can be said to encompass article 7(2), so that the latter seems

201 A trademark application must list all the goods for which trademark registration is sought, not a design application. See Carboni, 'The Overlap between Registered Community Designs and Community Trade Marks' (n 156) 262.

202 As will be seen in chs four and five, the Paris Court of Appeal and Court of Appeal of England and Wales take opposite views on the interpretation of the registered design infringement test.

203 As to Trademark Directive, art 7, see above section III.B(i). Article 15: 'Exhaustion of rights. The rights conferred by a design right upon registration shall not extend to acts relating to a product in which a design included within the scope of protection of the design right is incorporated or to which it is applied, when the product has been put on the market in the Community by the holder of the design right or with his consent'.

redundant.[204] But as is clearly explained by others, article 7(2) can still cover some other cases not covered by article 7(1):

> the technical function exception primarily deals with a product that works on its own and in relation to which design features are dictated by the technical function of that product, whereas the must fit exception deals with two products that need to be connected, etc, in order for them to work . . . The technical function exception on its own may not have been able to achieve this result, because the shape of the connector is not dictated solely by the product's technical function. Indeed, as the electrical plug and socket example shows, for example, different plugs and sockets can be devised, and are in use in the UK and continental Europe. The narrowly defined technical function exception would therefore not cover this example, because the design features of one system are not essential for any product to carry out its technical function.[205]

Thus, article 7(2) is crucial as it ensures that no single designer 'monopolises the connector system due to the fact that interoperability of products is a vital element to enhance competition'.[206] Must-fit aspects which may not be protected by design right should not normally be protected by trademarks either because of the sweeping effect of the interpretation of Trademark Directive, article 3(1)(e)(ii).

However, there can still be an overlap as there will be some two- or three-dimensional designs which are neither novel nor have individual character but which can be distinctive.

(b) Trademark Protection Unavailable

The definition of a trademark is so broad that it is difficult to think of subject matter which could not be a trademark but could be a design. It is not impossible to imagine cases where a sign would be novel and have individual character but would not be distinctive. This is because a design does not have to be distinctive of the products it attaches to. It is not a problem if a shape cannot be registered as a trademark because it gives substantial value to the good but can be protected under design law. In fact, this is the purpose of design and copyright law and the exclusion in trademark law has been included to reflect this. More problematic is the case where a design right could be available where a trademark could not because the exclusion as regards functional shapes in design law is interpreted less restrictively than under trademark law. But this has more to do with the patent/trademark overlap, so this is addressed in section VI.

(iii) A Posteriori *Overlap*

Similarly to the overlap between trademark and copyright, trademarks can artificially prolong the normal life of a registered or unregistered design. No rule directly regulates this overlap. However, Advocate-General Colomer in *Philips* was clearly of the opinion that the purpose of indents (ii) and (iii) of Trademark Directive, article 3(1)(e) was to prevent this from happening.[207] He specifically referred to patents and designs. Thus, no overlap will be allowed for those three-dimensional designs as a result of *Philips* and its

[204] W Cornish and D Llewelyn, *Intellectual Property: Patents, Copyright, Trade Marks and Allied Rights*, 6th edn (London, Sweet & Maxwell, 2007) 579, para 15-20, adding however straight afterwards (at 580) that 'perhaps it implies that the general exception of solely technical designs is not just for must fit cases'.

[205] Torremans, *Holyoak and Torremans Intellectual Property Law* (n 130) 329–30.

[206] Ibid 329. See also Cornish and Llewelyn, *Intellectual Property* (n 204) 580.

[207] See also the Court of Appeal in *Philips v Remington* (n 169) who shared the same idea. See chapter 5, section IV.B.

progeny. It should also be the case for copyright works, as it can very reasonably be argued that the Advocate-General meant also to encompass copyright and that design and patents were only examples.[208] There will thus be cases of *a posteriori* overlap for shapes which can be registered as designs but also as trademarks, so long as they do not fall within the exclusion of Trademark Directive, article 3, and of course for two-dimensional subject matter. It has been suggested that there is no policy reason for prohibiting the overlap.[209]

Unlike with the trademark/copyright overlap, there is, however, a partial convergence between trademark and design here in the sense that if the design is not re-registered every five years it will lapse, similar to the rule that if a trademark is not used continuously for five years and also re-registered every 10 years, it will also lapse. Finally, a design right cannot prolong a trademark right if the trademark has not been used or has lost distinctive character. The reason is that it will not be novel.

In conclusion, apart from the rules relating to the excluded subject matter and ownership, there is no rule in the European Union regulating the simultaneous overlap between trademark and designs at the other levels (subject matter, protection requirements, rights and exceptions). The negative overlap is partially resolved in the legislative texts (exclusion of purely functional marks and designs). The *a posteriori* overlap is partially resolved through case law. Therefore, all three types of overlaps occur at diverse degrees.

C Literature

Very few if any commentators have discussed the simultaneous overlap as regards subject matter, protection requirements, ownership, rights or exceptions. Instead, they have focused on the shapes exclusions. This is hardly surprising as these are the only provisions which organise the trademark/design overlap in trademark and design law. However, it is worrying as many problems arise out of cumulation of rights at the other levels and not only at the level of protection requirements, as has been identified above. The discussion below will thus review the arguments for the simultaneous and *a posteriori* overlaps concerning subject matter excluded by trademark law.

(i) Simultaneous Overlap: Excluded Subject Matter

First of all, it must be noted that the exclusion only applies for shapes consisting *exclusively* of the provisions in indents (i), (ii) and (iii) of Trademark Directive, article 3(1)(e). It is therefore somewhat narrow so that the overlap between trademarks and designs regarding shape is still alive and well.[210] Firth, Gredley and Maniatis submit that the following interpretation of the article is the most satisfactory:

[208] In the relevant paragraph of his Opinion, he uses the term 'specifically' and says clearly that the aim is 'to prevent the exclusive and permanent rights which a trademark confers from serving to extend the life of other rights which the legislature has sought to make subject to limited periods'. So this must also include copyright.

[209] Carboni, 'The Overlap between Registered Community Designs and Community Trade Marks' (n 156) 265.

[210] G Ghidini, 'From Here to Eternity? On the Overlap of Shape Marks with Design' in J Drexl (ed), *Technology and Competition: Contributions in Honour of Hanns Ullrich (Technologie et Concurrence, Mélanges en l'Honneur de Hanns Ullrich)* (Brussels, Larcier, 2009) 55, 68, noting that generally shape marks are always accompanied by a word mark. He gives the example of the Coca-Cola bottles: Coca-Cola is written everywhere, even on the cap.

> the sign consists exclusively of the shape of the goods (or of their packaging), i.e. it contains no element other than features of shape (such as words or logo) and the shape for which registration is sought (i.e. the combination of features making up the shape) conveys one (or more) of the 'forbidden' messages described in art. 3(1)(e)(i), (ii) or (iii), regardless of whether it also conveys other messages. On this construction, the shape would never be registrable, no matter how distinctive in practice of the applicant's goods.[211]

(a) Shapes Resulting Exclusively from the Nature of Goods

As Advocate-General Colomer in *Philips* well qualified it, the shape which results from the nature of the product (Trademark Directive, article 3(1)(e)(i)) is the natural shape of the product in question. In other words, it is 'that without which the product could not exist; . . . it is imperative for all products of the same kind';[212] or in yet other words, 'the designer of a product has no real or effective choice as to the shape that the product can take'.[213] A common example is the shape of a fruit or the round or oval shape of a ball (for tennis, rugby etc).[214] Such shapes can be said not to be registrable because in the vast majority of cases, they will not distinguish the product, as 'consumers will often see the shape of that product as an indication of what the product is, rather than of who makes it'.[215] In addition, and perhaps more importantly, allowing such shapes to become trademarks would greatly inhibit competitors wishing to sell the products as it would give a monopoly on the product themselves to the trademark holder.[216] Of course, it all depends on how 'the goods themselves' are defined. The narrower the definition, the more likely the shape will be excluded.[217] Even though a shape which results from the nature of a product could be distinctive, there is a higher interest which governs the prohibition of its registrability. Despite its arguable vagueness,[218] the exception serves a crucial purpose, like the others under article 3(1). Indeed, if, as has been argued, it could also exclude trivial technical shapes, ie shapes that the public sees as the standard appearance of the product, then the exception is even more useful in this respect.[219] In conclusion, despite its vagueness, for commentators, the exception seems uncontroversial as it is necessary to maintain competition.

(b) Technical Function Exclusion

This exclusion overlaps to some extent with the first indent of Trademark Directive, article 3(1)(e).[220] As we saw above, the exception has been interpreted in the *Philips* decision which has had a considerable impact on the clarification of the exact extent of the 'technical exclusion' in article 3(1)(e)(ii). Many commentators have argued that, as the Court

[211] Firth, Gredley and Maniatis, 'Shapes as Trade Marks' (n 160) 91.
[212] Folliard-Monguiral and Rogers, 'The Protection of Shapes by the Community Trademark' (n 192) 173.
[213] Bently and Sherman, *Intellectual Property Law* (n 82) 809.
[214] Quaedvlieg, 'Concurrence and Convergence in Industrial Design' (n 109) 64; Bently and Sherman, *Intellectual Property Law* (n 82) 808.
[215] Phillips, *Trade Mark Law* (n 86) 146.
[216] Bently and Sherman, *Intellectual Property Law* (n 82) 808.
[217] Ibid.
[218] Quaedvlieg, 'Concurrence and Convergence in Industrial Design' (n 109) 64.
[219] Ibid 67.
[220] Cornish and Llewelyn, *Intellectual Property* (n 204) para 18-44; Bently and Sherman, *Intellectual Property Law* (n 82) 810.

of Justice did not use the terms 'patents' and 'designs', unlike the Advocate-General, it must have meant that the exclusion applies even if a patent or design would not be available.[221] The terms 'technical result', 'technical solution' or 'functional characteristics of a product' embrace not only those shapes which can be patentable or registrable under design law but all shapes the essential functional features of which are attributable only to the technical result, be they patentable, protectable by designs, or not. This may even include other IPRs such as copyright and utility models. 'Consequently the exclusion should encompass shapes which facilitate convenient storage or transportation of the goods, all of which provide the purchaser with other "convenience features"'.[222] The *Philips* decision also means that the underlying public interest behind article 3(1) transcends trademark law.[223] The rationale behind the provision is market freedom or effective competition, not simply the prohibition of the overlap, ie that the overlap is objectionable per se.[224] Therefore, the interpretation of article 3(1)(e)(ii) given by the Court of Justice is a broad one, which will exclude many shapes from trademark protection. It has also been argued that the *Philips* decision implies that there is a relationship between the distinctiveness criterion and article 3(1)(e).[225] It is in fact a rational argument as the prior case law on indents (b) and (c), which both concern distinctiveness, has highlighted the same underlying rationale that applies to article 3(1)(e), ie effective competition in the (internal) market. The only difference is that as regards (b) and (c), it is thought not too restrictive of competition to make the trademark owner's brand recognition efforts prevail over the interest in having an effective competition, whereas effective competition weighs more in the balance under article 3(1)(e).[226]

Although the decision has tremendously clarified the scope of the exclusion for technical shapes, it remains unclear which evidence is relevant to decide 'whether a shape is attributable to a technical result'.[227]

> The inconsistent language used by the Court suggests that subsequent tribunals should form an overall conclusion taking account of a variety of perspectives. In particular: first, whether the shape actually achieves a technical result (as sine qua non to the operation of the exception); second, whether the shape was chosen by the designer to do so; third, whether the shape is one of a limited number that a competitor could use to achieve the function.[228]

Another criticism, not of the decision as such but of the law, is that, as for Trademark Directive, article 3(1)(e)(iii), 3(1)(e)(ii) does not apply to two-dimensional signs, although in all logic it should.[229] Finally, some have argued that trademark and design law should negatively converge as to the design exclusion for must-fit and (when the issue is harmonised)

221 Bently and Sherman, *Intellectual Property Law* (n 82) 810; Suthersanen, 'The European Court of Justice in *Philips v Remington*' (n 167) 268–70, noting that this view is not new and citing B Strowel, 'Benelux: A Guide to the Validity of Three-dimensional Trademarks in Europe' (1995) *European Intellectual Property Review* 154, 158; R Annand and H Norman, *Blackstone's Guide to the Trademarks Act 1994* (London, Blackstone, 1994) 84 *et seq*.

222 Bently and Sherman, *Intellectual Property Law* (n 82) 810.

223 Quaedvlieg, 'Concurrence and Convergence in Industrial Design' (n 109) 33. See also section VI.B.

224 Suthersanen, 'The European Court of Justice in *Philips v Remington*' (n 167) 282–83.

225 Ibid 274, 283. However, the Advocate-General did not think that the exclusion was based on the lack of distinctiveness of certain natural, functional or ornamental shapes (see para 16 of his Opinion).

226 Suthersanen, 'The European Court of Justice in *Philips v Remington*' (n 167) 273.

227 Bently and Sherman, *Intellectual Property Law* (n 82) 811.

228 Ibid.

229 Firth, Gredley and Maniatis, 'Shapes as Trade Marks' (n 160); Suthersanen, 'The European Court of Justice in *Philips v Remington*' (n 167) 281–82.

must-match shapes.[230] It seems that the broad interpretation of article 3(1)(e)(ii) in *Philips* should normally take care of the potential overlap for must-fit features, and arguably also for must-match ones on the basis of article 3(1)(e)(iii),[231] although for this exclusion, not entirely, as we saw above that the exclusion is less strict than for (ii). Hence it would not be a luxury to enact it in legislation, as the case law is more likely to change than legislation. This is even the more so for must-match features, as the extended protection for famous marks (action against unfair advantage under Trademark Directive, article 5(2)) may give the possibility to the trademark owner to override the must-match exclusion. As well explained by Kur:

> [t]he crucial question would then be whether the fact that . . . production and sales of must-match parts are legal business activities under design legislation, would furnish any 'due cause' that needs to be given full consideration also in the framework of trademark law. It is hardly conceivable that the question could be answered in the negative. However, as the ECJ has given no guidelines on that point, the issue is still open.[232]

(c) Signs which Consist Exclusively of the Shape which Gives Substantial Value to the Goods

The UK Trademarks Registry Work Manual describes the exception as applying to 'goods which are purchased primarily because of the eye appeal of the shape – such as the shape of novelty soap, or the shape of an ornament or figurine for those goods'.[233] A good example of such a shape is that of 'the famous lemon squeeze ("the juicy salif") designed by Philip Starck, where the squeezer component is suspended between three long legs to give the appearance of a space ship'.[234] This provision does not exclude all shapes which give substantial value to goods as those shapes which also indicate origin will be registrable. OHIM's Boards of Appeal have held that the simple fact that the shape is pleasing to the eye or aesthetic does not make it fall within the exception.[235] As stated by Bently and Sherman, 'the decisive question is therefore whether the shape performs a trademark function'.[236] As the exclusion is partial, it still allows an overlap between trademarks, on the one hand, and designs and copyright law on the other.[237] Commentators, like the EU courts, think that underlying the exception is the public

[230] Quaedvlieg, 'Concurrence and Convergence in Industrial Design' (n 109) 61.

[231] Kur, 'Cumulation of IP Rights Pertaining to Product Shapes' (n 43) 627, citing a decision of the German Federal Patent Court going in this direction.

[232] Ibid 628–29.

[233] Bently and Sherman, *Intellectual Property Law* (n 82) 813, citing the Trademark Registry Work Manual, ch 6, s 8, 175–76.

[234] Bently and Sherman, *Intellectual Property Law* (n 82) 813.

[235] 'If that were the case, it would be virtually impossible to imagine any trademark of shape, given that in modern business there is no product of industrial utility that has not been the subject of study, research and industrial design before its eventual launch on the market.' See BoA R 272/1999-3, 3 May 2000, s 34, R 164/1998-1, 12 April 1999, s 12. Phillips, *Trade Mark Law* (n 86) 149, shares the same opinion.

[236] Bently and Sherman, *Intellectual Property Law* (n 82) 813.

[237] Suthersanen, 'Breaking Down the Intellectual Property Barriers' (n 156) 291, citing C Gielen and B Strowel, 'The Benelux Trademark Act: A Guide to Trademark Law in Europe' (1996) 86 *The Trademark Reporter* 543, 553, para 40. See also Quaedvlieg, 'Concurrence and Convergence in Industrial Design' (n 109) 42. This interpretation has been confirmed by Jacob J's ruling in the *Philips v Remington* case (n 169) and is supported by Torremans, *Holyoak and Torremans Intellectual Property Law* (n 130) 389.

interest or policy reason that such shapes should be available to all traders,[238] and also that trademark law should not prolong copyright in a work.[239] It reflects negative convergence. Therefore, it has been submitted that to respect this public interest, the provision should only exclude signs which have already been protected by copyright and have fallen in the public domain and works of art existing in only one or very few copies.[240] Commentators think that the exclusion should be interpreted in this way, even if they have heavily criticised its current wording, ranging from finding it unclear[241] to 'particularly opaque',[242] wondering why it should limit itself to shapes and not also two-dimensional subject matter as there is no reason for such distinction,[243] or even advocating its repeal.[244] For instance, it is unclear how 'substantial value' should be determined. It has been suggested that it should be 'as "the quality prized by consumers" rather than as "the quality based on the *objective* usefulness of a product"'.[245] Others have suggested that 'the value of the goods over their lifetime' should be considered.[246] A decision of the Court of Justice on this exclusion is thus badly needed to clarify its meaning.[247]

In conclusion, as well summed up by Suthersanen:

> [t]he future boundaries of trademark protection of shape may thus be reliant on a myriad of factors including the information conveyed by the sign, the level of distinctiveness, the level of competing substitutes in a particular product market and the nature of the advertising employed for the product.[248]

(ii) Negative Overlap

Kur has discussed the potential negative overlap there could be if must-match parts are excluded at EU level (if and when the issue is finally harmonised) but could nevertheless be protected by trademark or even copyright law.[249] In the *Jeep* decision, the CFI accepted registration of such spare parts, so the issue is not moot.[250] The next question is whether their making and selling by independent manufacturers would be use of the mark and thus infringement.[251] According to *Opel/Autec*,[252] it would be use of the mark but as to

[238] Torremans, *Holyoak and Torremans Intellectual Property Law* (n 130) 389; Quaedvlieg, 'Concurrence and Convergence in Industrial Design' (n 109) 51–52.

[239] Quaedvlieg, 'Concurrence and Convergence in Industrial Design' (n 109) 43–44.

[240] Ibid 57.

[241] Ibid and see also Folliard-Monguiral and Rogers, 'The Protection of Shapes by the Community Trademark' (n 192) 178.

[242] Cornish and Llewelyn, *Intellectual Property* (n 204) para 18-45.

[243] Suthersanen, 'The European Court of Justice in *Philips v Remington*' (n 167) 267; Quaedvlieg, 'Concurrence and Convergence in Industrial Design' (n 109) 48.

[244] Quaedvlieg, 'Concurrence and Convergence in Industrial Design' (n 109) 57.

[245] Folliard-Monguiral and Rogers, 'The Protection of Shapes by the Community Trademark' (n 192) 174.

[246] Firth, Gredley and Maniatis, 'Shapes as Trade Marks' (n 160) 94.

[247] According to Musker, *Community Design Law* (n 54) 78, the Advocate-General in Case C-299/99 *Koninklijke Philips Electronics v Remington Consumer Products* [2002] ECR I-5475 also found (although it appears to have been obiter as the case turned on the interpretation of the functional exclusion only) that the exclusion of shapes which add value was intended to minimise the overlap with designs, and therefore to exclude protection for 'ornamental' shapes (see esp para 30). However, there was no further discussion as to how to interpret the term 'substantial value' so that a decision of the Court of Justice is still needed.

[248] Suthersanen, 'The European Court of Justice in *Philips v Remington*' (n 167) 283.

[249] Kur, 'Cumulation of Rights with Regard to Three-Dimensional Shapes' (n 45) 167.

[250] Case T-128/01 *Daimler Chrysler* [2003] ECR II-701 (Jeep grille).

[251] Kur, 'Cumulation of Rights with Regard to Three-Dimensional Shapes' (n 45) 168.

[252] Case C-48/05 *Adam Opel v Autec* [2007] ECR I-1017.

the question whether use of the mark is likely to affect the essential trademark function, EU jurisprudence has left national courts with a rather wide margin for discretion.[253] Factors that courts would take into consideration would be whether there is no confusion (ie the independent manufacturer also clearly affixes his or her mark) and whether the public expect that such spare parts are also available legally from third parties, ie because such production and sale is allowed by design law. However, the independent manufacturer would still need to pass one hurdle, namely that his or her use does not take unfair advantage of the mark's reputation.[254] The question would be whether the fact that it is legal to make must-match parts under the design legislation would be due cause in trademark law. Kur believes that the answer should be positive. Indeed:

> protection of the reputation as such – in the meaning that no one else should derive profit from the mark's power to attract enhanced interest and traffic – could hardly be considered to trump the competition-related considerations militating in favour of the repairs clause.[255]

The last question to be asked is whether the use as a mark for repair purposes would comply with Trademark Directive, article 6 (which allows use of the mark when this is necessary to indicate the intended purpose of products). However, the EU courts have given no guidelines on this issue yet and the *Opel/Autec* decision seems to go in the opposite direction.[256] In conclusion, at this stage, it seems likely that trademark law could cut across design law and that this negative overlap could well exist.

(iii) A Posteriori *Overlap*

Some authors have wondered whether the *a posteriori* overlap should be forbidden even when the shape does not fall within the exclusions of Trademark Directive, article 3(1)(e). For them, not only is a general ban on the registrability of attractive shapes not supported by the current case law or literature, it would also be inappropriate because it would not be practicable.[257] It could be done in at least three different ways: (1) decide that only banal shapes could be protected by trademark; (2) make the owner consciously choose between trademark and design (ie a shape that could have been registered as a design but was not could get trademark protection); or (3) the most radical solution, excluding all shapes from trademark protection (which was the situation in some Member States before the Trademark Directive and was rejected nearly unanimously as unsatisfactory and unrealistic).[258] This latter solution would also be in breach of TRIPs,

[253] Kur, 'Cumulation of Rights with Regard to Three-Dimensional Shapes' (n 45) 169–70.

[254] Ibid 170. See now also the *L'Oréal v Bellure* ruling (Case C-487/07 *L'Oréal SA, Lancôme Parfums et Beauté & Cie SNC and Laboratoire Garnier & Cie v Bellure NV, Malaika Investments Ltd and Starion International Ltd* [2009] ECR I-5185).

[255] Kur, 'Cumulation of Rights with Regard to Three-Dimensional Shapes' (n 45) 170 n 29.

[256] Ibid 170–71, noting that in 2000, the Italian Supreme Court gave a positive answer to this last question.

[257] Kur, 'Cumulation of IP Rights Pertaining to Product Shapes' (n 43) 618. For similar arguments, see Kur, 'Cumulation of Rights with Regard to Three-Dimensional Shapes' (n 45) 162–64, illustrating her argument with the decision in Case C-371/06 *Benetton Group v G-Star International* [2007] ECR I-7709. For Kur, 'if a shape is aesthetically appealing, but at the same time serves as a badge of origin – and if it is bought by consumers for exactly that reason, ie because they want to buy jeans of that particular origin – it cannot be claimed any longer that the value of the product is (only) determined by its aesthetic features'. This was in effect the position taken by the Court too and therefore Trademark Directive, art 3(1)(e) did not apply to exclude registrability.

[258] Kur, 'Cumulation of IP Rights Pertaining to Product Shapes' (n 43) 619–20.

Article 15.[259] However, the negative effects of such *a posteriori* overlap can nevertheless be minimised by interpreting the protection requirements for designs and trademarks strictly or, to put it more mildly, less generously than today.[260] Nevertheless, Kur is worried that the strong emphasis of the EU courts on consumer perception may lead to a reduction in competition in this area.[261] This is because this perception is subject to change, and such change may even be induced by the trademark owner's efforts to educate the public that the sign is his or her mark. The criterion of consumer perception therefore is to the advantage of already powerful brands, as they can afford to spend a great deal of money on promoting their signs to be seen as a trademark. The consequence of the application of this criterion is therefore not welcome from a competition point of view.[262] Kur thus advises that courts should carry on ensuring that trademark protection for shapes is difficult to acquire, with the criterion of consumer perception being only one, not the only one, to be considered in the registrability or validity assessment.[263] She also favours the use of the 'effects on competition' criterion as a tool to regulate the *a posteriori* overlap.[264] Finally, she adds one more caveat:

> Although protection . . . should not be excluded forever simply because a shape is attractive and therefore has commercial value, its monopolisation for one particular enterprise after the lapse of initial protection should be subject to a fairly high threshold – only a very high degree of public awareness should be able to tip the balance in favour of the proprietor's interest as opposed to those of his competitors.[265]

Torremans agrees with Kur.[266] It is often unnecessary that the investment in developing shapes be protected both by trademark and design. In the same vein as advocated by Feer Verkade that one law should not cut across another, for Torremans, if the law has given different duration and conditions of protection to designs and trademarks, it is for a reason.[267] Cumulation 'allows the right holder to pick the one that suits its needs best and to overrule restrictions which were deliberately included in the other regime'.[268] Adding that the way the 'gaps' in the system are (mis)used is worrying, he also hopes that the individual character requirement will be interpreted strictly to reduce the instances of cumulation until the legislature acts to address the problems caused by the trademark/design overlap.[269] Ghidini also mentions the principle of 'implicit abrogation' which exists in many legal systems to regulate the temporal succession of laws:

> According to this principle, the more recent regulation will prevail, if it applies to the same subject matter and is founded on the same basic criterion of access to legal protection, but adopts a normative solution and a justification that is acutely different from that expressed by the previous law.[270]

[259] Ibid 619.
[260] Ibid 620, although noting that for shape marks, current EU case law is already doing the job properly. See also Kur, 'Cumulation of Rights with Regard to Three-Dimensional Shapes' (n 45) 165–66.
[261] Kur, 'Cumulation of IP Rights Pertaining to Product Shapes' (n 43) 620.
[262] Ibid 620–21.
[263] Kur, 'Cumulation of Rights with Regard to Three-Dimensional Shapes' (n 45) 166.
[264] Ibid; Kur, 'Cumulation of IP Rights Pertaining to Product Shapes' (n 43) 621.
[265] Kur, 'Cumulation of Rights with Regard to Three-Dimensional Shapes' (n 45) 166.
[266] Torremans, 'Three Dimensional Trade Marks and Designs for Packaging' (n 29) 765–66.
[267] In the same vein, see Ghidini, 'From Here to Eternity?' (n 210) 63–64 ('one set of rules cannot circumvent another').
[268] Torremans, 'Three Dimensional Trade Marks and Designs for Packaging' (n 29) 765–66.
[269] Ibid.
[270] Ghidini, 'From Here to Eternity?' (n 210) 64.

However, he notes that it is doubtful that this principle forms part of the EU legal system.[271] He also notes, more generally, that the limited duration of one IPR is a signal that it cannot be prolonged by another IPR and acts as a pro-competitive and pro-innovative tool, and also at the same time preventing rent-seeking.[272] In the end for him, the conflicts created by the trademark/design overlap should be regulated through the principle of free competition.[273] An important and more general rule is also set out by Kur. She insists on the fact that when overlaps do occur, it would be a mistake to focus on the effect of the overlap as such, whereas most of the time the problem is in each right taken separately. As she notes, this is because 'the legal foundations and the requirements to be fulfilled are different, notwithstanding the fact that they may relate to the same physical product'.[274] This claim will be further examined in the concluding chapter as it is a fundamental one which can help find a solution to the problems caused by overlaps identified in this book, namely regime clashes and overprotection.

In conclusion, many of the rules and principles set out in the legislative texts and the case law and proposed by commentators to regulate the three types of overlaps between trademark/design (eg effective competition, market freedom, one law should not cut across another) are similar to those suggested in the previous sections.

V. DESIGNS AND PATENTS

A The Legal Framework

First of all, Design Directive, article 16 and Design Regulation, article 96(1) clearly allow the overlap between designs and patents. However, the overlap is not complete as Design Directive, article 7 regulates it (designs dictated by their technical function and designs of interconnections). In this respect, the patent/design overlap is clearly envisaged in the Green Paper on the Legal Protection of Industrial Design. The Green Paper refers to countries which give a 'negative' definition to the term 'design'. Such countries define design by providing that shapes which are exclusively dictated by the technical function of the product cannot be protected. The Green Paper appropriates this rule[275] and later explains it. If the designer retains some freedom for aesthetic features independently from the technical function, the overlap should be allowed so that the patent would protect the inventive aspects of the subject matter whilst the design right 'would only protect those features where the free action of the designer has manifested itself'.[276] For instance, a chair could have a specific function (better back/leg position for the user), and also a beautiful design.[277] To a lesser extent, European Patent Convention (EPC), article 52(2)

[271] Ibid refers to Case C-228/99 *Silos* [2001] ECR I-8401 for this proposition.

[272] Ghidini, 'From Here to Eternity?' (n 210) 67.

[273] Ibid 69.

[274] Kur, 'Cumulation of Rights with Regard to Three-Dimensional Shapes' (n 45) 157.

[275] Green Paper on the Legal Protection of Industrial Design, European Commission, June 1991, Working Doc. 111/F/51 31/9-EN, 60.

[276] Ibid 154, under the title 'Relationship to patent and utility model law'.

[277] For an example in French case law, the Court of Appeal of Paris held that if the interior shape of a lighter's case was dictated by its function (to contain the lighter), its external shape was independent and could have a configuration distinct from the external shape. CA Paris, 22 September 2000, PIBD, 2001, no. 713, III, 64 cited by F Pollaud-Dulian, *Le Droit d'Auteur* (Paris, Économica, 2005) 96.

(b), (3) also create a separation between designs and patents.[278] However, it seems more relevant to the patent/copyright overlap,[279] as the subsection excludes aesthetic creations as such from patentability so it does not cover functional designs.

B 'Content Overlap'

The general opinion is that functional subject matter should be protected under patent law. However, some functional elements incorporated in product designs can also be protected by design right.[280] Therefore, an overlap is possible.[281] Indeed, as stated above, Design Directive, article 16 clearly allows it.

(i) Simultaneous Overlap

(a) Subject Matter

There potentially could be an overlap, as both design and patent laws deal with functional subject matter. But because of Design Directive, article 7, it is difficult to see how there could be a 'proper' or full overlap. As designs totally dictated by their function are unprotectable by design right, they can only find protection through patent. What is possible, however, is to have (as in the example given above) a single object (eg a chair) on which two rights apply. Whilst the two rights will not cover the same intangible intellectual property, they will concern the same object.[282] As we shall see below (section VI.D), this neat separation is an illusion. So we shall still discuss simultaneous overlap here.

(b) Protection Requirements

A patent needs to be new, inventive and industrially applicable (EPC Articles 54, 56 and 57). A design needs to be new, have individual character and be visible (the latter requirement only applies if the design is claimed on a component part of a complex product). It will more often be the case that a patented product could also obtain design protection,

[278] Musker, *Community Design Law* (n 54) 75–76, notes that this does not exclude 'methods of achieving an aesthetic effect [which] may be patentable, and may provide protection for resulting designs' and that '[s]imilar exclusions are sometimes applied where the only novelty lies in an aesthetic feature, or the only benefit to a novel feature is the aesthetic effect'. He also refers to some relevant EPO Appeal Board cases: 'T 119/88: coloured disc sleeve was held unpatentable as being aesthetic (T 962/91 is similar); stained-glass provided by technical means was held patentable; T456/90 the only feature of a watch strap which was not obvious was merely aesthetic in effect, and the patent was found to lack inventive step'.

[279] Musker, *Community Design Law* (n 54) 76.

[280] Suthersanen, 'Breaking Down the Intellectual Property Barriers' (n 156) 268.

[281] Quaedvlieg, 'Concurrence and Convergence in Industrial Design' (n 109) 24, in footnote noting that 'some authors assert, however, that under European design law, design protection could in certain circumstances concur with patent protection'. See also M Schlötelburg, 'Design Protection for Technical Products' (2006) 1(10) *Journal of Intellectual Property Law and Practice* 675.

[282] For an example where three rights subsisted, see *Display Factory v Pejoine,* CA Paris, 4th ch, 28 January 2004 [2005] *Gazette du Palais*, 6 January 2005, no. 6, 24, holding that a model for a liquids distributor could be protected at the same time by design law and copyright law and that the objection that the model was already protected by a patent was irrelevant, as an object can be protected in its technical characteristics by patent law and in its shape by a design law under the condition of Books I and V of the Intellectual Property Code, so long as this shape is distinguishable from the technical elements.

rather than the converse.[283] This is because the patent requirements are obviously more stringent than the design ones. Not all designs will be 'entirely new' (as novelty is relative in design law and absolute in patent law) and even less often will they also be inventive, although they will most of the time be industrially applicable. Conversely, all patents will have to be absolutely new so a fortiori they will comply with the design law's condition of relative novelty; they often will also have individual character, as the informed user should normally have a different impression from the prior art since the subject matter will be new. The only hurdle would be the requirement of visibility, but again if the design is not for a component part of a complex product, this requirement is not applicable.

(c) Excluded Subject Matter

Patents and designs contrary to public policy and morality are excluded. Designs and patents exclude software, although patent law only excludes it as such. The two laws in the main converge on these points. The other exclusions in patent law are not relevant to design law (except for aesthetic creations discussed above). An overlap could occur if there is a design of an aesthetic feature as well as a patent, as long as the aesthetic feature is not claimed as such.

(d) Ownership and Dealings

As with the other overlaps discussed above, the provisions on ownership and dealings are national (except to some extent Design Regulation, article 14 and EPC, Article 60) and therefore, they will be discussed in the chapters on national law. However, suffice it to say here that there could be different owners as a result of diverging legal provisions on initial ownership, or otherwise as a result of a transfer.

(e) Rights and Infringement

The design and patent rights are in fact perfect twins, as the provisions of the Design Directive, article 12 and Design Regulation, article 19 have been modelled on the corresponding provision of the Community Patent Convention (Article 25). But this is, of course, as far as the Community Patent Convention is concerned (which is still not in force), as there are no provision as to rights in the EPC. So, once again, the overlap at the level of rights is a national issue rather than a European one. The only difference between patent law and design right is with the CUDR, as proof of copying is required in this case.

(f) Exceptions Including Exhaustion Principle

Some of the exceptions in design law (Design Directive, article 13(1)(a), (b), (2)) are derived from national patent laws and one from the Paris Convention (Article *5ter* which

[283] Musker, *Community Design Law* (n 54) 76, also notes that '[f]unctional designs would appear not to be excluded from protection by product patents where they meet the necessary criteria of absolute novelty, and inventive step'.

aims to facilitate foreign transport). Thus, there is some positive or symmetric convergence at this level. However, one exception coming from copyright law (reproduction for the purposes of making citations or of teaching) does not exist in national patent laws, so that in case of an overlap, the patent regime will trump it.

As a result of the case law on patents and of Design Directive, article 15, the principle of exhaustion applies in the same way for patents as for designs. There is one difference, however. The patent holder can block the marketing and the importations on the territory of a Member State B when the patent holder is forced into a compulsory licence by a Member State A, or more generally has a genuine legal obligation to market the product in Member State A, and the patented goods are imported on a territory where s/he also has a patent (Member State B).[284] It seems, however, that this case law would not apply to designs in the same situation simply because there are no provisions allowing the imposition of compulsory licences in design law. However, clashes on this aspect should normally be rare as compulsory licences in patent law apply in very few cases and in cases where the overlap is unlikely (eg in the field of pharmaceuticals).

(g) Literature

It needs to be first noted that the literature has in fact almost exclusively focused on excluded subject matter, and more specifically even on Design Directive, article 7(1) and the corresponding provision in the Design Regulation. There is virtually no literature on the negative and *a posteriori* overlaps.

But first, one commentator has made a general remark about the subject matter as such. He believes that the cumulative protection of patent and design is not problematic. This is because design law does not protect ideas, concepts or methods.[285] So, in fact, 'design law is only applicable to patentable subject matter where the invention has materialised a specific product'.[286] Nevertheless, this argument is weak as the overlap will be complete once the patented idea is put into practice (as it has to be industrially applicable). 'The patent will rarely dictate the appearance of the products it covers and so the scopes of protection of patent and design will be very different.'[287]

Some commentators have summarised the reasons which may underlie Design Directive, article 7(1). The first reason is obviously to avoid the overlap with patents 'as such'. However, as well noted, this contradicts Design Directive, article 16, which expressly allows the design/patent overlap, so that it is not possible to find that the EU legislature intended to (totally) separate designs from inventions.[288] Article 7(1) could also be indicating that dictated features lack individual character.[289] But there are cases where features solely dictated by function can also have individual character. Finally, article 7(1) can reflect a need for 'freedom to compete in must-copy situations'.[290] This concern is similar to that underlying Trademark Directive, article 3(1)(e).

[284] See Case 15/74 *Centrafarm v Sterling Drug* [1974] ECR 1147; Case 187/80 *Merck v Stephar* [1981] ECR 2063; Case 19/84 *Pharmon v Hoechst* [1985] ECR 2281; and Joined Cases C-267/95 and C-268/95 *Merck v Primecrown* [1997] 1 CMLR 83.

[285] Schlötelburg, 'Design Protection for Technical Products' (n 281) 676.

[286] Ibid.

[287] Musker, *Community Design Law* (n 54) 76.

[288] Ibid 42.

[289] Ibid.

[290] Ibid 43.

The patent/design interface was further elaborated in *Philips v Remington*, not by the Court but by the Advocate-General. Although his Opinion is not strictly the law, it can influence future case law. Also, both the Advocate-General's Opinion and the *Philips* decision have been criticised in many different ways in the literature. So what had the Advocate-General to say about the exclusion in Design Directive, article 7? His reasoning is contained in paragraphs 34–40 of his Opinion:

> The feature concerned must not only be necessary but essential in order to achieve a particular technical result: form follows function. This means that a functional design may, none the less, be eligible for protection if it can be shown that the same technical function could be achieved by another different form.[291]

For him, '[i]t is logical that the bar for assessing whether a ground for excluding a functional form applies is set higher for designs than for trademarks: the nature and scope of their protection are completely different from one another'.[292]

He gives three reasons for this:[293]

> First, a trademark seeks to protect the identity of the origin of the goods and, therefore, indirectly, the goodwill which the goods attract, whereas designs – like patents – seek to protect the goods, in their own right . . . In that sense, it is entirely logical that the legislature is less concerned by the strict delimitation between designs and patents than by that which ought to exist between the latter and trademarks. Secondly, whereas trademarks enjoy protection unlimited in time, rights in designs – like rights in patents – are limited in time. From that viewpoint, too, it is appropriate to use a stricter test for excluding functional or ornamental shapes from registration as trademarks than that to be used in separating designs from patents. If we were to accept Philips' argument, which consists in accepting evidence of the existence of other shapes capable of achieving the same technical performance with the aim of preventing the exclusion of a merely functional mark, nothing would stop an undertaking from registering as trademarks all imaginable shapes which achieved such a result, thus obtaining a permanent monopoly over a particular technical solution. Furthermore, the trademark court would have to carry out a comprehensive assessment concerning the equivalence of the performance of the different technical processes. Thirdly, even if it should be accepted that the restrictive test for the ground for refusal put forward by *Philips* carries only a slight risk that trademark rights might unduly encroach on the field of patents, I cannot see why the public interest should tolerate such a risk.

Several criticisms can be made on this reasoning. Quaedvlieg rightly says that the Advocate-General's arguments are flawed. If shapes not entirely dictated by function can nevertheless be registered as designs, it offers an 'alternative regime to patent protection which lasts considerably longer [and] can be acquired more easily; moreover, it will monopolise technical solutions on a sub-inventive level'.[294] For him, this is contrary to the public interest underlying patent law, ie that 'technical solutions either comply with all the requirements and safeguards of the patent system or will be free for all',[295] which again is linked to the idea of free or effective competition. He concludes and we agree that:

[291] At para 34.
[292] At para 36.
[293] At paras 37–40.
[294] Quaedvlieg, 'Concurrence and Convergence in Industrial Design' (n 109) 61.
[295] Ibid.

it would be incorrect to conclude, as did the Advocate General, from a comparison with trademark law, rather than patent law, that design protection as a less monopolising regime should enjoy freedom to offer supplementary protection in the technical domain.[296]

Indeed, the Advocate-General's first argument is flawed. It is not so logical that the legislature should be less concerned with the delimitation between patents and designs. As Quaedvlieg rightly says, if design law allows for the registration of technical subject matter (as it does under the current interpretation of Design Directive, article 7(1)) permitting therefore the circumvention of the patent law's stricter requirements, the legislature should be concerned. Similarly, his second argument is also defective, because if renewed, designs can last five years longer than patents. In fact, he fails to see that the same problem as under the patent/trademark overlap can occur in the design/patent overlap when he says 'nothing would stop an undertaking from registering as trademarks all imaginable shapes which achieved such a result, thus obtaining a permanent monopoly over a particular technical solution'. This is well noted by Cornish who sees in the Court of Justice's interpretation in *Philips* the dangerous possibility for designers to register a few more shapes covering the obvious alternatives so that 'he or she would have a monopoly on the practicable ways of giving effect to a clever technical idea without having to satisfy the requirements for patent'.[297]

Another problem with Design Directive, article 7 (literally read) is that it will allow monopolisation if the design is dictated by function but is also aesthetic and there is no other way to design the product. Simply because the design is also aesthetic, it is not entirely dictated by function and therefore is registrable.[298] In addition, article 7 also allows the following reasoning, as well put in evidence by Koschtial:

> It is also not sufficient to ask if a design could be patented under patent law to classify it as unprotectable under design law, as only 'principally' but 'not exclusively functional' elements of a product may very well be protected by patent law. It is therefore to be feared that the new European law may grant designs a patent-like protection without requiring the strict prerequisites that patent law does. This broad protection of designs that are also functional could considerably obstruct the market, as competitors could be blocked from using functional elements by the monopolisation of certain product features – and due to the protection of non-registered designs even without any prior registration.[299]

This quote's last few words are even more alarming, as indeed CUDR is available automatically; in addition, no description of the functionality is rendered public (as required under patent law) as there is no registration.[300] This interpretation of article 7(1), as well depicted by Koschtial, contradicts the aims of the EU legislature when adopting the Design Directive and Regulation.[301]

However, the last sentence of paragraph 34 of the Advocate-General's Opinion ('a functional design may, nonetheless, be eligible for protection if it can be shown that the

[296] Ibid.

[297] Cornish and Llewelyn, *Intellectual Property* (n 204) 579, para 15-19. *Contra*: Torremans, *Holyoak and Torremans Intellectual Property Law* (n 130) 329, who thinks that the current 'interpretation of the provision does . . . strike the correct competition-friendly balance between adequate design protection and the risk of competition excluding technical designs'.

[298] U Koschtial, 'Design Law: Individual Character, Visibility and Functionality' (2005) *International Review of Intellectual Property and Competition Law* 297, 306.

[299] Ibid 306–7.

[300] Musker, *Community Design Law* (n 54) 44.

[301] Koschtial, 'Design Law' (n 298) 307.

same technical function could be achieved by another different form') strikes the right chord as it addresses the problem of the literal interpretation of article 7 discussed above by Koschtial. In other words, if there are alternative designs which fulfil the same function, the design is registrable, otherwise not. Put differently, '[i]f there is only one possible technical composition, *however aesthetic or useful it may be*, protection would not only cover the design but also the product, and protection under design law could therefore not be granted' (emphasis added).[302] This interpretation integrates the free competition element that the *travaux préparatoires* of the Design Directive and Regulation stressed when discussing article 7(1). Koschtial argues that article 7(1) should ideally be modified to reflect this interpretation.[303]

Finally, it must also be stated that:

> the existence of a patent does not mean that the design is solely dictated by its technical function. If there is at least one alternative design that can achieve the same technical function and does not fall under the design registration, the registration cannot be invalidated on the ground of article 7.1 Design Directive. The fact that all possible design alternatives may be covered by the patent has no implication for the validity of the design registration. An enforceable protection right for an embodiment of an invention at hand, a long time before the corresponding patent is granted, is a valuable asset in an IP portfolio. The additional costs incurred by the design of this registration are insignificant in comparison with the cost of the patent.[304]

In conclusion, the Advocate-General's Opinion is to be commended and followed as regards paragraph 34, but taken very cautiously for the rest.

There are some (isolated) commentators, however, who disagree with Design Directive, article 7(1) altogether, arguing that denying protection to technically innovative design is 'as likely to hamper innovation as granting it would have done'.[305] For them, article 7(1)'s exclusion could be narrowly construed 'to exclude only those designs which would have the scope of protection equivalent to that of the corresponding patent (and not merely overlapping with it)'.[306]

[302] Ibid 308.

[303] Ibid 309–10 asks herself the same question as regards designs which are economically superior as well as solely dictated by function. Should such designs be excluded if the alternative designs are prohibitively expensive? She replies negatively as this would kill the incentive to create such designs in the first place ('Rewarding the designer via higher sales is a quid pro quo for the benefit the public receives through the better design'), citing A Kur, 'EG-Geschmacksmusterschutz und Kfz-Ersatzteile – Eine Erwiderung' (1993) *GRUR Int* 71, 73 *et seq*. Schlötelburg, 'Design Protection for Technical Products' (n 281) 677, notes that the UK Intellectual Property Office came to a similar conclusion in its practice of design examination: 'it may not be fatal therefore that all of the features of the design are dictated by function. The test would appear to be whether or not the technical function dictates the appearance of the product to the extent that there is no (or negligible) design freedom . . . This test has been applied by the invalidity division of OHIM in its decision regarding registered Community design number 225073-0001 for an underwater motive device. The validity of the registration has been contested inter alia with the argument that most features are necessary for technical function. The invalidity division found that the Community design does not subsist in features of appearance only dictated by a technical function of the underwater motive device. The device would still fulfil its function with a body of a different shape'.

[304] Schlötelburg, 'Design Protection for Technical Products' (n 281) 678.

[305] Musker, *Community Design Law* (n 54) 41.

[306] Ibid 42.

(ii) Negative Overlap

(a) Design Protection Unavailable

Design protection will be unavailable for subject matter not covered by design right, such as chemical compounds or living things. It will also be unavailable if the design is solely dictated by function, which is normal as this is the realm of patent law. If the design is not new, it will not be possible to patent it either. The unavailability of design right is one of the most perfect cases where there cannot possibly be a negative overlap, by contrast with the other negative overlaps examined above.

(b) Patent Protection Unavailable

It will sometimes be possible for a prospective patent applicant to file a design instead of a patent (unless his or her patent relates to chemicals or living things), and this will be much easier as novelty is only relative. The applicant will also have to prove individual character, so s/he must make sure that his or her invention has an appearance that is different from those in the prior art. This should not be difficult if s/he can prove his or her invention is (relatively) new, as there is considerable overlap between the requirements of novelty and individual character.[307] The applicant will also have to make sure his or her 'invention' is not solely dictated by function. That might well be the case, so that, in effect, in some cases a prospective patent applicant may well acquire design right instead of a patent. Thus, in contrast with the previous negative overlap (when design protection is not available), here design law could fill the gap left by patent law. However, the gap is not fully filled because design law cannot protect entirely technical designs.

(iii) A Posteriori *Overlap*

The *a posteriori* overlap is less problematic than in other cumulation scenarios. This is because the maximum length of a (registered) design right is 25 years and that of a patent is 20 (supplementary protection certificates are irrelevant as there cannot be designs on plants or chemical compounds). However, subject matter protected both by patent and design rights could still have its protection extended by five years, which is always useful to have. It is surprising that the commentators who have criticised the *Philips* decision have not also pointed out the problem that a monopolisation by design right of patentable subject matter can also be detrimental, as the duration of registered design right is five years longer.[308]

C 'Level Overlap'

There is no 'level overlap' when an overlap concerns patents. This is because national and European patents are alternatives, they cannot be cumulated. The reason is that European

[307] Massa and Strowel, 'Community Design: Cinderella Revamped' (n 31) 73.

[308] Note, however, G Zimmerman, 'Extending the Monopoly? The Risks and Benefits of Multiple Forms of Intellectual Property Protection' (2001) 17 *Canadian Intellectual Property Review* 345, 363 in relation to Canadian law.

patents do not give a patent for all the states parties to the EPC but only to the countries designated in the application, so those chosen by the applicant. They become national once granted. So, for instance, it is not possible to have a UK patent and a European patent designating the United Kingdom.[309] Thus, in this respect, the European patent does not compare to the Community trademark or design.

In conclusion, free competition and preventing the circumvention of the stricter patent requirements seem to be the main reasons for prohibiting the simultaneous patent/design overlap.

VI. TRADEMARKS AND PATENTS

A The Legal Framework

As we have seen above in section III (overlap between copyright and trademarks), both the Trademark Directive and Trademark Regulation allow cumulation with other IPRs. The EPC does not have a provision concerning cumulation.[310] Article 52 EPC does not even exclude trademarks. Therefore, it is assumed that there can be an overlap between trademarks and patents.

B 'Content Overlap'

(i) Simultaneous Overlap

(a) Subject Matter

The concept of trademark is very broad: it is any sign which can be graphically represented. The appearance of a patented product can therefore be a sign. This is, as we have seen, what happened in the *Philips* case. On the other hand, it is hard to imagine that a trademark could be the subject of a patent unless it is registered at the same time, as it will then be deemed new. Only signs (it is difficult to imagine other types of signs apart from shapes[311]) which solve a technical problem could be patented, so the possibility of an overlap will be very small.

However, registration of a concept is not possible, as the Court of Justice ruled in *Dyson* in 2007.[312] Since 1993, Dyson has manufactured bagless vacuum cleaners. In 1996, it filed a trademark application for a sign which was described as 'a transparent bin or collection chamber forming part of the external surface of a vacuum cleaner as shown in the representation'.[313] A picture was attached with two examples of currently manufac-

[309] Bently and Sherman, *Intellectual Property Law* (n 82) 372–73 (referring to UK Patents Act 1977, s 73(2)).

[310] Quaedvlieg, 'Concurrence and Convergence in Industrial Design' (n 109) 33, notes that 'there is no (key) provision in patent law which explicitly forbids the protection, by trademark law, of technically-inspired shapes'.

[311] It is thinkable, however. Take the example of a specific pattern (bar code or the like) which solves a technical problem in granting conditional access.

[312] Case C-321/03 *Dyson v Registrar of Trademarks* [2007] ECR I-687.

[313] At para 10 of judgment.

tured vacuum cleaners.[314] Dyson's application was refused and the refusal upheld, so Dyson appealed to the High Court of England and Wales. Dyson did not want to register a shape mark but the bin itself. This meant that the trademark applied for covered all the possible shapes of a transparent collecting bin forming part of the external surface of a vacuum cleaner. The High Court wondered whether such a sign can acquire distinctiveness through use and, in doubt, referred a question to the Court of Justice. The answer turned on whether it was possible to register all the possible shapes of a transparent collecting bin forming part of the external surface of a vacuum cleaner as a sign, rather than the question of distinctiveness. First, the Court held that even though Trademark Directive, article 2 is open in terms of what can be a sign, it cannot be that the subject matter of any trademark application is *necessarily* a sign, since otherwise article 2's condition would be deprived of all substance.[315] In other words, for the Court, not anything and everything can be a sign. As the application was for all possible shapes of transparent collecting bins, it could not be said that it could be perceived visually so the subject matter is not specific.[316] Thus, for the Court, a sign must be specific, otherwise it would give the trademark holder an unfair competitive advantage 'since it would be entitled to prevent its competitors from marketing vacuum cleaners having any kind of transparent collecting bin on their external surface, irrespective of its shape'.[317] Indeed, 'the shape, the dimensions, the presentation and composition of that subject-matter depend both on the vacuum cleaner models developed by Dyson and on technological innovations. Likewise, transparency allows for the use of various colours'.[318] The Court concluded that the subject matter of the application was not a sign but a mere property of the product and therefore could not be registered as a trademark.[319]

The Advocate-General had added a few arguments, some of which are worth recounting as they may continue to influence future legal developments and also deal specifically with the trademark/patent overlap. The Advocate-General first pointed out that what Dyson was trying to register was a new concept 'for collecting, storing and emptying waste'.[320] A concept is a general and abstract mental representation of an object.[321] Secondly, he said that the essential function of a trademark (to enable consumers to distinguish products from different traders without being confused) would not be respected if a concept could be registered as a trademark.[322] Thirdly, even if it was not so, a concept cannot be represented graphically because it is not precise enough. In this case, the appearance of the bin may change over the years.[323] Also, in this case the bin would not be able to pass Trademark Directive, article 3(1)(e)'s hurdle as the shape is necessary to obtain a technical result. Interestingly, the Advocate-General added that allowing registration in this case would harm competition, which would be contrary to TRIPs,

[314] See www.ipo.gov.uk, no 2118079, which can also be seen in the Advocate-General's Opinion at www.curia.europa.eu.

[315] Case C-321/03 *Dyson v Registrar of Trademarks* [2007] ECR I-687, para 33. The purpose of this requirement is to prevent the abuse of trademark law in order to obtain an unfair competitive advantage (para 34 citing Case C-49/02 *Heidelberger Bauchemie* [2004] ECR I-6129, para 24).

[316] Case C-321/03 *Dyson v Registrar of Trademarks* [2007] ECR I-687, paras 36 and 37.

[317] Ibid para 38.

[318] Ibid para 37. See also Advocate-General's Opinion in the same case, para 51.

[319] Case C-321/03 *Dyson v Registrar of Trademarks* [2007] ECR I-687, para 39.

[320] Advocate-General's Opinion in ibid, para 47.

[321] Ibid para 48.

[322] Ibid para 54.

[323] Ibid para 62.

Article 7.[324] Therefore, the Advocate-General considered TRIPs, Article 7 to be an important tool in the interpretation not only of international law but of EU law, which is similar to what we advocated in chapter one. Finally, and most importantly, the Advocate-General also noted that allowing registration of concepts as trademarks would give an exclusive right to inventions, which is not the purpose of trademark law.[325] It would allow the circumvention of patent law's stringent requirements in addition to giving the right-holder a protection (potentially) unlimited in time.

Although the Court of Justice did not mention the word 'patent' and therefore did not address the overlap head-on, the effect of the decision is that concepts and ideas cannot be registered as trademarks. In fact, it can be said that there is an idea/expression dichotomy also in trademark law. The term 'expression' can also be used here because the sign needs to be graphically represented, so in a way 'expressed'. If one wishes to have a trademark in a functional shape, one must claim one precise shape. The Advocate-General's Opinion also shows that the three requirements are linked: if it is not a sign, it also cannot be represented graphically and thus cannot be distinctive. Few commentators have discussed the decision; however, one does not agree with it because the Court could in any case have refused the registration on the basis of Trademark Directive, article 3 (which was the Registry's conclusion). For him:

> there seems no pressing need to develop an overly philological understanding of what can constitute a sign in order to achieve this result . . . Concepts come in many forms, some very specific and perceivable (by the senses) and other subject matter esoteric and abstract.[326]

He gives the example of colours. In our view, this reasoning is ill-conceived as it is clear from the EU case law that colours as such are rarely registrable, and in any case, like all signs, they must be clearly graphically represented. The colour blue will not do, it must be detailed and the colour code given.

(b) Protection Requirements

Of course, the sign (invention here) would also have to be distinctive of goods or services for which it is registered. It is not impossible for that to be the case. The trademark would not only have to be new but also inventive and industrially applicable. The latter requirement is not hard to fulfil, but inventiveness might be. Again a good example is the *Philips* shaver.

(c) Excluded Subject Matter

As we know, the Trademark Directive and Regulation exclude signs which consist exclusively of the shape of goods which are necessary to obtain a technical result. The *Philips* ruling and its progeny have rendered the trademark/patent overlap practically impossible in this respect. In *Lego Juris v Mega Brands*, the Grand Board of Appeal at OHIM dismissed Lego's appeal against cancellation of the CTM registration of its toy brick, noting that 'a prior patent is *practically* irrefutable evidence that features therein disclosed

[324] Ibid para 94.
[325] Ibid paras 95–97.
[326] S Godsell, 'Concepts and Signs' (2007) 196 *Trademark World* 15.

or claimed are functional' (emphasis added).[327] All instances decided the brick was unregistrable on the basis of CTMR, article 7(1)(e)(ii), including the Court of Justice. In its decision of September 2010, the Court of Justice followed the Advocate-General's Opinion and confirmed the previous case law, mainly *Philips,* and added a few more details.[328] The Advocate-General had said that the exclusion of functional features in trademark law is based:

> on a twofold premiss: first, that of preventing a monopoly on technical solutions for goods through trade-mark law, in particular where those solutions have previously enjoyed the protection afforded by another industrial property right, and, second, that of keeping separate trademark protection and the protection conferred by other forms of intellectual property.[329]

The Court of Justice echoed this statement by stating that CTMR, article 7(1)(e)(ii):

> ensures that undertakings may not use trademark law in order to perpetuate, indefinitely, exclusive rights relating to technical solutions. When the shape of a product merely incorporates the technical solution developed by the manufacturer of that product and patented by it, protection of that shape as a trademark once the patent has expired would considerably and permanently reduce the opportunity for other undertakings to use that technical solution. In the system of intellectual property rights developed in the European Union, technical solutions are capable of protection only for a limited period, so that subsequently they may be freely used by all economic operators. As OHIM pointed out in its argument summarised in paragraph 37 above, that consideration underlies not only Directive 89/104 and Regulation No 40/94, with regard to trademark law, but also Regulation No 6/2002, in relation to designs.[330]

To go back to the Grand Board of Appeal's statement that 'a prior patent is *practically* irrefutable evidence that features therein disclosed or claimed are functional', such was the case in *Philips* and *Lego*, and for that matter also *Dyson*, and the three registrations were void. The *Philips* ruling justifies trademark law's exclusion for technical subject matter not within trademark law itself but 'in considerations of public interest transcending trademark law'.[331] In effect, the ruling almost completely rules out the overlap by using the public interest which applies to both patent and trademark laws, namely that 'patent law alone should govern the field of technical subject matter and that no IP right should interfere with the domain which patent law consciously leaves unprotected and free for all'.[332] Therefore, it is not necessary to envisage how the overlap may work at the other levels (ownership, rights and exceptions).

[327] Case R 856/2004-G, Decision of the Grand Board of Appeal of OHIM of 10 July 2006, para 40.

[328] Case C-48/09 *Lego Juris v Mega Brands* (14 September 2010, nyr), available at www.curia.europa.eu. See also Advocate-General Mengozzi's Opinion, 26 January 2010 in Case C-48/09 *Lego Juris v OHIM*, available at www.curia.europa.eu.

[329] Advocate-General's Opinion, para 55.

[330] *Lego Juris v Mega Brands* (n 328), judgment of the Court of Justice, paras 45–46. For additional guidelines, see also paras 84–85. Unfortunately, at para 61, the Court issued the following cryptic statement: 'In those circumstances, the position of an undertaking which has developed a technical solution cannot be protected – with regard to competitors placing on the market slavish copies of the product shape incorporating exactly the same solution – by conferring a monopoly on that undertaking through registering as a trademark the three-dimensional sign consisting of that shape, but can, where appropriate, be examined in the light of rules on unfair competition. Such an examination is, however, outside the scope of these proceedings'. Whether this leaves national courts total freedom in applying unfair competition law (ie sanctioning pure slavish imitations where there is no (risk of) confusion) is not clear. We believe that only when there is (a risk of) confusion should unfair competition law apply in such a situation, see below section IX and chapter 7, section IV.

[331] Quaedvlieg, 'Concurrence and Convergence in Industrial Design' (n 109) 33.

[332] Ibid.

(ii) Negative Overlap

(a) Patent Protection Unavailable

As with the simultaneous overlap, the negative overlap will not be possible. If the subject matter is functional or is a concept or an idea, and is not new or is new but not inventive or industrially applicable, since concepts and shapes necessary to obtain a functional result are per se excluded from trademark protection, a negative overlap cannot occur. There is therefore total negative convergence.

(b) Trademark Protection Unavailable

If a sign is an idea or is a shape which is necessary to obtain a technical result, then trademark protection will not be available but patent law might be if the protection requirements can be fulfilled. This is entirely normal as it is the converse of the previous negative overlap. It is meant to be so. If the sign cannot obtain trademark or patent protection for these reasons, then it is meant to remain unprotectable by IPRs (if it cannot be protected by copyright or designs, and it should not normally if it is not an idea). However, some countries may offer some protection under their unfair competition laws.

(iii) A Posteriori *Overlap*

As well remarked by the Advocate-General in *Philips*, trademark protection could also be acquired after the expiry of the patent, so that the *a posteriori* overlap can occur. He rejected this possibility because it would circumvent patent law's requirements, is against the general interest behind Trademark Directive, article 3(1)(e), and also against the higher interest of free competition enshrined in the EC Treaty (now TFEU).[333] However, some have doubted that this part of the Advocate-General's reasoning is appropriate in some situations. For them, it can seem 'illogical and contrary to public policy to allow the acquired goodwill [of a patented shape] to be appropriated by all upon expiration of patent protection'.[334] However, it can be retorted that since the inventor has already had his or her reward under patent law, it would be overprotective to prolong it or have it a second time under trademark law (especially if it is unlimited in time).[335]

In conclusion, as a result of the statutory provisions and case law, none of the three overlaps between patents and trademarks is practically possible. Again, we see the effective or free competition principle permeating this overlap, just as for all of the other overlaps examined above.

[333] Advocate-General's Opinion in *Philips v Remington* (n 169), para 38.

[334] Suthersanen, 'The European Court of Justice in *Philips v Remington*' (n 167) 267.

[335] Dinwoodie, 'Copyright, Trade Marks and Trade Dress' (n 75) 519 (election of rights); E Derclaye, *The Legal Protection of Databases: A Comparative Analysis* (Cheltenham, Edward Elgar, 2008) ch 1 and ch 10 s 7.

VII. COPYRIGHT AND PATENTS

A The Legal Framework

EPC Article 52(2) provides that:

> the following in particular shall not be regarded as inventions within the meaning of paragraph 1 . . . (b) aesthetic creations; (c) schemes, rules and methods for performing mental acts, playing games or doing business, and programs for computers; (d) presentations of information.

Article 52(3) then provides:

> the provisions of paragraph 2 shall exclude patentability of the subject-matter or activities referred to in that provision only to the extent to which a European patent application or European patent relates to such subject-matter or activities as such.

Thus, provided that aesthetic creations, computer programs and presentations of information are not claimed as such, they are patentable.

Software Directive, article 9[336] clearly allows the cumulation by stating that:

> the provisions of this Directive shall be without prejudice to any other legal provisions such as those concerning patent rights.

It adds that:

> [a]ny contractual provisions contrary to Article 6 or to the exceptions provided for in Article 5(2) and (3) shall be null and void.[337]

This implies that if a technological protection measure (TPM) or a legal provision overrides these exceptions, imperativity does not kick in. So Software Directive, article 9 regulates the contract/copyright relationship not other overlaps.[338] As we said in the introduction, we are not envisaging the overlap between copyright and contract/TPMs here. However, where confidential information is achieved by contract, this provision will be relevant as trade secrets are part of unfair competition law. Software Directive, recital 14 is also interesting. It provides:

> Whereas, in accordance with this principle of copyright, to the extent that logic, algorithms and programming languages comprise ideas and principles, those ideas and principles are not protected under this Directive.

This means that algorithms (although probably neither logic nor programming languages as it is hard to see how they could be original expressions) may be protected by

[336] For the reference, see above chapter 3, section I.

[337] See also the related and almost identical recital 26: 'Whereas protection of computer programs under copyright laws should be without prejudice to the application, in appropriate cases, of other forms of protection; whereas, however, any contractual provisions contrary to article 6 or the exceptions provided for in article 5(2) and (3) should be null and void'.

[338] However, Infosoc Directive, recital 50 seems to mean that the imperativity of the exceptions applicable to computer programs also applies in case a technological protection measure is applied to a computer program. It provides that '[i]t should neither inhibit nor prevent the development or use of any means of circumventing a technological measure that is necessary to enable acts to be undertaken in accordance with the terms of Article 5(3) or Article 6 of Directive 91/250/EEC'.

copyright if they are original expressions and thus not mere ideas, reinforcing the overlap between copyright and patents for computer programs.

B 'Content Overlap'

(i) Simultaneous Overlap

(a) Subject Matter

As neither the Software Directive[339] nor the EPC defines 'computer program' or 'software', the overlap at the level of subject matter is flagrant. It is even more flagrant in view of the long-standing and constant case law of the European Patent Office (EPO)[340] admitting the patentability of computer programs,[341] and culminating with the *IBM* decisions which allow the patentability of computer programs as products, ie simply recorded on a medium (such as a disk) so long as they have the ability to produce a 'technical effect going beyond the normal physical interaction between the program and the computer when the program runs or is loaded on a computer'.[342] As many computer programs will generally comply with the conditions required by the EPO case law, the overlap will occur frequently.

It must be noted that this overlap should not normally exist because of the general, universal rule excluding technical subject matter from copyright law, as such subject matter is protected or protectable by patent law (TRIPs, Article 9(2) and WCT, Article 2). As Quaedvlieg puts it well:

[339] All the Software Directive notes is that '[f]or the purposes of this Directive, the term "computer programs" shall include their preparatory design material' (art 1(1)).

[340] D Pearce, 'Patentable Subject-matter: Where Are We Now?', 28 January 2010, available at http://ipkitten.blogspot.com/2010/01/Patentable_subject_matter_ where_are_we.html, noting that the early decisions of *Vicom* and *Koch and Sterzel* (1987 and 1988) 'are largely consistent with the case law that followed over the next 20 years. There is essentially not very much that has changed in the way that [computer-implemented inventions] have been dealt with by the EPO'.

[341] For a summary of the case on the patentability of computer programs, see M Singer and D Stauder, *The European Patent Convention: A Commentary*, 3rd edn (London, Sweet & Maxwell, 2003) vol I, 73–76.

[342] See Case T 1173/97 *IBM/Computer Program Product I and II* [1999] OJ EPO 609 and T 0935/97 [1999] RPC 861, quoted by Singer and Stauder, *The European Patent Convention* (n 341) vol I, 76. This case law has been codified in the EPO Guidelines for Examination, April 2009, Part C, ch IV, para 2.3.6, available at http://documents.epo.org/projects/babylon/eponet.nsf/0/1AFC30805E91D074C125758A0051718A/$File/guidelines_2009_part_C_en.pdf. Note that computer programs are intrinsically processes but the EPO has recognised the patentability also of computer programs as products. See R Hilty and C Geiger, 'Patenting Software? A Judicial and Socio-Economic Analysis' (2005) *European Intellectual Property Review* 615, 629–30; JP Martin, 'La protection des logiciels informatiques: droit d'auteur ou brevet d'invention?' (1990) *JCP E*, II, 15752, 270, 271; C Le Stanc, 'Logiciels entre droit d'auteur et brevet: implications juridiques et economiques' in G Ghidini and M Genovesi (eds), *Intellectual Property and Market Power, ATRIP Papers 2006–2007* (Buenos Aires, Eudeba, 2008) 295, 302, also noting that the distinction between product and process does not have much importance as far as the determination of the scope of protection of computer programs is concerned. The Enlarged Board of Appeal has recently held that the EPO decisions on the patentability of computer programs were not conflicting and therefore held the EPO President's referral on this matter inadmissible. See Decision of the EPO Enlarged Board of Appeal of 12 May 2010 in G3/08, available at:http://documents.epo.org/projects/babylon/eponet.nsf/0/DC6171F182D8B65AC125772100426656/$File/G3_08_Opinion_12_05_2010_en.pdf. See further M Leistner and M Kleinemenke, 'The Impact of Institutional Design on the Development of Patent Law: Patentability of Computer Programs and Business Methods in Europe and the United States of America as a Topical Example' (2010) 2 *Zeitschrift für Geistiges Eigentum/Intellectual Property Journal* 273, 304 *et seq*.

> copyright will typically have to surrender to the rule of patent law, such that technical subject matter is either protected by this law or not at all . . . Filling this 'gap' with protection by other intellectual property rights would therefore run counter to the policy of the legislator.[343]

Thus, the overlap between patent and copyright for software is clearly an exception to this rule (software being technical subject matter should not normally be protected by copyright). Nevertheless, the principle of prohibition of cumulation still applies to software and the overlap should not, at least in theory, normally pose a problem in the sense that patent right will protect functions and applications of ideas, and copyright will protect expressions, so that normally the scope of the two rights is clearly separate. But because of the nature of computer programs, it is often difficult to determine a program's form/expression and therefore, to trace the border between copyright and patents because the protectable form is imprecise.[344] Indeed, if the form is difficult to determine, it is not possible to know if it is separable from function so that it can escape the prohibition.[345]

The EPC does not define the terms 'aesthetic creation' or 'presentation of information' either, thus there is a possibility of overlap between copyright works, such as works of applied art and databases if they are not claimed 'as such' in a patent application. However, it should be noted at this stage that the overwhelming majority of patent applications for inventions embodying aesthetic creations or presentations of information have been refused protection by the EPO so that an overlap between copyright and patent for those will be rare.[346] However, patents could be granted for such inventions as the EPO case law is similar to that for software patents. Therefore, a presentation of information will not be excluded if it includes some technical means 'no matter how old, banal or trivial'.[347] This would mean that a book, a visual display or a database could be patented if the claim includes technical means. Thus, it is possible to have an overlap.

(b) Protection Requirements

One would have thought that the separation between ideas and expressions would neatly coincide with the realms of patent and copyright laws, thus embodying the general rule described above. Whilst it is true that ideas within a computer program will not be copyrightable, the original expressions of such a program may also constitute parts of the new and inventive aspects of the program, so there can be overlap between copyright and patent in the program. There is no reason why a computer program which is original cannot also be new and inventive if certain additional technical elements of the program establish the necessary inventive step. Conversely, and probably even more likely, new and inventive computer programs will be original. As regards aesthetic creations, although technical solutions can have aesthetic effects, 'whether a feature is technical or non-

[343] Quaedvlieg, 'Overlap/Relationships between Copyright and Other Intellectual Property Rights' (n 27) 491.

[344] C Caron, 'La coexistence du droit d'auteur et du droit des brevets sur un même logiciel' in JL Goutal (ed), *Brevetabilité des logiciels, travaux du CUERPI, droit des technologies avancées* (Paris, Hermes Science Publications, 2002) vol 9(1–2), 183, 196.

[345] Ibid.

[346] See Singer and Stauder, *The European Patent Convention* (n 341) vol I, 71 and 76–77. The applications for presentations of information which were rejected were so rejected because the presentations of information had no technical effect, they only triggered the performance of mental, and thus non-technical, acts, which are also excluded from patentability. See, however, the examples given in the EPO Guidelines for Examination, April 2009, Part C, ch IV, para 2.3.7, available at http://documents.epo.org/projects/babylon/eponet.nsf/0/1afc30805e91d074c125758a0051718a/$file/guidelines_2009_complete_en.pdf.

[347] Bently and Sherman, *Intellectual Property Law* (n 82) 434.

technical depends on the effect of the feature claimed. If the effects address the sense of shape or colour, they cannot be capable of establishing a patent'.[348]

(c) Excluded Subject Matter

Only aesthetic creations, computer programs and presentations of information *as such* are excluded from patentability, this is why an overlap with copyright is by definition possible. Apart from this exclusion, it will be rare that such copyright works, which could also attract patent protection, will be excluded on the basis that they are contrary to '*ordre public*' or morality (EPC, Article 53(a)).

(d) Ownership and Dealings

Since there are many different stages in the creation of a computer program (from the preparatory material up to the final step, the object code), it is possible that there are different persons involved and therefore that the patent and the copyright belong to different owners at the outset. Also, the owners of the patent and the copyright in the same computer program can be different as a result of a difference in the patent and copyright ownership rules.[349] This also applies for presentation of information and aesthetic creations. Otherwise, if the owner is the same for both the copyright and the patent, ownership can become split as a result of a transfer of the copyright and of the patent to different persons. Thus, as with other overlaps, conflicts of ownership can occur. The EPC is silent on ownership and the Software Directive by and large leaves the issue to the Member States,[350] so that the details of the overlap regarding ownership and dealings will be examined at national level.

(e) Rights and Infringement

European patents always designate (a) specific country(ies) where they will be applicable, as such patents are not granted automatically in all states parties to the EPC (ie there is no Single European Patent, or in other words Community patent). Accordingly, EPC Article 64 expressly states that a European patent will grant its owner:

> in each Contracting State in respect of which it is granted, the same rights as would be conferred by a national patent granted in that State.[351]

[348] See Singer and Stauder, *The European Patent Convention* (n 341) vol I, 71, referring to Case T 119/88, OG 1990, 395. For another example, see Case T 456/09, 25 November 1991 (patent was refused to the connection between a watch casing and the wrist strap of a wrist watch).

[349] As noted by J Reichman, 'Charting the Collapse of the Patent-Copyright Dichotomy: Premises for a Restructured International Intellectual Property System' (1995) 13 (2) *Cardozo Arts and Entertainment Law Journal* 475, 506–7; see also Quaedvlieg, 'Overlap/Relationships between Copyright and Other Intellectual Property Rights' (n 27) 514.

[350] Software Directive, art 2(2) requires that where a computer program is created by a group of natural persons jointly, the exclusive rights will be owned jointly. Article 2(3) requires that the economic rights in a program made by an employee in the course of his or her employment belong exclusively to the employer. However, the latter rule can be modified by contract.

[351] The EPC forces Member States to harmonise their patent laws but it does not harmonise the infringement acts nor acts amounting to indirect infringement. See G Tritton, R Davis, M Edenborough, J Graham, S Malinicz and A Roughton, *Intellectual Property in Europe* (London, Sweet & Maxwell, 2008) 86–87.

The question of the simultaneous overlap at the level of rights will therefore be addressed in the next chapters. However, it can already be mentioned that, as with other overlaps between a 'monopoly right' and an 'anti-copying' right, if there is an infringement of copyright (ie by copying), this will automatically infringe the patent. But this is so as long as what has been copied also reproduces what is claimed in the patent. This will have to be checked each time, but since copying copyright expressions includes copying the underlying ideas, the patent will typically be infringed. Conversely, if someone independently comes up with the same or similar invention, only the patent will be infringed not the copyright in the computer program.[352]

(f) Exceptions Including Exhaustion Principle

The exceptions to the economic rights of the owner of copyright in a computer program are namely: acts necessary for the normal use of the computer program (including error correction), the making of one back-up copy, certain acts in order to 'observe, study or test' the program, and certain acts in order to decompile it. Again, as far as European patent law is concerned, the EPC leaves the issue of exceptions to each Member State, so that the question of the overlap will be addressed in the chapters on national law. As has already been seen above (section II.B(i)), the exceptions to copyright's economic rights are numerous and will vary from Member State to Member State. Therefore, likewise, the question of overlap between copyright and patent for aesthetic creations and presentations of information at the level of exceptions will be addressed in the next chapters. However, it should already be noted that both patent and copyright laws can cancel out the benefits that each of their exceptions provides.[353] On the one hand, the patent owner could, thanks to his or her rights, restrict or completely prevent the interoperability established in Software Directive, article 6, as there is no corresponding exception in patent law.[354] On the other hand, the copyright holder can prevent the making of derivative software, something allowed under patent law provided the second invention is sufficiently important.[355] The overlap at the level of the exceptions is a classic case of asymmetric convergence. However, the patent owner's power to prevent interoperability is not total, as the Commission noted in its (now defunct) Proposal for a Directive on the patentability of computer-implemented inventions: 'as regards developing interoperable programs, the requirement for each patent to include an enabling disclosure should facilitate the task of a person seeking to adapt the

[352] The overlap at the level of rights was expressly mentioned by the Commission in its Consultation Paper, *The Patentability of Computer Implemented Inventions* (DG Internal Market, Brussels, October 2000) 5, and similarly in the Explanatory Memorandum of Directive Proposal 2002/0047 on the Patentability of Computer-Implemented Inventions, available at http://eur-lex.europa.eu/LexUriServ/site/en/com/2002/com2002_0092en01.pdf, which never saw the light of day. See also Moffatt, 'Mutant Copyrights and Backdoor Patents' (n 103) 1514.

[353] As noted by Quaedvlieg, 'Overlap/Relationships between Copyright and Other Intellectual Property Rights' (n 27) 513.

[354] J Weyand and F Haase, 'Patenting Computer Programs: New Challenges' (2005) *International Review of Intellectual Property and Competition Law* 647, 653–54. Note, however, that article 6 of the Proposal for a Directive on the Patentability of Computer-Implemented Inventions specifically provided that the copyright exceptions (provided in Software Directive, arts 5 and 6) were safeguarded where a copyrighted program was also patented.

[355] See TRIPs Art 31(l). G Ghidini and E Arezzo, 'One, None or A Hundred Thousand: How Many Layers of Protection for Software Innovations?' in J Drexl (ed), *Research Handbook on Intellectual Property and Competition Law* (Cheltenham, Edward Elgar, 2008) 358–59. Something also noted by Moffatt, 'Mutant Copyrights and Backdoor Patents' (n 103) 1513.

program to another, pre-existing one incorporating patented features'.[356] The Commission added that 'in the event that patent rights are exercised in an abusive way, compulsory licences may be available as a remedy, as well as possible recourse to competition law'.[357] The efficacy of these mechanisms, however, as has been seen in the case law, is not particularly good.

Finally, since the EU case law on exhaustion of copyright and patent rights concurs, there will be convergence between the two fields and no problems should occur.[358] Otherwise, the *Dior v Evora* case could surely apply by analogy in situations involving a computer program which is at the same time patented and protected by copyright.[359] It should be noted that there is so far no EU or EPO case law on this specific overlap or on the interpretation of the Software Directive.

(ii) Negative Overlap

(a) Patent Protection Unavailable

Patent protection is not available if a computer program is claimed as such, or if a computer program not claimed as such is nevertheless not new or not inventive. This can frequently happen. As we have seen, many computer programs can now be patented. However, often, a program which is not new or inventive may be original so that copyright will easily fill the gap left by patent law, albeit running counter to the general rule of exclusion of technical subject matter in copyright law. We have seen, however, that the European legislature has expressly made an exception to this rule for computer programs.[360] Nevertheless, copyright protection will not be available for ideas and functions so that it does not entirely fill the gap.

(b) Copyright Protection Unavailable

The converse will be rarer. If a computer program is not original, it will be difficult for it to be novel or inventive. This second negative overlap will therefore not be frequent.

(iii) A Posteriori *Overlap*

When the patent in a computer program has expired, copyright subsists. It might, depending on the program, not protect as much but it is still a non-negligible protection against piracy. Neither the EPC nor the Software Directive has rules organising this overlap. The reverse is not possible. If copyright subsisted in a program and expires, it is not possible to prolong it with a patent, as it will no longer be new.

[356] Proposal for a Directive of the European Parliament and of the Council on the Patentability of Computer-Implemented Inventions, COM(2002)92 final, 2002/0047 (COD), 9, available at http://eur-lex.europa.eu/LexUriServ/site/en/com/2002/com2002_0092en01.pdf.

[357] Ibid.

[358] See section V.B(i) above. Software Directive, art. 4(c) provides: 'The first sale in the Community of a copy of a program by the right-holder or with his consent shall exhaust the distribution right within the Community of that copy, with the exception of the right to control further rental of the program or a copy thereof'.

[359] Probably, however, such situations will be rare as it is often not necessary to show the source code or other protectable aspects of a computer program to advertise it.

[360] Quaedvlieg, 'Overlap/Relationships between Copyright and Other Intellectual Property Rights' (n 27) 481.

C Literature

In general, most commentators are very critical of the overlap between patent law and copyright regarding software. Some strongly disapprove the EPO case law 'which grants patents on the basis of the "program as a product", thereby contributing to the extension of the patent beyond its natural limits'.[361] Because of the messy situation created by the overlap between copyright and patent for computer programs,[362] others recommend abolishing copyright law for software and clearly allowing their patentability.[363] This is because software is intrinsically of a technical and not of a literary nature.[364] To reduce problems caused by the cumulation of rights, others propose that the source code of patented programs be published in the patent application.[365] However, some others believe that 'the dilemma about the choice of protection between copyright and patent protection does not exist', referring to an EU study which found that there is 'no evidence that European independent software developers have been unduly affected by the patent positions of large companies or indeed of other software developers'.[366]

In conclusion, the simultaneous overlap is alive and well, especially for computer programs. The negative overlap is also clearly possible when patent protection is not available but the converse is much less true. The *a posteriori* overlap can also help to prolong a patent, although of course only the expressions not the ideas will be protected. There are no rules organising any of the three types of overlap.

VIII. PATENTS AND PLANT VARIETY RIGHTS

A The Legal Framework

The best way to explain the legal framework regarding the overlap between patents and plant variety rights is to do so chronologically, as in some ways it has not changed, and in others it has evolved with time. First, EPC Article 53(b) excluded plant varieties from

[361] R Hilty and C Geiger, 'Patenting Software? A Judicial and Socio-Economic Analysis' (2005) *European Intellectual Property Review* 615, 630.

[362] Ghidini and Arezzo, 'One, None or A Hundred Thousand: How Many Layers of Protection for Software Innovations?' (n 355) 359, adding that 'the scope of each of these rights [not only copyright and patent but TPMs and trade secrets] is far from clear, and it is different in each Member State'.

[363] Ibid 372.

[364] Ibid 359.

[365] B Caillaud, 'La propriété intellectuelle sur les logiciels' in J Tirole, C Henry, M Trommetter, L Tubiana and B Caillaud (eds), *Propriété intellectuelle* (Paris, Conseil d'Analyse Economique, La Documentation Française, 2003) 154, 164; F Macrez, 'Les cumuls de droits intellectuels sur les créations informatiques' in S Dusollier and A Cruquenaire (eds), *Le cumul des droits intellectuels* (Brussels, Larcier, 2009) 87, 101; J Weyand and F Haase, 'Patenting Computer Programs: New Challenges' (2005) *International Review of Intellectual Property and Competition Law* 647, 660.

[366] G Casucci, 'Software and Computer Related Inventions: Protection by Patent and Copyright' in C Heath and A Kamperman Sanders (eds), *New Frontiers of Intellectual Property Law, IP and Cultural Heritage, Geographical Indications, Enforcement and Overprotection* (Oxford, Hart Publishing, 2005) 161, 178, citing R Hart, P Holmes and J Reid, *The Economic Impact of Patentability of Computer Programs,* Report to the European Commission (19 October 2000) 3, Conclusions 1, available at http://ec.europa.eu/internal_market/indprop/docs/comp/study_en.pdf.

patent protection, except where they are the result of microbiological processes.[367] Therefore, there was initially a clear separation between patents and plant variety rights. This was the result of the prohibition of double protection in the UPOV Convention, which was lifted in 1991 (see chapter two, section VIII.A).[368] Despite the lifting of the prohibition in the UPOV Convention, the European Union retained it.

In 1994, the European Union adopted a Regulation creating the Community plant variety right (CPVR).[369] Two things are worth noting. First, the CPVR Regulation conforms to the 1991 act of the UPOV Convention and generally follows its text closely.[370] Secondly, before the adoption of the CPVR Regulation, the EU Member States' plant variety rights varied considerably. The adoption of the CPVR Regulation seems to have led Member States to harmonise their national plant variety right laws.[371] Therefore, the legal provisions at the three levels (national, regional and international) are very similar. According to the CPVR Regulation, national plant variety rights subsist (article 3)[372] but, by contrast with trademark and designs, cannot be cumulated with the Community right (article 92). If a prior national plant variety right or patent for the variety is granted, the later CPVR will prevail and the national right(s) will be ineffective. In other words, the CPVR prevails. This is so for as long as the Community right is effective.[373] Therefore, if the CPVR is invalidated or expires, the national right(s) can be revived. As a result, the 'level overlap' is by definition excluded. The CPVR Regulation insists that the definition of plant variety is not intended to interfere with or exclude the application of other laws, and expresses the hope that states will arrive at a common definition at international level (recitals 9 and 10). Recital 29 states that the CPVR Regulation takes the EPC into account and 'consequently implements the ban on patenting plant varieties only to the extent that the European Patent Convention so requires, ie to plant varieties as such' (see also CPVR Regulation, article 92).[374] As seen above, the EPC does not provide that plant varieties are not patentable as such. But in practice that is what EPC Article 53(b) boils down to.

Finally, in 1998, the European Union adopted the Directive on the legal protection of biotechnological inventions, also called the Biotech Directive, which adapted the national

[367] The article reads as follows in relevant part: 'European patents shall not be granted in respect of: . . . (b) plant or animal varieties or essentially biological processes for the production of plants or animals; this provision shall not apply to microbiological processes or the products thereof'.

[368] Bently and Sherman, *Intellectual Property Law* (n 82) 601.

[369] Council Regulation (EC) 2100/94 of 27 July 1994 on Community plant variety rights [1994] OJ L227/1. The CPVR is completed by Commission Regulation (EC) 1768/95 of 24 July 1995 implementing rules on the agricultural exemption provided for in article 14(3) of Council Regulation (EC) 2100/94 on Community plant variety rights [1995] OJ L173/14 (provision regarding small farmers).

[370] T Millett, 'The Community System of Plant Variety Rights' (1999) *European Law Review* 231, 234; see also Tritton *et al*, *Intellectual Property in Europe* (n 351) 615 *et seq*.

[371] R Moufang, 'The Interface between Patents and Plant Variety Rights in Europe' in *WIPO/UPOV Symposium on Intellectual Property Rights in Plant Biotechnology*, Doc WIPO-UPOV/SYM/03/6 (Geneva, 24 October 2003) 6.

[372] M Llewelyn and M Adcock, *European Plant Intellectual Property* (Oxford, Hart Publishing, 2006) 205, note that the reason for keeping a choice between national and Community plant variety rights is that some varieties cannot grow in some countries and there would be little point in forcing a breeder to have a Community-wide right when the variety can only be commercialised in a couple of countries.

[373] Tritton *et al*, *Intellectual Property in Europe* (n 351) 629 ('There is nothing to stop the applicant from initially pursuing both routes. It is only upon grant of the CPVR that the national PVR becomes ineffective.').

[374] Llewelyn and Adcock, *European Plant Intellectual Property* (n 372) 224, also think that this is what art 92 means (ie prohibition of cumulative protection over a variety as such and not to the acquisition of any national rights over the constituent parts of the variety). However, they note that the article is not so clear and could be interpreted differently.

patent laws of Member States to biotechnological developments. It makes explicit what was already clear from the CPVR Regulation, namely that plants are patentable as long as 'the application of the invention is not confined to a single plant variety' (Biotech Directive, recital 29). This is reflected in Biotech Directive, article 4(2):

> Inventions which concern plants or animals shall be patentable if the technical feasibility of the invention is not confined to a particular plant or animal variety.

Also 'a plant grouping which is characterised by a particular gene (and not its whole genome) is not covered by the protection of new varieties and is therefore not excluded from patentability even if it comprises new varieties of plants' (recital 31). However, recital 32 sets a limit to recital 31:

> if an invention consists only in genetically modifying a particular plant variety, and if a new plant variety is bred, it will still be excluded from patentability even if the genetic modification is the result not of an essentially biological process but of a biotechnological process.

The Biotech Directive also ensures that where a patent is granted on a plant, an identical exception to that provided for in the CPVR Regulation, the so-called farmer's privilege, applies. The Directive also provides that when a breeder cannot acquire or exploit a plant variety right without infringing a patent, s/he can apply for a compulsory licence to the invention covered by the patent and then must grant a cross-licence on the plant variety right to the patentee. An identically phrased provision applies in the converse situation, ie when a patent holder cannot acquire or exploit a patent without infringing a plant variety right. Thus, the simultaneous overlap is quite substantially organised and is examined in more detail below.

B 'Content Overlap'

(i) Simultaneous Overlap

(a) Subject Matter

The EPC has a specific exclusion for plant varieties in Article 53(b).[375] It is even stronger than the exclusion in EPC Article 52, as Article 53 excludes subject matter whether the criteria are met or not.[376] This exclusion is also reflected in Biotech Directive, article 4, so that the two instruments' provisions match exactly.[377] On the face of it, this would mean that there could not be a simultaneous overlap at all, but Article 53(b) is so phrased that

[375] Cornish and Llewelyn, *Intellectual Property* (n 204) 230, para 5-81 (EPC Art 53(b)'s 'exclusion of essentially biological processes (other than microbiological) for the production of plants and animals is evidently related to the exclusion of varieties'). See also Llewelyn and Adcock, *European Plant Intellectual Property* (n 372) 316.

[376] J Funder, 'Rethinking Patents for Plant Innovation' (1999) *European Intellectual Property Review* 501, 514.

[377] Tritton *et al*, *Intellectual Property in Europe* (n 351) 197, para 2-207: 'many of the articles of the directive have been implemented into the EPC in order to ensure that the approach of the EPC to biotechnological inventions is the same as the directive. The difference of approach between the EPC and ECT would be intolerable because contracting states of the EPC are required to align their national patent laws with the EPC'. Ibid 200: 'The wording of article 4.2 has been incorporated into implementing regulations of the EPC. See EPC r.23.c.d'. See also Bently and Sherman, *Intellectual Property Law* (n 82) 445.

plant varieties cannot be patented *unless* they are the result of microbiological processes.[378] Therefore, a plant variety which has been produced by a 'microbiological process' is not within the scope of Article 53(b) and is patentable. So the exclusion is not total and simultaneous overlap is possible. Even if one of the Biotech Directive's goals was to 'promote the fruitful existence' of patents and plant variety rights, and indeed directly regulates some of the issues posed by the overlap, 'the European legal framework does not really reduce the area of possible overlap between the two systems, since the patent system remains capable of covering plant-related innovations'.[379] It is not the place to retrace the history and evolution of the interpretation of EPC Article 53(b)'s exclusion here, as the Biotech Directive has clearly put an end to the previous muddled case law.[380] Suffice it to say that both the case law and commentators agree that Article 53(b), being an exception, should be narrowly construed[381] and that the result of the Biotech Directive is that the areas of overlap have grown larger as compared with the situation in the 1970s.

In summary, there are three ways a simultaneous overlap can occur. According to both the Biotech Directive and the *Novartis* decision, as long as a claim encompasses more than one variety, it is potentially patentable.[382] Patents for plants are allowed 'even if they encompass a plant variety'.[383] However, if a patent application directly claims a plant variety, it will be rejected.[384] An example of this is if:

> a claim is directed to transgenic plants characterised by the insertion of a specific DNA sequence, it is considered not to be directed to plant varieties per se (and thus not hit by the patent exclusion of plant varieties) since plant varieties are defined by their whole genome and, hence, are characterised by a multiplicity of genetic traits. Nevertheless, the scope of protection of such claims may also encompass plant varieties, namely when those varieties contain the specific DNA sequence.[385]

[378] A Christie, 'Patents for Plant Innovation' (1989) *European Intellectual Property Review* 394, 397, thinks that 'the correct reading of the limitation is that it removes from the scope of the exclusionary provision *all* products of a microbiological process' (emphasis in original).

[379] Moufang, 'The Interface between Patents and Plant Variety Rights in Europe' (n 371) 3.

[380] For the evolution of the case law, see eg Christie, 'Patents for Plant Innovation' (n 378).

[381] See ibid; R Moufang, 'Protection for Plant Breeding and Plant Varieties: A Frontier of Patent Law' (1992) 3 *International Review of Intellectual Property and Competition Law* 328, 331, 345; Funder, 'Rethinking Patents for Plant Innovation' (n 376) 510; see also in the case law, T49/83 *Ciba-Geigy/Propagating Material* [1979–85] C EPOR 758; T320/87 *Lubrizol/Hybrid Plants* (TBA) [1990] EPOR 173, 178 ('whether or not a (non-microbiological) process is to be considered as "essentially biological" within the meaning of Article 53(b) EPC has to be judged on the basis of the essence of the invention taking into account the totality of human intervention and its impact on the result achieved').

[382] T1054/96 *Novartis/Transgenic Plant* (TBA) [1999] EPOR 123 (plants that were genetically modified to render them resistant to fungi). The board found that 'a claim wherein specific plant varieties are not individually claimed is not excluded from patentability under article 53(b), even though it may embrace plant varieties'. *Contra*: Funder, 'Rethinking Patents for Plant Innovation' (n 376) 512.

[383] Bently and Sherman, *Intellectual Property Law* (n 82) 446. See also Funder, 'Rethinking Patents for Plant Innovation' (n 376) 511, 513. Bently and Sherman (n 82) 447, also note that 'the *Novartis* decision . . . gives rise to a potential problem, similar to the problems that arose when the whole content approach was first adopted in relation to patenting of computer programs. This is the problem that patent claims will be dressed up to appear as if they do not fall within the exception. While the jurisprudence on the patentability of computer programs may provide guidance in this area, the different rationale behind the exclusion means that the whole contents – technical effect approach cannot be directly imported into . . . article 53(b)'.

[384] Bently and Sherman, *Intellectual Property Law* (n 82) 446. See also Funder, 'Rethinking Patents for Plant Innovation' (n 376) 511, 513.

[385] Moufang, 'The Interface between Patents and Plant Variety Rights in Europe' (n 371) 4. See also T Cook, 'Responding to Concerns about the Scope of the Defence from Patent Infringements for Acts done for Experimental Purposes relating to the Subject Matter of the Invention' (2006) 3 *Intellectual Property Quarterly* 193, 204 n 24: 'although a single variety may not be patented, a single variety may, for example, contain genes which are the subject of several different patents, and several different varieties may each contain genes which are the subject of a single patent'. Llewelyn and Adcock, *European Plant Intellectual Property* (n 372) 223.

The second possibility of overlap results from the distinction patent law makes between 'subject-matter eligible for protection as such and subject-matter falling under the scope of protection'.[386] Even if it is not possible to claim a plant variety (as a product), it is possible to indirectly protect the plant variety by applying for a process patent (as long as it is not essentially biological). The plant variety, being the resulting product of the patented process, will be protected as it falls within the scope of protection of the patent.[387] Furthermore, '[a]ccording to Art. 8(2) EU Biotech Directive, this extension not only comprises the first generation plants, but also the following generations (as long as they possess the same characteristics as the first generation plants)'.[388] The third possibility arises from patents claiming DNA sequences, such as genes or vectors. In this case, patent protection 'extends to any material into which the patented DNA sequence has been introduced and in which it functions. Such material may well be a plant variety'.[389]

The overlap's limits are well summarised in Biotech Directive, recitals 31 and 32:

> A plant grouping which is characterised by a particular gene (and not its whole genome) is not covered by the protection of new varieties and is therefore not excluded from patentability even if it comprises new varieties of plants.

And:

> If an invention consists only in genetically modifying a particular plant variety, and if a new plant variety is bred, it will still be excluded from patentability even if the genetic modification is the result not of an essentially biological process but of a biotechnological process.

So already at this level, the simultaneous overlap is broad.

(b) Protection Requirements

As long as the subject matter fulfils the requirements of both patent (novelty, inventiveness and industrial application) and plant variety rights (distinctiveness, uniformity, stability and novelty[390]), and this is not infrequent, the overlap is complete.

[386] Moufang, 'The Interface between Patents and Plant Variety Rights in Europe' (n 371) 3; N Brahy, 'Cumul et chevauchement du brevet et du certificat d'obtention végétale: beaucoup de droit . . . mais peu de faits' in S Dusollier and A Cruquenaire (eds), *Le cumul des droits intellectuels* (Brussels, Larcier, 2009) 107, 110; Christie, 'Patents for Plant Innovation' (n 378) 399.

[387] Moufang, 'The Interface between Patents and Plant Variety Rights in Europe' (n 371) 3–4; Funder, 'Rethinking Patents for Plant Innovation' (n 376) 509; Christie, 'Patents for Plant Innovation' (n 378) 404; Llewelyn and Adcock, *European Plant Intellectual Property* (n 372) 320. Indeed, EPC Art 64(2) provides that 'if the subject matter of the European patent is a process, the protection conferred by the patent shall extend to the products directly obtained by such process'.

[388] Moufang, 'The Interface between Patents and Plant Variety Rights in Europe' (n 371) 4. Christie, 'Patents for Plant Innovation' (n 378) 408, was also of this opinion before the Biotech Directive was adopted.

[389] Moufang, 'The Interface between Patents and Plant Variety Rights in Europe' (n 371) 4; Christie, 'Patents for Plant Innovation' (n 378) 396; Funder, 'Rethinking Patents for Plant Innovation' (n 376) 512; Brahy, 'Cumul et chevauchement du brevet et du certificat d'obtention végétale' (n 386) 107, 110 (also citing G 01/98 *Transgenic Plants/Novartis II* (EBA) [2000] EPOR 303).

[390] As noted by Tritton *et al*, *Intellectual Property in Europe* (n 351) 617: '[t]he regulation provides the same test of novelty under the 1991 Act, including the same "grace periods" whereby the applicant may test the commercial value of the variety prior to the date of application . . . However, unlike patent law, novelty is not destroyed by the fact that third parties are fully aware of the variety, its pedigree or its characteristics before the

(c) Excluded Subject Matter

Apart from EPC Article 53(b), EPC Article 53(a), CPVR Regulation, article 13(8) and Biotech Directive, article 6 converge to exclude subject matter contrary to morality or *ordre public*.[391] CPVR Regulation, article 13(8) adds that:

> the exercise of the rights conferred by Community plant variety rights may not violate any provisions adopted on the grounds of . . . the protection of health and life of humans, animals or plants, the protection of the environment, the protection of industrial or commercial property, or the safeguarding of competition, of trade or of agricultural production.

Broadly speaking, in practice, EPO case law excludes patents for the same reasons on the basis of EPC Article 53(a).[392] There is therefore virtually full convergence at this level.

(d) Ownership and Dealings

CPVR Regulation, articles 11 and 22–29 have detailed provisions on ownership, licences and transfers. Neither the EPC nor the Biotech Directive contains provisions concerning ownership, licences and transfers of patents. Therefore, the overlap only occurs at national level.

(e) Rights and Infringement

As we saw above, the question of the simultaneous overlap at the level of rights only occurs at national level because patent rights are only national and not regional.

(f) Exceptions Including Exhaustion Principle

The same comments as to ownership, rights and infringement apply to exceptions. They will therefore be analysed in each relevant national chapter. Exhaustion is a regional issue and is properly addressed here. The CPVR Regulation has a specific article on exhaustion (article 16). Exhaustion will occur when the right-holder has parted with the protected material and will not be able to control material derived from it. 'Thus, the CPVR holder has no rights against harvested products or products derived from harvested products or varieties placed on the market in the Community by themselves or with their consent.'[393] This provision was necessary because, if the normal exhaustion principle applied, each time a farmer sowed the protected seeds, s/he would reproduce them and therefore it would be an infringement.[394] There are two exceptions to this exhaustion principle. The first is when the user further propagates the material (unless the right-holder intended propagation was going to be the use of the material when s/he

date of application'.

[391] Llewelyn and Adcock, *European Plant Intellectual Property* (n 372) 229: 'but unlike in patent law, the issue of whether a plant variety or use made of that variety is immoral is not relevant for the purpose of either securing or of retaining a plant variety right. All it relates to is the exercise of the protected variety post-grant'.

[392] See *Harvard/Onco-Mouse* [1990] OJ EPO 451 (Examining Div); T19/90 [1990] EPOR 501; [1990] OJ EPO 490 (TBA); [1991] EPOR 525 (Examining Div) and T356/93 *Plant Cells/Plant Genetic Systems* [1995] OJ EPO 545 (TBA).

[393] Tritton *et al*, *Intellectual Property in Europe* (n 351) 625. Llewelyn and Adcock, *European Plant Intellectual Property* (n 372) 238, think that this wording is restricted to when the products have been *sold*.

[394] Brahy, 'Cumul et chevauchement du brevet et du certificat d'obtention végétale' (n 386) 107, 115–16.

put the material on the market[395]). The second exception is when s/he exports the material to a country which does not protect the plant variety in question, except when the material is exported for final consumption. In case of an overlap, the normal exhaustion rule in patent law[396] would also pose a problem, for the reason given above. Therefore, Biotech Directive, article 10 aligned the patent exhaustion rule in CPVR Regulation, article 16 for inventions covering biological material. Tritton *et al* give a concrete example of the application of this rule:

> The sale of such harvested wheat grains to a miller would not constitute an infringement of the patent. However, the sale of such harvested seed to another farmer as seed would constitute infringement as such would be for the purposes of subsequent propagation.[397]

The article thus only allows the first reproduction, ie multiplication or propagation.[398] This also implies that the farmer cannot use the seeds collected after the first harvest and replant them a second time, a fortiori sell them. This applies if the use is commercial. The exception for private use applies to use which is not commercial.[399] However, Biotech Directive, article 10 could prevent reproduction for the purposes of research. It is unclear whether article 10 supplants the research exemption or whether it has to be read alongside it.[400] Furthermore, the recitals do not explain article 10.[401] In conclusion, although the aim may have been to create perfect convergence between patents and plant variety rights, ambiguities in the law remain which do not allow us to draw this conclusion.

(g) No Overlap between Plant Variety Right Denomination and Trademark

Finally, it must be noted that there cannot be an overlap between a variety denomination and a trademark. There is a clear prohibition both in the UPOV Convention and the CPVR Regulation and it applies even after the plant variety right has expired.[402] What happens is simply coexistence between the two. The variety denomination is used as the generic name for the product, it is in the public domain and cannot be appropriated.[403] The trademark is just used alongside it. As well said by Piatti and Jouffray, the denomination has the role of identifying without confusion or ambiguity whilst the trademark has the role of 'competitive advertising within a liberal framework'.[404] This prevents all three types of overlaps, including the *a posteriori* overlap, ie where the trademark could

[395] Llewelyn and Adcock, *European Plant Intellectual Property* (n 372) 238.

[396] The exhaustion rule is absent from the EPC but arises as a result of the EU case law. See decisions cited above n 284.

[397] Tritton *et al*, *Intellectual Property in Europe* (n 351) 202–3.

[398] Llewelyn and Adcock, *European Plant Intellectual Property* (n 372) 381.

[399] Ibid 382.

[400] Ibid.

[401] Ibid 383.

[402] See the 1991 act of the UPOV Convention, Art 20(1) and CPVR, arts 17 and 18(1). For details, see S Butler, *A Guide to UK and EU Plant Variety Rights* (Rutland, Transpose Technology, 2005) 109–10. See the same rule in France: art L623-15, the plant variety right's denomination cannot be registered as a mark. On this, see MC Piatti and M Jouffray, 'Plant Variety Names in National and International Law, Part 2' (1984) *European Intellectual Property Review* 315. A similar rule also applies in the United Kingdom, Plant Varieties Act 1997, s 19(3) (a trade name or mark can be used in selling or marketing varieties only if it is juxtaposed to the registered variety name and the latter is easily recognisable).

[403] MC Piatti and M Jouffray, 'Plant Variety Names in National and International Law, Part 1' (1984) *European Intellectual Property Review* 283, 284.

[404] Piatti and Jouffray, 'Plant Variety Names in National and International Law, Part 2' (n 402) 316.

be the same as the denomination and thus prolong the plant variety right after its expiration through a trademark right. The CPVR Regulation is a little more lax than the UPOV convention in the sense that it is not strictly forbidden to use the denomination as the trademark, but if one does so it cannot hamper the free use of the denomination.[405] Rights-holders therefore have a strong incentive not to choose the same name for both the denomination and their trademark: the trademark would become generic and thus they would lose their trademark right.[406] This situation is similar to the patent/trademark overlap where case law also prevents all three types of overlap. However, the mark can serve as a substitute for breeders' rights,[407] thereby creating a negative overlap between trademark and plant variety right.

(ii) Negative Overlap

(a) Plant Variety Right Protection Unavailable

If the plant variety does not have one of the required characteristics (eg it is not uniform or stable), then the breeder can try and use the patent system if s/he can meet the requirements. Indeed, the EPO does not consider a plant variety to be one if it fits the definition of plant variety but does not meet the requirements for a plant variety right.[408] As Christie notes, this encourages breeders who prefer patent protection to 'create in the plant a genetic characteristic to ensure the unavailability of PVR protection (for example, insufficient uniformity), so as to avoid the application of the exclusionary provision'.[409] Another example is a modification of a plant of a purely chemical nature, thus not involving a genetic modification of the plant.[410] This modification of a chemical nature would not lead to a plant variety right. The fact that the innovation relates to a plant variety is irrelevant and does not prevent the grant of a patent. New species, because they constitute higher taxonomic units than varieties, are not protectable by plant variety right but should be patentable.[411] Some also think that patent protection should be available for 'plant varieties of a species to which the PVR legislation does not apply'.[412] This is because EPC Article 53(b) must be interpreted narrowly; Article 53(b)'s rationale 'is to avoid conflict between the patent and PVR systems, and . . . there are good policy reasons for ensuring that some intellectual

[405] See CPVR, arts 17 and 18(1), and Butler, *A Guide to UK and EU Plant Variety Rights* (n 402) 109. For an example, see A4/2004 re: CV No. 198/1034 *Ginpent/Gynosemma Pentaphyllum*, Board of Appeal of Community Plant Variety Office, and Tritton *et al*, *Intellectual Property in Europe* (n 351) 628 (The board of appeal held that even if the plant variety right-holder used the denomination as a trademark, 'it did not give grounds to require an amendment to the name of the variety denomination. However, the board of appeal did say that the variety denomination is a generic name which distinguishes one variety from another and as a designation describing the product could not fulfil the function of a trademark').

[406] Piatti and Jouffray, 'Plant Variety Names in National and International Law, Part 2' (n 402) rightly note that in this respect, it is better to use a very complicated non-memorable name (eg XPZ5245) for the variety name, and keep the memorable name as a trademark.

[407] Ibid 312.

[408] *Ciba-Geigy* (1984) 3 OJ EPO 112, 114; Case T 320/87 *Lubrizol Genetics* (1990) 3 OJ EPO 71.

[409] Christie, 'Patents for Plant Innovation' (n 378) 397.

[410] *Ciba-Geigy* (1984) 3 OJ EPO 112. Moufang, 'Protection for Plant Breeding and Plant Varieties' (n 381) 346, reports that most experts agree with this solution.

[411] Ibid 347.

[412] Christie, 'Patents for Plant Innovation' (n 378) 397.

property protection is potentially available'.[413] This ensures that there is no gap in the protection. But one thing the breeder cannot do is to avoid using the term 'plant variety' in the patent application (in other words avoid 'literally claiming a plant variety') where the application is in effect for a plant variety. In this case, the Article 53(b) exclusion bites.[414] 'Simply because the words "plant variety" are absent from the claim does not change the true nature of the subject matter included in the claim.'[415] In sum, claiming a plant variety which is one but never citing its name in the application does not make it patentable.

In short, both the law and the commentators seem to agree that there should be no gaps in protection: 'only where plant varieties are actually protected does Article 53(b) operate to exclude patents'.[416]

(b) Patent Protection Unavailable

As can now be seen from the above, patent and plant variety rights are almost perfect alternatives. If the inventor cannot obtain patent protection, for instance because his or her invention does not involve an inventive step, but can fulfil the requirements of plant variety right, this is what the latter is for. If patent protection is not available and the plant cannot be classed as a variety or is not stable, uniform or distinct, it is fair enough that it should not obtain any protection.

(iii) A Posteriori *Overlap*

As is well known, the term of a patent is 20 years from filing. Plant variety rights last a little longer: 25 years, and for vines and trees, 30 years. Moreover, unlike the term of patents, the protection period is counted from the year of grant (CPVR Regulation, article 19). The second paragraph of this article makes it possible for the Council to prolong these terms by five more years. This has so far been done only for potatoes, which benefit from a 30-year term.[417] If there is an overlap between a patent and a plant variety right, it is thus possible to enjoy a few more years of protection. However, this will not be very frequent as the commercial life of a variety is often less than 25 or 30 years.[418] In addition, it often takes a long time to obtain a marketable plant variety (on average 15 years following the initial invention). Thus, 'usually only five years of patent-protection remain once the variety reaches the market'.[419] The converse *a posteriori* overlap cannot happen, as for a patent to be granted the invention has to be new.

[413] Ibid. See also Moufang, 'Protection for Plant Breeding and Plant Varieties' (n 381) 347. Llewelyn and Adcock, *European Plant Intellectual Property* (n 372) 372, also think this is the interpretation that should probably be given to the exclusion in the current intellectual property law climate (ie 'because of the presumption of protectability which operates at all levels of intellectual property law').

[414] Christie, 'Patents for Plant Innovation' (n 378) 397.

[415] Ibid.

[416] Funder, 'Rethinking Patents for Plant Innovation' (n 376) 510, referring to Moufang, 'Protection for Plant Breeding and Plant Varieties' (n 413) 346. Funder (n 376) 515, however, notes that '[a]lternatively, it could be seen that the deliberate omission of certain varieties from PVR protection serves a specific policy objective in the context of each country's legal, scientific, industrial and agricultural objectives and does not imply the need for mandatory patent protection'. For a similar view, see chapter 4, section VIII.

[417] See Council Regulation (EC) 2470/96 of 17 December 1996 providing for an extension for the terms of a Community plant variety right in respect of potatoes [1996] OJ L335/10.

[418] Brahy, 'Cumul et chevauchement du brevet et du certificat d'obtention végétale' (n 386) 107, 121.

[419] M Kock, S Porzig and E Willnegger, 'The Legal Protection of Plant-Biotechnological Inventions and Plant Varieties in Light of the EC Biopatent Directive' (2006) *International Review of Intellectual Property and Competition Law* 135, 148.

C Literature

Commentators debate whether the historical reasons that have led to a differentiated system for plant varieties are still valid today and therefore some argue against the overlap ban. What were the reasons for a special system? Why were patents not adequate to protect plant varieties? The main arguments were that it is difficult for plant varieties to fulfil the novelty requirement and even more so the inventive step requirement.[420] There were also other objections, such as plants being products of nature or living things (where patent law is tailored to inanimate ones), lack of industrial applicability, impossibility of description or reproduction.[421] However, most of these arguments have now been refuted by the literature.[422]

Generally, in the biotechnological field, inventiveness derives not from the characteristics of a new product but from the process used to make this new product.[423] This is the main reason why it has been deemed appropriate to keep a specific intellectual property right for new plant varieties[424] and it should remain the preferred option of plant breeders.[425] Indeed, along with the lower level of novelty and the absence of the inventiveness requirement, the disclosure requirement is not as stringent as in patent law.[426] But as has been said, and as is almost the case now after a long evolution of the law over three decades:

> There is, however, no logical reason that plant breeders rights' systems should preclude the applicability of general patent law to those plant innovations which meet its requirements. It would be an untenable generalisation to consider patent law as ill suited for all types of plant genetic innovation only because a certain type is deemed not to fit properly into it.[427]

This comment goes further than the present state of the law, as it would require the abolition of the exclusion in EPC Article 53(b) to allow claims on plant varieties as such. It is arguable that this should be done, in view of the obscure legislative history surrounding the adoption of Article 53(b),[428] and also because scientific developments have made it 'possible to overcome the impediments of novelty and inventive step in many cases'.[429] Van Overwalle even proposes the abolition of the ban for conventional breeding techniques.[430]

[420] Millett, 'The Community System of Plant Variety Rights' (n 370); R Crespi, 'Patents and Plant Variety Rights: Is There an Interface Problem?' (1992) 23 *International Review of Intellectual Property and Competition Law* 173, 178; Funder, 'Rethinking Patents for Plant Innovation' (n 376) 504; Moufang, 'Protection for Plant Breeding and Plant Varieties' (n 381) 338 (however doubting this); G Van Overwalle, 'Patent Protection for Plants: A Comparison of American and European Approaches' (1999) 39(2) *IDEA* 143, 152.

[421] Van Overwalle, 'Patent Protection for Plants' (n 420) 148–53.

[422] Ibid 172–91, citing other commentators.

[423] Funder, 'Rethinking Patents for Plant Innovation' (n 376) 504, citing Christie, 'Patents for Plant Innovation' (n 378) 407 and I Purvis, 'Patents and Genetic Engineering: Does a New Problem Need a New Solution?' (1987) *European Intellectual Property Review* 347.

[424] Millett, 'The Community System of Plant Variety Rights' (n 370) 232.

[425] Crespi, 'Patents and Plant Variety Rights: Is There an Interface Problem?' (n 420) 178.

[426] Moufang, 'Protection for Plant Breeding and Plant Varieties' (n 381) 341 n 49; Funder, 'Rethinking Patents for Plant Innovation' (n 376) 505.

[427] Moufang, 'Protection for Plant Breeding and Plant Varieties' (n 381) 341. See also generally Van Overwalle, 'Patent Protection for Plants' (n 420).

[428] Moufang, 'Protection for Plant Breeding and Plant Varieties' (n 381) 343–46; Funder, 'Rethinking Patents for Plant Innovation' (n 376) 507.

[429] Van Overwalle, 'Patent Protection for Plants' (n 420) 182, 191–92.

[430] Ibid 192.

Even if the ban is not lifted, the very narrow construction of Article 53(b) in the case law, as well as technological developments, have pushed the boundaries and in effect, there is now considerable overlap between plant variety rights and patents. In other words, the exclusion of plant variety rights from patent law is 'more formal than substantial'.[431] Commentators do not see the overlap as a problem.[432] Because the two systems converge so much (at least in terms of rights and exceptions, namely dependency licensing, farmer's privilege, exhaustion) and patent protection is more attractive (except for the term), the overlap situations are rare, though where they exist they pose problems, albeit less frequently.[433] This state of affairs has caused some commentators to wonder whether plant variety rights are still really useful as patent protection does the trick in most cases, and provides stronger (although not longer) protection, so that there have been 'increased attempts to obtain patent protection for plant related products'.[434] Technology has advanced so much that we are now able to use microbiological or other technical processes to achieve what we need rather than doing it via a biological process. Technology may thus in fact have rendered plant variety rights outdated/obsolete.[435] Other commentators add that the cumulation of the two protections is not worthwhile as 'the additional social cost might not correspond with the level of public benefit derived from the innovation'.[436] Moreover, '[a]llowing both systems to operate to appropriate the same type of subject matter in plants might also reduce their respective efficiency'.[437]

But commentators also point out that plant variety rights remain useful for those plant varieties which are not novel or inventive in the patent sense,[438] and also because plant variety rights have advantages the patent system does not have: they are generally 'easier to administer, cheaper, better examined, more certain, easier to enforce and less prone to

[431] Moufang, 'The Interface between Patents and Plant Variety Rights in Europe' (n 371) 8.

[432] Crespi, 'Patents and Plant Variety Rights: Is there an Interface Problem?' (n 420) 183, who finds 'parallel planes at different levels' a better term to describe the relationship between plant variety rights and patents, a little like the possibility of having a patent and design in the same object, but where no overlap occurs as the two systems reward a different effort (function by patent and external aspect by design); Brahy, 'Cumul et chevauchement du brevet et du certificat d'obtention végétale' (n 386) 107, 123 ('the examination of the empirical data available reveals few overlap situations which are problematic'. He speculates that the reason is that where the two protections are available, breeders choose patents because it affords more extensive protection). However, Llewelyn and Adcock, *European Plant Intellectual Property* (n 372) 321, note that for process patents whose products include a variety, the EPO has left it to national courts to decide whether the patent's scope includes the variety. This is worrying, as national courts' opinions on this may diverge.

[433] As concrete overlaps happen at national rather than regional level, more detail on this convergence can be found in chapters four, five and six.

[434] Bently and Sherman, *Intellectual Property Law* (n 82) 601. See also Millett, 'The Community System of Plant Variety Rights' (n 370) 236, 258; Funder, 'Rethinking Patents for Plant Innovation' (n 376) 525.

[435] As hinted by Millett, 'The Community System of Plant Variety Rights' (n 370) 258 ('Whether plant variety rights continue to thrive as such or whether they may be displaced by patents is a matter which the future will tell but which will doubtless be influenced by the development of biotechnology which is currently advancing fast in relation to plants and other life forms').

[436] Funder, 'Rethinking Patents for Plant Innovation' (n 376) 526–27, and authors cited in his footnotes. See also Brahy, 'Cumul et chevauchement du brevet et du certificat d'obtention végétale' (n 386) 107, 121 ('if the immediate interest of an economic agent is to have the most extended protection, this interest does not coincide necessarily with that of society, the question whether a strong protection is preferable to more limited protection remains open in particular in the context of complementary and cumulative innovation').

[437] Funder, 'Rethinking Patents for Plant Innovation' (n 376) 526–27 and authors cited in his footnotes.

[438] Kock, Porzig and Willnegger, 'The Legal Protection of Plant-Biotechnological Inventions and Plant Varieties in Light of the EC Biopatent Directive' (n 419) 146, pointing at the fact that many conventionally bred plant varieties do not manage to meet the inventiveness criterion.

litigation than patent protection'.[439] Plant variety rights are therefore not per se unsuitable. For that reason, some commentators do not advocate the abolition of plant variety rights. Instead, they 'advocate . . . the coexistence of both protection systems, with the choice of which system to use left to the individual plant breeder'.[440] When the plant variety fulfils the conditions of patent law, the breeder could choose patent law if s/he wishes, but when it does not, s/he could just fall back on the plant variety right.[441] What seems clear here is that commentators do not see problems (such as hampering competition or free movement of goods) arising from the overlap, unlike in the case of the previous overlaps discussed. This may also be because, in practice, the overlap does not seem to have raised problems.

IX. INTELLECTUAL PROPERTY RIGHTS AND UNFAIR COMPETITION

A The Legal Framework

The European Union has passed only two Directives in the field of unfair competition law – the Misleading and Comparative Advertising Directive (MCAD)[442] and the Unfair Commercial Practices Directive (UCPD)[443] – and they only partially harmonise unfair competition law. Apart from the situations covered by those two Directives, national laws therefore still rule this area. The MCAD is interesting in two respects. First, it extends trademark protection for non-famous marks when they are used in comparative advertising. As such, it is not an overlap but an extension of protection in one particular situation. MCAD, article 4(f) does not allow comparative advertising which takes 'unfair advantage of the reputation of a trademark, trade name or other distinguishing marks of a competitor or of the designation of origin of competing products', whereas Trademark Directive, article 5(2) only gives the right to the owner of a famous trademark (a trademark which has reputation) to 'prevent all third parties not having his consent from using in the course of trade any sign which is identical with, or similar to, the trademark in relation to goods or services which are not similar to those for which the trademark is registered (but also similar or identical goods as per the case law[444]), where the latter has a reputation in the Member State and where use of that sign without due cause takes unfair advantage of, or is detrimental to, the distinctive character or the repute of the trademark'. Secondly, the MCAD is also interesting for a situation it does not envisage, but which gives rise to a conflict of regimes due to an overlap. What happens if a trademark is also protected by copyright and/or design law? Can comparative advertising,

[439] Funder, 'Rethinking Patents for Plant Innovation' (n 376) 525–26.

[440] Van Overwalle, 'Patent Protection for Plants' (n 420) 192.

[441] Ibid 193.

[442] Directive 2006/114/EC of the European Parliament and of the Council of 12 December 2006 concerning misleading and comparative advertising (codified version) [2006] OJ L376/21.

[443] Directive 2005/29/EC of the European Parliament and of the Council of 11 May 2005 concerning unfair business-to-consumer commercial practices in the internal market and amending Council Directive 84/450/EEC, Directives 97/7/EC, 98/27/EC and 2002/65/EC of the European Parliament and of the Council and Regulation (EC) 2006/2004 of the European Parliament and of the Council ('Unfair Commercial Practices Directive') [2005] OJ L149/22.

[444] See mainly Case C-408/01 *Adidas-Salomon AG and Adidas Benelux BV v Fitnessworld Trading Ltd* [2004] ECR I-12537.

which is legal under the MCAD, become illegal if the trademark is protected by copyright and/or design? In other words, do copyright/design laws trump comparative advertising? It could be argued that recital 10 of MCAD indirectly addresses the issue but this is far from clear. This will be explored under the 'content overlap' (section IX.B).

After the MCAD, the UCPD is the first real step in the harmonisation of unfair competition law in the European Union because it aims at total harmonisation by dealing with all types of unfair trading practices.[445] It only regulates unfair business-to-consumer (B2C) practices, but as stated in its recital 8, thereby the UCPD also 'indirectly protects legitimate businesses from their competitors who do not play by the rules in this Directive and thus guarantees fair competition in fields coordinated by it'. Two clear examples of this are comparative advertising[446] and passing off.[447] The same recital recognises that there are other practices which hurt competitors and asks the Commission to examine whether there is a need to legislate in this respect, and if so to make a legislative proposal. Recital 9, like most other secondary legislation in the field of IPRs as will be seen immediately below, also allows cumulation between IPRs and the regulation of B2C unfair practices. UCPD, article 5 is a general clause in the same vein as Article 10bis of the Paris Convention. It is entitled 'Prohibition of unfair commercial practices' and provides that:

1. Unfair commercial practices shall be prohibited.
2. A commercial practice shall be unfair if:
   (a) it is contrary to the requirements of professional diligence, and
   (b) it materially distorts or is likely to materially distort the economic behaviour with regard to the product of the average consumer whom it reaches or to whom it is addressed, or of the average member of the group when a commercial practice is directed to a particular group of consumers.

The Explanatory Memorandum to the UCPD suggests, however, that the general clause will be 'used infrequently because the two categories of misleading and aggressive commercial practices capture the vast majority of cases'.[448] Indeed, it is difficult to imagine

[445] R de Vrey, *Towards a European Unfair Competition Law: A Clash between Legal Families* (Leiden, Martinus Nijhoff, 2006) 57, 59.

[446] Ibid 62. At 62–63, the author poses the good question of what would happen if an advertisement is at the same time misleading and comparative and hurts both competitors and consumers. It is not clear whether both the UCPD and MCAD would be applicable.

[447] See U Bernitz, 'The Unfair Commercial Practices Directive: Its Scope, Ambitions and Relation to the Law of Unfair Competition' in S Weatherill and U Bernitz (eds), *The Regulation of Unfair Commercial Practices under EC Directive 2005/29: New Rules and New Techniques* (Oxford, Hart Publishing, 2007) 34, 42 and below next para.

[448] Proposal for a Directive of the European Parliament and of the Council concerning unfair business-to-consumer commercial practices in the Internal Market and amending Directives 84/450/EEC, 97/7/EC and 98/27/EC COM(2003)356 final, 2003/0134 (COD) (Brussels, 18 June 2003) 12, para 52. Aggressive and misleading practices are expressly regulated in UCPD, arts 6–9. See also G Howells, 'Unfair Commercial Practices Directive: A Missed Opportunity?' in S Weatherill and U Bernitz (eds), *The Regulation of Unfair Commercial Practices under EC Directive 2005/29: New Rules and New Techniques* (Oxford, Hart Publishing, 2007) 103, 108; G Abbamonte, 'The Unfair Commercial Practices Directive and its General Prohibition' in S Weatherill and U Bernitz (eds), *The Regulation of Unfair Commercial Practices under EC Directive 2005/29: New Rules and New Techniques* (Oxford, Hart Publishing, 2007) 11, 20. See also Bernitz, 'The Unfair Commercial Practices Directive' (n 447) 36, who thinks that '[p]rimarily, the general clause can be expected to cover practices which are well in line with such practices that fall under any of the two prohibitions on misleading and aggressive practices or the blacklisted practices, but do not fully fit the specific criteria of these provisions'. However, C Wadlow, 'The Case for Reclaiming European Unfair Competition Law from Europe's Consumer Lawyers' in S Weatherill and U Bernitz (eds), *The Regulation of Unfair Commercial Practices under EC Directive 2005/29: New Rules and New Techniques* (Oxford, Hart Publishing, 2007) 175, 180, notes that

that, for instance, slavish imitation, or in other words parasitism, is an unfair commercial practice towards consumers.[449] This is because the definition of 'materially distort the economic behaviour of consumers' in UCPD, article 2(e) is not broad enough to include it. It 'means using a commercial practice to appreciably impair the consumer's ability to make an informed decision, thereby causing the consumer to take a transactional decision that he would not have taken otherwise'. Also the Explanatory Memorandum clearly states that slavish imitation is outside the scope of the UCPD.[450]

UCPD, article 5(5) refers to the Annex to the Directive, which is a list of behaviours regarded as unfair and which all Member States must ensure are prohibited. However, as the list in the annex is not exhaustive, it is still left to Member States to choose to punish other behaviours which fulfil the conditions of article 5(2), although in practice it will often be difficult to justify national prohibitions on the basis of article 5(2). In this respect, harmonisation has not been effected and the overlap with IPRs can occur at national level. In particular, overlaps with parasitism or slavish imitations are allowed as these are practices which harm competitors rather than consumers, and are thus not regulated by the UCPD and in fact are left intact by recital 9. Item 13 of the Annex specifically refers to passing off,[451] a prohibited behaviour which is 'primarily directed at protecting the interests of competitors, not consumers'.[452] As per its article 6(2), the UCPD allows the overlap between trademark law and passing off, or else unfair competition, for risk of confusion at national level. In effect, this article codifies the *Beele* case.[453]

In addition to the provisions set out in the MCAD and UCPD, the Copyright, Trademark and Design Directives, along with the Trademark and Design Regulations, clearly allow cumulation between copyright, neighbouring rights, trademarks and designs, on the one hand, and unfair competition laws, on the other. Explicit cumulation is the rule but none of the texts regulates this specific overlap, leaving this task to the Member States. Typically, the texts use the formula: '[The provisions of] this Directive/ Regulation shall be without prejudice to provisions concerning in particular unfair competition'. The texts sometimes specifically add the term 'trade secrets', 'civil liability' and/or 'laws on restrictive practices' in addition to the terms 'unfair competition'.[454] The

'despite the clarity of the directive on this point, it is not surprising to find its general clause in danger of being misinterpreted (if not actually misappropriated) on behalf of brand owners to combat what is really, to their way of thinking, a case of unfair competition based on the "misappropriation of valuable intangibles", and having little or nothing to do with misrepresentation'.

[449] Abbamonte, 'The Unfair Commercial Practices Directive and its General Prohibition' (n 448) 11, 17, who definitely thinks that slavish imitation does not fall within the UCPD's scope. See also Bernitz, 'The Unfair Commercial Practices Directive' (n 447) 34, 42, who refers to recital 14 which may be an implicit indication of that.

[450] COM(2003)356 final, 10, para 40.

[451] It provides: 'Promoting a product similar to a product made by a particular manufacturer in such a manner as deliberately to mislead the consumer into believing that the product is made by that same manufacturer when it is not'.

[452] De Vrey, *Towards a European Unfair Competition Law* (n 445) 71, also states that this is another example, along with comparative advertising, 'of the way in which protection for honest traders is currently included in the UCPD'. Ibid 77: because the UCPD only deals with B2C relations, it has created more problems than it solves, and in his view 'will lead to a division of unfair competition that should be prevented at all costs'.

[453] Case 6/81 *BV Industrie Diensten Groep v JA Beele Handelmaatschappij BV* [1982] ECR 707 (holding that national unfair competition laws can prohibit imitation which causes confusion so long as they do not discriminate between domestic and imported (EU) goods). On this case, see A Arnull, 'Cassis de Dijon and Intellectual Property: A Case of Unfair Competition' (1983) *New Law Journal* 347.

[454] Software Directive, art 9: 'Continued application of other legal provisions. 1. The provisions of this Directive shall be without prejudice to any other legal provisions such as those concerning . . . unfair competi-

preparatory materials of the Directives and Regulations are also mostly silent on the overlap between IPRs and unfair competition law. Only the Green Paper on the Legal Protection of Industrial Design explains a little more why cumulation is allowed. For the Commission, cumulation is natural because the intellectual property and unfair competition rules have a different nature. Unfair competition laws 'tend to protect the fairness in the behaviour of the operators in trade and . . . require, next to objective acts of misbehaviour, the existence of a subjective element of fault on conditions on the side of the offender'.[455] The Commission also notes the differences between Member States which allow an unfair competition action against slavish imitations after the term of protection of the design has expired, and those which do not.[456] All it does then is to welcome comments from interested circles on this problem and how it should be resolved. The Green Paper does not venture further.

The other instruments, namely the EPC, the Biotechnology Directive 98/44/EC and the CPVR Regulation, do not envisage the overlap with unfair competition law.

It must be finally noted that there is no regulation of trade secrets/confidential information at EU level, which is not surprising as the UCPD only deals with B2C, and not B2B behaviours. This overlap will therefore be examined at national level.

B 'Content Overlap'

Apart from specific issues arising from the two Directives adopted in the field of unfair competition law, the overlap between IPRs and unfair competition law is to be envisaged at national level only. The two issues identified in section IX.A will be discussed here as they are part of the harmonisation efforts described above. A third issue has arisen from the case law as a result of the *L'Oréal* case.

tion, trade secrets'. . . . Database Directive, art 13: 'Continued application of other legal provisions. This Directive shall be without prejudice to provisions concerning in particular . . . laws on restrictive practices and unfair competition, trade secrets'.

Copyright Directive, art 9: 'Continued application of other legal provisions. This Directive shall be without prejudice to provisions concerning in particular . . . laws on restrictive practices and unfair competition, trade secrets'.

Design Regulation, art 96(1): 'Relationship to other forms of protection under national law. 1. The provisions of this Regulation shall be without prejudice to any provisions . . . of the law of the Member States concerned relating to . . . civil liability and unfair competition'.

Design Directive, art 16: 'Relationship to other forms of protection. The provisions of this Directive shall be without prejudice to any provisions . . . of the law of the Member State concerned relating to . . . civil liability or unfair competition'.

Trademark Directive, recital 6: 'Whereas this Directive does not exclude the application to trademarks of provisions of law of the Member States other than trademark law, such as the provisions relating to unfair competition, civil liability or consumer protection'.

Trademark Regulation, art 14(2): 'This Regulation shall not prevent actions concerning a Community trademark being brought under the law of Member States relating in particular to civil liability and unfair competition'.

[455] Green Paper on the Legal Protection of Industrial Design (n 17) 24, 156.

[456] It notes: 'This prohibition, based on the idea that the monopoly right should be entirely available to the public as soon as the exclusiveness period is over, (the "patent approach"), risks justifying unfair misappropriations of commercial goodwill attached to a well introduced design which comes to the expiry of its protection term'. Ibid 156. See also in similar terms ibid 25.

The first question concerns the simultaneous overlap: what happens if a trademark is also protected by copyright or design law? Can comparative advertising, which is legal under the MCAD, become illegal if the trademark is protected by copyright or design too? In other words, do copyright/design laws trump comparative advertising? There is no answer in the MCAD and its recital 10 does not seem to address the issue. It provides: 'The international conventions on copyright . . . should apply when the results of comparative tests carried out by third parties are referred to or reproduced in comparative advertising'. This recital seems to refer to results of tests which would be protected by copyright, not to the logo which is both a registered mark and a copyright work.[457] In addition, the recital does not address design rights at all. The Directive Proposal does not shed any light on this issue either.[458] Therefore, copyright or design rights could in theory trump the MCAD.

Commentators have discussed this issue. Most think that copyright should not trump trademark law in this situation, but find it difficult to find a rule in the existing corpus to prevent this from happening. Nonetheless, some others have proposed such rules. Feer Verkade thinks that '[w]here the compared trademark is subject to both the trademark rights and copyright, the trademark aspect takes precedence, also in comparative advertising. It is unlikely that the directive was intended to permit invoking the copyright as well'.[459] Ohly and Spence think that a principle analogous to that in *Dior v Evora* could be applied: 'If copyright is used to prevent comparative advertising it is used as a control on marketing, and it might be argued that the regime for regulating marketing constituted by the comparative advertising directive ought to prevail'.[460] However, Kur thinks that *Dior v Evora* cannot be applied, as the advertisement's purpose is not to sell the product depicted but to compare it with another product in order to sell that latter product. Kur notes further that none of the exceptions in Infosoc Directive, article 5(3) addresses this issue either.[461] She mentions the *IPC Magazines v MGN* case which addressed the issue but did not provide any solution to the problem,[462] and the *BMW/Blok* case decided by the Dutch Supreme Court ('a photograph of a BMW was displayed in an advertisement for accessories (rims) in order to demonstrate their visual effect on a car'[463]). The Court in this case held there was neither trademark nor copyright infringement, but as Kur notes, '[i]t is however not very easy to procure a solid and convincing basis for such a finding, once it is accepted that copyright does subsist in the shape of the car'.[464] One solution to the problem would be to raise the originality level for works of applied art so that they are not protected by copyright[465] but that does not solve the problem for two-dimensional works or designs. Discussing the *O2 v 3G* case, Trimmer thinks that the Advocate-General's reasoning implies that the MCAD should also trump copy-

[457] This seems to be also the opinion of Feer Verkade, 'The Cumulative Effect of Copyright Law and Trademark Law' (n 122) 69, 76.

[458] COM(77)724 final [1978] OJ C70/4.

[459] Feer Verkade, 'The Cumulative Effect of Copyright Law and Trademark Law' (n 122) 69, 76.

[460] A Ohly and M Spence, *The Law of Comparative Advertising, Directive 97/55/EC in the United Kingdom and Germany* (Oxford, Hart Publishing, 2000) 56. They say that the Court of Justice ruled in *Dior* as it did because copyright was effectively being used as 'a form of control on marketing . . . and . . . commercial exploitation of copyright raises the same issues as that of any other industrial or commercial property'.

[461] Kur, 'Exceptions to Protection Where Copyright and Trade Mark Overlap' (n 101) 593, 612.

[462] [1998] FSR 431. For a discussion of this case and other similar cases, see chapter 5, section IX.C.

[463] Kur, 'Exceptions to Protection Where Copyright and Trade Mark Overlap' (n 101) 593, 612.

[464] Ibid 612.

[465] Ibid 612 n 59.

right, design rights, passing off and unfair competition laws, even though he agrees that the MCAD only mentions trademark rights and not any other IPR.[466] But others think that even the MCAD can be interpreted to include other IPRs simply because the definition of comparative advertising is rather broad ('any advertising which explicitly or by implication identifies a competitor or goods or services offered by a competitor') and includes advertisements which use other things than a trademark (such as copyrighted works) to identify a competitor's goods or services.[467] Thus, '[i]f an advertisement reproduced enough of a competitor's product to constitute copyright infringement, and yet the comparison being made satisfied the eight conditions of the Directive, the . . . courts might be compelled to treat the advertisement as being lawful'.[468]

The second question concerns the three types of overlap and arises from MCAD, article 4(g), according to which comparative advertising must not 'present goods or services as imitations or replicas of goods or services bearing a protected trademark or trade name'. The Directive here gives some sort of unfair competition protection for subject matter whether or not protected by an IPR as long as there is a trademark or trade name affixed to the product (which will virtually always be the case), but only insofar as advertising is concerned. The competing product can still be sold but the way it is advertised cannot mention that it is an imitation or reproduction of the competitor's good. The protection given by MCAD, article 4(g) is strongest for subject matter which cannot be protected by IPRs at all (eg perfumes) or was once protected by an IPR (eg pharmaceuticals) because they cannot sue for IPR infringement in those cases.[469] In *L'Oréal v Bellure*, the Court of Justice held that:

> it is not only advertisements which explicitly evoke the idea of imitation or reproduction which are prohibited, but also those which, having regard to their overall presentation and economic context, are capable of implicitly communicating such an idea to the public at whom they are directed.[470]

So what did the Court of Justice decide in *L'Oréal*? This ruling creates a tort of parasitism for marks with a reputation. The problem is that the concept of 'mark with a reputation' has never been defined precisely.[471] In that case, Bellure (and some other companies) were selling imitations of some of L'Oréal's perfumes but it was clear that the public could not be confused. Bellure also established 'comparison lists which it provide[d] to [its] retailers and which indicate[d] the word mark of the fine fragrance of which the perfume being marketed [wa]s an imitation'.[472] One of the questions referred asked whether such behaviour infringed Trademark Directive, article 5(2). The Court interpreted the terms used in that article 'tak[ing] unfair advantage . . . of the distinctive character or repute of the trademark'. The Court held that:

466 B Trimmer, 'Comparative Advertising Trumps Trademarks Rights: *O2 Holdings Ltd v Hutchinson 3G UK Ltd*' (2008) *European Intellectual Property Review* 304.

467 J McCormick, 'The Future of Comparative Advertising' (1998) *European Intellectual Property Review* 41, 42.

468 Ibid.

469 F Henning-Bodewig, *Unfair Competition Law: European Union and Member States* (The Hague, Kluwer Law International, 2006) 49.

470 Case C-487/07 *L'Oréal SA, Lancôme Parfums et Beauté & Cie SNC and Laboratoire Garnier & Cie v Bellure NV, Malaika Investments Ltd and Starion International Ltd* [2009] ECR I-5185, para 75. For more details, see paras 76–80.

471 I Simon Fhima, '*L'Oréal v Bellure* at the ECJ', *Ipkat*, 18 June 2009, available athttp://ipkitten.blogspot.com/2009/06/loreal-v-bellure-at-ecj.html.

472 Case C-487/07 *L'Oréal v Bellure* (n 470) para 21.

> as regards the concept of 'taking unfair advantage of the distinctive character or the repute of the trademark', also referred to as 'parasitism' or 'free-riding', that concept relates not to the detriment caused to the mark but to the advantage taken by the third party as a result of the use of the identical or similar sign. It covers, in particular, cases where, by reason of a transfer of the image of the mark or of the characteristics which it projects to the goods identified by the identical or similar sign, there is clear exploitation on the coat-tails of the mark with a reputation.[473]

Consequently, such advantage 'may be unfair, even if the use of the identical or similar sign is not detrimental either to the distinctive character or to the repute of the mark or, more generally, to its proprietor'.[474] In conclusion, the Court decided that:

> where a third party attempts, through the use of a sign similar to a mark with a reputation, to ride on the coat-tails of that mark in order to benefit from its power of attraction, its reputation and its prestige, and to exploit, without paying any financial compensation and without being required to make efforts of his own in that regard, the marketing effort expended by the proprietor of that mark in order to create and maintain the image of that mark, the advantage resulting from such use must be considered to be an advantage that has been unfairly taken of the distinctive character or the repute of that mark.[475]

As the Court of Justice has clearly created a tort of parasitism for marks with a reputation, the question is: Does it replace Member States' laws on parasitism for such marks? The answer is probably in the affirmative so that there is no simultaneous overlap possible. But some national courts may not see this and may still wrongly cumulate the two and repair the same damage twice. Only the future will tell whether this actually happens. Secondly, the Court's ruling only (so far) recognises the tort of parasitism when the marks are actually registered and in use. Therefore, it does not affect the negative and *a posteriori* overlaps. Another similar simultaneous overlap between trademarks and unfair competition law can occur, however: it is between the other part of Trademark Directive, article 5(2) (use of a sign is 'detrimental to the distinctive character or repute of the trademark') and unfair competition law provisions which prevent denigration or discredit. To the extent that these two overlaps have occurred at national level, they will be examined in the chapters dealing with national laws.

One final but important point: under Software Directive, articles 6 and 9(1), decompilation is permitted under certain conditions. A contract, such as a confidentiality contract, cannot take this user's privilege away.[476] As these provisions are mandatory for the Member States, the same applies in France, Germany and the United Kingdom.[477] In addition, in France, the United Kingdom and Germany, the 'observe, study and test' exception cannot be overturned by contract (see IPC, article L122-6-1 *in fine*, CDPA 1988, section 50BA(2) and German Copyright Act, sections 69d(3) and 69g(2)).

In conclusion, the three types of overlaps are allowed. More specifically, EU law gives no answer as to whether copyright or other rights (such as passing off, design rights and unfair competition law) can trump the MCAD, whilst article 4(g) of the latter gives simultaneous and *a posteriori* overlap protection to protected and unprotected subject

[473] Ibid para 41.
[474] Ibid para 43.
[475] Ibid para 49. See also para 50.
[476] Note that the same cannot be said of Software Directive, art 5(1) (the exception for observing, studying and testing a program in order to discover the ideas and principles which underlie it when loading, displaying, running, transmitting or storing the program) because it begins with the words 'in the absence of specific contractual provisions'.
[477] See CDPA 1988, s 50B(4); IPC, art L122-6(1) *in fine*; and German Copyright Act, s 69e.

matter, although only where advertising is concerned. Finally, the *L'Oréal* ruling recognises simultaneous overlap with the tort of parasitism for marks which have a reputation.

C Literature

Even if, in the main, the overlap between IPRs and unfair competition law happens at national level, the following general considerations can already be made at this stage. Commentators agree that the lack of harmonisation in the field of unfair competition law is far from ideal.[478] There is a lack of certainty for competitors, sometimes even for users (depending how generous the national unfair competition law in question is and whether it punishes acts by consumers as well, not only those of competitors). Even if an IPR could not be obtained at all in the first place or if it has expired, copying is a risky affair as courts can punish the user's behaviour as parasitic or dishonest under unfair competition law.[479] To give just one example: Trademark Directive, article (3)(1)(e)(i) excludes certain trivial technical shapes, but it only makes sense if the makers of those shapes cannot use unfair competition law to fill the gap.[480] Commentators also agree that unfair competition law should not undermine national or EU trademark law,[481] and more generally should not disturb 'the delicate balance between the freedom of competition (and imitation) and the granting of exclusive rights'.[482]

X. CONCLUSION: IDENTIFICATION OF PRINCIPLES GOVERNING OVERLAPS IN EUROPEAN LAW AND REMAINING OPEN QUESTIONS

There is no general rule that forbids intellectual property overlaps in EU law, on the contrary EU secondary law provides that each IPR is without prejudice to any other and to unfair competition law. Therefore, the *acquis communautaire* 'supports the conclusion . . . that without special reason to the contrary, protective regimes will cumulate'.[483] It has also become apparent – and this will not surprise the European lawyers – that the main principles that pervade EU intellectual property law in general, and overlaps in particular, are free, undistorted, unhindered competition and the principle of the free movement of goods and services. Some overlaps are more heavily regulated than others, which also

478 W Cornish, 'Informal Rights in Industrial Design: Why Impose Community Constraints?' in J Kabel and G Mom, *Intellectual Property and Information Law: Essays in Honour of Herman Cohen Jeroham* (The Hague, Kluwer Law International, 1998) 259 (pointing out that trademark harmonisation has been achieved without harmonising passing off and unfair competition); C Gielen, 'Design Protection and Unfair Competition' in J Kabel and G Mom, *Intellectual Property and Information Law: Essays in Honour of Herman Cohen Jeroham* (The Hague, Kluwer Law international 1998) 261, 269 ('a situation in which a few countries exclude such protection [ie unfair competition] whereas the majority of the European Union allows cumulation should be avoided'); A Kamperman Sanders, 'Do Whiffs of Misappropriation and Standards for Slavish Imitation Weaken the Foundations of Intellectual Property Law?' in E Derclaye (ed), *Research Handbook on the Future of EU Copyright* (Cheltenham, Edward Elgar, 2009) 566.

479 Kur 'Cumulation of IP Rights Pertaining to Product Shapes' (n 43) 613, 614, referring to shapes.

480 Quaedvlieg, 'Concurrence and Convergence in Industrial Design' (n 109) 23, 67.

481 Henning-Bodewig, *Unfair Competition Law: European Union and Member States* (n 469) 4.

482 Ibid; see also A Kamperman Sanders, *Unfair Competition Law: The Protection of Intellectual and Industrial Creativity* (Oxford, Clarendon Press, 1997) 11 *et seq*.

483 Quaedvlieg, 'Overlap/Relationships between Copyright and Other Intellectual Property Rights' (n 27) 479, 484.

reflect the amount of harmonisation achieved so far (more so for copyright, trademarks, designs and plant variety rights than for patents and unfair competition law). Whereas there is no general prohibition of cumulation, some rules exist to prevent certain overlaps. Some are general and cut across various IPRs, and some are more particular and only concern a specific aspect. General rules are:

- the rule governing shape marks, which regulates the overlap between trademark, patents, designs and copyright;
- the *Dior v Evora* decision, which arguably can apply by analogy to similar situations in most intellectual property overlaps;
- the rules coming out of the *Dyson, Libertel* and *Heidelberger Bauchemie* cases that concepts should not be registrable as trademarks, and single or simple combinations of colours will very rarely be, which respectively regulate the trademark/patent overlap and preserve negative convergence.

Specific rules are:

- the prohibition on computer programs being designs;
- the conflict rule which prevents the registration of a copyright or industrial property right as a design and the registration of the same as a trademark;
- the rule which avoids clashing judicial decisions between national and Community designs and national and Community trademarks;
- the rule prohibiting the registration of designs entirely dictated by their technical function and designs of interconnections, which regulates the patent/design overlap;
- the high level of convergence achieved between patents and plant variety rights;
- the rule prohibiting the overlap between plant variety right denomination and trademarks.

On the other hand, there are no rules organising the overlap between copyright and patents although computer programs are of great practical relevance. However, one will note that the European Union once envisaged a few such rules, in the Proposal for a Directive on the patentability of computer-implemented inventions, which failed to be adopted. As regards this overlap, almost everything remains open (except that the idea/expression dichotomy is safeguarded). Likewise, the overlap between IPRs and unfair competition is generously allowed but no rule regulates it whereby such regulation is absolutely vital to preserve the coherence of both systems.

As to the level overlaps, some are allowed while some are not, without any apparent coherent reason. Registered designs can cumulate while unregistered designs cannot (except for those already in force, namely only the UK UDR). One can have both a CTM and a national trademark but one cannot have a CPVR and a national plant variety right.

In conclusion, EU law in the end contains quite a few rules across the vast majority of IPRs which attempt to avoid regime clashes and overprotection, which consequently prevent monopolisation and a corresponding lessening of competition. Exclusionary convergence, however, is rather well preserved (computer programs being a limited exception). On the other hand, as will become even more apparent at the conclusion of this book, many IPRs differ in their treatment of limitations and exceptions, leading to much asymmetric convergence. As we saw, some overlap areas are also almost totally unregulated, such as computer programs and unfair competition law. For the problematic overlaps caused by these, rules will need to be elaborated in the final chapter.

4

France

I. THE LEGAL FRAMEWORK

FRENCH LAW IS based on the principle of freedom to copy. This principle dates back to the Décret d'Allarde of 2–17 March 1791, also known as Loi le Chapelier,[1] which provides for the principle of freedom of commerce and industry. This rule means that undertakings are free to compete, so that competitive prejudice is in principle lawful. In practice, every competitor has the right to attract the customers of his or her competitors. The corollary of this principle is that everyone is free to sell similar or even identical products. Therefore, in the realm of intellectual products, it means that everyone is free to copy or imitate another's achievement. This principle is affirmed by courts and the vast majority of commentators.[2] The principle of the freedom to copy is subject to two exceptions. First, the legislature can grant certain intellectual property rights to certain deserving achievements. In this case, copying is no longer free but is an infringement of the right-holder's exclusive right. Secondly, the courts have declared certain types of copying contrary to honest practices in commercial matters on the basis of unfair competition law.

As to the first exception, French intellectual property law is regulated by a single piece of legislation enacted on 1 July 1992 (Law No 92-597), the Intellectual Property Code (IPC), which has been revised several times, inter alia, to implement the various European Directives.[3] Part I of the IPC deals with copyright and neighbouring rights and is subdivided into a number of 'books'. The first deals with author's rights, the second with neighbouring rights, whilst the third contains general provisions common to author's rights and neighbouring rights, including the database *sui generis* right. Part II deals with industrial property and is also subdivided into a number of 'books'. Book IV deals with professional and administrative organisation (eg the National Intellectual Property Institute (INPI)), Book V with designs, Book VI with inventions and know-how (this book includes the protection of trade secrets and plant varieties), and Book VII with trademarks and other distinctive signs. As to the second exception to the principle of

[1] J Huillier, 'Le parasitime parasite-t-il la propriété intellectuelle ?' (2001) 312 *Gazette du Palais* 6, who notes that free competition is also enshrined in the ECT (now TFEU). These premises are important and will be discussed again in the concluding chapter.

[2] E Golaz, *L'imitation servile des produits et de leur présentation, étude comparée des droits Français, Allemands, Belges et Suisses* (Genève, Droz, 1992) 105; JJ Burst, *Concurrence déloyale et parasitisme* (Paris, Dalloz, 1993) 1; M Buydens, *La protection de la quasi-création* (Brussels, Larcier, 1993) 655, 677, 683; J Passa, *Contrefaçon et concurrence déloyale*, Publications de l'IRPI no 15 (Paris, Litec, 1997) 13; ML Izorche, 'Les fondements de la sanction de la concurrence déloyale et du parasitisme' (1998) 51(1) *Revue Trimestrielle de Droit Commercial* 17, 19; A Bertrand, *Le droit Français de la concurrence déloyale* (Paris, Cedat, 1998) 16 *et seq*; P De Candé, 'L'action en concurrence déloyale est-elle menacée par l'evolution du droit de la propriété intellectuelle?' (2004) *Propriétés Intellectuelles* 492 and the authors and decisions cited by all these authors. *Contra*: P Le Tourneau, 'Retour sur le parasitisme' (2000) *Dalloz, Chronique* 403, 405.

[3] The Code is available in both French and English at www.legifrance.gouv.fr.

freedom to copy, French law has an unfair competition law (*concurrence déloyale*), which is regulated separately. It derives from articles 1382 and 1383 of the Civil Code, which sets out civil liability and the case law interpreting it, which has grown and developed over the years. The Misleading and Comparative Advertising Directive 2006/114/EC (MCAD) is implemented in another body of law, the Code de la Consommation (in its article L121-8 *et seq*).[4] Unless otherwise stated in this part, reference to articles starting with 'L' are always to the IPC. There are a great number of French books on IPRs and on unfair competition law, listed below.[5]

II. COPYRIGHT AND DESIGNS

A Simultaneous Overlap

(i) Subject Matter

French copyright law, enshrined in the first Book of the Intellectual Property Code, simply states that 'all works of the mind whatever their kind, form of expression, merit or purpose' are protected even though they are not fixed (articles L111-1 and L112-1). Article L112-2 then enumerates a long non-exhaustive list of works:

(1) books, pamphlets and other literary, artistic and scientific writings;
(2) lectures, addresses, sermons, pleadings and other works of such nature;
(3) dramatic or dramatico-musical works;
(4) choreographic works, circus acts and feats and dumb-show works, the acting form of which is set down in writing or in other manner;
(5) musical compositions with or without words;
(6) cinematographic works and other works consisting of sequences of moving images, with or without sound, together referred to as audiovisual works;
(7) works of drawing, painting, architecture, sculpture, engraving and lithography;
(8) graphical and typographical works;

[4] For a discussion of the French implementation of the Directive, see J Passa, 'Brève présentation du droit de la publicité comparative après la transposition de la Directive Communautaire' (2002) 3 *Propriétés Intellectuelles* 32.

[5] Copyright : A Lucas and HJ Lucas, *Traité de la propriété littéraire et artistique*, 3rd edn (Paris, Litec, 2006); PY Gautier, *Propriété littéraire et artistique*, 6th edn (Paris, Presses Universitaires de France, 2007); C Caron, *Droit d'auteur et droits voisins*, 2nd edn (Paris, Litec, 2010); F Pollaud-Dulian, *Le droit d'auteur* (Paris, Économica, 2005); M Vivant and JM Bruguière, *Droit d'auteur* (Paris, Dalloz, 2009); B Edelman, *La propriété littéraire et artistique*, 4th edn (Paris, Presses Universitaires de France, 2008); P Sirinelli, *Propriété littéraire et artistique*, 2nd edn (Paris, Dalloz, 2004). Trademarks: A Bertrand, *Droit des marques: signes distinctifs, noms de domaine*, 2nd edn (Paris, Dalloz, 2005); C Caron *et al*, *Droit des marques: stratégies et questions d'actualité: législation, doctrine, jurisprudence, bibliographie* (Paris, LexisNexis, 2007); J Schmidt-Szalewski, *Le droit des marques* (Paris, Dalloz, 1997). Designs: P Greffe, F Greffe and PB Greffe, *Traité des dessins et des modèles: France, Union Européenne, Suisse, USA, Amérique Latine*, 8th edn (Paris, Litec, 2008); D Cohen, *Le droit des dessins et modèles, droit communautaire, droit international, droit Français et autres droits etrangers*, 2nd edn (Paris, Economica, 2004); N Dreyfus and B Thomas, *Marques, dessins et modèles, protection, défense, valorisation*, 2nd edn (Paris, Delmas, 2006); N Hadjadj-Cazier, *Stratégies de protection du design: mieux protéger les créations esthétiques* (Paris, La Documentation Française, 2004). Industrial property : Burst, *Concurrence déloyale et parasitisme* (n 2); J Azéma and JC Galloux, *Droit de la propriété industrielle*, 6th edn (Paris, Dalloz, 2006); J Passa, *Traité de droit de la propriété industrielle* (Paris, LGDJ, 2006) vol I; J Schmidt-Szalewski and JL Pierre, *Droit de la propriété industrielle*, 4th edn (Paris, Litec, 2007); H Gaumont-Prat, *Droit de la propriété industrielle* (Paris, Litec, 2009). Unfair competition: Passa, *Contrefaçon et concurrence déloyale* (n 2); L Vogel, *Droit de la concurrence déloyale* (Paris, Lawlex, 2007); Bertrand, *Le droit français de la concurrence déloyale* (n 2).

(9) photographic works and works produced by techniques analogous to photography;
(10) works of applied art;
(11) illustrations, geographical maps;
(12) plans, sketches and three-dimensional works relative to geography, topography, architecture and science;
(13) software, including the preparatory design material;
(14) Creations of the seasonal industries of dress and articles of fashion. Industries which, by reason of the demands of fashion, frequently renew the form of their products, particularly the making of dresses, furs, underwear, embroidery, fashion, shoes, gloves, leather goods, the manufacture of fabrics of striking novelty or of special use in high fashion dressmaking, the products of manufacturers of articles of fashion and of footwear and the manufacture of fabrics for upholstery shall be deemed to be seasonal industries.

Book V of the IPC deals with designs. Its first article (L511-1) faithfully reproduces Design Directive 98/71/EC's definition of design and product. The possible overlaps are therefore between designs and two- and three-dimensional artistic works (article L111-2(7)–(12) and (14)) but not between designs and audiovisual works (6).[6] The overlap is expressly recognised in the theory of the unity of art (*unité de l'art*), which is enshrined in articles L112-1 and L513-2.[7] According to this theory, there should be no criterion to distinguish between art and industry because otherwise it would force courts to make subjective aesthetic judgements.[8] The theory of the unity of art thus implies that there is total cumulation between copyright and design laws.[9] It means that the owner of a registered model can invoke design and copyright laws separately or together so long as the protection requirements of both rights are fulfilled. It also implies that creations can be protected by copyright which could not attract design right.[10] As a result of the theory, the duration of the design right is prolonged by that of copyright if the two protections subsist.[11] But this does not mean that design protection can be sought at the expiry of the copyright.[12] In any case, the design would no longer be new.[13] In summary, the maximum length of protection possible is 70 years after the death of the designer.

As a result, courts have held a wide range of functional three-dimensional articles to be protectable by copyright. Examples include a salad basket,[14] a bottle opener,[15] a

[6] It is not clear from the INPI designs database or website if it accepts the registration of audiovisual works. However, French commentators claim that moving trademarks are not registrable in France. The INPI is very strict on the requirement of graphical representation. Even if the sequence of images could be reproduced by a series of photographs (which is difficult as French law requires it to be appear in a square of 8cm by 8cm), it is not clear that courts would consider the movement as such as protected (email from A Latreille, on file with the authors). Contrast with the OHIM's practice, see chapter 3, section II.B(i).

[7] See Greffe, Greffe and Greffe, *Traité des dessins et des modèles* (n 5) 50, 62; Lucas and Lucas, *Traité de la propriété littéraire et artistique*, 3rd edn (n 5); Pollaud-Dulian, *Le droit d'auteur* (n 5) 123–24 ; C Caron, *Droit d'auteur et droits voisins* (Paris, Litec, 2006) 81; Passa, *Traité de droit de la propriété industrielle* (Paris, LGDJ, 2006) vol I, 903–5, paras 672–75. See also Cohen, *Le droit des dessins et modèles* (n 5) 127–29, citing a number of decisions from the 1990s and 2000s involving the shape of a car, shoe, stairs, armchair, and illustrating the theory.

[8] U Suthersanen, *Design Law in Europe* (London, Sweet & Maxwell, 2000) 137.

[9] Greffe, Greffe and Greffe, *Traité des dessins et des modèles* (n 5) 49 *et seq*.

[10] Caron, *Droit d'auteur et droits voisins* (n 7) 82, para 108.

[11] Dreyfus and Thomas, *Marques, dessins et modèles* (n 5) 280.

[12] Gautier, *Propriété littéraire et artistique*, 6th edn (n 5) 130.

[13] On this obvious fact, see eg *Verceral v Faience et Cristal de France*, Cass com, 22 March 2005 [2005] PIBD, III, 372.

[14] Cass crim, 2 May 1961 [1961] JCP G, II, 12242, comment Aymond; Cass crim, 30 October 1963 (1964) *Dalloz* 678, comment Françon.

[15] Cass crim, 9 October 1974 [1976] JCP G, II, 18311, comment AC; (1975) 3 *Revue Internationale du Droit d'Auteur* 176; (1974) *Dalloz*, Inf Rap 228.

signalisation mast, packaging for quail's eggs,[16] hair styles,[17] a jumper,[18] and a model's make-up.[19] The limit of copyright protection is 'purely' functional articles. This limit is reflected in the field of designs in Design Directive, article 7, which excludes designs solely dictated by function and interconnection features.[20] This theory is explained below in the discussion of excluded subject matter.

(ii) Protection Requirements

Copyright law's requirement of originality is not stated in the IPC but in the case law. Originality means that the author must have expressed the stamp of his or her personality in the work.[21] Merit or an artistic or aesthetic aspect is not required.[22] Commentators have reported that courts lower the criterion of originality for works of applied art generally. They ask only for the trace of a personal effort of creation and aesthetic research in the combination of characteristic elements.[23] On the other hand, article L511-2–511-6 implemented the Design Directive's requirements of individual character and novelty, and visibility for component parts. This was not clear for a while, but now French case law and literature both clearly agree that the copyright and design laws' protection requirements are different.[24] However, some think that novelty is redundant because individual character includes novelty.[25] Some courts even confuse the two criteria.[26]

[16] For references, see A Lucas and HJ Lucas, *Traité de la propriété littéraire et artistique*, 2nd edn (Paris, Litec, 2001) 75 n 40.

[17] See CA Aix-en-Provence [1957] RD Propriété Industrielle 151, 189; Tribunal Correctionnel, Paris, 11th ch, 12 July 1977 (1978) 1 *Gazette du Palais* 41. Lucas and Lucas, *Traité de la propriété littéraire et artistique*, 2nd edn (n 16) 116, citing CA Aix, 11 June 1987 [1988] Cahiers de Droit d'Auteur 23.

[18] Civ 1st, 8 December 1987, Bulletin Civil I, no 341.

[19] CA Paris, 1995, cited by A Kerever in (1995) *Revue Internationale du Droit d'Auteur* (October) 241.

[20] Pollaud-Dulian, *Le droit d'auteur* (n 5) 98, para 126, thinks that the multiplicity of shapes is the criterion that the European Union meant to choose. He refers to the *travaux préparatoires* but without citing from them.

[21] For recent decisions, see *X v Compagnie Francaise des Eaux Spiritueux*, Cass com, 20 March 2007 (2007) *Propriétés Intellectuelles* 469, comment P De Candé (bottle cap unprotectable for lack of originality); *SA La Redoute v Sarl J Martin Trepointes*, CA Bordeaux, 1st ch, 28 June 2007, Jurisdata no. 2007-346021; *H&M v Scooter*, CA Paris, 4th ch, A, 7 November 2007 (2007) 229 *Revue Internationale de la Propriété Industrielle et Artistique* 35 (earring combining corals and shells); *Amatai Services v Jean Cassegrain and Longchamp SAS*, CA Paris, 4th ch, 23 November 2007 [2008] PIBD no 866, III, 51; (2008) *Propriété Industrielle* (June) 41, comment Gasnier (bags) and *D Murat et DLM v H&M*, CA Paris, 4th ch, A, 16 April 2008, RG no 07/1890 (five models of socks (mini-socks) made by a fashion designer (D Murat) were copied by H&M); *SA Lamarthe v SA Monoprix*, Cass 1st civ, 14 February 2008, Jurisdata no 2008-042726 [2008] PIBD no 872, III, 266 (bag), reported by AE Kahn 'Un an de droit de la mode' (2008) *Communication Commerce Electronique* (September).

[22] For an isolated decision, see, however, *Marcal v Pardo*, CA Paris, 4th ch, A, 14 September 2005, (2006) *Propriétés Intellectuelles* 455, comment P De Candé.

[23] See eg VL Benabou, 'Les rapports entre droit d'auteur et droit des marques et de la concurrence déloyale, Rapport national, France' in J Ginsburg and J Besek (eds), *Adjuncts and Alternatives to Copyright, Proceedings of the ALAI Congress, June 13–17, 2001, New York, USA* (New York, Columbia University School of Law, 2002) 3, citing Cass civ, 1st ch, 10 May 1995, (1995) *Revue Internationale du Droit d'Auteur* (October) 291.

[24] P Kamina, 'Le nouveau droit Français des dessins et modèles' (2001) 40 *Dalloz*, Affaires 3258, para 40; 2003, para 28; Lucas and Lucas, *Traité de la propriété littéraire et artistique*, 2nd edn (n 16) 93; MA Pérot-Morel 'A propos du maintien de l'unité de l'ait dans le nouveau droit des dessins et modèles' (2005) *Propriété Industrielle*, Avril, Etudes, 9; ME Piatti, 'Autonormisation du droit français des dessins et modèles' (2004) *Propriété Industrielle*, Décembre, Etudes, 7. *X v Compagnie Francaise des Eaux Spiritueux*, Cass com, 20 March 2007 (2007) *Propriétés Intellectuelles* 469, comment P De Candé.

[25] P De Candé, 'Dessins et modèles' (2003) 9 *Propriétés Intellectuelles* 396, citing B Humblot in (2003) 24 *JCP E* 990; CH Massa and A Strowel, 'Community Design: Cinderella Revamped' (2003) *European Intellectual Property Review* 68, 73.

[26] Cohen, *Le droit des dessins et modèles* (n 5) 67–68, citing Court of First Instance (TGI) Paris, 15 February 2002 [2002] PIBD 377, holding that this overall visual impression, which cannot be found in any of the cited prior art, gave individual character to the furniture.

Commentators also think that as regards constraints on the freedom of the designer, if the sector is crowded, even slight differences will be enough to confer individual character on the design and that the freedom of the designer is appreciated only by objective and not subjective criteria.[27] This is in accordance with the General Court's recent *Grupo Promer* decision.[28] French courts have interpreted the concept of informed user similarly to the UK courts, and now the General Court. Accordingly, the informed user is not an expert. It is a user not with an average attention but a special vigilance, because of his or her personal experience or extended knowledge of the sector in question;[29] or as the General Court put it:

> The informed user is particularly observant and has some awareness of the state of the prior art, that is to say the previous designs relating to the product in question that had been disclosed on the date of filing of the contested design, or, as the case may be, on the date of priority claimed.[30]

Both in copyright and design law, the combination of public domain, banal or known elements does not exclude creativity or individual character per se.[31] It is interesting to note that when copyright and design laws are both invoked to protect a product, most of the time, novelty and originality are recognised together or rejected together.[32] Cohen even notes that when a design is new and has individual character, it is by definition original, and vice versa. To be convinced of this, it is sufficient to note that after a hundred years of case law in which protection under Books I and V has been invoked cumulatively, in no decision has the court considered that the design fulfilled the condition of protection under Book V but not Book I, and vice versa.[33] For Cohen, it is therefore statistically certain that if the words describing the criteria are different, the thing is the same: novelty and individual character, on the one hand, and originality, on the other, represent purely and simply the same concept.[34] So there seems to be convergence at this

[27] N Hadjadj-Cazier, *Stratégies de protection du design: mieux protéger les créations esthétiques* (Paris, La Documentation Française, 2004) 29. Cohen, *Le droit des dessins et modèles* (n 5) 66, also cites CA Aix-en-Provence, 15 December 2000 [2001] PIBD 224, which held that the reference to visual impression refers only to the external appearance of the design. No other parameter, such as flexibility to touch, technical function, resistance to use or difference in terms of weight, can be taken into consideration.

[28] Case T-9/07 *Grupo Promer Mon Graphic v OHIM*, especially para 72, available at www.curia.europea.eu.

[29] See *Zygote et M. Fabry v Habitat France*, Court of First Instance (TGI) of Paris, 15 February 2002 (2002) *Propriété Industrielle* Comm 80; TGI Paris, 15 February 2002 [2002] PIBD 377. See also French literature, Cohen, *Le droit des dessins et modèles* (n 5) 65 and below, chapter 5, section II.A.

[30] Case T-9/07 *Grupo Promer Mon Graphic v OHIM*, para 62, available at www.curia.europea.eu, also adding that 'the informed user is neither a manufacturer nor a seller of the products in which the designs at issue are intended to be incorporated or to which they are intended to be applied'.

[31] *Santoni Calzatore v Hermes Sellier and others*, CA Paris, 4th ch, B, 1 December 2006 [2007] PIBD no 847, III, 187; *Tulipe v Ubu*, CA Paris, 4th ch, A, 27 September 2006 [2006] PIBD no 840, III, 748. See also *Mosaic v Opium and S. Prunet*, CA Paris, 4th ch, B, 23 May 2008 [2008] PIBD, no 880, III, 516; *Lignes Ambiance and Vide Central v Nuera Solutions*, CA Paris, 4th ch, B, 30 May 2008 [2008] PIBD no 881, III, 552 and *Nelson v Etam*, CA Paris, 4th ch, B, 4 March 2005 [2005] PIBD III, 406; CA Paris, 4th ch, A, 1 February 2006 [2006] PIBD no 828, III, 298 (shoes' models); CA Paris, 4th ch, A, 27 September 2006 [2006] PIBD no 840, III, 748. See also Gautier, *Propriété littéraire et artistique*, 6th edn (n 5) 133, citing Civ 1st, 20 March 2001 (2001) *Revue Internationale du Droit d'Auteur* (July) 347; Com 17 March 2004 (2004) *Revue Internationale du Droit d'Auteur* (July) 263. See also Cohen, *Le droit des dessins et modèles* (n 5) 68, speaking of designs and citing as examples *La Redoute v Laurence Tavernier*, CA Paris, 3 July 2002; *Cassegrain v Renault*, TGI Paris, 13 September 2002.

[32] AE Kahn, 'Un an de droit de la mode' () (2006) *Communication Commerce Electronique* (September)22. See eg CA Paris, 4th ch, A, 9 February 2005 [2005] PIBD III, 375 (bag). For comments, see Dreyfus and Thomas, *Marques, Dessins et Modèles* (n 5) 284.

[33] Cohen, *Le droit des dessins et modèles* (n 5) 129–30.

[34] Ibid

level of the overlap. However, a difference with design law is that components of complex products can be protected by copyright even if they are hidden (not visible).[35]

(iii) Excluded Subject Matter

As mentioned above, copyright does not protect ideas, genre or style. The same applies in design law.[36] The other main exclusion in both rights is that of functional shapes. In France, the exclusion of purely functional shapes is known as the theory of multiplicity of shapes, which applies to both copyright and design right and is enshrined in article L511-8 (which faithfully implements Design Directive, article 7). So the exclusion curiously only appears in Book V of the Code, but in the nineteenth century, courts had without hesitation extended the theory to copyright.[37] The prohibition of the protection of functional forms aims to avoid that the latter be protected by copyright or designs rather than patents, whose requirements and regime are stricter.[38] The theory means that once there is place for arbitrary shapes, copyright protection is possible. In other words, if several shapes can obtain the same functional result, the shape is dissociable from this utilitarian result.[39] However, courts are not always consistent in their application of the theory of multiplicity of shapes.[40] Some even seem to have abandoned it altogether.[41] Many courts derive originality from the simple fact that the form is not functional or hold that if the shape is separable from the function, it is necessarily original.[42] But commentators think that it should not mean that as long as it is possible to conceive several possible shapes, copyright subsists.[43] What is relevant is the functional aim not the utilitarian result. Thus, copyright can subsist, and overlap can occur, only if the author is

[35] Caron, *Droit d'auteur et droits voisins* (n 7) 53, para 59.

[36] Greffe, Greffe and Greffe, *Traité des dessins et des modèle* (n 5) 27. For a recent decision, see *Hermes Sellier v Pier Import*, CA Paris, 4th ch, B, 17 March 2006 (2006) *Propriétés Intellectuelles* 459, comment P De Candé.

[37] Caron, *Droit d'auteur et droits voisins* (n 7) 55.

[38] Ibid.

[39] Vivant and Bruguière, *Droit d'auteur* (n 5) 109, para 121 .

[40] PY Gautier, *Propriété Littéraire et Artistique*, 4th edn (Paris, Presses Universitaires de France, 2001) 119. However, Cohen, *Le droit des dessins et modèles* (n 5) 23, notes that today the dominant French case law considers that all designs whose shape obeys a technical and non-aesthetic logic (ie if the shape results from a utilitarian imperative rather than being inspired by a purely aesthetic research) must be excluded. He cites examples: *Aerazur v Transaco*, CA Paris, 13 November 2002 (clothes) and CA Paris, November 2001 [2002] PIBD 446 (waterproof pocket).

[41] For instance, two decisions of the Paris Court of Appeal led one commentator to write in 2006 that the theory of multiplicity of shapes had been abandoned because in these decisions, the court held that the shape is not dissociable from its function and the technical result sought, and thus rejected the protection of the design. It added that it did not matter that the shape in question can vary. See C Caron, 'Droit de la propriété intellectuelle' (2006) 30 JCP G, I, 162, 1504, commenting on *Pall France v Fim medical*, CA Paris, 4th ch, A, 12 October 2005, Jurisdata no 2006-285031 and *Decathlon v Ste Francaise de Judo et d'Arts Martiaux*, 28 September 2005, Juridata 2005-287639. Azéma and Galloux, *Droit de la propriété industrielle* (n 5) 634, suggest that the theory has been abandoned, the latter citing Cass com, 20 October 1998 [1999] PIBD III, 51. But Azéma and Galloux believe that if one thinks in terms of juxtaposition of the two rights instead of cumulation between copyright and design right, there could be a place for a rebirth of the criterion of multiplicity of forms. *Contra*: Vivant and Bruguière, *Droit d'auteur* (n 5) 109, para 121 (not proposing to abandon it).

[42] C Bernault, 'La protection des formes fonctionnelles par le droit de la propriété intellectuelle' (2003) *Dalloz* 957, 958–59.

[43] Lucas and Lucas, *Traité de la propriété littéraire et artistique*, 3rd edn (n 5) 108, para 125. They note, however, that this on the contrary can apply in design law so design right would subsist in such a case but not copyright. See also Caron, *Droit d'auteur et droits voisins* (n 7) 55.

animated by aesthetic preoccupations.[44] As a result, a shape, without being exclusively functional, may nevertheless not reveal the personality of the author and thus may not be protected by copyright.[45] As has been well said, originality does not mean arbitrariness.[46] In sum, in order to obtain copyright protection a functional shape must fulfil two cumulative conditions: it must not be dictated by its function and it must be original. This analysis means that a lot of works of applied art cannot benefit from copyright law's protection and that there will not be any simultaneous overlap.[47] Similarly, it is not because the shape is separable from function that it is automatically new and has individual character.[48]

French law also faithfully implemented the Design Directive's morality provision (article L511-7). By contrast, there is no morality and public policy clause in the copyright provisions of the IPC. Thus, French courts do not tend to deny copyright to immoral works and apply article L112-1 strictly,[49] although some criminal courts have considered that if a work is particularly degrading, it should not be protected.[50] There could therefore be a clash if the same subject matter is protected by copyright and design. French intellectual property law does not provide rules to solve this clash. However, the exercise/enforcement of copyright can be prohibited by other legal rules, such as eg criminal provisions which protect minors against violent and pornographic messages, and privacy rules.[51] Therefore in practice, in most cases, the result of the application of the several laws will be converging.

(iv) Ownership and Dealings

In copyright law, the provisions on ownership and dealings are quite detailed. In principle, ownership goes to the author even if the author is employed or is a civil servant (article L111-1).[52] A contract can always provide to the contrary. Special rules exist for works of collaboration, composite, collective and audiovisual works.[53] Works of collaboration

[44] Lucas and Lucas, *Traité de la propriété littéraire et artistique*, 3rd edn (n 5) 108, para 125, and 109.

[45] Ibid 109, citing other authors. See also Bernault, 'La protection des formes fonctionnelles par le droit de la propriété intellectuelle' (n 42) 959.

[46] Bernault, 'La protection des formes fonctionnelles par le droit de la propriété intellectuelle' (n 42) *Dalloz* 959.

[47] See for examples, Caron, *Droit d'auteur et droits voisins* (n 7) 54, para 6, citing CA Paris, 11 October 2000 (2001) 188 *Revue Internationale du Droit d'Auteur* 367 (shape of a windsurfer only justified by his function of being stable on water); Cass 1st civ, 28 November 2000, Bull civ, I, no 309 (kitchen utensil). See also more recently *Borelly v NCMv*, CA Paris, 4th ch, B, 28 March 2008 (2008) *Propriétés Intellectuelles* 445, comment P De Cancé; CA Paris, 4th ch, A, 28 September 2005 [2005] PIBD no 820, III, 747 (design of a karate glove held unprotectable because the shape chosen could not be dissociated from the aim pursued).

[48] Bernault, 'La protection des formes fonctionnelles par le droit de la propriété intellectuelle' (n 42) 960.

[49] Pollaud-Dulian, *Le droit d'auteur* (n 5) 119–20, para 158; Vivant and Bruguière, *Droit d'auteur* (n 5) 151, para 186.

[50] Ibid. Pollaud-Dulian, however, thinks that copyright should not be denied for immoral works. The situation is similar in Germany. Contrast with the situation in the United Kingdom, which has specific copyright case law refusing protection to such works, see chapter 5, section II.A.

[51] Pollaud-Dulian, *Le droit d'auteur* (n 5) 120, para 158.

[52] See also IPC, art L113-1 which establishes a rebuttable presumption of ownership by the person(s) under whose name the work has been disclosed.

[53] These are defined in art L113-2: '"Work of collaboration" shall mean a work in the creation of which more than one natural person has participated. "Composite work" shall mean a new work in which a preexisting work is incorporated without the collaboration of the author of the latter work. "Collective work" shall mean a work created at the initiative of a natural or legal person who edits it, publishes it and discloses it under his direction and name and in which the personal contributions of the various authors who participated in its

belong jointly to all the authors who contributed. Authors need to agree together how they will exercise their rights. If the authors cannot agree, the civil courts will decide for them. Where the contribution of each of the joint authors is of a different kind, each may, unless otherwise agreed, separately exploit his or her own personal contribution without, however, prejudicing the exploitation of the common work (article L113-3). A composite work is the property of the author who has produced it, subject to the rights of the author of the pre-existing work (art. L 113-4) whilst collective works are the property of the natural or legal person under whose name they have been disclosed, unless proved otherwise (article L113-5). Article L113-7 lays down the special rules applying to audiovisual works.

As to dealings, article L122-7 lays down the principle that the two rights (reproduction and representation[54]) can be transferred. Transfers are subject to a formality: each right must be separately mentioned in the contract and the field of exploitation of the assigned rights must be defined as to its scope and purpose, as to place and as to duration (article L131-3). In addition, article L131-6 mandates that:

> any assignment clause affording the right to exploit a work in a form that is unforeseeable and not foreseen on the date of the contract shall be explicit and shall stipulate participation correlated to the profits from exploitation.

Yet more special rules apply to audiovisual works. Because of the rule in article L131-3, everything that is not expressly transferred is presumed to remain the property of the author.[55]

Rules in the field of designs are, in contrast, almost non-existent and in fact are much simpler. Article L511-9 simply provides that the design right goes to the designer and there is a rebuttable presumption that the person applying to register the design is considered the beneficiary of the protection. A legal person can be the owner of a design right.[56] No rules exist on joint ownership so the common property regime should apply. As to dealings, all rights are transferable; no rules other than those of contract law are imposed for exploitation acts.[57] There is no particular formality except that, as for patents, article L513-3 requires that the transfers be registered in the national registry of designs in order for them to be enforceable against third parties.[58]

As a result, the most stringent regime, copyright, will prevail. For instance, in all cases (except collective works) a natural person must be the owner *ab initio*.[59] Because of the principle of the unity of art, it is not possible to transfer the design rights without the

production are merged in the overall work for which they were conceived, without it being possible to attribute to each author a separate right in the work as created'.

[54] On this see below.

[55] Benabou, 'Rapport national, France' (n 23) 19.

[56] Azéma and Galloux, *Droit de la propriété industrielle* (n 5) 674; Gaumont-Prat, *Droit de la propriété industrielle* (n 5) 144.

[57] Azéma and Galloux, *Droit de la propriété industrielle* (n 5) 638.

[58] Ibid 638. Passa, *Traité de droit de la propriété industrielle* (n 5) vol I, 1017: 'The article has been modified and the act is however before its registration enforceable to third parties who have acquired rights after the date of the act but who knew of the act when acquiring these rights . . . Therefore if a right holder transfers its rights to two different persons, it is the first who registered the contract who wins unless he or she was of bad faith at the moment of the transfer. If a design is protected by copyright, the question is what the exact scope of the publicity obligation is'.

[59] Gaumont-Prat, *Droit de la propriété industrielle* (n 5) 144.

copyright.[60] This rule helps to avoid conflicts in case of overlap to keep the rights in the hands of only one person. A problem occurs, however, when there is cumulation between copyright and a Community design because the rules on employment are reversed (the rules relating to joint authorship are identical).[61] Probably in most cases, however, a problem will not occur as the employee will have transferred his or her copyright to his or her employer, but potentially clashes could occur whereby two different persons own the rights to the copyright and the Community design right.

Finally, as Community designs are deemed national rights for the purpose of transfers and licences, and other minimal provisions of Design Regulation 6/2002 on this issue add to or do not differ from the French ones (Design Regulation, articles 27–28, 32), what has been said above as regards national designs applies. The more restrictive rule of article 32(3) will apply to exclusive licences as French law does not appear to have any rule on this.[62]

(v) Rights and Infringement

The economic right of the copyright owner is the right of exploitation which comprises the right of representation and the right of reproduction. These are very broad and include the communication of the work to the public in any form and the physical reproduction of the work, including alterations such as adaptations and translations in whole or in part (article L122-1–122-4). As ideas are not protected, there cannot be infringement if the defendant takes an idea from the claimant's work. Another principle is that the more original a work is, the more protection it receives.[63] Courts determine infringement by looking at the similarities.[64] After having done that, they look at differences. A total resemblance is not needed; what is important is the overall impression.[65] If the differences do not destroy the overall impression, there is infringement. On the other hand, if the second work presents differences that are characteristic to it, then there is no infringement.[66] But there can be partial infringement when the infringer has added some personal creation to the unlawful copying.[67] There is infringement if the characteristic

[60] Kahn 'Un an de droit de la mode' (2008) (n 21) (mentioning certain commentators who interpret the evolution of design right and its 'autonomisation' as allowing the transfer, separately from copyright, of industrial property rights covering the same work but noting that the principle of unity of art prohibits such interpretation).

[61] Design Regulation, art 14 provides: 'Right to the Community design. 1. The right to the Community design shall vest in the designer or his successor in title. 2. If two or more persons have jointly developed a design, the right to the Community design shall vest in them jointly. 3. However, where a design is developed by an employee in the execution of his duties or following the instructions given by his employer, the right to the Community design shall vest in the employer, unless otherwise agreed or specified under national law'. See also M Portron, 'Table ronde' (2000) 55 *Gazette du Palais* (February) 23, pointing out that not all the rules are the same in copyright law and the Community design right.

[62] Design Regulation, art 32(3) provides: 'Without prejudice to the provisions of the licensing contract, the licensee may bring proceedings for infringement of a Community design only if the right holder consents thereto. However, the holder of an exclusive licence may bring such proceedings if the right holder in the Community design, having been given notice to do so, does not himself bring infringement proceedings within an appropriate period'.

[63] Lucas and Lucas, *Traité de la propriété littéraire et artistique*, 2nd edn (n 16) 242.

[64] Gautier, *Propriété littéraire et artistique*, 6th edn (n 5) 831–36.

[65] Dreyfus and Thomas, *Marques, Dessins et Modèles* (n 5) 334; Gautier, *Propriété littéraire et artistique*, 4th edn (n 40) 708, citing cases.

[66] Gautier, *Propriété littéraire et artistique*, 4th edn (n 40) 709.

[67] Ibid 710.

elements of the work have been copied.[68] Resemblances arising from the functional elements are not relevant. Confusion is an indication that there can be copyright infringement but it is not one of its conditions.[69] Copyright also gives moral rights but design right does not (except the right of paternity in Design Regulation, article 18). Therefore, most copyright moral rights can block the exploitation of the product protected by design right.[70]

Articles L513-4 (rights) and L513-5 (scope of protection/test of infringement) substantially provide the same as the Design Directive. Under the old design provisions, advertising in a catalogue was held to constitute an act of infringement.[71] Since the Directive's list of rights is open, this case law could be upheld. As regards the infringement test, the terms used by the French Act differ slightly from those of the Directive. The text of Design Regulation, article 10 and Design Directive, article 9 does not include the term 'visual', whilst the IPC states that:

> the protection given by the registration of a design extends to all designs which do not produce on the informed observer a different global visual impression. (emphasis added)

However, it is now clear that the only impression that counts is visual.[72] The French courts have not elaborated much on the test of infringement. However, the two decisions handed down on the basis of the new law seem to use the old test rather than the new one. The first is the litigation involving Procter & Gamble's Community registered design right for its air freshener Febreze, a cylindrical sprayer with a trigger, copied by Reckitt Benckiser's Air Wick Odour Stop, which was litigated in different European jurisdictions, including France and the United Kingdom.[73] The Court of Appeal of Paris found there was infringement on the basis of reproduction of essential elements, rather than on the basis of a 'similar global visual impression'. According to the court, the design has to be scrutinised with attention in order to see that the superior part of Procter & Gamble's sprayer is slightly curved while it is flat on Reckitt's model.[74] The second decision by the French Supreme Court (the Court of Cassation) does not shed much light on whether the Court has endorsed the new test. The Court agreed with the test of infringement used by the Court of Appeal of Paris, which simply held that the reproduction of the original characteristics of the design and the irrelevance of minor differences did not affect the visual resemblance.[75] This test seems to be a combination of

[68] Gautier, *Propriété littéraire et artistique*, 6th edn (n 5) 831; Lucas and Lucas, *Traité de la propriété littéraire et artistique*, 2nd edn (n 16) 242, 250, para 287.

[69] Lucas and Lucas, *Traité de la propriété littéraire et artistique*, 2nd edn (n 16) 243. See also *Chaumet v Camille and Lucie*, CA Paris, 4th ch, B, 11 April 2008 (2008) *Propriétés Intellectuelles* 446, comment P De Candé.

[70] Passa, *Traité de droit de la propriété industrielle* (n 5) vol I, 1119.

[71] CA Paris, 21 March 2001 [2001] PIBD, II, 510.

[72] This has been confirmed in Case T-9/07 *Grupo Promer Mon Graphic v OHIM*, para 50, available at www.curia.europea.eu. The Design Regulation was also clear on this point. See also D Stone, 'Some Clarity, Some Confusion: 12 P&G v Reckitt Benckiser Decisions Help Explain Registered Community Designs' (2008) *Journal of Intellectual Property Law and Practice* 376, 384.

[73] *Reckitt v Procter & Gamble*, CA Paris, 14th ch, A, 17 January 2007, available at http://oami.europa.eu/pdf/design/cdcourts/Air_Wick.pdf. For a discussion of the litigation, see Stone, 'Some Clarity, Some Confusion' (n 72).

[74] Note that the Paris Court of Appeal's ruling is in total contrast with that of the Court of Appeal of England and Wales in the same case, [2007] EWCA Civ 936. See also chapter 5, section II.A.

[75] Cass, 1 July 2008, available at www.legifrance.gouv.fr/affichJuriJudi.do?oldAction=rechJuriJudi&idTexte=JURITEXT000019127786&fastReqId=789785982&fastPos=1 (perfume flasks).

the old and the new test and, if the accent is on the visual impression, then it accords with the new law.

Commentators are of the opinion that since the new law has not changed a great deal on the issue of infringement, the latter will be determined as before, taking into account the similarities and not the differences.[76] Generally, courts refer to the differences only to reject them by stating that they do not prevent infringement.[77] However, the applicability of the old test is doubtful, as during the elaboration of the Design Directive, part of its article 11 which said: 'to determine the scope of protection, the appreciation is based in principle more on the common characteristics than on the differences' was deleted.[78] Therefore, insisting on the similarities rather than the differences is arguably no longer part of the infringement test. Otherwise, as in copyright law, partial reproduction can also be infringement.[79] Of course, if there is only similarity in the genre, functions or ideas, there is no infringement. In other words, there is only infringement if the parts that are new and have individual character also appear in the infringing design.[80] The quantity, quality or merit of the infringing products and the commercial prejudice are all irrelevant in the appreciation of infringement.[81] The process, material, medium or destination is also irrelevant.[82] If all this is right, then the tests are similar or even identical in both copyright and design right and there should be no regime clashes. However, it is doubted that the new infringement test amounts to the same rules as the previous one. A clarification from the EU courts will be needed to resolve the current differences of interpretation that already exist in the French and UK case law.

Finally, as in copyright law, the risk of confusion is not an element taken into consideration. After a period of contradictory decisions among the lower French courts,[83] the Court of Cassation clearly stated in 2008 that the risk of confusion must not be checked to determine infringement of a registered design.[84] The case law now accords with the views of the literature.[85] The risk of confusion is a criterion qualifying an unfair competition act

[76] Dreyfus and Thomas, *Marques, dessins et modèles* (n 5) 334; Greffe, Greffe and Greffe, *Traité des dessins et des modèles* (n 5) 442 *et seq.*

[77] For instance, in a recent case, the only difference between the claimant's and defendant's bags was their dimensions. See *Cassegrain v Cecop*, CA Paris, 7 February 2003, cited by Dreyfus and Thomas, *Marques, dessins et modèles* (n 5) 335.

[78] De Candé, 'L'action en concurrence déloyale est-elle menacée par l'evolution du droit de la propriété intellectuelle?' (n 2) 502 n 56.

[79] Greffe, Greffe and Greffe, *Traité des dessins et des modèles* (n 5) 442.

[80] Ibid 446–49.

[81] Ibid 439–41; Dreyfus and Thomas, *Marques, dessins et modèles* (n 5) 335.

[82] Dreyfus and Thomas, *Marques, dessins et modèles* (n 5) 335.

[83] For examples, see the decisions commented on by J Passa in (2006) 18 *Propriétés Intellectuelles* 85.

[84] *FS-P+B, Frendo v Ets Tarrerias Bonjean* (knives), Cass com, 26 March 2008, Jurisdata no 2008-043353 (2008) *Propriété Industrielle* (June) 38, comment F Greffe. See also P De Candé, 'Dessins et modèles' (2008) 29 *Propriétés Intellectuelles* 447. See also *Manufacture Générale Horlogerie v G Ellia, Auchan France, Générale de marques (Suisse) et LGE*, Cass com, 23 September 2008 [2008] PIBD no. 883, III, 608, in which the court set aside a decision holding that there was infringement because the global visual impression could create a risk of confusion. The Court of Appeal of Paris has since followed the Supreme Court. See *Chaumet v Camille and Lucie*, CA Paris, 4th ch, B, 11 April 2008 (2008) *Propriétés Intellectuelles* 446, comment P De Candé. See also *Cashtex-Popny v Memo France*, CA Paris, 4th ch, B, 18 April 2008 (2008) *Propriétés Intellectuelles* 447, comment P De Candé and *Amatai v Jean Cassegrain*, CA Paris, 4th ch, B, 23 November 2007 [2008] PIBD no 866, III, 51 (copyright infringement).

[85] P De Candé, 'Dessins et modèles' (2004) 13 *Propriétés Intellectuelles* 940; Kahn, 'Un an de droit de la mode' (2006) (n 32) 24; Passa, *Traité de droit de la propriété industrielle* (n 5) vol I, para 751; J Passa, 'Les Ddvergences dans la définition de l'acte de contrefaçon dans les différentes branches du droit de la propriété intellectuelle. Plaidoyer pour une clarification' (2004) 10 *Propriétés Intellectuelles* 513, 516.

distinct from the infringement act, or an element that aggravates the prejudice suffered by the victim of the infringement of the design.[86] It is, as some have argued, dangerous to use this criterion because it prevents the claimant from using the action in unfair competition, which requires confusion.[87] This overlap will be analysed in detail in section IX. It can already be said that with regard to this particular aspect, the legal situation is the same as in copyright law so there should not be any regime clashes.

(vi) Exceptions Including Exhaustion Principle

Exceptions to copyright are numerous and very detailed (article L122-5). To summarise article L122-5, copyright owners cannot prevent:

- private and gratuitous performances carried out exclusively within the family circle;
- private copying;
- analyses and short quotations justified by the critical, polemic, educational, scientific or informatory nature of the work in which they are incorporated; press reviews including speeches in political, administrative, judicial or academic gatherings, as well as in public meetings of a political nature and at official ceremonies; reproductions of works of graphic or three-dimensional art intended to appear in the catalogue of a judicial sale held in France, in the form of the copies of the said catalogue made available to the public prior to the sale for the sole purpose of describing the works of art offered for sale. These three exceptions apply on condition that the name of the author and the source are clearly stated;
- use of extracts of most works to illustrate teaching and research under certain conditions;
- parody, pastiche and caricature, as long as the rules of the genre are observed;
- acts necessary to access the contents of an electronic database for the purposes of and within the limits of the use provided by contract;
- temporary reproduction (faithful implementation of Infosoc Directive 2001/29/EC, article 5(1));
- reproduction and communication by establishments open to the public only in order for disabled persons to consult works for their private use;[88]
- reproduction and communication of works for preservation purposes by libraries, museums and archives as long as they do not seek an economic or commercial advantage;
- reproduction and communication of an artistic work by the press exclusively for information purposes and in direct relation with the work and indicating clearly the name of the author, except works which themselves aim to give an account of information.

[86] De Candé, 'Dessins et modèles' (2004) (n 85); De Candé, 'Dessins et modèles' (2008) (n 84). *Contra*: CH Massa and A Strowel, 'Le cumul du dessin ou modèle et du droit d'auteur: orbites parallèles et forces d'attraction entre deux planètes indépendantes mais jumelles' in S Dusollier and A Cruquenaire (eds), *Le cumul des droits intellectuels* (Brussels, Larcier, 2009) 21, 82, citing a Belgian decision which held that the defendant's product produces the same general impression to the point of causing confusion to the non-informed eye, and commenting that this does not affect the final decision; its effect seems purely ornamental.

[87] C Caron, comment, Cass, 19 September 2006 (2007) *Communication Commerce Electronique* (February) 31; Kahn, 'Un an de droit de la mode' (2006) (n 32) 24; P De Candé, 'Dessins and modèles' (2005) 17 *Propriétés Intellectuelles* 454; Kahn 'Un an de droit de la mode' (2008) (n 21). For more details, see below on unfair competition.

[88] The conditions of application of this exception are set out in detail in art L122-5.

Article L122-5 *in fine* subjects all exceptions to the three-step test. The exceptions in design law are copied from the Design Directive (article L513-6–513-7). Therefore, except for the private copying and teaching and research exceptions,[89] the two regimes do not converge in respect of their exceptions because the other two exceptions in design law originate from patent law. Also, as design law does not allow for more than the four exceptions mentioned, it trumps all the other copyright exceptions.[90] The French Intellectual Property Code does not have a rule to regulate this conflict.

The exhaustion principle made its appearance extremely late in French copyright law, as it was included only in 2006 in article L122-3(1) (as a result of the belated implementation of the 2001 Infosoc Directive).[91] Previously, it was only recognised for software and databases. Article L513-8 enshrines the exhaustion principle for designs. However, the right of destination which exists only in copyright law restricts the exhaustion principle.[92] According to this right, the copyright owner has the right to control the use of the copies of his or her work after they have been put on the market, so s/he can prevent their destination from being changed. For instance, if an artist creates a poster for a film for it to be posted in public, that does not mean s/he has accepted the sale of these posters in a shop.[93] The basis of the right is in article L131-3 and commentators agree that it is weak.[94] Courts have nevertheless upheld the right.[95] As can be seen, however, the right in effect goes against the exhaustion principle recognised at EU level[96] and, moreover, it openly contradicts article L111-3.[97] This is even more the case now that the exhaustion principle has been explicitly included in the Intellectual Property Code. In sum, the questions of relations between exhaustion, the right of distribution and the right of destination are not yet solved but some commentators advocate a repeal of the destination right.[98]

In conclusion, convergence occurs either de jure or de facto in respect of protection requirements and excluded subject matter, but in the areas of ownership, dealings, rights, infringement, exceptions and exhaustion, the two intellectual property rights diverge quite a bit so that this represents a case of asymmetric convergence – the more restrictive right will prevail.

[89] And in fact the convergence in respect of these exceptions is not perfect as noted by Passa, 'Les divergences dans la définition de l'acte de contrefaçon' (n 85) 516: 'The exception of article L513-6 IPC for acts accomplished privately and to non-commercial ends is drafted in broader terms than the exception for private copying in copyright law so that an act which is lawful within Book V can however be unlawful under copyright law. Concerning the exception for acts of reproduction for illustration of teaching in design law it seems delicate to articulate with the rules of copyright. On the one hand, these rules authorise only short citations to very specific ends, whilst article L513-6 speaks more broadly of reproduction for illustration purposes without any other precision'.

[90] On this see also Passa, *Traité de droit de la propriété industrielle* (n 5) vol I, 1119.

[91] Vivant and Bruguière, *Droit d'auteur* (n 5) 334, para 494; Caron, *Droit d'auteur et droits voisins* (n 7) 256, para 321.

[92] C Le Stanc, 'Interferences entre droit d'auteur et droit des brevets quant à la protection du logiciel: approche Française' in S Verma and R Mittal (eds), *IP Rights: A Global Vision, ATRIP Papers 2002–03* (New Delhi, Indian Law Institute, 2004) 162, 169–70.

[93] Example given by Pollaud-Dulian, *Le droit d'auteur* (n 5) 476, para 730 *et seq* and cases cited.

[94] Vivant and Bruguière, *Droit d'auteur* (n 5) 335, para 495; Caron, *Droit d'auteur et droits voisins* (n 7) 255, para 320; 467, para 594, thinks that the right of reutilisation of the database maker is some sort of right of destination.

[95] See eg *Lucky Luke*, Cass civ I, 27 November 2001, Bull civ, I, no 296, 187 (on the basis of the destination right, the use of comic books as vouchers for gasoline was not allowed).

[96] Vivant and Bruguière, *Droit d'auteur* (n 5) 334, para 494.

[97] Ibid 335, para 495.

[98] Ibid 334, para 494.

B Negative Overlap

(i) Copyright Protection Unavailable

As discussed in chapter three, this situation will be rare.

(ii) Design Protection Unavailable

As also mentioned in chapter three, this situation will happen more frequently as designs may not be novel or have the required individual character. However, designs purely dictated by function will not be able to obtain copyright protection because of the theory of the multiplicity of shapes. Another way copyright can fill the gap is when a claimant is unable to win his or her infringement case on design law because the design was not published before defendant's use. If the subject matter also attracts copyright, the claimant wins on that basis.[99] This shows that in France, copyright law in fact absorbs in large part design law. The only two advantages of design law over copyright are the monopoly right it gives (no need to prove copying in an infringement action), and fewer and narrower exceptions.

Finally, it must be noted that there is no French unregistered design right.

C *A Posteriori* Overlap

There is here no difference with what has been said in chapter three, as the rules in France are the same as at EU level.[100] Copyright therefore can prolong a national or Community registered design right (CRDR), as well as a Community unregistered design right (CUDR), or rather, will survive the expiry of the design right (as generally both rights will be cumulated from day one because copyright arises without formality from the moment of creation). Design law cannot prolong a copyright, as by definition a work which has fallen into the public domain cannot be then registered or protected (if it is a CUDR) as a design, since it will not be new.[101]

[99] See for an example *Free and others v Magaprice*, CA Paris, 4th ch, 11 June 2003(2005) 6 *Gazette du Palais* (6 January) 24 (military trousers model).

[100] Compare with the United Kingdom where copyright protection can be shortened in some cases. See chapter 5, section II.C.

[101] Gautier, *Propriété littéraire et artistique*, 6th edn (n 5) 466. Passa, *Traité de droit de la propriété industrielle* (n 5) vol I, 921–22, para 689, also notes that the new conception of novelty excludes that a registration can be validly made at the expiry of the duration of copyright which has benefited a design that has been divulged, whereas such a conjunction of duration of protection was not formally prohibited by the previous statute. In 1999, the Supreme Court held that a work fallen into the public domain could not be validly registered as a design by the copyright holder. See Cass com, 19 October 1999 [2000] PIBD no. 690, III, 48; (2000) *Revue Trimestrielle de Droit Commercial* 85, comment Azéma and Galloux; (2000) *Communication Commerce Electronique* Comm 3, comment C Caron. The solution, which was surely questionable under the old law because of the declarative character of the right to the registration, seems appropriate today because of the 'absolute' novelty requirement at the date of the registration.

D Literature

Some commentators think that the cumulation of copyright and design is overprotective and propose to get rid of design right altogether.[102] Cumulation became unnecessary with the law of 1957, so already at that point French law could have done away with it and, a fortiori, the European Union could have just rejected the protection by design instead of harmonising it.[103] Other commentators question the usefulness of design law since copyright grants a longer and more efficient protection.[104] However, other commentators think that the European harmonisation has further distanced design right from copyright and predict that in future the overlap will be very theoretical.[105] This seems to be the case in France, at least as to infringement and exceptions.[106] Nevertheless, this does not prevent the overlap since the subject matter and protection requirements still converge quite closely. Only future French and European case law will confirm or deny this.

In the meantime, Gautier has proposed an interpretation of article L513-2 to make copyright prevail over design right in case of conflicts. Indeed, article L513-2 can mean that when there is a cumulation between copyright and designs, it must be without prejudice to the rights under Books I and III, namely copyright and general provisions applying to copyright and neighbouring rights. This should allow copyright to prevail when there is a doubt, rather than hold that Book V is an exception to principles and an autonomous sector.[107] Nevertheless, this would not solve one important problem created by the botched harmonisation of designs. As Passa notes, when a Community design right expires, copyright law will still protect the creation in many Member States but not all, because some require a high threshold of originality.[108] Therefore, the right-holder in a Member State where the creation is still protected can prevent importation into that country of the products lawfully made by a third party in another Member State where protection no longer exists.[109] Furthermore, third parties cannot easily know where the creation previously covered by the design right can be freely exploited.[110] Passa concludes that 'these obstacles to the application of provisions of the Regulation result inevitably from the consecration by EU law of the principle of cumulation of protections'.[111]

[102] Gautier, *Propriété littéraire et artistique*, 6th edn (n 5) 128, para 100.

[103] Ibid.

[104] Bernault, 'La protection des formes fonctionnelles par le droit de la propriété intellectuelle' (n 42) 962. Azéma and Galloux, *Droit de la propriété industrielle* (n 5) 638, also note that generally, copyright seems more advantageous than design right.

[105] Portron, 'Table ronde' (n 61); Azéma and Galloux, *Droit de la propriété industrielle* (n 5) 636–38.

[106] Azéma and Galloux, *Droit de la propriété industrielle* (n 5) 636–38, also note that, as examined above, several categories of creations that can be protected by copyright are today expressly excluded from protection by design right: the appearance generated by computer programs, creations contrary to public policy and morality, divulged creations, hidden aspects of a complex product.

[107] Gautier, *Propriété littéraire et artistique*, 6th edn (n 5) 129, para 101.

[108] Passa, *Traité de droit de la propriété industrielle* (n 5) vol I, 1118–19. This is unless the *Infopaq* ruling (Case C-5/08 *Infopaq International AS v Dankse Dagblades Forening* [2009] ECR I-6569) has solved this problem, which is far from certain because of Design Regulation, art 96(2). See chapter 3, section II.B(i).

[109] This is unless the *Peek and Cloppenburg* ruling can be extended to cover this situation. See Case C-456/06 *Peek and Cloppenburg v Cassina* [2008] ECR I-2731.

[110] Passa, *Traité de droit de la propriété industrielle* (n 5) vol I, 1119.

[111] Ibid.

III COPYRIGHT AND TRADEMARKS

A Simultaneous Overlap

(i) Subject Matter

The French Intellectual Property Code is more specific than European trademark law as it lists examples of signs which can be protected as a trademark and similarly gives a long non-exhaustive list of works which can be protected by copyright (see articles L111-1, L112-1 and L112-2, at IIA(i)). Article 711-1 provides that:

> A trademark or service mark is a sign capable of graphic representation which serves to distinguish the goods or services of a natural or legal person. The following, in particular, may constitute such a sign:
>
> (a) denominations in all forms, such as: words, combinations of words, surnames and geographical names, pseudonyms, letters, numerals, abbreviations;
> (b) audible signs such as: sounds, musical phrases;
> (c) figurative signs such as: devices, labels, seals, selvedges, reliefs, holograms, logos, synthesized images; shapes, particularly those of a product or its packaging, or those that identify a service; arrangements, combinations or shades of colour.

French courts have recognised copyright protection for single words.[112] In any event, the *Infopaq* decision has now ruled this out completely for all Member States.[113] On the other hand, French law specifically provides that titles can be protected by copyright law. Article L112-4 states that:

> The title of a work of the mind shall be protected in the same way as the work itself where it is original in character. Such title may not be used, even if the work is no longer protected under articles L123-1 to L123-3, to distinguish a work of the same kind if such use is liable to create confusion.

There is therefore a first possible overlap between copyright and trademark on titles. Until recently, the majority of the commentators and courts seemed to be in agreement that the protection by copyright should only be granted exceptionally to titles because they are necessarily brief.[114] However, in 2006, the Court of Cassation twice clearly affirmed this overlap in one case for a very short title (two words) and in the other case for a single word itself.[115]

[112] S Thierry, 'La protection des marques verbales par le droit d'auteur', in *Droits de Propriété Intellectuelle, Liber Amicorum Georges Bonet* (Litec, Paris 2010), 515–16 and decisions cited; Caron, *Droit d'auteur et droits voisins* (n 7) 100–1 says that single words can be protected if they are original but adds that protection should only be granted parsimoniously in order not to sacrifice the principle of freedom of commerce and industry; JM Bruguière, 'Du droit des marques dans le droit d'auteur', in *Droits de Propriété Intellectuelle, Liber Amicorum Georges Bonet* (Litec, Paris 2010), 90 (also recommending at 99 that titles, slogans and names should be protected by trademark law or unfair competition law not copyright).

[113] Case C-5/08 *Infopaq International AS v Dankse Dagblades Forening* [2009] ECR I-6569, para 45.

[114] J Passa, 'Titres et slogans: entre marque et droit d'auteur' (2005) 14 *Propriétés Intellectuelles* 31, 32. However, for Pollaud-Dulian, *Le droit d'auteur* (n 5) 151, even banal titles can be protected under the article so long as they are not totally banal (eg 'Histoire de France').

[115] *Sté Colmax v Ste Archange International*, Cass 1st civ, 4 April 2006, Jurisdata no 2006-033037, comment C Caron, 'L'empilement des propriétés intellectuelles: le droit d'auteur ne chasse pas la marque' (2006) 6

French courts also protect slogans by copyright in addition to trademark law. As early as 1963, the Paris Court of Appeal held that an advertising slogan can, like any other intellectual creation, benefit from the protection of copyright law but only if there is some originality.[116] Later, some courts have been rather generous and protected slogans which were barely original[117] or applied the trademark protection criteria to find a slogan original and thus protected by copyright,[118] although some other courts are stricter in their application of the copyright criteria.[119] It seems that the protection afforded by article L112-4 is not based on copyright but on unfair competition law, and therefore that an action in unfair competition can be launched if the work identified by the title is protected but also when it is no longer protected.[120] Finally, some commentators also think that it will be more difficult to register a trademark for a single work than for a periodical, series or collection. Courts have also excluded trademark protection of the title because a work which does not belong to a collection is not a product and, thus, its title cannot be protected as a mark.[121] In this case, through article L112-4, copyright can fill the gap.

As we have seen in chapter three on Europe, a third overlap can occur with two- and three-dimensional artistic works. French courts have admitted cumulation between

Communication Commerce Electronique (June) Comm 88 (use of claimant's book title 'Angélique' by defendant as title for its film); Cass com, 4 July 2006, no 03-13.728, [2006] PIBD no 838, III, 645, comment JP Doat, 'La marque, création objet de droit d'auteur: portée et limites de l'application' (2007) 23 *Revue Lamy Droit de l'Immatériel* 6; (2006) 31–35 JCP G IV, no 2715 (the term used was 'High Score').

[116] CA Paris, 30 April 1963 [1963] JCP II, 13243, cited by Passa, 'Titres et slogans' (n 114) 39. Caron, *Droit d'auteur et droits voisins* (n 7) 100–1, also thinks that slogans can be protected by copyright as long as they are original.

[117] Passa, 'Titres et slogans' (n 114) 39, reports that some decisions held the slogan original only because its wording was not in itself perfectly usual, or that the originality of the slogan could be found in the idea that it expresses, implying that the originality was in the idea not the expression. See also J Klink, 'Titles in Europe: Trade Names, Copyright Works or Title Marks' (2004) *European Intellectual Property Review* 291, 295, discussing titles and criticising this trend as leading to overprotection.

[118] Passa, 'Titres et slogans' (n 114) 39–40. See also Lucas and Lucas, *Traité de la propriété littéraire et artistique*, 3rd edn (n 5) 92n 254, citing CA Versailles, 12th ch, 11 January 2001 [2001] JCP E 496; (2001) *Communication Commerce Electronique* Comm 97, 2, comment C Caron. See also A Bertrand, *Le droit d'auteur et les droits voisins*, 2nd edn (Paris, Dalloz, 1999) 172 ; JM Bruguière, 'Du droit des marques dans le droit d'auteur', in *Droits de Propriété Intellectuelle, Liber Amicorum Georges Bonet* (Litec, Paris 2010), 92.

[119] Passa, 'Titres et slogans' (n 114) 41.

[120] Caron, *Droit d'auteur et droits voisins* (n 7) 103, para 133. See also Lucas and Lucas, *Traité de la propriété littéraire et artistique*, 3rd edn (n 5) para 108 and Pollaud-Dulian, *Le droit d'auteur* (n 5) 150–51, para 205, who also think that this article does not provide an infringement action but instead an unfair competition action, even though it does not refer to it explicitly.

[121] Passa, 'Titres et slogans' (n 114) 37–38. Ibid 36: he explains that 'it is certain in fact that the mark can be registered for any product whatever its nature. The only reserve is that the designated object consists in a product or service. Now, if the newspaper is in itself a work, it is also a product. It is however not a product because it is a work: it is the two together on different levels. One needs here to distinguish the content – intellectual – of the newspaper, which constitutes the work, and the 'containing' – the material support (medium) – which constitutes a product, and editorial product, whose successive copies come from the same origin'. He also summarises what the Paris Court of Appeal said: 'it doesn't matter that the work is embodied in a material object proposed to the public (the book), susceptible to be qualified as a product, so long as the title does not identify this product, but the work, with which it is un-dissociable or with which it is an integral part, independently of its marketing in the form of a book'. On this see also Pollaud-Dulian, *Le droit d'auteur* (n 5) 154–55, para 210; trademark law only covers the title as a sign used to distinguish products (art L711-1) and not to identify a particular work, and a work is not a product. He cites as an example CA Paris, 2 October 1996 (1997) *Revue Internationale du Droit d'Auteur* (April) 280 ; (1997) *Dalloz*, Som com 93, comment Colombet; S Thierry, 'La protection des marques verbales par le droit d'auteur', in *Droits de prorpiété intellectuelle, Liber Amicorum Georges Bonet* (Litec, Paris 2010), 517.

copyright and trademark law for products' labels[122], logos,[123] and names and likenesses of fictitious characters.[124] A famous such example is Michelin's Bibendum.[125] A court has even recognised trademark rights in the shape of a building.[126] However, some commentators think that trademark law should not be used to systematically protect buildings because this would be a diversion of trademark protection.[127] In fact, the INPI refuses to register fashion products and furniture as marks because of the substantial character or value of the shape so that only design or copyright can protect those.[128] Finally, there can also be an overlap between musical works and music marks, but not sounds as they are not protectable by copyright. However, in France, because the mark has to fit in a square of 8cm by 8cm for the purposes of registration, only five staves of music will be able to be protected as a trademark.[129]

(ii) Protection Requirements

The protection requirements for trademarks are dictated by EU law. As examined above at IIA(ii), originality means that the author must have expressed his or her personal stamp in the work. As discussed in chapter three, it will not be rare that there is an overlap between the two rights at this level.

(iii) Excluded Subject Matter

As far as trademarks are concerned, EU law dictates excluded subject matter (see article L711-2–711-4) and reference is made to section III.B of chapter three. As in all EU Member States, ideas are not protectable by copyright. In France, unfair competition law not trademark law protects unregistered trademarks (see below section IX).

(iv) Ownership and Dealings

According to article L711-1, both natural and legal persons can acquire a trademark right. Article L712-1 provides that:

> Ownership of a mark shall be acquired by registration. A mark may be acquired under joint ownership.

Therefore, the owner of the mark is the person who registered it. There is no specific regime of co-ownership as in patent law, however. Therefore, it is the common regime that applies, ie Civil Code, article 1873-1 *et seq.*[130] In copyright law, only a natural person can be the author *ab initio* and collaborative works are the joint property of its authors (IPC, article L113-3).

[122] For a rather old decision, see CA Paris, 7 April 1843, cited by Benabou, 'Rapport national, France' (n 23) 12.
[123] For a logo, see Cass com, 4 July 2006, Jurisdata no 2006-034458, cited by Caron, *Droit d'auteur et droits voisins* (n 7) 19, para 23.
[124] Benabou, 'Rapport national, France' (n 23) 11.
[125] CA Riom, 15 September 1994 (1995) *Dalloz*, Juris 429, comment B Edelman.
[126] Com 11 January 2000, Chron Azéma, Galloux (2000) *Revue Trimestrielle de Droit Commercial* no 2, 352–61.
[127] Benabou, 'Rapport national, France' (n 23) 12.
[128] Ibid.
[129] Ibid 13.
[130] Azéma and Galloux, *Droit de la propriété industrielle* (n 5) 816.

Article L714-1 provides that:

> The rights under a mark may be transferred in whole or in part, independently of the company that exploits them or has them exploited. Assignment, even where in part, may not comprise territorial limitation. The rights under a mark may be wholly or partially licensed on an exclusive or non-exclusive basis or pledged. A non-exclusive licence grant may result from an unwritten agreement concerning its use.

The IPC also requires that transfers be recorded in writing, otherwise they are null (article L714-1 *in fine*). As seen above, in copyright law, transfers always need to precisely describe the uses, media, duration and geographical scope envisaged (article L131-3). In addition, it is generally admitted that the distinction between transfers and licences which exists in industrial property law does not hold in copyright law, despite the terminology used.[131] Any transfer or modification of the rights attached to the registered trademark must be recorded in the national register of trademarks in order to be enforceable against third parties (article L714-7). This requirement does not exist in copyright law. The more restrictive regime will thus command the overlap, for certain aspects it will be copyright (description) and for others, trademark law (registration of transfers, geographical scope).

(*v*) *Rights and Infringement*

The provisions on rights and infringement (article L713-1–713-6) mimic those of the Trademark Directive 2008/95/EC, except for article L713-5 which is more generous than the corresponding article 5(2) of the Directive. It provides that:

> Any person who uses a mark enjoying repute for goods or services that are not similar to those designated in the registration shall be liable under civil law if such use is likely to cause a prejudice to the owner of the mark or if such use constitutes unjustified exploitation of the mark.

It is more generous because it potentially covers more than article 5(2) of the Directive (any type of prejudice to the mark will do) and also because the action seems to be based on civil liability, not the property right conferred by the Intellectual Property Code.[132] The problem with article L713-5 is that it does not cover similar signs but only identical signs. However, the Court of Cassation in the *Olymprix* case held that when a sign is only imitated, ie not copied identically, the protection is that of civil liability.[133] The economic right of the copyright owner is the right of exploitation which comprises the right of representation and the right of reproduction (see at II.A above). As stated in chapter three on Europe, in trademark law, infringement can arise without copying so the right is stronger than copyright in this respect.

As to infringement, trademark law is less protective than copyright as it applies only within the limit of the principle of speciality. A decision of the Court of Cassation involving the famous comic book characters Obélix and Astérix illustrates this.[134] Despite their fame, trademark law did not give them a right to a protection extending to all

[131] Benabou, 'Rapport national, France' (n 23) 19.

[132] Bertrand, *Le droit Français de la concurrence déloyale* (n 2) 56, para 2.53, thinks that art L713-5 embodies the theory of parasitic acts, and that to act on the basis of it, one must launch an unfair competition action.

[133] Cass, 30 October 2006 (2007) *Propriétés Intellectuelles* 10, cited by Schmidt-Szalewski and Pierre, *Droit de la propriété industrielle* (n 5) para 594.

[134] Cass com, 7 March 1995, cited by Benabou, 'Rapport national, France' (n 23) 12.

classes of products and services. Also, by contrast with copyright law, trademark protection does not normally extend to the character if it is depicted in attitudes different from that under which it has been registered.[135] As a result, if copyright and trademark protect the same sign, copyright will override the limitations of trademark law (principle of speciality, use in the course of trade and requirement of confusion in some cases) and trademark law will override the limitations of copyright law (requirement of copying). The owner of the rights therefore gets the best of both worlds. This is well illustrated by the following case. The trademark 'L'avenir au présent' was registered for lighting and heating installations, and the like.[136] There was no trademark infringement because of the principle of speciality (the third party used 'L'avenir au présent' for totally different products, namely painter's knives) but the court held that even if the slogan was composed of two words of the current vocabulary, the combination and the non-necessary relationship between them showed the stamp of the personality of the author and therefore found it was original. So even if there was no trademark infringement, there was infringement of copyright. The court added in relation to the copyright infringement that the defendant could complain that consumers could be misled as to the origin of products or the relationships that exist between the parties. The slogan was also depreciated by the banalisation resulting from the abusive use by the third party. Amazingly, the court used trademark law reasoning to establish copyright infringement.

(vi) Exceptions Including Exhaustion Principle

As has been seen in chapter three, and this is not different in French law, there are no exceptions to the rights in trademark law. There are free uses, however: when the mark is used outside the course of trade, for dissimilar goods or services if the mark is not famous or for similar goods or services as long as there is no risk of confusion. French copyright law has a long list of exceptions, as has been seen at II.A above. For the most part, there is convergence between copyright and trademark law as far as the exceptions are concerned. This is because most copyright exceptions are allowed when the use is private or non-commercial. Another interesting convergence is noted by Pollaud-Dullian.[137] The Supreme Court has admitted that the composer of the music of films adapted for a series of novels, who exploited this music separately through phonograms, could freely use the title of the novel in its own works or on the jacket of the phonograms. It held that the authors of the original literary work could not prevent him from using the titles nor require from him remuneration for this exploitation as it was necessary. This idea of necessary relation or reference conjures up the trademark law exception at article L713-6, allowing the use of the mark by someone else than the trademark owner as a reference necessary to indicate the destination of a product or service.

However, there are some uses allowed by copyright law which can involve use of the trademark in the course of trade. These are: short citations for criticism, scientific, pedagogic information aims (article L122-5(3)(a)), press reviews (article L122-5(3)(b) and (9)) and parody, caricature and pastiche (article L122-5(4)). So a problem arises when one

[135] Ibid 12, citing CA Chambéry, 10 December 1951 ('Professor Nimbus', in a different position and without mention of the name).

[136] CA Paris, 26 January 1989 [1989] PIBD no 457, III, 330, cited by Doat, 'La marque, création objet de droit d'auteur' (n 115).

[137] Pollaud-Dulian, *Le droit d'auteur* (n 5) 775, para 1312.

regime allows the use (copyright) and the other does not (trademark). A typical example is the parody exception which exists in copyright law but not in trademark law. Several courts have had to decide which regime prevails. Most of the time, courts have held that the most restrictive regime (trademark law) prevails; in other words, they do not admit a parody exception in trademark law.[138] For instance, the character 'Titi Fricoteur' was not held to infringe the copyright in 'Bibi Fricotin', but held to infringe the trademark right in the same.[139] Whilst courts generally do not accept a parody exception in trademark law, sometimes they have done so. In the *Bibendum* case,[140] where the Michelin 'mascot' was represented bearded, carrying a club and wearing an animal skin, the court held that despite his economic and moral rights, the owner and author of the copyright cannot prohibit parody. There was no copyright infringement for that reason nor any trademark infringement, because there was no prejudice. According to the court, the trade union's parody was not denigrating the mark but in fact honoured it; it presented an ironic but not demeaning image of it.

In 2000, the full assembly of the Supreme Court had to decide a case concerning some words uttered during a programme of *Les Guignols de l'info*, a satirical French television show criticising political figures as well as prominent French companies. The court held that the words used in this episode of the show, which criticised Peugeot vehicles, could not be dissociated from the caricature made of Peugeot's President so that these words were properly classed as free speech and could not create any confusion between reality and the satirical work.[141] Certain commentators have seen in this case an embryonic recognition of a parody exception in trademark law.[142] Later decisions seem to confirm this prediction, at least implicitly. In the case parodying the 'ESSO' trademark with the symbol 'E$$O', use of the trademark was held not to infringe copyright (the parody exception was applicable) but was not permitted under trademark law as it could damage the trademark's reputation.[143] But in another case, the same court held there was no infringement when the claimant's logo was used with skull-and-crossbones.[144] The reasons were, inter alia, that:

> the parody was in relation to the trademark owner's industrial nuclear activities and not in relation to the services in class 38 for which it was registered; and that . . . given the notoriety of Greenpeace, no one seeing the logo on its website would believe that the trademark owner had anything to do with the information sitting next to it on the same page.[145]

[138] Benabou, Rapport national, France' (n 23) 18; Caron, *Droit d'auteur et droits voisins* (n 7) 299, citing TGI Paris, 30 January 2004 (2004) *Communication Commerce Electronique* Comm 39, comment Caron (trademark law does not recognise the exception of parody, therefore one cannot export this copyright concept into trademark law as it is foreign to trademark law).

[139] CA Paris, 12 July 1993, cited by Benabou, 'Rapport national, France' (n 23) 12.

[140] *Synd. Dptel CFDT des Industries Chimiques du Puy de Dome v Cie générale des Ets Michelin et Cie*, CA Riom, 1st ch civ, 15 September 1994, Jurisdata no 049661 [1995] JCP G, no 48, no 2598, 324 ; (1995) *Dalloz*, Juris 429, comment B Edelman.

[141] Cass, 12 July 2000 [2000] JCP II, 10439, note A Lepage, cited by Benabou, 'Rapport national, France' (n 23) 18–19. This case was, however, decided under art 1382 of the Civil Code (civil liability) and not trademark law.

[142] See B Edelman, 'Vers une reconnaissance de la parodie de marque' (2001) *Dalloz* 259, comment AP, 12 July 2000.

[143] *Esso SA Francaise v S Ossetian Greenpeace France and Société Internet.fr*, CA Paris [2003] ETMR 867.

[144] *Société des Participations du Commissariat à l'Energie Atomique v Greenpeace France and others* (2 August 2002, unreported, TGI) affirmed by CA Paris [2003] ETMR 870.

[145] For a discussion, see J Phillips, *Trade Mark Law: A Practical Anatomy* (Oxford, Oxford University Press, 2003) 239, para 8.68.

Perhaps the different result compared to the *Esso* decision comes from these two factors: use for different services/goods and a less famous mark. In many cases, however, it will be possible to mock a mark because often the imitation will not be in the course of trade and will therefore escape the control of the trademark owner.[146]

Thus, in France, there seems to be a convergence between copyright and trademark laws at least as regards the parody, caricature and pastiche exception, although it rests on shaky grounds. It cannot, however, be said that there is a full convergence as the other exceptions cited above involving use in the course of trade have not been tested in the courts.

As far as exhaustion is concerned, article L713-4 reproduces Trademark Directive, article 7, and as we saw at IIA above, the exhaustion principle also applies in copyright law, although with the problem caused by the right of destination (see also at II.B above).

B Negative Overlap

(i) Copyright Protection Unavailable

Copyright protection is rarely available for *de minimis* works such as words or short titles. In addition, *Infopaq* now prevents the protection of single words by copyright law. But trademark protection is well suited for such short signs.

(ii) Trademark Protection Unavailable

In France, claimants have been successful in obtaining copyright protection where trademark protection failed. The Court of First Instance of Paris held that 'soie et moi' ('silk and me') was an invalid trademark for clothing but considered the term original and thus protected by copyright law. The competitor who obtained the cancellation of the mark nevertheless could not use the terms because they were protected by copyright.[147] A commentator has added that, paradoxically, slogans could be more easily protected by copyright than by trademark law, even if trademark law, because of the principle of speciality, is not an absolute right.[148] As with the simultaneous overlap, copyright can easily fill the gaps left by trademark law.

C *A Posteriori* Overlap

French law has a rule for one particular aspect: article L122-4 provides that even if the copyright in the title has expired, if the use by another person of the title for a work of the same kind creates confusion with the (once copyright protected) work to which it relates, it will be an infringement. This rule prevents the *a posteriori* overlap by another person than the copyright holder but allows the overlap by the copyright holder. The moral right of integrity, which in France is perpetual, could be used to the same effect but

[146] Caron, *Droit d'auteur et aroits voisins* (n 7) 299.
[147] Doat, 'La marque, création objet de droit d'auteur' (n 115), citing TGI Paris, 10 April 1986.
[148] Passa, 'Titres et slogans' (n 114) 44.

for all kinds of works and even if there is no similarity. The right could be invoked to prevent the trademark registration of any work by other persons than by its author.[149] The latter rule therefore partially prevents the overlap *a posteriori*. Indeed, it is only a partial prohibition because, as in the situation of article L122-4, it does not prevent the owner of the copyright work prolonging the 'life' of the right on his or her work by registering the latter as a trademark him- or herself. Courts are divided on the issue whether registration of a work as a trademark should be allowed when the copyright on the said work has expired. Some allow it,[150] some don't.[151] Likewise, commentators are divided on the issue. Some think there is a pacific coexistence between the two rights. Trademark law can prolong copyright: since their aims are different, there are no interferences between the two rights.[152] Others think the contrary: because in their opinion there is a hierarchy of rights, trademark law cannot be used to perpetually prolong an exclusive right on a literary or artistic creation which has fallen into the public domain.[153] This latter argument has its problems, as such hierarchy would violate international law. The merits of these arguments will be discussed in the final chapter.

Courts and literature have not addressed the converse situation, namely where copyright is used to protect a mark which has become generic or otherwise lost its protection, eg by non-use, but nothing in French law prevents it.

D Literature

Some commentators have tried to find solutions when there is a clash of regimes in case of simultaneous overlaps. A criterion of intention, main purpose or function has been proposed. According to such criterion, if the work has been created to serve as a trademark (thus serve a commercial interest not an artistic one) from day one, the trademark regime would have priority over the copyright one.[154] The vast majority of commentators

[149] Benabou, 'Rapport national, France' (n 23) 13, mentions that some commentators hold this opinion.

[150] See Cass, 13 January 1904 [1904] Ann Prop Ind 26, cited by Gautier, *Propriété littéraire et artistique*, 6th edn (n 5) 467: a drawing or photograph can in general, even if they have fallen into the public domain as artistic works, constitute a trademark, albeit according to an old obiter dictum; TGI Paris, 20 March 1975 [1976] Ann Prop Ind 55; CA Paris, 6 July 1989 [1990] PIBD, III, 112, cited by Benabou, 'Rapport national, France' (n 23) 13. However, ibid 8, reports that judges are generally against using trademarks to perpetuate copyright. However, she does not cite decisions for the overlap copyright/trademark but only for the overlap copyright/patent on this.

[151] See Caron, 'L'empilement des propriétés intellectuelles' (n 115) 88, noting that some courts, including the Court of Cassation, have showed some hostility to the reappropriation by trademark law of the public domain of copyright, and citing CA Besancon, 5 June 1970 [1972] Ann Prop Ind 20, comment Dusolier, also cited by Gautier, *Propriété littéraire et artistique*, 6th edn (n 5) para 409 (refusing the protection of an architectural work as a trademark on the basis that one should not be able to appropriate for an unlimited time a shape which belongs to the public domain or has a likelihood to fall into it); *SARL J. Pironin v SA Thiers Virole*, Cass com, 19 October 1999, (2000) *Communication Commerce Electronique* Comm 3; CA Paris, 4th ch, 25 June 1997 (1998) 1 *Gazette du Palais* Somm 63 ('one cannot, because it diverts trademark rights from their aim, protect as a trademark the arrangement and interior decoration of a shop, which cannot be protected by copyright'), cited by Bertrand, *Droit des marques* (n 5) 20, para 1.141.

[152] Benabou, 'Rapport national, France' (n 23) 1; PY Gautier, *Propriété Littéraire et Artistique*, 5th edn (Paris, Presses Universitaires de France, 2004) para 226, who says that there should be proof of fraud to contest the registration of the work as a mark in such circumstances cited by Caron, 'L'empilement des propriétés intellectuelles' (n 115).

[153] Bertrand, *Droit des marques* (n 5) vol 41, para 2.512(a)).

[154] Doat, 'La marque, création objet de droit d'auteur' (n 115) 8–9, states that the trademark regime has priority and that copyright law can remedy a lack or punish a breach which escapes trademark law.

are also against the protection of slogans and titles by copyright law because it seriously mistreats the copyright concepts and threatens copyright.[155] For them, it is even more reprehensible as it results in absolute and thus excessive protection.[156] A quasi-unanimous literature has criticised this trend, insisting that trademark law is better suited for slogans so that copyright should not come into play.[157] This doctrinal criticism meets the position of the nineteenth century's expert Pouillet, who said that a title by itself is not a work of the mind and can never be protected by copyright, and envisaged a protection of titles essentially against the risk of confusion through unfair competition law.[158] Indeed, slogans are so brief that it is very difficult to find them to be original so that copyright is not adapted to protect slogans.[159] The same criticism is made about decisions relating to titles.[160] If their originality results from the relationship with the content of the work, it is not right as copyright protects originality without any relationship. If originality depends on the content of the work, trademark law is the appropriate protection not copyright. In conclusion, for many French authors, copyright can also protect slogans and titles but this should be the exception rather than the rule, trademark law being the natural protection of such items.[161]

IV. TRADEMARKS AND DESIGNS

Both trademark and design rights are heavily harmonised by EU law. Therefore, what has been said in chapter three applies in France too. Only ownership and dealings are not, or very partially, harmonised by the Trademark and Design Directives and Regulations. This section will therefore concentrate on the differences between EU and French law. This means that only the simultaneous overlap will be discussed. French courts have expressly recognised cumulation between the two rights,[162] but strangely, decisions on this overlap seem rather rare.

As has been seen in sections II and III, ownership rules in trademark and design law are minimal. They are similar in the sense that the applicant is presumed to be the owner of the right. The trademark provisions mention the possibility of joint ownership whilst the design ones do not, but one can imagine that the common property law regime applies. The trademark regime of dealings is more elaborate than that of designs, so

[155] Passa, 'Titres et Slogans' (n 114) 34, 40.

[156] Ibid 40, adding that it is difficult to accept that because the slogan 'A fond la forme' was a work, its use as an element of a legend in a photograph in a magazine dedicated to celebrities was infringing, as the Court of First Instance of Paris decided. He makes the same remark for titles at 35.

[157] Benabou, 'Rapport national, France' (n 23) 11, citing S Durrande, JCl Marques, fasc 7100; Passa, 'Titres et slogans' (n 114) 39–41; Lucas and Lucas, *Traité de la propriété littéraire et artistique*, 3rd edn (n 5) paras 107–8; Pollaud-Dulian, *Le droit d'auteur* (n 5) 147; no. 197; Passa, *Contrefaçon et concurrence déloyale* (n 2) para 324, cited by Pollaud-Dulian, *Le droit d'auteur* (n 5) 155, para 197; Gautier, *Propriété littéraire et artistique* (n 5) 65 ('original book titles and names of characters can be protected by copyright. It is not excluded that they can be registered as trademarks although the public domain risks being misappropriated').

[158] Pollaud-Dulian, *Le droit d'auteur* (n 5) 147, para 197.

[159] Passa, 'Titres et slogans' (n 114) 39–40; Lucas and Lucas, *Traité de la propriété littéraire et artistique*, 3rd edn (n 5) paras 107–8; Pollaud-Dulian, *Le droit d'auteur* (n 5) 147 para 197.

[160] Passa, 'Titres et slogans' (n 114) 33 ('copyright does not aim to ensure the protection of the relation between a sign and the object it designates').

[161] Ibid 35. See also Klink, 'Titles in Europe' (n 117) 301 (also noting that in reality the majority of titles are neither distinctive nor original).

[162] For an example, see CA Paris, 8 April 1998 [1998] PIBD, III, 419, cited by Benabou, 'Rapport national, France' (n 23) 9.

there again the most restrictive regime, here trademark law, will prevail. Therefore, transfers will have to be in writing and territorial limitations will not be possible even if these are allowed in design law. One area where both rights converge is the requirement to record transfers and modifications of rights attached to the trademark and design in order for them to be enforceable against third parties.

Further complications arise from a level overlap, namely between a Community design and a national trademark or Community trademark and a national design, as the rules are also different. In addition, strangely enough, the provisions on ownership and dealings in the Community Trademark Regulation (CTMR) and Design Regulation are not identical. First, the CTMR does not have a provision on ownership, in contrast to Design Regulation, article 14. However, since trademarks are generally registered by the employer or the self-employed person, few conflicts should arise with designs because the rule of article 14 is a default rule in favour of the employer. Community trademarks can be transferred with or without the goods or services attached to them. A similar provision does not exist for designs. Transfers of Community trademarks must be in writing with the signature of the parties (CTMR, article 17) otherwise they are null. A similar requirement does not exist for Community designs. The provisions on licences, however, are more or less identical (compare CTMR, article 22 with Design Regulation, article 32). One main difference is that the grant or transfer of a licence must be entered in the register for Community trademarks but is not mandatory and may be entered at the request of one of the parties for Community designs. Both Regulations provide that so long as the transfer was not entered in the register, the successor in title may not invoke the rights arising from the registration of the Community design or trademark (CTMR, article 17 and Design Regulation, article 28). Again, in case of overlap, the most restrictive regime, generally the CTMR, will prevail.

There is little comment in the literature on this overlap. A commentator notes that regime clashes are inevitably even more frequent if the overlap concerns three rather than two rights. Such overlap often occurs between copyright, trademarks and designs. Whilst copyright has an exception for parody, and one is being slowly recognised by the French courts in the area of trademarks, as the design provisions do not include it, simply asserting one's design would trump the parody. This commentator hopes that courts will extend the parody exception to design right by applying the constitutional value of freedom of expression to it.[163] This would certainly respect the articles relating to exceptions to the three rights in the TRIPs Agreement (Articles 13, 17 and 26(2)).[164]

As to the negative overlap, it is very obvious. As Cohen notes, the registration of a design as a mark can sometimes be very precious. Indeed, to escape condemnation, an alleged infringer under IPC, Books I and V often does not have any alternative apart from discovering prior art to destroy the validity of the design. If such prior art exists, protection by design right and copyright will not be available.[165] But the registration as a mark will be useful. This is because the mark does not have to be new or be original but only distinctive of the products or services. And to establish distinctive character, the existence of a prior design which is similar or identical to the market does not matter. The mark may be valid even if there is prior art.[166]

[163] N Binctin, 'Le cumul d'appropriation: du parfum au *logiciel*' (2006) 12 *Communication Commerce Electronique* (December) no 36, para 10.

[164] Ibid.

[165] Cohen, *Le droit des dessins et modèles* (n 5) 133–34.

[166] Ibid.

As to the *a posteriori* overlap, some commentators think that a trademark should not be able to 'prolong' a design right.[167]

V. TRADEMARKS AND PATENTS

As with the previous overlap (trademarks and designs), this overlap is heavily harmonised at European level. Once again, the discussion in chapter three on Europe also applies in France. Provisions concerning ownership, dealings, rights, infringement and exceptions have for the most part not been harmonised, so these will be discussed. In addition, there has been extensive comment by courts and commentators about the *a posteriori* overlap, which is not clearly forbidden at EU level as a result of the lack of decision on this point in *Philips*, although it could be argued to have been forbidden because of the Advocate-General's Opinion in the same case, which has been endorsed by the Advocate-General in *Lego*.[168]

A Simultaneous Overlap

(i) Ownership and Dealings

The rules concerning ownership in patent and trademark law are to some extent converging, most probably because they are both industrial property rights and also because both are registered rights. Nevertheless some differences subsist. Whilst patent rights go to the inventor and there is a rebuttable presumption that the person applying to register the design or patent is considered the beneficiary of the protection, ownership of a trademark is acquired by registration. The rules on joint ownership in patent law are quite detailed whilst the trademark provisions only say that a mark 'may be acquired under joint ownership'. Since a mark will be registered by a company and therefore the employer or else a person who is self-employed, there should be few clashes with the patent provisions. Nevertheless, there could be a clash if the owner of the patent is the employee not the company. Patent transfers and licences must be in writing (article L613-8(5)). Trademark law is less rigid in some ways (only transfers must be in writing) but more so in others (assignments, even in part, may not be territorially limited) (article L714-1). But both patent and trademark provisions allow transfers and licences in whole or in part, and exclusively or non-exclusively, and with or without the business.[169] Another identical provision is that any transfer or modification of the rights attached to the registered trademark or patent must be recorded, respectively, in the national register of trademarks and the national register of patents in order to be enforceable against third parties (articles L613-19 and L714-7).

[167] Bertrand, *Droit des Marques* (n 5) 20, para 1.141. Azéma and Galloux, *Droit de la propriété industrielle* (n 5) 634, note that for some commentators, protection by trademark is no longer be possible when the shape constitutes the essential value of the product.

[168] On this see chapter 3, section VI.B(i)(c) .

[169] Azéma and Galloux, *Droit de la propriété industrielle* (n 5) 276.

(ii) Rights and Infringement

Neither patent nor trademark provisions require copying so, on this aspect, they converge. In case of overlap, the patent regime will prevail over that of trademark as the patentee's rights are not restricted to use in trade for identical or similar goods or services (with the exception of famous marks).

(iii) Exceptions Including Exhaustion Principle

As has been seen in chapter three, trademark law does not have exceptions but any use which is not in trade for goods which are not identical or similar will be free (except for well-known marks). Patent law, as will be seen below, has exceptions which include uses in trade (eg acts done for experimental purposes, extemporaneous preparation for individual cases in a pharmacy of a medicine in accordance with a medical prescription). Therefore, trademark law will trump these exceptions in case of an overlap. There is, however, convergence as regards the exhaustion principle.

One commentator reports that apart from the prohibition in article L711-2(c), which corresponds to Trademark Directive, article 3(1)(e)(ii), French courts are generally hostile to the protection of a patented product by trademark.[170] There do not seem to be any reported cases dealing with simultaneous overlap in this area, which may suggest that owners do not try to enforce this overlap, and may also be because of its near impossibility due to the EU rules prohibiting almost all the overlap.

As regards the negative overlap, we refer the reader to chapter three.

B *A Posteriori* Overlap

Courts have generally not allowed the *a posteriori* overlap, so that a trademark right cannot 'prolong' an expired patent.[171] As early as 1933, the Court of Appeal of Paris rejected it.[172] Later decisions followed this ruling, culminating with the *Lego* case in the 1990s. The Court of Appeal of Paris held in 1986 that:

> as trademark law is an occupation right conferring, by exception to the principle of freedom of commerce, a monopoly of a duration determined by the only will of the registrant, it would be inadmissible that, by the registration of a functional form, therefore a necessary form, the registrant could prevent competitors from using an object which is in the public domain.[173]

This decision hints at the rationale behind the rejection, which is freedom to compete. In the *Lego* case, the court held that the sign which was the shape itself (a rectangular brick comprising cylindrical protuberances) was not distinctive of the goods in question. In addition, the mark reproduced exactly the patent which had then fallen into the public domain, and its shape was to procure the industrial result which was sought.[174] Nevertheless,

[170] Benabou, 'Rapport national, France' (n 23) 8, 15.

[171] Ibid 15.

[172] CA Paris, 4th ch, 24 April 1933 [1934] Ann Propr Ind 9, note FJ, cited by Bertrand, *Droit des marques* (n 5) 25, para 1.312.

[173] *Cebal v Natrial*, CA Paris 4th ch, 28 October 1986 [1987] PIBD, III, 137 (Banana case).

[174] *Kirby and Lego v Fryd*, TGI Bobigny, 5th ch, 21 January 1992 [1992] PIBD, III, 559, cited by Bertrand, *Droit des marques* (n 5), affirmed by CA Versailles, 7 November 1994, cited by Benabou, 'Rapport national,

one court has held that one cannot prevent the inventor from protecting as a mark the name given by him to a new product (in this case 'Cellophane') and this well beyond the duration of the patent which protected the making of that product.[175] While for one commentator, the 'Cellophane' decision flagrantly violates the elementary principles of both trademark and patent laws,[176] others seem to agree with the 'Cellophane' court's view. Thus, for Galloux, the cancellation or expiration of the patent does not have any consequence on the validity of the mark, and conversely. During the whole period when the patent produces its effects, consumers will have become used to the name of the product, and when the patent expires, even if others can commercialise the patented product they must do it under another name, which is a great advantage for the patentee because of the ingrained habits of consumers.[177] Azéma and Galloux, however, note that this link between the protection by patents and the knowledge of a product under the trademark constitutes an obstacle in particular to the development of generic medicines, which the legislature has tried to avoid by allowing the pharmacist, in the execution of a prescription under the trademark, to substitute a generic medicine without this being infringement under trademark law (article L716-10, introduced by a Law of 1998).[178] The commentator who disagrees with the 'Cellophane' decision believes that there is a hierarchy between intellectual property rights and that trademark law is lower in this hierarchy than patent law.[179] According to him:

> the hierarchy of exclusive rights works equally in the two directions, so the deposit of an invention or a creation as mark is not valid if this deposit registration's sole objective is to create an exclusive right on any design or model which would not be protectable as a design or by copyright.[180]

France' (n 23) 15. See also a similar case a few years later involving Meccano: CA Versailles, 25 November 1998 [1999] Ann Propr Ind 239; CA Versailles, 12 January 2006 [2006] PIDB no 828, III, 295 cited by Y Reboul, 'Dessins ou Modèles et Marques: A la Recherche d'une Coexistence entre Deux Droits de Propriété Intellectuelle', 465, also mentioning at 466 that the French courts have followed the Court of Justice's *Philips v Remington* ruling. See TGI Paris, 13 June 2003 [2003] PIBD no 776, III, 612; CA Paris, 16 February 2005, [2005] PIBD no 808, II, 312.

[175] CA Nancy, 1st ch, 12 June 1963 [1963] Ann Prop Ind 159, cited by Bertrand, *Droit des marques*(n 5) 66, para 3.222.

[176] Ibid 66, para 3.222.

[177] JC Galloux, *Des possibles cumuls de protection par les droits de propriété intellectuelle* (Paris, Litec, Coll IRPI, 2003) vol 23, 86. See in the same vein, Azéma and Galloux, *Droit de la propriété industrielle* (n 5) 745.

[178] Azéma and Galloux, *Droit de la propriété industrielle* (n 5) 745.

[179] Bertrand, *Droit des marques* (n 5) 66, para 3.222.

[180] Ibid 25, para 1.312, citing CA Paris, 4th ch, 27 January 1994. Benabou, 'Rapport national, France' (n 23) 10, 15, has suggested that one *a posteriori* overlap is legitimate. Indeed at first sight, the rule that a trademark cannot prolong a patent that has expired only applies if products previously patented and now registered as a trademark are identical. The French Supreme Court has validated this statement. See CA Paris, 4 July 1989 (1990) *Revue Trimestrielle de Droit Commercial* 577, affirmed by Cass com, 19 November 1991 [1992] PIBD, III, 226 cited by Benabou, ibid. Accordingly, it could be possible to register as a trademark a shape that was once protected by patent to identify products or services which are totally different, eg a Lego brick for a company providing IT services, as the trademark would not prevent the reproduction of Lego bricks after the expiration of the patent (except in this example for IT services, of course). However, this argument is flawed for the following simple reason. If the IT company were to become famous and the sign also (here, the Lego brick which serves to distinguish the services of the IT company) and thus benefit from extended trademark protection by the normal effect of the law, this would reinstate protection for the mark (the Lego brick) as such, as it does not need to be used with similar goods/services.

VI. PATENTS AND DESIGNS

As with the above two overlaps, as patents and designs are substantially harmonised at EU level, what has been said in chapter three therefore applies in France too. Again, only the provisions on ownership, dealings, rights and exceptions remain mainly national, so that a discussion follows regarding the simultaneous overlap only.

A Simultaneous Overlap

(i) Ownership and Dealings

The rules concerning ownership in design and patent law are to some extent converging. Both the design and patent rights go to the 'creator' and there is a rebuttable presumption that the person applying to register the design or patent is considered the beneficiary of the protection. However, in design law, there are no rules on joint ownership or on the employer-employee relationship whereas there are very detailed rules in this respect in patent law (articles L613-29 and L611-7; for details see section VIII.A(i) below). Therefore, the patent regime will prevail over the flexibility of the design regime.[181] Also, there may be a clash if the employer has not obtained the design rights as a contract is needed, in contrast with patent law where the transfer is automatic.

As to dealings, there is no particular formality except that, as for patents, article L513-3 requires that the transfers of design rights be registered in order for them to be enforceable against third parties. The patent regime will again prevail, since for patents, assignments and licences must be in writing and registered (article L613-8–613-9).

(ii) Rights and Infringement

The patent and design rights are very similar: the making, offering, putting on the market, importation and use are prohibited without the consent of the right-holder. Article L513-4 adds exportation, which does not appear in the patent provision (article L613-3). Article L613-4 also prohibits, in some conditions, offering the means to make the invention, whilst this provision does not exist in designs law. The patent regime therefore will trump the more lenient design regime on this point.

Under article L613-2, the scope of patent protection is determined by the claims which can, however, be interpreted by the description and drawings. The theory of equivalents also applies in accordance with the Protocol on the interpretation of EPC Article 69.[182] The test in design law is different as it has to do with visual impression (article L513-5 provides that the scope of protection extends to all designs which do not produce on the informed observer a different global visual impression). This means that even if the patent would not be infringed, the design could be, and vice versa.

[181] Note, however, that the employer ownership rule is the same for Community designs and for French patents (the employer is the owner unless there is a contract to the contrary).

[182] As amended by the Administrative Council of the EPO in its decision of 28 June 2001 [2001] OJ EPO, Special edn, no 4, 55.

(iii) Exceptions Including Exhaustion Principle

In patent law, the following are exempted: (1) acts done privately and for non-commercial purposes; (2) acts done for experimental purposes relating to the subject matter of the patented invention; (3) extemporaneous preparation for individual cases in a pharmacy of a medicine in accordance with a medical prescription or acts concerning the medicine so prepared, studies and trials required in order to obtain a marketing authorisation for a medicine, as well as acts necessary to the realisation and obtaining of the authorisation; and finally (4) objects introduced on French territory whose purpose is to be launched in the extra-atmospheric space (article L613-5). The first two and the fourth exceptions also exist in design law, as they have been modelled on the equivalent provisions. However, the exception for teaching and citation purposes (article L513-6(c)) which applies in design law does not exist in patent law and therefore it will be trumped by the patent regime, and the design regime will trump the fourth patent exception. Finally, there is convergence as to the principle of exhaustion.

VII. COPYRIGHT AND PATENTS

The obvious overlap here, as in European law, is the overlap concerning computer programs. However, there are other possibilities of overlap, including the overlap between patent and copyright for aesthetic creations and presentations of information, as well as the drawings and/or text of a patent application and the invention covered by it. There are some rules organising the overlap between copyright and patents, mainly mimicking those existing in the EPC, namely: aesthetic creations and presentations of information as such cannot be considered as inventions (article L611-10(2), (3)). As has been already noted in chapter three, in short, any cumulation between copyright and patent is forbidden unless the appearance of the work is not exclusively imposed by the technical function of the product. There is also article L511-8, which reproduces Design Directive, article 7, which organises the patent/design interface.[183] Courts have also prohibited cumulation between copyright and patent on a similar basis as Design Directive, article 7 since the nineteenth century and have interpreted this rule extensively.[184] Accordingly, cumulation is prohibited when the invention is patented but also when it is not patented but is nevertheless patentable.[185]

[183] C Le Stanc, 'Logiciels entre droit d'auteur et brevet: implications juridiques et economiques' in G Ghidini and M Genovesi (eds), *Intellectual Property and Market Power, ATRIP Papers 2006–2007* (Buenos Aires, Eudeba, 2008) 295, 301 n 22, citing C Caron, 'La coexistence du droit d'auteur et du droit des brevets sur un même logiciel' in JL Goutal (ed), *Brevetabilité des logiciels, travaux du CUERPI, droit des technologies avancées* (Paris, Hermes Science Publications, 2002) vol 9 (1–2) 183, 184, notes that art L511-8-1 does not apply to software. This is because the provision is limited to shapes which manifest themselves in space and therefore language works are not concerned.

[184] Caron, 'La coexistence du droit d'auteur et du droit des brevets sur un même logiciel'(n 183) 192, citing Cass civ, 30 March 1858 [1858] DP, 1, 100.

[185] Caron, 'La coexistence du droit d'auteur et du droit des brevets sur un même logiciel' (n 183) 192–93, noting however that the case law on this issue has been confused and contradictory.

A Simultaneous Overlap

(i) Subject Matter, Protection Requirements and Excluded Subject Matter

As, by definition, the rules on subject matter, protection requirements and excluded subject matter are the same as at European level, what has been said in chapter three applies here too. So we refer the reader to chapter three, and discuss here only idiosyncrasies existing in French statutory and case law applying the same principles.

Computer programs are protected by copyright under article L112-2(13) and are excluded from patentability only if they are claimed as such under article L611-10. French case law follows that of the European Patent Office. The French Supreme Court held as early as 1975 that it is sufficient to insert a computer program inside a technical 'whole' (set) for it to be patentable.[186] The same solution applies when the claims cover an industrial process: the fact that certain steps use hardware which itself uses a computer program does not prevent patentability.[187] The problem highlighted in chapter three on Europe, namely that it is often difficult to trace the border between copyright and patents because the protectable form/expression is imprecise,[188] has recently been illustrated in a dispute opposing Microsoft and Cuadros, although the question was easily resolved because of the facts of the case. The French Supreme Court had to decide whether functionalities executed by a computer program could be protected by copyright. The Court held that functionalities cannot in themselves benefit from copyright law if they correspond to an idea. In the case, the judicial expert had considered there to be an identity in the results, which only corresponded to the actual objective of the functionality, but he did not consider there to be any similarity of form. There was therefore no copyright infringement.[189] It is unclear whether programming languages can or cannot be protected by copyright as there is no case law on the issue, and the literature is divided.[190]

French law, like the EPC, excludes aesthetic creations as such from patentability (article L611-10(2)). So if the effect sought is only aesthetic, it is not patentable.[191] French courts have interpreted the exclusion broadly, so that the prohibition applies if the shape is patented, but also if it is patentable[192] or simply utilitarian.[193] It suffices therefore that the shape espouses the function for copyright protection to be refused even if this function is not susceptible to be patented. But as both the EPO guidelines and French case law allow,[194] a process which produces an aesthetic creation can include a technical innova-

[186] Cass com, 28 March 1975 [1975] PIBD, 155, III, 149, cited by Schmidt-Szalewski and Pierre, *Droit de la propriété industrielle* (n 5) para 83.

[187] Ibid, citing *Schlumberger*, CA Paris, 15 June 1981 (1982) *Dalloz*, Inf Rap 23, comment Mousseron; (1982) 2 *Gazette du Palais* 368, comment Le Tourneau; TGI Paris, 10 June 2005, [2005] PIBD no 815, III, 541.

[188] See chapter 3, section VII.B(i).

[189] *Microsoft v Cuadros*, Cass 1st civ, 13 December 2005, no 03-21.154, comment P Belloir, 'L'exclusion de la protection des fonctionnalités d'un logiciel par le droit d'auteur' (2006) 14 *Revue Lamy Droit de l'Immateriel* 15.

[190] Contrast Caron, *Droit d'auteur et droits voisins* (n 7) 132 with Gautier, *Propriété littéraire et artistique*, 5th edn (n 152) para 85.

[191] Azéma and Galloux, *Droit de la propriété industrielle* (n 5) 123, citing TGI Paris, 13 May 1992 [1992] PIBD no 532, III, 574; TGI Paris, 19 December 1990 [1991] PIBD no. 501, III, 335.

[192] Caron, *Droit d'auteur et droits voisins* (n 7) 56, citing Cass com, 22 February 1966 [1967] JCP G, II, 1596, comment Gegout.

[193] Ibid 56, citing Cass com, 21 October 1980 (1982) *Revue Trimestrielle de Droit Commercial* 36, comment Chavanne and Burst.

[194] See ch C.IV.2.1 of the guidelines.

tion and be patentable. Likewise, if an object is an aesthetic creation but also presents particularities of technical character or particularities which can render it functional, it can be patentable. Accordingly, a French court has held that a technical process allowing the building of sloping surfaces which also have an aesthetic aspect is patentable because the object of the patent is not purely ornamental.[195] Likewise as regards presentations of information, French judges are of the view that as long as the method of presenting information is distinct from the content of the information, it can perfectly well constitute a patentable technical characteristic.[196]

Finally, at least one French court has held that the text of patent applications is not protectable by copyright.[197] This decision takes into consideration the objective or aim of the work and we suspect would also apply by analogy to any drawings contained in the application. But this absence of protection is purely jurisprudential and openly contradicts article L112-1. In addition, it prevents the exercise of moral rights which could be useful.[198] There are no other decisions on this issue[199] and not much other commentary exists. Le Stanc thinks that even if the drawings and text of the patent are published officially, copyright still subsists (as long, of course, that there is originality). It is not because the text becomes official that copyright loses its force, especially if it is for a use different from that of the patent. According to him, the issue in France is currently obscure but the English *Catnic* decision (which held that copyright does not subsist in such a case[200]) seems to make good sense.[201] Latreille thinks that most patent applications will not be original because the drawings and text describe the invention in a largely standardised form.[202] If there is originality, it is in the described invention not in its description, therefore there will rarely be an overlap.

(ii) Ownership and Dealings

The default rule in copyright law is that the author is the owner (article L111-1). The same rule applies in patent law, but if two persons have invented the same invention independently, only the first one who has filed it is entitled to the right. In addition, the first registrant is not necessarily the inventor and can be a legal person (article L611-6(1), (2)).[203] Therefore, because this latter rule does not exist in copyright law, in respect of the same subject matter (computer programs, aesthetic creations and presentations of information), the copyright and patent rights can be owned by different persons at the outset.

[195] Azéma and Galloux, *Droit de la propriété industrielle* (n 5) 124, citing TGI Paris, 13 May 1992 [1992] PIBD no 532, III, 574.

[196] CA Paris, 31 March 1977, Dossiers Brevets, 1977, V Dec, no 1 and Cass com, 22 May 1979, Dossiers Brevets, 1979, VI, Dec no 1 (the print-out allowing the gathering and expressing of the result of an automatic analysis is patentable because the direct and immediate reading of the data gives an industrial result), cited by Azéma and Galloux, *Droit de la propriété industrielle* (n 5) 123. See also CA Paris, 26 March 1971 [1971] PIBD, III, 279, affirmed by Cass com, 13 February 1973 [1974] JCP, 2, 17626, comment Pérot-Morel.

[197] TGI Paris, 17 January 1968 (1968) 1 *Gazette du Palais* 197; (1968) *Revue Trimestrielle de Droit Commercial* 1037, comment Chavanne, cited by Caron, *Droit d'auteur et droits voisins* n 7) 83, para 109.

[198] Ibid.

[199] To Latreille's knowledge.

[200] See *Catnic Components v Hill and Smith* [1982] RPC 183 (High Court affirmed by Court of Appeal). See chapter 5, section VII.A(i).

[201] Email of 21 May 2009 from C Le Stanc, on file with the authors.

[202] Email of 19 May 2010 from A Latreille, on file with the authors.

[203] Caron, 'La coexistence du droit d'auteur et du droit des brevets sur un même logiciel' (n 183) 199.

A second divergence occurs if the author/inventor is an employee, as the rules are different in copyright and patent law.[204] The problem is posed for all three types of inventions but the example of computer programs is taken to illustrate it below. French law faithfully implemented Software Directive 2009/24/EC, article 2(3) in IPC, article L113-9, so that when a computer program is created in the course of employment, the copyright's economic rights belong to the employer unless there is a contract to the contrary. The same rule applies in patent law if the program was made by a civil servant in the course of his or her duties, and to employed inventors if their role includes an inventive mission (article L611-7(1)).[205] All other patented inventions belong to the employees. However, if the employee invents something not strictly in the course of his or her employment, but in the course of the execution of his or her functions, in the field of the company's activities or through knowledge or use of techniques or means specific to the company or of data given by the company, the employer has the right to acquire the property of the invention and the employee has the right to obtain a just price for it (article L611-7(2)). A parallel provision does not exist in copyright law. This poses the following problem. An employee will have the copyright in a computer program s/he has authored if it was created not strictly in the course of his or her employment. But if it nevertheless was created in the course of the execution of his or her functions, in the field of the company's activities or through knowledge or use of techniques or means specific to the company or of data given by the company, s/he may not own the patent.

Another divergence occurs in the rules on co-ownership. Article L113-3 provides that:

> A work of collaboration shall be the joint property of its authors. The joint authors shall exercise their rights by common accord. In the event of failure to agree, the civil courts shall decide. Where the contribution of each of the joint authors is of a different kind, each may, unless otherwise agreed, separately exploit his own personal contribution without, however, prejudicing the exploitation of the common work.

By contrast, article L613-29 provides that each co-owner of a patent can alone decide to exploit the invention so long as s/he equitably indemnifies the other co-owners who have not worked the invention or granted a licence. If the co-owners do not agree on the sum, it is decided by the Court of First Instance. However, exclusive licences can only be granted with the agreement of all co-owners or else by judicial authorisation. Each co-owner can sue alone for infringement, but if s/he does, s/he must notify the other co-owners. Articles L613-29–613-31 have detailed rules which allow each co-owner to transfer his or her share or abandon it to his or her co-owner's benefit. Co-owners can derogate to the rules set out in articles L613-29–613-31 at any time by agreement (article L613-32). So in sum, each co-owner of a patent can alone decide to exploit the invention as long as s/he indemnifies the others equitably. But the converse is true in copyright law: the co-authors must exercise their rights together unless the judge grants permission to by-pass the resistance of one or more of them.[206]

Yet another divergence concerns formalities for transferring the rights or granting a licence. Such contracts must be in writing if they concern a patent, otherwise they are

[204] Caron, *Droit d'auteur et droits voisins* (n 7) 152.

[205] Schmidt-Szalewski and Pierre, *Droit de la propriété industrielle* (n 5) para 58: the employer can decide to patent these inventions or keep them secret.

[206] Le Stanc, 'Interférences entre droit d'auteur et droit des brevets quant à la protection du logiciel' (n 92) 166–67.

null (article L613-8) and they must also be registered to be enforceable against third parties (article L613-9).[207] In copyright law, a transfer of the right of representation or reproduction must determine the exploitation modes in the contract (articles L122-7 and L131-3) but a contract is not strictly necessary, it only serves for evidential purposes.

(iii) Rights and Infringement

Again, software will be taken to illustrate the differences between patent and copyright at this level. Under article L613-3, the patent owner has the right to prevent:

(a) Making, offering, putting on the market or using a product which is the subject matter of the patent, or importing or stocking a product for such purposes;
(b) Using a process which is the subject matter of the patent or, when the third party knows, or it is obvious in the circumstances, that the use of the process is prohibited without the consent of the owner of the patent, offering the process for use on French territory;
(c) Offering, putting on the market or using the product obtained directly by a process which is the subject matter of the patent or importing or stocking for such purposes.

This is an exhaustive not indicative list of rights so there is no general right against exploitation of the invention.[208] 'Making' is the material realisation of a product object of the patent whether the product is sold or not; 'offering for sale' includes advertising.[209] In copyright law, the rights are prescribed by the Software Directive, and in substance identical to the rights of other copyright owners, namely: permanent or temporary reproduction in any form, translation, adaptation, arrangement or any other alteration and the placing on the market for consideration or gratuitously, including rental, of the software or of copies thereof by any process (article L122-6). The simple deliberate offer of a product infringing a patent will be per se an infringement. This does not seem to be the case for the offer of an infringing copy of a work.[210] Also in patent law, a third party who procures the means to make the invention knowingly or when it is obvious that this means will be used to make the invention will infringe (article L613-4). Copyright law does not have a similar provision.[211] The main difference between the two regimes, however, is that copyright gives a right to prohibit reproduction whilst patent gives a stronger right, since even if there is no copying, the making or using of the patented product will infringe. Therefore, if a patent and a copyright subsist in the same computer program, by copying, the defendant will generally infringe both the patent and the copyright (unless s/he copies only the ideas not the expressions). But when a defendant makes or uses the computer program without having copied it, it will only infringe the patent, not the copyright. Also of course, under patent law, by application of the theory of equivalents, a person would infringe even if s/he wrote the code in a different way.[212] In copyright law, in most cases, writing the code in a different way may well not be infringing as

[207] On this, see eg Schmidt-Szalewski and Pierre, *Droit de la propriété industrielle* (n 5), paras 251–53 and Gaumont-Prat, *Droit de la propriété industrielle* (n 5) 120–23.

[208] Schmidt-Szalewski and Pierre, *Droit de la propriété industrielle* (n 5) para 162.

[209] See Gaumont-Prat, *Droit de la propriété industrielle* (n 5) 102 and Schmidt-Szalewski and Pierre, *Droit de la propriété industrielle* (n 5) para 171, citing case law holding that advertising is included in the patentee's scope of protection.

[210] Le Stanc, 'Interférences entre droit d'auteur et droit des brevets quant à la protection du logiciel' (n 92) 172.

[211] Ibid.

[212] Ibid 171.

the defendant can use the ideas and express them differently in writing. Finally, in patent law, *mens rea* is necessary to proceed against the seller (but not the maker) whilst not in copyright law (article L615-1). Thus, if a program is protected by both rights, the infringer will not be able to use his or her good faith to escape infringement.[213]

(iv) Exceptions Including Exhaustion Principle

The exceptions in patent and copyright law also differ quite a bit. In patent law, the following are exempted: acts done privately and for non-commercial purposes; acts done for experimental purposes relating to the subject matter of the patented invention; extemporaneous preparation for individual cases in a pharmacy of a medicine in accordance with a medical prescription or acts concerning the medicine so prepared; studies and trials required in order to obtain a marketing authorisation for a medicine, as well as acts necessary to the realisation and obtaining of the authorisation; and finally objects introduced on French territory whose purpose is to be launched in the extra-atmospheric space (article L613-5). The exceptions in copyright law are those of the Software Directive, namely: normal use, including error correction, observe study and test, back-up copy and decompilation (article L 122-6(1)). Since the exceptions are quite different, the cumulation of protections will have as a consequence that the users' privileges in a computer program which is protected by both copyright and patent will be more restricted than if the computer program was simply covered by patent or by copyright.[214] For instance, the user will not be able to make a back-up copy or decompile a program which is protected both by copyright and patent.[215] There is a strong argument to interpret the exceptions cumulatively rather than restrictively however, as article 6 of the failed Proposal for a Directive on the Patentability of Computer-Implemented Inventions provided that where a computer program is protected by the two types of protection, the existence of a patent on the program cannot prejudice the exceptions which apply by virtue of copyright law to the same program.[216] Also, it seems that copyright law should normally not prevent the application of the patent exceptions permitting acts accomplished privately or for non-commercial ends and acts for experimental purposes.[217] Note, however, that there is no private copying exception for computer programs in copyright law, so that a clash exists in this case.

Finally, the principle of exhaustion is similar in both patent and copyright law (articles L613-6 and L122-6(3)) but the right of destination which exists in copyright law restricts the principle.[218]

In conclusion, if the computer program is protected both by copyright and patent, and both rights are owned by the same person, depending on his or her interest, the owner will be able to benefit from the most advantageous regime of the two (eg act

[213] Ibid 172–73.

[214] Ibid 169.

[215] On the overriding of the decompilation exception because a patent covers the programme, see J Weyand and F Haase, 'Patenting Computer Programs: New Challenges' (2005) *International Review of Intellectual Property and Competition Law* 647, 653–54.

[216] Proposal 2002/0047 for a Directive on the Patentability of Computer-Implemented Inventions, available at http://eur-lex.europa.eu/LexUriServ/site/en/com/2002/com2002_0092en01.pdf.

[217] Caron, 'La coexistence du droit d'auteur et du droit des brevets sur un même logiciel' (n 183) 201.

[218] Le Stanc, 'Interférences entre droit d'auteur et droit des brevets quant à la protection du logiciel' (n 92) 169–70.

against non-slavish copies by using the patent right), even if s/he will have to comply with the strictest regime, namely patent (formalities such as contracts in writing, registration, payment of fees) to safeguard all his or her rights.[219] When the copyright and the patent belong to separate persons, French law does not lay down any rules to regulate the conflict. Whereas there will most of the time be no problem for the owner of the patent as s/he can exploit it without infringing the copyright, the converse is not true – exploiting the work will imply exploitation of the invention.

B Negative and *A Posteriori* Overlaps

As the rules are dictated by European law, there is no difference between French law and European law, so the reader is referred to the discussion in chapter three.

C Literature

Notably, the Commission did not think that the cumulation of copyright and patent protections on software caused any problems when it proposed its Directive on the protection of computer-implemented inventions.[220] But most French commentators generally criticise the overlap as overprotective and thus economically undesirable,[221] even though competition law may sometimes solve some problems.[222] This had led some commentators to prefer a single regime (namely patent law[223]) and to reject a *sui generis* right to replace both copyright and patent.[224] However, some others think that copyright is necessary to combat piracy and patent is necessary, at least for fundamental or pioneering innovations.[225] Therefore, they are not against cumulation if it is well organised to avoid overprotection.[226] Accordingly, and based on economic theory, patent protection should be rather rare as the criteria of novelty and inventiveness would be applied strictly, but would be deep (protection would cover downstream developments and applications)

[219] Ibid 175; Le Stanc, 'Logiciels entre droit d'auteur et brevet' (n 183) 304.

[220] COM(1999)42 final, 5 February 1999, para 3.2.2. See also R Hart, P Holmes and J Reid, *The Economic Impact of Patentability of Computer Programs,* Report to the European Commission (19 October 2000) 3 Conclusions 1, available at http://ec.europa.eu/internal_market/indprop/docs/comp/study_en.pdf, cited by G Casucci, 'Software and Computer Related Inventions: Protection by Patent and Copyright' in C Heath and A Kamperman Sanders (eds), *New Frontiers of Intellectual Property Law, IP and Cultural Heritage, Geographical Indications, Enforcement and Overprotection* (Oxford, Hart Publishing, 2005) 161, 178.

[221] Le Stanc, 'Logiciels entre droit d'auteur et brevet' (n 219) 309; F Macrez, 'Les cumuls de droits intellectuels sur les créations informatiques' in S Dusollier and A Cruquenaire (eds), *Le cumul des droits intellectuels* (Brussels, Larcier, 2009) 87, 106 (also adding that overlaps bring far too much complexity). See also chapter 3, section VII.C.

[222] Le Stanc, 'Logiciels entre droit d'auteur et brevet' (n 219) 309.

[223] Ibid 301 (recognising the patentability of programs allows the better definition of the contours of the protection of the substance and of the form). Outside France, see G Ghidini and E Arezzo, 'One, None or A Hundred Thousand: How Many Layers of Protection for Software Innovations?' in J Drexl (ed), *Research Handbook on Intellectual Property and Competition Law* (Cheltenham, Edward Elgar Publishing, 2008) 372.

[224] Caron, 'La coexistence du droit d'auteur et du droit des brevets sur un même logiciel' (n 183) 203.

[225] B Caillaud, 'La propriété intellectuelle sur les logiciels' in J Tirole, C Henry, M Trommetter, L Tubiana and B Caillaud (eds), *Propriété intellectuelle* (Paris, Conseil d'Analyse Economique, La Documentation Française, 2003) 154, 164. See also Macrez, 'Les cumuls de droits intellectuels sur les créations informatiques' (n 221) 102.

[226] Caillaud, 'La propriété intellectuelle sur les logiciels' (n 225) 154, 164–65.

albeit relatively narrow (it would not serve as an excessive leverage to other markets in particular through interfaces).[227] As already stated in chapter three, section VII.C, this coexistence between patent and copyright would be more balanced if the source codes of patented computer-implemented inventions were made public.[228]

In any case, it is not currently possible to do away with either copyright or patent as the protection of computer programs by copyright and patent laws is mandated by both European and international law.[229] So in the meantime, as we have to live with the overlap and French law does not contain rules that regulate it, commentators have proposed some to avoid regime clashes. One such rule is *accessorium sequitur principale*, or *major pars trahit ad se minorem*.[230] According to this principle, one would need to determine if the form of a computer program protected by copyright is or not the accessory of the invention protected by the patent. Once this is determined, the principal would communicate its regime to the accessory. Nonetheless, it can be difficult to determine the accessory and the principal in practice.[231] In conclusion, for Caron, the best we can do is to trust the wisdom of judges and practitioners to organise the coexistence in the best way possible. There is no perfect remedy as each presents advantages and disadvantages.[232] Another proposed solution is using a hierarchical principle.[233] Where a program is protected by both a patent and copyright, patent would be the only protection available or would trump copyright. This is because, according to that opinion, in this situation, copyright becomes in practice useless. If not de lege, copyright is de facto inferior to patent in cases of a simultaneous overlap. Indeed, all the program codes which can realise a given function would be covered by the patent.[234] The complementary character of the two monopolies is in fact frequently put forward to defend the prevalence of patent rights in computer programs.[235] Another way to organise regime clashes is clearly to do so by contract; one obvious application is to concentrate the two rights in one and the same person.[236] But this is a private remedy not a legislative one, and therefore it does not avoid all clashes. Finally, others have proposed a harmonisation of the regimes to avoid conflicts, in short, convergence.[237]

VIII. PATENTS AND PLANT VARIETY RIGHTS

As has been seen in chapter three, the simultaneous overlap regarding ownership, dealings, rights and exceptions must be examined at national level because patent rights are

[227] Ibid 164.

[228] Ibid. See also Macrez, 'Les cumuls de droits intellectuels sur les créations informatiques' (n 225) 101 and Weyand and Haase, 'Patenting Computer Programs: New Challenges' (n 215) 660, adding that 'it should not be only the pure text of the program listing that is submitted, but also a commentary and explanations sufficient to enable a knowledgeable person to follow the program in detail'.

[229] Caron, 'La coexistence du droit d'auteur et du droit des brevets sur un même logiciel' (n 183) 202.

[230] Ibid. See also *Electronic Techniques (Anglia) v Critchley Components* [1997] FSR 401, 413, per Laddie J.

[231] Caron, 'La coexistence du droit d'auteur et du droit des brevets sur un même logiciel (n 183) 202–3.

[232] Ibid.

[233] Macrez, 'Les cumuls de droits intellectuels sur les créations informatiques' (n 225) 99, quickly admitting that the existence of a hierarchical principle cannot cover all possible situations and one will have to examine the way overlaps can be organised without the principle.

[234] Ibid 101.

[235] Ibid 102, citing Lucas and Lucas, *Traité de la propriété littéraire et artistique*, 3rd edn (n 5) 13.

[236] Macrez, 'Les cumuls de droits intellectuels sur les créations informatiques' (n 225) 106.

[237] Binctin, 'Le cumul d'appropriation: du parfum au *logiciel*' (n 163) para 35.

not harmonised on those aspects, even if plant variety rights are. What will be said here regarding the provisions on ownership, dealings, rights and exceptions relating to plant variety rights will often not be restated in the chapters on British and German law, because some aspects are similar and reference will accordingly be made to this section. The French plant variety right is codified in IPC, article L623–1–623-25.[238] Before examining the provisions on ownership and dealings, it is interesting to note that French law incorporates the prohibition of EPC Article 53(b)[239] in a less rigid way. Article L623-2 states:

> Any new plant variety belonging to a genera or species *enjoying the system of protection instituted by the provisions of this Chapter* [ie the chapter of the IPC on plant variety rights] shall not be patentable. (emphasis added)[240]

This means that if a plant variety cannot be protected by the plant variety right, it could potentially be patentable. 'Such modifications of the exclusionary norm reveal one of the principal reasons for its existence which consists in the double protection prohibition enshrined in' Article 2(1) of the 1978 Act of the UPOV Convention.[241] Article L611-19 implemented Biotech Directive 98/44/EC, article 4 (exclusions as to plant varieties) in a faithful way.[242] However, some argue that a plant variety is excluded from French patent protection when it corresponds to the definition in the Community Plant Variety Right (CPVR) Regulation 2100/94 whether or not it is protected or protectable by plant variety right.[243] In addition, it must be noted that the CPVR Regulation excludes protection for plant varieties which would violate public morality, public policy, public security, the protection of health and life of humans, animals or plants, the protection of the environment, the protection of industrial or commercial property, or the safeguarding of competition, of trade or of agricultural production (CPVR Regulation, article 13(8)). Accordingly, CPVR Regulation, article 13(8) probably converges with the application of EPC Article 53(a), which is reflected in IPC, article L611-17 (morality and *ordre public* exclusion) and TFEU Articles 101 and 102(competition law provisions).

[238] Note that as of 22 October 2009, France was still only a party to the 1978 act of UPOV, see www.upov.int/export/sites/upov/en/about/members/pdf/pub423.pdf.

[239] As a reminder, EPC Art 53(b) states that 'European patents shall not be granted in respect of: . . . (b) plant or animal varieties or essentially biological processes for the production of plants or animals; this provision shall not apply to microbiological processes or the products thereof'.

[240] Article 7(b) of the old French Patent Act already had this wording (Patent Act no 68-1 of 2 January 1968 modified by Act no 78-742 of 13 July 1978 and then integrated in the 1992 Intellectual Property Code) cited by R Moufang, 'Protection for Plant Breeding and Plant Varieties: A Frontier of Patent Law' (1992) 3 *International Review of Intellectual Property and Competition Law* 328, 345; A Christie, 'Patents for Plant Innovation' (1989) *European Intellectual Property Review* 394, 395.

[241] Moufang, 'Protection for Plant Breeding and Plant Varieties' (n 240) 345–46.

[242] See in relevant part art L611-19:

> 'I The following shall be unpatentable: . . . (2) plant varieties as defined in Article 5 of Regulation (EC) No 873/2004 introducing new rules governing intellectual property ownership of Community plant variety rights;
>
> (3) essentially biological processes for the production of plants and animals. A process that consists entirely of natural phenomena such as crossing or selection shall be regarded as biological process . . . II Notwithstanding the provisions of (I) above, inventions which concern plants or animals shall be patentable if the technical feasibility of the invention is not confined to a particular plant or animal variety. III The provisions of I (3) shall be without prejudice to the patentability of inventions which concern a technical process, in particular a microbiological one, or a product obtained by means of such a process; any process involving or resulting in or performed upon a microbiological material shall be regarded as microbiological process'.

[243] See art L611-19; Azéma and Galloux, *Droit de la propriété industrielle* (n 5) 137; Schmidt-Szalewski and Pierre, *Droit de la propriété industrielle* (n 5) para 69.

A Simultaneous Overlap

(i) Ownership and Dealings

(a) French Plant Variety Right and French Patent

There is a perfect convergence between patents and plant variety rights in relation to co-ownership and dealings. This is largely because the Intellectual Property Code itself refers to the patent provisions, which are meant to apply mutatis mutandis to plant variety rights (see article L623-24, which states that the provisions of articles L613-8 and L613-29–613-32 are applicable to applications for plant variety rights and to plant variety rights; for details, see above section VII.A(ii)).[244] Also, article L623-14 provides that acts delivering the certificate, transferring property or conceding the right of exploitation or pawning are only enforceable against third parties if they have been published under conditions regulated by a decree in the Council of State. In short, such contracts have to be registered in the national register of plant variety rights.[245] The similar patent provision states that the acts modifying or transferring rights in a patent application or a patent are only enforceable against third parties if they are recorded in the register of patents (article L613-9). Thus, if there is an overlap between a French patent and a French plant variety right, there are no regime clashes in this respect.

However, as regards the main ownership rules, including those regarding employees, the two rights differ somewhat. As has been seen above, the right to the patent goes to the inventor, qualified by the rule of first to file (article L611-6). In patent law, there are also very specific provisions for employee inventions (see above section VII.A(ii)). But the French plant variety right provisions have very little to say on this topic. Article L623-4 simply states that the plant variety right belongs to its right-holder, but does not set out a rule as to who is the right-holder (see also article L623-6). But as in patent law, the right belongs to the first to file, which can be a natural or legal person.[246] However, if the first to file is not the breeder, s/he must indicate who the breeder is when applying for the certificate.[247] There are also no rules about plant varieties discovered and developed or bred by employees, nor any case law, and since the patent rules do not state that they also apply to the plant variety right, one cannot apply them by analogy.[248]

(b) Community Plant Variety Right and French Patent

The rules as to entitlement are laid down in CPVR Regulation, article 11. Its first paragraph provides that:

The person who bred, or discovered and developed the variety, or his successor in title, both – the person and his successor – referred to hereinafter as 'the breeder', shall be entitled to the Community plant variety right.

[244] See also Schmidt-Szalewski and Pierre, *Droit de la Propriété Industrielle* (n 5) paras 317, 326.
[245] Ibid para 326; Azéma and Galloux, *Droit de la propriété industrielle* (n 5) 581.
[246] Gaumont-Prat, *Droit de la propriété industrielle* (n 5) 130.
[247] Azéma and Galloux, *Droit de la propriété industrielle* (n 5) 518–82.
[248] Ibid 583.

There can be several discrepancies as to the persons who will own the patent and the plant variety right. This can occur because a plant variety right can be owned by the person who bred the variety, or alternatively by the person who discovered and developed it, and these three types of activities do not necessarily imply inventing.[249] Another instance is when 'A has a patent on a gene and B a plant variety right on a variety which includes this gene'.[250] However, if these persons are the same then differences are slight in terms of joint ownership because CPVR Regulation, article 11(2) provides that the right vests jointly in them even if those who bred and those who discovered the variety are different. Nevertheless, the problem will be the same as with the overlap between a French patent and a French plant variety right when a breeder is an employee and a patent also exists in addition to the plant variety right, because CPVR Regulation, article 11(4) provides that the national provisions on plant variety rights apply and French law is silent on this.

French patent law allows transfers and licences in whole or in part. The licences can be exclusive or non-exclusive. Both transfers and licences must be recorded in writing, otherwise they are null (article L613-8). CPVR Regulation, article 27 provides that licences can be in whole or in part and exclusive or non-exclusive. CPVR Regulation, article 23 also requires that transfers be in writing, further adding the signature of the parties, otherwise they are void. Accordingly, if the subject matter is protected by both rights, the signature of the parties will be necessary on the transfer document even if patent law does not require it. Finally, the CPVR Regulation requires transfers to be entered in the register of Community plant variety rights in order for them to be enforceable against third parties, which is similar to article L613-9 which also stipulates that patent licences must be recorded in the national register of patents. These rules are identical or similar in the two rights and there is therefore almost complete convergence at this level. There is one difference: as the CPVR is a Community unitary right (CPVR Regulation, article 2), it can only be transferred for the whole of the European Union. Therefore, a subject matter protected at the same time by a patent and a CPVR cannot be transferred for one Member State only.

[249] The Board of Appeal of the Community Office said 'breeding . . . does not necessarily imply inventing something totally new but includes the planting, selection and growing on of pre-existing material and its development into a finished variety'. *Sakata Seed Corporation*, A 017/2002, 3 April 2003, 8–9. And in another decision, the Board said that 'discover' means that 'somebody comes across a variety either by search or chance, being conscious of the fact that it is a new variety, which was unknown to him before and which in his opinion is unknown to other persons as well'. See *Canna Phasion*, A 001/2004, 6. Both decisions discussed by L Bently and B Sherman, *Intellectual Property Law*, 3rd edn (Oxford, Oxford University Press, 2009) 597. See also M Llewelyn and M Adcock, *European Plant Intellectual Property* (Oxford, Hart Publishing, 2006) 239–40: 'The fact that the first type of activity [breeding] indicates an active, breeding role in producing the plant grouping which is a distinct, uniform and stable variety, would seem to suggest that the latter activity, does not. In theory therefore, developing a variety could simply mean doing that which is necessary to bring the discovered variety to the European market. On this basis, protection is secured by showing that the discovered variety is distinct, uniform and stable. What does not appear necessary is that the discoverer/developer has to show that, through breeding activity, he was responsible for producing the distinct, uniform and stable characteristics which distinguish a plant grouping from others within the same species – such an applicant could be a seed merchant. Protection is therefore conferred for the act of bringing a commercially new variety to the Community marketplace. This is underlined by article 7'.

[250] N Brahy, 'Cumul et chevauchement du brevet et du certificat d'obtention végétale: beaucoup de droit . . . mais peu de faits' in S Dusollier and A Cruquenaire (eds), *Le cumul des droits intellectuels* (Brussels, Larcier, 2009) 107, 110.

(ii) Rights and Infringement

As has been seen in section VII.A(iii), article L613-3 provides that the patent owner has the right to prevent:

(a) Making, offering, putting on the market or using a product which is the subject matter of the patent, or importing or stocking a product for such purposes;
(b) Using a process which is the subject matter of the patent or, when the third party knows, or it is obvious in the circumstances, that the use of the process is prohibited without the consent of the owner of the patent, offering the process for use on French territory;
(c) Offering, putting on the market or using the product obtained directly by a process which is the subject matter of the patent or importing or stocking for such purposes.

It is also an infringement for someone to sell or offer to sell the means to make an essential element of the invention if the person knows or it is evident from the circumstances that this element will be used to make the invention (article L613-4). In addition, French law has faithfully incorporated Biotech Directive, articles 8 and 10 in articles L613-2(3) and (4).[251] Therefore, as per respectively Biotech Directive, articles 8 and 10:

> the protection conferred by a patent on a biological material possessing specific characteristics as a result of the invention shall extend to any biological material derived from that biological material through propagation or multiplication and possessing those same characteristics; the protection conferred by a patent on a process that enables a biological material to be produced possessing specific characteristics as a result of the invention shall extend to biological material directly obtained through that process and to any other biological material, derived from the latter, by reproduction or multiplication and possessing those same characteristics.

Also:

> the protection referred to in Articles 8 and 9 shall not extend to biological material obtained from the propagation or multiplication of biological material placed on the market in the territory of a Member State by the holder of the patent or with his consent, where the multiplication or propagation necessarily results from the application for which the biological material was marketed, provided that the material obtained is not subsequently used for other propagation or multiplication.

Under article L623-4, the French plant variety right grants the following rights to the breeder: production, sale, offer for sale and importation of:

> all or part of the plant or any element for the reproduction or vegetative propagation of the variety or of varieties derived from it by hybridization where their reproduction requires the repeated use of the original variety.

The rights are the same as under patent law except that stocking is not included and that the plant variety right includes the production of hybrids (on this see next paragraph). The rights conferred by a CPVR are also almost identical to those of a patent owner. The CPVR holder has two more rights, that of conditioning for the purpose of propagation and of exportation outside the European Union (CPVR Regulation, article 13). CPVR Regulation, article 13(3), however, adds that the rights:

[251] Only the terms 'in an identical or divergent form' used in the Biotech Directive are missing but since this omission does not entail any difference, in practice the texts have the same meaning.

shall apply in respect of harvested material only if this was obtained through the unauthorised use of variety constituents of the protected variety, and unless the holder has had reasonable opportunity to exercise his right in relation to the said variety constituents.[252]

Both the French and Community plant variety rights extend to essentially derived varieties (EDVs) although the CPVR Regulation is a little more precise as to what an essentially derived variety is (article L623-4 and CPVR Regulation, article 13(5)–(7)[253]). A question poses itself: has the extension to EDV the same effect in practice as the principle of equivalents? If the answer is positive, then the rights are converging on the test of infringement as France applies the theory of equivalents, in accordance with the Protocol on the interpretation of EPC Article 69, because it is desirable that the French judges interpret in the same way both European and French patents.[254] Likewise, the question is: has the extension to EDV the same effect in practice as the patent infringement test which stipulates that infringement is appreciated by similarities not differences, that simple differences of detail do not take away the infringing character of the reproduction of a protected invention,[255] and that there is infringement where all the essential elements of the claim are taken either identically or by equivalent?[256] If so, there is also convergence. If not, it is unclear if there is convergence, because there is no reported case law on infringement of a French plant variety right.

[252] See also para 4: 'In the implementing rules pursuant to Article 114, it may be provided that in specific cases the provisions of paragraph 2 of this Article shall also apply in respect of products obtained directly from material of the protected variety. They may apply only if such products were obtained through the unauthorised use of material of the protected variety, and unless the holder has had reasonable opportunity to exercise his right in relation to the said material. To the extent that the provisions of paragraph 2 apply to products directly obtained, they shall also be considered to be "material"'.

[253] See para 5–7: '5. The provisions of paragraphs 1 to 4 shall also apply in relation to: (a) varieties which are essentially derived from the variety in respect of which the Community plant variety right has been granted, where this variety is not itself an essentially derived variety; (b) varieties which are not distinct in accordance with the provisions of Article 7 from the protected variety; and (c) varieties whose production requires the repeated use of the protected variety.

6. For the purposes of paragraph 5(a), a variety shall be deemed to be essentially derived from another variety, referred to hereinafter as "the initial variety" when: (a) it is predominantly derived from the initial variety, or from a variety that is itself predominantly derived from the initial variety; (b) it is distinct in accordance with the provisions of Article 7 from the initial variety; and (c) except for the differences which result from the act of derivation, it conforms essentially to the initial variety in the expression of the characteristics that result from the genotype or combination of genotypes of the initial variety.

7. The implementing rules pursuant to Article 114 may specify possible acts of derivation which come at least under the provisions of paragraph 6.'

[254] CA Paris, 6 March 1975 [1975] Ann Prop Ind 118, comment Burst; Cass com, 6 November 1984 [1985] Ann Prop Ind 77, comment Mathély; CA Paris, 11 October 1990 [1991] PIBD III, 2; [1990] Ann Prop Ind 235, comment Mathély, all cited by Azéma and Galloux, *Droit de la propriété industrielle* (n 5) 367. For more details and case law on the theory of equivalents, see ibid 372–74.

[255] Cass civ, 5 July 1878 [1878] Ann Prop Ind 33; Cass com, 5 May 1971 [1971] Ann Prop Ind 102; CA Paris, 20 June 1969 [1971] Ann Prop Ind 89; CA Paris, 6 January 1965 [1966] Ann Prop Ind 14; CA Paris, 6 March 1975 [1975] Ann Prop Ind 113, comment Burst; CA Grenoble, 24 February 1969 [1969] PIBD, III, 64, cited by Azéma and Galloux, *Droit de la propriété industrielle* (n 5) 371.

[256] Cass com, 24 September 2002 [2002] PIBD, III, 33; TGI Paris, 30 November 2004 [2005] PIBD no 803, 134; TGI Paris, 10 December 2004 [2005] PIBD no 805, 203, cited by Azéma and Galloux, *Droit de la propriété industrielle* (n 5) 371, also noting that an element or means is essential when it is necessary to solve the technical problem posed.

(iii) Exceptions

(a) CPVR and French Patent

As has been seen in section VII.A(iv) above, there are five exceptions to the patent right, namely: acts done privately and for non-commercial purposes; acts done for experimental purposes relating to the subject matter of the patented invention; extemporaneous preparation for individual cases in a pharmacy of a medicine in accordance with a medical prescription or acts concerning the medicine so prepared; studies and trials required in order to obtain a marketing authorisation for a medicine, as well as acts necessary to the realisation and obtaining of the authorisation; and finally objects introduced on French territory whose purpose is to be launched in the extra-atmospheric space. In addition, when vegetal reproduction material is patented, the same exception as under Community plant variety rights applies, namely the farmer can use his or her harvest for further reproduction or multiplication on his or her own farm. This comes from the Biotech Directive (recital 47 and article 11) which aligned the two regimes to avoid a patent on a plant or plant gene (which is a not plant variety) preventing the application of the farmer's privilege because the subject matter of the patent overlaps with the variety covered by the plant variety right. Article L613-5-1 adds, like Biotech Directive, article 11, that the conditions of such use are those of CPVR Regulation, article 14 (article 14(2) lists the only plant varieties for which farmers can benefit from the exemption, namely several types of fodder plants, cereals, potatoes and oil and fibre plants; and article 14(3) bans quantitative restrictions and introduces special provisions for small farmers). Like patent law, CPVR Regulation, article 15 also exempts acts done privately and for non-commercial purposes; acts done for experimental purposes; and acts done for the purpose of breeding, or discovering and developing other varieties, except EDVs.[257] Indeed, the French legislature introduced this latter exception (ie for acts done for the purpose of creating or discovering and developing other plant varieties) in its patent provisions too (article L613-5(3)).[258] Therefore, there is on this aspect almost total convergence between patent and Community plant variety rights (because the exceptions concerning medicines and objects in outer space should not normally concern plant varieties[259]). However, as Cook explains further, article L613-5(3) is the 'minimum required to maintain the integrity of the plant variety rights system against the consequences of overlap with the patent system'.[260] Indeed, there could still be clashes in some cases. This is because article L613-5(3) does not:

[257] To be precise, CPVR Regulation, art 15(d) states 'The Community plant variety rights shall not extend to: . . . acts referred to in Article 13(2) to (4), in respect of such other varieties, except where the provisions of Article 13(5) apply, or where the other variety or the material of this variety comes under the protection of a property right which does not contain a comparable provision'.

[258] This exception also exists in German law, see chapter 6, section VI. See also T Cook, 'Responding to Concerns about the Scope of the Defence from Patent Infringements for Acts Done for Experimental Purposes relating to the Subject Matter of the Invention' (2006) 3 *Intellectual Property Quarterly* 193, 206–7 ('The reasoning for inserting such a defence is explained in the report on the measure. This states that art L613-5-3 constitutes a third derogation to the right of the patentee, which it calls a "privilège du sélectionneur" (privilege of the plant breeder). According to the report, the insertion of this derogation should ensure a greater consistency as between patent protection and plant variety protection [ie art L623-25(2)]').

[259] But what if a plant variety must be used to prepare a medicine? If both patent and plant variety rights cover the same subject matter, the plant variety right will take over and the patent exception will not be applicable.

[260] Cook, 'Responding to Concerns about the Scope of the Defence from Patent Infringements' (n 258) 207.

go so far as to provide any sort of defence in relation to the subsequent commercial exploitation of the varieties produced by acts which have been the subject of the defence. No such defence is needed if the resultant variety lacks the patented gene sequence, as the resultant variety cannot itself infringe. If, however, the resultant variety contains the patented gene sequence, then it will infringe, irrespective of whether (depending on the question of 'essential derivation') the plant variety system treats its commercial exploitation as infringing.[261]

In addition to exceptions, French patent law and the CPVR Regulation also contain provisions on compulsory licences. First, both the CPVR Regulation and patent law have parallel provisions to enable a breeder who cannot obtain or exploit a plant variety right without breaching a patent, and a patent owner who cannot obtain or exploit a patent without breaching a plant variety right, to obtain licences. The owner of the plant variety right can request a licence from the patent owner as long as the variety represents, in relation to the patented invention, significant technical progress and demonstrates a considerable economic interest, and the breeder has applied unsuccessfully to the patent owner to obtain a contractual licence. If the licence is granted, then the patent owner has the right to obtain a cross-licence to use the variety in question (article L613-15(1)). The same rule applies for the patent owner in the converse situation (CPVR Regulation, article 29(5a)[262]). These two compulsory cross-licensing provisions are derived from Biotech Directive, article 12.[263] The reason for the modification of CPVR Regulation, article 29 in 2004 is clearly set out in recitals 6 to 8 of the amending Regulation, namely to align its provisions with those of the Biotech Directive. Again, the two legal regimes converge on this point,[264] although some have criticised the vagueness of the terms 'considerable', 'significant', 'technical' and 'progress'.[265] Also, 'compulsory licenses against dominant patents do not solve the issue completely since they presuppose the very existence of a *new* plant variety'[266] (emphasis added). Therefore, in many cases, the breeder will thus have to rely on the patent research exemption to perform breeding activities.[267]

In the end, the two regimes may not converge totally because of some differences in the provisions concerning other compulsory licences. However, as will be seen, in the main, these differences may not be as big as they seem. CPVR Regulation, article 29(1)–(5) provides for a very general compulsory licence, stating that such a licence can be granted by the Community Plant Variety Office to anyone on the grounds of public

[261] Ibid 207. This is also valid for the German defence.

[262] As amended by Council Regulation (EC) 873/2004 of 29 April 2004 amending Regulation (EC) 2100/94 on Community plant variety rights [2004] OJ L162/38.

[263] See also Biotech Directive 98/44/EC, recitals 52 and 53.

[264] On the problems caused by the different territorial jurisdiction which arises in case of cross-licences between a CPVR and a patent, see M Boizard, 'Licence de dépendance entre brevet et certificat d'obtention végétale' (2005) *Propriété Industrielle* no 24, 25. Indeed, the PVR being a Community title, only the Community Plant Variety Office is competent to grant a reciprocal licence for a dependent PVR, whereas it is the TGI in France which grants the patent licence to the breeder. The author notes that 'At the end, it is two very different authorities which will decide in the framework of the same file, which is not necessarily appropriate for the balance of the interests at stake'. The converse situation is also complex because the national authority can only grant a licence to the patent for one country. Thus, the breeder who has a CPVR will have to ask for a licence in all the states parties to both the EPC and the European Union.

[265] Llewelyn and Adcock, *European Plant Intellectual Property* (n 249) 384, who also ask 'considerable economic interest of whom?'. But this term is not new as it was used in TRIPs Art 31(l).

[266] R Moufang, 'The Interface between Patents and Plant Variety Rights in Europe' in *WIPO/UPOV Symposium on Intellectual Property Rights in Plant Biotechnology*, Doc WIPO-UPOV/SYM/03/6 (Geneva, 24 October 2003) 5.

[267] Ibid.

interest.[268] Reasonable conditions such as time limitation, payment of an equitable remuneration and certain obligations must be attached to these licences. Each year, any of the parties can ask that the licence be amended or cancelled if the circumstances have changed. French patent law also contains compulsory licence provisions but they are less broad than the general provision under the CPVR Regulation, so that convergence is not total. The first circumstance is when the patent owner fails to put his or her invention into use and does not have legitimate reasons to do so.[269] In this case, anyone may be granted a compulsory non-exclusive licence on expiry of a period of three years from the grant of a patent or four years from the filing date of the application. Conditions are necessarily attached to such compulsory licence as to the duration, field of application and amount of the royalties (article L613-11, 613-12 and 613-13). Secondly, article L613-16 allows the state, in order to safeguard public health and when an agreement has not been reached with the patent owner, to subject patents on medicines and processes to obtain them, as well as *ex vivo* diagnostic methods, to a compulsory licence. Thirdly, article L613-18 allows the state to subject patents to a compulsory licence if patent owners who have been summoned to make products or processes to satisfy the national economy's needs, refuse to do so. Finally, the French state can also obtain a compulsory licence to meet its national defence requirements (article L613-19–613-20).

(b) French Plant Variety Right and French Patent

The picture is patchier for the overlap between the national rights. Sometimes the two systems converge, sometimes they don't. First, the convergences: as in patent law, the plant variety right provides for similar or identical compulsory licences on the grounds of public health and national defence (article L623-17–623-22). Article L623-22(1) and (2) are the symmetrical provisions to article L613-15(1) (compulsory cross-licence).[270] However, there is a 'hidden' discrepancy that puts the patentee in a better position than the holder of a plant variety right, as is well explained by Boizard.[271] France introduced in its patent provisions (article L613-5(3)) an exception similar to the breeder's privilege, which is provided for at article L623-25 in the provisions on the (French) plant variety

[268] G Tritton, R Davis, M Edenborough, J Graham, S Malinicz and A Roughton, *Intellectual Property in Europe* (London, Sweet & Maxwell, 2008) 623, note that this compulsory licence provision mirrors art 17 of the 1991 act of the UPOV Convention.

[269] This compulsory licence originates from Art 5A of the Paris Convention.

[270] Azéma and Galloux, *Droit de la propriété industrielle* (n 5) 324, note, however, that if the regime of dependent licences from patents to plant variety rights is well explained, this is curiously not the case for licences from plant variety rights to patents (art L613-15(1)), the legislature simply referring back to conditions of the common regime, namely arts L613-12– 613-14.

[271] M Boizard 'Licence de dépendance entre brevet et certificat d'obtention végétale' (2005) *Propriété Industrielle* no 24, 24, who explains that the perfect symmetry of the provisions organising the regime of licences is in fact illusory. To understand one needs to go back to the content of art L623-22(1). This article gives to the patent owner the possibility to obtain a licence to exploit a protected plant variety. It sets out the principle of the dependent licence and indicates generally the cases in which such licence is to be requested. It is stated that this provision will apply when the owner of a patent on a biotech invention cannot exploit it without breaching a prior plant variety right. The determination of the scope of this provision implies returning to the definition of plant variety right. That is where the problem lies. The right of the breeder, as described in art L623-4, has not changed. We must deduce that the principle of free access is still in force in French law, which leads one to ask oneself about the usefulness of art L623-22(1), but especially and consequently about the balance between patentee and breeder. Today as yesterday in French law, the owner of a patent including a protected plant variety can exploit it within the limits of art L623-4 – ie rather broadly – without any right for the owner of the plant variety right.

right. Thus, anyone can use a protected variety as a source to create a new variety without committing an infringement, whether the plants are protected by the plant variety right or the patent.[272] Now for the divergences: unlike patents, the plant variety right does not have a similar compulsory licence if the breeder fails to put its variety to use, or a compulsory licence to meet the national economy's requirements. In addition, the French plant variety right does not have exceptions parallel to those existing in patent law, namely: acts done privately and for non-commercial purposes and acts done for experimental purposes. Therefore, the plant variety right will trump those exceptions if there is an overlap.[273] On the other hand, the farmer's privilege is still absent from the French plant variety right.[274]

B *A Posteriori* Overlap

The *a posteriori* overlap between a patent and a national plant variety right in France is stronger than with a CPVR, as article L623-13 grants the 30-year term also to 'perennial fodder grass and vegetables and to endogamic lineages used for the production of hybrid varieties'.

In conclusion, in French law, there is quite a lot of convergence in the area of ownership, dealings, rights, infringement and exceptions but it is far from total and it is greater between French patent law and the CPVR Regulation.

IX. INTELLECTUAL PROPERTY RIGHTS AND UNFAIR COMPETITION

As stated above as regards the legal framework (section I), French unfair competition law is based on civil liability, which is itself contained in two very general provisions, namely articles 1382 and 1383 of the Civil Code. Accordingly, case law regulates the area. Several acts of unfair competition are prohibited by courts on this basis, namely defamation, causing confusion, individual obstruction, parasitism, misleading practices and breach of an agreement to keep know-how or business secrets confidential.[275] Other behaviours are also regulated, such as sales at a loss, lotteries and indications of origin.[276] Only slavish imitation (also called parasitism), causing confusion and breach of confidentiality are

[272] Azéma and Galloux, *Droit de la propriété industrielle* (n 5) 396, however, note that 'the compatibility of this article [L613-5(3)] with EU law depends logically on the compatibility of article 613-2-1. It [which article is intended is unclear from the sentence] is badly articulated with the provisions of the CPVR which, by contrast with the French PVR, provides a form of dependency for essentially derived varieties (article 13(5)(a) CPVR)'.

[273] See also Brahy, 'Cumul et chevauchement du brevet et du certificat d'obtention végétale' (n 250) 107, 114, saying, whilst discussing patents and plant variety rights, that in practice, when there is cumulation of two IPRs, only the exceptions common to the two rights can be invoked.

[274] Azéma and Galloux, *Droit de la propriété industrielle* (n 5) 396. This is as long as the text reforming the French plant variety right has not been definitively adopted. X Buffet-Delmas and A Doat, 'La protection des plantes: entre brevet et certificat d'obtention végétale' (2004) *Propriété Industrielle* no 8, 12, also state that in France, the farmer's privilege is not recognised by any text. Decisions on this issue are also scarce. To these authors' knowledge, only the TGI Nancy has ever ruled on it. It held on 15 May 1987 that the monopoly of the breeder extends to the use of a part of the harvest as new seed. Therefore, the exception is not recognised by the courts either.

[275] Henning Bodewig, *Unfair Competition Law: European Union and Member States* (The Hague, Kluwer Law International, 2006) 114, 124.

[276] Ibid 114.

likely to overlap with most IPRs, whereas comparative advertising can sometimes cause a problem if a sign is protected both as a trademark and a copyright or design right.[277] Overlaps between unfair competition and IPRs only occur if they protect the same effort. If unfair competition law punishes slavish imitation, it will overlap with all IPRs as they all give a right to the right-holder to prevent copying (for industrial property rights, copying is not even required). If unfair competition law punishes the risk of confusion, it will only overlap with the IPRs which require such risk as a condition of infringement. This is only the case of trademark law. Finally, if unfair competition law punishes the breach of a confidentiality agreement protecting a trade secret or know-how in a product which is or was also protected by copyright or patent, there is also an overlap. French courts' decisions have continuously oscillated between admitting and not admitting these overlaps. Each subsection of each 'overlap section' (simultaneous, negative and *a posteriori*, sections IX.B, IX.C and IX.D) will focus on the three relevant unfair competition torts parasitism, risk of confusion and breach of confidentiality. These three unfair competition torts are based on the same conditions which are detailed in the next section (section IX.A).

A Conditions of the Unfair Competition Action

The three requirements of any civil liability action (breach or wrong (in French, *faute*[278]), damage and causal link) must be proven to establish that an act of unfair competition occurred. The breach will either be slavish imitation, the risk of confusion or the breach of confidentiality. Good faith is not an excuse because the breach required by the action in unfair competition can consist in a simple negligence or imprudence; there is no need for an intentional element.[279] Courts generally infer damage from the breach itself. Damage usually consists in the vague notion of 'commercial turmoil'[280] or can simply be a moral prejudice,[281] or even only a risk of prejudice.[282] It is not necessary to prove a loss of turnover or of clients[283] unless the claimant wants damages.[284] Sometimes, courts grant damages even if the claimant does not prove any damage at all.[285] It is possible to take

277 See chapter 3, section IX.

278 The main element of the tort is that there must be a '*faute*'. This more or less corresponds to the breach of the duty of care in the British tort of negligence. The term 'breach' will be used throughout to designate the *faute*.

279 Greffe, Greffe and Greffe, *Traité des dessins et des modèles* (n 5) 485–86.

280 See eg Cass com, 22 February 2000 [2000] *Contrats Concurrence Consommation* com 81, comment Malaurie-Vignal; Cass com, 25 April 2001 [2001] PIBD no 726, III, 451; *Guerlais v Tillaud Boisouvres*, Cass com, 1 July 2003, Jurisdata no 2003-019892, comment J Schmidt-Szalewski in (2003) *Propriété Industrielle* (November) 29; Golaz, *L'Imitation servile des produits et de leur présentation* (n 2) 105; Burst, *Concurrence déloyale et parasitisme* (n 2) 64; ML Izorche, 'Concurrence déloyale et parasitisme economique' in Y Serra, *La concurrence déloyale, permanence et devenir* (Paris, Dalloz, 2001) 27, 31–32.

281 Cass, 22 May 2002, case no 99-21579, available at www.legifrance.gouv.fr, cited by J Passa, 'Responsabilité civile: concurrence' (2003) *Propriétés Intellectuelles* 84, 85.

282 Greffe, Greffe and Greffe, *Traité des dessins et des modèles* (n 5) 486.

283 Cass com, 22 October 1985, Bull civ IV, no 245. See also J Passa, 'Responsabilité civile: distribution' (2002) *Propriétés Intellectuelles* 100.

284 Cass com, 16 January 2001 [2001] *Contrats Concurrence Consommation* Com 59, comment Malaurie-Vignal, cited by Passa, 'Responsabilité civile: distribution' (n 283).

285 See eg *Vente.privée.com v Kalypso*, CA Paris, 24 September 2008 (2009) 3 *Communication Commerce Electronique* (March) Comm 25, comment A Debet. In this case, the claimant was 10th in the ranking of e-commerce sites the most visited during the third trimester of 2005 according to the classification Médiamétrie/

legal action before the damage has happened (ie when the defendant is merely attempting to commit the act of unfair competition) to prevent it from happening.[286] Finally, since acts of unfair competition do not only lead to a decreased turnover, courts are flexible on the certainty of the causation and often skip the requirement altogether.[287] The courts' loose interpretation of the action's requirements over the years has led some commentators to say that there is no need to prove any of the three requirements to win the action.[288] Indeed, because in practice damage and causation need not be established, the action is used more to prevent the behaviour complained of[289] and has come to resemble a prohibitory injunction.

Since the unfair competition and infringement actions are distinct and have a different cause and object, they can be cumulated.[290] This possibility to cumulate is expressly provided for in articles L331-1, L341-1 *et seq*, L615-19(2), L521-3(1) and L716-3, which state that actions in infringement of copyright, patents, designs or trademarks that also raise an unfair competition question are brought exclusively before the Court of First Instance.[291] The two actions are subject to the fulfilment of their respective conditions.[292] The unfair competition action thus complements the infringement action.[293] This complementary nature means that there can be cumulation as long as the acts of unfair competition complained of are distinct from the infringement acts. Therefore, there can only be a condemnation for unfair competition if a breach distinct from infringement can be established.[294] If not, the unfair competition action will be rejected. Courts and commen-

NetRatings, and kept its ranking. There was no taking over of the clients or prejudice in terms of reputation. The claimant could not even exactly say which investment it had made in drafting the general conditions of sale.

[286] See eg P Le Tourneau, 'Le bon vent du parasitisme' (2001) *Contrats Concurrence Consommation* (January) 4, 6.

[287] JM Mousseron, 'Entreprise: parasitisme et droit' (1992) 6 JCP E 14, 24; Burst, *Concurrence déloyale et parasitisme* (n 2) 182.

[288] Golaz, *L'Imitation servile des produits et de leur présentation* (n 2) 105; Burst, *Concurrence déloyale et parasitisme* (n 2) 64.

[289] P Roubier, 'Théorie générale de l'action en concurrence déloyale' (1948) *Revue Trimestrielle de Droit Commercial* 541, 589; Golaz, *L'imitation servile des produits et de leur présentation* (n 2) 105; Burst, *Concurrence déloyale et parasitisme* (n 2) 63, 154, 174, citing CA Douai, 21 December 1989 [1990] PIBD, III, 316; Passa, 'Responsabilité civile: distribution' (n 283).

[290] Passa, *Contrefaçon et concurrence déloyale* (n 2) 73; Golaz, *L'imitation servile des produits et de leur présentation* (n 2) 105; Burst, *Concurrence déloyale et parasitisme* (n 2) 84.

[291] Curiously, a similar provision is not envisaged for plant variety rights. Note that the unfair competition action is the sole action available to certain persons because they are not eligible to sue for infringement (eg the person who cannot prove ownership of the IPR or the licensee of a design right). See Benabou, 'Rapport national, France' (n 23) 15.

[292] Passa, *Contrefaçon et concurrence déloyale* (n 2) 73.

[293] Roubier, 'Théorie générale de l'action en concurrence déloyale' (n 289) 555; Passa, *Contrefaçon et concurrence déloyale* (n 2) 2, 73; Bertrand, *Le droit français de la concurrence déloyale* (n 2) 25. However, the Court of Cassation has held that the action in unfair competition requires a breach while the action in infringement sanctions the infringement of a privative right. The two actions have different causes and have different aims; one does not complement the other. See Cass com, 22 September 1983 (1984) *Dalloz* 187 and also Golaz, *L'imitation servile des produits et de leur présentation* (n 2) 84 (the action in unfair competition is independent from the infringement action; it is not the accessory, the complement nor the consequence of the infringement action; however, courts cumulate the actions as long as there are facts distinct from infringement).

[294] J Passa, 'Heurts et malheurs du fait de concurrence déloyale distinct de la contrefaçon: panorama de jurisprudence récente' (2005) 15 *Propriétés Intellectuelles* 210, 211, explains this concept with utmost precision: the action in unfair competition is not an action in liability for a fact, even a damageable one, but for *breach*. So it is not a distinct fact that one must look for but a distinct *breach*, which embodies itself in a fact distinct from that of infringement. To keep things simple, in this book, we will use those terms (breach, act and fact) interchangeably to convey the same idea.

tators are unanimous on this point.[295] The existence of a distinct breach can be explained by the fact that the damages for infringement must be granted on the principle of integral reparation of the prejudice. The same act cannot serve as the basis of an unfair competition action because there would be no prejudice to repair.[296] The claimant cannot ask a single global reparation since the two prejudices are different but he or she must ask for the reparation of two distinct prejudices.[297] In spite of this rule, many judges often grant a global sum.[298] The unfair competition breach can also be based on the same material fact as the infringement act whilst still being legally distinct from it.[299] This is the case when the behaviour infringing the right in the achievement, be it copyright, design or patent but not a trademark, is itself the source of a risk of confusion. The qualification of infringement of such a right is not subordinated to the existence of a risk of confusion by the public, and therefore when likelihood of confusion exists, it is not the sign that infringement exists.[300]

The problem is that neither courts nor commentators agree as to what constitute acts, facts or breach distinct from infringement. For some commentators, only facts without any link with the achievement (or sign) infringed, such as disparagement, misleading advertising, copying secret know-how or risk of confusion, can constitute distinct acts.[301] For others, parasitism as such can be a distinct act.[302] In many cases involving infringement of subject matter protected by patent, design, trademark or copyright, the Court of Cassation and many appellate courts have held that slavish copying, because it allows the copier to save costs and market the product at a reduced price, is a fact distinct from infringement.[303] The majority of appellate and first instance courts have traditionally

[295] See eg Cass com, 23 May 1973, Bull civ, IV, no 182; *Villeroy and Bosch*, CA Paris, 16 November 2001, Jurisdata no 2001-170988; Roubier, 'Théorie générale de l'action en concurrence déloyale' (n 293) 557; Burst, *Concurrence déloyale et parasitisme* (n 2) 2, 146; A Kamperman Sanders, *Unfair Competition Law: The Protection of Intellectual and Industrial Creativity* (Oxford, Clarendon Press, 1997) 25; Bertrand, *Le droit français de la concurrence déloyale* (n 2) 153–54 ; Passa, *Contrefaçon et concurrence déloyale* (n 2) 2; Golaz, *L'imitation servile des produits et de leur présentation* (n 2) 84–85; Burst, *Concurrence déloyale et parasitisme* (n 2) 84–85; X Desjeux, 'La reproduction ou copie servile et l'action en concurrence déloyale dans la jurisprudence Française' (1976) 17 *Juris-Classeur Périodique* 240; Izorche, 'Concurrence déloyale et parasitisme economique' in Y Serra, *La concurrence déloyale, permanence et devenir* (n 280) 27, 33; R Clauss, 'The French Law of Disloyal Competition' (1995) *European Intellectual Property Review* 550, 552–53; J Schmidt-Szalewski 'La distinction entre l'action en contrefaçon et l'action en concurrence déloyale dans la jurisprudence' (1994) *Revue Trimestrielle de Droit Commercial* 455, 456; M Malaurie-Vignal, 'Le parasitisme des investissements et du travail d'autrui' (1996) *Dalloz* 177, 178; De Candé, 'L'action en concurrence déloyale est-elle menacée par l'evolution du droit de la propriété intellectuelle?' (n 2) 493; N Mallet-Poujol, 'Protection des bases de données' (2003) *Ed Jurisclasseur* no 8, fasc 6080; Cohen, *Le droit des dessins et modèles* (n 5) 236.

[296] Passa, *Contrefaçon et concurrence déloyale* (n 2) 73.

[297] TGI Paris, 6 December 1988 (1989) *Revue du Droit de la Propriété Intellectuelle* nos 23–24, 72.

[298] Passa, *Contrefaçon et concurrence déloyale* (n 2) 73 *et seq*.

[299] J Passa, 'Heurts et malheurs du fait de concurrence déloyale distinct de la contrefaçon: panorama de jurisprudence recente' (2005) 15 *Propriétés Intellectuelles* 210, 212.

[300] Ibid.

[301] Passa, *Contrefaçon et concurrence déloyale* (n 2) 73 *et seq*; Bertrand, *Le droit français de la concurrence déloyale* (n 2) 154; Gautier, *Propriété littéraire et artistique*, 4th edn (n 40) 186, para 114; Mallet-Poujol, 'Protection des bases de données' (n 295).

[302] X Desjeux, 'La reprise de la prestation d'autrui: l'idée commerciale et l'investissement économique (esquisse d'un projet de loi)' (1992) *Gazette du Palais*, Doctrine 973.

[303] See eg Cass com, 30 November 1966, Bull no 460, Bull civ, III, 407; Cass, 2 January 1969 (1969) *Revue Internationale de la Propriété Industrielle et Artistique* 13, cited by Desjeux, 'La reproduction ou copie servile et l'action en concurrence déloyale dans la jurisprudence française' (n 295); Cass com, 25 October 1977 (1978) *Dalloz*, Inf Rap 164; Bull civ, IV, 245; Malaurie-Vignal, 'Le parasitisme des investissements et du travail d'autrui' (n 295) 178; CA Paris, 20 December 1989 (1991) *Dalloz*, Somm 91, comment Colombet; CA Paris, 1 October 1992 [1993] PIBD no 535, III, 35, cited by Schmidt-Szalewski, 'La distinction entre l'action en contrefaçon et

been in favour of the tort of parasitism.[304] This is the case for all three types of overlap (simultaneous, negative and *a posteriori*). But the Supreme Court has oscillated between recognising and rejecting the tort, and so have the lower courts.[305] Therefore, as will be seen below, the case law is still unsettled for all overlaps between IPRs and unfair competition law.

B Simultaneous Overlap

(i) Parasitism

(a) General Considerations

Parasitism occurs when a third party, without incurring any expenditure, uses the fruit of another's efforts by following in his or her wake. In other words, it is the act of copying another's achievement, even if the copy is not slavish,[306] and does not create a risk of confusion, by which someone (the parasite) benefits unduly from the achievement, efforts, investments or know-how of another person without him- or herself making any

l'action en concurrence déloyale dans la jurisprudence' (n 295) 462–63; CA Paris, 7 April 1993 [1993] PIBD no 548, III, 462; CA Paris, 21 June 1994 [1994] PIBD, III, 583; CA Versailles, 5 April 2001 [2002] PIBD no 734, III, 38, cited by Passa 'Responsabilité civile: distribution' (n 283) 81; Cass 1st civ, 19 October 2004, case no 02-16057, reported by Passa, 'Heurts et malheurs du fait de concurrence déloyale distinct de la contrefaçon' (n 299) 217. For more decisions, see Golaz, *L'imitation servile des produits et de leur présentation* (n 2) 106 nn 268–72; Burst, *Concurrence déloyale et parasitisme* (n 2) 241 n 872; Passa, *Contrefaçon et concurrence déloyale* (n 2) 248, 274–75 ; Passa 'Responsabilité civile : distribution' (n 283). For the most recent decisions, see below.

[304] Golaz, *L'imitation servile des produits et de leur présentation* (n 2) 106; Passa, *Contrefaçon et concurrence déloyale* n 2) 267 *et seq*; Bertrand, *Le droit français de la concurrence déloyale* (n 2) 47 nn 122, 123; 48 n 124, and decisions cited; Benabou, 'Rapport national, France' (n 23) 14. Very few lower courts have rejected the tort of parasitism. See Passa, *Contrefaçon et concurrence déloyale* (n 2) 58–59, 286, who identified only a couple of decisions.

[305] For instance, a chamber of the Court of Appeal of Paris is reluctant to punish parasitism but another chamber of the same court takes the opposite stance. See J Passa, 'Propos dissidents sur la sanction du parasitisme économique' (2000) 25 *Dalloz,* Chronique 297, 306; Passa 'Responsabilité civile : distribution' (n 283) 112–13; Passa 'Responsabilité civile: concurrence' (2003) (n 281) 448–49 and decisions cited. See also Passa, 'Heurts et malheurs du fait de concurrence déloyale distinct de la contrefaçon' (n 299) 213–17, reporting that the same two chambers of the Paris Court of Appeal continued to swing in 2004 and 2005, sometimes recognising, sometimes rejecting that argument that a lower price is a distinct fact. We concentrate below on the most recent case law as it is the most relevant in illustrating the current trend and what may hold for the future.

[306] The act of copying another's achievement is also referred to as slavish or quasi-slavish copying. Slavish or quasi-slavish copies are simply identical or quasi-identical copies of another person's achievement protected or unprotected by an intellectual property right. Passa, *Contrefaçon et concurrence déloyale* (n 2) 242. *Contra*: A Strowel and JP Triaille 'De l'équilibre entre le droit de la concurrence et la propriété intellectuelle. A propos de la proposition de loi Godfrain sur les "créations réservées"' (1993) 2 *Droit de l'Informatique et des Télécoms* 25, 26 (slavish copies are those which create a risk of confusion). The notion of parasitism requires the avoidance of efforts and does not require that the copy be slavish or quasi-slavish, although it will generally be the case. Y Saint-Gal, 'Concurrence parasitaire ou agissements parasitaires' (1956) *Revue Internationale de la Propriété Industrielle et Artistique* 37. It is not the slavish character of the copy which constitutes the breach; the breach is the avoidance of efforts. Passa, *Contrefaçon et concurrence déloyale* (n 2) 249 *et seq*; ML Izorche, 'Les fondements de la sanction de la concurrence déloyale et du parasitisme' (1998) 51(1) *Revue Trimestrielle de Droit Commercial* 17 and decisions cited. However, generally, when one slavishly or quasi-slavishly copies something, one inevitably avoids efforts. Slavish copying therefore always has as a consequence that the copying product will be cheaper, since the copier by definition always avoids the research and presentation costs. Parasitism and slavish copying can therefore be said to be synonyms or quasi-synonyms. Consequently, when we refer to parasitism, this will be synonymous with slavish and quasi-slavish copying.

such efforts and thereby saving the costs necessary for the creation of the original product.[307] It can now be understood why courts called the tort 'parasitism'; the copier acts like a parasite, nourishing him- or herself from the efforts of another person without making any efforts him- or herself.[308] However, the Court of Cassation has sometimes ruled that it is not necessary for the victim of parasitism to prove s/he made efforts or investments.[309] It was the Court of Appeal of Paris in the 1960s and 1970s which set the trend of holding that simply selling a similar or identical product to that of the IPR owner at a lower price (than the price the IPR owner charges) was unfair competition.[310] The notion of parasitism encompasses parasitic competition (*concurrence parasitaire*) and parasitic acts (*actes parasitaires*). The difference between the two is that, in the first case, the two parties are in competition with one another, but in the second, they are not. So the action is available not only to competitors but to anyone who justifies an interest. The copied achievement must not be banal, nor be a necessary and functional form; in other words, resemblances imposed by functional constraints or norms are not reprehensible; only the copying of 'arbitrary' forms is parasitic.[311] In yet other words, the compatibility of products, free of intellectual property rights, does not constitute in itself an unfair practice as long as there is no risk of confusion between the products.[312] The action for parasitic acts or competition boils down to an action for dilution in some way.[313] Recently, decisions of the French Supreme Court seem to suggest that the tort of

[307] See eg A Puttemans, *Droits intellectuels et concurrence déloyale* (Brussels, Bruylant, 2000) 236; Golaz, *L'imitation servile des produits et de leur présentation* (n 2) 228. There are two notions of parasitism, a broad one (parasitism exists if the copied achievement necessitated some effort or investment) and a narrow one (parasitism exists only if the copied achievement necessitated important efforts). See eg Malaurie-Vignal, 'Le parasitisme des investissements et du travail d'autrui' (n 295) 180.

[308] Sometimes parasitism is also referred to as 'economic parasitism' to distinguish it from parasitism occurring in nature. The term 'parasitism' will be used throughout the book to describe economic parasitism.

[309] Contrast Cass com, 26 January 1999 (2000) *Dalloz*, Jurisp 87, cited by B Dutoit, 'Concurrence déloyale et droit comparé' in Y Serra (ed), *Concurrence déloyale, permanence et devenir* (Paris, Dalloz, 2001) 57, 61 and P Le Tourneau, 'Folles idées sur les idées' (2001) 4 *Communication Commerce Electronique, Chronique* 8, 12; Cass com, 30 January 2001 (2001) *Dalloz* no 24, 1939, Bull civ, IV, 27; (2001) JCP G, I, 340, no 29, comment Viney; (2001) *Dalloz*, Jurisp 1939, comment Le Tourneau; (2002) 3 *Propriétés Intellectuelles* 101, comment J Passa with Cass com, 20 May 2003, case no 01-11212, available at www.legifrance.gouv.fr, cited by Passa, 'Responsabilité civile: concurrence' (2003) (n 281) 448–49 (claimants have to establish the amount of the investment necessary to make the copied product and show the extent to which the relevant behaviour has allowed the other party to benefit from it).

[310] Greffe, Greffe and Greffe, *Traité des dessins et des modèles*' (n 5) 500.

[311] Buydens, *La protection de la quasi-création* (n 2) 707, 721; Passa, *Contrefaçon et concurrence déloyale* (n 2) 272; Schmidt-Szalewski, 'La distinction entre l'action en contrefaçon et l'action en concurrence déloyale dans la jurisprudence' (n 295) 466–67; Henning Bodewig, *Unfair Competition Law* (n 275) 123; Greffe, Greffe and Greffe, *Traité des dessins et des modèles* (n 5) 498–500, citing numerous decisions only one of which goes in the opposite direction; Bertrand, *Le droit français de la concurrence déloyale* (n 2) 65–66, citing inter alia, *Sodima v Chambourcy*, CA Paris, 4th ch, 26 November 1982 [1983] PIBD, III, 78 (shapes of yoghourt pots); *Ise v Omni pac*, CA Paris, 4th ch, 22 February 1989, CDA 1989, no 20, 15 (shape of containers for steaks); *Guérault v Nathan*, CA Paris, 1st ch, 9 November 1988 (1989) *Dalloz*, Inf Rap 294; (1990) *Dalloz*, Som 58, comment Colombet (booklets' presentation dictated by the content of the programmes); *Café Grand Mère v Vaudour Danon*, Cass com, 24 May 1976, Bull civ, IV, no 172; CA Paris, 4th ch, 22 March 1988 (1988) 5 *Cahiers du Droit d'Auteur* 25 (colour black for coffee packaging). Bertrand, *Le droit français de la concurrence déloyale* (n 2) 68, also notes that unfair competition will nevertheless be found if there is reproduction not only of the functional parts where similarities are necessary by the application of standards, but also when the parts and shapes which are non-functional and even simply decorative are copied and create confusion even for customers who are informed: citing *Siedma v Lamarque*, CA Paris, 4th ch, 10 April 1962 [1962] Ann. 1962, 240; *Dylon France v LJW*, CA Paris, 4th ch, 20 June 1985 [1986] PIBD, III, 33.

[312] Greffe, Greffe and Greffe, *Traité des dessins et des modèles* (n 5) 499.

[313] Benabou, 'Rapport national, France' (n 23) 14.

parasitism is now defunct, but nothing is less certain as the Court has constantly changed its mind on the topic during the last 10 years and many Courts of Appeal still continue to punish parasitic behaviours. The courts' trend to accept the tort of parasitism has moved away from the traditional foundation of the action in unfair competition, and is now close to an action in protection of property.[314]

(b) Copyright and Neighbouring Rights

Apart from one decision,[315] from 2003 until mid-2007, the Supreme Court has been consistent and rejected the tort of parasitism in cases involving infringement of copyright.[316] However, in June 2007, the Supreme Court handed down a rather contradictory decision which has left the law uncertain.[317] Solstiss argued that its lace, which was protected by copyright, was copied. The Court of Cassation set the decision aside, arguing that the Court of Appeal of Lyon should not have allowed the unfair competition action in addition to the copyright one because there was only slavish imitation. But then the Court added that there is unfair competition when either there is confusion or the defendant benefits from the investments or reputation of another. However, copying always implies benefiting from the investments of another, and copying is no different from the actions punished in an infringement action. Similarly, the reasoning of the highest court in a decision in 2008 involving a 'Longchamp' bag is puzzling.[318] There was held to be copyright infringement but no unfair competition, because there was no risk of confusion *nor intention to benefit from the reputation* of the trademark 'Longchamp'. Again benefitting from the reputation of a competitor is not a fact distinct from copyright infringement. It therefore seems that the French Supreme Court continues to swing between recognising and rejecting the tort of parasitism, with the trend now seeming to recognise the tort.

In two other cases, the Supreme Court correctly held that copyright was infringed and there was unfair competition because there was a risk of confusion.[319] In this situation, there is no simultaneous overlap with copyright, as the copyright infringement test does

[314] Ibid 14.

[315] *SA Conception de Presse v Ste Playboy Enterprises Inc,* Cass 1st civ, 25 May 2004, Jurisdata no 2004-023791 [2004] JCP G, no 29, IV, no 2461, 1340–41 (copies of photographs of Pamela Anderson from the magazine *Playboy*: copyright infringement and also unfair competition simply on the basis of the fact that the defendant wanted to benefit from the reputation of the claimant).

[316] *Movitex and Daxon v Fuego*, Cass com, 23 January 2007, case no 03-13338 [2007] PIBD no 849, III, 258; (2007) 24 *Propriétés Intellectuelles* 357, comment J Passa (sale of infringing clothes at a lower price or lower quality (acrylic against wool) to that of those covered by the exclusive rights not a distinct act of unfair competition); Cass com, 20 February 2007, case no 04-19671 [2007] PIBD no 853, III, 380; (2007) 24 *Propriétés Intellectuelles* 357, comment J Passa (copyright infringed on jacquard designs used for ornamentation of clothes but acts allowing defendant to benefit from the reputation and investments of the copyright holder were not unfair competition); see also Cass com, 20 February 2007, case no 05-13927 [2007] PIBD no 851, III, 304; (2007) 24 *Propriétés Intellectuelles* 357, comment J Passa.

[317] *Solstiss v Erco Pizzi*, Cass com, 12 June 2007 (2007) 30 *Revue Lamy Droit de l'Immatériel* 18.

[318] *Cassegrain and Longchamp v Normal*, Cass com, 2 December 2008 (2009) 45 *Revue Lamy Droit de l'Immatériel* 18.

[319] Cass com 14 January 2003, case no 01-01759 (2003) 7 *Propriétés Intellectuelles* 227, comment J Passa (copyright and design right infringed in the design of a tool used to cultivate vines and risk of confusion); *Sté Rayure v Sté Infinitif*, Cass com, 28 November 2006, case no 04-20555 (2007) 22 *Propriétés Intellectuelles* 120, comment J Passa (copyright infringed in model blouses and risk of confusion resulting from the presentation of blouses following identical modalities, use of the same busts, imitation of the arrangement of the claimant's shops, claimant's advertising boards including the deletion of the claimant's name from them).

not require risk of confusion. 'The two qualifications of infringement and confusion do not overlap even if they result from the same material fact.'[320] Some Courts of Appeal have also ruled in the same way where the defendant affixed the claimant's trademark or other sign in addition to copying the copyrighted work,[321] or because the copyright work was used on the same or similar products, thereby creating a risk of confusion.[322] But otherwise, appellate courts remain split on whether to recognise the tort of parasitism or not, including in the field of the protection of databases by the *sui generis* right,[323] with the majority still in favour of the tort of parasitism.[324]

(c) Designs

A similar picture as that for the overlap between copyright and unfair competition is revealed when one analyses the case law concerning designs. Between 2001 and 2003, the Supreme Court rejected the tort of parasitism and only accepted the action in unfair competition if there was a risk of confusion.[325] Then between 2004 and 2007, the Court

[320] See J Passa in (2003) 7 *Propriétés Intellectuelles* 227.

[321] CA Paris, 4th ch, A, 27 October 2004, RG no 03/16035 (infringement of copyright on olive oil bottle shape and condemnation for unfair competition because the product's labels, although not invoked as infringed under copyright, had been used by the defendant so that it created a risk of confusion); CA Paris, 9 June 2004 [2005] PIBD no 801, III, 95 (infringement of copyright in a computer program and unfair competition because of risk of confusion created by the reproduction of denomination); CA Paris, 4th ch, A, 10 November 2004, RG no 04/13547 (several blouse models protected by copyright were infringed and there was also unfair competition because the defendant sold the products in shops whose arrangements indicated those of the claimant and therefore created a risk of confusion), all three decisions reported by Passa, 'Heurts et malheurs du fait de concurrence deloyale distinct de la contrefaçon' (n 299) 211.

[322] CA Paris, 4th ch, A, 19 January 2005, RG no 03/18891, comment Passa, 'Heurts et malheurs du fait de concurrence déloyale distinct de la contrefaçon' (n 299) 212 (infringement of two drawings protected by copyright by their production on T-shirts; as the claimant produced these designs on products of the same type, the court also concemned on the basis of unfair competition because of a risk of confusion between the products).

[323] *GPSPrevent v Coyote System and others*, TGI Lille, 19 November 2009 and *Xooloo v Optenet Center, Optenet, France Telecom*, Trib Com Paris, 17 December 2009 (*sui generis* right infringed and condemnation for parasitism); compare with *Europages v Ewaycom*, TGI Paris, 3 November 2009, and *AFP v Topix Technologies, Topix Presse*, Trib Com, Paris, 5 February 2010, all available at www.legalis.net (infringement of *sui generis* right and rejection of parasitism).

[324] *SARL Euro 2000 v SA Vog'fournitures and Ste Toupy*, CA Paris, 4th ch, B, 2 July 2004 (2004) 13 *Propriétés Intellectuelles* 968, comment J Passa (jumper design); *SARL K.A. France v SA Citec Environnement and SA SSI Schaeffer*, CA Paris, 4th ch, B, 2 July 2004 (2004) 13 *Propriétés Intellectuelles* 968, comment J Passa. Unclear decisions: *SAS Solune v Sarl Maroquinerie Lafayette*, CA Paris, 4th ch, A, 9 November 2005 (2006) 18 *Propriétés Intellectuelles* 87 (copyright in bag infringed; the court held that the reproduction of the bag in the same range and colours could create a risk of confusion but then added that the defendants willingly followed in the footsteps of the claimants and benefited from important advertising investments). *Contra*: *SA Loubsol Ets Loubeyre v Bollé*, CA Besancon, Ch com, 10 December 2002, Jurisdata no 2002-200815 [2003] JCP G no 25, IV, 2129, 1175 (the copyright in glasses was infringed; the two parties had the same distribution channels and clients; consumers can still be mislead even if the defendant's trademark is different so there was unfair competition as well). Rejecting parasitism: *H&M v Scooter*, CA Paris, 4th ch, A, 7 November 2007 (2007) 229 *Revue Internationale de la Propriété Industrielle et Artistique* 35 (copyright-protected earring design infringed but action in unfair competition for slavish imitation and sale at a lower price rejected as they were not distinct facts).

[325] *SA Jonelli v SA Fuego*, Cass 1st civ, 3 April 2001, Jurisdata no 009007, JCP G no 23, IV, 2015, 1128–29 (the design right on T-shirts was infringed but selling at half price is not unfair competition); Cass com, 17 June 2003, case no 01-17242; Cass com, 17 June 2003, case no 01-12280, available at www.legifrance.gouv.fr; (2003) 9 *Propriétés Intellectuelles* 447, comment J Passa (selling at lower price not a distinct fact); *SA Diffusion des Ebénistes Contemporains dite Romeo v SARL Gelineau Xavier*, Cass com, 3 June 2003, Jurisdata no 2003-019289 [2003] JCP no 30, IV, no 2352, 1432 (chairs and sofas models were infringed, not unfair competition simply to copy them); *Cave v* Y, Cass com, 14 January 2003, case no 01-01759 (design infringement and unfair competition because the slavish copying of the model created a risk of confusion in the mind of the public).

accepted the tort.[326] On 1 July 2008, in a decision where a design and trademark were infringed on a perfume bottle, the Court accepted the tort[327] but the same day rejected it in a case concerning the lay-out of a magazine's front page, requiring that there be a risk of confusion.[328] In December the same year, the Court again rejected the tort.[329]

Courts of Appeal have not fared any better. They are split, although more of them have recognised and still do recognise the tort.[330] Appellate courts also remain split as to whether

[326] Cass com, 17 March 2004 [2004] PIBD no 788, III, 366; (2004) *Propriété Industrielle* (December) 26; (2004) 12 *Propriétés Intellectuelles* 800, comment J Passa (Waterman pen covered by copyright and design right was infringed and selling imitations of a bad quality at a low price leading to lessening the value of the design and banalising its image were facts distinct from infringement); *Chaumet v Diperi*, Cass com, 26 May 2004, case no 03-11030, comment P De Candé in (2004) 13 *Propriétés Intellectuelles* 943 (design infringement and unfair competition because of slavish copying); *Mr X, Sté Maison du Kelsh and Sté Alscacienne de Maroquinerie v Sté Création Li Yi Sa Lys*, Cass com, 28 November 2006 (2007) *International Review of Intellectual Property and Competition Law* 739 (using a colour not described in the registration documents but identical to that in which the bag was marketed was a fact distinct from design infringement).

[327] *Sté Senteur Mazal v SA BPI*, Cass com, 1 July 2008, Jurisdata no 2008-044659 [2008] JCP G no 36, IV, 2429, 53 (trademark and design right in the shape of a perfume bottle infringed and there was parasitism because defendant, by selling similar non-confusing goods, tried to benefit from the investments of the claimant).

[328] *1633 v Sté Conception de presse et d'édition (SCPE)*, Cass com, 1 July 2008 [2008] PIBD no 885, III, 674; (2008) 29 *Propriétés Intellectuelles* 449, comment P De Candé (design right in magazine's cover page layout infringed; court rejected parasitism but accepted unfair competition if there was a risk of confusion).

[329] *SA La Redoute v Sarl J Martin Trepointes*, Cass com, 2 December 2008, Jurisdata no 2008-046115; RLDI 2009/45, no 1478, obs LC (there was infringement of copyright but no unfair competition as simple copying is not a distinct fact).

[330] Decisions rejecting the tort: CA Lyon, 15 May 2003 (2003) 9 *Propriétés Intellectuelles* 447, comment J Passa (selling at lower price not a distinct fact); *Free v C&A France*, CA Paris, 4th ch, A, 25 June 2003, unpublished; *Cassegrain v Hpo*, CA Paris, 4th ch, A, 2 July 2003, unpublished; *Guenoun v Coblentz*, CA Paris, 4th ch, A, unpublished, comment P De Candé in (2003) *Propriétés Intellectuelles* 401 (all three courts rejecting the action in unfair competition, in addition to the infringement action, when products are sold at an inferior price and material used is of mediocre quality); *SAS Nemery v Enesco France,* CA Paris, 4th ch. B, 28 April 2004, comment P De Candé in (2004) 13 *Propriétés Intellectuelles* 943 (rejects the parasitism action in addition to infringement action for copying of figurines); *AGLO v SNCF and others*, CA Paris, 4th ch, B, 4 March 2005 (2005) 17 *Propriétés Intellectuelles* 455, comment P De Candé (the simple fact of commercialising a competing product which is not protected by an exclusive right is not in itself an act of unfair competition unless there is a risk of confusion as to the origin of the products. To make savings to the detriment of the competitor is not in itself a breach and derives from the freedom of commerce and free competition. But in this case, there was also a risk of confusion); *Jade v Rautureau*, CA Paris, 4th ch, A, 1 February 2006, (2006) 21 *Propriétés Intellectuelles* 463, comment P De Candé (admits unfair competition in addition to infringement action because the defendant had copied eight models of goods and it could create a risk of confusion); *Alain Manoukian v Laury Jim*, CA Paris, 4th ch, B, 5 May 2006 (2006) 21 *Propriétés Intellectuelles* 462, comment P De Candé (infringement of jumper design but copying the same range of colours is not a distinct fact); *Santoni Calzatore v Hermès*, CA Paris, 4th ch, B, 1 December 2006 [2007] PIBD no 847, III, 187 (selling infringing shoes in shops close to that of Hermes' shops were not acts of unfair competition because Hermes' clients were very particular and would not confuse shoes distributed by Hermes with shoes from another origin); *Chaumet v Camille and Lucie*, CA Paris, 4th ch, B, 11 April 2008 (2008) *Propriétés Intellectuelles* 451, comment P De Candé (range effect does not constitute unfair competition). See also TGI Paris, 9 September 2003, [2004] PIBD 178; CA Paris, 9 April 1999, [2000] PIBD 298; *Snera v Stand 21*, CA Paris, 4 December 1990, cited by Cohen, *Le droit des dessins et modèles* (n 5) 237 and CA Paris, 16 January 2004, [2004] PIBD 207; CA Paris, 21 March 2001, [2001] PIBD 286; CA Paris, 22 September 2000, [2000] PIBD 64; CA Paris, 12 June 2002, [2003] PIBD 110, cited by Cohen, *Le droit des dessins et modèles* (n 5) 243–44, holding that simply selling at a low price is not a distinct fact. Decisions accepting the tort: *SARL DSL Textiles v SA Sprintex and others*, CA Paris, 4th ch, B, 20 February 2004 (2004) 13 *Propriétés Intellectuelles* 943, comment P De Candé (condemnation for infringement and slavish copying of cloth); *Practidose v Holdiplast*, CA Paris, 4th ch, A, 22 June 2005 (2005) 17 *Propriétés Intellectuelles* 455, comment P De Candé (adopting the same dimensions, the same shades of colours presented in the same way is a fact distinct from design infringement); *Bouchara v Siretext*, CA Paris, 4th ch, A, 29 June 2005 (2005) 17 *Propriétés Intellectuelles* 455, comment P De Candé (affixing the drawing on a similar product in the same cloth, with the same colours and lower price is a fact distinct from design infringement); *Cama v PBI Follies Diffusion You*, 19 January 2005 and *Diramode Boutique v Stock J Boutique*, 22 June 2005 (2005) 17 *Propriétés Intellectuelles* 455, comment P De Candé (copying the drawings on the same range of

using the same colours, dimensions and/or material (ie a 'range effect') entails liability, some requiring, some not requiring a risk of confusion.[331] Finally, some decisions are confusing or contradictory, adding to the already generally messy state of the case law.[332]

(d) Patents

Case law on the overlap between patents and unfair competition is scarce but orthodox. A fairly old decision of the Court of Cassation set aside a decision which held that there was unfair competition without stating what the distinct facts were.[333] The Court of Appeal of Paris seems to have followed this view.[334] For instance, recently, the Court of Appeal of Paris rejected the action in unfair competition for slavish imitation of a patent holder whose patent was held valid and infringed, stating that slavish imitation is not an act distinct from infringement.[335] In a previous case, the Court of Appeal of Paris held there was infringement of a patent on the interior mechanism of a foldable food trolley and also unfair competition because the infringing trolley reproduced slavishly the exterior aspect of the product, its metallic structure, the plasticised squared cloth, and the notice of use of the carriage also reproduced the eight images illustrating the claimant's trolley.[336] Other appellate courts also punished defendants because they created a risk of confusion.[337] Therefore, it seems that at least in the field of patents, the courts do not admit the tort of parasitism at all.

(e) Plant Variety Rights

Decisions on this overlap appear to also be rare. In a decision of 2002, the Court of Appeal of Paris held that a plant variety right was infringed and that it was unfair competition to

clothing and same range of colours is a fact distinct from design infringement); *Auchan France v Comptoir Lux, Maghill and Hexagona*, CA Paris, 4th ch, B, 24 November 2006 (2007) 25 *Propriétés Intellectuelles* 477, comment P De Candé (simple copying is a fact distinct from infringement). For more decisions, see Greffe, Greffe and Greffe, *Traité des dessins et des modèles* (n 5) 488–91, citing a long list of decisions which have held that the simple imitation of packaging can be unfair competition, even if there was infringement of either copyright or design right. Few require a risk of confusion. See ibid 494–97, citing decisions stating that slavish imitation is a breach. The decisions accept the action whether the design was or not protected and infringed.

[331] *C&A France v Eurl HG*, CA Paris, 4th ch, A, 16 January 2008; CA Paris, *Sarl Trading European Company v SAS Guy Degrenne*, 4th ch, A, 16 January 2008; *Consortium Ménager Parisien v EPB*, CA Paris, 4th ch, A, 20 February 2008 (range effect constitutes unfair competition); and *Dessange International v Denaive*, CA Paris, 4th ch, A, 21 November 2007 (2008) *Propriétés Intellectuelles* 451, comment P De Candé. See also Cohen, *Le droit des dessins et modèles* (n 5) 238–40, citing decisions condemning range effects mostly without checking whether there is a risk of confusion.

[332] *Ukal v LND*, CA Paris, 4th ch, A, 20 December 2006 (2007) 5 *Propriétés Intellectuelles* 477, comment P De Candé (unfair competition because of a range effect even if the infringer only reproduced two models(!)); *Proconect and Ametek v Albright France & Prestolite*, CA Paris, 4th ch, A, 7 November 2007, (2008) 87 *Gazette du Palais* (27 March) 28 (court held that slavish copying cannot constitute a distinct fact of unfair competition, but then defines parasitism and decides that Albright France does not prove investments so that parasitic acts are not characterised. This seems to mean that if it had proved investments simple copying would have been punished).

[333] Cass com, 23 May 1973, Bull civ, IV, no 182, cited by Schmidt-Szalewski and Pierre, *Droit de la propriété industrielle* (n 5) para 228 n 455.

[334] See CA Paris, 27 May 1993 [1993] PIBD no 553, III, 609; CA Paris, 29 November 1995 [1996] PIBD no606, III, 109, cited by Schmidt-Szalewski and Pierre, *Droit de la propriété industrielle* (n 5) para 228 n 455.

[335] *SSI Schaeffer v Sté Citec Environnement*, CA Paris, 4th ch, B, 26 October 2007, RG no 06/05972 (2008) 27 *Propriétés Intellectuelles* 263, comment J Passa.

[336] CA Paris, 4th ch, A, 8 December 2004 [2005] PIBD no 804, III, 166, comment J Passa, 'Heurts et malheurs du fait de concurrence déloyale distinct de la contrefaçon' (n 299) 15 *Propriétés Intellectuelles* 210.

[337] CA Lyon, 15 February 1990 [1990] PIBD no 477, III, 282; CA Lyon, 13 January 2000 [2000] PIBD no 696, III, 183; CA Paris, 21 October 2005 [2006] PIBD no 822, III, 43.

sell infringing strawberries without indicating the exact denomination as it appears in the plant variety right certificate.[338] This decision has been criticised because the indication is only mandated for the commercialisation of authentic products (see article L623-15(5)). Here, the products were not authentic. The infringer does not make a distinct breach by not using the denomination of the infringed variety.[339] By analogy with this case, the infringer of a patent or a design right does not commit a distinct breach of unfair competition when it does not use the commercial name of the product, whether or not it is registered as a trademark, under the pretext that the denomination used can give the impression that the new products are comparable.[340] As Passa points out, conversely, selling the infringing strawberries under the denomination of the infringed variety would have led to a real risk of confusion and therefore of capture of the sales. Such a risk of confusion, not covered by the qualification of infringement of a plant variety right, would have justified a condemnation in addition for unfair competition.[341]

(ii) Risk of Confusion

For a trademark right to be infringed, in most cases, a likelihood of confusion is required, ie when there is no identity but only similarity between the sign and the products or services.[342] Therefore, risk of confusion is not an act distinct from infringement. This is so for acts which relate to the trademark itself. If other aspects of the products which are not part of the trademark are copied or imitated and from this, an increased risk of confusion results, then this is a fact distinct from infringement. Risk of confusion is not required when dissimilar goods or services are sold and the mark has reputation. It is sufficient that the reproduction or imitation of the mark causes a prejudice to the trademark holder or constitutes an unjustified exploitation of the mark (article L713-5). This article says 'it gives rise to the civil liability of the defendant' rather than saying it is a trademark infringement. So it is much wider than the corresponding Trademark Directive, article 5(2), which simply provides that there is infringement if the use of the sign without due cause takes unfair advantage of, or is detrimental to, the distinctive character or the repute of the trademark. The problems associated with this article are discussed under the negative overlap as this is where they have occurred.

Again, as for the previous simultaneous overlaps with unfair competition law, the Court of Cassation is inconsistent in the way it punishes infringers for unfair competition. In one case, it held that benefiting from the investments of the trademark holder or prejudicing a trademark holder's reputation or image justifies an additional condemnation,[343] whereas this is not a fact distinct from infringement (for the latter, if the mark is not well-known). In another case two months later, the Court held that imitation of a trademark is a fact distinct from trademark infringement.[344] In yet another dispute, the owner of the marks 'Le Ruban Bleu' and 'Le Fil Bleu' ('The Blue Ribbon' and 'The Blue Thread') used to des-

[338] See comment J Passa in (2002) 5 *Propriétés Intellectuelles* 111.

[339] Ibid.

[340] Ibid.

[341] Ibid.

[342] According to the Supreme Court's case law, the risk of confusion is determined by reference to the consumer of average attention who does not see the relevant products simultaneously. See *Nathan v Hachette*, Cass com, 3 July 2001, cited by Greffe, Greffe and Greffe, *Traité des dessins et des modèles* (n 5) 487.

[343] Cass com, 14 January 2003 [2003] PIBD no 60, III, 156.

[344] *Comité national olympique et sportif français v Groupement d'achat des centres Leclerc*, Cass com, 11 March 2003 (2003) *Contrats Concurrence Consommation* (August/September) 24.

ignate a ribbon and a thread of the colour blue which allied plastic and metallic threads and used mainly to make electric fences, launched trademark and unfair competition actions because the defendant used these terms. The Supreme Court set aside the judgment of the Court of Appeal which held that there was no infringement or unfair competition.[345] Nevertheless, the decisions of the French Supreme Court against the use of the unfair competition action to repair the same prejudice as under trademark infringement seem more abundant and also more recent.[346] The Court has also approved appellate courts which held that there was unfair competition when the acts were distinct (eg selling the infringing goods in a shop very close to that of the claimant and using a sticker stating that the goods are controlled by the trademark owner[347]). This does not punish the same act twice as the confusion does not arise from the mark itself but from other acts. The risk of confusion is aggravated by these distinct acts. In one case, however, the Supreme Court went too far and prevented the use of the action where it was legitimate. Copying the essential characteristics of a product's shape where the trademark is not the shape and the said shape is arbitrary are facts distinct from infringement, which aggravate the risk of confusion, but the Court of Cassation did not think so.[348] Nevertheless, later the Court handed down a decision in the opposite direction.[349]

[345] Cass com, 4 June 2002 [2002] PIBD no 752, III, 510, briefly reported in (2003) 7 *Propriétés Intellectuelles* 223, comment J Passa.

[346] *Christian Marry v Creations LTN*, Cass com, 11 February 2003 [2003] *PIDB* no 762, III, 214, comment P De Candé, L'action en concurrence déloyale est-elle menacée par l'evolution du droit de la propriété intellectuelle?' (2004) *Propriétés Intellectuelles* 492, 500. The Supreme Court set aside the appellate court's decision because it did not indicate precisely which other facts were distinct from infringement of the trademark. For De Candé, this decision means that all the demonstrative elements of a risk of confusion, which can be taken into account to hold that there is infringement, cannot be invoked to base the unfair competition action; *Trader Classified Media France v Atemi & Liins*, Cass com, 6 November 2007, case no 06-16189 (2008) 27 *Propriétés Intellectuelles* 263, comment J Passa (setting aside Court of Appeal's decision which had allowed the additional claim in unfair competition because the defendant had tried to follow in the footsteps of the owner by profiting from the reputation of its trademarks, which were held infringed); *M6 v LPG Systems*, Cass com, 30 May 2007, case no 06-13830 [2007] PIBD no. 857, III, 507; (2007) 25 *Propriétés Intellectuelles* 499, comment J Passa (setting aside decision concerning massage machines); *Auchan France v Leonidas*, cass com, 20 February 2007, Jurisdata no 037494 [2007] JCP G, IV, no 13, no 1670, 48 (the Court of Appeal held there was infringement of the trademark 'Leonidas' by mark 'Belidas' and unfair competition for taking away Leonidas' clients and benefitting from its investments. The Supreme Court sets aside the decision because there were no distinct facts).

[347] Cass com 22 October 2002, case no 00-19701. For other examples, see Cass com, 24 January 1995 [1995] JCP E, Pan 329 (infringer used same colour as used by trademark owner to present its products to the public); Cass com, 6 April 1999 [1999] PIBD no 678, III, 254; Cass com, 29 January 2002 [2002] PIBD no 744, III, 277; CA Colmar, 20 February 2002 [2002] JCP E, 1742 (use of similar graphics in commercial documents); CA Paris, 7 September 2005 [2006] PIBD no 823, III, 96 and CA Paris, 7 December 2005 [2006] PIBD no 823, III, 90 (confusion with the claimant's undertaking); CA Paris, 18 January 2006 [2006] PIBD no 829, III, 327 (use of the claimant's trade name to distribute the products under the imitated mark), cited by Schmidt-Szalewski and Pierre, *Droit de la propriété industrielle* (n 5) para 634.

[348] Cass com, 11 February 2003 [2003] PIBD no 762, III, 213.

[349] *Sté Colmar v Sté Archange International*, Cass 1st civ, 4 April 2006, Jurisdata no. 2006-033037, comment Caron, 'L'empilement des propriétés intellectuelles' (n 115) (defendant infringed trademark 'Angélique' (registered for books) by using it as the title of its film. There was unfair competition because there was a risk of confusion because of the similarity of graphics and images between the pages of the cover of certain 'Angelique' books and the titles of the defendant's film). See also *SA Streibig and others v Streibig AG*, an earlier decision of CA Colmar, 1st ch, 20 February 2002, Jurisdata no 2002-188465 [2002] JCP G no 49, IV, no 2980, 2202–3 (it is an act of unfair competition which aggravates the risk of confusion to reproduce a distinctive character which does not appear in the trademark registration. This is the case when a competitor reproduces on the machines and commercial documents similar graphics, which aggravates the risk of visual confusion. There was no slavish copying of the machines but some similarities existed with the claimant's machines and therefore that also aggravated the risk of confusion. However, the court adds that there was parasitism because these acts allowed the defendant to attract clients without paying anything).

The Courts of Appeal have been equally inconsistent but recently, like the Court of Cassation, seem to have rejected the overlap.[350] Those which accept the overlap hold that benefiting from the reputation of the mark and the trademark owner's commercial efforts is a distinct act and that there is unfair competition in addition to trademark infringement. However, as we have said, trademark infringement already repairs this prejudice.[351] Although the case law has been inconsistent, recently both the highest and the appellate courts seem to reject unfair competition if the acts are not distinct from trademark infringement.

(iii) Trade Secrets and Know-How

Not surprisingly, the decisions relating to the overlap between patent and trade secret protection are rare. Several recent decisions have punished under unfair competition law acts which exploit the fruit of another's work, whether or not covered by exclusive rights, in the particular circumstance where it has been rendered accessible during a prior contractual or pre-contractual relationship. In one of the cases, the Court of Appeal underlined that the infringing behaviour was the misappropriation of know-how made possible because of the prior contractual relationship. Even though the Court of Appeal added that this behaviour resulted in important savings to the detriment of the claimants, which naturally conjures up parasitism, the court's reasoning, however, went on to make clear that the breach resides not only in the fact of exploiting the achievement and benefiting from the investments, but in disloyal behaviour which consists in exploiting elements transmitted during the previous contractual relationship.[352] If prior relations allowed infringement, breaching the obligation of loyalty arising from these relations constitutes a breach which is separable and therefore distinct from the exploitation itself.[353] Therefore, after having held that the company committed patent infringement, the Court of Appeal of Paris, in the decision of 7 October 2005, added that this company and one of its employees should be punished under civil liability.[354] The Supreme Court in the same type of situation had already approved an appellate court which had punished the patent infringer for unfair competition because he had hired a former employee of

[350] See in this latter respect, *LFDL v Pasquier*, CA Angers, Ch com, 25 November 2008 [2009] JCP G no 21, IV, no 1883, 51 ('Chinois des rois' as a trademark for a cake (gateau des rois) infringed but unfair competition action rejected because benefiting from trademark holder's investments, reputation and success, and diverting its clients, are not distinct facts); *WMF France v SA Maj and others*, CA Paris, 4th ch, A, 28 January 2009 (2009) 90 *Gazette du Palais* (31 March) 37.

[351] See eg CA Versailles, 5 April 2001 [2002] PIBD no 734, III, 38, comment J Passa in (2002) 4 *Propriétés Intellectuelles* 81; *Com v Microsoft and others*, CA Paris, 4th ch, 9 March 2005, case no 04-0552, Jurisdata no 267711 (2005) 7 *Revue Lamy Droit de l'Immatériel* 25 (copyright and trademark infringement and unfair competition for profiting from claimant's investments and reputation and selling at cheaper price); *Sté Editions KL et les Epoux L v SAS Carboatmedia*, CA Paris, 4th ch, B, 21 March 2008, case no 06-20647, Jurisdata no 364580 (2008) 42 *Revue Lamy Droit de l'Immatériel* 26.

[352] Cass 1st civ, 13 December 2005, case no 03-21154 [2006] PIBD no 823, III, 110 (parasitism for know-how hijacking. Defendant had a contractual relationship with claimant but later denounced it. It used the know-how divulged by claimant in its computer program during the contractual negotiations to create its own computer program and thereby made important savings); CA Paris, 4th ch, B, 7 October 2005 [2005] PIBD no 819, III, 685; CA Paris, 4th ch, B, 4 November 2005 [2006] PIBD no 823, III, 103; CA Paris, 4th ch, B, 17 February 2006, RG no 04/21739 (2006) 19 *Propriétés Intellectuelles* 226, comment by J Passa.

[353] J Passa, 'Responsabilité civile : concurrence' (2006) 19 *Propriétés Intellectuelles* 227.

[354] Ibid. For another example see *ADM v Rozenthal*, CA Paris, 10 March 1995 and *Leblon-Delienne v Sarl Pylones*, CA Rouen, 5 January 1995 (taking advantage of pre-commercial relations during which a trade secret or know-how is revealed is a distinct fact), cited by Cohen, *Le droit des dessins et modèles* (n 5) 236.

the patentee and had irregularly obtained manufacturing precisions and results of research work.[355]

To close this subsection on simultaneous overlaps, unlike the United Kingdom but like Germany, it must be noted that there is apparently no decision involving a sign in which there is a trademark as well as a copyright or design right, and which has been compared, therefore giving rise to the application of the Misleading and Comparative Advertising Directive (MCAD).[356] However, in some cases it could be that criticism, review or parody permitted under French copyright law (IPC, article L122-5) could coincide with comparative advertising allowed by the MCAD.

In conclusion, the situation in France as to whether a simultaneous overlap between unfair competition and intellectual property rights is allowed is unclear. This is so for all simultaneous overlaps except the patent/unfair competition one. The Court of Cassation's most recent decisions seem to accept the tort of parasitism for most overlaps, but in view of its other recent conflicting decisions, the status of the tort of parasitism is uncertain. Additionally, Courts of Appeal remain split and the majority of them favour cumulation. Since France has a long tradition approving the prevention of parasitism, it is very likely that the tort is still alive.

C Negative Overlap

As far as unprotected achievements are concerned, the Court of Cassation continually contradicts itself. Generally, it is clearly in favour of the notion of parasitism.[357] Thus, it is unlawful to reproduce an unprotected achievement (eg a catalogue, a trademark) even if this reproduction does not entail a risk of confusion. The position of the Court more recently, however, has been that there is no parasitism when the copier also invested him- or herself, or has made some (even minor) differences to his or her product, even if s/he copied to avoid the need to make his or her own efforts.[358] Nevertheless, in other decisions from the end of the 1990s and until recently, the Court did not accept that parasitism

[355] Cass com, 18 December 1957, Bull civ, III, no 355; Cass com, 25 April 1967, Bull civ, IV, no 164, cited by Passa, 'Responsabilité civile: concurrence' (2006) (n 353).

[356] Compare with chapter 5, section IX.C.

[357] See eg Cass com, 21 June 1994 [1994] PIBD, III, 514 cited by Passa, *Contrefaçon et concurrence déloyale* (n 2) 273; Cass com, 27 June 1995 (1995) *Revue de Jurisprudence de Droit des Affaires* 1129 (parasitism does not require proof of confusion), cited by Malaurie-Vignal, 'Le parasitisme des investissements et du travail d'autrui' (n 295) 181; Cass com, 26 January 1999 (2000) *Dalloz*, Jurisp 87, cited by Le Tourneau, 'Folles idées sur les idées' (n 309) 12; Cass com, 30 January 2001 (2001) *Dalloz*, no 24, 1939, comment Le Tourneau; Bull civ IV, 27; [2001] JCP G, I, 340, no 29, comment Viney; [2002] Prop Int 101, comment J Passa (plagiarism of a catalogue); Cass com, 27 March 2001 (2001) 123 *Contrats Concurrence Consommation* 4, comment Malaurie; [2001] PIBD no 725, III, 408; Passa 'Responsabilité civile: distribution' (n 283) *Propriétés Intellectuelles* 100 *et seq*; Cass, 15 January 2002, 22 May 2002, 18 June 2002 and 8 October 2002, cited by Passa, 'Responsabilité civile : concurrence' (2003) (n 281) 85; Cass, 8 July 2003, case no 01-13293, cited by Passa, 'Responsabilité civile: concurrence' (2003) (n 281); Cass com, 29 October 2003 [2004] PIBD no 778, III, 47, cited by J Passa, 'Responsabilité civile : concurrence' (2004) 11 *Propriétés Intellectuelles* 683; Cass, 1 July 2003, case no 01-00628, available at www.legifrance.gouv.fr.

[358] Cass com, 18 June 2002 [2003] PIBD no 755, III, 22, cited by Passa, 'Responsabilité civile : concurrence' (2003) (n 281) 85; Cass com, 17 December 2002 [2003] PIBD no 764, III, 278, cited by Passa 'Responsabilité civile: concurrence' (2003) (n 281). Thus, the Court of Cassation limits the hypotheses of parasitism to pure slavish imitations. That was not the position of the previous case law. Ibid 449.

alone is an act of unfair competition; instead it required a risk of confusion.[359] And in two decisions of 2002, the Court held that it is not unlawful to sell products identical to those of another undertaking which are unprotected by an intellectual property right.[360] These decisions are difficult to reconcile with the other decisions of the Court of the same period (2001–2003) which are clearly in favour of preventing parasitism.[361]

(i) Copyright and Neighbouring Rights

The case law relating to the possibility of a negative overlap between copyright and neighbouring rights, on the one hand, and unfair competition law, on the other hand, is confusing. More decisions of the Supreme Court accept the overlap[362] than reject[363] it but the most recent cases are contradictory or unclear. In the 2007 *Bollé* case, the claimant argued that the defendant copied models of glasses and thereby infringed its copyright. The Court of Appeal of Lyon held that copyright was not infringed and also rejected the action in unfair competition as there were no facts distinct from copying. The Court of Cassation set the decision aside.[364] The Court said that the unfair competition action can be launched by someone who cannot benefit from an exclusive right; it does not matter that the facts are materially the same as those alleged to support an infringement action which has been rejected and originality of the product is not a condition of unfair competition. It added that this circumstance is only one possible factor to determine the existence of a breach by creating a risk of confusion. The ruling is not clear, in at least two respects. First, it is unclear whether the Court requires risk of confusion or not. A

[359] Cass com, 21 October 1997 [1998] PIBD no 645, III, 21; Cass com, 27 January 1998 [1998] PIBD no 657, III, 362; Cass com, 5 October 1999 [2000] PIBD no 691, III, 75, cited by Passa, 'Propos dissidents sur la sanction du parasitisme économique' (n 305) 306; Cass com, 16 January 2001 [2001] Bull civ, IV, no 13; (2001) *Contrats Concurrence Consommation* Comm 43, comment Malaurie-Vignal; JCP, IV, 1421; Cass com, 13 February 2001 [2001] PIBD no 723, III, 354. See also Passa, 'Responsabilité civile: distribution' (n 283).

[360] Cass com, 18 June 2002 [2002] PIBD no 754, III, 578, cited by Passa, 'Responsabilité Civile: concurrence' (n 357) 684; *Distribution Casino France v Ratureau*, Cass com, 9 July 2002 (2003) *Contrats Concurrence Consommation* (January) 11; [2003] *Propriétés Intellectuelles* 82, comment J Passa.

[361] See above.

[362] *Microsoft v Cuadros*, Cass 1st civ, 13 December 2005, case no 03-21.154, comment P Belloir, 'L'exclusion de la protection des fonctionnalités d'un logiciel par le droit d'auteur' (n 189) 17 (functionalities of a computer program were not protected by copyright because they were only ideas, but there was parasitism. It is not clear what is meant by parasitism in the Court of Cassation's decision as it is laconic. The appellate court had said there was parasitism because the defendant had used the know-how of the software's creators); *Lausecker v Karelis*, Cass 1st civ, 5 July 2006, Jurisdata no 2006-034428 [2006] JCP G, no 31-35, IV, no 2686, 1608 (no copyright in a chalet for want of originality but the Supreme Court sets aside the Court of Appeal's decision that there was no unfair competition although the Court of Appeal recognised that the defendant had benefited from the efforts of the claimant); *Janssens v CFEVS*, Cass civ, 1st ch, 20 March 2007, Jurisdata no 2007-038076 [2007] JCP G, IV, no 17, no 1859, 42 (similarly, no copyright in a bottle top for want of originality. The Court of Appeal's decision held that there was no unfair competition for want of distinct facts. The Supreme Court sets it aside because the Court of Appeal should have checked whether there was parasitic behaviour by the defendant).

[363] Cass com, 8 July 2003, case no 01-13293, available at www.legifrance.gouv.fr and (2003) 9 *Propriétés Intellectuelles* 448, comment J Passa (not unfair competition to copy products unprotected by IPR and sell them at lower price (board games)); Cass, 14 November 2006 (2007) *Propriétés Intellectuelles* 118, comment J Passa; see also AE Kahn, 'Un an de droit de la mode' (2007) *Communication Commerce Electronique* (September) 26 (tort of parasitism rejected for Scottish patterns on which no IPR subsisted or at least the claimant did not sue on that basis); *Sté Martin v La Redoute*, Cass com, 2 December 2008, case no 07-19.436 (2009) 45 *Revue Lamy Droit de l'Immatériel* 19 (reproducing a bag and selling it cheaper at a lower quality is not a fact distinct from copyright infringement so there was no unfair competition).

[364] *Bollé v Euro Protection*, Cass com, 12 June 2007 (2007) 31 *Revue Lamy Droit de l'Immatériel*, comment E Arnaud. See also Kahn 'Un an de droit de la mode' (2008) (n 21).

possible reading is that copying a product can constitute a breach on the basis of unfair competition law, even if the copy served as the basis of an infringement action (which failed), as long as it creates a risk of confusion in the consumer's mind.[365] Secondly, the ruling does not clarify whether the action in unfair competition would also have been allowed if there was infringement (so allowing the simultaneous overlap).

A year or so later, the Court allowed the protection of perfumes through an action for parasitism.[366] The owner of a trademark and design right in the shape of perfume bottles ('Le Mâle' of J-P Gaultier and also the female equivalent) sued for infringement. The Court of Appeal held that the designs were valid and infringed. It also held that copyright protected the fragrance. On this latter point, the Supreme Court set aside the decision. But in addition, the Court of Appeal held that copying the fragrance was parasitic behaviour because the defendant tried to benefit from the investments of the claimant. No risk of confusion existed. If consumers using the website eBay searched for 'J-P Gaultier', they would find the infringing goods as well as the original (advertised as perfumes 'of Gaultier type'). These were sold for 7 euros rather than 40–60 euros. On this point, the Supreme Court upheld the decision. This decision recognises a simultaneous overlap (parasitism/designs/trademark) and implicitly also a negative overlap (absence of copyright/parasitism). Indeed, it may well be that if the claimant could not sue on the basis of trademark, copyright or designs in respect of his perfume/perfume bottle/logo/name, s/he could sue on the basis of parasitism. Finally, in February 2009, the Supreme Court confirmed its *Bollé* jurisprudence, repeating the same formula and thus leaving the case law in a confused state on the issue of negative overlaps.[367]

The same confusion reigns within appellate courts, with again more decisions accepting[368] than rejecting[369] the overlap. Furthermore, some appellate courts adopt a slightly

[365] See comment E Arnaud in (2007) 31 *Revue Lamy Droit de l'Immatériel*.

[366] *Sté Senteur Mazal v SA BPI*, Cass com, 1 July 2008, Jurisdata no 2008-044659 [2008] JCP G no. 36, IV, 2429, 53; see also AE Kahn 'Un an de droit de la mode' (2009) *Communication Commerce Electronique* (September).

[367] *Parisac SARL v Louis Vuitton Malletier SA*, Cass com, 10 February 2009, Jurisdata no 2009-047000 [2009] PIBD no 893, III, 921; [2009] JCP G no 12, IV, 1437, 72 (bags reproducing the 'Louis Vuitton' marks but no other IPR subsisted on the bags themselves. The trademark infringement did not concern the combination of colours, so for the court these were distinct facts which had not been punished).

[368] *SA Pall France v Sté Fim Medical*, CA Paris, 4th ch, A, 12 October 2005, RG no 04/14848 (2006) 18 *Propriétés Intellectuelles* 87 (no copyright infringement but parasitism because of similarities of shape and colour between the products); *Vente.privée.com v Kalypso*, CA Paris, 24 September 2008, available at www.legalis.net; (2009) 3 *Communication Commerce Electronique* (March) Comm 25, comment A Debet (no copyright in general conditions of sale, no risk of confusion but condemnation of the defendant for parasitic acts). See also *Agatha v Din Vanh*, CA Paris, 4th ch, B, 18 January 2008 (action based solely on unfair competition not copyright; similar jewels sold by defendant at one-tenth of the price. The Court of Appeal condemned for parasitism because the sale at an inferior price could only create a risk of confusion. De Candé thinks that it was improbable that there was a risk of confusion); *SARL Domoti v EPB*, CA Paris, 4th ch, B, 14 December 2008 (claimant also deliberately chose to use unfair competition), both reported in (2008) 29 *Propriétés Intellectuelles* 449, comment P De Candé; *Sté IIEESS, Ditel v Société*, CA Paris, 14th ch, B, 23 January 2009, affirming Trib Com Paris (réf), 18 June 2008 (defendant copied database, claimant deliberately chose to use the unfair competition action, court declared itself competent and condemned on parasitism alone. Defendant also used the name of the claimant to sell its software. It is unclear from the decision why this is an act of parasitism rather than risk of confusion).

[369] *Clanet, es qual and others v SA Etoile du Vercors*, CA Grenoble, Ch com, 12 September 2002, Jurisdata no 2002–190571, JCP nos 51–52, IV, 3085, 2305 (packaging design for cheese not original therefore not protected. Defendant used the same packaging but the labelling was totally different so there was no unfair competition); *Direct Line v Rabbit Tanaka Corp*, CA Colmar, 1st civ, 31 January 2006, Jurisdata no 2006-293618, JCP no 18, IV, no 2068, 931–32 (lamp not considered original; defendant's importation of lamps from China at a cheaper price was not unfair competition since the model was regularly commercialised in China and the Chinese provider of the competitor had a design right for China for the relevant lamp); see also a decision of

more restrictive version of parasitism, requiring the claimant to prove his or her investments to win the action and/or the defendant to prove investments of his own to escape condemnation on this basis.[370]

(ii) *Designs*

Unsurprisingly, courts are also split in relation to the negative overlap concerning design rights. Some courts only accept the unfair competition action if the reproduction of designs or models which are in the public domain create a possible confusion between the objects, although nothing justifies this requirement of confusion.[371] Some courts do not find risk of confusion because the trademark of the defendant was clearly affixed on the product.[372] But other courts grant the unfair competition action simply for copying, even if there is no risk of confusion.[373] In the same way as with the negative overlap between copyright and unfair competition, some courts require that the defendant proves investments of its own to win the action in parasitism.[374]

(iii) *Trademarks*

The situation relating to negative overlap between trademark and unfair competition is less critical. Indeed, unfair competition has always acted as a way of protecting unregistered signs. Therefore, several rulings of the Court of Cassation in 2003 requiring risk of confusion to punish a defendant using a claimant's unregistered sign make perfect sense.[375] As very clearly summarised by Passa, when an operator claims that the denomination or an element of the presentation of these products, not covered by exclusive rights, has been reproduced or used by a competitor, s/he must launch an unfair competition action whose success supposes proof of a risk of confusion between the products and the anteriority of his or her exploitation on the market of the element allegedly copied. The copied element must be arbitrary, ie not dictated by the nature or function of the product or other technical or commercial necessities.[376] These decisions have the merit of reminding us clearly of this rule. Reinforcing this position, in a 2008 decision, the Supreme Court clearly showed its hostility towards the tort of parasitism when a competitor copies an unprotected sign. This case concerned the protection of the domain name 'gay.fr' against the use of 'gay.com' for a website offering similar services. The

the Court of Appeal of Aix-en-Provence regarding a model for underwear in which no IPR subsisted, comment J Passa in (2006) 18 *Propriétés Intellectuelles* 88: the court held that advertising investments made by an economic agent to promote his product cannot in themselves prevent another agent from selling a similar product and therefore benefiting from his advertising investments).

[370] See CA Paris, 4th ch, A, 18 October 2006; CA Paris, 4th ch, A, 27 September 2006 and CA Paris, 4th ch, A, 29 November 2006 (2007) 22 *Propriétés Intellectuelles* 122, comment J Passa.

[371] Greffe, Greffe and Greffe, *Traité des dessins et des modèles:* (n 5) 492–94.

[372] Ibid 492–94.

[373] Ibid 494–97. See eg CA Paris, 8 June 1989 [1989] PIBD III, 645, cited by Burst, *Concurrence déloyale et parasitisme* (n 2) 121.

[374] *SARL Oscar and Lola v Société Codico and Codico International*, CA Paris, 4th ch, A, 17 December 2008, (2009) 90 *Gazette du Palais* (March) 40.

[375] Cass com, 20 May 2003, case no 01-11212; Cass com, 3 June 2003, case no 01–15740, Cass com, 1 July 2003, case no 99-18590; Cass com, 8 July 2003, case no 01-18023; CA Douai, 9 September 2002 [2003] PIBD no 766, III, 332, (2003) 9 *Propriétés Intellectuelles* 451, comment J Passa.

[376] Passa, 'Responsabilité civile: concurrence' (n 281).

Court of Appeal of Paris held that the principle of freedom of commerce implies that achievements which cannot or can no longer attract an intellectual property right can be freely reproduced as long as there is no risk of confusion. The court said that there was no risk of confusion: the term 'gay' was banal because it was used very frequently on the Internet. The Supreme Court confirmed the decision.[377]

However, it makes little sense for the courts to declare a trademark invalid for lack of distinctiveness but then punish the defendant on the basis of parasitism. Some courts have handed down decisions doing just that. This is the case of a 2004 decision of the Court of Appeal of Paris concerning a three-dimensional mark comprised of a bottle characterised by the combination of its shape (long-necked) and giving an impression of icing, registered for beer (it was held that the long-necked shape had been used for a long time by brewers generally and that the icy aspect, conjuring up freshness, could not be protected because it would prevent competition on an element allowing the designation of a characteristic of the beverage (freshness)).[378] In another dispute, the Court of Appeal of Paris allowed the claimant to sue on the basis of unfair competition rather than trademark law and found infringement on the basis of parasitism.[379] However, these decisions predate the 2008 Court of Cassation ruling firmly rejecting the tort of parasitism in the field of trademarks. Therefore, if the Supreme Court sticks to its latest case law, and lower courts follow it, the negative overlap unfair competition/trademark seems to be the clearest so far.

Finally, a few brief words need be added about a specific French trademark law 'problem'. IPC, article L713-5 implements Trademark Directive, article 5(2), which protects marks with a reputation against tarnishment and dilution. However, the French legislature did not implement the Trademark Directive properly, for two reasons: the action is not an intellectual property action but a civil liability one, and it is possible to sue only if the well-known trademark as such is used not a sign similar to it. This is not in line with the Directive, which includes protection against the use of a similar sign. After hesitations in the case law,[380] it seems now that courts are complying with the provisions of the Directive despite the French legislation's different wording.[381]

[377] *Neocom Multimédia v Stés PlanetOut*, Cass com, 8 April 2008, case no 07-11385 (2008) 28 *Propriétés Intellectuelles* 359, comment J Passa. See also in the same vein, *Stés Thermohauser, Mallard Ferriere and Matfer*, CA Paris, 4th ch, B, 22 February 2008 [2008] PIBD no 872, III, 244 (2008) 28 *Propriétés Intellectuelles* 359, comment J Passa.

[378] CA Paris, 4th ch, B, 14 May 2004 [2004] PIBD no 791, III, 447; (2004) 13 *Propriétés Intellectuelles* 966, comment J Passa. For a similar earlier decision, see Cass com, 6 November 1984 [1985] Ann. Prop. Ind. 146 (it was a breach to use a mark, which had been invalidated because it was generic ('Super glue'), because the defendant tried to follow in the wake of a known appellation), cited by Schmidt-Szalewski and Pierre, *Droit de la propriété industrielle* (n 5) para 634.

[379] *SCPE v Metropolitan Film Export and FKGB Agence de Communication*, CA Paris, 4th ch, B, 14 January 2005 (2006) 17 *Gazette du Palais* (17 January) 34 (the cover of the defendant's journal had a similar layout, similar colour, an identical typography and an evident connotation between its titles, *Entrevue* and *Entrejambes*. For the Court of Appeal, this showed that the defendant wanted to divert to its profit, without paying and without the preliminary authorisation of the claimant, the reputation of the claimant's magazine).

[380] See Cass, 29 June 1999 (*Olymprix* case). For comments, see De Candé, 'L'action en concurrence déloyale est-elle menacée par l'evolution du droit de la propriété intellectuelle?' (n 2) 498–99; CA Paris, 1st ch, 8 November 2000 [2001] JCP E, 227, comment C Caron.

[381] CA Paris, 27 March 2002 (2003) 21 *Dalloz* 1428. But see Cass com, 11 March 2003, case no 00-22722, which held that for sign imitation the owner of a well-known mark can act under art 1382 of the Civil Code not under IPC, art L713-5 (action by the owner of the name 'olympique' and 'jeux olympiques' against Olymprix); for comments see (2003) 7 *Propriétés Intellectuelles* 229 and De Candé, 'L'action en concurrence déloyale est-elle menacée par l'evolution du droit de la propriété intellectuelle?' (n 2); for subsequent case law, see (2005) 16

(iv) Patents

There have not been many decisions, but yet again the courts are split. Some courts admit the action when there is a risk of confusion[382] and reject it when there isn't.[383] Others allow the action to succeed when there is only simple copying.[384] A very confusing recent decision of the Court of Appeal of Paris is worth noting, and also shows the mess the case law is in concerning overlaps between IPRs and unfair competition in general. The Court of Appeal of Paris held that there was no patent infringement but admitted the unfair competition action because there were similarities in the shape of the products and the defendants willingly followed in the footsteps of the claimants in order to create confusion as to the origin of the products.[385] As Passa notes, this reasoning is disputable for two reasons. First, if the court finds that the behaviour generates a risk of confusion, this is enough to justify a condemnation for unfair competition. Therefore, it is not necessary to find that the behaviour is also parasitic as it does not add anything.[386] Furthermore, the superfluous allusion to the parasitic character of the behaviour gives the impression that parasitism in itself constitutes a breach.[387]

There appear to be no reported decisions on the negative overlap plant variety right/unfair competition. As for trade secrets, the negative overlap was discussed with the simultaneous overlap in section IX.B(iii) above.

In conclusion, the negative overlap between IPRs and unfair competition is as messy, if not more so (because the situation as to patents is confusing for the negative overlap whereas it does not appear so for the simultaneous overlap), as the simultaneous overlap.

D *A Posteriori* Overlap

Compared to the simultaneous and negative overlaps, claimants do not seem to have claimed protection through *a posteriori* overlaps as extensively. In some decisions, courts have allowed the action for slavish imitation where a design was no longer protected by design right.[388] The Court of Cassation has twice pronounced on the issue concerning a design for a famous Cartier watch (the 'Tank' watch). In the first case, the Court held that it was wrong to reduce the watch to the status of an advertising gimmick by repro-

Propriétés Intellectuelles 360, comment J Passa and *Gpt d'Achat E Leclerc v Cté National Olympique et Sportif Francais*, Cass com, 31 October 2006, Jurisdata no 2006-035-696, reported by C Caron, 'Droit de la propriété intellectuelle' [2007] JCP G no 1–2, I, 101 (the Supreme Court held that the Court of Appeal was right to sanction the use of the term 'Olymprix' in an advertising campaign for parasitism).

382 CA Aix-en-Provence, 22 February 1989, Dossiers Brevets, 1990, II, 4 (patent registered but not yet granted), cited by Schmidt-Szalewski and Pierre, *Droit de la propriété industrielle* (n 5) para 228 n 457.

383 CA Paris, 4th ch, A, 9 June 2004 [2005] PIBD no 800, III, 67; CA Aix-en-Provence, 2nd ch, 28 November 2004, case no 2004/735, comment Passa, 'Heurts et malheurs du fait de concurrence déloyale distinct de la contrefaçon' (n 299) 220. These courts held that the simple commercialisation of a similar product which is not protected by an exclusive right (in these two cases a patent) does not constitute an act of unfair competition.

384 CA Paris, 9 April 1992 [1992] PIBD no 532, III, 570 (patent was cancelled); Cass com, 8 October 2002 [2002] PIBD no 754, III, 564 (the breach can be the act of following in the wake of the right-holder), both cited by Schmidt-Szalewski and Pierre, *Droit de la propriété industrielle* (n 5) para 228 n 458.

385 *SA Rapidex SM v Ste Simca SPA and others*, CA Paris, 4th ch, A, 9 November 2005, RG no 04/15195 (2006) 18 *Propriétés Intellectuelles* 87, comment J Passa.

386 Passa, 'Responsabilité civile : concurrence' (n 353).

387 Ibid 87–88.

388 See decisions cited by Greffe, Greffe and Greffe, *Traité des dessins et des modèles* (n 5) 494–97.

ducing it in a leaflet and distributing copies of it to the public.[389] For the Court, to publish a slavish copy of the watch in an advertisement was an act of unfair competition because it depreciated the image of the watch, which was a luxurious object, and relegated it to a simple advertising gimmick. However, it is not clear whether simple copying is punishable per se because the Court seemed to imply a depreciation of the image of the watch as an additional condition. Some commentators have argued that if this is a new criterion, it is reprehensible. Only the risk of confusion seems to be able to justify the condemnation of the reproduction or imitation of a achievement not covered by an exclusive right.[390]

Four years later, the highest court clarified its position on the matter in a second ruling. Again, Cartier obtained condemnation for the slavish copy of its famous 'Tank' watch. But here the defendant was a watchmaker who was making good-quality watches. The Court held that there is parasitism when someone takes inspiration unjustifiably and for commercial purposes from another's economic value, which is individualised and procures a competitive advantage, and which is the fruit of know-how, intellectual work and investments.[391] The Court insisted on the high reputation of the watch and also said that it did not matter that the trademark 'Raymond Weill' was affixed on the dial since the entire appearance was the same, the consumer being able to identify the shape and aspect of the well-known 'Tank' watch. For the Court, the defendant was attempting to benefit from the defendant's investments and from the reputation of the watch, and this was a parasitic behaviour which diverted the attractive and prestigious power of the watch. Thus, as has been argued, this case basically boils down to saying that the simple reputation of a product suffices to remedy the absence of an IPR, with the consequence that the notion of public domain would no longer make any sense.[392] Other commentators, on the other hand, have applauded the decision.[393]

In another ruling in 2005, concerning a storage lorry the patent in which had expired, the Supreme Court approved the decision of the appellate court which had punished simple copying under unfair competition law.[394] The trend is therefore for the protection of expired IPRs through parasitism.

E Literature

French literature is divided between those who advocate the recognition of the tort or theory of parasitism and those who reject it. This section summarises the two camps' arguments and evaluates their merit.

The majority of commentators believe that there is nothing reprehensible in slavishly copying another's achievement unless it is accompanied by a fact distinct from infringement

[389] *Metro v Cartier*, Cass com, 22 October 2002, case no 00-12914 (2003) *Contrats Concurrence Consommation* (January) 11; [2003] JCP E, 563, comment Mainguy.

[390] (2003) 6 *Propriétés Intellectuelles* 85, comment J Passa.

[391] *Cartier v Raymond Weill*, CA Paris, 4th ch, A, 14 June 2006 [2006] PIBD no 837, III, 639; (2007) 22 *Propriétés Intellectuelles* 124, comment J Passa; (2006) 21 *Propriétés Intellectuelles* 463, comment P De Candé.

[392] J Passa, 'Responsabilité civile: concurrence' (2007) 22 *Propriétés Intellectuelles* 125.

[393] P De Candé, 'Dessins et Modèles' (2006) 21 *Propriétés Intellectuelles* 463.

[394] Cass com, 25 January 2005, case no 03-11770, comment Passa, 'Heurts et malheurs du fait de concurrence déloyale distinct de la contrefaçon' (n 299) 221.

of the IPR, eg a risk of confusion.[395] Therefore, they are against the concept of parasitism.[396] There are several reasons for this. First, it is contrary to unfair competition and intellectual property law and the principle of pre-emption to consider the simple copying of another's efforts unlawful.[397] The principle of the freedom to copy means that copying per se is lawful. The theory of parasitism (whether it condemns copying of achievements which required efforts or not) advocates the contrary. It negates this principle.[398] Thereby, parasitism creates an intellectual property right by the back door – in fact, a right even stronger than an intellectual property right (since the conditions are easier to fulfil), a power which should be left to the legislature.[399] Thus, parasitism goes against the legislature's intentions behind the unfair competition and intellectual property systems. This is valid for parasitism in general; in other words, it applies to achievements whether they are protected or unprotected by an intellectual property right (either because they cannot be or because they were but have fallen into the public domain).[400]

A consequence of parasitism's negation of the principle of the freedom to copy is that it also breaches the principle of freedom to compete.[401] Thereby, it hinders competition and creation, and this is also contrary to the legislators' intent.[402] It is inherent to the mechanism of competition to try to win one's competitors' customers and try to appropriate economic value unprotected by an intellectual property right.[403] Such behaviour

[395] Roubier, 'Théorie générale de l'action en concurrence déloyale' (n 289) 556; B Dutoit, 'Exposé de synthèse sur la concurrence parasitaire' in *La concurrence parasitaire en droit comparé, Actes du colloque de Lausanne* (Genève, Droz, 1981) 159, 160; S Durrande, 'Les rapports entre contrefaçon et concurrence déloyale' (1984) *Dalloz*, Chronique 187, 190; Passa, 'Responsabilité civile: concurrence' (2003) (n 281); De Candé, 'L'action en concurrence déloyale est-elle menacée par l'évolution du droit de la propriété intellectuelle?' (n 2) 495; Greffe, Greffe and Greffe, *Traité des dessins et des modèles* (n 5) 494–97, 500; Bertrand, *Droit des Marques* (n 5) 261, para 11.342.

[396] Some recent theses are unfavourable to the theory: Golaz, *L'imitation servile des produits et de leur présentation* (n 2); Burst, *Concurrence déloyale et parasitisme* (n 2); Buydens, *La protection de la quasi-création* (n 2); Passa, *Contrefaçon et concurrence déloyale* (n 2) 278 n 3 and authors cited, and 57; Puttemans, *Droits intellectuels et concurrence déloyale* (n 307). Other authors opposed the theory of parasitism: see eg Malaurie-Vignal, 'Le parasitisme des investissements et du travail d'autrui' (n 295), citing J Azéma, *Le droit français de la concurrence*, 2nd edn (Paris, Presses Universitaires de France, 1989) para 165 and Lucas and Lucas, *Traité de la propriété littéraire et artistique*, 2nd edn (n 16) para 18; *Protection Against Unfair Competition*, no 725(E) (Geneva, WIPO, 1994) para 107; Lucas and Lucas, *Traité de la propriété littéraire et artistique*, 3rd edn (n 5) 22–23, para 20; Caron, *Droit d'auteur et droits voisins* (n 7) 270, para 341 and 391, para 492.

[397] Buydens, *La protection de la quasi-création* (n 2) 714; R Van den Bergh, 'Parasitaire mededinging en artikel 54, Wet Handelspraktijken, comment on CA Gent, 9 November 1978' (1978–79) *Rijkskundig Weekblad* 1717.

[398] Burst, *Concurrence déloyale et parasitisme* (n 2) 118–19, 217, 298; Buydens, *La protection de la quasi-création* (n 2) 704, 752; Passa, *Contrefaçon et concurrence déloyale* (n 2) 218, 276.

[399] A Lucas, 'Comment on CA Rouen 13 January 1981' (1983) *Dalloz* 53; A Lucas, *Le droit de l'informatique* (Paris, Presses Universitaires de France, 1987) para 307; Lucas and Lucas, *Traité de la propriété littéraire et artistique*, 2nd edn (n 16) para 18; Burst, *Concurrence déloyale et parasitisme* (n 2) 231; A Delcorde, 'Droits intellectuels et pratiques du commerce' in *Liber Amicorum Aimé De Caluwé* (Brussels, Bruylant, 1995) 107, 114; Passa, *Contrefaçon et concurrence déloyale* (n 2) 279.

[400] Delcorde 'Droits intellectuels et pratiques du commerce' in *Liber amicorum Aimé de Caluwé* (n 399) 107, 114; Passa, *Contrefaçon et concurrence déloyale* (n 2) 275–76; Durrande 'Les rapports entre contrefaçon et concurrence déloyale' (n 395) 190; A Bonnefont, 'Parasitisme et concurrence déloyale: il faut garder le cap' (2001) *Contrats Concurrence Consommation* (March) 4–5.

[401] Passa, *Contrefaçon et concurrence déloyale* (n 2) 283.

[402] Lucas, 'Comment on CA Rouen 13 January 1981' (n 399) 55, cited by JM Mousseron, 'Entreprise: parasitisme et droit' (1992) 6 *JCP E* 14, 22; Burst, *Concurrence déloyale et parasitisme* (n 2) 100; Clauss, 'The French Law of Disloyal Competition' (n 295)554.

[403] Buydens, *La protection de la quasi-création* (n 2) 661; W Cornish, 'Nouvelles technologies et naissance de nouveaux droits' in *L'avenir de la propriété intellectuelle*, Colloque IRPI (Paris, Litec, Paris, 1993) 5, 13.

inevitably allows each competitor to benefit without paying from the efforts of others. The damage suffered is only a consequence of the principle of free competition. Furthermore, if parasitism, as some propose,[404] is used to protect ideas and all activities, it could restrict creation and the free circulation of ideas and consequently the public domain.[405]

Secondly, parasitism threatens the intellectual property system as a whole because it renders intellectual property rights useless, in other words redundant.[406] There is an important risk that courts solve everything through civil liability and no longer resort to intellectual property rights. Civil liability would replace or absorb intellectual property rights. This is already happening.[407] In fact, there are now two means to protect intellectual achievements, by intellectual property rights which are subject to strict conditions and by the tort of parasitism, which has less stringent conditions. Paradoxically, parasitism's effect is that the lesser the efforts, the less stringent the conditions and the longer the protection. Why then bother to meet the protection requirements of intellectual property rights, eg register a patent or a design, if one can have the equivalent or even better (because unlimited) protection at a lesser cost?[408] Article 12(2) of the Civil Procedure Code obliges the judge to recategorise an unfair competition action into an action for infringement of an intellectual property right if the unfair competition action is alleged instead of the infringement action.[409] Thus, an IPR holder who is the victim of an infringement cannot choose one or the other action. S/he must proceed under the infringement action. The majority of commentators also believe that the unfair competition action is not, or should not be, a substitute for the infringement action.[410] Despite the prohibition in Civil Procedure Code, article 12(2), a number of courts have in fact accepted that claimants may use the unfair competition action for parasitism rather than the infringement action, and also when infringement has not been established.[411] The

[404] P Le Tourneau, 'Le parasitisme dans tous ses états' (1993) *Dalloz*, Chronique 310, 313; Le Tourneau, 'Folles idées sur les idées' (n 309) 8.

[405] Passa, *Contrefaçon et concurrence déloyale* (n 2) 6, 55–56; Passa 'Propos dissidents sur la sanction du parasitisme économique' (n 305) 297, 298–99, 303–4.

[406] Lucas, 'Comment on CA Rouen 13 January 1981' (n 399); Lucas and Lucas, *Traité de la propriété littéraire et artistique*, 2nd edn (n 16) para 18; Buydens, *La protection de la quasi-création* (n 2) 661, 681; Passa, *Contrefaçon et concurrence déloyale* (n 2) 280 ; J Huillier, 'Le parasitime parasite-t-il la propriété intellectuelle ?' (2001) 312 *Gazette du Palais* 6.

[407] Passa, 'Propos dissidents sur la sanction du parasitisme économique' (n 305) 302 and cases cited. For a recent case, see *Sté IIEESS, Ditel v Société*, CA Paris, 14th ch, B, 23 January 2009, affirming Trib Com Paris (réf), 18 June 2008, available at www.legalis.net (defendant copied database, claimant deliberately chose to use the unfair competition action, the court declared itself competent and condemned on parasitism alone. Defendant also used the name of the claimant to sell its software. It is unclear from the decision why this is an act of parasitism rather than risk of confusion).

[408] Passa 'Propos dissidents sur la sanction du parasitisme économique' (n 305) 301; Bonnefont, 'Parasitisme et concurrence déloyale' (n 400) 4–5, citing critics of parasitism.

[409] Passa, *Contrefaçon et concurrence déloyale* (n 2) 72 (except for trademarks: the victim of a trademark infringement can, under certain conditions, act under unfair competition rather than trademark law).

[410] Schmidt-Szalewski 'La distinction entre l'action en contrefaçon et l'action en concurrence déloyale dans la jurisprudence' (n 295) 456, 458, citing Cass com, 23 May 1973, Bull civ, IV, no 182; Clauss, 'The French Law of Disloyal Competition' (n 295) 552–53; Passa, *Contrefaçon et concurrence déloyale* (n 2) 72; Le Tourneau, 'Retour sur le parasitisme' (n 2); Le Tourneau, 'Le bon vent du parasitisme' (n 286) 5.

[411] Desjeux, 'La reproduction ou copie servile et l'action en concurrence déloyale dans la jurisprudence Française' (n 295). See eg TGI Paris, 19 March 1993 [1993] PIBD no 548, III, 439, cited by Schmidt-Szalewski 'La distinction entre l'action en contrefaçon et l'action en concurrence déloyale dans la jurisprudence' (n 295) 465 (infringement action for copyrighted software was rejected because there were not enough similarities between the two programs, but the court condemned the defendant for parasitism). In *ABC Rénovation v Les Maisons Barbey Maillard*, CA Paris, 10 December 2003, RG no 2003/17581, cited by Passa, 'Responsabilité

Court of Cassation validated this choice between the two actions. In 2001, it held that the plagiarism of a catalogue, which imitates both substance and form, is parasitic.[412] Plagiarism can exist when there is no confusion, and parasitism can subsist even if the parasitic acts do not concern elements which cost the maker of the catalogue efforts and investments. No mention was made of copyright or the *sui generis* right. Recently, the Paris Commercial Court and Paris Court of Appeal have again accepted jurisdiction when the claimant brought an unfair competition action for extraction of data from a database without looking into the question whether a *sui generis* right subsisted and whether it was infringed.[413]

Thirdly, when courts condemn both for infringement and parasitism, they grant two sets of separate damages which repair the same damage, thereby punishing the defendant twice for the same act. This amounts to double indemnification of the same prejudice and can even be seen as disguised punitive damages.[414]

The converse problem also arises where courts repair the two prejudices with a global sum, in cases where the unfair competition action is justified (ie there is a risk of confusion in addition to the infringement of the IPR, except trademark rights).[415] The two acts are distinct so two sets of damages are legitimate as they do not repair the same damage.[416] It is hard to understand, therefore, when courts which allow the two actions for infringement and unfair competition sometimes award a global sum without distinguishing the part relevant to infringement and that to unfair competition.[417] As Passa comments, this practice should be avoided, in particular because a decision awarding a global amount cannot be appealed separately on the question of infringement or unfair competition.[418] If the appellate court were to decide that there was either no infringement or no unfair competition, what would be the amount that the defendant would have to pay? And if the Court of Appeal were to confirm the decision which was referred to it, it

civile: concurrence' (n 357), the Paris Court of Appeal allowed a claim exclusively based on parasitism and condemned defendant on this count only, although the subject matter (a catalogue of drawings) was protected by copyright.

412 *Glock France v Bécheret*, Cass com, 30 January 2001 (2001) 24 *Dalloz* 1939, comment Le Tourneau; Bull civ, IV, 27; JCP G, I, 340, no 29, comment Viney; (2002) *Propriétés Intellectuelles* 101, comment J Passa.

413 *Sté IIEESS, Ditel v Société*, CA Paris, 14th ch, B, 23 January 2009, affirming Trib Com Paris (réf), 18 June 2008, available at www.legalis.net.

414 Passa, 'Heurts et malheurs du fait de concurrence déloyale distinct de la contrefaçon' (n 299) 210. For example, see CA Versailles, 5 April 2001 [2002] PIBD no 734, III, 38; (2002) 4 *Propriétés Intellectuelles* 81, comment J Passa (trademark infringement and unfair competition for benefitting from the reputation of the mark and the claimant's commercial efforts. Damages of 200,000 French francs for each. But trademark infringement includes benefitting from the reputation of the mark and the claimant's commercial efforts, thus one sum was sufficient to repair the damage). For a similar case, see *Sté Editions KL et les Epoux L v SAS Carboatmedia*, CA Paris, 4th ch, B, 21 March 2008, case no 06-20647, Jurisdata no 364580 (2008) 42 *Revue Lamy Droit de l'Immatériel* 26 (trademark infringement and unfair competition found for the same reasons, same damage repaired twice). See also CA Paris, 4th ch, A, 29 November 2006, RG no 05/23887. See also CA Paris, 30 March 2001 [2002] PIBD no 733, III, 19, comment J Passa in (2007) 22 *Propriétés Intellectuelles* 120.

415 See eg CA Paris, 4th ch, A, 29 November 2006, RG no 05/23887; CA Paris, 30 March 2001 [2002] PIBD no 733, III, 19, reported in (2007) 22 *Propriétés Intellectuelles* 120, comment J Passa.

416 For a correct application, see *Sté Rayure v Sté Infinitif*, Cass com, 28 November 2006, case no 04-20555 (2007) 22 *Propriétés Intellectuelles* 120, comment J Passa.

417 Passa, 'Heurts et malheurs du fait de concurrence déloyale distinct de la contrefaçon' (n 299) 211. For an example, see *Com v Microsoft and others*, CA Paris, 4th ch, 9 March 2005, case no 04-0552, Jurisdata no 267711 (2005) 7 *Revue Lamy Droit de l'Immatériel* 25 (a single sum was awarded to Microsoft for the two prejudices under infringement and unfair competition).

418 Passa, 'Responsabilité civile: concurrence' (2007) (n 392).

would clearly be badly placed to award (as it should in principle always be able to do) an inferior or superior amount, according to its appreciation of the prejudice, because it would have to ignore the amount awarded by the first instance court.[419] The same difficulty would also arise for the Court of Appeal on remand, where the Supreme Court, to which a question only of infringement or of unfair competition has been referred, sets aside the decision.[420]

Those who are in favour of the tort of parasitism think that one must reverse or at least restrict the principle of the freedom to copy and fully prevent parasitism.[421] Every copy (of the achievement which cannot be protected by an intellectual property right[422] and of one whose intellectual property protection has expired[423]) would be presumed unlawful and it would be up to the copier to justify his or her behaviour. The main advocates of this solution are Desjeux and Le Tourneau.[424] Other French and foreign commentators follow Desjeux and Le Tourneau's ideas and are thus in favour of the concept of parasitism.[425] Commentators in favour of this solution justify their position by citing the case law which has for 20 years affirmed that creators who cannot secure an intellectual property right can be protected against parasitism.[426] For these authors, the reason for allowing the tort of parasitism is that the intellectual property system does not ensure sufficient protection; many achievements remain unprotected by intellectual property laws. If indirectly the theory of parasitism constituted a new property right, according to

[419] Ibid.

[420] Ibid.

[421] Note that according to Strowel and Triaille, 'De l'équilibre entre le droit de la concurrence et la propriété intellectuelle' (n 306) 26–27, parasitism does not reverse the principle of the freedom to copy, it only restricts it. For them, the tort of parasitism can be justified because of another principle of competition law, the principle of equality. Parasitism breaks the equality between competitors and should be prohibited. Buydens, *La protection de la quasi-création* (n 2) 704–5 (parasitism does not lead to complete reversal of freedom to copy if important efforts are required).

[422] Lucas and Lucas, *Traité de la propriété littéraire et artistique*, 2nd edn (n 16) 636, paras 817–21; JM Mousseron, 'Recherche, dévelopement et parasitisme économique' in *Le parasitisme économique* (Paris, Gazette du Palais Editions Techniques, 1988) 29; Desjeux, 'La reprise de la prestation d'autrui' (n 302); Le Tourneau, 'Le parasitisme dans tous ses états' (n 404); Le Tourneau, 'Retour sur le parasitisme' (n 2); Le Tourneau, 'Folles idées sur les idées' (n 309) 13; Malaurie-Vignal, 'Le parasitisme des investissements et du travail d'autrui' (n 295); M Malaurie-Vignal, 'Réflexions sur la théorie du parasitisme économique' (2001) *Contrats Concurrence Consommation* (October) 4, 5 (although her position is less clear-cut than the previous authors').

[423] Le Tourneau, 'Retour sur le parasitisme' (n 2) (the goods protected by the action must not have fallen into the public domain nor be an act authorised by statute, eg an exception to copyright). However Le Tourneau, 'Folles idées sur les idées' (n 309) 13, seems to contradict his previous writings: the action for parasitism can succeed when the achievement which fulfils its conditions has fallen into the public domain. See also Malaurie-Vignal, 'Réflexions sur la théorie du parasitisme économique' (n 422) 5 (although her position is less clear-cut than the previous authors').

[424] Cited by Buydens, *La protection de la quasi-création* (n 2) 753 *et seq*.

[425] See the authors cited by Passa, *Contrefaçon et concurrence déloyale* (n 2) 257 and 262 n 3; Strowel and Triaille, 'De l'equilibre entre le droit de la concurrence et la propriété intellectuelle' (n 306) 26–27; Puttemans, *Droits intellectuels et concurrence déloyale* (n 307) 240, citing Y Saint-Gal, 'Concurrence et agissements parasitaires en droit français et belge' in *La concurrence parasitaire en droit comparé, Actes du colloque de Lausanne* (Genève, Droz, 1981) 133, 142; De Candé, 'L'action en concurrence déloyale est-elle menacée par l'evolution du droit de la propriété intellectuelle?' (n 2); P De Candé commenting on *Free v C&A France*, CA Paris, 4th ch, A, 25 June 2003, unpublished; *Cassegrain v Hpo*, CA Paris, 4th ch, A, 2 July 2003, unpublished; *Guenoun v Coblentz*, CA Paris, 4th ch, A, unpublished, (2003) 9 *Propriétés Intellectuelles* 401. For P De Candé, anything that does not constitute reproduction of the design or model, be it an inferior price, bad quality materials, or a range effect, should qualify as an act of unfair competition.

[426] See eg Cass com, 3 October 1978, Bull civ, IV, 208; CA Toulouse, 11 September 1997 (1997) 2 *Gazette du Palais* Somm 402; CA Rennes, 28 January 1998 [1998] JCP E 195.

these commentators, this would not be a relevant argument to reject its application.[427] Le Tourneau's view is that it should be unlawful to copy achievements unprotected by an intellectual property right which have an economic value and are the result of some effort.[428] In his view, there would be no need for a specific law since parasitism could be prevented through civil liability.

Those arguments will be examined in the final chapter against the criteria developed to determine the appropriateness, or not, of the three types of overlaps.

X. CONCLUSION: IDENTIFICATION OF PRINCIPLES GOVERNING OVERLAPS IN FRENCH LAW AND REMAINING OPEN QUESTIONS

Just as in EU law, there is no general rule in French law banning overlaps. The fundamental principle on which both intellectual property and unfair competition law are based is the principle of the freedom to copy and its corollary freedom of commerce and competition. Of course, like all EU Member States, French intellectual property and unfair competition laws are in great part harmonised and the EU rules governing the overlaps will apply as well (as to which we refer the reader to chapter three). French law does not have many rules regulating the overlaps. One important rule is that of the unity of art, which clearly mandated the overlap between copyright and design before the EU legislature provided for it. The consequence is that it is not possible to transfer the design right without the copyright. This rule helps to avoid conflicts in case of overlap by keeping the rights in the hands of only one person. However, this rule does not seem to apply for Community designs. Another rule (albeit a flimsy one as it relies on an isolated decision) is that preventing the text of a patent application from being protectable by copyright. What is interesting is the rationale for the decision, which takes into consideration the destination or objective of the work. As we shall see, this could be a useful rule to govern some problematic overlaps, and has also been proposed by commentators. The very high degree of convergence, over and above that required by EU law, in the field of patents and plant variety rights is also to be commended. Finally and most ironically, even if freedom to copy is at the root of the French system, many courts including the Supreme Court do not apply it by the letter, leaving much of IPR/unfair competition law dishevelled, to say the least.

In sum, French law does not add much to the EU rules, and when it does, the picture is very mixed: France's few additional rules are useful to regulate some overlaps but the main principle, which regulates the IPR/unfair competition overlap, is continuously violated by its courts. Most of the overlaps which are not regulated at EU level, therefore, also remain unregulated under French law.

[427] Le Tourneau, 'Le bon vent du parasitisme' (n 286).

[428] Le Tourneau, 'Retour sur le parasitisme' (n 2) 404; Schmidt-Szalewski, 'La distinction entre l'action en contrefaçon et l'action en concurrence déloyale dans la jurisprudence' (n 295) 46,6 citing F Lasserre-Jeannin, *L'acte de concurrence déloyale* (Thesis, Montpellier, 1992) para 135 (the achievement copied must have a competitive value).

5

United Kingdom

I. THE LEGAL FRAMEWORK

AS IN FRANCE, freedom of competition pervades the IPR framework. It is a paramount yet implicit principle of UK law, which is nevertheless often cited in intellectual property judgments to curb the overprotective effects of IPRs or passing off.[1] All IPRs are regulated in separate instruments, unlike in France where they are all codified in one single statute. Copyright and unregistered designs are dealt with in the Copyright, Designs and Patents Act (CDPA) 1988 (as amended).[2] In the United Kingdom, the term copyright includes neighbouring rights. Database rights are regulated separately in the Copyright and Rights in Databases Regulations 1997.[3] The Trademark Act (TMA) 1994 regulates trademarks, whilst the Registered Design Act (RDA) 1949 (as amended) deals with registered designs.[4] The Patents Act 1977 (as last amended by the Patents Act 2004) implements the changes effected by the European Patent Convention (EPC) 2000, which itself amends the original EPC of 1973.[5] Plant variety rights are regulated in a separate instrument, the Plant Varieties Act 1997.[6] In the United Kingdom, 'the law of unfair competition is not recognised in the sense that there is no general principle that underlies a body of law governing competition'.[7] Therefore, the law can be described 'as a patchwork of various torts and regulations'.[8] While there is no general civil liability statutory provision, as in France, courts have developed a series of different unfair competition torts to which they have applied different rules. These common law torts are injurious falsehood, defamation, passing off interference with contractual relations, interference with trade by unlawful means, deceit, conspiracy, intimidation and breach of confidence.[9] As will be seen in section IX, only passing off and breach of confidence are able to create overlaps between IPRs and unfair competi-

[1] See eg Jacob J in *RoHo/Hodgkinson & Corby v Wards Mobility Services* [1995] FSR 169, 173: 'Certainly it is not the law that copying as such is unlawful: the common law . . . leans against monopolies'.

[2] Copyright, Designs and Patents Act (CDPA) 1988 (c 48).

[3] SI 1997/3032.

[4] Trademark Act (TMA) 1994 (c 26) and Registered Design Act (RDA) 1949 (c 88). Consolidated versions are available from the Intellectual Property Office at www.ipo.gov.uk.

[5] The EPC 2000 came into force on 13 December 2007.

[6] Brought into force by SI 1998/1028.

[7] A Kamperman Sanders, *Unfair Competition Law: The Protection of Intellectual and Industrial Creativity* (Oxford, Clarendon Press, 1997) 52.

[8] Ibid.

[9] P Burns, 'Unfair Competition: A Compelling Need Unmet' (1981) *European Intellectual Property Review* 311; A Robertson and A Horton, 'Does the UK or the EC Need an Unfair Competition Law?' (1995) *European Intellectual Property Review* 568; *Protection Against Unfair Competition*, WIPO doc 725(E) (Geneva, WIPO, 1994).

tion. Finally, the Misleading and Comparative Advertising Directive 2006/114/EC (MCAD) and Unfair Commercial Practices Directive 2005/29/EC (UCPD) are implemented respectively in the Business Protection from Misleading Marketing Regulations 2008 (which replace the Control of Misleading Advertising Regulations)[10] and in the Consumer Protection from Unfair Trading Regulations 2008.[11]

II. COPYRIGHT AND DESIGNS

First of all, it must be noted that in addition to copyright law, the United Kingdom has two types of protection for designs: registered design right and unregistered design right. There can therefore be an overlap between copyright, Community unregistered design right (CUDR), UK unregistered design right (UK UDR), Community registered design right (CRDR) and UK registered design right (UK RDR). As the Community design rights are modelled on the Design Directive 98/71/EC, what is said of the susbtantive (as opposed to procedural) provisions of the national RDR applies to the Community designs rights too (except for the small differences with CUDR, eg term). The RDA 1949 (as amended following the Design Directive) faithfully incorporates the provisions of the Directive, so that there is nothing specific or different to mention in this section, except that the United Kingdom has opted to have a must-match exclusion, as allowed by the Directive since the issue was left unharmonised (RDA 1949, section 7A(5)). The case law developed on the RDR will of course be reviewed. The three rights (RDR, UDR and copyright) will be compared together in this section. UDR is regulated in CDPA 1988, sections 213–64. It was introduced in 1988 to remedy the absence of copyright protection for functional articles abolished by the *British Leyland* decision.[12] Like copyright, and as its very name indicates, the right arises automatically without the need to complete any formality. As will be seen below, UK provisions imply that there can be an overlap between both types of design rights and copyright and often even set out specific rules to regulate this overlap.

A Simultaneous Overlap

(i) Subject Matter

(a) Copyright

UK law protects literary, dramatic, musical and artistic works, sound recordings, films, broadcasts and typographical arrangements of published editions (CDPA 1988, sections

[10] These replace the Control of Misleading Advertisements Regulations 1988, SI 1988/915, as amended by the Control of Misleading Advertisements (Amendment) Regulations 2000, SI 2000/914 (which implemented Directive 97/55/EC which amended Directive 84/450/EEC) and by the Control of Misleading Advertisements (Amendment) Regulations 2003, SI 2003/3183.

[11] SI 2008/1277, in force 26 May 2008. J Davis, 'Unfair Competition Law and its Protection under English Law', paper presented at 'Unfair Competition: Where are We Now and Where are We Going?' Conference, Cambridge, 14 March 2009, noting that it is a consumer protection law rather than a law against unfair competition.

[12] *British Leyland Motor Corp and others v Armstrong Patents Co Ltd* [1986] RPC 279.

1–8). However, the main difference between UK and continental copyright law is the requirement of categorisation, which narrows down copyrightable subject matter. If a work does not fall within one of the eight categories stated in the CDPA 1988, namely literary, dramatic, musical and artistic works, sound recordings, films, broadcasts and typographical arrangements of published editions, it cannot be protected, even though it is an original expression.[13] The lack of protection arising due to the categorisation requirement is famously illustrated in *Merchandising Corporation of America v Harpbond*[14] and *Creation Records and others v News Group Newspapers*.[15] In the first case, the artwork in question was a few lines of make-up in the American-Indian style, which were painted on the artist's (Adam Ant of the pop group Adam and the Ants) face. The main reason why it was not protectable was that it could not be considered a painting, as it needed to be fixed on a surface and as the marks would disappear when the artist washed.[16] The second case dealt with a scene for the cover of a pop music album. An uninvited journalist took a photograph of the scene, which was virtually identical to the one that would appear a few weeks later on the album cover. Since the album photograph was not copied, the journalist's photograph having been taken independently, the claimant had to qualify the scene as a copyright work. It consisted of a number of *objets trouvés* (including a Rolls-Royce in a swimming pool, a scooter, a clock, a phonograph) placed in the grounds of a hotel with the artists standing by them. As the scene was static, it could not be a dramatic work. It also could not be an artistic work as it could not be said to come under the normal meaning of the term 'sculpture', nor a 'collage' (as the court restrictively interpreted the term as necessitating the objects to stick together), nor a work of artistic craftsmanship as there was no craftsmanship involved. Thus, make-up or fashion, which would consist in non-permanent body art, would arguably not be protectable in the United Kingdom. Purely static scenes would not be protectable either but shows could be classed as dramatic works. This is because shows generally involve some sort of action or convey a story.[17]

British categorisation also prevents the protection of some artistic works, such as clothes and furniture. This is because these fall under the category of works of artistic craftsmanship which requires a higher threshold of protection, namely that the work be artistic, which is in addition to being original (in the UK sense of the term, ie skill, labour, judgement and/or capital, but does not equate with creative. Other artistic works such as photographs, graphic works and sculptures do not need to meet this higher threshold. In short, in relation to works of artistic craftsmanship, only works of art can be protected

[13] The effect of the Court of Justice's *BSA* judgment may well be that the categorization requirement is now a thing of the past. Case C-393/09, *Bezpečnostní softwarová asociace – Svaz softwarové ochrany v Ministerstvo kultury*, 22 December 2010, nyr, available on www.curia.europa.eu, paras 46, 51 (concerning whether a graphical user interface is protected as a computer program or as another type of work).

[14] [1983] FSR 32.

[15] [1997] EMLR 444.

[16] This reasoning can be criticised as a 'surface' can be anything and the act does not require permanence for a work to be fixed. The unnamed reason for the decision seems to have been a lack of originality as the design was very simple. On this latter point, see H Laddie, P Prescott, M Vitoria, A Speck and L Lane, *The Modern Law of Copyright*, 3rd edn (London, Butterworths, 2000) paras 4.20 and 4.37.

[17] The definition of dramatic work arises from two cases: *Green v Broadcasting Corporation of New Zealand* [1989] 2 All ER 1056 and *Norowzian v Arks Ltd (No 2)* [2000] FSR 363 (CA) and is a work of action, with or without words or music, capable of being performed before an audience and which has sufficient unity to be able to be performed again.

because the requirement of 'artistic' is still set by a House of Lords decision[18] in which their Lordships could not agree, so that the more stringent requirements set out by some of them won the day. Their Lordships gave three main criteria: namely, the work must be considered a work of art or something artistic by the judge, by the public or by experts. Whether one criterion was applied rather than another depended on the Law Lord involved. Several Law Lords referred to another test which has been followed in several later cases, the criterion of intention and/or result. The creator must have intended to create something artistic and, for some Law Lords, the result must also be artistic. How to decide whether it is artistic was not stated by the Law Lords but, presumably, one must fall back on one of the three criteria stated above. What is clear from the subsequent case law is that functional, although original, works of craftsmanship are much less likely to be protected simply because they are not artistic.[19] Indeed, not only must the works be artistic, they must generally be hand-made.[20] However, *Infopaq* might have changed this.[21] The Court of Justice's decision requires that all original works meet the threshold of being the author's own intellectual creation, which is obviously a less stringent requirement than 'work of art'. The ruling's force is somewhat reduced because Design Regulation (EC) 6/2002, article 96(2) and the corresponding Design Directive, article 17, specifically leave the Member States a choice as to the level of originality for designs. The *Infopaq* decision is in contradiction with those articles and arguably for this reason not applicable as against the clear intention of the EU legislature. However, it may be argued that while the term 'own intellectual creation' has now been set as the EU threshold of protection, the specification of that term (and arguably even a different specification for different categories of works) is still left to the national courts.

(b) (C)RDR/CUDR

The Design Directive and the RDA 1949 define a design as 'the appearance of the whole or a part of a product resulting from the features of, in particular, the lines, contours, colours, shape, texture and/or materials of the product itself and/or its ornamentation'. Computer programs are excluded but not graphic symbols such as computer icons. Indeed, Jacob J was prepared to say they were protected under the new law.[22] In addition, in February 2001 the Patent Office (now Intellectual Property Office (IPO)) in its Consultation Paper on the implementation in the United Kingdom of the Design Directive confirmed that the definition of 'product' was broad and could include icons. For the IPO, 'computer program' means only the actual code not the icon or graphical user interface.[23] In any case, the Explanatory Memorandum to the Design Directive expressly stated that computer menus and icons should be registrable.

[18] *George Hensher v Restawile Upholstery (Lancs)* [1976] AC 64 (HL).

[19] For an example, see *Merlet v Mothercare* [1986] RPC 115 (baby and mother rain cape).

[20] *George Hensher v Restawile Upholstery (Lancs)* [1976] AC 64 (although not required, it was stated that it would be very difficult for mass-produced objects to qualify). See also *Guild v Eskandar* [2001] FSR 38.

[21] See Case C-5/08 *Infopaq International AS v Dankse Dagblades Forening* [2009] ECR I-6569 and E Derclaye, 'Wonderful or Worrisome? The Impact of the ECJ Ruling in *Infopaq* on UK Copyright Law' (2010) *European Intellectual Property Review* 247.

[22] *Apple Computer Inc v Design Registry* [2001] All ER (D) 336 (October); [2002] FSR 38 (RDAT).

[23] As referred to by D Brown and E Cameron, 'Designing the Interface' (2005) 19(1) *International Review of Law, Computers and Technology* 65, 73.

(c) UDR

'Design' means the design of any aspect of shape or configuration (whether internal or external) of the whole or part of an article. No eye appeal is required. Therefore, both functional and aesthetic designs are covered.

The conclusion of this overview of subject matter is very interesting. As a result of the legal rules governing the three rights, there will be few products which will cumulate all three rights at the same time. Generally, already at this stage the overlap will be limited; it will be only double not triple. Indeed, copyright law will rarely protect works of artistic craftsmanship. This gap is filled by RDR and UDR. In addition, UDR does not protect surface decoration, therefore most[24] two-dimensional products can only obtain copyright and RDR protection. The area of overlap between the three rights and also the CUDR and CRDR is constituted by sculptures, etchings and engravings, which are in three dimensions and do not fall under the strict provisions governing works of artistic craftsmanship. Buildings should also be protectable by the three (or five) rights, although the literature is divided on whether they need to be artistic, as for works of artistic craftsmanship, to be protected.[25]

(ii) Protection Requirements

(a) Copyright

Like France, the United Kingdom obviously adheres to the idea/expression dichotomy as it is mandated by the TRIPS Agreement.[26] As in France, the requirement of originality is not laid down in the statute but in the case law. First of all, the work must not be copied from another work and must originate from the author.[27] Then, what is required is sufficient skill, judgement, labour or capital,[28] which is less than the requirements in France and Germany as no creativity is required.[29] However, the *Infopaq* decision has arguably now raised the bar so that the level of originality is the same as in France (although this should not change the position as regards works of artistic craftsmanship, as noted above).

(b) (C)RDR/CUDR

As we saw in chapter three, the requirements are novelty and individual character, the latter being decided by the informed user. The decision in *WoodHouse UK plc v*

[24] Indeed some products in two dimensions have a shape, for instance, the shape of a paper star (simply paper cut in the shape of star).

[25] W Cornish and D Llewelyn, *Intellectual Property: Patents, Copyright, Trade Marks and Allied Rights*, 6th edn (London, Sweet and Maxwell, 2007, para 10-16, think that there should be some artistic quality, while L Bently and B Sherman, *Intellectual Property Law*, 3rd edn (Oxford, Oxford University Press, 2009) 77, think probably not.

[26] The most recent judgment of the highest court applying it is *Designers Guild v Russell Williams (Textiles)* [2001] FSR 11 (HL).

[27] *University of London Press v University Tutorial Press* [1916] 2 Ch 601.

[28] *Ladbroke v William Hill* [1964] 1 WLR 273, 291 (HL).

[29] Note that in Germany, a higher level of originality nevertheless applies for works of applied art. Also note that the UK courts have so far abided by the new requirement set out in *Infopaq*. See *SAS Institute v World Programming* [2010] ECDR 15; *NLA et al v Meltwater et al*. [2010] EWHC 3099.

Architectural Lighting Systems (t/a Aquila Design),[30] which gave (obiter dictum) a definition of the informed user, accords with the more recent General Court decision in *Grupo Promer*.[31] The British decision provides a few more details than the EU decision, so these will be stated here. According to the High Court, the informed user must be a regular user of the sort of product registered, thus it could be a consumer or buyer or s/he could otherwise be familiar with the subject matter, ie through use of it at work. S/he is not a manufacturer nor the average man in the street but a person to whom the design is directed. S/he must not have:

> an archival mind (or eye) or more than an average memory but it does . . . demand some awareness of product trend and availability and some knowledge of basic technical considerations (if any) . . . Focus on eye appeal seems more pertinent than familiarity with the underlying operational or manufacturing technology (if any).

On the facts, which involved the design of a street lamp, that meant that the informed user was 'a regular member of an urban development team (typically in a council) who is primarily interested in the appearance of street furniture but who also has a basic grasp of a product's technical underlay – and maybe, cost'.[32] Jacob LJ, who delivered the Court of Appeal judgment in *Procter & Gamble v Reckitt Benckiser*, basically confirmed *Woodhouse* on this point and held that the informed user is not a person skilled in the art as in patent law or the average consumer of trademark law. In addition, he took the view that the test for individual character is that the impression produced on the informed user by the design must be *clearly* different from that produced on him or her by prior designs, as opposed to simply different.[33] According to him, 'smaller differences will be enough to create a different overall impression where freedom of design is limited'.[34] Again, this latter statement is accordance with the General Court's *Grupo Promer* decision.[35] Consequently, as Jacob LJ says, 'protection for a striking novel product will be correspondingly greater than for a product which is incrementally different from the prior art, though different enough to have its own individual character and thus be validly registered'.[36]

(c) UDR

The requirements are identical to those in copyright law. Therefore, the design must be fixed and original (CDPA 1988, section 213(1), (4)), ie not be copied and display sufficient skill, judgement and labour.[37] But there is an additional requirement, namely non-commonplaceness. The test of 'commonplaceness' was given by the Court of Appeal per

[30] [2006] ECDR 11, paras 50–52.

[31] Case T-9/07 *Grupo Promer Mon Graphic v OHIM*, available at www.curia.europea.eu. On this case, see chapter 4, section II.A. As a reminder, the General Court held that '[t]he informed user is particularly observant and has some awareness of the state of the prior art, that is to say the previous designs relating to the product in question that had been disclosed on the date of filing of the contested design, or, as the case may be, on the date of priority claimed'.

[32] [2006] ECDR 11, para 51.

[33] [2007] EWCA Civ 936, paras 16–19.

[34] Ibid para 30.

[35] Case T-9/07 *Grupo Promer Mon Graphic v OHIM*, available at www.curia.europea.eu, especially para 72.

[36] [2007] EWCA Civ 936, para 35.

[37] *C&H Engineering v Klucznik & Sons* [1992] FSR 421. Note that now the requirement of originality is higher in copyright law than in UDR because of *Infopaq* (Case C-5/08 *Infopaq International AS v Dankse Dagblades Forening* [2009] ECR I-6569).

Mummery LJ in *Farmers Build v Carrier Bulk Materials*.[38] After establishing that the design is original, the court should compare the design of the article in which design right is claimed with the design of other articles in the same field, including the alleged infringing article, as at the time of its creation. Then, it must ascertain how similar that design is to the design of similar articles in the same field of design. The comparative exercise has to be carried out objectively in the light of the evidence from experts in the relevant field, pointing out the similarities and the differences and explaining the significance of them. Experts must not evaluate the factual evidence but only point out the similarities and differences and their significance, without concentrating on the similarities alone or the differences alone, as it would give an unbalanced view.[39] In the end, however, it is for the court to decide whether the design was commonplace. That judgement is one of fact and degree according to the evidence in each particular case:

> The closer the similarity of the various designs to each other, the more likely it is that the designs are commonplace, especially if there is no causal link, such as copying. If a number of designers working independently of one another in the same field produce very similar designs by coincidence the most likely explanation of the similarities is that there is only one way of designing that article. Then the design in question can reasonably be seen as 'commonplace' . . . If however, there are aspects of the plaintiff's design of the article which are not to be found in any other design in the field in question, and those aspects are found in the defendant's design, the court would be entitled to conclude that the design in question was not 'commonplace'.[40]

In conclusion, the requirements in the three rights somewhat overlap so that often a design will at the same time be original, non-commonplace, novel and have individual character. It is more likely, however, that a design which is novel and has individual character or is not commonplace will also be original than that a work which is original will also be novel or not commonplace.

(iii) Excluded Subject Matter

(a) Copyright

Copyright excludes from protection ideas (as seen above under protection requirements), purely functional shapes (through CDPA 1988, section 51) and immoral works (through case law). A few words must be said about these two last excluded subject matters. A bit of history is needed to understand the rationale behind section 51. As copyright infringement extends to indirect copying, the making of things depicted in drawings amounts to infringement (CDPA 1988, section 17(3)). The corresponding predecessor of this section led to the indirect protection of many functional articles that would otherwise not qualify as works of artistic craftsmanship or sculptures, and therefore with it, to an abuse or distortion of copyright law (functional articles that should have been protected under registered design or patent law could obtain copyright protection without passing the hurdles of registration and were protected for a much longer time). This trend culminated and was abolished in the famous *British Leyland v Armstrong* case.[41] There, the

[38] [1999] RPC 461.

[39] As was recently added to the test in *Virgin Atlantic Airways v Premium Aircraft Interiors Group* [2009] ECDR 11.

[40] [1999] RPC 461, 482.

[41] [1986] RPC 279 (HL).

House of Lords invented a right of repair to curb the abuses to which the string of cases had led. This judge-made defence was shortly thereafter overridden by the introduction in 1988 of the section 51 defence in the new CDPA 1988. The section provides that:

> It is not an infringement of any copyright in a design document or model recording or embodying a design for anything other than an artistic work or a typeface to make an article to the design or to copy an article made to the design.

In short, this means that when a design document (which can be a literary or artistic work such as a drawing, a photograph or even something in three dimensions) depicts something that is not an artistic work, making articles to this depiction will not infringe the copyright in the drawings. Thus, indirect infringement of the drawing of an exhaust pipe by building exhaust pipes based on the drawing will fall within this defence. But if the design document depicts a sculpture or a work of artistic craftsmanship (a beautiful jewel or *haute couture* clothes), then it will be an infringement to make those articles. Therefore, under section 51, copyright normally cannot protect 'non-artistic' functional products. However, as the meaning of the term 'artistic' is unclear (the case law on artistic works is not yet settled), it is not always clear when the defence applies and the overlap can still happen in some cases involving 'borderline artistic works' (namely sculptures, woodcuts, etchings and engravings).[42] The *Infopaq* ruling should result in the overlap occurring less frequently by requiring the author's own intellectual creation for such works.[43] Of course, the overlap between UDR and copyright will still be possible for artistic works.

Finally, UK courts have consistently held that copyright protection will not be granted for obscene, blasphemous, libellous, irreligious or immoral works.[44] While few works will be considered as such, the notion of morality will accord with that in RDR since both rights will use the current notion of morality not that of a previous era. There is therefore convergence in this respect.

(b) (C)RDR/CUDR

RDR provisions were discussed in sections III.B(i) of chapter three and II.A of chapter four. In short, ideas, purely functional shapes and designs of interconnections are not protectable. Immoral designs are also unprotectable.

(c) UDR

Four types of designs are excluded from protection. Section 213(3) provides that design right does not subsist in:

- (a) methods or principles of construction;
- (b) features of shape or configuration of an article, which:
  - (i) enable the article to be connected to, placed in, around or against, another article so that either article may perform its function, or

[42] For details, see E Derclaye, '*Flashing Badge v Groves*: A Step Forward in the Clarification of the Copyright/Design Interface' (2008) *European Intellectual Property Review* 251.

[43] For details, see Derclaye, 'Wonderful or Worrisome?' (n 21).

[44] *Glyn v Weston Feature Film Co* [1916] 1 Ch 261; *A-G v Blake* [2001] 1 AC 268; [2000] EMLR 949 (HL). As a result of this latter case it is still unclear whether the court meant that copyright cannot subsist or rather that copyright will not be enforced. In any case, one thing is clear: even if copyright subsists, it cannot be enforced.

(ii) are dependent upon the appearance of another article of which the article is intended by the designer to form an integral part; or

(c) surface decoration.

Paragraph (b)(i) is often referred to as the 'must-fit' exclusion and paragraph (b)(ii) as the 'must-match' exclusion. They correspond more or less to the same exclusions in RDR. The objective of the exclusion for methods or principles of construction is to exclude features which should be protected by patent law.[45] It broadly corresponds to the idea/expression dichotomy. As to surface decoration, by definition two-dimensional patterns are per se excluded. But this is not to say that all surface decoration will be two-dimensional. Some decoration, like embroidery on garments, will be in three dimensions but will still be excluded,[46] further reducing the instances of overlap between copyright and UDR.

As the method or construction exclusion does not equate with the exclusion of designs solely dictated by function, sometimes a design may be excluded from UDR but still be protected by CRDR or CUDR. This is well illustrated in the *Bailey* case.[47] The claimants' design was a ladder–resistant PVA micromesh for a bait bag for use in fishing. The court held that the design was a method or principle of construction because the appearance of the design was generated by the stitch method used.[48] But it held that it was not dictated solely by function because it was 'not the only design . . . capable of achieving *to a degree* this useful function for anglers'.[49] It was thus protected by CUDR but not UK UDR. This narrow view of the CUDR/CRDR exclusion was later endorsed by the Court of Appeal in *Landor*.[50]

In conclusion, the exclusions in the three rights are broadly the same, although in UDR there is no morality exclusion. In addition, copyright law excludes non-artistic functional shapes and leaves them to design rights. UDR excludes surface decoration, so the vast majority of two-dimensional and decorative three-dimensional designs will be excluded, leaving an overlap only between RDR and copyright. The overlap between the three rights is therefore further reduced at this level.

(iv) Ownership and Dealings

(a) Copyright

The author of a copyright work is the first owner (CDPA 1988, section 11(1)). Author means the person who creates the work, here the design. If the author is an employee, then the employer is the first owner unless there is an agreement to the contrary (section

[45] For cases applying this exclusion, see *Parker v Tidball* [1997] FSR 680 (concerned the design of mobile phone cases; held that stitching in seams was a method of construction); *A Fulton Co v Grant Barnett & Co* [2001] RPC 257 (umbrella case); *Landor and Hawa International v Azure Designs* [2006] ECDR 31 (CA) (the way the zippers and piping for the expansion section of a suitcase were arranged was not a method or principle of construction).

[46] See eg *Mark Wilkinson v Woodcraft Designs* [1998] FSR 63 (engraving, painting); *Jo-Y-Jo v Matalan Retail* [2000] ECDR 178 (embroidery on a garment was surface decoration since it was comprised of stitches added to the garment after it was made).

[47] *Bailey (t/a Elite Angling Products) v Haynes (t/a RAGS)* [2007] FSR 10.

[48] Ibid para 68.

[49] Ibid para 75, (emphasis in original).

[50] *Landor and Hawa International v Azure Designs* [2006] ECDR 31 (CA).

11(2)). Commissioned designs are subject to the principle (section 11(1)) and thus belong to the author unless a contract provides for the contrary.

Dealings with copyright are regulated in CDPA 1988, sections 90–93 and 101–102. Assignments can be in whole or part (ie not all the copyright needs to be transferred and not necessarily for the whole period when copyright subsists). For the assignment to be valid, it must be in writing and signed by or on behalf of the assignor. It is possible to assign future copyright. There is no need to register the assignment for it to be valid. The first buyer in time has priority over subsequent purported transferees. As to licences, they can be exclusive or non-exclusive, in whole or part. Generally the successors in title of the licensor are bound by the licence (section 90(4)). Only exclusive licences have to be in writing and the exclusive licensee can sue even without the copyright owner.

(b) RDR

The designer is the author and first owner (RDA 1949, sections 2, 3). 'Author' means the person who creates the design. A commissioned design (for money or money's worth) belongs to the commissioner. The original proprietor of a design created by an employee in the course of employment is the employer.[51] However, the Act does not specify whether this rule can be varied by contract. Probably it can, as in copyright law.

Dealings are regulated in RDA 1949, sections 15B and 15C. Assignments must be in writing and signed by or on behalf of the assignor. Any transfer is subject to any rights vested in another person of which notice is entered in the register of designs. The provisions for exclusive licences are the same as those provided for copyright in the CDPA 1988.

(c) UDR

UDR provisions mimic the corresponding RDA 1949 ones. Therefore, the author of the design is the person who creates it and s/he is the first owner (CDPA 1988, sections 214 and 215(1)). If the design is made in pursuance of a commission, the commissioner is the first owner (section 215(2)). If the design is made by an employee in the course of employment, the employer is the first owner (section 215(3)). Neither section 215(2) nor (3) states 'unless provided otherwise'. Probably again, it is possible to derogate from these provisions. The provision on joint designs is the same as for copyright works (CDPA 1988, section 259).

Provisions regarding assignments and licences (CDPA 1988, sections 222–225) are also the same as those provided in the CDPA 1988 in relation to copyright. There is one more provision which regulates regime clashes, namely CDPA 1988, section 224. It provides:

> Assignment of rights in registered design is presumed to carry with it design right. Where a design consisting of a design in which design rights exist is registered under the Registered Designs Act 1949 and the proprietor of the registered design is also the design right owner, an assignment of the right in the registered design shall be taken to be also an assignment of the design right, unless a contrary intention appears.

[51] *Coffey's Registered Design* [1982] FSR 227, cited by Bently and Sherman, *Intellectual Property Law* (n 25) 661, suggests that the employer is only first owner 'when employment carries with it a duty to make the design for the benefit of the employer'.

A corresponding section exists in the RDA 1949, namely section 19(3B).[52] These provisions apply only if the registered and unregistered designs are identical.[53] They do not oblige parties to transfer the two rights to the same person but if nothing contrary is stated in the contract, then they are. According to some, the assignment does not have to be in writing in this case.[54] CDPA 1988, section 224 and RDA 1949, section 19(3B) only apply to assignments and therefore not to other forms of transmission such as testamentary disposition:[55]

> Where a registered design consists of a number of design features, in each of which a separate design right exists, assignment of the registered design does not automatically take with it each of the design rights for the individual features nor does an assignment of the design right in one feature take with it an assignment of the registered design.[56]

If this was not the case, strange consequences would ensue.[57] However, the same authors note that in some cases a court may hold that 'as a matter of business efficacy an assignment of a registered design will impliedly include an assignment of all design rights with it'.[58] Therefore, the law attempts to avoid regime clashes but the system is imperfect because it does not impose that the same person must at all times be the proprietor of both the registered and unregistered design rights. Nevertheless, retention of some of the rights by the assignor may frustrate the agreement so that courts may decide that the assignment (of the registered or unregistered design according to the case in question) 'carries with it by implication a license to the assignee to use, and license others to use, such of the assignor's residual rights as are inevitably used when the [registered or unregistered according to the case] design is exploited'.[59] Finally, there are licences of right after five years since the start of the design right (CDPA 1988, section 237), something neither copyright nor (C)RDR provide.

(d) CRDR/CUDR

As to ownership, article 14 of the Design Regulation accords with UK copyright and design provisions, but has nothing to say about commissioned designs. Therefore, national law will apply and the same problems described above may occur between copyright and design rights for commissioned designs. As Community designs are deemed national rights for the purpose of transfers and licences, and other minimal provisions of the Regulation on this issue do not differ from the British ones (Design Regulation, articles 27–28, 32), what has been said above in respect of national designs applies. There is only one slight difference as regards exclusive licensees in that the conditions to sue for infringement are slightly more restrictive in the Regulation. Article 32(3) provides that:

[52] RDA 1949, s 19(3B) provides 'Where national unregistered design right subsists in a registered design and the proprietor of the registered design is also the design right owner, an assignment of the national unregistered design right shall be taken to be also an assignment of the right in the registered design, unless a contrary intention appears'.

[53] Laddie *et al*, *The Modern Law of Copyright* (n 1) 2035, para 46.11 and 2203, para 55.2.

[54] Ibid para 46.11.

[55] Ibid.

[56] Ibid.

[57] Ibid 2036, para 46.12. The authors give an example to illustrate this.

[58] Ibid 2204.

[59] Ibid.

> Without prejudice to the provisions of the licensing contract, the licensee may bring proceedings for infringement of a Community design only if the right holder consents thereto. However, the holder of an exclusive licence may bring such proceedings if the right holder in the Community design, having been given notice to do so, does not himself bring infringement proceedings within an appropriate period.

In conclusion, since copyright law and design law differ as to commissioned designs, there will often be regime clashes unless contracts are drawn to cede the designer's copyright to the commissioner.[60] The provisions regarding dealings are quasi-identical in the four types of rights so problems will rarely happen (transfers will be entered in the register if there is an overlap with RDR). In addition, CDPA 1988, section 224 and RDA 1949, section 19(3B) attempt to avoid inevitable regime clashes when design rights are transferred but do not include copyright, so that even if design rights should generally vest in the same person, copyright may not.

(vi) Rights and Infringement

(a) Copyright

The CDPA 1988 grants holders of copyright in most works the same set of rights, namely the rights of reproduction, issuing copies of the work to the public, rental, public lending, performing, showing or playing in public, communicating the work to the public and adaptation (sections 16–21). Indeed, holders of copyright in artistic works do not enjoy the rights of performance, showing or playing in public, nor of adaptation. The test of infringement is stated in CDPA 1988, section 16(3) and consists of taking the whole or a substantial part of the work, directly or indirectly. Thus, a causal connection must be proved – in other words, access to the copyright work.

As to rights, while the lack of a right of adaptation is not really problematic in practice as reproduction should always encompass adaptation, the fact that artists do not enjoy the performance right is a problem. Nothing could be done to prevent a competitor showing the protected artistic work in public, for instance in a show, or extracting a licence fee from this activity. This difference from the position of other copyright works is explained with difficulty, especially as artistic works benefit from the right of communication to the public, which includes showing the same work online or through traditional broadcast rather than live. As to infringement, first, copying must be proved. If there is no direct proof of access, one has to identify the similarities and differences between the two works to ascertain copying. Secondly, it needs to be established whether a substantial part has been taken. It does not matter at this second stage whether there are similarities between the two works, and therefore whether or not they look similar, provided that one finds that a substantial part has been taken.[61] What constitutes a substantial part is evaluated qualitatively rather than quantitatively.[62] After *Infopaq*, a 'substantial part' now means a part which comprises the author's own intellectual creation. Thus, taking a commercially significant or even small but important part will no longer

[60] As the case law shows, contracts are not always clear on who obtains the ownership of what. See for copyright commissioned works, *Robin Ray v Classic FM* [1998] FSR 622; *Warner v Gestetner* [1988] EIPR D-89 and *Griggs v Evans* [2005] EWCA Civ 11.

[61] *Designers Guild v Russell Williams (Textiles)* [2001] FSR 11 (HL).

[62] *Ladbroke (Football) Ltd v William Hill (Football) Ltd* [1964] 1 WLR 273.

amount to infringement if the condition of comprising the author's own intellectual creation is not fulfilled.[63] The work cannot be dissected but must be looked at as a whole.[64] Lord Mummery in *Baigent v Random House* usefully summarised the test as follows. Although he clearly stated it was not an 'exhaustive checklist', the following six steps

> will usually need to be considered, preferably in a chronological setting:
>
> (1) What are the similarities between the alleged infringing work and the original copyright work? Unless similarities exist, there is no arguable case of copying.
> (2) What access, direct or indirect, did the author of the alleged infringing work have to the original copyright work? . . .
> (3) Did the author of the alleged infringing work make some use in his work of material derived by him, directly or indirectly, from the original work?
> (4) If the defendant contends that no such use was made, what is his explanation for the similarities between the alleged infringing work and the original copyright work? Are they, for example, coincidental? Or are they explained by the use of similar sources? If the latter, what are the common sources that explain the similarities? How were the sources used by the authors of the respective works?
> (5) If, however, use was made of the original copyright work in producing the alleged infringing work, did it amount, in all the circumstances, to 'a substantial part' of the original work? . . .
> (6) What are the circumstances or factors that justify evaluating the part copied in the alleged infringing work as 'a substantial part' of the original copyright work?[65]

(b) (C)RDR/CUDR

As we have seen, Design Directive, article 9 and the corresponding RDA 1949 provision provide that:

> [t]he scope of the protection conferred by a design right shall include any design which does not produce on the informed user a different overall impression.

This test of infringement was interpreted by Jacob LJ in *Procter & Gamble v Reckitt Benckiser*. He held that 'what matters is what strikes the mind of the informed user *when* it is carefully viewed',[66] as opposed to *after*, when the informed user no longer has the design in front of him or her. The informed user will examine the products with a reasonable degree of care: 'In this exercise the level of generality to which the court must descend is important . . . The appropriate level of generality is that which would be taken by the notional informed user'.[67] Contrary to the individual character test, however, the test at the level of infringement is that the impression must be 'different' not 'clearly different'.[68] It will therefore be difficult to establish infringement, since provided the defendant's design is different, it will escape liability, as happened in the case, although Procter & Gamble's design was very different from anything that had been designed in the field previously.

[63] See eg *BBC v Time Out* [1984] FSR 64.
[64] [2001] FSR 11 (HL).
[65] *Baigent v Random House Group Ltd* [2007] EWCA Civ 247, para 124.
[66] [2007] EWCA Civ 936 (CA), para 25 (emphasis added).
[67] Ibid 35.
[68] Ibid.

In addition, CPDA 1988, section 53 ensures that there is no double protection, ie by copyright and RDR.[69] Section 53 provides that if someone does an act restricted by copyright in pursuance of an assignment or licence under registration of a corresponding design, it does not infringe any copyright in that design. However, as soon as this person is on notice that the RDR's validity is in danger (there are cancellation or rectification proceedings), copyright infringement is 'revived'. The copyright infringement immunity kicks in only if the assignment or licence has been granted by the proprietor of the RDR:

> Presumably the immunity only relates to those features of the corresponding design which are the subject of the registration. Therefore, for example, if a design monopoly is only sought for part of what is shown on the registration filed at the registry, it is just that part in respect of which no copyright infringement can be asserted.[70]

(c) UDR

The owner of UDR in a design has the exclusive right to reproduce the design for commercial purposes, inter alia, by making articles to that design (CDPA 1988, section 226(1)). Both copyright and UDR prohibit primary and secondary infringement and these concepts are the same in the two rights. 'The only difference is that the concept of primary infringement by breach of the rental right is unknown in design right law.'[71] Reproduction of a design by making articles to that design is defined by section 226(2) as meaning: 'copying the design so as to produce articles exactly or substantially to that design'. The test is therefore different from that of copyright law, which requires copying of a substantial part. As the test is substantial similarity, it tends to protect less than copyright law, as well stated in *L Woolley Jewellers v A&A Jewellery*: '[I]t may not be enough to copy a part, even a substantial part. Regard has to be had to the overall design which enjoys design right.'[72] Thus, it is a test of overall impression, as for RDR. However, if the claimant is wise enough to rely only on the part of the article in which his or her UDR resides and which is allegedly infringed, s/he can circumvent the UDR infringement test and the result will be the same as in copyright law, as the whole or a substantial part of that part of the article will have been copied. If the claimant acts this way, the test of infringement is the same as in copyright law.

UK law establishes a rule in cases where both copyright and UDR are infringed in the same subject matter: if an article is protected both by copyright and UDR, at the stage of infringement, copyright prevails (CDPA 1988, section 236).[73] UDR does not disappear but yields at the infringement stage, thereby avoiding cumulation of the rights. This provision applies to both primary and secondary infringement of design right.[74] But when there is no copyright infringement, eg because the work is not artistic, UDR can be infringed if UDR subsists.

[69] On this section, see Bently and Sherman, *Intellectual Property Law* (n 25) 685; Laddie *et al*, *The Modern Law of Copyright* (n 16) para 59.47.

[70] Laddie *et al*, *The Modern Law of Copyright* (n 16) para 59.47.

[71] Ibid 1574, para 32.63.

[72] [2003] FSR 15 (CA), para 19.

[73] CPDA 1988, s 236 provides that '[w]here copyright subsist in a work which consists of or includes a design in which design right subsists, it is not an infringement of design right in the design to do anything which is an infringement of the copyright in that work'.

[74] Laddie *et al*, *The Modern Law of Copyright* (n 16) 2220, para 56.16.

In conclusion, because copyright only requires an original part of the work to be copied, its more lenient regime will prevail over that of RDR. There will be no double compensation where both copyright and UDR are infringed, because of CDPA 1988, section 236. There is, however, no equivalent provision preventing the coincidence of UDR and RDR infringement so that the owner can sue on both counts and arguably double compensation can be obtained[75] (but note the effect of CDPA 1988, section 53 discussed above).

(vii) Exceptions Including Exhaustion Principle

The UK CDPA 1988 contains no less than 59 exceptions (sections 28A–75 and 171). RDR has four exceptions: acts done privately and for non-commercial purposes; acts done for experimental purposes; acts of reproduction for the purposes of making citations or of teaching under certain conditions; and the exception to facilitate international transport (Design Directive, article 13 which corresponds to RDA 1949, section 7A(2) and (3)). UDR has no exceptions but its scope of protection only encompasses commercial activities. In addition, in UDR acquiescence is a defence, but it is not in copyright law.[76] Therefore, in case of cumulation, the more restrictive regime will prevail, thus RDR for exceptions and copyright for acquiescence.

Exhaustion applies in the same way for both copyright and RDR. No corresponding provision exists in the CDPA 1988 for UDR. On the other hand, UDR does not include a right of distribution. It would not be surprising, however, if courts require that the principle of exhaustion also applies to subject matter protected by UDR, since otherwise it would be blatantly contrary to the case law of the EU courts.

B Negative Overlap

(i) Copyright Protection Unavailable

Because of the categorisation requirement, it is possible that certain creations may not be able to gain copyright protection, such as in the *Creation Records* case.[77] Therefore, (C) UDR or (C)RDR may be useful in those cases. This is the only case where copyright protection would be unavailable. Indeed, the change in the originality requirement, which makes it closer to the requirements in RDR and UDR, means that often both protection will be available together or not available together, preventing a negative overlap. Nevertheless, presumably works of artistic craftsmanship will still have to meet the higher threshold of originality so that UDR and RDR will also be useful in this case, although of course relative novelty and/or non-commonplaceness will need to be proved.

[75] Ibid.
[76] *Fisher v Brooker* [2009] UKHL 41.
[77] It is arguable, however, that this sort of creation may be now classed as a database (the *sui generis* right was not yet applicable when the litigation took place), but other types of artistic works may not be able to be so classified and therefore may be uncopyrightable.

(ii) UDR/RDR Protection Unavailable

If the design is not new or is commonplace, copyright will easily fill the gap as long as the design is original in the sense of the author's own intellectual creation. But if the work is of craftsmanship and cannot be said to be artistic, then copyright will not be available either.

C *A Posteriori* Overlap

Copyright lasts for 70 years after the author's death or 50 years from the triggering event in case of a non-original work, while (C)RDR lasts for a maximum of 25 years and CUDR for three years. UDR lasts generally 10 years from the date when a product incorporating the design is first marketed.[78] Copyright can therefore prolong all design rights. However, UK law has a special rule which prevents the prolongation of RDR by copyright in some cases. CDPA 1988, section 52 provides that if a copyright-protected artistic work (with some exceptions, namely sculptures, wall plaques, medals, medallions and printed matter primarily of a literary or artistic character) is produced by an industrial process and exploited commercially (ie more than 50 copies are exploited commercially or it consists of goods manufactured in lengths or pieces not being hand-made), the duration of the copyright is no longer 70 years after the author's death but 25 years from the first marketing of the industrially produced articles in question. This can happen during the life of the designer or after.

III. COPYRIGHT AND TRADEMARKS

To our knowledge there is virtually no case law on this overlap. However, it is not impossible for it to occur and a relevant case is *IPC Media v News Group Newspapers* which will be reviewed in section X.

A Simultaneous Overlap

(i) Subject Matter

The Trademark Act 1994 reproduces almost word for word the definition of a trademark found in the Trademark Directive 2008/95/EC. Therefore, a trademark may consist of words (including personal names), designs, letters, numerals or the shape of goods or their packaging. As in France, the overlap is therefore clear between literary, musical and artistic works and word, figurative and aural marks. In addition, audiovisual marks can be protected in the United Kingdom.[79] However the overlap is not total. Single words[80]

[78] For the full explanation of the rule, see CDPA 1988, s 216. It varies between from 10 years to just under 16 years depending whether or not creation of the design coincides with the first marketing of articles made to the design.

[79] At least a series of images can be registered, which amounts to a moving mark in practice. See eg the registrations by O2, the telecommunications company, nos 2417895B, 2417895C, 2417895F and 2417895G from 2006 and 2509058–2509065 registered in 2009, available at www.ipo.gov.uk/types/tm/t-os/t-find/t-find-adp.

[80] *Exxon Corp v Exxon Insurance Consultants* [1982] RPC 69 (CA).

and titles[81] are not normally protected by copyright. In fact, the *Infopaq* decision has completely ruled out for all Member States that single words can be protected by copyright so that the overlap in this respect is impossible.[82] Courts rarely allow the trademark registration of characters (ie names or likenesses of real or deceased persons) because generally the public does not regard them as indications of origin or they lack distinctive character.[83] The overlap will therefore be rare in this respect, if copyright happens to subsist. It is easier for fictitious characters to obtain trademark or copyright protection.[84] UK law may protect titles and therefore slogans if they are particularly original. Whether this means that the threshold of originality has to be higher than the author's own intellectual creation remains to be seen, as the *Francis Day* case[85] was decided under the old originality requirement and required something more than the latter, but it is unclear how high the threshold might be. Therefore, the overlap is possible. Often, however, as the EU case law illustrates well, it is difficult for slogans to obtain trademark protection in the first place so that the overlap is rare. But a UK example is interesting in this respect. For many years, Nestlé marketed its 'Kit Kat' chocolate bar in the United Kingdom under the slogan 'Have a break, have a Kit Kat'. It had a trademark in 'Kit Kat'. Nestlé then applied to register the first half of the slogan as a trademark. Although the words 'Have a break' were well known to the relevant public, it was held that they were not inherently distinctive of Nestlé's chocolate bar.[86] In other words, 'there was nothing to show that "Have a break" when not followed by "Have a Kit Kat", had acquired its own independent distinctiveness through use'.[87] But the Court of Justice reversed this finding and held it did: distinctive character may be acquired in consequence of the use of that mark as part of or in conjunction with a registered trademark mark.[88] Therefore, the slogan 'Have a break, have a Kit Kat' was a valid mark.

Book titles are very rarely regarded as indicating origin and therefore rarely registrable.[89] In essence, a book title describes the contents of the book to which it relates.[90] Besides, the trademark registry considers that 'use of words as a title of a publication

[81] *Francis Day & Hunter v 20th Century Fox* [1940] AC 112 (PC).

[82] Case C-5/08 *Infopaq International AS v Dankse Dagblades Forening* [2009] ECR I-6569, para 45. In an article preceding the *Infopaq* ruling, M Richardson had, however, argued that single words should be able to attract copyright protection because lack of originality was not the reason for denying copyright protection to the word 'Exxon'. See M Richardson, 'Copyright in Trademarks? On Understanding Trademark Dilution' (2000) *Intellectual Property Quarterly* 66, 71–76.

[83] See A Firth, 'National Report, Reply to the Questionnaire for the United Kingdom, ALAI 2001 Sessions IIA and IIB: The Relationship of Copyright and Trademarks' in J Ginsburg and J Besek (eds), *Adjuncts and Alternatives to Copyright, Proceedings of the ALAI Congress, June 13–17, 2001, New York, USA* (New York, Columbia University School of Law, 2002) 4, citing *Elvis Presley* [1999] RPC 567. Laddie *et al*, *The Modern Law of Copyright* (n 16) 1727–28, paras 37.11–37.12.

[84] 'In *Mirage Studios v Counter-feat Clothing* [1991] FSR 145 the copyright claims probably reinforced the passing off claims.' See Firth, 'National Report, Reply to the Questionnaire for the United Kingdom' (n 83) 4. See also section X.

[85] *Francis Day & Hunter v 20th Century Fox* [1940] AC 112 (PC) (the song's title 'The Man Who Broke the Bank at Monte Carlo' was held not original enough because the words 'to break the bank' are hackneyed and Monte Carlo is an obvious place at which that event can occur).

[86] See *Nestlé v Mars UK* [2003] FSR 37 (HC) and [2004] FSR 2 (CA), comment J Phillips, *Trade Mark Law: A Practical Anatomy* (Oxford, Oxford University Press, 2003) 141.

[87] Phillips, *Trade Mark Law* (n 86) 141.

[88] Case C-353/03 *Nestlé v Mars UK* [2005] ECR I-6135.

[89] S Jennings and C Donovan, 'Trade Marks and Book Titles' (1994) *Entertainment Law Review* 38, 38–41.

[90] Ibid 38; J Klink, 'Titles in Europe: Trade Names, Copyright Works or Title Marks' (2004) *European Intellectual Property Review* 291, 293. This is comparable to the situation in France, see section III.A.

does not amount to use of those words as a trademark'.[91] Therefore, someone using a mark in the title of a book does not infringe the trademark[92] and prolonged use of the title by the would-be trademark owner will only very exceptionally make the title acquire secondary meaning. Things may be different for titles of periodicals, however, as people carry on buying the following issues of the same magazine on the basis of origin.[93]

As to artistic works, first of all, as the Paris Convention prescribes, emblems and flags cannot be registered (at least without the authorisation of the country concerned). Shapes are registrable only if they do not fall within the exclusions of Trademark Directive, article 3(1)(e) (TMA 1994, section 3(2)). Case law has not been abundant apart from the famous *Philips* case which gave rise to the Court of Justice decision on the topic. Other examples of three-dimensional subject matter which can be protectable as trademarks include uniforms as they can be distinctive.[94]

(ii) Protection Requirements

EU law dictates the protection requirements for trademarks and copyright. As examined in the chapters on France and the European Union, it will not be rare that there is an overlap between the two rights at this level.

(iii) Excluded Subject Matter

As far as trademarks are concerned, excluded subject matter is dictated by EU law (see TMA 1994, sections 3–5) and reference is made to section III.C of chapter three. As in all EU countries, ideas are not protectable by copyright. UK trademark law does not protect unregistered trademarks but passing off can protect them (see below section X). TMA 1994, section 5(4)(b) reproduces the Trademark Directive's provision so that a mark may not be registered if its use in the United Kingdom is liable to be prevented by copyright or design laws. More details on the overlap are therefore found in section IV.B(i) of chapter three.

(iv) Ownership and Dealings

Copyright provisions have been examined above at IIA. The relevant provisions of the TMA 1994 are sections 22–31. Under section 23(1), a trademark can be co-owned and in this case, each co-owner 'is entitled, subject to any agreement to the contrary, to an equal undivided share in the registered trademark'.

The consent of all co-owners is required to license use of the trademark or assign the trademark. A trademark can be assigned with or without the business or goodwill and for all or part of the goods or services and limited or not in its geographical scope (section 24). It must be in writing signed by or on behalf of the assignor. A licence can also

[91] Jennings and Donovan, 'Trade Marks and Book Titles' (n 89). See also Klink, 'Titles in Europe' (n 90).

[92] See *Mothercare v Penguin Books* [1988] RPC 113.

[93] Jennings and Donovan, 'Trade Marks and Book Titles' (n 89) 40–41, citing *John Leng v Gold Star Publications* [1967] FSR 75.

[94] Firth, 'National Report, Reply to the Questionnaire for the United Kingdom' (n 83) 4, citing Wadlow, who cites *Knott v Morgan* (1836) 48 ER 610.

be for all or part of the goods or services, limited or not in its geographical scope, can be exclusive or non-exclusive and must also be in writing and signed by or on behalf of the assignor (section 28). Unless the licence states otherwise, it is binding on a successor in title to the grantor's interest. Assignments and licences need to be recorded in the trademark register (section 25). The provisions on transfer and licensing for the Community trademark (CTM) (Community Trademark Regulation (EC) 207/2009 (CTMR)), articles 16–18, 22–23) are very similar or identical to those for the Community design;[95] ie joint ownership, CTMs are deemed national rights for the purpose of transfers and licences unless otherwise stated, transfers must be in writing with the signature of *both* parties, CTMs may be licensed for some or all of the goods or services for which they are registered, for the whole or part of the European Union and may be exclusive or non-exclusive, and CTMR, article 22(5) (conditions for exclusive licensee to sue) reproduces Community Design Regulation (EC) 6/2002, article 32(3)). In addition, the CTMR provides that the trademark can be transferred with or without the business and for all or some of the goods/services for which it is registered. Entry in the register of transfers and licences is not required but if transfers are not registered, the successor in title may not invoke the rights arising from the registration of the Community trademark. Licences and transfers only have effect vis-à-vis third parties if they are entered in the register.

The overlap does not create many problems as the provisions are very similar or identical in the three rights. When there is a difference, the stricter regime will prevail (eg entries in the register).

(v) Rights and Infringement

Section 9 provides that the mark is infringed if it is used in the course of trade in the United Kingdom without the owner's consent (TMA 1994, section 9(4) lists a series of acts which amount to use). Infringement is different for marks with or without a reputation and depends whether the sign or good/service is identical or similar (section X). Again UK law reproduces the Trademark Directive in this respect. The main differences between the two rights is that in trademark law the sign does not have to be copied to infringe, and use in the course of trade is necessary for trademark infringement. Trademark law will trump copyright in the first case and copyright will trump trademark law in the second.

(vi) Exceptions Including Exhaustion Principle

As we have seen above at IIA(vi), UK copyright law has no less than 59 exceptions. Trademark law has no relevant one[96] but as we saw in the preceding paragraph, its scope of protection only extends to use of the mark in the course of trade. As we saw in the chapter on Europe, there is convergence between copyright and trademark law when copyright exceptions allow use for private and non-commercial purposes. Otherwise, copyright prevails as some uses are infringing even if they are not commercial (eg criticism or review which does not comply with all the conditions of the exception (namely section 30, parody) as it is not an exception in UK law; private copying as such as opposed

[95] On these see section II.A.
[96] On this see Trademark Directive, art 6 and the discussion in chapter 3, section III.B(i).

to private study). But if the use fell within copyright law's criticism and review defence,[97] would courts allow a similar (parody) defence in trademark law? There has been virtually no decision involving parodied trademarks. If there is no risk of confusion and it is required, then parody will be implicitly allowed as there will be no infringement. But where risk of confusion is not required (identity of goods/signs or dissimilar goods and a mark with reputation), some think a defence is probable if it is truly parodic or satirical as the use would be with cause.[98] But if the use causes detriment to the trademark owner or provides an advantage to the alleged infringer, courts will be more reluctant to admit such a defence.[99] 'Since trade mark infringement inevitably involves commercial speech, the courts have shown less tolerance of parody in trade mark cases than in copyright cases.'[100] Thus the parody argument will only work when the parody 'is a vehicle for "non-commercial speech" for the primary purpose of political or satirical comment'.[101]

Exhaustion provisions are regulated by EU law so we refer the reader to the discussion of this point in chapter three (section IV.B(i)). In addition, CDPA 1988, section 63(1) provides that:

> it is not an infringement of copyright in an artistic work to copy it or to issue copies to the public, for the purpose of advertising the sale of the work.

The rest of the article considers it an infringement to deal subsequently with these copies of the work for other purposes than advertising. This provision is close to the *Dior v Evora* ruling, although it does not imply that if the copyright work is also a trademark, the trademark would not be infringed. Thanks to *Dior*, this is also covered. In addition, *Dior* arguably covers any copyright work, not just artistic works.

B Negative Overlap

(i) Copyright Protection Unavailable

As for the overlap between copyright and designs, there may be some creations which cannot fall within one of the categories of the CDPA 1988 or do not reach the level of originality but which can be trademarks (eg all *de minimis* works, works of artistic craftsmanship). What has been said in chapter three therefore applies.

[97] Courts may use CDPA 1988, s 30 to allow parodies but the defence will work only if there is sufficient acknowledgement which will often not be the case. In addition, courts feel that the purpose and intention, as well as the originality of the parodying work, are important factors for the exception to apply. Finally, in some cases, authors could use their right of integrity to trump the parody. On this see S Maniatis and E Gredley, 'Parody: A Fatal Attraction' (1997) *European Intellectual Property Review* 339, 341–42.

[98] D Kitchin, D Llewelyn, J Mellor, R Meade, T Moody-Stuart and D Keeling, *Kerly's Law of Trade Marks and Trade Names,* 14th edn (London, Sweet and Maxwell, 2005) 386; Maniatis and Gredley, 'Parody: A Fatal Attraction' (n 97) 419.

[99] Kitchin *et al*, *Kerly's Law of Trade Marks and Trade Names* (n 98) 386–87, referring to the French 'E$$O' case; on this see chapter 4, section III.A.

[100] Firth, 'National Report, Reply to the Questionnaire for the United Kingdom' (n 83) 6, citing Maniatis and Gredley, 'Parody: A Fatal Attraction' (n 97) 412.

[101] Maniatis and Gredley, 'Parody: A Fatal Attraction' (n 97) 418, noting, however, at 420 that 'There is no freedom of expression defence in UK trade mark law'.

(ii) Trademark Protection Unavailable

We refer the reader to section IV.B(ii) of chapter three on this point as there is no case law in the United Kingdom.

C *A Posteriori* Overlap

We again refer the reader to section IV.B(iii) of chapter three on this point as there is no case law in the United Kingdom. Some commentators, however, have discussed this issue in relation to book titles. They report that publishers try to acquire trademark rights in book titles and book characters to extend the copyright protection once it has expired.[102] As we have seen above as regards the simultaneous overlap (at IIIA), the Trademark Registry's position will normally prevent this from happening. Passing off will be a better bet for established book titles and characters, as goodwill will have had the time to grow. This will be further explored in section X.

IV. TRADEMARKS AND DESIGNS

EU law almost entirely regulates both trademark and designs, only ownership and dealings are slightly harmonised by the Trademark and Design Directives and Regulations, so this section will concentrate on ownership and dealings only. In addition, apart from the *Philips v Remington* decision, there have not been any decisions as yet on this overlap in the United Kingdom, so we refer the reader to the corresponding section in chapter three. A few words will be said also about the *a posteriori* overlap as the Court of Appeal and other UK courts expressed similar concerns as those voiced by the Advocate-General and Court of Justice in the *Philips* case.

A Simultaneous Overlap

We have already had the chance to discuss the provisions regarding ownership and dealings for both trademarks and designs when discussing the overlap between copyright and trademarks and copyright and designs in the preceding sections. The following ensues. As to ownership, there might be a problem as a trademark belongs to the person who registers it and that might not be the owner of the (C)RDR or (C)UDR, who will generally be the creator. However, often a logo or other design will have been made under commission or by an employee and therefore will also belong to the company registering the trademark. In addition, a trademark cannot be registered if it infringes a design, and vice versa, so that this problem is avoided. As to transfers and licences, provisions are quasi-identical for both national and Community trademark and design rights,[103] so problems will rarely happen and convergence is quasi-perfect on this aspect. Even with this high convergence, problems can still occur, however, mainly if the design is not transferred to the same person as the trademark (be it a national or Community right).

[102] Jennings and Donovan, 'Trade Marks and Book Titles' (n 89) 41–42.

[103] What is different mainly is that a trademark can be transferred or licensed for just some of the goods or services for which it is registered, something which is not provided for designs.

B *A Posteriori* Overlap

As we saw in section V.B(iii) of chapter three, the Advocate-General in *Philips v Remington* was of the clear opinion that trademarks, at least three-dimensional ones, cannot artificially prolong designs and patents. The Court of Appeal of England and Wales in the same case was also of this opinion, but went even further, as Aldous LJ (who delivered the judgment) held that TMA 1994, section 3(2)(b) and (c) appeared to seek 'to exclude from registration certain shapes which are protectable under patents, registered designs, copyright and other such intellectual property rights'.[104] It then added:

> For many years it has been recognised that monopoly rights, other than trademarks, granted by the state are anti-competitive and can only been justified for a limited term and on well-known grounds. Trademarks have been seen as an exception provided they only monopolise indications of origin and not inventions and designs. To enable monopolies granted in respect of patents, registered designs and the like to be extended by trademark registrations would be contrary to the public interest unless justifiable on grounds of the public good.[105]

Thus, Aldous LJ seems to have expressed this opinion in a broader sense than the Court of Justice so as to exclude the *a posteriori* overlap for all sorts of subject matter not only three-dimensional. At around the same time, the Trademarks Registry, and on appeal, Neuberger J, expressed similar views in *Interlego's Application* (concerning the trademark registration of the Lego brick).[106] In conclusion, the UK courts seem to be even more strongly against the *a posteriori* overlap in general than the Court of Justice.

V. TRADEMARKS AND PATENTS

Like the previous overlap (trademark/design), this overlap is heavily harmonised at European level so that the discussion in chapter three on Europe also applies in the United Kingdom. As a result of the excluded subject matter provisions and EU case law, it is practically impossible for any of the three different overlaps (simultaneous, negative and *a posteriori*) to occur. Therefore, it is not necessary to examine the rest of the national provisions (namely, ownership, dealings, rights, infringement and exceptions) for this overlap.

One thing is interesting to note in relation to the *a posteriori* overlap. In a decision of 2002, the High Court had to decide whether a trademark application is to be considered made in bad faith if the applicant's aim when registering a product's shape as a trademark is to prolong his or her patent monopoly.[107] The court rejected this argument and construed bad faith narrowly as to include only cases where:

[104] [1999] ETMR 816, 824.

[105] Ibid.

[106] [1998] RPC 69, cited by A Firth, E Gredley and S Maniatis, 'Shapes as Trade Marks: Public Policy, Functional Considerations and Consumer Perception' (2001) *European Intellectual Property Review* 86, 90. Neuberger J said at 114: 'the decision whether to register a trade mark can, at least in some cases, involve a balancing exercise, particularly in light of the very substantial benefit accorded to a proprietor if he succeeds in registering his mark and the public interest against monopolies in products (as opposed to marks) . . . the fact that an applicant has, or has had, the benefit of the protection of a registered patent in respect of the very thing which (or part of which) he seeks to register as a trade mark is a factor, which, *at least in some cases,* ought to be taken into account' (emphasis added).

[107] Phillips, *Trade Mark Law* (n 86) 455, para 13.104, discussing *Nestlé v Unilever* [2002] EWHC 2709 ('Viennetta' ice cream's shape).

dishonesty or something approaching it (such as conduct falling short of acceptable commercial behaviour) can properly be alleged with full particulars. It is a serious addition, not one to be thrown in the pot along with other, more conventional points . . . Not surprisingly it failed in this case.[108]

VI. PATENTS AND DESIGNS

As we saw in the chapter on France, the provisions regarding patents are partly harmonised at European level through the EPC. Provisions concerning ownership and dealings, rights, infringement and exceptions have in most part not been harmonised so that these will be discussed. As the provisions relevant for the negative and *a posteriori* overlaps are identical they will not be repeated here and can be found in chapter three.[109]

A Simultaneous Overlap

(i) Ownership and Dealings

Ownership and dealings are regulated in Patents Act 1977, sections 30–38. Patents can be co-owned and in this case, unless the co-owners agree otherwise, each co-owner is entitled to an equal undivided share in the patent and can exploit the patent without the other's consent without it being an infringement (section 36). Sections 39–41 contain detailed provisions on employee inventions. In sum, they provide that the employer owns the patent of the employee if:

(a) it was made in the course of the normal duties of the employee or in the course of duties falling outside his normal duties, but specifically assigned to him, and the circumstances in either case were such that an invention might reasonably be expected to result from the carrying out of his duties; or
(b) the invention was made in the course of the duties of the employee and, at the time of making the invention, because of the nature of his duties and the particular responsibilities arising from the nature of his duties he had a special obligation to further the interests of the employer's undertaking.

In all other cases, the patent belongs to the employee. Patents Act 1977, section 39(3) further provides that if the invention belongs to the employee:

nothing done

(a) by or on behalf of the employee or any person claiming under him for the purposes of pursuing an application for a patent, or
(b) by any person for the purpose of performing or working the invention,

shall be taken to infringe any copyright or design right to which, as between him and his employer, his employer is entitled in any model or document relating to the invention.

This provision prevents regime clashes in this particular situation. If an invention and/or a patent has brought an outstanding benefit to the employer, the employee may be

[108] See *Nestlé v Unilever* [2002] EWHC 2709, para 7.

[109] An exception is when there is an *a posteriori* overlap between patent and UDR. In this case, it is the patent which will prolong the life of the UK UDR by five or 10 years, not vice versa.

especially compensated (Patents Act 1977, section 41). This section is imperative (ie it overrides any agreement between the inventor and employer except collective agreements made by or on behalf of a trade union to which the employee belongs, and by the employer).

Transfers must be in writing and signed by or on behalf of the assignor. Under Patents Act 1977, sections 32 and 33, rules were made in relation to the registration of patents.[110] These provide that registration is not required for validity but only for evidential purposes. Surprisingly, there are no specific provisions regarding licences. Common contract law will thus apply.

If a design and a patent subsist on the same object, the stricter patent regime will apply in terms of employee inventions, unless the design and the invention are clearly separable. The Patents Act 1977 does not deal with commissioned patents. This is probably because these cases are rather rare. Nevertheless, then the default rule will be that the owner will be the inventor. A clash may thus exist if there is also a design involved. As to transfers and licences, as we saw, patent provisions are minimal. The only difference that may exist between patents and designs in this respect is that design exclusive licences must be in writing, whereas patent licences need not be as the Act is silent. As to transfers, the Patents Act 1977 does not provide that they can be in whole or part but, as for designs, they have to be signed by the assignor or on his or her behalf. Regime clashes should therefore be rather rare in case of overlap. Commentators note that there is no provision equivalent to CDPA 1988, section 224 applying to the assignment of patents.[111] Therefore, they recommend that the 'assignee of a patent . . . ensure that his assignment at least conveys all design rights owned by the assignee and which are included with the patent specifications and drawings'.[112] However, as we shall see in section VII, this may not even be necessary because of the ruling in the *Catnic* case.

(ii) Rights and Infringement

The patent owner has the following rights: to dispose of, offer to dispose of, use or import the patented product or keep it, whether for disposal or otherwise. Thus, it is an infringement to do any of those acts. If the invention is a process, intention or reason to believe that use of the process would infringe is required except when dealing with products resulting from the process (Patents act 1977, section 60(1)). In addition, it is also an infringement to supply or offer to supply a person with any means (relating to an essential element of the invention) for putting the invention into effect when knowing, or when it is obvious to a reasonable person in the circumstances, that those means are suitable for putting, and are intended to put, the invention into effect in the United Kingdom (there is a qualified exception for staple commercial products) (section 60(2), (3)). The test of infringement incorporates EPC 2000, article 69 in Patents Act 1977, section 125, so that the doctrine of equivalents is part of UK law. Therefore, the patent's scope is that provided in the claims but the drawings and description must be used to interpret the

[110] See Patent Rules 2007, SI 2007/3291, rule 47.

[111] As a reminder, CPDA 1988, s 224 provides: 'Where a design consisting of a design in which design rights exist is registered under the Registered Designs Act 1949 and the proprietor of the registered design is also the design right owner, an assignment of the right in the registered design shall be taken to be also an assignment of the design right, unless a contrary intention appears'.

[112] Laddie *et al*, *The Modern Law of Copyright* (n 16) 2203, para 55.2 n 3.

claims.[113] When comparing the strict overall impression test as interpreted in *Procter & Gamble v Reckitt Benckiser*,[114] it seems more likely, because of the doctrine of equivalents, that the patent will be infringed but not the RDR.

(iii) Exceptions

There are six exceptions to patent infringement (Patents Act 1977, section 60(5)(a)–(i)). They are: acts for private and non-commercial purposes; experimental purposes; extemporaneous preparation in a pharmacy of a medicine for an individual in accordance with a prescription; the exception which aims at facilitating international transport; the farmer's privilege (in relation to plants and animals); and acts done in conducting a study, test or trial which is necessary for and is conducted with a view to the application of the directives on the Community codes relating to veterinary medicinal products and medicinal products for human use.[115] In addition, the Patents Act 1977 provides for several compulsory licences (sections 48, 48A, 48B, 49 and 50). After three years from grant, and after having unsuccessfully sought a licence from the patent owner at reasonable conditions, anyone may apply to the Comptroller of Patents for a compulsory licence in the following cases:

(1) a demand in the United Kingdom for the patented product is not being met on reasonable terms;
(2) the unreasonable refusal of the patent owner prevents another patented invention which involves an important technical advance of considerable economic significance in relation to the invention for which the patent concerned was granted;
(3) the unreasonable refusal of the patent owner unfairly prejudices the establishment or development of commercial or industrial activities in the United Kingdom;
(4) the patent owner's acts unfairly prejudice the manufacture, use or disposal of materials not protected by the patent, or the establishment or development of commercial or industrial activities in the United Kingdom.

These compulsory licences apply as regards WTO members; section 48B has a similar set of compulsory licences for non-WTO members (some other cases are also added). Sections 49 and 50 list factors to be taken into account by the Comptroller when imposing a licence. Finally, the Crown may make use of a patented invention for several purposes (eg defence, wars, emergencies) (sections 55–59).

The exceptions in RDR are less extensive than those in patent law so that the (C)RDR/(C)UDR regime will trump that of patent and also of UK UDR which has no exceptions but whose scope of protection only encompasses commercial uses. However, the farmer's privilege and exceptions for the making of a drug and drug trials would not in the vast majority of cases apply in case of an overlap, so that in fact it is the patent regime which will trump the additional exception in RDR, namely use for teaching and citation purposes. Finally, the design regime will trump the patent regime in relation to compulsory licences.

[113] *Kirin-Amgen v Transkaryotic Therapies* [2005] RPC 9 (HL).
[114] See the above discussion, section II.A.
[115] Directive 2001/82/EC, art 13(1)–(5) or Directive 2001/83/EC, art 10(1)–(4).

VII. COPYRIGHT AND PATENTS

A Simultaneous Overlap

As we saw in the chapters on French and EU Law, the most obvious overlap here, is the overlap concerning computer programs. The other overlaps are those concerning aesthetic creations, presentations of information and the drawings and/or text of a patent application. There are some rules organising the overlap between copyright and patents, mainly reproducing those existing in the EPC, namely: computer programs, aesthetic creations and presentations of information as such cannot be considered as inventions (Patents Act 1977, section 1(2)).

(i) Subject Matter, Protection Requirements and Excluded Subject Matter

As, by definition, the rules on subject matter, protection requirements and excluded subject matter are the same as at European level, what has been said there applies here too. So we refer the reader to them and add here only case law applying the same principles and also idiosyncrasies applying in UK law.

Only computer programs as such are excluded by Patents Act 1977, section 1(2). Following the Software Directive, computer programs are copyrightable under CDPA 1988, section 3(1)(b). Copyrightability of computer programs has not posed problems. The result of the decisions is that many features are excluded because they are functional so the protection will not be very strong in case of infringement by similar copying rather than identical copying.[116] On the other hand, the history of the UK case law on the patentability of computer programs is chequered. There are now five Court of Appeal decisions which set out different rules to determine software patentability, and the Technical Board of Appeal of the EPO recently held that the last one (*Aerotel/Macrossan*[117]) does not conform to the EPC.[118] All but one of the UK Court of Appeal cases dealt with business methods or rules for performing mental acts implemented by software rather than computer programs used in connection with hardware. *Symbian* is really the only one which deals with such type of invention so that its ruling may be more relied upon in similar cases.[119] In the four cases dealing with business methods,[120] the latter were all held unpatentable. In *Symbian*, the computer program could be patentable. Even if the test is not the same in the UK courts and at the EPO, often times, the result will be the same.[121] Lately, the High Court restated that *Aerotel* did not change the 'old law' (ie that conforming to the EPO case law) and the latest Intellectual Property Office

[116] See eg *Cantor v Tradition* [1999] All ER (D) 389.

[117] *Aerotel v Telco & Neal, Macrossan's Application (Aerotel/Macrossan)* [2006] EWCA Civ 1371.

[118] See Case T-154/04, discussed by D Pearce, 28 January 2010, available at http://ipkitten.blogspot.com/2010/01/patentable-subject-matter-where-are-we.html.

[119] *Symbian Ltd v Comptroller General of Patents* [2008] EWCA Civ 1066.

[120] *Merrill Lynch's Application* [1989] RPC 561; *Gale's Application* [1991] RPC 305; *Fujitsu Ltd's Application* [1997] RPC 608; *Aerotel v Telco & Neal, Macrossan's Application* [2006] EWCA Civ 1371.

[121] Kitchin J in *Astron Clinica v Comptroller General of Patents* [2008] EWHC 85 (Pat). See also D Pearce, 28 January 2010, available at http://ipkitten.blogspot.com/2010/01/patentable-subject-matter-where-are-we.html.

practice guidelines continue to follow the latter.[122] The overlap between patent and copyright for computer programs is thus alive and well in the British Isles.

The final overlap is that concerning the text and drawings (and when disclosed a computer program's source code) disclosed in a patent application. The High Court, per Whitford J, ruled on this issue as follows in *Catnic Components v Hill and Smith*:

> In my view, by applying for a patent and accepting the statutory obligation to describe and if necessary illustrate embodiments of his invention, a patentee necessarily makes an election accepting that, in return for a potential monopoly, upon publication, the material disclosed by him in the specification must be deemed to be open to be used by the public, subject only to such monopoly rights as he may acquire on his application for the patent and during the period for which his monopoly remains in force, whatever be the reason for the determination of the monopoly rights. If this be correct, . . . upon publication, the plaintiffs must be deemed to have abandoned their copyright in drawings the equivalent of the patent drawings.[123]

In the Court of Appeal, Buckley LJ found no copyright infringement and so did not have to revisit Whitford J's view. He therefore did not rule on the matter and nor did the House of Lords. The *Catnic* decision is still good law so that it may be said that not only drawings but also copyright in any subject matter contained in the patent application becomes unenforceable at the moment the patent application is published. One Canadian decision, in which the claimant argued both copyright infringement of mechanical drawings and patent infringement when the defendant used drawings to rebuild the claimant's products, applied *Catnic* and further stated that otherwise the time limitation set out in the Patents Act 1977 would be defeated.[124] For the Canadian judge, however, it seems that the moment when copyright should expire in this precise case is at the end of the patent term.[125] He added:

> I strongly believe that it was not the intention of Parliament nor from a practical view is it desirable that the Patent Act, the Copyright Act, and the Industrial Design Act be interpreted so as to give overlapping protection.[126]

This decision could be relied upon in the United Kingdom to extend the *Catnic* ruling to designs in addition to copyright. This overlap between patents and copyright at this level is therefore not possible in the United Kingdom.

(ii) Ownership and Dealings

The copyright and patent rules relating to ownership, dealings, rights and infringement have been exposed in the previous sections and we refer the reader to them. The following

[122] See Bently and Sherman, *Intellectual Property Law* (n 25) 429.

[123] [1982] RPC 183, 206 (the case went to the House of Lords but the latter did not revisit the issue). For the position in French law on this issue, see chapter 4, section VII.A(i).

[124] See *Rucker Co v Gavel's Vulcanising Ltd* (1985) 7 CPR (3d) 294 (FCTD). See also G Zimmerman, 'Extending the Monopoly? The Risks and Benefits of Multiple Forms of Intellectual Property Protection' (2001) 17 *Canadian Intellectual Property Review* 345, 353, discussing this and other Commonwealth decisions on the matter.

[125] Welsh J said: 'mechanical patents have drawings in connection therewith and the drawings can readily be copyrighted, but when patent infringement protection is no longer available to the owner of the patent it is not desirable that he should be able to extend this protection by application of the copyright act to drawings from which the physical object covered by the patent was constructed, and thereby prevent anyone else from manufacturing the same device, even without the use of the drawings'.

[126] Ibid.

subsections will only draw conclusions from these rules for the overlap in question. Both copyright and patent law have the same rule as to initial ownership of works and inventions: the IPR belongs to the creator/inventor. If a copyright and a patent subsist in the same product, the stricter patent regime will apply in terms of employee inventions, unless the copyright and the invention are clearly separable. The silence of the Patents Act 1977 as to commissioned patents coincides with the default copyright rule: the creator/inventor will be first owners in this case. As to transfers and licences, patent provisions are minimal. The only difference that may exist is that copyright exclusive licences must be in writing whereas patent exclusive licences need not be as the Act is silent. As to transfers, the Patents Act 1977 does not provide that they can be in whole or part but, as for copyright, they have to be signed by the assignor or on his or her behalf. Regime clashes should therefore be rather rare in case of overlap.

(iii) Rights and Infringement

As we saw in chapter three, the main difference is that patent law does not require copying whereas copyright does. Therefore, if there is copying, both patent and copyright will be infringed provided a substantial (ie original) part of the work has been taken and the invention or an equivalent has been used. If there is no copying, the patent may still be infringed.

(iv) Exceptions

As seen in section VI above, there are six exceptions to patent infringement and a number of compulsory licences, whereas copyright has a great number of exceptions. The patent regime will therefore trump the copyright regime. Special exceptions exist for computer programs deriving from the Software Directive, namely: back-up copy, observe-study-test, normal use and decompilation (CDPA 1988, sections 50A–50C). Since none of these are provided in the Patents Act 1977, they will be inapplicable in case of an overlap (unless the user contract provides otherwise, of course).

B Negative and *A Posteriori* Overlaps

As European law dictates the rules, there is no difference between UK law and European law so that the reader is referred to the discussion in chapter three.

VIII. PATENTS AND PLANT VARIETY RIGHTS

As has been seen in chapter three, the simultaneous overlap regarding ownership, dealings, rights and exceptions must be examined at national level because patent rights are not harmonised on those aspects even if plant variety rights are. The overlap between UK patents and UK plant variety rights, as well as UK patents and Community plant variety rights, will both be examined, as in chapter four. Unlike France, the United Kingdom is a party to the 1991 act of the UPOV Convention. The Plant Variety Rights Act (PVRA) 1997 regulates the UK plant variety right. The negative overlap has been dealt with in chapter three so the discussion will not be repeated.

The exclusion of plant varieties in EPC Article 53(b) is implemented in Patents Act 1977, section 1(3)(b). The rule in Community Plant Variety Right (CPVR) Regulation (EC) 2100/94, article 92, that a grant of a Community right leads to the suspension of any equivalent national rights that may exist is faithfully implemented in PVRA 1997, section 11(3). A provision identical to Biotech Directive 98/44/EC, article 4(2) has been introduced in Patents Act 1977, Schedule A2, para 4.

A Simultaneous Overlap

(i) Ownership and Dealings

(a) UK Plant Variety Right and UK Patent

The person entitled to the grant of the plant variety right is the person who breeds the plant variety or discovers and develops it (PVRA 1997, section 4(3)). In patent law, it is the inventor and more precisely the first inventor to file. As breeding, discovering and developing are not the same as inventing, there is not always correspondence between these persons. However, the employment rules are identical in the patent and plant variety right laws the employer obtains the right unless otherwise agreed (Patents Act 1977, section 39 and PVRA 1997, section 4(4)).

The only plant variety rights provision regarding dealings is PVRA 1997, section 12 which states that:

> Plant breeders' rights shall be assignable like other kinds of proprietary rights, but in any case rights under section 6 above and rights under section 7 above may not be assigned separately.

This means that the rights in the variety and in dependent varieties cannot be transferred separately. This provision therefore avoids clashes. There are no other provisions regarding transfers and licences (so for licences this is the same as in patent law[127]). Therefore, the common property and contract regimes will apply. As transfers of patent rights must be in writing and signed by or on behalf of the assignor, although not those of plant variety rights, the patent regime will prevail.

(b) Community Plant Variety Right and UK Patent

We saw the ownership and dealings rules regarding the CPVR in section VIII.A(i) of chapter four. As to ownership, the provision (CPVR Regulation, article 11) is the same as in the PVRA 1997 and it also refers to the national provisions for employees. Therefore, we refer the reader to the discussion in the preceding paragraphs on the overlap between UK PVR and UK patent. As to dealings, again provisions are almost identical, with the CPVR regime being slightly stricter (signature of both parties for transfers and licences, recording in the Register of Community Plant Variety Rights to make transfers and licences enforceable against third parties, whereas this is only necessary for evidential

[127] PVRA 1997, s 6(2) simply states that '[t]he holder of plant breeders' rights may give authority for the purposes of subsection (1) [ie his or her rights] above with or without conditions or limitations'.

purposes in patent law).[128] Finally, of course, the CPVR can only be transferred for the whole of the European Union.

(ii) Rights and Infringement

(a) UK Plant Variety Right and UK Patent

The rights of the breeder are set out in PVRA 1997, sections 6 and 7. S/he can prevent the following acts: production or reproduction (multiplication), conditioning for the purpose of propagation, offering for sale, selling or other marketing, exporting, importing, stocking for any of these purposes the variety and dependent varieties (section 6). The patentee's rights are identical except that exportation is not covered. As far as the scope is concerned, patents and plant variety rights do not differ greatly because dependent varieties[129] are within the breeder's scope of protection (PVRA 1997, section 7) and patent law's doctrine of equivalents include 'dependent patents' (see also Patents Act 1977, Schedule A2, para 7).

(b) CPVR and UK Patent

CPVR Regulation, article 13 is virtually identical to PVRA 1997, sections 6 and 7, so that the paragraph above equally applies.

(iii) Exceptions Including Exhaustion Principle

(a) UK Plant Variety Right and UK Patent

Patent law has six exceptions and a number of compulsory licences. The only two exceptions which are potentially applicable in the field of plant varieties, namely acts for private and non-commercial purposes and acts for experimental purposes, also exist in the plant variety rights regime (PVRA 1997, section 8).[130] In addition, as we saw in section VI, patent law also has a farmer's privilege corresponding to that in the plant variety right (Patents Act 1977, section 60(5)(g), Schedule A1 and PVRA 1997, section 9). The PVRA 1997 has a third exception which extends to acts done for the purpose of breeding another variety. This latter exception may clash with the patent regime.[131] Also, if it is possible that a plant variety can be used to prepare a medicine in a pharmacy, this patent law exception will be trumped, as a corresponding exception does not exist in the UK plant variety rights regime. Nonetheless, for most practical purposes, in respect of exceptions, there is almost total convergence.

[128] See above in this section and section VII.A(ii).

[129] These include essentially derived varieties.

[130] The exception which aims at facilitating international transport and that for acts done in conducting a study, test or trial which is necessary for and is conducted with a view to the application of the directives on the Community codes relating to veterinary medicinal products and medicinal products for human use, will generally not be applicable to plant varieties so their non-existence in the plant variety rights regime does not pose a problem (although the second one might if the medicine involves using a plant variety).

[131] As N Brahy, 'Cumul et chevauchement du brevet et du certificat d'obtention végétale: beaucoup de droit . . . mais peu de faits' in S Dusollier and A Cruquenaire (eds), *Le cumul des droits intellectuels* (Brussels, Larcier, 2009) 107, 115, notes that patent law does not have an equivalent of the selection exception but there is, however, the research exception which may somewhat cover it.

There is only one compulsory licence in the PVRA 1997 (section 17), which is in some ways broader than those in the Patents Act 1977 combined. Therefore, in case of overlap, the Patents Act 1977 will usually prevail. But since there are more compulsory licences in the Patents Act, when they do not correspond to the wording of the plant variety right compulsory licences, the latter regime will prevail. In addition, the patent system will trump the plant variety rights system in terms of the period after which a compulsory licence can be ordered (three years in the patent regime against two years in the plant variety rights regime[132]). Finally, under Biotech Directive, article 12, both the patents and plant variety rights laws have set up compulsory cross-licences for interdependent inventions and new plant varieties so that the two regimes converge on this point.[133] The regimes converge even in terms of the timing, as in France.

Finally, exhaustion is regulated in the same way in the two regimes, although PVRA 1997, section 10 is a little bit more detailed than Patents Act 1977, Schedule 2A (exports of material enabling propagation of the variety to a non-qualifying country otherwise than for final consumption are not within the exhaustion principle in the PVRA 1997).

(b) CPVR and UK Patent

Most provisions of the CPVR Regulation are reproduced in those of the UK PVR. The exceptions in the CPVR Regulation are the same as in the UK plant variety right regime. There is one slight difference: CPVR Regulation, article 15, only exempts acts done for the purpose of breeding, or discovering and developing other varieties, if they are not essentially derived varieties (EDVs). The compulsory licences for interdependent patents and plant variety rights are also quasi-identical (compare Patents and Plant Variety Rights (Compulsory Licensing) Regulations 2002, regulation 15 and CPVR Regulation, article 29(5a)).[134] As we saw in the chapter on France, the CPVR also has quite a number of other compulsory licences. They do not entirely match those found in the Patents Act 1977. Therefore, the stricter regime (here patents[135]) will prevail in case of overlap. Finally, the exhaustion principle is phrased in the same way as in the PVRA 1997. The convergence at this level is therefore quite high.

B *A Posteriori* Overlap

The *a posteriori* overlap is the same as described in chapter three as no special regulation has been made as yet to increase the length of protection to 30 or 35 years for some varieties, this option being provided for in PVRA 1997, section 11(1).

[132] See Plant Breeders' Rights Regulations 1998, SI 1998/1027, cited by Bently and Sherman, *Intellectual Property Law* (n 25) 600.

[133] The compulsory cross-licence was implemented by the Patents and Plant Variety Rights (Compulsory Licensing) Regulations 2002, SI 2002/247, as amended by SI 2007/3293. See regs 3–10 (compulsory patent licences) and 11–16 (compulsory plant variety licences).

[134] Brahy, 'Cumul et chevauchement du brevet et du certificat d'obtention végétale' (n 131) 107, 118, notes that to his knowledge, no such licence has ever been granted.

[135] Compulsory licences can only be granted three years after the patent has been granted and the grounds are much less broad than those of the CPVR Regulation, which provides for the granting of a very general compulsory licence to anyone on the ground of public interest (CPVR Regulation, art 29(1)–(5)). For the compulsory licences in patent law, see above section VI.

In conclusion, in UK law, there is a high degree of convergence both between the UK PVR and patents, and the CPVR and patents (because most provisions in the two plant variety rights laws are almost identical) in the area of ownership, dealings, rights, infringement and exceptions. Sometimes the patent system is stricter (for licences and transfers in comparison to the UK PVR), sometimes it is the plant variety rights system which is stricter (the CPVR Regulation is stricter for licences and transfers than the patent regime). At the level of rights and exhaustion, the convergence is almost perfect. At the level of exceptions and compulsory licences, the plant variety rights regime is generally more generous to users.

Note that there could in theory be an overlap between the UK PVR or CPVR and UDR. Indeed, UK courts have held that an article in UDR could also be a plant or (a part of) the human body. UDR is therefore capable of protecting any aspect of the shape or configuration of the whole or part of a plant variety. And it is possible that new varieties also differ in terms of their external appearance.

IX. INTELLECTUAL PROPERTY RIGHTS AND UNFAIR COMPETITION

As we saw in section I above (legal framework), there is no such thing as unfair competition law in the United Kingdom. Despite the obligation under Article 10*bis* of the Paris Convention[136] and calls from many authors for a law against unfair competition,[137] the United Kingdom has continuously rejected the legal concept of unfair competition as such,[138] as well as a general clause establishing a tort of unfair competition.[139] Besides intellectual property rights, the only way to protect intellectual assets is through the tort of passing off and the law on confidential information,[140] which are based on the common law. There is therefore no statutory law regulating this area of the law, so that pass-

[136] It is arguable that the United Kingdom complies with Art 10*bis* of the Paris Convention because it is unclear whether Art 10*bis*(2) requires other acts than those enumerated in Art 10*bis*(3) to be considered unfair. See Robertson and Horton, 'Does the UK or the EC Need an Unfair Competition Law?' (n 9)572.

[137] W Cornish, 'Unfair Competition? A Progress Report' (1972) 12 *Journal of the Society of Public Teachers of Law* 126; G Dworkin, 'Unfair Competition: Is the Common Law Developing a New Tort?' (1979) *European Intellectual Property Review* 241; H Brett, 'Unfair Competition: Not Merely an Academic Issue?' (1979) *European Intellectual Property Review* 295; Burns, 'Unfair Competition: A Compelling Need Unmet' (n 9); A Booy, 'A Half-Way House for Unfair Competition in the United Kingdom: A Practitioner's Plea' (1991) *European Intellectual Property Review* 439; Robertson and Horton 'Does the UK or the EC Need an Unfair Competition Law?' (n 9) 581–82.

[138] G Schricker, 'Twenty-Five Years of Protection Against Unfair Competition' (1995) *International Review of Intellectual Property and Competition Law* 782, 785; Robertson and Horton, 'Does the UK or the EC Need an Unfair Competition Law?' (n 9) (during the passing of the Trademark Act 1994 there was lobbying for an unfair competition law but the government resisted it).

[139] W Cornish 'Unfair Competition and the Consumer in England' (1974) *International Review of Intellectual Property and Competition Law* 73, 74; Dworkin 'Unfair Competition: Is the Common Law Developing a New Tort?' (n 137) 242; F Beier 'The Law of Unfair Competition in the European Community, Its Development and Present Status' (1985) *International Review of Intellectual Property and Competition Law* 139, 156; Robertson and Horton, 'Does the UK or the EC Need an Unfair Competition Law?' (n 9). One reason for the lack of unfair competition and misappropriation in the United Kingdom is the low threshold of originality in copyright law (sufficient skill, judgement and labour), the effect of which is to protect creations which would not be protectable by continental copyright laws but may be protected by parasitism. However, this has now changed with the *Infopaq* case (Case C-5/08 *Infopaq International AS v Dankse Dagblades Forening* [2009] ECR I-6569) and may trigger renewed calls for an unfair competition law.

[140] There is also malicious falsehood but it is not widely used because courts are reluctant to find malice for fear of interfering with legitimate competition.

ing off and confidential information are entirely based on judge-made law.[141] English courts are conservative and are reluctant to create new causes of action,[142] especially a general unfair competition cause of action,[143] and accordingly they have still not recognised a tort of misappropriation or parasitism[144] and are unlikely to do so.[145] Therefore, in the United Kingdom, misappropriation as such is not unlawful.[146] In sum, since there is no British tort of misappropriation or parasitism, no simultaneous, negative or *a posteriori* overlap can occur for any IPR, with the exception of registered trademarks which can also be protected under passing off.[147] The section will therefore envisage the three overlaps in relation to passing off and trademarks and IPRs/confidential information. Case law has also been developed on the interface between copyright, trademarks and misleading and comparative advertising.

It must already be noted that in comparison with France and Germany, the focus of UK 'unfair competition law' is the consumer, not the aggrieved competitor.[148] Therefore, only if the consumer is deceived by a competitor's misrepresentation or misconduct will there be an actionable tort. If there is not, only rarely can there be a remedy under one of the so-called 'economic torts'.[149] Therefore, as we shall see from the case law, the overlaps are much less likely than in France and Germany. Another important aspect is that the regulations implementing both the MCAD and UCPD, whose provisions sometimes overlap with trademark law and passing off,[150] have not reinforced the remedies available for private parties under these two causes of action. This is because these remedies are mainly criminal and only enforceable by state agencies (eg Office of Fair Trading (OFT) and local authority trading standards services).[151]

[141] Of course, as we saw in section I on the legal framework, the United Kingdom is bound by the Directives in the field of unfair competition law, mainly the Unfair Commercial Practices Directive and the Misleading and Comparative Advertising Directive.

[142] Burns 'Unfair Competition: A Compelling Need Unmet' (n 9); Cornish and Llewelyn, *Intellectual Property: Patents, Copyright, Trade Marks and Allied Rights* (n 25) para 1-22; Davis, 'Unfair Competition Law and its Protection under English Law' (n 11). Courts believe this power exclusively belongs to Parliament.

[143] G Dworkin, 'Unfair Competition: Is it Time for European Harmonisation?' in D Vaver and L Bently (eds), *Intellectual Property in the New Millennium, Essays in Honour of William R. Cornish*, (Cambridge, Cambridge University Press, 2004) 175, 177.

[144] An attempt to establish a general tort of unfair competition and misappropriation was killed off by the Privy Council in *Cadbury Schweppes v Pub Squash* [1981] 1 All ER 213, comment G Dworkin, 'Passing Off and Unfair Competition: An Opportunity Missed' (1981) *Modern Law Review* 564, 566–67. The defendant had reaped where he had not sown but there was no misrepresentation. The court stuck to the strict conditions of passing off and the claimant lost. The Privy Council (per Lord Scarman) refused to create a tort of misappropriation because it had encountered criticism in the United States and Australia. Lord Scarman also emphasised the need to preserve the freedom to compete: 'A defendant, however, does no wrong by entering a market created by another and there competing with its creator. The line may be difficult to draw; but unless it is drawn, competition will be stifled'.

[145] Davis, 'Unfair Competition Law and its Protection under English Law' (n 11).

[146] J Adams, 'Unfair Competition: Why a Need is Unmet' (1992) *European Intellectual Property Review* 259, 260.

[147] As will be seen, there is one exception to this (namely the overlap between the author's rights of attribution and against false attribution and passing off).

[148] See also C Wadlow, 'The Case for Reclaiming European Unfair Competition Law from Europe's Consumer Lawyers' in S Weatherill and U Bernitz (eds), *The Regulation of Unfair Commercial Practices under EC Directive 2005/29: New Rules and New Techniques* (Oxford, Hart Publishing, 2007) 175, 178, adding that English law equates 'fairness' with 'honesty' and 'honesty' with 'truthfulness' so that it is the consumer who determines what is honest, and therefore what is fair.

[149] Ibid 177.

[150] As we have seen in chapter 3, section IX.

[151] Davis, 'Unfair Competition Law and its Protection under English Law' (n 11). F Henning Bodewig, *Unfair Competition Law: European Union and Member States* (The Hague, Kluwer Law International, 2006)

A Passing Off

(i) Simultaneous Overlap

To win an action in passing off, the claimant must show s/he gained goodwill (ie reputation) over his or her product, that the defendant made a misrepresentation and that, as a consequence (causal link), the claimant suffers damage (although as long as the two first conditions are fulfilled, damage will often be presumed).[152] The claimant can obtain an injunction or declaration that the defendant has ceased activity and has a choice between receiving damages or an account of profits.[153] Goodwill can be in names, slogans, images (such as those used in advertising campaigns[154]) get-up or packaging. Therefore two- and three-dimensional[155] objects can be protected. There must also be goodwill in time and space (ie the trader's reputation must have existed for a certain amount of time and must exist over a certain territory). These two requirements have been stretched so much that they are easily fulfilled.[156] However, passing off will hardly protect subject matter that has just been launched on the market. A month or so is generally required for goodwill to exist. There is a tendency not to find goodwill if the name or get-up adopted is descriptive, although a strict requirement of distinctiveness as in trademark law is certainly not required.[157] There must normally be a common field of activity in the sense that the defendant's and claimant's goods or services must be similar.[158] However, if the claimant's sign is well known, the similarity of the goods or services is generally irrelevant. The concept of misrepresentation implies the creation of a false belief of connection between the two products in the mind of consumers. There has to be a representation made to consumers that leads to confusion and thereby becomes a misrepresentation, which by definition deceives the public. In short, confusion is essential and will generally suffice.[159]

140, adds as regards misleading and comparative advertising that '[t]he OFT generally intervenes only if the protection through the local governmental institutions and self regulation bodies fails and if it is in the best interests of the general public . . . Once the OFT takes on a case, it generally tries to settle the case with the advertiser before bringing a suit for a cease and desist order. Consequently such suits are rare'.

[152] *Draper v Trist and Tristbestos Brake Lining* [1939] 56 RPC 429 and *Procea Products v Evans & Sons* [1951] 68 RPC 210.

[153] P Torremans, *Holyoak and Torremans Intellectual Property Law,* 5th edn (Oxford, Oxford University Press, 2008) 483.

[154] See *Cadbury Schweppes v Pub Squash* [1981] RPC 429.

[155] The most famous case in this respect is certainly the so-called 'Jif Lemon' case (*Reckitt & Colman Products v Borden* [1990] 1 All ER 873) where the goodwill resided in a lemon-shaped container containing lemon juice.

[156] See *BBC v Talbot Motor Co Ltd* [1981] FSR 228 (goodwill held to subsist for 'carfax' service (radio traffic information) even though the service had not yet been launched because the BBC had done a lot of advertising); *Chelsea Man Menswear v Chelsea Girl* [1987] RPC 189 (claimant sold clothes in Leicester, Coventry and London but obtained injunction for all of England and Wales because people and goods move around the country).

[157] *Phones 4U v Phone4u.co.uk Internet* [2007] RPC 5 (CA). See also Torremans, *Holyoak and Torremans Intellectual Property Law* (n 153) 459–60.

[158] See eg *Harrods v R Harrod* (1923) 41 RPC 74.

[159] Robertson and Horton, 'Does the UK or the EC Need an Unfair Competition Law?' (n 9) 569; Adams, 'Unfair Competition: Why a Need is Unmet' (n 146); Beier 'The Law of Unfair Competition in the European Community, Its Development and Present Status' (n 139) 156; S Byrt, 'Le *passing-off* au Royaume-Uni: des leçons à tirer?' (2003) 213 Revue Internationale de la Propriété Industrielle et Artistique, 55, para 213; Torremans, *Holyoak and Torremans Intellectual Property Law* (n 153) 473–74.

Misrepresentation subsists when a substantial part[160] of the relevant public is deceived (ie has bought the goods of the defendant thinking they were those of the claimant) or is likely to be deceived.[161] The average consumer who is reasonably attentive and circumspect is also the test in passing off.[162] Merely enticing is not considered passing off if the wrong impression is corrected before the sale. 'Therefore look-a-likes (same get-up but distinct different marks) are largely considered legal.'[163] Indeed, as the case law and literature suggests, passing off is not of much help to creators and innovators and therefore overlaps are rather infrequent.

(a) Names,[164] Titles and Slogans

The best avenue to protect titles, especially book and periodical titles, is the law of passing off.[165] Copyright and trademark laws generally do not help (as we have seen, copyright does not protect titles unless they are highly original and trademark law requires distinctiveness[166]). The majority of cases on this subject matter have thus been brought on the basis of passing off.[167] Actions are not often successful because, as in trademark law, the customer may not rely on the character, title, slogan as indication of origin[168] or because it is rather banal.[169] If the name or title is relatively descriptive, then small differences between the products will be sufficient for the defendant to escape passing off.[170] Although courts agreed there was no reason why a slogan should be by definition denied protection by passing off,[171] in the few cases which were brought to court, the claimants failed on the facts.[172] As for book titles, the literature doubts that even a totally arbitrary title can be distinctive of the publisher. It is only distinctive of the book's content, so passing off is not well adapted to protect the titles of individual literary works.[173] Therefore, the overlap between trademark, passing off and copyright for this type of subject matter is rare.

[160] See *Neutrogena v Golden* [1996] RPC 473 and Bently and Sherman, *Intellectual Property Law* (n 25) 757–58. A substantial part does not mean a majority but it must be more than *de minimis*.

[161] See *Lego Systems Aktieselskab v Lego M Lemelstrich* [1983] FSR 155; *Irvine v Talksport* [2002] FSR 943, confirmed on appeal [2003] FSR 619.

[162] Henning Bodewig, *Unfair Competition Law: European Union and Member States* (n 151) 148.

[163] Ibid 148.

[164] These include characters and likenesses.

[165] Jennings and Donovan, 'Trademarks and Book Titles' (n 89) 39.

[166] Laddie *et al*, *The Modern Law of Copyright* (n 16) 1727, para 37.11.

[167] Jennings and Donovan, 'Trademarks and Book Titles' (n 89) 39.

[168] Laddie *et al*, *The Modern Law of Copyright* (n 16) 1728, para 37.12.

[169] For instance, newspaper titles. Kitchin *et al*, *Kerly's Law of Trade Marks and Trade Names* (n 98) 506–7, para 15-170, reports that 'the case law shows that it has become difficult, though not impossible, to persuade a court that the use of similar or even closely similar names for rival newspapers or periodical publications will result in passing off'. Most courts in these cases rejected the claims.

[170] For instance in the newspaper cases, 'the respective periodicals were too different in terms of appearance, presentation, content, price, readership or other matters for either deception or damage to occur'. See C Wadlow, *The Law of Passing-Off: Unfair Competition by Misrepresentation*, 3rd edn (London, Sweet and Maxwell, 2004) 652. Two other factors may explain why claimants are unsuccessful in newspapers cases. First, readers are loyal. Secondly, periodicals are bought regularly and frequently so that readers who buy another one by error will not repeat the mistake. Thus, the claimant's damage is slight. Ibid.

[171] *Schweppes v Pub Squash* [1981] RPC 49.

[172] Wadlow, *The Law of Passing-Off* (n 170) 651.

[173] Ibid 658. As we saw, the same applies in both French and UK trademark law.

(b) Two-Dimensional (Visual) Aspects

Passing off, like trademark law, more easily protects two-dimensional visual aspects such as labels, logos, symbols, pictures, photographs, portraits or the design of words (ie words written in a special way). Of course, what is common in the trade in question or otherwise not distinctive cannot be protected by passing off.[174] There is another type of double protection that can occur between passing off and copyright. It is the overlap between the author's right of attribution (CDPA 1988, sections 77–79) and anyone's right against false attribution (CDPA 1988, section 84) and passing off. Both copyright law and passing off prohibit the use of any person's name on another work/product not authored by him or her and the omission or substitution of an author's name on a work authored by him or her.[175] The overlap is not complete as the conditions in the two rights differ somewhat (eg in copyright law, there are some exceptions to the right of attribution).

(c) Three-Dimensional Articles

Passing off rarely succeeds when three-dimensional aspects (mainly get-up and packaging) are involved. Indeed, traders rarely rely solely on get-up to distinguish their products or services. They also use words or names in addition to packaging. Therefore, a different name is sufficient to distinguish the goods of one trader from another's despite the similarity of get-up or packaging.[176] The overlap between passing off, on the one hand, and trademark, copyright and design laws, on the other, is therefore rare. Most decisions have rejected passing off claims in relation to furniture and architectural designs.[177] The resemblance must be extremely close so as to confuse consumers even if the name used in addition on the product is different.[178] As in trademark law, features of the goods dictated solely by function cannot be protected by passing off.[179] In addition, the reluctance of courts to find passing off for shapes is based on the shape's lack of trademark function, ie typically it does not indicate commercial origin.[180] The last nail in the coffin is that courts seem to be generally disinclined to regard get-up or packaging as distinctive in both passing off[181] and trademark law actions.[182]

[174] Ibid 694–95.

[175] See eg *Bristol Conservatories v Conservatories Custom Built* [1989] RPC 455, cited by Firth, 'National Report, Reply to the Questionnaire for the United Kingdom' (n 83) 6 (it was passing off for the defendants to use photographs of conservatories built by the claimants to illustrate the defendants' brochure).

[176] Kitchin *et al*, *Kerly's Law of Trade Marks and Trade Names* (n 98) 509.

[177] *George Hensher v Restawile Upholstery (Lancs)* [1976] AC 64 (furniture); *Jarman and Platt* [1977] FSR 200 (furniture); *Charles Church v Cronin* [1990] FSR 1 (architectural design), cited by Firth, 'National Report, Reply to the Questionnaire for the United Kingdom' (n 83) 5.

[178] Rare examples of such situation are the 'Jif Lemon' case (*Reckitt & Colman (Products) v Borden* [1990] RPC 341, where the shape of the lemon juice container had become distinctive on its own); *Edge v Nicholls* [1911] AC 693 (the claimant sold bags of laundry, each bag holding a stick of a particular form. The evidence showed that customers' decisions were made entirely by the appearance of the goods; they relied in particular on the stick. The defendants adopted a similar stick. The court held that the presence on defendants' goods of defendants' name was in these circumstances an insufficient distinction); and *United Biscuits v Asda Stores* [1997] RPC 513.

[179] Kitchin *et al*, *Kerly's Law of Trade Marks and Trade Names* (n 98) 510.

[180] Firth, 'National Report, Reply to the Questionnaire for the United Kingdom' (n 83) 4.

[181] See Firth, 'National Report, Reply to the Questionnaire for the United Kingdom' (n 83) 4, citing *RoHo/Hodgkinson & Corby v Wards Mobility Services* [1995] FSR 169.

[182] See *Philips v Remington* [1998] RPC 283, [1999] RPC 809; *Dualit* [1999] RPC 304, 890.

Finally, whether there is also convergence between passing off and trademark law as regards tarnishment and dilution is not clear, as there is passing off case law in both directions. Whereas the Court of Justice implicitly ruled in *Davidoff* that unfair competition law can protect against non-confusing use of similar goods and services, and some UK courts also think so,[183] other UK decisions go in the opposite direction.[184] 'In summary, the case-law provides no clear guidance on the capacity of the law of passing off to provide dilution protection.'[185] But note that in *Irvine v Talksport*,[186] it was decided that it is not necessary to show a common field of activity, what is essential is to show misrepresentation. It must also be noted that there are cases (many involving domain name cybersquatting) in which the courts have ruled that there was both passing off and trademark infringement on the basis of TMA 1994, section 10(2) (risk of confusion)[187] or (3) (dilution/tarnishment provision).[188] In conclusion, one can say that in the majority of cases, passing off and trademark infringement normally go hand in hand, although it is less true than it used to be that when there is no passing off there is no trademark infringement either.[189]

(ii) Negative Overlap

The new Trademark Act 1994 seems to have filled many gaps but, following case law over the years, it appears that it has not filled them all. Thus, passing off still plays a role in filling the remaining ones.[190] In many ways passing off is less constraining, more flexible than trademark law. Therefore, negative overlap can occur when the effect of trademark law is to reject protection of a sign. Conversely, passing off will be available more often than trademark law so that the other negative overlap will be much rarer. There are instances where claimants have argued both trademark and passing off and the court has only used passing off to condemn defendants.[191]

For instance, smells are not registrable because they cannot be graphically represented. Therefore, so long as there is goodwill in smells and they are not merely descriptive, passing off can fit the bill. The standard of descriptiveness is also much woollier than in trademark law, thus single colours may be sufficiently distinctive in passing off, although not under trademark law. 'The English . . . courts have [also] shown considerable lenience towards plaintiffs seeking to rely on passing off as against the use by others of descriptive or generic names.'[192] Passing off also protects place names and celebrity names better than trademark law.[193] Finally, passing off can also cater for images and

[183] See eg *Taittinger v Allbev* [1993] FSR 641; Case C-292/00 *Davidoff & Cie SA v Gofkid* [2003] ECR I-389.

[184] M Ni Shuilleabhain, 'Common-Law Protection of Trade Marks: The Continuing Relevance of Passing Off' (2003) 34(7) *International Review of Intellectual Property and Competition Law* 722, 741–42.

[185] Ibid 744.

[186] [2002] FSR 943.

[187] *Wagamama v City Centre Restaurants* [1997] FSR 713 (Ch D).

[188] See eg *British Telecommunications and others v One in a Million and others* [1998] 1 WLR 903 (CA); *Harrods v UK Network Services* (unreported 1996, Ch D), comment in [1997] EIPR D106-107; *Neutrogena v Golden (No 2)* (unreported, 1995, Ch D), comment in [1995] EIPR D231-232, affirmed [1996] RPC 473 (CA); *Colgate-Palmolive v Markwell Finance* [1989] RPC 497 (CA).

[189] We would like to thank Jacob LJ for confirming this statement.

[190] Ni Shuilleabhain, 'Common-Law Protection of Trade Marks' (n 184) 34(7) 724–25.

[191] See eg *Direct Line Group v Direct Line Estate Agency* [1997] FSR 374 (Ch D).

[192] Ni Shuilleabhain, 'Common-Law Protection of Trade Marks' (n 184) 726.

[193] Ibid 730 and 733. The landmark trademark case on place names is *Windsurfing Chiemsee*.

themes which cannot be graphically represented because they are not 'capable of concise expression (in the manner of a word or a logo)'.[194] Passing off can thus protect advertising campaigns and advertisements whilst trademark law will often not be able to. Thus, generally, passing off is more generous than trademark law and the negative overlap can occur.

Nevertheless, courts have been very sensitive not to (re)create monopolies by using passing off and have rejected such claims in cases involving the shapes of goods.[195] Some have gone as far as stating that 'the mere copying of goods as distinct from the copying of something capricious added to the good can never amount to passing off'.[196] On the other hand, courts have generally 'shown a complementary tendency to treat as inherently unlawful the copying of fanciful characteristics of goods or packaging'.[197] These trends depart from the previous case law. Normally, if there is no IPR on a feature, fanciful or not, copying should be allowed so long as the second trader clearly distinguishes his or her goods or services from those of the previous one.[198] In the *RoHo* case:

> Jacob J expressed the view that a defendant may still commit passing off even if all he has copied are the functional features of the plaintiff's product. If the copying of functional features will deceive the public, then the onus is on the defendant to use other distinguishing indicia so that his product is not confused with the plaintiff's. It follows that the courts may often allow an action in passing off for the protection of a get-up that would not be registrable as a trade mark.[199]

In conclusion, the case law is a little unclear, although the most recent trend is not to permit the negative overlap when there is mere copying without any risk of confusion.

(iii) A Posteriori *Overlap*

Passing off can be useful when copyright or design protection has expired but again, only as long as there is (a risk of) confusion. This is well illustrated in the *Fearns (t/a Autopaint International) v Anglo-Dutch Paint and Chemical Co.*[200] In this case, the claimant (Fearns) alleged passing off, trademark and copyright infringement (among other claims such as malicious falsehood and breach of contract). The defendant started to sell the claimant's Autopaint (paint for spray painting cars) to the claimant's franchisees without permission so that the claimant lost its franchisees' business. The court held this was trademark infringement and passing off but not copyright infringement. This was because Trademark Act 1994, section 52 applied so copyright protection of the logo and design appearing on the Autopaint paint tins was limited to 15 years and did not fall in

[194] Ni Shuilleabhain, 'Common-Law Protection of Trade Marks' (n 184) 736.

[195] Kitchin *et al*, *Kerly's Law of Trade Marks and Trade Names* (n 98) 510, para 15-177.

[196] Ibid, citing *Terrapin v Ariston* [1964] FSR 218; *Benchairs v Chair Centre* [1974] RPC 429; *Hawkins v Flude's* [1957] RPC 8.

[197] Kitchin *et al*, *Kerly's Law of Trade Marks and Trade Names* (n 98) 511, citing *New Way v Lucking* [1960] RPC 147.

[198] See eg *Dunhill v Bartlett and Bickley* (1922) 39 RPC 426, 438, and more recently, *RoHo/Hodgkinson & Corby v Wards Mobility Services* [1995] FSR 169, 173 ('Certainly it is not the law that copying as such is unlawful: the common law . . . leans against monopolies' per Jacob J).

[199] *RoHo/Hodgkinson & Corby v Wards Mobility Services* [1995] FSR 169, 176–77. See Ni Shuilleabhain, 'Common-Law Protection of Trade Marks' (n 184) 737.

[200] [2007] EWHC 955 (Ch D), reversed in part by [2008] EWCA Civ 99 (CA) but the discussion of the overlap between different IPRs was not reconsidered in the Court of Appeal's judgment.

the exception for printed matter of a primarily literary or artistic character. Although there was no overlap as far as subject matter was concerned (the name is not the same as the once copyrighted logo, and copyright protects mere copying whilst trademark law/passing off generally require risk of confusion), the effect of the overlap is that the claimant could prevent the sale of its products all the same. As we have seen at IX.A(i), however, it is nearly impossible to protect once-protected inventions or functional designs by passing off.

In conclusion, there is a considerable degree of convergence between the passing off action and trademark law. A further proof that trademark law and passing off are converging derives from the Court of Justice decision in *O2 Holdings v Hutchison 3G UK*.[201] Indeed, the Court ruled that when assessing likelihood of confusion under Trademark Directive, article 5(1)(b), the context in which the mark is used needs to be considered. Therefore, '[l]ooking at the defendant's use of his sign in context will entail a more "holistic" approach to assessing confusion under art 5(1)(b), bringing it closer in nature of an action for passing off'.[202] However, passing off is more generous than trademark law and thus fills the gaps left by it so that the negative overlap still subsists. In addition, there is often a simultaneous overlap. Finally, passing off can provide some *a posteriori* overlap. As Ni Shuilleabhain has noted, passing off's supplementary role is sometimes justifiable, sometimes not, and in this latter case, clarity and thus legal certainty suffer.[203] Therefore, she concludes that '[w]hilst respecting the separate roles that they may play, [passing off and trademark law] should be harmoniously developed insofar as they do pursue a common goal'.[204]

B Trade Secrets/Confidential Information

As we saw in section I, in the United Kingdom, trade secrets are protected under the common law breach of confidence which protects confidential information. Like the tort of passing off, breach of confidence is thus based on precedent. There are three elements to the action for breach of confidence.[205] First, the information must be capable of being protected. This means that it cannot be trivial (in other words, it must be original or novel but not as strictly as the intellectual property laws), immoral, vague (it must be detailed enough, ie not be a simple concept) or in the public domain. Secondly, the defendant must owe the claimant an obligation to keep the information confidential; and thirdly, the defendant must have used the information in breach of that obligation. The defendant can raise defences, the main one being that the disclosure was in the public interest.

[201] Case C-533/06 *O2 Holdings v Hutchison 3G UK* [2008] ECR I-4231.

[202] I Simon Fhima, 'Trade Mark Infringement in Comparative Advertising Situations' (2008) *European Intellectual Property Review* 420, adds that 'further guidance from the ECJ as to which contextual factors to take into account and at what stage will be needed in due course'.

[203] Ni Shuilleabhain, 'Common-Law Protection of Trade Marks' (n 184) 34(7) 749.

[204] Ibid 750.

[205] On breach of confidence, see Bently and Sherman, *Intellectual Property Law* (n 25) 1003 *et seq*; Torremans, *Holyoak and Torremans Intellectual Property Law* (n 153) 495 *et seq*; Cornish and Llewelyn, *Intellectual Property: Patents, Copyright, Trade Marks and Allied Rights* (n 25) para 8-01 *et seq*.

(i) Simultaneous Overlap

So how does this pan out in relation to the overlap between confidential information and IPRs? First, it is clear that the information will be original in the sense of the law on confidential information (subject matter protected by IPR has to fulfil higher criteria to be protected in the first place). It will also not be vague for the same reason. It must not be in the public domain; so to be protected by both IPR and confidential information, a copyright work (eg a literary work), a trademark, a design, a plant variety right, a patent must not yet be published or disclosed to the public (such as through sales of a trademarked or patented product).

In the case of a design, trademark or copyright work, if the work or design is not yet published, the overlap is broader because confidential information will protect not only the form but also the very information, the ideas behind the work, trademark or design. Once the trademark, design or copyright work is published, confidential information ceases to have effect. Therefore, the simultaneous overlap is not as strong, as much of this subject matter is in the end published. In case of a patented invention, which is by definition disclosed to the public through the publication of the application, the information disclosed in the application is no longer confidential.[206] So what about the source code of a computer program which is generally not disclosed in a patent application? If the patented product is sold on the market, it seems that the source code is in the public domain as it can be reverse-engineered through legitimate access to the object code. This appears to be the consequence of the ruling in *Mars v Teknowledge*.[207] In that case, the High Court held that encrypted information which is in the public domain (ie freely available on the market because the machine containing the encryption system was so available) was not confidential.[208] So, even if a person is bound by a contract with an obligation of confidence as to the source code of a patented program, the contract must be disregarded because the information is in the public domain. However, there is older case law which could be interpreted as leading to the opposite conclusion. *Ackroyds v Islington Plastics* suggests that if the information which is in the public domain needs to be reverse-engineered it ought to be treated as relatively secret and therefore protectable.[209] What is clear, of course, is that if someone steals confidential information embodied in a product which has not been put on the market yet, there is definitely a breach.

If the patented computer-implemented invention is also protected by copyright along with a confidentiality contract, the situation is easier. CDPA 1988, sections 50B(4) and 50BA(2) provide that confidential information cannot trump copyright. According to these provisions, decompilation is permitted under certain conditions and observing, studying and testing a program in order to discover the ideas and principles which underlie it (when loading, displaying, running, transmitting or storing the program) is allowed. A contract cannot take these users' privileges away. The same applies, of course, if the program is simply copyrighted and not patented. No simultaneous overlap can occur here.

[206] Thus, confidence can only play a role here with respect to implementing (complementary) know-how and in the rare case of secret patents for military inventions and the like.

[207] [2000] FSR 138.

[208] For similar reasoning, see also *Saltman* (1948) 65 RPC 203.

[209] [1962] RPC 97, 104.

(ii) Negative Overlap

Confidential information is the protection of choice for things which are not protectable by IPRs because they do not pass the stricter criteria. However, as we saw above, courts generally require some originality or novelty for the information to be protected. Thus, television formats which are not copyrightable or protectable by any other IPR can be protected through confidentiality agreements. Of course, most of the elements of a TV-format will become public once it is first broadcast.

Conversely, if the information is in the public domain, a patent or plant variety right (and sometimes a design) cannot be obtained. And if it is just information which the person wants to protect, it cannot be through copyright or design laws, rarely through trademark law unless it can be graphically represented and is distinctive.

(iii) A Posteriori *Overlap*

No *a posteriori* overlap between confidential information and any IPR will be possible as confidential information cannot be protected for ever[210] (by the end of the IPR's term, the information will already have been discoverable by competitors and in many cases it may very well already be obsolete). Confidential information can subsequently be protected by an IPR (it then loses its quality of confidentiality because of the necessary publication that ensues) if it fulfils the IPR's conditions, so that the subject matter protection can be in effect much longer than that provided by the IPR's term.

In conclusion, the simultaneous overlap will be rare, whilst the negative overlap will be more frequent, except for patents, plant variety rights and some designs. The *a posteriori* overlap is possible only to extend the protection of confidential information by an IPR.

C Comparative and Misleading Advertising, Trademark and Copyright Laws

As we stated above, there is case law on the overlap between comparative and misleading advertising, trademark and copyright laws. The two cases involved magazines. In the first, *IPC Magazines v MGN*,[211] the defendant had broadcast the front page of the claimant's women's magazine (*Woman*), featuring also its price and comparing it to its own women's magazine (*Personal*), stating that it was free when people bought its newspaper, the *Sunday Mirror*. The claimant argued that there was infringement of the logo, layout and photographs of the page of its magazine broadcast by the defendant.[212] The court held that copyright subsisted and that there was infringement. Although the MCAD was not yet in force at the time, as the defendant made the point that its actions were permitted comparative advertising, the court briefly addressed the issue. It thought that the defendant was taking the Directive too far and therefore did not think that the defendant's actions fell within allowed comparative advertising. Not much more can be found in the case.

[210] As a result of the springboard doctrine. On this doctrine, see eg Bently and Sherman, *Intellectual Property Law* (n 24) 1016–17.

[211] [1998] FSR 431.

[212] It also claimed there was trademark infringement but did not make this claim during the summary proceedings so the trademark issue was not discussed in the judgment.

The second case, *IPC Media v News Group Newspapers*,[213] does shed a little more light on the issue whether the MCAD also trumps copyright law and not only trademark law. It involved similar facts. The claimant published a television listings magazine (*What's on TV*) and had copyright in the logo and cover layout. The defendant, the *Sun*, ran an advertisement for its own free television listings magazine (*TV Mag*). This advert contained a reproduction of the front page of an issue of *What's on TV* and stated that *TV Mag* was free whilst *What's on TV* was not. The court held, first, that the regulations did not give a civil remedy to private parties (as we saw above). It went on to state, however, that the MCAD only mentioned trademark law, not copyright law; but even if it had mentioned it, it was not indispensable for the defendant to use the claimant's copyrighted works to perform the comparison. The court performed a quick balance between the values of competitiveness, including the right of consumers to information, and copyright law. It concluded that while competitiveness necessarily implies that one competitor has the right to make advertisements at the expense of his or her competitors, this competitiveness cannot transform 'an activity which might otherwise be a fair dealing into an unfair one', copyright being valued highly to the point that its infringement is criminalised.[214] As the defendant could not find any example that it is a common practice to use copyright material in comparative advertising, the court concluded that the use of the claimant's work was infringing.

Therefore, the court interpreted the Directive strictly and it seems that comparative advertising does not trump copyright law, at least in the United Kingdom, perhaps also because the practice of using copyright material to compare products is not (yet) established in the United Kingdom. However, it could also be said that the ruling is really confined to its facts. Probably using the whole cover was too much, using the trademark only may have been sufficient. Later, Jacob LJ, in the O2 appeal, felt that sooner or later a court would need to refer this issue (whether compliance with MCAD, article 3a, provides an automatic defence to all intellectual property rights) to the Court of Justice for clarification.[215] In this connection, there is case law suggesting that it is difficult to win on the basis of passing off when a defendant compares its product or service to that of the claimant simply because often there is no (risk of) confusion.[216] One commentator has deduced from the Court of Justice's *Pippig Augenoptik v Hartlauer* decision[217] that reproducing the copyrighted logo of a competitor is allowed, and therefore that the Directive also trumps copyright.[218] The argument is that MCAD, article 15's words 'other distinguishing marks' cannot be construed as covering only trademarks *sensu stricto*, otherwise they would be redundant.[219] He thus concludes that in light of this, UK law should be modified accordingly.[220] However, the ruling is not as clear because its paragraph 84 states that:

[213] [2005] FSR 35.

[214] Ibid para 18.

[215] Simon Fhima, 'Trade Mark Infringement in Comparative Advertising Situations' (n 202) 422. This could include not only copyright but also design rights and passing off.

[216] See eg *Ciba-Geigy v Parke Davis & Co* [1994] FSR 8, discussed by P Stephenson, 'Comparative Advertising and Intellectual Property Rights' (2006) *European Intellectual Property Review* 182.

[217] Case C-44/01 *Pippig Augenoptik v Hartlauer* [2003] ECR I-3095.

[218] Stephenson, 'Comparative Advertising and Intellectual Property Rights' (n 216) 190.

[219] MCAD, article 15 provides 'Whereas such use of another's trade mark, trade name *or other distinguishing marks* does not breach this exclusive right in cases where it complies with the conditions laid down by this Directive, the intended target being solely to distinguish between them and thus to highlight differences objectively' (emphasis added).

[220] Stephenson, 'Comparative Advertising and Intellectual Property Rights' (n 216) 190–91.

> Article 3a(1)(e) of Directive 84/450 does not prevent comparative advertising, in addition to citing the competitor's name, from reproducing its logo and a picture of its shop front, *if that advertising complies with the conditions for lawfulness laid down by Community law* (emphasis added).

As regards copyright, it could be that in some cases, permitted criticism or review (CDPA 1988, section 30) could coincide with comparative advertising allowed by the MCAD.

Finally, one must not forget the Court of Justice's ruling in *L'Oréal v Bellure*[221] which extends trade mark law's scope into the realm of unfair competition. Although the Court of Appeal followed the Court of Justice's ruling, it strongly disapproved it and called for the EU courts and the legislature to reverse this dangerous trend as contrary to freedom of competition and of expression.[222]

X. CONCLUSION: IDENTIFICATION OF PRINCIPLES GOVERNING OVERLAPS IN UK LAW AND REMAINING OPEN QUESTIONS

As in France and the European Union, there is no general rule banning intellectual property overlaps in the United Kingdom and freedom of competition is also strongly embedded in UK law.

By contrast, unlike France and the European Union, UK intellectual property laws contain quite a few rules banning some overlaps, albeit not totally perfectly. These rules are all concentrated in the overlap between copyright and registered and unregistered designs. Despite the reasons being probably mostly historical, these rules still make good sense and could well serve to regulate the problems caused by this overlap at EU and even international level. We will not repeat them all here, but in summary, they avoid both overprotection and regime clashes at several levels, namely subject matter, ownership and dealings, infringement and duration.

Apart from these rules, as in France, the British have a few additional rules to regulate some overlaps. Interestingly, one rule is similar to a French one and is equally case-based. It prevents the protection of drawings by copyright if they are part of a patent application. Another, CDPA 1988, section 63(1), is similar but slightly less generous than the *Dior v Evora* ruling. As in France, owing to EU harmonisation, the degree of convergence between patents and plant variety rights is also quite high. The remaining overlaps, as in all Member States, are regulated by EU law. Finally, even if freedom of competition is almost sacrosanct, the overlap between trademark law and passing off is generously allowed, which in fact is in total contradiction with this overarching principle. However, UK courts are generally reluctant to allow a posteriori overlaps. The House of Lords' statement in *In re Coca-Cola Co*[223] that it is undesirable to expand the boundaries of intellectual property rights to allow a perpetual monopoly was relayed by the Privy

[221] Discussed in chapter 3, section IX.B.

[222] *L'Oréal v Bellure* [2010] EWCA Civ 535, esp paras 10, 16, deciding the case after the Court of Justice gave its answers in the preliminary ruling.

[223] [1986] 1 WLR 695, 697-98 (concerning the attempt by Coca-Cola to register a trade mark for its iconic Coca-Cola bottle for which the design right had expired). The precedent is overruled by the current Trade Mark Act but the statement arguably still stands because of its generality.

Council in *Interlego v Tyco Industries et al*[224] and in *Philips v Remington*, both the High Court and the Court of Appeal also expressed their disapproval of the a posteriori IPR/trade mark overlap.[225] To that can be added the recent call of Jacob J against creating a tort of unfair competition law by the back door or at least extending trade mark protection to that effect as it can create monopolies.[226]

[224] [1989] AC 217, 255-56 (a decision which rejected the protection by copyright of slightly amended previous drawings of Lego bricks for which the patent had expired). Lord Templeman, who delivered the ruling, also referred to the *British Leyland* case (*British Leyland Motor Corporation v Armstrong Patents Co* [1986] 2 WLR 400) in support of this statement.

[225] [1998] RPC 283, 287; [1999] ETMR 816, 824.

[226] *L'Oréal v Bellure* [2010] EWCA Civ 535, esp paras 4-20, 50 following reluctantly the Court of Justice's answers to the Court of Appeal's questions in the same case.

6

Germany

I. THE LEGAL FRAMEWORK

A Relevant Intellectual Property Statutes in German Law

IN THIS CHAPTER, first, the intellectual property statutes most relevant to the issue of IPR overlaps in German law will be briefly outlined.[1] The statutory basis of German copyright law is the Act on Copyright and Neighbouring Rights of 1965 (Urheberrechtsgesetz, Copyright Act), as last amended in 2008.[2] German trademark law is primarily governed by the Act on the Protection of Trademarks and other Signs of 1994 (Markengesetz, Trademark Act), as last amended in 2009.[3] The Act is the result of a fundamental revision of German trademark law in 1994 in order to implement the Trademark Directive 2008/95/EC. Besides the protection afforded by the Community Design Regulation (EC) 6/2002, the German Act on the Protection of Designs and Models of 2004 (Geschmacksmustergesetz, Design Act), as last amended 2009, provides for an independent German registered design right.[4] The Act was fundamentally revised in 2004 in order to implement the Design Directive 98/71/EC. The statutory basis of German patent law is the Patent Act of 1981 (Patentgesetz, Patent Act), as last amended in 2009.[5] In the field of green biotechnology, patent protection overlaps with the *sui generis* protection afforded to plant varieties by the Plant Variety Protection Act of 1997

[1] See F Mächtel, R Uhrich and A Förster (eds), *Geistiges Eigentum – Vorschriftensammlung Gewerblicher Rechtsschutz, Urheber- und Wettbewerbsrecht*, 2nd edn (Tuebingen, Mohr Siebeck, 2009).

[2] A consolidated version of the German Copyright Act is available at http://bundesrecht.juris.de/bundesrecht/urhg/gesamt.pdf as last amended by the Gesetz zur Reform des Verfahrens in Familiensachen und in Angelegenheiten der freiwilligen Gerichtsbarkeit of 17 December 2008, BGBl (Bundesgesetzblatt, Federal Law Gazette) I/2008, 2586 and the Sechstes Gesetz zur Änderung des Urheberrechtsgesetzes of 7 December 2008, BGBl (Bundesgesetzblatt, Federal Law Gazette) I/2008, 2349. A translation of the German Copyright Act by the International Bureau of WIPO completed by the German authorities as last amended on 22 December 1997 is available at www.wipo.int/clea/en/text_pdf.jsp?lang=EN&id=1032.

[3] A consolidated version of the German Trademark Act is available at http://bundesrecht.juris.de/bundesrecht/markeng/gesamt.pdf as last amended by the Gesetz zur Vereinfachung und Modernisierung des Patentrechts of 31 July 2009, BGBl I/2009, 2521. A translation of the German Trademark Act by the International Bureau of WIPO as last amended on 16 July 1998 is available at www.wipo.int/clea/en/text_pdf.jsp?lang=EN&id=1011.

[4] A consolidated version of the German Design Act is available at http://bundesrecht.juris.de/bundesrecht/geschmmg_2004/gesamt.pdf as last amended by the Gesetz zur Vereinfachung und Modernisierung des Patentrechts of 31 July 2009, BGBl I/2009, 2521.

[5] A consolidated version of the German Patent Act is available at http://bundesrecht.juris.de/bundesrecht/patg/gesamt.pdf as last amended by the Gesetz zur Vereinfachung und Modernisierung des Patentrechts of 31 July 2009, BGBl I/2009, 2521. A translation of the German Patent Act by the International Bureau of WIPO as last amended on 6 August 1998 is available at www.wipo.int/clea/en/text_pdf.jsp?lang=EN&id=1035.

(Sortenschutzgesetz, Plant Variety Protection Act), as last amended in 2008,[6] which latter was fundamentally revised in 2005 to implement the Biotechnology Directive 98/44/EC into German law. Finally, the new German Act against Unfair Competition of 2004 (Gesetz gegen den unlauteren Wettbewerb, Unfair Competition Act)[7] was amended extensively in 2008 to implement the Unfair Commercial Practices Directive 2005/29/EC (UCPD) into German law.

B Overview and General Principles Governing Overlaps

The initial principle governing overlaps in German law is the cumulative application of overlapping IPRs if their respective conditions are met.[8] However, statutory bases for this principle have emerged only lately in Trademark Act, section 2 (for trademarks) and Design Act, section 50 (for designs), partly going back to the implementation of the respective European Directives in German law.[9] Nonetheless, as a general starting point, the principle of cumulative application is acknowledged beyond these specific statutory provisions. The fundamental background of this legal situation is the traditional acknowledgement of the (formerly common) fact that different IPRs serve different purposes, ie protect a different immaterial subject matter, and therefore overlap problems in the strict sense cannot exist.[10]

However, more recent German literature increasingly emphasises that this traditional assessment of most overlap situations as a justified cumulation of several 'insulated' IPRs has become doubtful as a result of the expansion of several IPRs beyond their traditional immaterial subject matter.[11] The consequence is an increasing number of genuine overlaps where the legislative balances of comparable interests, crafted differently with respect to different IPRs, come into conflict because the specifically protected immaterial subject matter of the respective IPRs overlaps, ie a single unitary human

[6] A consolidated version of the Plant Variety Protection Act is available at http://bundesrecht.juris.de/bundesrecht/sortschg_1985/gesamt.pdf as amended by the Gesetz zur Verbesserung der Durchsetzung der Rechte des geistigen Eigentums of 7 July 2008, BGBl I/2008, 1191, and the Gesetz zur Reform des Verfahrens in Familiensachen und in Angelegenheiten der freiwilligen Gerichtsbarkeit of 17 December 2008, BGBl I/2008, 2586.

[7] A consolidated version of the Unfair Competition Act is available at http://bundesrecht.juris.de/bundesrecht/ uwg_2004/gesamt.pdf, BGBl I/2004, 1414. An English translation is available at http://bundesrecht.juris.de/englisch_uwg/index.html.

[8] See on different categories of overlaps, eg H-P Götting, *Gewerblicher Rechtsschutz*, 9th edn (Munich, Beck, 2010) s 5 VI; O Sosnitza, 'Konvergenz und Interferenz der Schutzrechte' in E Keller, C Plassmann and A von Falck (eds), *Festschrift für Winfried Tilmann* (Cologne/Berlin/Bonn/Munich, Heymanns, 2003) 896; R Jacobs, 'Die Himmelsscheibe von Nebra – Gedanken zum Verhältnis von Urheberrechtsschutz und Markenschutz' in A Ohly, T Bodewig and T Dreier (eds), *Perspektiven des geistigen Eigentums und des Wettbewerbsrechts, Festschrift für Gerhard Schricker zum 70. Geburtstag* (Munich, Beck, 2005) 807; A Ohly, 'Areas of Overlap Between Trade Mark Rights, Copyright and Design Rights in German Law' (2007) *GRUR Int* 704, 706.

[9] See recital 7 of Directive 2008/95/EC of the European Parliament and of the Council of 22 October 2008 to approximate the laws of the Member States relating to trademarks (codified version) [2008] OJ L299/25, and arts 16 and 17 of Directive 98/71/EC of the European Parliament and of the Council of 13 October 1998 on the legal protection of designs [1998] OJ L289/28.

[10] See Sosnitza, 'Konvergenz und Interferenz der Schutzrechte' (n 8) 897; A Kur, 'Funktionswandel von Schutzrechten: Ursachen und Konsequenzen der inhaltlichen Annäherung und Überlagerungen von Schutzrechtstypen' in G Schricker, T Dreier and A Kur (eds), *Geistiges Eigentum im Dienst der Innovation* (Baden-Baden, Nomos, 2001) 34.

[11] Kur, 'Funktionswandel von Schutzrechten' (n 10) 33.

effort is protected by different IPRs. Moreover, as a result of the recent proliferation of IPRs, situations where different IPRs overlap with respect to a unitary good or service, although the specifically protected immaterial subject matter is (at least terminologically) different, have become more frequent. These overlaps in a wider sense will very often pose similar problems to the genuine overlaps, in particular in the area of adjusting the different exceptions to protection.[12]

Consequently, the specific rules of conflict governing certain overlaps beyond the general principle have lately attracted more attention in German case law[13] and literature.[14] In fact, the general principle of cumulative application has never been without exceptions and qualifications. However, explicit statutory delineation rules are rare in German law. In a strict sense, only Patent Act, section 2a (providing for a delineation of patent protection and plant variety protection in German law) and Design Act, section 1(2) (excluding the design of computer programs from the scope of design protection in delineating the latter from copyright law) deserve to be mentioned here. Both of these provisions are of European origin.[15]

Beyond explicit hard and fast conflict rules, different mechanisms in the statutory framework and in case law serve to delineate and adjust different IPRs in overlap situations. Thus, the principle of cumulative application is no more than a starting point, while courts have developed more specific conflict rules to delineate different IPRs from each other or to adjust conflicting IPR provisions on the basis of certain statutory provisions, in particular in the framework of conditions and scope of protection of the respective IPRs. These rules may widely exclude certain kinds of overlaps and in fact frequently do so. Where such 'IP internal' instruments do not suffice or where appropriate solutions cannot be reached on the basis of (too rigidly drafted) statutory IP provisions, the application of certain general doctrines of German law has been considered to avoid unbalanced results in overlap situations. Thus, the application of fundamental rights, competition law, unfair competition law, tort law (Civil Code (BGB), section 826) and the general principle of good faith (anchored in Civil Code, section 242) have been considered

[12] Ibid 34.

[13] See for the overlap between trademarks and copyright especially *Parfumflakon*, Federal Court of Justice (Bundesgerichtshof) (2000) *Neue Juristische Wochenschrift* 3783, and *Mona Lisa*, Federal Patents Court (Bundespatentgericht) (1998) *Gewerblicher Rechtsschutz und Urheberrecht* 1021. For the potential overlap between works of applied art and the protection of designs, see *Silberdistel*, Federal Court of Justice (1995) *Gewerblicher Rechtsschutz und Urheberrecht* 581. For the overlap between trademarks and unfair competition law see *MAC Dog*, Federal Court of Justice (1999) *Gewerblicher Rechtsschutz und Urheberrecht* 161. For the overlap between the unregistered Community design right and unfair competition law, see *Jeans*, Federal Court of Justice (2006) *Gewerblicher Rechtsschutz und Urheberrecht* 79. Comprehensive references beyond these landmark cases will be given in context below.

[14] See eg Ohly, 'Areas of Overlap Between Trade Mark Rights, Copyright and Design Rights in German Law' (n 8); Jacobs, 'Die Himmelsscheibe von Nebra' (n 8) 801; C Krüger, 'Zur Konvergenzdiskussion im gewerblichen Rechtsschutz und Urheberrecht' in A Ohly, T Bodewig and T Dreier (eds), *Perspektiven des geistigen Eigentums und des Wettbewerbsrechts, Festschrift für Gerhard Schricker zum 70. Geburtstag* (Munich, Beck, 2005) 69; A Ohly, 'Von einem Indianerhäuptling, einer Himmelsscheibe, einer Jeans und dem Lächeln der Mona Lisa – Überlegungen zum Verhältnis zwischen Urheber- und Kennzeichenrecht' in L Pahlow and J Eisfeld (eds), *Grundlagen und Grundfragen des Geistigen Eigentums, Festgabe für Diethelm Klippel zum 65. Geburtstag* (Tuebingen, Mohr Siebeck, 2008) 203; Sosnitza, 'Konvergenz und Interferenz der Schutzrechte' (n 8) 897; Kur, 'Funktionswandel von Schutzrechten' (n 10) 33.

[15] Design Directive 98/71/EC, art 1(b) and Art 53(b) of the Convention on the Grant of European Patents concluded at Munich on 5 October 1973 as revised by the act revising the EPC dated 29 November 2000 (European Patent Convention, EPC), respectively.

in case law[16] and literature[17] as 'IP external' solutions to prevent certain overlaps from resulting in unjustified restrictions on free competition or the freedom of expression. All these unwritten conflict rules with respect to different kinds of overlap situations will be discussed in what follows.

So far, situations have been described where the overlapping IPRs are owned by the same person or entity (single right-holder situations). However, as a matter of course, overlaps can also lead to a situation of conflict when IPRs of *different* owners overlap each other. On principle, it is acknowledged in German law that in these situations IPRs may overlap as well. This can obviously lead to outright conflicts between the different right owners. Generally, such conflicts are accepted, resulting in a certain danger of hold-up. Where explicit conflict rules exist for such situations (in particular in trademark[18] and design law[19] with regard, inter alia, to earlier copyright or neighbouring rights) the governing principle in German law for solving such conflicts is the principle of priority.[20] Only in exceptional cases (in particular involving bad faith on the part of the earlier applicant) will the later IPR prevail. Apart from these clear-cut solutions, in several situations a certain degree of co-existence of the overlapping rights is regulated by the law.[21] In the following, such 'multiple right-holder situations' will be discussed where they are relevant to the topic.

It is increasingly acknowledged in recent German literature that the governing principle for developing detailed solutions to overlap problems on a case-by-case basis should be an appropriate balancing of exclusive IPR protection and the remaining realm of the public domain, fundamentally underpinned by the framework of fundamental rights and the principle of free competition.[22] Against such background, the main function of conflict rules is regarded as to avoid that specific overlap situations lead to an exclusion of effective competition with respect to a certain protected subject matter or to unjustified curtailments of fundamental rights, namely the right to freedom of expression. Moreover, inter alia, the discussion on inner conflicts in the system of different IPRs has led to significant legal research projects with the goal to develop what might be called a

[16] See especially on the application of German Constitution (Grundgesetz), art 5(3) concerning freedom of arts when using a reputed trademark for the purposes of parody, *Lila-Postkarte*, Federal Court of Justice (2005) *Gewerblicher Rechtsschutz und Urheberrecht* 583. See (sceptical) on a potential application of good faith (Civil Code (BGB), art 242) in extreme cases, *Johann Sebastian Bach*, Higher Regional Court (Oberlandesgericht) Dresden (2001) *Neue Juristische Wochenschrift* 615, 617 *et seq* (obiter). See on the application of unfair competition law (on the grounds of interfering with a competitor's trade) in the slightly different context of 'domain-grabbing' cases generally, *cyberspace.de*, Higher Regional Court Dresden (1999) *Computer und Recht* 589, 592; *zwilling.de*, Higher Regional Court Karlsruhe (1998) *Zeitschrift für Urheber- und Medienrecht* 944; *buecherde.com*, Higher Regional Court Munich (2000) *Gewerblicher Rechtsschutz und Urheberrecht* 518; *deta.com*, Regional Court (Landgericht) Braunschweig (1998) *Computer und Recht* 364, 366; *epson.de*, Regional Court Duesseldorf (1998) *Gewerblicher Rechtsschutz und Urheberrecht* 159, 164 . See on the application of the general tort of intentional damage against public policy, *weideglueck.de*, Higher Regional Court Frankfurt aM (2000) *Computer und Recht* 615.

[17] See eg G Schricker, 'Anmerkung zu BGH 4.5.2000 I ZR 256/97 – *Parfumflakon*' (2001) *Juristenzeitung* 463, 463 *et seq* (on a possible application of unfair competition law on the grounds of interfering with a competitor's trade).

[18] See Trademark Act, s 13.

[19] See Design Act, s 34.

[20] Sosnitza, 'Konvergenz und Interferenz der Schutzrechte' (n 8) 902 *et seq.*

[21] Ibid 906 *et seq.*

[22] See eg Kur, 'Funktionswandel von Schutzrechten' (n 10) 42; Ohly, 'Von einem Indianerhäuptling, einer Himmelsscheibe, einer Jeans und dem Lächeln der Mona Lisa' (n 14) 203 *et seq*; cf gradually more restrictive, Sosnitza, 'Konvergenz und Interferenz der Schutzrechte' (n 8) 896 *et seq.*

'general part' of German intellectual property law overarching specific provisions on different IPRs.[23]

II. COPYRIGHT AND DESIGNS

A General Principles

The potential overlap of copyright and design protection for the two- or three-dimensional appearance of the whole or part of a product (cf Design Act, section 1(1)) is evident.

Traditionally, in German law the relationship of copyright and design rights was expressly regarded as a relationship between two genuinely overlapping IPRs.[24] As the condition of 'individuality' (*Eigentümlichkeit*) in (old) German design law was originally essentially similar to the assessment of individuality with respect to works of art in copyright law, the two rights were regarded as protecting the essentially same immaterial subject matter, ie the same creative effort. From this inevitably followed the need for a clarification of the relationship of the two rights in case law. According to the so-called 'two-level theory' of protection of designs (*Stufentheorie*[25]), copyright was regarded as the further reaching, higher-level protection system, applicable in the field of utilitarian designs and creations only subject to additional qualifications. Thus, according to the German courts, the difference between the two systems was of a gradual nature, concerning the necessary threshold of respective individual creativity.[26] Consequently, German courts have established particularly restrictive conditions with regard to the necessary degree of individual creativity for the area of the so-called 'applied arts'. While no specific conditions apply to works of 'pure' art (without any utilitarian purpose), a particular 'level of creativity' (*Schöpfungshöhe*) is required for copyright protection for works of 'applied art', ie utilitarian designs or works of craftsmanship, and so forth.[27] For the establishment of the level of creativity, the Federal Court of Justice has applied the test of a level of creativity, substantially beyond the area of the average standard of

[23] See V Jänich, *Geistiges Eigentum: eine Komplementärerscheinung zum Sacheigentum* (Tuebingen, Mohr Siebeck, 2002) 373; H-J Ahrens, 'Brauchen wir einen Allgemeinen Teil der Rechte des Geistigen Eigentums?' (2006) *Gewerblicher Rechtsschutz und Urheberrecht* 617.

[24] See especially E Ulmer, *Urheber- und Verlagsrecht*, 3rd edn (Berlin, Springer, 1980) s 25 III 3; cf U Loewenheim, in G Schricker and U Loewenheim (eds), *Urheberrecht*, 4th edn (Munich, Beck, 2010) s 2, para 33 and 159, for comprehensive further references.

[25] See ibid.

[26] See unambiguously *Silberdistel*, Federal Court of Justice (1995) *Gewerblicher Rechtsschutz und Urheberrecht* 581.

[27] See for the oldest authority Reichsgericht, RGZ 76, 339 (1911), 344 (on the design and copyright protection of typefaces). See from the case law of the Federal Court of Justice especially the controversial landmark judgment in *Silberdistel (Carline Thistle)*, Federal Court of Justice (1995) *Gewerblicher Rechtsschutz und Urheberrecht* 581. In the judgment, the Federal Court of Justice denied protection to the replica of a thistle which had been created for use as an ear clip. According to the court, a very natural and adept figuration of the original, natural thistle did not suffice for protection. Instead, an additional element of artistry, in particular a certain degree of artistic transfiguration, was needed to trigger copyright protection in the area of utilitarian designs. This has been criticised, as it will usually be almost impossible to establish criteria in order to assess what constitutes 'artistic character' in comparison to mere highly adept craftsmanship; moreover, the distinction between 'pure' and 'applied' arts will at times be equally hard to make (see G Schricker, 'Der Urheberrechtsschutz von Werbeschöpfungen, Werbeideen, Werbekonzeptionen und Werbekampagnen', (1996) *Gewerblicher Rechtsschutz und Urheberrecht* 815, 818 *et seq*).

creations in the relevant sector.[28] Therefore, a specific creative achievement substantially beyond the usual average craftsmanship or design is required. According to the Federal Court of Justice, the artistic value of the creation as such is irrelevant.[29] However, presentation of a design in museums and art exhibitions has been acknowledged as an indicator of an above-average creation, as well as the attention a particular design has raised among experts and the public at large.[30]

From this it follows that the overlap of copyright and design protection is possible in German law, but that the area for such overlap has effectively been limited by the courts to those 'artistic' creations which are not just new and of individual character, compared to already existing designs, but also *substantially* above the level of the average standard of existing achievements of normal craftsmanship in the field in question.[31] Thus, the *Stufentheorie* (two-level theory) and the condition of *Schöpfungshöhe* (level of creativity) amount to a genuine conflicts rule, regulating the boundaries of legally accepted overlap of copyright and design protection.[32] The additional condition of *Schöpfungshöhe* (level of creativity) has been maintained until today,[33] although the new conception of European unitary and harmonised design protection arguably puts the 'two-level theory' in question.[34]

Mainly for this latter reason, the conflicts rule has recently been increasingly criticised in literature.[35] Apart from the (older) argument of impending legal uncertainty,[36] the

[28] See *Silberdistel*, Federal Court of Justice (1995) *Gewerblicher Rechtsschutz und Urheberrecht* 581.

[29] See *Rosenthal-Vase*, Federal Court of Justice (1959) *Gewerblicher Rechtsschutz und Urheberrecht* 289, 290.

[30] See *Le Corbusier Möbel*, Federal Court of Justice (1987) *Gewerblicher Rechtsschutz und Urheberrecht* 903, 905. See for further references Loewenheim in Schricker and Loewenheim (eds), *Urheberrecht* (n 24) s 2, para 159 *et seq*.

[31] Superior achievements in industrial design or other fields of design will, however, regularly reach that threshold before German courts, see eg *Le Corbusier Möbel*, Federal Court of Justice (1987) *Gewerblicher Rechtsschutz und Urheberrecht* 903 (concerning an armchair and a couch designed by Le Corbusier). For comprehensive references from German case law see G Schulze, in T Dreier and G Schulze, *Urheberrechtsgesetz*, 3rd edn (Munich, Beck, 2008) s 2, para 161 *et seq*.

[32] See Kur, 'Funktionswandel von Schutzrechten' (n 10) 40; Ohly, 'Von einem Indianerhäuptling, einer Himmelsscheibe, einer Jeans und dem Lächeln der Mona Lisa' (n 14) 215.

[33] See most recently eg *Panther mit Smaragdauge*, Higher Regional Court Frankfurt aM (2006) *GRUR-RR* 43, 44, maintaining the argument that there is only a gradual difference of copyright and design protection and not a difference with respect to the objectives and the character of these two rights, and consequently applying the restrictive condition of a 'substantial level of creativity'. In legal doctrine see especially A Ohly, 'Designschutz im Spannungsfeld von Geschmacksmuster-, Kennzeichen- und Lauterkeitsrecht' (2007) *Gewerblicher Rechtsschutz und Urheberrecht* 731, 733; Schulze, in Dreier and Schulze, *Urheberrechtsgesetz* (n 31) s 2, para 174. Moreover, recently, the Federal Constitutional Court (Bundesverfassungsgericht) has affirmed the relevant case law of the civil courts in *Laufendes Auge*, Federal Constitutional Court (2005) *Gewerblicher Rechtsschutz und Urheberrecht* 410.

[34] See immediately below in the text.

[35] See G Schricker, 'Farewell to the Level of Creativity' (1995) *International Review of Intellectual Property and Competition Law* 41; U Loewenheim, 'Höhere Schutzuntergrenze des Urheberrechts bei Werken der angewandten Kunst?' (2004) *GRUR Int* 765; A Nordemann and N Heise, 'Urheberrechtlicher Schutz für Designleistungen in Deutschland und auf europäischer Ebene' (2001) *Zeitschrift für Urheber- und Medienrecht* 128; Schricker, 'Der Urheberrechtsschutz von Werbeschöpfungen, Werbeideen, Werbekonzeptionen und Werbekampagnen' (n 27) 818 *et seq*; U Koschtial, 'Zur Notwendigkeit der Absenkung der Gestaltungshöhe für Werke der angewandten Kunst im deutschen Urheberrecht' (2004) *Gewerblicher Rechtsschutz und Urheberrecht* 555; H Haberstumpf, 'Urheberrechtlich geschützte Werke und verwandte Schutzrechte' in F-K Beier, A Kraft, G Schricker and E Wadle (eds), *Gewerblicher Rechtsschutz und Urheberrecht in Deutschland – Festschrift zum hundertjährigen Bestehen der Deutschen Vereinigung für Gewerblichen Rechtsschutz und Urheberrecht und ihrer Zeitschrift* (Weinheim, Wiley-VCH, 1991) 1125, 1159 *et seq*; H Ahlberg, in P Möhring and K Nicolini (eds), *Urheberrechtsgesetz* (Munich, Vahlen, 2000) s 2, para 111; Schulze, in Dreier and Schulze, *Urheberrechtsgesetz* (n 31) s 2, para 153.

[36] See Schricker, 'Der Urheberrechtsschutz von Werbeschöpfungen, Werbeideen, Werbekonzeptionen und Werbekampagnen' (n 27) 819.

critics[37] rely upon the fundamental reform of the German Design Act (Geschmacksmustergesetz) in 2004,[38] implementing the Design Directive.[39] According to the Explanatory Memorandum to the new law and in line with the Design Directive, German harmonised design law is now conceived as an *independent* protection system which follows its own autonomous objectives and conditions of protection and is no longer characterised by its specifically close relationship to copyright law.[40] In particular, the condition of 'individual character' (*Eigenart* in the sense of originality) is now arguably closer to comparable requirements with regard to unfair competition law protection against direct imitations,[41] than to the requirement of (creative) individuality in copyright law.[42] It has thus been argued that the older 'two-level theory', according to which there is only a *gradual* difference between design protection and copyright, can no longer justify the perpetuation of particularly restrictive conditions for copyright protection in the field of utilitarian designs (the 'applied arts').[43] However, this argument is not self-evident. In particular, the shift in design law from the requirement of individuality to the requirement of individual character (in the sense of originality), now characterised by elements concerning abstract distinctiveness by assessing the 'difference' between the overall impression of the new design compared to already existing designs, is a merely gradual, nuanced change. The remarkable convergence with regard to the conditions of protection therefore still partly exists, since a higher degree of individuality (in the sense of copyright law) will typically result in a higher capability to identify a particular design because of its difference in overall impression compared to existing product shapes. Moreover, the unitary Community design, as well as harmonised German design law, now provide for a tailor-made protection system for product designs (namely including unitary Community design protection for non-registered designs). Hence the need for a conflicts rule, preventing copyright from entirely undermining the carefully balanced differentiations and limitations of that system, has become even more urgent.[44] A departure from the 'two-level theory' would also substantially undermine the objectives of European harmonisation in this field.[45] Therefore, it is proposed that the 'old' additional requirement of a specific, substantial 'level of creativity' (*Schöpfungshöhe*) should be maintained as a condition of copyright protection in the area of applied arts. This effectively amounts to an appropriate conflicts rule with regard to the copyright/design overlap.[46] In fact, the

[37] See eg Loewenheim, in Schricker and Loewenheim (eds), *Urheberrecht* (n 24) s 2, para 33, with comprehensive further references.

[38] See BGBl I/2004, 390.

[39] Directive 98/71/EC.

[40] See the official Explanatory Memorandum to the German Design Protection Act in 2004, BT-Drs (Bundestagsdrucksache, Official Records of Parliament) 15/1075, 69.

[41] See below, section VIII.A.

[42] See in particular A Kur, 'Die Auswirkungen des neuen Geschmacksmusterrechts auf die Praxis' (2002) *GRUR Int* 661, 662 and 665 *et seq*.

[43] See Kur, 'Funktionswandel von Schutzrechten' (n 10) 41 *et seq*.

[44] Cf Ohly, 'Von einem Indianerhäuptling, einer Himmelsscheibe, einer Jeans und dem Lächeln der Mona Lisa' (n 14) 216; similarly A Mahr, 'The Relationship Between Design Protection Law and Copyright Law in Europe from a German Perspective' in *Prace Instytutu Prawa Wlasnosci Intelektualnej UJ, Jagiellonen-University Krakow* (Krakow 2007) vol 99, 103 *et seq*.

[45] See M Leistner *Konsolidierung und Entwicklungsperspektive des Europäischen Urheberrechts*, Zentrum für Europäisches Wirtschaftsrecht, Vorträge und Berichte no 167 (2008) 50, available at www.jura.uni-bonn.de/fileadmin/Fachbereich_Rechtswissenschaft/Einrichtungen/Lehrstuehle/Zivilrecht4/Publikationen/ZEW_167_Leistner.pdf.

[46] See especially Ohly, 'Designschutz im Spannungsfeld von Geschmacksmuster-, Kennzeichen- und Lauterkeitsrecht' (n 33) 733; Ohly, 'Von einem Indianerhäuptling, einer Himmelsscheibe, einer Jeans und dem

proposed adherence to the 'two-level theory' seems to be in line with the trend in recent German case law.[47] Hence, it is submitted that the relationship of German copyright law and German harmonised design law will continue to be governed by the requirement of a substantial 'level of creativity' (*Schöpfungshöhe*) as an additional condition of copyright protection in the area of potential overlap. With regard to the relationship between copyright and the *unitary* Community design right, in particular the unregistered Community design, this solution applies equally. The conflicts rule in Design Regulation, article 96 effectively leaves the controversial issue of delineating copyright from design protection to the Member States and thus allows the necessary leeway for German law.[48]

A particular conflicts rule of European origin is provided for by Design Act, section 1(2), implementing Design Directive, article 1(b).[49] The provision excludes 'designs' of computer programs from the ambit of design protection, thus effectively excluding design protection for the internal 'look and feel' of computer programs and reserving this area for copyright protection.[50]

B Simultaneous Overlap

(i) Single Right-Holder

With regard to the remaining simultaneous protection overlap, the consistent 'two-level' delineation of copyright and design law in German case law and literature has prevented the emergence of specifically problematic overlap issues.

As a matter of course, issues such as the incongruous design of exceptions will be of certain relevance in this field in the future. For instance, the question of whether a future (and controversially discussed) mandatory 'repair exception'[51] in harmonised European design law would have to be extended to copyright law is already discussed in German literature.[52] However, it is submitted that the consistent delineation of the two protection systems, requiring a higher degree of artistic creativity in copyright law, reduces the need for respective transpositions of certain limitations from design law to copyright law to a minimum, if necessary at all.

In theory, the comparatively limited exceptions to design protection might trump broader copyright exceptions in situations of parallel copyright and design protection. According to German literature, the analogous transposition of copyright exceptions to

Lächeln der Mona Lisa' (n 14) 215 *et seq*; Schulze, in Dreier and Schulze (eds), *Urheberrechtsgesetz* (n 31) s 2, para 174.

[47] Cf *Panther mit Smaragdauge*, Higher Regional Court Frankfurt aM (2006) *GRUR-RR* 43, 44; see further Schulze, in Dreier and Schulze, *Urheberrechtsgesetz* (n 31) para 158 *et seq*.

[48] See chapter 3, section II.B above (also on the controversial *Infopaq* case which in our view, should not change Design Regulation, art 96(2)'s application).

[49] See chapter 3, section II.B(i) above.

[50] See chapter 3, section II.B(i) above.

[51] With respect to the Community design, such 'repair clause' is provided for by Design Regulation, art 110(1). See on the ongoing discussion regarding a 'repair clause' in a future reform of the Design Directive eg J Drexl, R Hilty and A Kur, 'Designschutz für Ersatzteile – Der Kommissionsvorschlag zur Einführung einer Reparaturklausel' (2005) *GRUR Int* 449.

[52] Krüger, 'Zur Konvergenzdiskussion im gewerblichen Rechtsschutz und Urheberrecht' (n 14) 69 *et seq*. Cf also art 5 (3)(k) Infosoc Directive 2001/29/EC which provides for an optional exception for use in connection with the demonstration or repair of equipment.

design law is not possible in such situations.[53] Thus, in principle, the comparatively limited exceptions to copyright will prevail.

(ii) Multiple Right-Holders

Conflicts can arise in the remaining area of accepted overlap (with regard to particularly artistic designs), when copyright and design rights are held by different persons or entities. Generally speaking, in these situations the *principle of priority* applies.

Thus, the holder of a previous copyright can claim the cancellation of a registered German design under Design Act, section 34(2).[54] Conversely, if someone uses a registered design to create a copyright protected work, such use will usually infringe the design right (see Design Act, section 38(1)) if it is not justified by the private use exception or by the exception for quotations (see Design Act, section 40(no 1) and (no 2)).

However, where creative use of the design is inevitably necessary to achieve the desired artistic result (eg a satirical treatment of a famous design), it is submitted that such use should be justified on the grounds of German Constitution (Grundgesetz), article 5(3) (fundamental right to freedom of the arts).[55] Hence, in such exceptional cases, a *principle of co-existence* would apply.[56]

C Negative and *A Posteriori* Overlaps

Neither decisions nor literature on negative or *a posteriori* overlap issues with regard to copyright and designs currently exist in German law.[57]

III. COPYRIGHT AND TRADEMARKS

A Simultaneous Overlap

In general, copyright and trademark rights may overlap in German law.[58] Given the unlimited ambit of signs potentially protectable in trademark law,[59] such overlaps are (theoretically) possible with regard to word marks (which may consist of non-generic words or advertising slogans which are at least potentially eligible for copyright protection as works of language, such as writings, under Copyright Act, section 2(1)(no 1)), sound marks (potentially eligible for copyright protection as works of music under Copyright Act, section 2(1)(no 2)), and in particular picture marks, designs or the shape of goods or their packaging (potentially eligible for copyright protection as works of

[53] See H Eichmann, in H Eichmann and R von Falckenstein, *Geschmacksmustergesetz*, 4th edn (Munich, Beck, 2010) s 38, para 32.

[54] The provision makes use of the relevant option for the Member States, provided for in Design Directive, art 11(2)(b). See also chapter 3, section II.B(i) above.

[55] See also below section III.A(i) for relevant case law of the Federal Court of Justice with regard to trademark protection.

[56] See further Sosnitza, 'Konvergenz und Interferenz der Schutzrechte' (n 8) 906 *et seq*.

[57] Therefore, see chapter 3, section II.B(i) above.

[58] See Ohly, 'Areas of Overlap Between Trade Mark Rights, Copyright and Design Rights in German Law' (n 8) 706, with further references.

[59] See Trademark Act, s 3 (1), going back to Trade Mark Directive, art 2.

art, including applied arts and architecture, as photographic works or as scientific or technical illustrations including three-dimensional representations under Copyright Act, section 2(1)(no 4), (no 5) and (no 7)).[60]

(i) Protection Requirements

In theory, the respective main substantive *conditions* for protection in copyright and trademark law, ie individuality, on the one hand, and distinctiveness, on the other, are fundamentally different.[61] However, as a higher degree of creative individuality compared to the existing words, designs and shapes will increase the distinctive character of a sign, as a matter of course, a certain partial convergence of these conditions cannot be denied.[62] In practice, the field of prospective simultaneous overlaps depends mainly upon the respective interpretation of the substantive conditions of protection, namely the condition of individuality in copyright law with respect to certain relevant categories of works and the main condition of distinctiveness in trademark law.[63] The interpretation of the condition of individuality in German copyright case law expressly varies throughout the different categories of works.[64] As regards trademark law, while in principle the assessment of the element of distinctive character follows the same unitary criteria throughout the different sorts of trademarks, in practice this yardstick is evidently adjusted to the different perceptions of the public with regard to different categories of signs.

With regard to word marks, ie non-generic words and advertising slogans,[65] the area of potential simultaneous protection overlap is very small. This is because in German case law, copyright protection, although theoretically available and approved in older authorities,[66] will for all practical purposes not be granted to creative word-combinations or slogans because such 'creations' usually fail to reach the threshold of substantial individuality required by the courts as a condition of protection with respect to practical writing.[67] In fact, there is no Federal Court of Justice judgment granting protection for

[60] See comprehensively with regard to the different trade, A-A Wandtke and W Bullinger, 'Die Marke als urheberrechtlich schutzfähiges Werk' (1997) *Gewerblicher Rechtsschutz und Urheberrecht* 573, 574 *et seq.* Ohly, 'Areas of Overlap Between Trade Mark Rights, Copyright and Design Rights in German Law' (n 8) 711, moreover mentions smells as a potential field of overlap, however also emphasises that in German copyright law, unlike in the Netherlands, there is no case law on copyright protection for smells and therefore overlaps in this area seem 'highly unlikely'.

[61] See Ohly, 'Areas of Overlap Between Trade Mark Rights, Copyright and Design Rights in German Law' (n 8) 706.

[62] See especially B von Linstow, 'Motezuma, Himmelsscheibe und das System der Schutzrechte' in H-J Ahrens, J Bornkamm and H Kunz-Hallstein (eds), *Festschrift für Eike Ullmann* (Saarbrücken, Juris, 2006) 297, on the practically comparable assessment of the conditions of protection. Basically, although individuality in copyright is not an 'objective' criterion, it is, as a matter of course, assessed by comparison to existing creations, in particular in the field of the applied arts (ie utilitarian designs, etc). Cf also Ohly, 'Areas of Overlap Between Trade Mark Rights, Copyright and Design Rights in German Law' (n 8) 706 and 708 *et seq.*

[63] See further Wandtke and Bullinger, 'Die Marke als urheberrechtlich schutzfähiges Werk' (n 60) 574 *et seq.*

[64] See especially Loewenheim, in Schricker and Loewenheim (eds), *Urheberrecht* (n 24) s 2, para 23 *et seq*, with comprehensive further references.

[65] See eg W Erdmann, 'Schutz von Werbeslogans' (1996) *Gewerblicher Rechtsschutz und Urheberrecht* 550.

[66] See eg *Biegsam wie ein Frühlingsfalter bin ich im Forma-Büstenhalter*, Higher Regional Court Cologne (1934) *Gewerblicher Rechtsschutz und Urheberrecht* 758, 759; *Buchstabenschütteln*, Superior Court of Justice Berlin (Kammergericht) (1971) *Gewerblicher Rechtsschutz und Urheberrecht* 368, 370.

[67] Ohly, 'Areas of Overlap Between Trade Mark Rights, Copyright and Design Rights in German Law' (n 8) 708. However, slightly more optimistic with regard to the potential of copyright protection in this area, Wandtke and Bullinger, 'Die Marke als urheberrechtlich schutzfähiges Werk' (n 60) 576. See further M Dallmann, *Nachahmungsschutz für Werbeschlagwörter und Werbeslogans* (Baden-Baden, Nomos, 2005) 56 *et seq.*

such word creations or slogans,[68] and in more recent case law of the lower courts, protection has constantly been denied.[69] As, therefore, simultaneous overlap will be rare, the main issue which is discussed in this field concerns certain negative and *a posteriori* overlap situations with regard to the protection of work *titles* in trademark law, where trademark law actually threatens to undermine limitations of copyright protection with regard to the respective underlying *work*, in particular the limited term of protection of copyright law. These cases will be considered in detail below (section III.B).

In harmonised German trademark law, all kinds of pictures and graphic-designs, such as labels, logos or logotypes, can be protected.[70] This includes applied art, in particular utilitarian designs, such as logos, logotypes, labels and tags of all sorts. Also, genuine works of art, such as paintings, or photographic representations of copyrighted works, such as buildings, might be registered as trademarks if the crucial threshold of distinctiveness is established.[71] In German copyright law, traditionally, the threshold of protection differs between works of applied art, such as utilitarian designs, and genuine 'pure' art, such as paintings or artistic sculptures: Whereas with regard to 'pure' art the protection threshold is comparatively low, concerning applied art, German courts demand a particular 'level of creativity' (*Schöpfungshöhe*), ie a creation of genuinely artistic character well above usual routine designs.[72] As this latter category plays the dominant role in the field of trademark protection, the area of potential overlap is limited.[73] Only unusually creative and outstanding 'iconic' symbols which can be regarded as genuinely artistic will qualify for copyright protection. An example might be the fanciful 'international style' representation of a shell in the Shell logo which was designed by the famous industry designer Raymond Loewy and is established as a piece of art, exhibited in various museums and presented in pictorials.[74] By contrast, a usual logo or logotype will typically not reach the artistic 'level of creativity' required for copyright protection. Thus, an older judgment of the Federal Court of Justice denied protection for the title logotype of a newspaper.[75]

[68] The only (older) judgment of the Federal Court of Justice on the protection of advertising slogans as such (see Federal Court of Justice (1966) *Gewerblicher Rechtsschutz und Urheberrecht* 691, 692, on the slogan 'Ein Himmelbett als Handgepäck'), left the question of copyright protection open in an *obiter dictum,* thereby departing from the positive assessment of the Higher Regional Court Duesseldorf (1964) *Betriebsberater* 447. The older judgment, *Pfiffikus-Dose* (1961) *Gewerblicher Rechtsschutz und Urheberrecht* 85, quoted by Wandtke and Bullinger, 'Die Marke als urheberrechtlich schutzfähiges Werk' (n 60), in fact related to the protection of an advertising folder as a whole.

[69] Protection denied for simple word creations by *Minicar*, Higher Regional Court Munich (1968) 51 *Archiv für Urheber- und Medienrecht* 375, 388; *Orgware*, Higher Regional Court Frankfurt (1973) *Wettbewerb in Recht und Praxis* 162, 163; for an even more original combination copyright protection denied by the court, see *Heidelbär*, Regional Court Mannheim (1999) *Zeitschrift für Urheber- und Medienrecht* 659, 660. As for advertising slogans, copyright protection has been denied in *Hamburg geht zu E*, Higher Regional Court Braunschweig (1955) *Gewerblicher Rechtsschutz und Urheberrecht* 205, 206; *JA . . . JACoBI*, Higher Regional Court Stuttgart (1956) *Gewerblicher Rechtsschutz und Urheberrecht* 481, 482. See further Dallmann, *Nachahmungsschutz für Werbeschlagwörter und Werbeslogans* (n 67) 56 *et seq.*

[70] K-H Fezer, *Markenrecht*, 4th edn (Munich, Beck, 2009) s 3, para 525.

[71] See further below section III.B(i).

[72] See further above section II.A.

[73] In fact the main issue in this field is the possible overlap with design protection, see section IV.

[74] See Jacobs, 'Die Himmelsscheibe von Nebra' (n 8) 801.

[75] See *Morgenpost/Europapost*, Federal Court of Justice (1957) *Neue Juristische Wochenschrift* 220. See for more recent lower court decisions Higher Regional Court Hamburg (2004) *Multimedia und Recht* (MMR) 607 (mobile phone logo not protected by copyright); Regional Court Hamburg (2005) *GRUR-RR* 106 (logo of the former East German communist party representing an only slightly stylised handshake not protected by copyright).

Given that pictures of 'pure' art, as well as graphic representations of sculptures or even buildings, are also capable of being protected in German trademark law, there is nonetheless an area of potential overlap. In fact, pieces of 'pure' art, such as famous paintings,[76] portrait photographs[77] or photographs of copyright protected buildings[78] can be registered as trademarks subject to the general conditions of protection.[79] However, the condition of distinctiveness will very often not be fulfilled in this area.[80] Nonetheless, in the field of picture marks for artistic objects, simultaneous overlap of copyright and trademark protection is practically relevant.[81] With regard to the latter cases, ie trademark registrations of famous paintings, iconic photographs, and so forth, the potential negative and *a posteriori* overlaps when famous paintings or cultural treasures which are in the public domain are subsequently registered as trademarks have occupied the German courts and legal literature. This specifically problematic issue is discussed below (section III.B).

While in principle, three-dimensional 'signs' are eligible for trademark protection according to the general conditions, and while as a starting point the assessment of the element of distinctive character follows the same unitary criteria as with respect to other categories of trademarks, in following the Court of Justice's case law in this area[82] German courts have recently[83] emphasised that concrete distinctiveness in terms of Trademark Act, section 8(2)(no 1) presupposes a substantial departure from usual shapes when product design in itself is concerned and the customers in the relevant market are already used to a certain standard.[84] However, in this regard a gradual difference between

[76] See below section III.B(i) on the important judgment *Mona Lisa*, Federal Patents Court (1998) *Gewerblicher Rechtsschutz und Urheberrecht* 1021, where protection was denied because of lack of distinctiveness.

[77] See *Marlene-Dietrich-Bildnis*, Federal Court of Justice (2008) *Gewerblicher Rechtsschutz und Urheberrecht* 1093.

[78] See *Bürogebäude*, Federal Court of Justice (2005) *Gewerblicher Rechtsschutz und Urheberrecht* 257; see also for the lower court decision *Bürogebäude*, Federal Patents Court (2004) *Gewerblicher Rechtsschutz und Urheberrecht* 334.

[79] Jacobs, 'Die Himmelsscheibe von Nebra' (n 8) 801 *et seq*; Ohly, 'Areas of Overlap Between Trade Mark Rights, Copyright and Design Rights in German Law' (n 8) 708 *et seq*.

[80] See further below section III.B(i).

[81] Jacobs, 'Die Himmelsscheibe von Nebra' (n 8) 802.

[82] See Joined Cases C-468/01 P–C-472/01 *P Procter & Gamble Company v OHIM* [2004] ECR I-5141; Joined Cases C-456/01 P and C-457/01 *P Henkel KGaA v OHIM* [2004] ECR I-5089; Case C-136/02 P *Mag Instrument Inc v OHIM* [2004] ECR I-9165; Case C-173/04 *Deutsche SiSi Werke v OHIM* [2006] ECR I-551; Case C-25/05 P *August Storck KG v OHIM* [2006] ECR I-5719, para 75 *et seq*; Case C-24/05 P *August Storck KG v OHIM* [2006] ECR I-5677; Case C-286/04 P *Eurocermex SA v OHIM* [2005] ECR II-1391. See further M Leistner, 'Harmonization of Intellectual Property Law in Europe: The European Court of Justice's Trade Mark Case Law 2004–2007' (2008) *Common Market Law Review* 69, 79.

[83] Earlier judgments of the Federal Court of Justice have applied a slightly more liberal attitude, see eg *Käse in Blütenform*, Federal Court of Justice (2004) *Gewerblicher Rechtsschutz und Urheberrecht* 329; *Gabelstapler II*, Federal Court of Justice (2004) *Gewerblicher Rechtsschutz und Urheberrecht* 502 (fork-lift truck); *Rado Uhr II*, Federal Court of Justice (2004) *Gewerblicher Rechtsschutz und Urheberrecht* 505; *Stabtaschenlampen II*, Federal Court of Justice (2004) *Gewerblicher Rechtsschutz und Urheberrecht* 506 (flashlight). See on the most recent developments the case law reports by M Grabrucker and E Fink, in (2007) *Gewerblicher Rechtsschutz und Urheberrecht* 267, 268; M Grabrucker and E Fink, in (2008) *Gewerblicher Rechtsschutz und Urheberrecht* 371, 373; M Grabrucker and E Fink, in (2009) *Gewerblicher Rechtsschutz und Urheberrecht* 429, 432.

[84] See *Waschmitteltablette*, Federal Patents Court (2005) *Gewerblicher Rechtsschutz und Urheberrecht* 327 (detergent tab); *Taschenlampen II*, Federal Patents Court (2006) *Wettbewerb in Recht und Praxis* 1533 (flashlight), following the restrictive line of the Court of Justice's case law in this field. See on the most recent practice of the Federal Patents Court, M Grabrucker and E Fink, in (2007) *Gewerblicher Rechtsschutz und Urheberrecht* 267, 268 *et seq*; M Grabrucker and E Fink, in (2008) *Gewerblicher Rechtsschutz und Urheberrecht* 371, 373 *et seq*; and M Grabrucker and E Fink, in (2009) *Gewerblicher Rechtsschutz und Urheberrecht* 429, 432

the (slightly) more restrictive attitude of the Federal Patents Court along the lines of the Court of Justice's approach and the (slightly) more liberal line of the Federal Court of Justice is arguably still noticeable.[85] In any case, often such signs will be of descriptive character (Trademark Act, section 8(2)(no 2)[86]), in particular where they need to be kept free in order to safeguard sufficient leeway for future creations in the field of relevant product design.[87] However, these absolute grounds of refusal can be overcome by distinctive character acquired through use under Trademark Act, section 2(3),[88] and the Federal Court of Justice has applied this provision readily, in particular where extensive advertising campaigns or media coverage accompanied the introduction of new or the marketing of established products.[89] The most relevant issue in this field is the imminent overlap with design rights, which is partly regulated by Trademark Act, section 3(2)(no 1)–(no 3);[90] however this provision (probably due to its rigid consequence of entire exclusion from protection, which in contrast to Trademark Act, section 8(2)(no 1)–(no 3) cannot be overcome by acquired distinctive character) has hitherto been of rather limited relevance in practice.[91] By contrast, overlap with copyright protection will be rare as trademarks concerning product shapes or packaging of a product will usually represent utilitarian designs and hence be assessed due to the restrictive protection threshold of substantial 'level of creativity' (*Schöpfungshöhe*) which is applicable with regard to the applied arts.[92] Only if an outstanding iconic product design has reached the level of a genuine artistic creation will copyright protection be triggered.[93] Apart from such rare cases, as a matter of course, overlap with copyright can occur with regard to three-dimensional trademarks of genuine, purely artistic character. These cases have to be assessed along the lines of the general principles which will be outlined here for the trademark/copyright overlap with regard to works of 'pure' art.[94]

et seq. Most recently, the Federal Court of Justice has also slightly adapted its standards and now also tends to apply rather restrictive criteria with regard to the capability of product designs to genuinely serve as identification of origin from the viewpoint of the customers in the relevant markets, see *Fronthaube*, Federal Court of Justice (2008) *Gewerblicher Rechtsschutz und Urheberrecht* 71, with further references.

[85] See especially Ohly, 'Areas of Overlap Between Trade Mark Rights, Copyright and Design Rights in German Law' (n 3) 710. The difference is clearly noticeable in earlier judgments of the Federal Court of Justice (see the references at n 83). Lately, the Federal Court of Justice has applied even more differentiated, and arguably slightly more restrictive, criteria, thus implementing the more restrictive European standard, see n 84.

[86] See Trademark Directive, art 3 (1)(c).

[87] See *Porsche Boxster*, Federal Court of Justice (2006) *Gewerblicher Rechtsschutz und Urheberrecht* 679 (on the shape of the Porsche Boxster sports-car where the absolute ground of refusal under Trademark Act, s 8(2) (no 3) was, however, overcome by distinctive character acquired through use (under s 8(3)) on the basis of the extensive advertising campaign which had accompanied the market introduction of the new model). More liberal in the field of watches because of the nearly infinite range of design possibilities, *Rado Uhr III*, Federal Court of Justice (2007) *Gewerblicher Rechtsschutz und Urheberrecht* 973. See also below section IV.A(i).

[88] See Trademark Directive, art 3(3).

[89] See *Porsche Boxster*, Federal Court of Justice (2006) *Gewerblicher Rechtsschutz und Urheberrecht* 679; *Milchschnitte*, Federal Court of Justice (2008) *Gewerblicher Rechtsschutz und Urheberrecht* 510.

[90] See Trademark Directive, art 3(1)(e).

[91] See further below section IV.A(i).

[92] See above section II.A.

[93] See eg *Stahlrohrstuhl*, Federal Court of Justice (1961) *Gewerblicher Rechtsschutz und Urheberrecht* 635; *Stahlrohrstuhl II*, Federal Court of Justice (1981) *Gewerblicher Rechtsschutz und Urheberrecht* 820. See recently also the problematic judgment of the Higher Regional Court Hamburg (2002) *Zeitschrift für Urheber- und Medienrecht: Rechtsprechungsdienst* 181, granting protection for the product design of the popular 'Tripp Trapp' baby high chair by the Norwegian manufacturer Stokke. See further above section II.A.

[94] See below section III.B(i).

Finally, as regards sounds, the condition of protection in German copyright law is constructed rather extensively. The so-called 'small coin' (*kleine Münze*) of copyright protection, ie the protection of works representing a low degree of individual creativity, also protects simple commonplace melodies.[95] In trademark law, apart from the general conditions, the main threshold for protection is the graphic representation of the sound in question.[96] In German law such graphic representation will usually take the form of the conventional occidental music notation[97] which meets the requirements of the Court of Justice with regard to graphic representations,[98] whereas a mere sequence of notes is not regarded as sufficient.[99] Obviously, on the one hand, because of the rather low threshold of copyright protection in this field, there is considerable room for simultaneous overlap. On the other hand, negative and *a posteriori* overlap situations can occur in this field, in particular when famous works of music which are in the public domain are registered as trademarks.[100] The problems in this regard are comparable to the similar problems concerning 'purely' artistic picture marks and will be discussed below (section III.B).

(ii) Resulting Area of Overlap

From the preceding analysis it follows that while in theory the purpose and conditions of protection are different, there is nonetheless considerable room for simultaneous overlap of copyright and trademark protection. It has already been remarked that such cumulative application of copyright and trademark protection is generally accepted in German law.[101]

The main theoretical argument for the acceptance of overlapping copyright and trademark protection is the essentially different character and scope of protection.[102] While

[95] *Dirlada*, Federal Court of Justice (1981) *Gewerblicher Rechtsschutz und Urheberrecht* 267, 268; *Ein bißchen Frieden*, Federal Court of Justice (1988) *Gewerblicher Rechtsschutz und Urheberrecht* 812, 814; *Brown Girl II*, Federal Court of Justice (1991) *Gewerblicher Rechtsschutz und Urheberrecht* 533.

[96] See on German trademark law, *SWF-3 Nachrichten*, Federal Patents Court (1997) *Gewerblicher Rechtsschutz und Urheberrecht* 60; see also Case C-283/01 *Shield Mark v Kist* [2003] ECR I-14313.

[97] See Markenverordnung, s 11(2). Additionally, a sound record has to be filed (Markenverordnung, s 11(3) and (5)).

[98] See further Case C-283/01 *Shield Mark v Kist* [2003] ECR I-14313, para 62. Still more sceptical because of possible variations of interpretation, *SWF-3 Nachrichten*, Federal Patents Court (1997) *Gewerblicher Rechtsschutz und Urheberrecht* 60. This part of the judgment, however, had been criticised in literature (see eg R Ingerl and C Rohnke, *Markengesetz – Kommentar,* 2nd edn (Munich, Beck, 2003) s 8, para 105) and is now clearly overruled by the judgment of the Court of Justice on the Trademark Directive.

[99] See Case C-283/01 *Shield Mark v Kist* [2003] ECR I-14313, para 61. The alternative of filing sonograms has been abolished in German law (see Markenverordnung, s 11(2)). Actually, this possibility had been criticised very early in German literature, see eg P Ströbele, 'Die Eintragungsfähigkeit neuer Markenformen' (1999) *Gewerblicher Rechtsschutz und Urheberrecht* 1041, 1044.

[100] There is no German case law in this field. However, Ohly, 'Areas of Overlap Between Trade Mark Rights, Copyright and Design Rights in German Law' (n 8) 711, rightly remarks that the Court of Justice's *Shield Mark/Kist* judgment in fact is an example in question although the Court of Justice only laid down (restrictive) requirements for graphical representation.

[101] See Ohly, 'Areas of Overlap Between Trade Mark Rights, Copyright and Design Rights in German Law' (n 8) 706, who mentions one of the 'Harry Potter' cases which were decided by German courts as an example in point (see *Literatur-Werkstatt-Grundschule*, Regional Court Hamburg, (2004) *GRUR-RR* 65): the claimant in this case had in fact relied on both copyright protection for the novel, and trademark protection for the sign 'Harry Potter', and was successful on both claims. See also below section III.B.

[102] See comprehensively Sosnitza, 'Konvergenz und Interferenz der Schutzrechte' (n 8) 898; critically Wandtke and Bullinger, 'Die Marke als urheberrechtlich schutzfähiges Werk' (n 60) 577 *et seq*, who argue in favour of a *de lege ferenda* limitation of the possibility to register formerly copyright protected works which have become part of the public domain. See further below section III.B.

copyright law in principle grants the right-holder an exclusive right to control any use of the work, trademark protection is limited to the use of the protected sign *as a trademark in the course of trade*.[103] Moreover, in most cases trademark protection will be limited to uses with respect to similar goods or services as the registered trademark subject to the general condition of likelihood of confusion.[104] Hence, copyright and trademark law have even been characterised as 'complementary' protection systems.[105]

However, the general acceptance of cumulative applicability in Germany makes it necessary, first, to further analyse conflict rules for cases where copyright and trademark rights are held by different parties. Secondly, from the 'complementarity' of copyright and trademark protection it follows that both protection systems tend to undermine the respective limitations of each other.

(iii) Multiple Right-Holders

A person who registers or uses a copyright protected two- or three-dimensional representation or a sound as a trademark needs the authorisation of the copyright holder.[106] However, the German Trademark Office does not examine the issue of copyrights in its registry proceedings.[107] Hence, in the case of a conflicting earlier copyright, a trademark application by a third party will be registered, but will be subject to cancellation under

[103] The consequence of this restriction of the scope of protection is controversial in German trademark law. Under pre-Directive German law, a 'trademark use' was required by German courts and the prevailing opinion in German literature. A 'trademark use' was understood as use of another trader's mark as a designation for the infringer's own products (see *REHAB*, Federal Court of Justice (1985) *Gewerblicher Rechtsschutz und Urheberrecht* 41). After the adoption of the Trademark Directive, German courts still require a 'trademark use' in addition to the statutory elements of infringement in Trademark Act, s 14(2) (see *Partnerprogramm*, Federal Court of Justice (2009) *Gewerblicher Rechtsschutz und Urheberrecht* 1167) while parts of German literature refuse to adapt the old term in reference to the statutory provisions of Trademark Directive, art 5 (see eg A Kur 'Confusion Over Use? – Die Benutzung "als Marke" im Lichte der EuGH-Rechtsprechung' (2008) *GRUR Int* 1, 11). The development of the jurisdiction has to be carefully observed, particularly considering the guidelines set out by the Court of Justice (see eg Case C-487/07 *L'Oréal SA, Lancôme Parfums et Beauté & Cie SNC and Laboratoire Garnier & Cie v Bellure NV, Malaika Investments Ltd and Starion International Ltd* [2009] ECR I-5185, emphasising the other protective functions of a trademark besides the essential function to guarantee to consumers the origin of the goods or services). However, many voices in German literature still regard the requirement of 'trademark use' as the main criterion to differentiate between copyright and trademark law and as the main reason why the overlap in the scope of protection is a priori limited, for example with regard to ornamental use of a picture mark on T-shirts, etc (see Jacobs, 'Die Himmelsscheibe von Nebra' (n 8) 810; A Nordemann in U Loewenheim (ed), *Handbuch des Urheberrechts*, 2nd edn (Munich, Beck, 2010) s 83, para 51; Ohly, 'Von einem Indianerhäuptling, einer Himmelsscheibe, einer Jeans und dem Lächeln der Mona Lisa' (n 14) 208; Sosnitza, 'Konvergenz und Interferenz der Schutzrechte' (n 8) 898 *et seq*).

[104] In German trademark law, well-known marks are protected against use of an identical or similar sign for products of any kind where use of that sign without due cause takes unfair advantage of, or is detrimental to, the distinctive character or the repute of the trademark, see Trademark Act, s 14(2)(no 3). The German legislator has thus implemented the optional protection of well-known marks under Trademark Directive, art 5(2).

[105] See Sosnitza, 'Konvergenz und Interferenz der Schutzrechte' (n 8) 899.

[106] See Jacobs, Die Himmelsscheibe von Nebra' (n 8) 805. See especially on problems which might follow from the fact that according to German law, licences with respect to moral rights can be granted only subject to certain specific conditions and that the very 'core' of moral rights cannot be subject to licences at all, Wandtke and Bullinger, 'Die Marke als urheberrechtlich schutzfähiges Werk' (n 60) 579 *et seq*. A case in point might be the degrading use of a copyright protected picture for a 'murky' category of products or services. Such use might violate the author's moral right to integrity of the work (see Copyright Act, s 14).

[107] Jacobs, 'Die Himmelsscheibe von Nebra' (n 8) 806. Acknowledged for a work in the public domain in *Mona Lisa*, Federal Patents Court (1998) *Gewerblicher Rechtsschutz und Urheberrecht* 1021, 1023.

Trademark Act, section 13(1), (2)(no 3).[108] Both the unauthorised registration of the trademark and its unauthorised use will amount to infringement of the earlier copyright.[109] The copyright holder can bring an action for a prohibitory injunction, damages, and for the other claims provided for in Copyright Act, section 97 and in general civil law in cases of copyright infringement, subject to their respective general conditions.

In the reverse case, ie the use of a protected trademark for the subsequent creation of a copyright protected work, the earlier trademark rights also prevail.[110] Thus, if the trademark included in the copyright protected work is used in the course of trade as a trademark, this will make the user liable for trademark infringement subject to the general conditions and limitations, in particular likelihood of confusion.[111] However, in these cases the fundamental rights to freedom of expression and freedom of art (German Constitution, article 5(1), (3)) might provide a defence for the copyright holder.[112] In particular, if the copyright protected creation aims at an ironic, satiric representation of a well-known trademark, as a general rule such satiric expressions will be justified by German Constitution, article 5(1).[113]

(iv) Incongruous Exceptions to Protection

The general acceptance of trademark/copyright overlap in German law brings about another problem when both rights are applied cumulatively to a certain use and when relevant exceptions to the rights are drafted differently.[114] The background to this problem is the legal doctrine that exceptions to IPRs in favour of certain uses do generally not grant subjective rights to the beneficiaries of such provisions. Instead, such exceptions only *justify* the uses in question according to the prevailing opinion in German law.[115] However, from this follows the general principle that exceptions to one IPR can be undermined by the application of another if the latter does not provide for comparable exceptions. Thus, as a general rule, conflicts between different outcomes of weighing of interests concerning the exceptions to several IPRs always tend to be decided in favour of the right-holder if the latter relies upon the right with the narrowest exceptions.

[108] The provision makes use of the optional possibility for the Member States to provide for such a ground of cancellation, provided for in Trademark Directive, art 4(4)(c)(iii). See chapter 3, section III.B(i) above.

[109] See Ohly, 'Areas of Overlap Between Trade Mark Rights, Copyright and Design Rights in German Law' (n 8) 706.

[110] See ibid 706.

[111] See further Sosnitza, 'Konvergenz und Interferenz der Schutzrechte' (n 8) 909.

[112] See on German Constitution, art 5(3), Ohly, 'Areas of Overlap Between Trade Mark Rights, Copyright and Design Rights in German Law' (n 8) 707; see on German Constitution, art 5(1), Sosnitza, 'Konvergenz und Interferenz der Schutzrechte' (n 8) 910.

[113] See especially Sosnitza, 'Konvergenz und Interferenz der Schutzrechte' (n 8) 911. See also below section III.A(iv).

[114] The problem was first clearly described in German literature by Kur, 'Funktionswandel von Schutzrechten' (n 10) 42 and 46 *et seq*.

[115] See ibid 47. See further G Hohagen, 'Überlegungen zur Rechtsnatur der Kopierfreiheit' in A Ohly, T Bodewig and T Dreier (eds), *Perspektiven des Geistigen Eigentums und des Wettbewerbsrechts, Festschrift für Gerhard Schricker zum 70. Geburtstag* (Munich, Beck, 2005) 354; E Obergfell, 'Freier Werkzugang versus Urheberrechtsschutz – Zur Legitimität und Durchsetzung urheberrechtlicher Schranken' in A Halfmeier, P Rott and A Colombi Ciacchi (eds), *Zugang und Ausschluss als Gegenstand des Privatrecht, Jahrbuch Junger Zivilrechtswissenschaftler 2005* (Stuttgart, Munich, Boorberg, 2006) 110; H Schack, 'Zur Rechtfertigung des Urheberrechts als Ausschließlichkeitsrecht' in O Depenheuer and K-N Peifer (eds), *Geistiges Eigentum: Schutzrecht oder Ausbeutungstitel?* (Berlin, Heidelberg, Springer, 2008) 135; H Schack, *Urheber- und Urhebervertragsrecht*, 5th edn (Tuebingen, Mohr Siebeck, 2010) paras 100 and 539; B Stickelbrock, 'Die Zukunft der Privatkopie im Digitalen Zeitalter' (2004) *Gewerblicher Rechtsschutz und Urheberrecht* 736, 740.

The phenomenon becomes particularly problematic when, during phases of proliferation of IPRs, several IPRs tend to expand beyond their traditional subject matter (as regards conditions of protection), while the exceptions to the rights, laid down in the statute, are not adjusted to this extended field of application.[116] Therefore, the problem has also been characterised as a problem of 'asymmetric convergence' (inter alia by German scholars).[117] However, it follows from this that in principle the cumulative application of several IPRs to the same situation is acceptable as far as these IPRs *in themselves* provide for an appropriate balance of the interests of the right-holder, on the one hand, and the interests of users and the general public, on the other. Hence, the problem of 'asymmetric convergence' is rather a problem of *inner* imbalance of extensive IPRs than a genuine overlap problem. Strictly speaking, the connection with overlap situations is merely incidental. As a matter of course such inner imbalances might typically be relevant with respect to subject matter at the very boundaries of the field of application of a certain IPR. Therefore, overlaps with a second IPR which will be typical in such borderline areas might particularly highlight the inner inconsistency *within* the system of the first IPR if this inconsistency *really* follows from the extension of the right to subject matter formerly outside the field of its application.[118] However, many of the cases discussed in this category do not even have this inner connection with overlap situations because the inner imbalance *within* one IP right is not limited to subject matter at the very boundaries of possible protection but instead is an inner imbalance of horizontal character, ie an inconsistency which exists *throughout* the whole field of application. Accordingly, they tend to emerge on the occasion of an overlap situation while not being genuine overlap problems.

The most prominent example in this latter group of cases is the *Parfumflakon* judgment of the Federal Court of Justice.[119] The facts of the case were similar to the facts in *Dior v Evora*.[120] The manufacturer of a perfume relied upon copyright to prevent the marketing of his (genuine) perfumes by a retailer who was not a member of the manufacturer's selective distribution system. However, trademark rights were exhausted because the perfume flacons in question had been put on the market with the consent of the manufacturer. In this situation, the manufacturer resorted to copyright with respect to the (outstandingly artistically creative) flacon in which the perfume was sold and argued that the photographs of the flacon, reproduced in the advertising folders of the retailer, infringed the reproduction right under Copyright Act, section 16. Due to the first marketing in the European Union, however, the distribution right was also exhausted under Copyright Act, section 17(2). In this situation, the application of Copyright Act, section 16 in order to prevent reproductions accessory to a perfectly legal distribution of the perfumes undermined the principle of exhaustion even *within* the inner system of copyright law in itself. Thus, the inconsistency highlighted by this case was not just in the 'external' relationship

[116] See especially Kur, 'Funktionswandel von Schutzrechten' (n 10).

[117] Ibid 42 *et seq*; following Kur see also Ohly, 'Areas of Overlap Between Trade Mark Rights, Copyright and Design Rights in German Law' (n 8) 707; Ohly, 'Von einem Indianerhäuptling, einer Himmelsscheibe, einer Jeans und dem Lächeln der Mona Lisa' (n 14) 204.

[118] See further on such cases below section VI.A(v).

[119] *Parfumflakon*, Federal Court of Justice (2000) *Neue Juristische Wochenschrift* 3783.

[120] See chapter 3, section III.B(i) above. See further on *Parfumflakon* G Schricker, 'Anmerkung zu BGH 4.5.2000 I ZR 256/97 – *Parfumflakon*' (2001) *Juristenzeitung* 463; A Kur, 'Mehr als nur ein "Hauch von Dior"? – Das Urheberrecht und die Präsentation von Waren' in G Schricker, C Heath and P Ganea (eds), *Festschrift für Adolf Dietz* (Munich, Beck, 2001) 253; Ohly, 'Areas of Overlap Between Trade Mark Rights, Copyright and Design Rights in German Law' (n 8) 707; briefly Krüger, 'Zur Konvergenzdiskussion im gewerblichen Rechtsschutz und Urheberrecht' (n 14) 70.

between copyright and trademark law but rather affected the 'inner' relationship of the doctrine of exhaustion, limited in German copyright law to the distribution right, and the right of reproduction which was not covered by that doctrine. From this followed the obvious potential of an untrammelled application of the reproduction right to effectively undermine the effect of the doctrine of exhaustion in practice. This problem, and the inner inconsistency of copyright law, is not limited to subject matter at the borderline of trademark law but is indeed a problem of a general nature. Within German law, as a typical example of a continental European *droit d'auteur* system with an enumerative catalogue of statutory exceptions, this problem was not easy to solve. In particular, all arguments to extend other statutory provisions on exceptions to the facts of the case were (rightly) dismissed by the court;[121] in this respect, the judgment is an exemplary case to illustrate the disadvantages of a rigid statutory system of exceptions without a broadly formulated 'fair use' provision.[122] However, as the problem was due to an inconsistency *within* the inner system of copyright as such and as the problem was *not* limited to trademark protected subject matter, consequently, the German Federal Court of Justice had nonetheless to rely upon a copyright 'internal' solution. Thus, while upholding the principled limitation to acts of distribution, the court effectively *extended* the copyright doctrine of exhaustion to reproductions merely accessory to legal distribution acts, such as reproductions needed for offers to the public or advertising activities of all sorts. This extension was based upon an essentially teleological argument with respect to the general objective of the principle of exhaustion, ie to allow the free movement of goods which have been put on the market with the initial consent of the right-holder.[123] While the prevailing opinion in German literature agreed with this teleological copyright 'internal' approach,[124] some authors have argued that a copyright 'external solution', based upon the application of unfair competition law to the attempt of the right-holder to directly interfere with the legal business activities of his or her competitors (on a lower market level), would have been the more consistent approach.[125] However, it might be doubted whether such an unfair competition law defence would be equally effective as the copyright 'internal' solution chosen by the Federal Court of Justice. Besides, whenever an inconsistency within the inner system of an IPR has a structural basis and therefore exists independently from particular market situations, such mischief should ideally be corrected *within* the system of this IPR. In contrast, the (less effective) application of competition and unfair competition law as an 'external' means of correcting dysfunctional effects of IPRs in the market should only be applied in cases where restrictions on freedom of competition follow from the exercise of the IPR in particular market situations. Therefore, it is submitted that the Federal Court of Justice's IPR 'internal' solution was actually correct and consistent.

Although the Federal Court of Justice therefore (correctly) did not treat the case as an overlap case in the strict sense, some general conclusions can certainly be drawn for genuine overlap problems with regard to the principle of exhaustion from the argumen-

[121] See *Parfumflakon*, Federal Court of Justice (2000) *Neue Juristische Wochenschrift* 3783, 3784.

[122] See Kur, 'Mehr als nur ein "Hauch von Dior"?' (n 120) 253 *et seq*; Ohly, 'Areas of Overlap Between Trade Mark Rights, Copyright and Design Rights in German Law' (n 8) 707.

[123] See *Parfumflakon*, Federal Court of Justice (2000) *Neue Juristische Wochenschrift* 3783, 3784.

[124] See especially Kur, 'Mehr als nur ein "Hauch von Dior"?' (n 120) 256: commendable approach in need (and capable) of further differentiation.

[125] Schricker, 'Anmerkung zu BGH 4.5.2000 I ZR 256/97 – *Parfumflakon*' (n 120) 463.

tative underpinnings of the decision. While the exhaustion principle exists throughout the different IPRs, its theoretical foundations and particular conditions and scope differ considerably. However, the formulation of the teleological underpinnings of the general principle by the Federal Court of Justice in *Parfumflakon* and other cases[126] make it clear that whenever a physical product has been put into circulation with the consent of the right-holder at a first stage of distribution, the subsequent free movement of that object must not be controlled or impeded by the holder of an IPR in that object. Hence, in German law the general principle of exhaustion prevails over attempts to undermine the objective of free movement of goods by misusing the system of overlapping IPRs. The solution of the Federal Court of Justice even goes beyond the *Evora* judgment by applying that principle also to purely national situations.

Apart from the issue of exhaustion, comparable problems can arise with respect to all those overlap situations where inconsistencies emerge between the different systems of exceptions to trademark law, on the one hand, and copyright law, on the other.[127] A case in point is the legal treatment of parody in German trademark and copyright law.[128] The underlying fundamental rights to freedom of the arts (German Constitution, article 5(3)) and freedom of speech (German Constitution, article 5(1)) provide the essential underpinning for the development of similar results in both trademark and copyright law. However, the doctrinal ways to reach these results differ considerably. In trademark law, the parody of well-known trademarks has been justified by the courts on the basis of a direct recourse to the freedom of the arts under German Constitution, article 5(3). By contrast, in copyright law, the provision on free transformative adaptations (Copyright Act, section 24) has been extended to cases where the underlying work is clearly identifiable in the satirical adaptation insofar as the satirical treatment establishes an 'inner distance' to its object.[129] Again, an underlying fundamental principle (ie the fundamental rights to freedom of expression and freedom of the arts) is thus implemented throughout the different IPRs, thereby bridging potential 'overlap gaps'.

B Negative and *A Posteriori* Overlaps

As has already been remarked here, trademark protection tends to undermine certain limitations of copyright protection (cf in particular above III.A(iv)). Above all, while the term of copyright protection is limited, trademark law can provide for unlimited protection of registered or unregistered marks which consist of previously copyright protected works (*a posteriori* overlap). The overlap is accepted because the scope of trademark protection is limited to particular uses[130] compared to the broader ambit of copyright protection.[131]

[126] See eg *OEM-Version*, Federal Court of Justice (2001) *Gewerblicher Rechtsschutz und Urheberrecht* 153 (on exhaustion of copyright).

[127] See further Ohly, 'Areas of Overlap Between Trade Mark Rights, Copyright and Design Rights in German Law' (n 8) 707.

[128] Ibid.

[129] *Gies-Adler*, Federal Court of Justice (2003) *Gewerblicher Rechtsschutz und Urheberrecht* 956 (on a satirical treatment of the German heraldic animal, the *Bundesadler*, which indeed is copyright protected).

[130] See with an example in point in the follow-up to the *Sky-Disk of Nebra* decision, von Linstow, 'Motezuma, Himmelsscheibe und das System der Schutzrechte' (n 62) 309. See further on the *Sky-Disk of Nebra* case below, n 134.

[131] See above section III.A(ii).

However, in parts of German literature it has been argued that in practice the trademark holder of a formerly copyright protected sign could easily try to prohibit uses beyond the limited scope of trademark protection by way of over-broad unjustified warnings against alleged infringers and could thus cause considerable chilling effects in the markets. For this reason a respective change of German law has been called for which would entirely exclude the trademark registration of formerly copyright protected works after the term of protection has expired.[132] However, even the proponents of this opinion predominantly accept the *de lege lata* position that copyright and trademark law protection may overlap with respect to formerly copyright protected works which have lapsed into the public domain.[133] This is consistent with the almost unanimous position in German case law and literature, which on principle accepts such overlaps, however seeks certain adjustments in particular situations where the two protection systems tend to undermine vital limitations of the other.

The cases in which trademarks partly remonopolise works or other creations and expressions (such as famous names, objects of cultural heritage, and so forth) which are in the public domain can be categorised in two main groups. First, there are situations where creations, as well as (pre)historic cultural artefacts[134] or other expressions, which

[132] Wandtke and Bullinger, 'Die Marke als urheberrechtlich schutzfähiges Werk' (n 60) 577.

[133] However, F Klinkert and F Schwab, 'Markenrechtlicher Raubbau an gemeinfreien Werken – ein richtungsweisendes Machtwort durch den Mona Lisa-Beschluß des Bundespatentgerichts?' (1999) *Gewerblicher Rechtsschutz und Urheberrecht* 1067, 1070, as well as partly (for merely descriptive signs) R Osenberg, 'Markenschutz für urheberrechtlich gemeinfreie Werke' (1996) *Gewerblicher Rechtsschutz und Urheberrecht* 101, 102, have argued that the registration of a work in the public domain would amount to a violation of public policy and would therefore have to be rejected under Trademark Act, s 8(2) (no 5). Against this see *Mona Lisa*, Federal Patents Court (1998) *Gewerblicher Rechtsschutz und Urheberrecht* 1021, 1023, arguing in an *obiter dictum* that such solution would also deprive the copyright holder of registering his own copyright protected work (during the protection term) as a trademark and that this result would be intolerable. Cf against the opinion of Klinkert and Schwab also W Nordemann, 'Mona Lisa als Marke – Re-Monopolisierung gemeinfreien Geistesgutes mit Hilfe des Markenrechts' (1997) *Wettbewerb in Recht und Praxis* 389, 391; F Seifert, 'Markenschutz und urheberrechtliche Gemeinfreiheit' (2000) *Wettbewerb in Recht und Praxis* 1014; L Kouker, 'Markenrechtlicher Schutz gemeinfreier Werke' in U Loewenheim (ed), *Urheberrecht im Informationszeitalter, Festschrift für Wilhelm Nordemann* (Munich, Beck, 2004) 394; Ohly, 'Von einem Indianerhäuptling, einer Himmelsscheibe, einer Jeans und dem Lächeln der Mona Lisa' (n 14) 207. Cf also against a violation of public policy in such cases, *Fr Marc*, Federal Patents Court (2000) 42 *Entscheidungen des Bundespatentgerichts* 275, 282.

[134] A case in point which stirred considerable debate in Germany was the conflict concerning the so-called *Sky-Disk of Nebra*, Regional Court Magdeburg (2004) *Gewerblicher Rechtsschutz und Urheberrecht* 672. The town of Querfurt, on whose territory the artefact had been found, and the German Federal State of Saxony-Anhalt filed conflicting applications for trademarks consisting of more or less abstract pictures of the disk. In this conflict, the right of Saxony-Anhalt prevailed because the state had earlier acquired a neighbouring right (under Copyright Act, s 71) through the first public presentation of the artefact and could hence claim the cancellation of the trademark of Querfurt according to the priority principle laid down in Trademark Act, s 13. However, the alleged existence of this neighbouring right was grounded on a broad construction of Copyright Act, s 71, which has widely been criticised in literature, see W Eberl, 'Himmelsscheibe von Nebra' (2006) *Gewerblicher Rechtsschutz und Urheberrecht* 1009; R Jacobs, 'Die Himmelsscheibe von Nebra' (n 8) 811 *et seq*. Nonetheless, the same result would arguably have followed from the physical property right to the Sky-Disk which the State of Saxony-Anhalt had acquired due to provisions of public law on prehistoric or cultural artefacts first discovered in the territory of the state; see especially on this aspect Eberl, 'Himmelsscheibe von Nebra' (above); Jacobs, 'Die Himmelsscheibe von Nebra' (n 8) 811 *et seq*. See most recently on the vaguely formulated and ambivalent provision of Copyright Act, s 71, *Motezuma*, Federal Court of Justice (2009) *Gewerblicher Rechtsschutz und Urheberrecht* 942. See further on the *Sky-Disk* case, the *Motezuma* case and Copyright Act, s 71, H-P Götting and A Lauber-Rönsberg, 'Der Schutz nachgelassener Werke' (2006) *Gewerblicher Rechtsschutz und Urheberrecht* 638.; H-P Götting and A Lauber-Rönsberg, 'Noch einmal: Die Himmelsscheibe von Nebra' (2007) *Gewerblicher Rechtsschutz und Urheberrecht* 303 (against Eberl); von Linstow, 'Motezuma, Himmelsscheibe und das System der Schutzrecht' (n 62) 303 *et seq*.

have never been copyright protected and thus are in the public domain, are registered as trademarks (negative overlap, see below section III.B(i)). Secondly, trademarks might be registered for copyright protected works (by the copyright holder if they are still protected or by any third person after expiry of the term of protection) in order to monopolise copyright protected works beyond their *term* of protection (*a posteriori* overlap, see below section III.B(ii)). Both these situations have been considered in German case law and literature.

(i) Negative Overlap

As regards the first situation, the most cited case in this respect is the *Mona Lisa* decision of the Federal Patents Court[135] which has sparked a lively discussion in the literature.[136] In its decision, the Federal Patents Court rejected the registration of a sign consisting of a photographic reproduction of the 'Mona Lisa' because, according to the court, the famous painting was already intensively used as a mere product decoration or for the sake of raising the general attention of the public and was therefore not capable of being perceived as an indication of origin (cf Trademark Act, section 8(2)(no 1) = Trademark Directive, article 3(1)(b)).[137] Moreover, the fact that the painting was widely used in marketing with regard to almost all categories of products and services would additionally trigger the absolute ground of refusal (Trademark Act, section 8(2)(no 3) = Trademark Directive, article 3(1)(d)) because the sign had therefore already become customary in the established practice of trade.

From this decision which has (at least in result) been widely accepted in legal doctrine,[138] a rule of thumb can be derived: the more famous a work of art is, the less likely it is to reach the threshold of distinctiveness.[139] However, such a rule of thumb leads to practically workable results only with respect to very famous works of art. Moreover, in a recent decision, the Federal Court of Justice has effectively overruled the rather restrictive attitude of the Federal Patents Court with regard to the registration of famous works of art or pictures of famous personalities. The case concerned the registration of an iconic photograph of German singer and actress Marlene Dietrich for a

135 *Mona Lisa*, Federal Patents Court (1998) *Gewerblicher Rechtsschutz und Urheberrecht* 1021.

136 See eg Klinkert and Schwab, 'Markenrechtlicher Raubbau an gemeinfreien Werken' (n 133) 1067 *et seq*; Kouker, 'Markenrechtlicher Schutz gemeinfreier Werke' (n 133) 385. See also the references in the following footnotes.

137 *Mona Lisa*, Federal Patents Court (1998) *Gewerblicher Rechtsschutz und Urheberrecht* 1021, 1022 *et seq*.

138 See eg Klinkert and Schwab, 'Markenrechtlicher Raubbau an gemeinfreien Werken' (n 133) 1067 *et seq*; F Klinkert and F Schwab, 'Signaturmarken: Ein Phänomen zwischen Urheberrecht, Persönlichkeitsrecht und Markenrecht' in C-O Lenz, W Thieme and F v Westphalen (eds), *Beiträge zum deutschen und europäischen Recht, Freundesgabe für Jürgen Gündisch* (Cologne/Berlin/Munich, Heymanns, 1999) 35; Kouker, 'Markenrechtlicher Schutz gemeinfreier Werke' (n 133) 385; Jacobs, 'Die Himmelsscheibe von Nebra' (n 8) 808; Ohly, 'Areas of Overlap Between Trade Mark Rights, Copyright and Design Rights in German Law' (n 8) 709; Ohly, 'Von einem Indianerhäuptling, einer Himmelsscheibe, einer Jeans und dem Lächeln der Mona Lisa' (n 14) 206 *et seq*; on the basis of a slightly different, more flexible argument, see also Sosnitza, 'Konvergenz und Interferenz der Schutzrechte' (n 8) 899 *et seq*; however, criticised as being undifferentiated (and in the result too restrictive) by Fezer, *Markenrecht* (n 70) s 8, para 292. To the contrary and (erroneously) criticising the Federal Patents Court for not applying Trademark Act, s 8(2)(no 5) (on public policy) to the application of famous works of art (which would result in a total exclusion of protection), Klinkert and Schwab, 'Markenrechtlicher Raubbau an gemeinfreien Werken' (n 133) 1070 *et seq*, 1073; against Klinkert and Schwab, see Seifert, 'Markenschutz und urheberrechtliche Gemeinfreiheit' (n 133) 1014.

139 Jacobs, 'Die Himmelsscheibe von Nebra' (n 8) 809; see also Ohly, 'Areas of Overlap Between Trade Mark Rights, Copyright and Design Rights in German Law' (n 8) 709.

broad variety of products and services. The Federal Patents Court had rejected the application entirely on the grounds of lack of distinctiveness (cf Trademark Act, section 8(2) (no 1)[140]) partly because of mere descriptive character with regard to certain kinds of products (Trademark Act, section 8(2)(no 2)[141]), and partly because the relevant public would regard this very famous photograph only as a means of raising general attention.[142] With regard to particular products, such as picture postcards and other reproductions of the photographic image, according to the Federal Patents Court, the sign would be identical to the marketed product and therefore not be capable of trademark protection under Trademark Act, section 3(2)(no 1).[143] The Federal Court of Justice only partly upheld this decision.[144] First, the application of Trademark Act, section 3(2)(no 1) to certain kinds of products which in fact essentially consisted of mere reproductions of the photograph, such as picture postcards, was (rightly) not accepted by the Federal Court of Justice. Other than with respect to three-dimensional marks, the sign in this case, ie the representation of the picture of Marlene Dietrich as such, could be distinguished from the concrete products, and therefore could not be regarded as consisting exclusively of a shape which resulted from the nature of the good itself. Secondly, with regard to distinctiveness and descriptive character, the Federal Court of Justice further differentiated the restrictive views of the Federal Patents Court concerning pictures of famous personalities: With respect to certain categories of products without any inner relationship to the fame and background of the person in question, the sign could well be used in a way which would make it capable of being perceived as an identification of origin. For example, the use of the sign as a label on the inside of garments could be understood by the relevant public as an identification of origin. Therefore, distinctive character could not be denied a priori with regard to such classes of products or services, where uses as an identification of origin were at least realistically conceivable.

As this *ratio decidendi* can obviously be transposed to signs which consist of more or less famous works of art, a differentiated position of German courts can be expected in the future. Applications will tend to fail for all those classes of products where the use of the sign amounts to a mere descriptive use or is only capable of raising the public's general attention. However, for other categories of products or services, where use of the sign as an identification of origin is practically conceivable, such signs might reach the minimum level of (concrete) distinctive character needed for registration. Against this background, certain public domain uses of works of art or cultural artefacts can obviously be impeded by trademark holders under German trademark law. Nevertheless, where famous works of art are systematically registered for the sole purpose to extract licence fees for uses already established in the markets, this might in extreme cases amount to bad faith and such applications should be rejected on the grounds of

[140] See Trademark Directive, art 3(1)(b).

[141] Ibid art 3(1)(c).

[142] See *Porträtfoto Marlene Dietrich*, Federal Patents Court (2006) *Gewerblicher Rechtsschutz und Urheberrecht* 333.

[143] See Trademark Directive, art 3(1)(e).

[144] See *Marlene-Dietrich-Bildnis*, Federal Court of Justice (2008) *Gewerblicher Rechtsschutz und Urheberrecht* 1093, with critical annotation by H-P Götting. See further on trademark applications concerning names and pictures of famous personalities on the basis of the acknowledgment of a property right to one's personality the older landmark case, *Marlene Dietrich*, Federal Court of Justice (2000) *Neue Juristische Wochenschrift* 2195; H-P Götting, 'Persönlichkeitsmerkmale von verstorbenen Personen der Zeitgeschichte als Marke' (2001) *Gewerblicher Rechtsschutz und Urheberrecht* 615.

Trademark Act, section 8(2)(no 10) or be cancelled subject to the general conditions of Trademark Act, section 50(3) (if the trademark was already registered).[145] Moreover, arguably, in such extreme cases the defendant in infringement proceedings could raise the general civil law defence of abuse of rights under Civil Code, section 242.[146] In addition, systematic interference with the trade of other companies might amount to unfair competition under Unfair Competition Act, sections 3, 4(no 10).

While this provisional result might not seem entirely satisfying, it also has to be considered that trademarks consisting of famous works of art, even when they are registered in the first place, will typically be of very little distinctive character. Therefore the scope of protection, typically limited in these cases to use of the sign where likelihood of confusion is established,[147] will be correspondingly narrow.[148] In particular with regard to outstandingly famous works, the fame of the work as such will usually outshine the use as an identification of origin; if such works are successfully registered as trademarks at all, the scope of protection will actually be limited to identical or almost identical use of the sign as an identification of origin for identical or very similar products and services.[149] Moreover, the scope of protection may also be limited by the requirement of a 'trademark use' in cases of an ornamental use of picture marks, for example on T-shirts, etc.[150]

(ii) A Posteriori *Overlap*

Basically, the same principles apply to situations where a work was registered as a trademark during copyright protection, and where trademark law is subsequently used by the right-holder to perpetuate protection beyond the limited term of copyright (*a posteriori* overlap).[151] Again, the overlap is accepted by the predominant opinion in German case law and literature because of the comparatively limited applicability and scope of trademark protection.[152] Some authors have argued that trademark protection should be further limited in this field by way of an analogy to Trademark Act, section 23, which

[145] See Ohly, 'Areas of Overlap Between Trade Mark Rights, Copyright and Design Rights in German Law' (n 8) 709; Ohly, 'Von einem Indianerhäuptling, einer Himmelsscheibe, einer Jeans und dem Lächeln der Mona Lisa' (n 14) 207. See in German case law *Classe E*, Federal Court of Justice (2001) *Gewerblicher Rechtsschutz und Urheberrecht* 242 on trademark registrations in bad faith in a case where a private person had systematically registered certain already established signs in order to demand money from certain large companies, such as DaimlerChrysler; see also the brief *obiter* remarks in *Mona Lisa*, Federal Patents Court (1998) *Gewerblicher Rechtsschutz und Urheberrecht* 1021, 1023.

[146] Considered and (sceptically) left open in *Johann Sebastian Bach*, Higher Regional Court Dresden (2001) *Neue Juristische Wochenschrift* 615, 617, in a case where the right-holder had systematically registered names and pictures of famous personalities (inter alia of the famous composer Johann Sebastian Bach) and had no discernible own business activity at all, apart from the practice of sending warnings to third parties using these names in the course of trade.

[147] Because of its little distinctive character, such trademarks will very seldom qualify for protection as a well-known trademark under Trademark Act, s 14(2)(no 3). See Ohly, 'Von einem Indianerhäuptling, einer Himmelsscheibe, einer Jeans und dem Lächeln der Mona Lisa' (n 14) 208.

[148] See especially *Johann Sebastian Bach*, Higher Regional Court Dresden (2001) *Neue Juristische Wochenschrift* 615, 617. See also Ohly, 'Areas of Overlap Between Trade Mark Rights, Copyright and Design Rights in German Law' (n 8) 708.

[149] See Ohly, 'Von einem Indianerhäuptling, einer Himmelsscheibe, einer Jeans und dem Lächeln der Mona Lisa' (n 14) 208.

[150] See above n 103.

[151] See Jacobs, 'Die Himmelsscheibe von Nebra' (n 8) 807 *et seq*.

[152] See already Nordemann, 'Mona Lisa als Marke – Re-Monopolisierung gemeinfreien Geistesgutes mit Hilfe des Markenrechts' (n 133) 389.

implements Trademark Directive, article 6(1) on the limitation of the effects of trademark protection with respect to certain necessary indicative uses where these are in accordance with honest practices in industrial or commercial matters.[153] From this it follows that all 'public domain' uses which are in compliance with honest practices and which do not lead to a risk of confusion or detriment to the repute of the trademark will be deemed justified by the fact that the work had previously lapsed into the copyright public domain. However, it is very doubtful whether such broad, analogous application of Trademark Act, section 23 would be accepted by the Court of Justice. Moreover, as the scope of protection of trademarks consisting of copyright protected works will very often be rather limited, it seems that there is in any event little room for the additional application of Trademark Act, section 23 in this field. The benefit from the doubtful analogy to Trademark Act, section 23 would therefore be very limited.[154] Consequently, the predominant opinion in German doctrine is opposed to this solution. Instead, the general principles which have been described aboveare applied.

The most relevant German case on *a posteriori* overlap situations in German law concerned a particularity of German trademark law, ie the *sui generis* protection of work titles under Trademark Act, section 5(3). Trademark Act, section 5(3) provides for protection of titles of print media, films, musical works (including sound broadcastings of all sorts[155]) or dramas, as well as any comparable work,[156] on the condition that the title possesses a (very low) minimum degree of distinctiveness.[157] Such title protection might obviously outlast the limited term of copyright protection of an *underlying* (titled) work as such. Thus, in the often-quoted *Winnetous Rückkehr* (*Winnetou's Return*) case of the Federal Court of Justice,[158] the claimant relied upon title protection for the work title 'Winnetou', who is a famous literary character in the novels by Karl May, a popular writer of adventure stories for young people in Germany. The defendant had published an adaptation of the novels about the Indian chief Winnetou under the title *Winnetous Rückkehr* (*Winnetou's Return*). The underlying novels by Karl May were already part of the public domain since Karl May died in 1912. However, according to the Federal Court of Justice, title protection was still available for the work title 'Winnetou'. In the opinion of the Federal Court of Justice, such protection would not be in conflict with the fact that the underlying work had lapsed into the public domain because German title protection was limited to the title in its function as an identification *of the underlying work*. Hence, the identical work could in fact be published by any third person under the original title after expiry of copyright protection because such publication would *not* violate the title protection right, as the original work would indeed be published under the original title. According to the court, the scope of protection of work titles would usually be extremely narrow because of the low level of distinctiveness represented by such titles.

[153] A Nordemann in U Loewenheim (ed), *Handbuch des Urheberrechts*, 2nd edn (Munich, Beck, 2010) s 83, para 55.

[154] See Jacobs, 'Die Himmelsscheibe von Nebra' (n 8) 808; see also Nordemann, 'Mona Lisa als Marke – Re-Monopolisierung gemeinfreien Geistesgutes mit Hilfe des Markenrechts' (n 133) 392.

[155] See *Radio Stuttgart*, Federal Court of Justice (1993) *Gewerblicher Rechtsschutz und Urheberrecht* 769.

[156] According to German case law work title protection might eg also cover titles of games, see *Zappel-Fisch*, Federal Court of Justice (1993) *Gewerblicher Rechtsschutz und Urheberrecht* 767.

[157] See eg *1, 2, 3 im Sauseschritt*, Federal Court of Justice (2002) *Gewerblicher Rechtsschutz und Urheberrecht* 1083, 1084; *Auto Magazin*, Federal Court of Justice (2002) *Gewerblicher Rechtsschutz und Urheberrecht* 176.

[158] *Winnetous Rückkehr* (*Winnetous Return*), Federal Court of Justice (2003) *Gewerblicher Rechtsschutz und Urheberrecht* 440, 441.

Thus, the title of the adaptation in question in the *Winnetou* case, ie '*Winnetous Rückkehr*', was held not to infringe the titles '*Winnetou I–III*' of the original *Winnetou* series because even a minimal addition (such as 'Return of . . .') sufficed to be outside the scope of protection of the original work title, limited to identical or almost identical titles. In sum, the Federal Court of Justice, while accepting the *a posteriori* overlap of protection in principle, limited its consequences to an acceptable minimum of identical uses of the title for different works leading to manifest risk of confusion of the public with respect to the represented work.

Another question relating to the *sui generis* protection of work titles after the expiry of copyright protection of the underlying work is whether it is permissible to use a still protected work title not only for the originally titled work itself but for other works with a close or loose connection to the original work, such as translations, screen or theatre adaptations or any other modification. This question is of particular relevance for free uses of a work in the public domain which are regarded as promoting cultural development and whose proliferation is therefore intended through the legislator's limiting of the time of copyright protection. In a case concerning the screen adaptation of Jack London's *The Sea-Wolf*, the Higher Regional Court Munich ruled that the use of the German translation of the original title *Der Seewolf* for a movie which was an adaptation of the original novel was covered by the exception in Trademark Act, section 23(no 2) as a descriptive use and therefore does not violate the work title protection.[159] This result, according to which the use of a still protected work title is descriptive as long as it can be considered as informative of a central characteristic of the new work due to its connection to the original work, is entirely satisfactory. By this means, on the one hand, a confusion of the association of the still protected work title can be avoided, while it is possible, on the other hand, to use the title for free uses of the work in the public domain.

The same problem might arise when work titles or famous characters of a film or a novel are registered as trademarks, as it is still common practice.[160] Such trademark protection would certainly be broader than the *sui generis* title protection right, as it would, first, not be limited to the identification of the underlying work but would also serve as an identification of origin; and secondly, it would arguably be broader in scope with regard to likelihood of confusion of the public in certain cases.[161] In these cases, trademark law might indeed undermine inherent limitations of copyright protection to a certain extent. This is not only as regards the limited term of protection (as the most striking example), but also limitations on copyright such as free (transformative) use under Copyright Act, section 24, if an adaptation (for example a satirical treatment) totally and creatively deviates from the original work (therefore as a free use not violating copyright under Copyright Act, section 24), nonetheless making use of the same fictitious characters in the title (and therefore potentially infringing trademark rights).[162] Again, the Federal Court of Justice tries to limit such problems to a minimum by taking a rather restrictive attitude with respect to applications for registration of work titles. However,

[159] See *Der Seewolf*, Higher Regional Court Munich (2009) *Zeitschrift für Urheber- und Medienrecht* 654.

[160] See Sosnitza, 'Konvergenz und Interferenz der Schutzrechte' (n 8) 899.

[161] See Ohly, 'Areas of Overlap Between Trade Mark Rights, Copyright and Design Rights in German Law' (n 8) 708; Ohly, 'Von einem Indianerhäuptling, einer Himmelsscheibe, einer Jeans und dem Lächeln der Mona Lisa' (n 14) 211 *et seq*.

[162] See further on this issue of differently drafted exceptions to protection in the two fields of law below section III.A(iv).

the standards have recently become more liberal in this area. Thus, in a case related to the *Winnetous Rückkehr* case, the court rejected an application for the trademark 'Winnetou' on the grounds of the *generic character* of the name (which had in fact become the established symbol for a reputable Indian chief because of the outstanding popularity of the novels among German youngsters and was therefore devoid of distinctive character under Trademark Act, section 8(2)(no 1)).[163] More recent case law along these lines suggests that non-generic work titles might well be registered as trademarks subject to the general conditions.[164] Hence, the older (more restrictive) position that work titles, as a rule, have to be regarded as descriptive per se because the general public does not understand them as indications of origin but rather as mere (albeit distinctive) descriptions of the work *as such*[165] has not been upheld.[166] The resulting overlap problem cannot be denied.[167] It is submitted that the area of prospective overlap should be reduced as far as possible by a rather restrictive practice with regard to the registration of work titles or fictitious characters as trademarks. Moreover, restrictive standards with respect to the assessment of the distinctiveness of such signs can help to reduce inner contradictions between the systems of copyright and trademark law as they will lead to an extremely limited scope of protection of such trademarks. In German literature, it has even been suggested to categorically deny trademark protection to work titles under Trademark Act, section 8(2)(no 2) because of their per se descriptive character with regard to the category of respective works, such as books, films, and so forth, and to rely exclusively on the *sui generis* title protection right in this field.[168]

IV. TRADEMARKS AND DESIGNS

A Simultaneous Overlap

(i) General Principles

The high practical relevance of the overlap of design protection and trademark protection for the two- or three-dimensional appearance of the whole or part of a product (cf Design Act, section 1(no 1)) is obvious.

[163] See *Winnetou*, Federal Court of Justice (2003) *Gewerblicher Rechtsschutz und Urheberrecht* 342. Critically with regard to this argument, see Ohly, 'Von einem Indianerhäuptling, einer Himmelsscheibe, einer Jeans und dem Lächeln der Mona Lisa' (n 14) 213 *et seq*.

[164] See recently *Der kleine Eisbär*, Federal Patents Court (2006) *Gewerblicher Rechtsschutz und Urheberrecht* 593; *Petterson und Findus*, Federal Patents Court, 29 W (Pat) 179/04 (available at www.juris.de).

[165] *Sherlock Holmes*, Federal Court of Justice (1958) *Gewerblicher Rechtsschutz und Urheberrecht* 354; *POINT*, Federal Court of Justice (1982) *Gewerblicher Rechtsschutz und Urheberrecht* 431; *Guldenburg*, Federal Court of Justic, (1993) *Gewerblicher Rechtsschutz und Urheberrecht* 692; see Ohly, 'Von einem Indianerhäuptling, einer Himmelsscheibe, einer Jeans und dem Lächeln der Mona Lisa' (n 14) 213.

[166] Critically Ohly, 'Von einem Indianerhäuptling, einer Himmelsscheibe, einer Jeans und dem Lächeln der Mona Lisa' (n 14) 213 *et seq*.

[167] The Federal Court of Justice considered to solve the problem by applying Trademark Act, s 23(no 2) in infringement cases when use of a title, registered as a trademark, was merely indicative. See *Bücher für eine bessere Welt*, Federal Court of Justice (2000) *Gewerblicher Rechtsschutz und Urheberrecht* 882, 883.

[168] Ohly, 'Von einem Indianerhäuptling, einer Himmelsscheibe, einer Jeans und dem Lächeln der Mona Lisa' (n 14) 214. However, clearly against such an approach in principle, *Bücher für eine bessere Welt*, Federal Court of Justice (2000) *Gewerblicher Rechtsschutz und Urheberrecht* 882.

The objectives and conditions of protection of both areas of law differ only in theory. In design law the crucial condition of protection (besides novelty) is 'individual character'. This presupposes the existence of creative elements which are different from the existing average standard of the overall appearance of products in the relevant sector of the market and which therefore allow for a certain distinctive originality of the protected product design. In trademark law, the main condition of protection is the 'distinctive character' of the protected sign. In practice, the potential convergence of these criteria cannot be denied. While in design law, the analysis of differences with regard to the overall impression of the object in question amounts to a certain extent to an assessment of (abstract) distinctive quality,[169] in certain fields of trademark law practice tends to assess distinctive character based on the criteria of originality and individual creativity which, strictly speaking, rather belong to the area of design protection.[170] Although, according to the essential function of trademark protection, the decisive criterion would have to be the perception of the relevant public (respectively resulting from previous formative influences on the consumer habits in the relevant sector), in practice, the criteria of originality or substantial difference, compared to average day-to-day design, play an important role to establish distinctive character.

Whilst the objectives and conditions of protection thus tend to overlap to a certain extent, the scope of protection is clearly different in the two fields of law. In particular, again (potentially perpetual) trademark protection threatens to undermine the limitations of the term of protection in design law, ie a (harmonised) maximum term of 25 years for registered German designs under Design Act, section 27(2).[171] This situation calls for a delineation rule with regard to the imminent overlap of trademark and design protection.

However, the (harmonised) provisions of Trademark Act, section 3(2)(no 1)–(no 3) (exclusion of shapes, resulting from the nature of, or giving substantial value to, the goods)[172] which could at least partly serve this purpose are of comparatively little relevance in German trademark practice.[173] The very objective of these provisions – ie the protection of the interest of the general public to prevent potentially perpetual restrictions to freedom of competition with regard to whole categories of products as a consequence of trademark rights being extended to the category of a product as such or its essential value for the public[174] – is exactly in line with the fundamental balance of inter-

169 See Schulze, in Dreier and Schulze, *Urheberrechtsgesetz* (n 31) s 2, para 177. Eichmann, in Eichmann and von Falckenstein, *Geschmacksmustergesetz* (n 53) s 2, para 12 *et seq*.

170 Kur, 'Funktionswandel von Schutzrechten' (n 10) 43.

171 See Design Directive, art 10.

172 See Trademark Directive, art 3(1)(e).

173 See rejecting the application of Trademark Act, s 3(2), eg *Stabtaschenlampen*, Federal Court of Justice (2001) *Wettbewerb in Recht und Praxis* 265; *Rado-Uhr*, Federal Court of Justice (2001) *Wettbewerb in Recht und Praxis* 269; *Gabelstapler*, Federal Court of Justice (2001) *Gewerblicher Rechtsschutz und Urheberrecht* 334; *Gabelstapler II*, Federal Court of Justice (2004) *Gewerblicher Rechtsschutz und Urheberrecht* 502; *Stabtaschenlampen II*, Federal Court of Justice (2004) *Gewerblicher Rechtsschutz und Urheberrecht* 506; *Fronthaube*, Federal Court of Justice (2008) *Gewerblicher Rechtsschutz und Urheberrecht* 71; and most recently *Milchschnitte*, Federal Court of Justice (2008) *Gewerblicher Rechtsschutz und Urheberrecht* 510 (rejecting the application of Trademark Act, s 3(2)(no 1) with regard to the specific shape of a light brown sponge cake with a creamy white milk filling which is extremely popular in Germany and had indeed acquired distinctive character in consequence of use).

174 See most recently *Milchschnitte*, Federal Court of Justice (2008) *Gewerblicher Rechtsschutz und Urheberrecht* 510, 511, referring to the Court of Justice's case law on Trademark Directive, art 3(1)(e). See further on the situation in chapter 3, section IV.B(i) above.

ests underpinning the overlap of trademark and design protection. However, from the perspective of German doctrine, the main practical problem of the provision is its rigid legal consequence:[175] if a sign consists exclusively of a shape which results from the nature of the goods themselves or which gives substantial value to the goods, trademark registration is *entirely* excluded. In particular, this consequence cannot be overcome by establishing distinctive character in consequence of use[176] (cf Trademark Act, section 8(3)).[177] It is this very inflexibility which has crucially limited the practical impact of this provision in German law.[178] In fact, only the alternative on the exclusion for shapes of products which are necessary to obtain a *technical* result (see Trademark Act, section 3(2)(no 2)[179]), has hitherto been effectively applied by the German Federal Court of Justice and the Federal Patents Court,[180] following the Court of Justice.[181] However, a recent decision of the Federal Court of Justice on trademark protection of Lego bricks has denied trademark registration for the square form of these bricks on the grounds of Trademark Act, section 3(2)(no 1) because, according to the court, the square form as such was characteristic for any such toy. Moreover, the court held that the 'pimple' structure on the upper side of the bricks was determined by the technical interlocking function of the bricks, and therefore excluded from trademark protection under Trademark

[175] See Kur, 'Funktionswandel von Schutzrechten' (n 10) 35 *et seq*. From recent German literature see especially T Sambuc, 'Designschutz mit Markenrecht?' (2009) *Gewerblicher Rechtsschutz und Urheberrecht* 333, 337.

[176] See Trademark Directive, art 3(3).

[177] The recent *Milchschnitte* decision (Federal Court of Justice (2008) *Gewerblicher Rechtsschutz und Urheberrecht* 510) provides an excellent example: trademark registration for the immensely popular *Milchschnitte* sponge-cake would have been excluded totally had the Federal Court of Justice applied Trademark Act, s 3(2) to a trademark application with regard to the three-dimensional shape of this product. However, the court did not apply this provision to the application. By contrast, the subsequent assessment of the case with regard to the element of *distinctive character* allowed the court to take into account the distinctive character which the particular shape of the *Milchschnitte* cake had acquired through use in the German market, where the cake is heavily advertised and extremely popular among the relevant public (cf Trademark Act, s 8(3)). See along the same lines with regard to Trademark Act, s 8(2)(no 2), *Porsche Boxster*, Federal Court of Justice (2006) *Gewerblicher Rechtsschutz und Urheberrecht* 679 (on the shape of the *Porsche Boxster* sports-car where the absolute ground of refusal of descriptiveness was again overcome by use on the basis of the extensive advertising campaign which had accompanied the market introduction of the new model). See also with a very similar reasoning (rejecting the application of Trademark Act, s 3(2), while in this case restrictively applying Trademark Act, s 8(2)(no 1) on distinctive character) *Motorhaube*, Federal Court of Justice (2008) *Gewerblicher Rechtsschutz und Urheberrecht* 71 (on the trademark application for the typical shape of the car bonnets of a German producer of luxury cars).

[178] See Ohly, 'Designschutz im Spannungsfeld von Geschmacksmuster-, Kennzeichen- und Lauterkeitsrecht' (n 33) 733 *et seq*. See also Sambuc, 'Designschutz mit Markenrecht?' (n 175) 337, who deplores the paradigm shift towards Trademark Act, s 8(2)(no 1), (no 2) and argues in favour of a more principled solution on the level of general eligibility of designs for trademark protection.

[179] See Trademark Directive, art 3(1)(e) second alternative.

[180] See *Scherkopf* and *Rasierer mit drei Scherköpfen*, Federal Court of Justice (2006) *Gewerblicher Rechtsschutz und Urheberrecht* 588 and 589, implementing the Court of Justice's decision in *Philips/Remington*. See also *Lego-Baustein*, Federal Patents Court (2007) *Gewerblicher Rechtsschutz und Urheberrecht* 786, denying registration of the shape of the Lego brick because this shape was essentially necessary to obtain a technical result. A decision of the Federal Patents Court, in which the registration of a three-dimensional trademark was (also) cancelled due to the provisions of Trademark Act, s 3(2)(no 3) (*Kraftfahrzeugteile*, Federal Patents Court (2005) *Gewerblicher Rechtsschutz und Urheberrecht* 333, 335) was specifically not upheld insofar as it was based on this provision; see Federal Court of Justice (2008) *Gewerblicher Rechtsschutz und Urheberrecht* 71, 73. See also chapter 3, section IV.B(i) above.

[181] See Case C-299/99 *Koninklijke Philips Electronics v Remington Consumer Products* [2002] ECR I-05475. See further chapter 3, section IV.B(i) above.

Act, section 3(2) (no 2).[182] If this decision marks the beginning of a more vital role for Trademark Act, section 3(2) in the regulation of the trademark/design overlap, this development should be met with approval.

While Trademark Act, section 3(2) has hitherto been of only limited relevance for the regulation of the overlap of trademark and design protection in German law, German courts, acting along the lines of the leading judgments of the Court of Justice in this field,[183] attempt to take into account the interests of the general public in freedom of competition by applying rather strict criteria to the assessment of distinctiveness, and in particular to the element of potentially descriptive character of signs consisting of the shape or packaging of a good[184] (cf Trademark Act, section 8(2)(no 1) and (no 2)).[185] The main advantage of this solution lies in the possibility to overcome these grounds of refusal on the basis of the relevant consumers' perception in the relevant sector when signs have acquired distinctive character *through use* (Trademark Act, section 8(3)) and German courts have in fact readily applied this provision.[186]

Hence, in practice, generally speaking, the threshold of protection in German trademark law[187] is distinctly above the level of 'distinctive character' in German design protection.[188] However, with regard to designs, which have actually acquired distinctive character among the relevant consumers through use, advertising campaigns, media coverage, and so forth, this more restrictive threshold does not apply. In more recent German literature it has correctly been argued that this rather liberal attitude concerning the general eligibility of established product designs for trademark protection has to be balanced in subsequent infringement cases by the application of consistent and strict criteria with regard to the elements of use of the sign in the course of trade,[189] and in particular of the likelihood of confusion.[190] Beyond cases of identical use, these

[182] Decision of 16 July 2009 – I ZB 53/07 and 55/07, Federal Court of Justice (2010) *Markenrecht* 131; see further on the decision L Jaeschke, 'Kein Markenschutz für den Legostein' (2010) *Markenrecht* 167. See also below section VIII.B(ii) on the issue of (recently denied) unfair competition protection against the imitation of Lego bricks by competitors. See chapter 3, section IV.B(i) and VI.B(i) above.

[183] See chapter 3, section IV.B(i) above.

[184] See Trademark Directive, art 3(2)(b) and (c).

[185] See *Käse in Blütenform*, Federal Court of Justice (2004) *Gewerblicher Rechtsschutz und Urheberrecht* 329, 330; *Transformatorengehäuse*, Federal Court of Justice (2004) *Gewerblicher Rechtsschutz und Urheberrecht* 507, 509; *Porsche Boxster*, Federal Court of Justice (2006) *Gewerblicher Rechtsschutz und Urheberrecht* 679; *Motorhaube*, Federal Court of Justice (2008) *Gewerblicher Rechtsschutz und Urheberrecht* 71; *Milchschnitte*, Federal Court of Justice (2008) *Gewerblicher Rechtsschutz und Urheberrecht* 510. From recent German literature see especially Sambuc, 'Designschutz mit Markenrecht?' (n 175) 336. See also above section III.A(i).

[186] See eg *Porsche Boxster*, Federal Court of Justice (2006) *Gewerblicher Rechtsschutz und Urheberrecht* 679; *Milchschnitte*, Federal Court of Justice (2008) *Gewerblicher Rechtsschutz und Urheberrecht* 510.

[187] See also above section III.

[188] See Ohly, 'Areas of Overlap Between Trade Mark Rights, Copyright and Design Rights in German Law' (n 8) 710.

[189] H Köhler, 'Der Schutz vor Produktnachahmung im Markenrecht, Geschmacksmusterrecht und neuen Lauterkeitsrecht' (2009) *Gewerblicher Rechtsschutz und Urheberrecht* 445, also emphasises the strict condition of the necessary use of the protected three-dimenional sign by the infringer as a trademark in the course of trade. See further S Zöllner, 'Wann wird eine dreidimensionale Marke markenmäßig verwendet, wenn sie selbst das Produkt ist? Überlegungen zu einem blauen Schaf' (2010) *Gewerblicher Rechtsschutz und Urheberrecht Praxis im Immaterialgüter- und Wettbewerbsrecht* 144. Concerning the use of a product design 'as a trademark in the course of trade' and the relevance of the degree of distinctiveness of the protected trademark in that regard, see *Rillenkoffer*, Federal Court of Justice (2008) *Gewerblicher Rechtsschutz und Urheberrecht* 793. See further on the element of use as a trademark in German trademark law above at n 103.

[190] See especially Sambuc, 'Designschutz mit Markenrecht?' (n 175) 337.

conditions of the protection of three-dimensional trademarks regarding product designs should indeed be consistently and strictly applied; in particular, the specific distinctive elements of such three-dimensional marks should be identified very thorougly by the infringement courts in order to prospectively guarantee a reasonable leeway for free competition in the area of product design.

(ii) Multiple Right-holders

With regard to the remaining field of overlap, ie distinctive product designs, the conflict rules for multiple right-holder situations in harmonised German law again follow the general *principle of priority*. Under Trademark Act, section 13(2)(no 6),[191] if a registered trademark infringes an earlier design right as one of the 'other industrial property rights' in the sense of that provision,[192] the holder of this right can claim the cancellation of that mark. Consequently, the registration of a protected design as a trademark requires the acquisition of the necessary rights of use.

Conversely, if a registered design infringes an earlier distinctive sign, the owner of that sign can claim for the cancellation of the subsequent design right under Design Act, section 34(no 1).[193]

B Negative and *A Posteriori* Overlaps

It is submitted that the application of strict criteria with regard to distinctiveness and descriptive character is at least in principle capable of regulating the overlap of trademark and design law in a balanced way if the scope of protection in infringement cases is correspondingly limited.[194] This takes into account that usually the public will not perceive the average design of a typical product as an identification of origin, and is at the same time balanced by the possibility to overcome this a priori rule through establishing actual distinctive character as a consequence of use.

In particular, the *a posteriori* overlap issue in this field, ie the fundamental difference with regard to the respective term of protection, can be consistently resolved on this basis. Thus, for new designs of mere 'individual character', German design protection provides for a registered investment protection right with a 25 year term of protection, while the potentially perpetual protection of trademark law is reserved for designs which can indeed serve as an identification of origin due to their significant departure from the usual average designs in the relevant sector, or which in fact already do so due to the actual establishment of distinctive character through use in the relevant market.

[191] The provision makes use of the optional possibility for the Member States to provide for such a ground of cancellation, provided for in Trademark Directive, art 4(4)(c)(iv).

[192] The Explanatory Memorandum to the German trademark law explicitly mentions design rights as one of the 'other rights' which may conflict with a trademark registration, see Explanatory Memorandum, BT-Drs 12/6581 of 14 January 1994, 74.

[193] The provision makes use of the option for the Member States provided for in Design Directive, art 11(2)(a).

[194] See also Ohly, 'Areas of Overlap Between Trade Mark Rights, Copyright and Design Rights in German Law' (n 8) 710.

V. TRADEMARKS AND PATENTS

Usually, trademarks and patents do not overlap as the registration of a patent for a technical invention does not necessarily coincide with corresponding trademark protection.

A Simultaneous Overlap

In fact, the only genuine overlap problem in this field can result from the attempt to register certain product shapes which are necessary to obtain a *technical* result (a patentable invention) as a three-dimensional mark. However, in these situations Trademark Act, section 3(2)(no 2)[195] (on the exclusion of trademark protection for shapes of products which are necessary to obtain a technical result) has been effectively applied by the German Federal Court of Justice and the Federal Patents Court[196] of late, following the relevant case law of the Court of Justice.[197] Thus, the overlap is effectively regulated by this specific provision in (harmonised) German trademark law.[198]

B Negative Overlap

There are no specific cases or literature on negative overlap issues between trademarks and patents in German law.

C *A Posteriori* Overlap

However, other protection overlaps can occur (incidentally) when trademark protection is acquired for a sign which is used for the marketing of an inventive product or process. In these situations, such a sign can particularly easily develop into a common denomination of the patented product or service, if due to patent protection the product or service as such is not subject to effective competition.[199] Patent protection thus effectively becomes a springboard for establishing the sign as a denomination of the patented product or service. After expiry of patent protection, the question arises whether trademark protection has to end accordingly.[200]

[195] See Trademark Directive, art 3(1)(e) second alternative.

[196] See *Scherkopf* and *Rasierer mit drei Scherköpfen*, Federal Court of Justice (2006) *Gewerblicher Rechtsschutz und Urheberrecht* 588 and 589, implementing the Court of Justice's decision in *Philips/Remington*. See also *Lego-Baustein*, Federal Patents Court (2007) *Gewerblicher Rechtsschutz und Urheberrecht* 786, denying registration of the shape of the Lego brick because this shape was essentially necessary to obtain a technical result. This decision was upheld by the Federal Court of Justice in the very recent decision of 16 July 2009 – I ZB 53/07 and 55/07 (2010) *Markenrecht* 131. See also chapter 3, section IV.B(i) above.

[197] See Case C-299/99 *Koninklijke Philips Electronics v Remington Consumer Products* [2002] ECR I-05475. See chapter 3, section IV.B(i) above.

[198] See further Kur, 'Funktionswandel von Schutzrechten' (n 10) 37 *et seq*; see further chapter 3, section IV.B(i) above.

[199] See Sosnitza, 'Konvergenz und Interferenz der Schutzrechte' (n 8) 897; Götting, *Gewerblicher Rechtsschutz* (n 8) s 5, para 46.

[200] See in particular the old authority of the *Antiformin*, Imperial Court (Reichsgericht), RGZ 100, 3, 8.

This is because otherwise there might be situations in which the (time-limited) monopoly of the former patent holder for offering the product or service is extended by way of trademark protection for the established denomination of the product. However, in principle, after expiry of patent protection competitors are at liberty to offer the same product or service under another name. Therefore, competition with regard to the product or service in question will in most cases only be restrained effectively by trademark protection when the sign has also developed into a generic denomination of the product or service as such. Thus, for most cases the solution to these overlaps lies in substantive trademark law, because if the sign develops into a generic term, trademark protection lapses and the cancellation of the trademark can be ordered under Trademark Act, section 49(2)(no 1).[201]

VI. COPYRIGHT AND PATENTS

The issue of a potential overlap of copyright and patent protection has been discussed in German literature, mainly[202] in relation to computer programs.[203]

A Simultaneous Overlap

(i) Subject Matter of Protection

At the outset, it has been remarked in German literature that from a theoretical viewpoint, copyright protection and patents in this area do not overlap in a strict sense as they have different objects of protection.[204] While (harmonised) copyright law protection of computer programs as works of literature, under Copyright Act, section 69a, protects the concrete *expression* of a computer program in any form, software patents for computer program related inventions protect the underlying technical functionality, including equivalent solutions to reach the same functional result.[205] Indeed, it was the limitation of copyright protection with regard to more abstract procedures, ideas and

[201] See Götting, *Gewerblicher Rechtsschutz* (n 8) s 5, para 46.

[202] Another specific issue is the question of copyright protection for patent applications and specifications. In German law, copyright protection is granted to the applications and patent specifications if the protection requirements are met. The overlap is accepted as the subject matter of copyright and patent protection is different in this field. However, for use of copyright protected material in the context of a patent application, as a general rule, the exception in favour of use in the framework of administrative proceedings (Copyright Act, s 45) will apply. Once the application is published by the Patent Office, it is regarded as an 'official work' in the sense of Copyright Act, s 5(2) and thus copyright protection lapses entirely.

[203] See Kur, 'Funktionswandel von Schutzrechten' (n 10) 39 *et seq*; T Dreier, 'Sinnvolle Reichweite des Patentschutzes – Software' in M Eifert and W Hoffmann-Riem (eds), *Geistiges Eigentum und Innovation* (Berlin, Duncker & Humblot, 2008) 245; M Leistner, 'Computerimplementierte Erfindungen im System des "Geistigen Eigentums"' in O Depenheuer and K-N Peifer (eds), *Geistiges Eigentum: Schutzrecht oder Ausbeutungstitel?* (Berlin, Heidelberg, Springer, 2008) 188, 192; M Hoffmann, *Mehrfachschutz geistigen Eigentums im deutschen Rechtssystem* (Munich, Utz, 2008) 141.

[204] See Kur, 'Funktionswandel von Schutzrechten' (n 10) 39; see also Leistner, 'Computerimplementierte Erfindungen im System des "Geistigen Eigentums"' (n 203) 188, 195.

[205] See Leistner, 'Computerimplementierte Erfindungen im System des "Geistigen Eigentums"' (n 203) 195 *et seq*.

principles[206] which put some pressure on patent law practice to gradually extend the realm of patent protection with regard to computer programs.[207] Thus, from a theoretical viewpoint, the object of protection is straightforwardly different.

However, the *factual* overlap of copyright and patents in this area leads to certain inconsistencies. These inconsistencies, caused by this overlap in a wider sense, mainly concern the issues of the object and the resulting scope of protection, ownership of rights, and the respective provisions on exceptions to protection. In all these areas, the two fields of law differ substantially.

(ii) Protection Requirements and Resulting Area of Overlap

In German copyright law, the main condition of protection for computer programs as works of literature is simple individuality of the program (Copyright Act, section 69a(3)). As a result of the full harmonisation of the condition of protection through the Software Directive 2009/24/EC, the protection threshold in German case law is decidedly low.[208] For more complex computer programs, simple individuality is even prima facie assumed by the courts.[209] As a result, copyright protection for computer programs is the rule, while non-eligibility for protection is the exception.[210] In light of this low threshold for protection in copyright law, the area of potential overlap mainly depends on the specific conditions of protection for computer program related inventions in patent law.

In German patent law, the condition of the necessary technical character of a patentable invention (Patent Act, section 1(1)),[211] and the exclusion of 'computer programs as such' from patent protection in Patent Act, section 1(3) (no 3),[212] are interpreted in a way which leads to practical results, essentially similar to the European 'middle course' of the EPO Boards of Appeal with respect to the eligibility of inventions related to computer programs for patent protection. However, the theoretical paths to reach this result differ substantially. After the initially very reserved attitude of the German Federal Court of Justice towards the eligibility of computer programs for patent protection due to their lack of technical character,[213] later decisions took a more liberal attitude. Effectively they adopted the theory of the EPO Boards of Appeal that with regard to technical character the claim should be considered 'as a whole' in such a way that it would not be possible to interpret the claim by focussing on the *essence* of the invention for the sake of assessing its technical character (*Gesamtbetrachtungslehre*).[214] This approach would in fact have

[206] In German law, the idea/expression dichotomy of Anglo-American copyright (underlying the Software Directive's definition of the object of protection) is mirrored by the doctrine of the dichotomy of content and concrete form. See eg T Dreier, in T Dreier and G Schulze, *Urheberrechtsgesetz*, 3rd edn (Munich, Beck, 2008) s 69a, para 20.

[207] See also ibid s 69a, para 2.

[208] See especially *Buchhaltungsprogramm*, Federal Court of Justice (1994) *Gewerblicher Rechtsschutz und Urheberrecht* 39, adjusting the threshold of protection to the European standard even before the explicit implementation of the Directive in Copyright Act, s 69a(3); *Programmfehlerbeseitigung*, Federal Court of Justice (2000) *Gewerblicher Rechtsschutz und Urheberrecht* 866, 868.

[209] See *Fash 2000*, Federal Court of Justice (2005) *Gewerblicher Rechtsschutz und Urheberrecht* 860.

[210] See Dreier, in Dreier and Schulze, *Urheberrechtsgesetz* (n 206) s 69a, para 26, referring to the Explanatory Memorandum to Copyright Act, s 69a.

[211] Corresponding to EPC Art 52(1).

[212] Corresponding to EPC Art 52(2)(c).

[213] See eg *Flugkostenminimierung*, Federal Court of Justice (1986) *Gewerblicher Rechtsschutz und Urheberrecht* 531.

[214] See eg *Tauchcomputer*, Federal Court of Justice (1992) *Gewerblicher Rechtsschutz und Urheberrecht* 430.

led to a very broad patentability for software related inventions, because merely minor and incidental technical elements, which do not constitute the main core of the invention, could thus have fulfilled the condition of the technical character of the computer program related invention as a whole. However, more recent decisions emphasise that, because of the explicit exclusion of computer programs as such from patent protection, the *characteristic* elements of an invention related to computer programming have to contribute to the *solution of a concrete technical problem*[215] in order to fulfil the requirement of technical character. This slightly resembles the differentiated attitude of the later EPO jurisdiction which applies similar criteria by focussing on the technical elements of the invention when assessing the necessary inventive step in the area of computer programs. In any event, the practical results are similar: computer program related inventions can be patented (as product and also as process patents) if they involve a genuine, and not merely incidental, technical element, such as in the area of computer controlled industrial process and control technology,[216] or if they at least simulate a traditionally technical process,[217] or if they involve an additional technical element, using the system resources of the programmed computer itself in a technically more effective way than before. In these areas of more or less 'technical' computer programs, protection by patent and by copyright law will very often factually overlap.

(iii) Scope of Protection

The object and consequently the scope of protection in copyright law is limited to the concrete form of the computer program as such. Consequently, the different programming of similar technological or functional routines will usually be outside the scope of copyright protection as it does not constitute an 'adaptation' of the concrete form of the original. In German law, an adaptation of a computer program will only be covered by copyright if essential structural elements, fulfilling the requirement of individual character, have been used by the infringer and can still be clearly distinguished in the adaptation. From this it follows that a certain inner relation between the *degree of individuality* of the computer program and the resulting scope of protection with regard to more or less direct adaptations exists in German copyright law: a higher degree of individuality will lead to a broader scope of copyright with regard to the distinction between free use and adaptations which violate the copyright of the original right-holder.

By contrast, patent protection for inventions relating to computer programs will usually be broader. Depending on the formulation and interpretation of the patent claims, patent protection will often cover a broad array of functional equivalents to the inventive elements

[215] See eg *Suche fehlerhafter Zeichenketten*, Federal Court of Justice (2002) *Gewerblicher Rechtsschutz und Urheberrecht* 143; *Elektronischer Zahlungsverkehr*, Federal Court of Justice (2004) *Gewerblicher Rechtsschutz und Urheberrecht* 667; *Anbieten interaktiver Hilfe*, Federal Court of Justice (2005) *Gewerblicher Rechtsschutz und Urheberrecht* 141; *Rentabilitätsermittlung*, Federal Court of Justice (2005) *Gewerblicher Rechtsschutz und Urheberrecht* 143.

[216] See very early decision in *Antiblockiersystem*, Federal Court of Justice (1980) *Gewerblicher Rechtsschutz und Urheberrecht* 849.

[217] See *Logikverifikation*, Federal Court of Justice (2000) *Gewerblicher Rechtsschutz und Urheberrecht* 498. For a comprehensive analysis of the patentability of computer programs and business methods in Germany, Europe and the US, see M Leistner and M Kleinemenke, 'The Impact of Institutional Design on the Development of Patent Law: Patentability of Computer Programs and Business Methods in Europe and the United States of America as a Topical Example' (2010) 2 *Zeitschrift für Geistiges Eigentum/Intellectual Property Journal* 273, 300 *et seq*.

of a computer program. Therefore, arguably, patent protection for incrementally small inventive steps in the area of computer programs leads to counter-productive overprotection, inhibiting technological progress in the field. Compared to copyright law, which in German practice essentially provides for an effective anti-piracy protection against identical copying, patents on software are therefore more problematic from an economic viewpoint, in particular with regard to the field of open source software development.[218]

The general discussion of the resulting controversy concerning the pros and cons of software patents in Germany and Europe is far beyond the limited topic of protection overlaps in the field and will therefore not be considered here. However, it has to be remarked that with regard to the theoretically different delineation of the object and scope of protection in the two areas of law, German authors have argued that patent law's doctrine on equivalents could indeed draw some inspiration from the flexible and proportional relationship between the degree of individuality and the scope of protection in copyright law. Similarly, the interpretation of patent claims of computer program related patents with regard to functional equivalents could at least be constructed more in light of the *degree* of the inventive step involved in the underlying patents. Consequently, the claims should be constructed rather narrowly in many cases, thereby gradually reducing the problems which patents for very small, incremental technological developments in the field might cause.[219]

(iv) Ownership of Rights

From a practical viewpoint, the factual overlap of copyright and patents with regard to 'technical' computer programs also causes some problems concerning the ownership of the respective rights. Implementing Software Directive, article 2(3), Copyright Act, section 69b provides for a comprehensive transfer of economic copyrights to the employer with regard to computer programs made for hire. Consequently, an additional compensation for the creation of copyright protected computer programs by employees in the course of their employment is not provided for in copyright law.[220]

By contrast, if the invention underlying a computer program, developed by an employee, is also eligible for patent protection, the German Employees' Inventions Act 2002 (Arbeitnehmererfindungsgesetz, last revised in 2009[221]) applies. Under section 9 of the Act, an employee has a right to additional compensation for inventions, made in the course of his or her employment, provided the employee has notified the invention to his or her employer and the employer has subsequently claimed the invention for its own use. Thus, under certain conditions the Employees' Inventions Act breaches the rule in

[218] See specifically from German economic literature B Brügge, D Harhoff and A Picot *et al*, *Open Source Software – Eine ökonomische und technische Analyse* (Berlin, Springer, 2004); A Picot and M Fiedler, 'Open Source Software und proprietäre Software' in O Depenheuer and K-N Peifer (eds), *Geistiges Eigentum: Schutzrecht oder Ausbeutungstitel?* (Berlin, Heidelberg, Springer, 2008) 165, both on the problematic implications of patent protection for the open source sector. See also Leistner, 'Computerimplementierte Erfindungen im System des "Geistigen Eigentums"' (n 203) 188, 190 and 209 *et seq*, with more comprehensive references.

[219] Dreier, 'Sinnvolle Reichweite des Patentschutzes – Software' (n 203) 245, 265; Leistner, 'Computerimplementierte Erfindungen im System des "Geistigen Eigentums"' (n 203) 188, 220.

[220] See *Wetterführungspläne I*, Federal Court of Justice (2001) *Gewerblicher Rechtsschutz und Urheberrecht* 155; *Wetterführungspläne II*, Federal Court of Justice (2002) *Gewerblicher Rechtsschutz und Urheberrecht* 149. See further A Brandi-Dohrn, 'Arbeitnehmererfindungsschutz bei Softwareerstellung' (2001) *Computer und Recht* 285; F Bayreuther, 'Zum Verhältnis zwischen Arbeits-, Urheber- und Arbeitnehmererfindungsrecht – Unter besonderer Berücksichtigung der Vergütungsansprüche des angestellten Softwareerstellers' (2003) *Gewerblicher Rechtsschutz und Urheberrecht* 570.

[221] Gesetz zur Vereinfachung und Modernisierung des Patentrechts of 31 July 2009, art 7, BGBl I/2009, 2521.

Copyright Act, section 69b, namely, that the creation of copyright protected computer programs is already compensated by the employees' salary. Instead, if such computer program is also eligible for patent protection, and is claimed by the employer, an additional compensation will have to be paid to the employee, according to the detailed provisions of the Employees' Inventions Act.[222] Moreover, according to the legal fiction in Employees' Inventions Act, section 6(2),[223] inventions made in the course of an employment will be regarded as claimed by the employer, if the employer has not expressly released the invention in text form within a period of four months beginning with the date on which the invention was notified to the employer. Consequently, if a computer program eligible for patent protection is notified to the employer by an employee, a claim for additional compensation will arise if the employer remains inactive.

Finally, Employees' Inventions Act 2009, section 20 provides for an additional claim for extra compensation in cases of certain so-called 'working improvements at operational level' (*betriebliche Verbesserungsvorschläge*) which are developed by employees.[224] In these cases, the creation of certain 'improvements', suggested by an employee, would entitle the employee to additional compensation on the condition that the employer subsequently uses this particularly suggested working improvement in his or her operations, and that the position which results from this use is 'comparable' to the position of an IP right-holder. However, if such suggested working improvements consist of computer programs, in the light of the work made for hire rule in copyright, the employer comprehensively acquires the economic rights to use such solutions in any case. Therefore, the Federal Court of Justice has clarified in two more recent judgments that if such suggestions for working improvements in the form of copyright protected computer programs are used by the employer, an additional claim of the employee for particular compensation is not justified.[225] According to that case law, a claim for additional compensation can only arise if the computer program incorporates specific technical contributions by the employee which go beyond the mere programming effort which is protected by copyright.

(v) Incongruous Exceptions to Protection

Undoubtedly, the overlap of copyright and patents with regard to computer programs eligible for patent protection has its most problematic implications in the area of exceptions to protection. On the one hand, the tailor-made European and German provisions on copyright protection for computer programs provide a comparatively wide array of mandatory exceptions to protection, partly reiterating the numerous general exceptions to copyright protection, partly reflecting specific interests of the users, the competitors and the general public in the area of computer program protection.[226] On the other hand, specific provisions on the exceptions to patent protection are rare in German, European and international patent law. In fact, specific interests of users, competitors and the

[222] See further Bayreuther, 'Zum Verhältnis zwischen Arbeits-, Urheber- und Arbeitnehmererfindungsrecht' (n 220) 578.

[223] This new provision is the core part of the recent 2009 revision of the Employees' Inventions Act 2002, see Gesetz zur Vereinfachung und Modernisierung des Patentrechts of 31 July 2009, art 7, BGBl I/2009, 2521.

[224] See further Bayreuther, 'Zum Verhältnis zwischen Arbeits-, Urheber- und Arbeitnehmererfindungsrecht' (n 220) 580.

[225] See *Wetterführungspläne I*, Federal Court of Justice (2001) *Gewerblicher Rechtsschutz und Urheberrecht* 155; *Wetterführungspläne II*, Federal Court of Justice (2002) *Gewerblicher Rechtsschutz und Urheberrecht* 149.

[226] Such as the exception in favour of decompilation, necessary to achieve interoperability (under Copyright Act, s 69e).

general public are hardly reflected in the system of patent law by way of exceptions,[227] while the exceptions to copyright, in principle, reflect such interests in a differentiated, sector-specific way.

Nonetheless, at the moment it can hardly be argued (and indeed it has not been argued in German literature) that the exceptions to copyright are undermined entirely by the overlapping system of patent protection with its narrower and less developed provisions on exceptions. This is mainly because the overlap clearly covers only certain computer program related inventions on the condition that they involve a more or less distinct technical element. Thus, it has been argued that in the area of patent law, the principal way to take specific interests of competitors, users and the general public into account is by constructing the conditions of patentability rather narrowly, in order to prevent patent protection from essentially undermining the comparatively more balanced and differentiated system of copyright protection.[228] A further extension of patentability in this area would dramatically increase the danger of unintended patent infringement, while copyright protection does not pose this danger because of the comparatively limited scope of protection with regard to adaptations. Thus, the danger of undermining the balanced system of exceptions to copyright by extensively granting patents for software related inventions adds an argument against a further broadening of patent protection in the field to the ongoing heated discussions about the pros and cons of patents for computer program related inventions. By contrast, it clearly does not justify the (analogous) transposition of certain computer program specific exceptions from copyright to the field of patent law.

From a policy perspective, recent contributions in German literature on overlaps between patents and other areas of IPR protection have raised the question of whether the system of exceptions in patent law should be expanded *de lege ferenda*, either horizontally or specifically with regard to computer program related inventions and other specific sectors.[229] Hitherto, the only really relevant exception to patent protection for computer program related inventions is the exception in favour of certain experimental uses under Patent Act, section 11(no 2). However, this provision is constructed rather narrowly because it is only applicable for research purposes relating to further research into the very essence of the patented invention. In certain sector-specific areas, such as drug patents and 'green' biotechnology, the exception has therefore already been adjusted and cautiously expanded to cover certain specific research interests of competitors, beyond mere research into the very essence of the invention.[230] In general, it has been argued in German literature that a cautious broadening of the exception with regard

[227] Instead, in patent law, the comparatively short term of protection, as well as the obligation to disclose the invention as a condition of patentability, take the interests of competitors, users and the general public into account. Against this background, it seems particularly problematic that patent protection for computer related inventions usually does not require the disclosure of the source code of a computer program because the program as such is not the object of the patented invention. See further Leistner, 'Computerimplementierte Erfindungen im System des "Geistigen Eigentums"' (n 203) 188, 220.

[228] See ibid 183, 205 *et seq*, 221 *et seq*.

[229] See Dreier, 'Sinnvolle Reichweite des Patentschutzes – Software' (n 203) 245, 265; Leistner, 'Computerimplementierte Erfindungen im System des "Geistigen Eigentums"' (n 203) 188, 221 *et seq*; see also K Blind, J Edler, R Nack and J Straus (eds), *Softwarepatente – Eine empirische Analyse aus juristischer und ökonomischer Perspektive* (Heidelberg, Springer, 2003) 207, proposing further research into a possible future need for a specific exception in favour of OSS-development in patent law.

[230] See Patent Act, s 11(no 2)(a) and (b). See further M Haedicke, 'Biotechnologische Erfindungen und patentrechtliche Schrankenregelungen – ein Statement' in M Eifert and W Hoffman-Riem (eds), *Geistiges Eigentum und Innovation* (Berlin, Duncker & Humblot, 2008) 239 *et seq*.

to certain research activities, not limited to research relating to the very essence of the patented invention as such, possibly combined with a remuneration claim for the right-holder, should be considered for the future, at least insofar as such a solution could be achieved within the framework of international conventions.[231]

In fact, the inspiration for these suggestions has been drawn from the comparatively further developed system of limitations and exceptions in favour of certain non-commercial research and other activities in German copyright law.[232] Thus, from a policy perspective, the system of exceptions to copyright distinguishably influences the system of exceptions to patent law because of the factual overlap of the two IPRs. Hence, instead of solving the overlap issue by strictly delineating both areas of law, from the perspective of German doctrine, the overlap helps to identify and possibly correct certain (sector-specific) imbalances within the patent system by changing that system itself.

B Negative and *A Posteriori* Overlaps

There is no case law or specific literature on negative or *a posteriori* overlap issues between copyrights and patents in German law.

VII. PATENTS AND PLANT VARIETY RIGHTS

Concerning the potential overlap of patent protection and plant variety protection, Patent Act, section 2a provides for an explicit delineation of both areas of law: In principle, patent protection is not available for biological processes to breed individual plant varieties (Patent Act, section 2a(1)). However, according to the 2005 implementation of the Biotechnology Directive into German patent law, and following the *Novartis II* ruling by the European Patent Office,[233] patents which embrace plant varieties can be granted if the claimed invention is not limited to an *individual* plant variety (Patent Act, section 2a(2)(no 1)).[234] Thus, patent protection and plant variety protection overlap with regard to such broader claims, in particular in the field of 'green' biotechnology. While with regard to ownership and exhaustions, no specific overlap problems have been identified for that field in German literature or case law, the overlap clearly leads to frictions[235] concerning the different scope of exceptions to protection in the two systems.

[231] Dreier, 'Sinnvolle Reichweite des Patentschutzes – Software' (n 203) 245, 263 *et seq*; Leistner, 'Computerimplementierte Erfindungen im System des "Geistigen Eigentums"' (n 203) 188, 221 *et seq*; see also Haedicke, 'Biotechnologische Erfindungen und patentrechtliche Schrankenregelungen – ein Statement' (n 230) 239, 243.

[232] Dreier, 'Sinnvolle Reichweite des Patentschutzes – Software' (n 203) 245, 251; Leistner, 'Computerimplementierte Erfindungen im System des "Geistigen Eigentums"' (n 203) 188, 221 *et seq*.

[233] *Novartis II*, EPO Enlarged Board of Appeal of 20 December 1999, G 1/98, OJ EPO 2000, 111.

[234] M Haedicke, 'Die Harmonisierung von Patent- und Sortenschutz im Gesetz zur Umsetzung der Biotechnologie-Richtlinie' (2005) *Mitteilungen der deutschen Patentanwälte* 241, 242; see further M Kock, S Porzig and E Willnegger, 'The Legal Protection of Plant-Biotechnological Inventions and Plant Varieties in Light of the EC Biopatent Directive' (2006) *International Review of Intellectual Property and Competition Law* 135, 146; K-J Mellulis, in G Benkard (ed), *Patentgesetz*, 10th edn (Munich, Beck, 2006) s 2a, para 16 *et seq*; see also R Anderson and W Tilmann, 'Patent Protection for Plants: The Novartis Ruling by the European Patent Office' (2000) *Mitteilungen der deutschen Patentanwälte* 192.

[235] See Haedicke, 'Die Harmonisierung von Patent- und Sortenschutz im Gesetz zur Umsetzung der Biotechnologie-Richtlinie' (n 234) 242. See further Kock, Porzig and Willnegger, 'The Legal Protection of Plant-Biotechnological Inventions and Plant Varieties in Light of the EC Biopatent Directive' (n 234).

In fact, the German legislator of 2005 has partly aligned the provisions on exceptions to plant variety rights and to patents. The so-called 'farmer's privilege' which is traditionally provided for in the area of plant variety protection (see Plant Variety Protection Act, section 10(4)–(6))[236] and which entitles the farmer under certain conditions to use the harvested seeds on his or her own land for the next crop,[237] has been transposed to patent law, where Patent Act, section 9c now provides for a corresponding exception to patent protection.[238]

By contrast, the breeders' exception (Plant Variety Protection Act, section 10a(1)(no 3)), according to which plant variety protection does not cover the use of protected varieties for breeding, developing or discovering *other* plant varieties and their commercialisation, on the condition that the new varieties are not essentially derived varieties,[239] has not been transposed to patent law. Instead, in an attempt to balance the involved interests, the German legislator provided for a new exception to patent protection in favour of the *use* of biological material for breeding, discovering or developing new plant varieties (Patent Act, section 11(no 2a)). The new exception is provided for in the systematic context of the traditional patent law privilege for research relating to the subject matter of the invention (cf Patent Act, section 11(no 2)). The general exemption of such experimental uses from the scope of patent protection is expressly broadened by the new provision to cover uses which are not limited to further research into the subject matter of the invention. Instead, *any* use of the patented biological material (even as a research tool or as a mere basic material) for the breeding, discovering or developing of new plant varieties is exempted.[240] Thus, the new exception also covers commercial development of a new variety *with* (ie merely making use of) the subject matter of the patent protected invention.[241] In this respect, the exception to patent protection is even broader than the traditional exception to plant variety protection.[242] However, in contrast to the breeders' privilege in the area of plant variety protection, the exception to patent law does not cover the commercialisation of the resulting newly developed plant varieties. While the commercial development of new plant varieties as such is broadly exempted from the scope of patent protection, the commercial use of such new varieties will fall within the scope of patent protection of the initial varieties, used for their breeding, discovering or developing, on the condition that the new variety represents a dependent invention.

[236] The provision corresponds to art 14 of Council Regulation (EC) 2100/94 of 27 July 1994 on Community plant variety rights [1994] OJ L227/1.

[237] See further Kock, Porzig and Willnegger, 'The Legal Protection of Plant-Biotechnological Inventions and Plant Varieties in Light of the EC Biopatent Directive' (n 234) 144 *et seq*.

[238] See critically (because of the detrimental effect on the incentives for innovation in the area of plant varieties and because of the systematic argument that subsidies for farmers should, if at all, rather be granted in a more direct way by the state) Haedicke, 'Biotechnologische Erfindungen und patentrechtliche Schrankenregelungen – ein Statement' (n 230) 239, 243; see also Haedicke, 'Die Harmonisierung von Patent- und Sortenschutz im Gesetz zur Umsetzung der Biotechnologie-Richtlinie' (n 234) 245 *et seq*.

[239] See Plant Variety Protection Act, s 10(2) on essentially derived varieties, which essentially genetically conform with the initial variety. See further Haedicke, 'Die Harmonisierung von Patent- und Sortenschutz im Gesetz zur Umsetzung der Biotechnologie-Richtlinie' (n 234) 244; Kock, Porzig and Willnegger, 'The Legal Protection of Plant-Biotechnological Inventions and Plant Varieties in Light of the EC Biopatent Directive' (n 234) 142 *et seq*.

[240] See Haedicke, 'Die Harmonisierung von Patent- und Sortenschutz im Gesetz zur Umsetzung der Biotechnologie-Richtlinie' (n 234) 244 *et seq*.

[241] See Kock, Porzig and Willnegger, 'The Legal Protection of Plant-Biotechnological Inventions and Plant Varieties in Light of the EC Biopatent Directive' (n 234) 142 *et seq*.

[242] See critically ibid 150 *et seq*; Haedicke, 'Biotechnologische Erfindungen und patentrechtliche Schrankenregelungen – ein Statement' (n 230) 242.

Undoubtedly, this new specific provision of German patent law, exempting any use of the patented invention for breeding, discovering or developing new plant varieties, is hard to justify with respect to any technological, economic or ethical conditions, specific to that particular area of technology.[243] Consequently, the Biotechnology Directive had not provided for any such specific exception.[244] In particular, it seems hardly justifiable that patent law should exempt uses of the patented biological material as a mere *tool* for the development, breeding or discovery of new plant varieties. This indeed amounts to a royalty free compulsory licence for this specific area of innovative activity.[245] However, there is no sound reason for such subject matter specific research-tool privilege[246] in patent law.[247]

The resulting inconsistency within the current system of German patent law follows from the fact that the new specific exemption from patent protection only for uses in the context of breeding activities is an ad hoc legislative reaction, attempting to reach a balanced compromise between the system of exceptions to patent law and the differently drafted exceptions to plant variety protection. Therefore, from a more general viewpoint, the legal situation in this area is typical of an overlap situation which identifies certain more general inconsistencies in a particular area of intellectual property: This is because the system of exceptions to protection in patent law is in general remarkably underdeveloped compared to other branches of intellectual property. Similar to the situation with regard to the overlap between copyright law and patent law in the field of computer program protection, the overlap between patents and plant variety protection, and in particular the legislator's attempt to bridge the gap between both systems in that specific area, thus underlines a more general systematic shortcoming of the patent system. It might well be considered whether exceptions in favour of certain privileged research uses, beyond the traditional 'experimental use' exception, limited to research into the subject matter of the invention, should be generally provided for in patent law.[248] In particular, if a carefully delineated research exception were combined with a statutory claim for remuneration, such carefully balanced limitation of exclusive patent protection with regard to certain research activities might arguably better serve the main objective of patent law, ie to foster technological innovation, than the current state of the law.

However, this question is of a general nature and more (empirical) research is needed to answer it profoundly.[249] Therefore, the attempt of the German legislator to provide for a subject matter specific balancing of interests in order to bridge the gap between the exceptions to plant variety protection and the exceptions to patent protection, respectively, was bound to fail, and is correctly criticised as being inconsistent with the systematic framework of patent law.[250] From a more general viewpoint, however, the overlap

[243] Haedicke, 'Biotechnologische Erfindungen und patentrechtliche Schrankenregelungen – ein Statement' (n 230) 243.

[244] See Kock, Porzig and Willnegger, 'The Legal Protection of Plant-Biotechnological Inventions and Plant Varieties in Light of the EC Biopatent Directive' (n 234) 152.

[245] See ibid 152.

[246] See in general on the problem of research tools and patent law, H Holzapfel, 'Die patentrechtliche Zulässigkeit der Benutzung von Forschungswerkzeugen' (2006) *Gewerblicher Rechtsschutz und Urheberrecht* 10.

[247] See Haedicke, 'Biotechnologische Erfindungen und patentrechtliche Schrankenregelungen – ein Statement' (n 230) 243.

[248] See ibid 244.

[249] See ibid.

[250] See ibid 243; cf Kock, Porzig and Willnegger, 'The Legal Protection of Plant-Biotechnological Inventions and Plant Varieties in Light of the EC Biopatent Directive' (n 234) 150, contrary to Haedicke, proposing a careful legislative limitation of the new breeders' exception in patent law.

with plant variety protection, which has led to this premature legislative activity, helps to identify a possible imbalance *within* the patent system as such.

VIII. INTELLECTUAL PROPERTY RIGHTS AND UNFAIR COMPETITION

A Protection Against Unfair Product Imitation in German Unfair Competition Law

The German Act against Unfair Competition of 2004 (Giesetz gegen den unlauteren Wettbewerb, UWG) has been revised in 2008 to implement the Unfair Commercial Practices Directive 2005/29/EC (UCPD).[251] The Act combines a wide umbrella general clause on the prohibition of unfair competition with different specific torts of unfair competition which constitute 'examples' of such unfair commercial practices.[252]

Among these examples, the Act contains a specific tort of unfair imitation of products or services of a competitor (Unfair Competition Act, section 4(no 9)). In fact, Unfair Competition Act, section 4(no 9) represents the statutory codification of the traditional 'German' tort of unfair product imitation, while the European consumer protection requirements of the UCPD have been implemented into German law in a different provision.[253] Under Unfair Competition Act, section 4(no 9), protection against unfair imitation is granted to products or services which feature a certain minimum degree of so-called 'competitive originality', ie which are perceived as a distinct product or service by the customers. However, the identification of a specific origin is not a precondition of competitive originality in that sense; instead, a certain minimum degree of distinctive originality or quality of the product or service is sufficient.[254] Whenever this general condition is fulfilled, the offer of imitations of a competitor's products or services is regarded as unfair if it either encompasses an element of customer confusion as to the commercial origin of the imitated product or service (Unfair Competition Act, section 4(no 9)(a)); or if it unfairly utilises or damages the goodwill of the imitated product or service (section 4(no 9)(b)); or if the basic material or knowledge, required for the imitation, has been acquired by illicit or dishonest means, such as the breach of trade secrets, confidentiality agreements and the like (section 4(no 9)(c)). The three additional elements of unfair imitation apply alternatively, ie if only one of the elements is present, the imitation will be regarded as unfair. Moreover, according to the so-called 'theory of interdependency', the degree of competitive originality and the intensity of one of the additional elements of unfairness, embodied in a particular case, are interdependent in the sense that a lower degree of one of the additional elements of unfairness can be compensated by a higher degree of competitive originality, and vice versa.[255]

[251] See BGBl I/2008, 2949.

[252] Moreover, in the 2009 revision, an Annex to Unfair Competition Act, s 3(3) has been introduced which implements Annex I to the Unfair Commercial Practices Directive on per se prohibited misleading and aggressive commercial practices.

[253] Unfair Competition Act, s 5(2). See Begründung zum Regierungsentwurf des UWG 2008 (Explanatory Memorandum to the 2008 Act), BT-Drs 16/10145, 17.

[254] See Ohly, 'Areas of Overlap Between Trade Mark Rights, Copyright and Design Rights in German Law' (n 8) 706.

[255] H Köhler, in H Köhler and J Bornkamm, *Gesetz gegen den unlauteren Wettbewerb*, 28th edn (Munich, Beck, 2010) s 4, para 9.69.

Furthermore, the list of additional factors in Unfair Competition Act, section 4(no 9) is non-exhaustive: Even if none of the additional elements of unfairness is present in a particular case, an imitation can still be regarded as unfair under Unfair Competition Act, sections 3, 4(no 10) because of the resulting unfair interference with a competitor's trade.[256] In fact, in this latter group of cases, the older case law of the Federal Court of Justice repeatedly granted protection against the unjustified, and in particular direct[257] and systematic imitation[258] of products or services, featuring a certain degree of competitive originality, even without any additional element of unfairness present.[259] Thus, German unfair competition case law granted protection against the imitation of products of high quality or originality *as such* in certain sectors. On that basis, unfair competition, for example, played a vital role for the seasonal protection of fashion novelties against imitation without an element of confusion.[260] In later cases, the Federal Court of Justice has constructed this latter group of cases very narrowly, although it has upheld the existence of such a tort of mere misappropriation in principle.[261] Nonetheless, it has to be noted that on the basis of the protection of goodwill (Unfair Competition Act, section 4(no 9)(b)), and also because of the theory of interdependency in the construction of the different elements of section 4(no 9), the tort of unfair imitation in German unfair competition law is still capable of protecting certain products or services of substantial quality or originality against imitations by competitors, even if such imitations do not cause any confusion in the marketplace.

In addition to Unfair Competition Act, section 4(no 9)(a), Unfair Competition Act, section 5(2) will (cumulatively) apply to cases which embody an element of risk of confusion of the customers. The provision prohibits the marketing of a product which creates confusion with a product, trademark, or trade name of a competitor and implements UCPD, article 6(2)(a) on certain misleading commercial practices. In German law, the provision is not limited to B2C relationships; instead, the German legislator extended the Directive's provisions on misleading commercial practices to B2B relationships. Thus, the provisions on misleading advertising in German law are of a general nature and equally encompass commercial practices, directed to private consumers or commercial customers. However, as a matter of course in assessing the element of misrepresentation, the standards in the two areas may still differ if the advertisement is directed to a certain, distinguishable public. Finally, Unfair Competition Act, section 6 provides for the conditions of admissible comparative advertising, and thus implements the mandatory requirements of Directive 2006/114/EC concerning misleading and comparative advertising in this area.

[256] See *Handtaschen*, Federal Court of Justice (2007) *Gewerblicher Rechtsschutz und Urheberrecht* 795, para 50.

[257] The main example is identical imitation by technical means without any substantial change by the infringer, see eg *Kunststoffzähne*, Federal Court of Justice (1969) *Gewerblicher Rechtsschutz und Urheberrecht* 618, on the imitation of artificial dents by recasting them.

[258] This was particularly the case if a large variety of the products of a competitor was imitated systematically, see eg *Similischmuck*, Federal Court of Justice (1960) *Gewerblicher Rechtsschutz und Urheberrecht* 244, on the systematic imitation of a variety of pieces of jewellery by a competitor.

[259] Ohly, 'Areas of Overlap Between Trade Mark Rights, Copyright and Design Rights in German Law' (n 8) 706; see further Köhler, in Köhler and Bornkamm, *Gesetz gegen den unlauteren Wettbewerb* (n 255) s 4, para 9.63 *et seq*.

[260] See *Modeneuheit*, Federal Court of Justice (1973) *Gewerblicher Rechtsschutz und Urheberrecht* 478. See further below section VIII.B(iii).

[261] See *Handtaschen*, Federal Court of Justice (2007) *Gewerblicher Rechtsschutz und Urheberrecht* 795, para 50. See further below section VIII.B(iii).

B Overlap Between Unfair Competition and Intellectual Property Rights

(i) General Principles

In theory, IPRs and unfair competition do not overlap. While genuine IPRs are exclusive property rights which grant protection *erga omnes,* the tort of unfair competition is limited to actions against certain practices of competitors.[262] Therefore, a genuine overlap does not exist in this field.

Undoubtedly, however, there is a wide area of *factual* overlap between IPRs and unfair competition.[263] This is, first, because unfair competition protection against unfair imitations has developed undeniable property rights characteristics in German case law.[264] In the framework of an action under Unfair Competition Act, sections 3, 4(no 9), damages will be granted to the plaintiff according to the criteria developed for IPRs.[265] Secondly, while in theory protection should only be granted with respect to certain unfair acts of competitors in cases which contain an extra element of unfairness or confusion, in German court practice, protection has also been granted in cases where no extra element of unfairness, breach of contract or other dishonest practice, or misrepresentation, was present at all.[266] Thus, on the basis of the theory of interdependency,[267] the action has actually been used by the courts to grant quasi-property protection to certain original or investment intensive subject matter beyond the reach of the established system of IPRs. At times this has even paved the way for the subsequent legislative development of neighbouring rights protecting certain investments,[268] such as the protection of record producers or database makers,[269] which was provided for by unfair competition before the respective IPRs were introduced in German law. Hence, the overlap issue has to be addressed.

The German Federal Court of Justice has repeatedly emphasised the principle of freedom of competition, encompassing freedom to compete by imitation outside the boundaries of the system of existing IPRs.[270] While the prevailing opinion in legal doctrine has

[262] See A Ohly, in H Piper, A Ohly and O Sosnitza, *Gesetz gegen den unlauteren Wettbewerb*, 5th edn (Munich, Beck, 2010) s 4, para 9/12.

[263] See ibid.

[264] See further ibid paras 9/83, 9/88 and 9/89.

[265] However, this is not the case with regard to the consumer protection orientated provision of Unfair Competition Act, s 5(2), see especially H Köhler, 'Der neue Schutz vor Produktnachahmung im Markenrecht, Geschmacksmusterrecht und neuen Lauterkeitsrecht' (2009) *Gewerblicher Rechtsschutz und Urheberrecht* 445, 447.

[266] See with a comprehensive overview of German case law T Sambuc, in H Harte-Bavendamm and F Henning-Bodewig (eds), *Gesetz gegen den unlauteren Wettbewerb*, 2nd edn (Munich, Beck, 2009) s 4(no 9), para 28 *et seq*. The most prominent example in this field is the seasonal protection of fashion novelties, developed by the courts in the framework of the tort of unfair competition (see *Modeneuheit*, Federal Court of Justice (1973) *Gewerblicher Rechtsschutz und Urheberrecht* 478). Meanwhile, protection by the unregistered Community design does indeed fill this former gap in the system of IPRs, see further below section VIII.B(iii).

[267] See above section VIII.A.

[268] See Ulmer, *Urheber- und Verlagsrecht* (n 24) 40.

[269] See eg *Tele-Info-CD*, Federal Court of Justice (1999) *Gewerblicher Rechtsschutz und Urheberrecht* 923, 926, granting unfair competition law protection against the direct copying of a CD containing the 'white pages' telephone directory of Deutsche Telekom, which would today be protected by the *sui generis* database protection right. In fact, the Federal Court of Justice also additionally considered the case with regard to the *sui generis* right in the decision.

[270] For classic authorities see *Schallplatten*, Imperial Court, RGZ 73, 294, 297, concerning the first cases of record piracy; *Apfel-Madonna*, Federal Court of Justice (1966) *Gewerblicher Rechtsschutz und Urheberrecht* 504, 506, on the overlap between copyright and unfair competition.

approved of this principle as a starting point for the delineation of unfair competition protection against misappropriation of competitors' materials,[271] critics have argued that a one-sided principle is not capable of serving as an appropriate basis for the process of comprehensively balancing different competitive interests in unfair competition law which is needed to reasonably balance competition by innovation and competition by imitation.[272] As for the principle of freedom of imitation as a teleologic principle, this criticism is partly justified. Indeed, the repeated practice of the courts to initially pronounce the principle of freedom to imitate, while subsequently granting protection against acts of mere imitation without any real additional element of unfair competition involved, impressively shows that the principle is inapt to encompass the intricate balance of interests needed in cases of unfair imitation. Consequently, the principle of freedom to imitate was temporarily seriously undermined (in particular in older German case law).

However, there is also a systematic element to the principle of freedom of imitation.[273] The argument follows from the normative pre-emption of unfair competition actions by the boundaries of the existing IPR system. In fact, where IPRs, as the result of a subject matter specific legislative process of balancing of the involved interests, set statutory limits to IPR protection in certain areas, whether with regard to the condition of protection or with regard to the scope or term of protection, such limits must not be generally undermined by the tort of unfair imitation in unfair competition law.[274] Therefore, in our opinion, unfair competition protection should only be granted to entirely new subject matter, which is beyond even the potential reach of the existing IPR system (subject matter test), or in cases where a genuine extra element of unfair competition, such as a danger of confusion, an illicit obtaining of the necessary source material, or a systematic and repeated free-riding concerning particularly time-sensitive products or services, is involved (extra element test).

Indeed, on the basis of the declaratory adherence to the principle of freedom of imitation, German courts traditionally require such additional extra elements of unfair competition as a precondition of the action against unfair imitation. However, in the past this element of unfair competition actions has repeatedly been ignored in the courts' practice. Consequently, parts of German legal doctrine call for what might be characterised as the 'additional element taken seriously' approach.[275] According to this approach, unfair competition protection against unfair imitation should only be granted in the future if genuine extra elements, which have not been taken into account in the balancing of interests underlying the entire system of the several existing IPRs, are embodied in a case. This opinion comes very close to the systematic pre-emption approach followed by us.

However, other authors argue differently, and favour a genuinely 'unfair competition' orientated balancing of interests, specific to the objectives of unfair competition law, which are independent from the objectives of intellectual property law according to the

[271] See Ohly, in Piper, Ohly and Sosnitza, *Gesetz gegen den unlauteren Wettbewerb* (n 262) s 4, paras 9/2 and 9/13, with further references to the ongoing discussion in German legal doctrine.

[272] Köhler, in Köhler and Bornkamm, *Gesetz gegen den unlauteren Wettbewerb* (n 255) s 4, para 9.3.

[273] Ohly, in Piper, Ohly and Sosnitza, *Gesetz gegen den unlauteren Wettbewerb* (n 262) s 4, paras 9/2 and 9/15.

[274] See clearly *Apfel-Madonna*, Federal Court of Justice (1966) *Gewerblicher Rechtsschutz und Urheberrecht* 504, 506, and many further decisions.

[275] Ohly, in Piper, Ohly and Sosnitza, *Gesetz gegen den unlauteren Wettbewerb* (n 262) s 4, para 9/14.

opinion of these authors.[276] While these arguments seem justifiable with regard to cases embodying an element of risk of confusion (which are mainly covered in Unfair Competition Act, section 5(2)),[277] in cases of mere imitation without any element of confusion or any other genuine extra element of unfair competition, the factual overlap of unfair competition law and IPRs cannot be denied. Therefore, unfair competition law has to take the value judgements embodied in the system of different IPRs into account, and must not undermine the objectives underpinning the particular limits to IPR protection. This concerns mainly the limits of the existing IPRs with regard to the conditions of protection, as well as the limitations to the scope of protection, and the limits of the term of protection. In fact, more recent court decisions have increasingly taken into account these aspects, as the following overview of case law on the overlaps with different branches of IPRs will show.

(ii) Overlap Between Unfair Competition, Copyright and Patents

(a) Overlap with Copyright Protection

According to German case law and legal doctrine, unfair competition protection against imitations is excluded if parallel copyright protection subsists.[278] Therefore, overlaps between copyright and unfair competition law protection will typically be negative or *a posteriori* overlaps. That is, overlap cases can only arise in cases where copyright protection is not available. This can be due to the fact that the partly strict conditions of German copyright protection, in particular the threshold of 'level of creativity' (*Schöpfungshöhe*) with regard to the 'applied arts' and non-literary texts, are not fulfilled; or copyright protection might not be available because of certain limitations of the scope of protection, in particular the limited protection term (*a posteriori* overlap).

However, the limitations of copyright protection must not be unduly undermined by the application of unfair competition law.[279] In particular, the Federal Court of Justice held that unfair competition law protection must not set limits to the use of formerly copyright protected works which have fallen into the public domain due to the lapse of the protection period. Therefore, in its *Notenstichbilder* judgment the court refused to grant unfair competition law protection against the identical reprint of sheet music after the expiry of copyright protection for the piece of music.[280] In the remaining area of overlap, ie mainly the unfair competition protection of certain achievements which do not fulfil the strict conditions of copyright protection, the Federal Court of Justice has of late applied the 'extra element' test more consistently. Thus, following the recent *Michel Nummern* judgment of the Federal Court of Justice, the tort of unfair imitation does

[276] Köhler, in Köhler and Bornkamm, *Gesetz gegen den unlauteren Wettbewerb* (n 255) s 4, para 9.6 *et seq*, with comprehensive further references. See recently very clearly Köhler, 'Der Schutz vor Produktnachahmung im Markenrecht, Geschmacksmusterrecht und neuen Lauterkeitsrecht' (n 189) 446.

[277] See further on the particularly intricate overlap between unfair competition and trademark law in this area below section VIII.B(iv).

[278] See Köhler, in Köhler and Bornkamm, *Gesetz gegen den unlauteren Wettbewerb* (n 255) s 4, para 9.7.

[279] See *Schallplatten*, Imperial Court, RGZ 73, 294, 297; *Apfel-Madonna*, Federal Court of Justice (1966) *Gewerblicher Rechtsschutz und Urheberrecht* 504, 506.

[280] See *Notenstichbilder*, Federal Court of Justice (1986) *Gewerblicher Rechtsschutz und Urheberrecht* 895, 896. See also eg *Apfel-Madonna*, Federal Court of Justice (1966) *Gewerblicher Rechtsschutz und Urheberrecht* 504, 506.

require a genuine extra element, ie an element of unfairness in competition, which is not encompassed in the usual copyright law action.[281]

The *Michel Nummern* judgment is also interesting from another point of view because it concerned the protection of a database structure against acts of extraction and re-utilisation. This raises the issue of overlap between *neighbouring* and *sui generis* rights in copyright law and additional unfair competition law protection against imitations. In general, the criteria for the delineation of copyright and unfair competition also apply with regard to the delineation of neighbouring rights and unfair competition,[282] that is, an extra element of unfairness will be needed to trigger additional unfair competition protection against imitations of a product or service.[283] While this result is plausible for rights neighbouring copyright, protecting certain attainments with an element of creativity involved, such as the protection of performing artists, it is submitted that with regard to investment protecting neighbouring rights, such as the rights for record and film producers and the *sui generis* right for database makers, even stricter criteria should apply. This is because these rights already encompass a comprehensive balancing of interests by the legislator, guided by the objective of *investment protection*. Consequently, any element of protecting investments against free-riding of any kind by a competitor cannot be regarded as an 'extra element' of unfair competition in these fields. In fact, German law with respect to the investments protecting neighbouring rights has often crystallised in statute the criteria of unfair competition case law on investment protection against free-riding in particular sectors. Therefore, the resulting statutory provisions already comprehensively balance the interests of the involved competitors and the general public, and any additional unfair competition law protection would threaten to unbalance these considerations of the legislator, as far as they are held to be conclusive. It is therefore submitted that with regard to these investment protection rights, additional unfair competition law protection can only be granted if an additional and specific element of unfairness vis-à-vis consumers is involved. This leaves only a small leeway for additional unfair competition law actions in those areas, mainly where danger of confusion in the marketplace is caused.

As regards copyright protection for creative works, apart from cases which involve an element of confusion or damage to goodwill, a potential field of application for unfair competition law actions remains with regard to entirely new products or services of the information society, formerly unknown to and beyond even the potential scope of copyright. With regard to such new subject matter, unfair competition law actions still can and should establish flexible protection against economically detrimental free-riding by competitors, thereby ideally operating as a 'laboratory', paving the way for the appropriate design of new specific intellectual property legislation. As has already been pointed out, unfair competition law protection beyond an element of confusion has played that role in the past.[284] However, given the recent proliferation of IPRs, the remaining area for application of such flexible unfair competition law protection as an instrument of invest-

[281] See *Michel Nummern*, Federal Court of Justice (2006) *Gewerblicher Rechtsschutz und Urheberrecht* 493, para 28.

[282] See M Leistner, *Der Rechtsschutz von Datenbanken im deutschen und europäischen Recht* (Munich, Beck, 2000) 346, for the rights of database makers.

[283] See Köhler, in Köhler and Bornkamm, *Gesetz gegen den unlauteren Wettbewerb* (n 255) s 4, para 9.7; Ohly, in Piper, Ohly and Sosnitza, *Gesetz gegen den unlauteren Wettbewerb* (n 262) s 4, para 9/17.

[284] See above section VIII.B(i).

ment protection for new market products or services of the information society is certainly rather small.[285] Moreover, as a matter of course, unfair competition actions cannot play such a subsidiary role where copyright protection for subject matter potentially already within the scope of copyright has been explicitly denied by the courts because it failed to fulfil the protection requirements; otherwise, the specific conditions of protection in copyright law would be undermined.

(b) Overlap with Patent Law

The general principles outlined above also apply to the overlap of unfair competition protection and patent law. However, due to the particular subject matter of patent protection, ie the claimed (technical) invention, the overlap issue only arises if the imitation concerns technically determined features of the imitated product where the implementation of the technical functionality leaves no substantial leeway for different product designs.[286] Only with regard to these patent protected 'technical' features of the product design are additional 'extra elements' required for unfair competition law actions against imitations of patented products if patent protection is exhausted or has expired.[287]

Such 'extra elements' have repeatedly been recognised in case law, in particular in cases where the imitation of the patented product was likely to cause confusion in the marketplace, resulted in free-riding on or damaging of the goodwill of a competitor.[288] In particular, further criteria have been developed to assess the offer of products or services complementary to patented products or services of a competitor from the angle of unfair competition law.[289] In principle, such marketing and sale of complementary products is admissible, if the different origin of the products is clearly indicated.

However, in the past the Federal Court of Justice had made an important exception to that principle when complementary pieces to modular products (such as Lego bricks) were offered. The so-called 'squeezing' of own products into the modular series of a competitor was regarded as an 'extra element', characterising such practice as unfair because of the resulting free-riding on the competitor's goodwill in cases where the original product was intended to be continuously extended by the customers as part of the business model of the claimant.[290] However, reacting to determined and justified criticism in literature,[291] more recent judgments of the Federal Court of Justice have first tried

285 See Ohly, in Piper, Ohly and Sosnitza, *Gesetz gegen den unlauteren Wettbewerb* (n 262) s 4, para 9/17.

286 Köhler, in Köhler and Bornkamm, *Gesetz gegen den unlauteren Wettbewerb* (n 255) s 4, para 9.12.

287 See instructively *Prospekthalter*, Federal Court of Justice (1997) *Gewerblicher Rechtsschutz und Urheberrecht* 116, 118; see Köhler, in Köhler and Bornkamm, *Gesetz gegen den unlauteren Wettbewerb* (n 255) s 4, para 9.12.

288 See eg *Verbrauchsmaterialien*, Federal Court of Justice (1996) *Gewerblicher Rechtsschutz und Urheberrecht* 781, 782.

289 See eg ibid on the unfair competition law limitations to the marketing of toner products for photocopiers of a competitor.

290 See *Klemmbausteine* (*Interlocking Bricks*), Federal Court of Justice (1964) *Gewerblicher Rechtsschutz und Urheberrecht* 621; *Klemmbausteine II* (*Interlocking Bricks II*), Federal Court of Justice (1992) *Gewerblicher Rechtsschutz und Urheberrecht* 619, 620, both on the protection of the famous Lego brick system. See further Köhler, in Köhler and Bornkamm, *Gesetz gegen den unlauteren Wettbewerb* (n 255) s 4, para 9.56 *et seq*.

291 See eg A Kur, 'Wettbewerbsrechtlicher Nachahmungsschutz gegen kompatible Produkte? – Zugleich Anmerkung zu den Entscheidungen des BGH, der Cour de Cassation und des Hoyesterett (norw Oberster Gerichtshof) in Sachen LEGO/TOMY-Train' (1995) *GRUR Int* 469; Köhler, in Köhler and Bornkamm, *Gesetz gegen den unlauteren Wettbewerb* (n 255) s 4, para 9.57 *et seq*, with further references.

to distinguish current cases from the older precedents,[292] and then narrowed the doctrine considerably: Hence, according to the most recent judgment in *Klemmbausteine III* ('Interlocking Bricks III'), unfair competition protection must at least not undermine the limited term of patent and design protection in such cases.[293] Therefore, if a modular product has been marketed for 45 years, unfair competition law protection against the 'squeezing into the series of a competitor' will not be granted, because the limited term of the existing (and expired) IPRs for the modular construction inherently limits the tort of unfair competition if no element of confusion in the marketplace is present.

While the judgment has even been criticised by some authors as not going far enough in the abandonment of the older doctrine,[294] it does nonetheless restate an important general principle: This is because the *ratio decidendi* of *Klemmbausteine III* can be generalised with regard to the term of protection of the unfair competition tort: Where an element of confusion is and remains present, the term of protection of the tort is potentially unlimited.[295] However, where no such element is present in a case (ie in the remaining cases of free-riding on a competitor's goodwill, illicit acquirement of the original material, and with regard to systematic and identical copies), unfair competition protection for certain products or services is inherently limited by the protection term of the IPRs which were originally available for the protection of these products or services.[296]

As for the conceivable overlap between plant variety protection and unfair competition, there is no specific case law or literature to be reported from Germany.

(iii) Overlap Between Unfair Competition and Design Protection

In the past, the main area of application for the German tort of unfair competition was the imitation of certain designs by competitors, in particular in the area of fashion novelties.[297] So-called 'seasonal' (short-term) protection was granted against systematic and identical imitations by competitors.[298] Fashion designs of a particularly high degree of competitive originality and distinction were even protected for a potentially unlimited

[292] See *Modulgerüst*, Federal Court of Justice (2000) *Gewerblicher Rechtsschutz und Urheberrecht* 521, 526, on a modular scaffold system, where the court tried to distinguish modular products where later extensions were merely 'incidental' (such as the modular scaffold system) from modular systems such as Lego where the later extension was allegedly part of the business concept. However, this distinction has been criticised with good cause as being artificial, see Köhler, in Köhler and Bornkamm, *Gesetz gegen den unlauteren Wettbewerb* (n 255) s 4, para 9.58.

[293] See *Klemmbausteine III (Interlocking Bricks III)*, Federal Court of Justice (2005) *Gewerblicher Rechtsschutz und Urheberrecht* 349, 352. See also above section IV.A(i) on the most recent Decision of the Federal Court of Justice of 16 July 2009 – I ZB 53/07 and 55/07, (2010) *Markenrecht* 131, on the denial of trademark protection for the three-dimensional shape of Lego bricks.

[294] In fact the unfair competition doctrine against the 'squeezing' of products into the modular series of a competitor should be given up entirely. This is because the mere business idea to offer a modular system, intended to create complementary needs on the part of customers, is in principle not protection-worthy as such (beyond available IPR protection for certain technical or aesthetic features of the product), see Köhler, in Köhler and Bornkamm, *Gesetz gegen den unlauteren Wettbewerb* (n 255) s 4, para 9.58. Moreover, the modularity of an imitated product cannot as such constitute an extra element of the unfair competition action, as it does not relate to the practice of the alleged infringer but is inherent to the imitated product.

[295] See further below section VIII.B(iii) on the differentiated case law in the practically important area of fashion novelties.

[296] See also Ohly, 'Areas of Overlap Between Trade Mark Rights, Copyright and Design Rights in German Law' (n 8) 706.

[297] See also above section VIII.A.

[298] See *Modeneuheit*, Federal Court of Justice (1973) *Gewerblicher Rechtsschutz und Urheberrecht* 478, on common fashion novelties.

term as long as they were still perceived as an identification of commercial origin in the markets.[299] The practical relevance of unfair competition in this area has meanwhile declined in Germany due to the fact that the protection needs of the fashion industry are (at least partly) met by the unregistered Community design right.[300] In fact, both protection systems serve a similar practical protection need in the area of product design, which makes the resulting overlap particularly intricate.

According to recent case law of the Federal Court of Justice, unfair competition law and design protection can still overlap.[301] The general criteria, ie in particular the requirement of an 'extra element' of unfair competition, do apply. Hence, according to the landmark *Jeans* case of the Federal Court of Justice, products of sufficient 'competitive originality' (such as a highly original and distinctive jeans design) can still be protected against imitations by competitors under German unfair competition law, notwithstanding the existence and availability of Community unregistered design protection, at least if there is a risk of confusion as to the commercial origin of the product.[302] Under these circumstances, even the expiry of the term of unregistered design protection will not foreclose the application of the unfair competition law action, according to the court. Apart from the reference to Design Regulation, article 96(1),[303] the court justified this cumulative application of design protection and the unfair competition action mainly with recourse to the different objectives of the two protection systems in such cases. According to the court, design law protects certain new and individual designs, while unfair competition law protects against causing confusion in the markets as to the commercial origin of imitated goods.

However, following the *Klemmbausteine III* judgment, the differentiated limitations of design protection law, and in particular the limited term of protection, have to be accepted in the framework of the unfair competition action against imitations if no element of confusion is present in a case. Therefore, it is submitted that the remaining leeway for protection against product imitations beyond an element of consumer confusion (which was allegedly present in the landmark *Jeans* case) is decidedly small if the product design is or has been protected by (registered or unregistered) design protection right.[304] In fact, unfair competition protection for such designs is hardly conceivable at all for future cases, which do not involve an element of confusion.

The main crux of the *Jeans* decision for the remaining cases involving an element of consumer confusion is that, through assessing the overlap with design protection in an isolated way, the Federal Court of Justice failed to discover the obvious additional overlap of the case with trademark law and therefore ended up with a somewhat lopsided analysis of the overlap issue.[305] Indeed, while it was defensible that the case involved an

[299] See *Trachtenjanker*, Federal Court of Justice (1998) *Gewerblicher Rechtsschutz und Urheberrecht* 477, 478, on the particularly original design of a traditional Bavarian costume.

[300] See Ohly, in Piper, Ohly and Sosnitza, *Gesetz gegen den unlauteren Wettbewerb* (n 262) s 4, para 9/18, with further references.

[301] *Gebäckpresse*, Federal Court of Justice (2009) *Gewerblicher Rechtsschutz und Urheberrecht* 79, para 26.

[302] *Jeans*, Federal Court of Justice (2006) *Gewerblicher Rechtsschutz und Urheberrecht* 79.

[303] See also above section II.A.

[304] Similarly Ohly, in Piper, Ohly and Sosnitza, *Gesetz gegen den unlauteren Wettbewerb* (n 262) s 4, para 9/18; Köhler, in Köhler and Bornkamm, *Gesetz gegen den unlauteren Wettbewerb* (n 255) s 4, para 9.8, both with further references; A Träger, 'The Additional Protection of the Shape of Goods Through German Law Against Unfair Competition (UWG)' in *Prace Instytutu Prawa Wlasnosci Intelektualnej UJ, Jagiellonen-University Krakow* (Krakow, 2007) vol 99, 113.

[305] See Ohly, 'Areas of Overlap Between Trade Mark Rights, Copyright and Design Rights in German Law' (n 8) 710 *et seq*, with further references.

element of consumer confusion, and that in fact the defendant had (also) tried to misappropriate the goodwill of the claimant's distinctive jeans design, the crucial question would have been whether the resulting protection interest of the claimant in a distinctive product shape was not sufficiently and exhaustively protected by the available instruments of trademark protection. This leads on to the discussion of the overlap between unfair competition and trademark law in Germany.

(iv) Overlap Between Unfair Competition and Trademarks

Trademark law and unfair competition law mainly overlap in two areas of German unfair competition law: First, Unfair Competition Act, section 5(2) prohibits misleading advertisements which create confusion with a product, trademark or trade name of a competitor (thereby implementing UCPD, article 6(2)(a)).[306] Secondly, under Unfair Competition Act, section 4(no 9)(a) and (b), the offer of imitations of a competitor's product or service (vested with a certain minimum of competitive originality) will be regarded as unfair if it leads to confusion in the marketplace or if it free-rides on or damages the goodwill of another competitor. Both these aspects are also present in trademark law.

As for Unfair Competition Act, section 5(2), due to the European ('consumer protection') background of the provision, it is acknowledged in German legal doctrine that in principle the unfair competition action applies independently from trademark law when an element of consumer confusion is present in a case, and that consumer councils or associations and other 'qualified entities' can bring the action before the court.[307] However, certain trademark law directions have to be accepted in unfair competition law to avoid inner incoherencies of the legal system. Thus eg if a trademark owner licenses the sign to a licensee in compliance with the relevant requirements of trademark law, consumer associations normally cannot bring unfair competition actions against the subsequent use of the licensed sign by the licensee, even if consumers would expect that the underlying product's direct origin is the licensor.[308]

As regards Unfair Competition Act, section 4(no 9), the 'traditional' German unfair competition tort of unfair product imitations which mainly protects the interests of competitors,[309] the rules governing the overlap with trademark law are highly differentiated and partly uncertain. Unfair Competition Act, section 4(no 9)(c) (the provision on

[306] Moreover, in this context Unfair Competition Act, para 13 of the Annex to s 3(3) implements para 13 of Annex I to the Unfair Commercial Practices Directive and per se prohibits the promotion of a product similar to a product made by a particular manufacturer in such a manner as *deliberately* to mislead consumers with regard to the commercial origin of the product.

[307] See H Köhler, 'Die Unlauterkeitstatbestände des § 4 UWG und ihre Auslegung im Lichte der Richtlinie über unlautere Geschäftspraktiken' (2008) *Gewerblicher Rechtsschutz und Urheberrecht* 841, 846; J Bornkamm, in H Köhler and J Bornkamm, *Gesetz gegen den unlauteren Wettbewerb* 28th edn (Munich, Beck, 2010) s 5, paras 1.86 and 4.211a.

[308] Example by Bornkamm, in Köhler and Bornkamm, *Gesetz gegen den unlauteren Wettbewerb* (n 307) s 5, para 1.86. See comprehensively on this necessary alignment with certain directions of trademark law J Bornkamm, 'Der lauterkeitsrechtliche Schutz vor Verwechslungen: Ein Kuckucksei im Nest des UWG?', in W Erdmann, M Leistner, W Rüffer and T Schulte-Beckhausen (eds), *Festschrift für Michael Loschelder zum 65. Geburtstag* (Köln, Verlag Dr. Otto Schmidt, 2010), 31.

[309] See Ohly, in Piper, Ohly and Sosnitza, *Gesetz gegen den unlauteren Wettbewerb* (n 262) s 4, no 9, para 9/19; however disputed by H Köhler, 'Das Verhältnis des Wettbewerbsrechts zum Recht des geistigen Eigentums – Zur Notwendigkeit einer Neubestimmung auf Grund der Richtlinie über unlautere Geschäftspraktiken' (2007) *Gewerblicher Rechtsschutz und Urheberrecht* 548, para 30.

illicit acquirement of source material, required for unfair product imitations) undoubtedly applies independently from trademark law because the provision clearly follows a different objective and therefore does not directly overlap with trademark law.[310] With regard to section 4(no 9)(a) and (b), which do indeed overlap with trademark protection, German courts have traditionally followed what was called the doctrine of 'priority of trademark law', under which trademark law in principle takes precedence over unfair competition law.[311] Subject to some qualifications,[312] this doctrine is indeed still applied more or less consistently in the area of word marks and other 'traditional' signs.[313] However, in particular in the area of product designs, the principle of 'priority of trademark law' protection has never been consistently applied by the courts in practice.[314] Especially in more recent judgments of the Federal Court of Justice, the scope of the doctrine has been narrowed down considerably.[315] Therefore, some authors have called for an abandonment of the 'principle of priority', and instead argued in favour of a 'principle of parity', emphasising the independence of the balance of interests underpinning unfair competition law.[316] However, the prevailing opinion in German law adheres to the doctrine of 'priority of trademark law', while emphasising necessary qualifications, in particular in the area of unfair product imitation.[317]

Hence, following more recent judgments of the Federal Court of Justice, the existence of trademark protection for three-dimensional product designs (with its strict requirements concerning distinctiveness or the acquirement of distinctive character through use[318]) does not in principle exclude the parallel application of Unfair Competition Act, section 4(no 9) with regard to three-dimensional product shapes which do not (yet) fulfil the strict requirements of trademark protection.[319] According to section 4(no 9)(a), such

[310] See Köhler, in Köhler and Bornkamm, *Gesetz gegen den unlauteren Wettbewerb* (n 255) s 4, para 9.9.

[311] See eg *MAC Dog*, Federal Court of Justice (1999) *Gewerblicher Rechtsschutz und Urheberrecht* 161, 162; *Tupperwareparty*, Federal Court of Justice (2003) *Gewerblicher Rechtsschutz und Urheberrecht* 973, 974; see also Ohly, 'Areas of Overlap Between Trade Mark Rights, Copyright and Design Rights in German Law' (n 8) 711.

[312] Thus according to *Tupperwareparty*, Federal Court of Justice (2003) *Gewerblicher Rechtsschutz und Urheberrecht* 973, 974, unfair competition law protection will not be excluded if no trademark has been registered for a sign consisting of words even if the word mark could have been registered.

[313] For further qualifications and differentiations, see Bornkamm, in Köhler and Bornkamm, *Gesetz gegen den unlauteren Wettbewerb* (n 307) s 4, para 9.11, with comprehensive references.

[314] See J Bornkamm, 'Markenrecht und wettbewerbsrechtlicher Kennzeichenschutz – Zur Vorrangthese der Rechtsprechung' (2005) *Gewerblicher Rechtsschutz und Urheberrecht* 97; Ohly, in Piper, Ohly and Sosnitza, *Gesetz gegen den unlauteren Wettbewerb* (n 262) s 4, para 9/19, with further references.

[315] See *Abschlussstück*, Federal Court of Justice (2003) *Gewerblicher Rechtsschutz und Urheberrecht* 332, 333; *Stufenleitern*, Federal Court of Justice (2007) *Gewerblicher Rechtsschutz und Urheberrecht* 339, para 23; *Rillenkoffer*, Federal Court of Justice (2008) *Gewerblicher Rechtsschutz und Urheberrecht* 793, para 26.

[316] See Köhler, in Köhler and Bornkamm, *Gesetz gegen den unlauteren Wettbewerb* (n 255) s 4, para 9.6a, with further differentiations and comprehensive references.

[317] See Ohly, in Piper, Ohly and Sosnitza, *Gesetz gegen den unlauteren Wettbewerb* (n 262) s 4, para 9/19.

[318] See above section III.A(i).

[319] See clearly *Stufenleitern*, Federal Court of Justice (2007) *Gewerblicher Rechtsschutz und Urheberrecht* 339, para 23, on the three-dimensional shape of a particular ladder. The court distinguished between trademark protection for distinctive signs and unfair competition protection for 'concrete achievements' by the claimant, and held that while for the protection of signs trademark law did indeed take precedence, for the protection of 'concrete achievements' against imitation in competition, Unfair Competition Act, s 4(no 9) should remain applicable cumulatively. It has to be noted that the judgment has been criticised justifiedly in literature because of the artificiality of this distinction and the resulting legal uncertainty (see Ohly, in Piper, Ohly and Sosnitza, *Gesetz gegen den unlauteren Wettbewerb* (n 262) s 4, para 9/19). See also more recently *Rillenkoffer*, Federal Court of Justice (2008) *Gewerblicher Rechtsschutz und Urheberrecht* 793, para 26, on the particular product design of a Rimowa suitcase series.

protection will be triggered if the product design fulfils the requirement of certain 'competitive originality', and if the offer of the imitated product leads to the confusion of customers as to the commercial origin of the imitations. Although the requirements and legal consequences of the unfair competition action are indeed independent and partly different from trademark law in this field,[320] it cannot be denied that the resulting unfair competition law protection for product designs below the strict threshold of trademark protection for (distinctive) three-dimensional signs leads to the danger that the specific requirements and limitations of European trademark law (and European design protection[321]) could be undermined in this area by the application of German unfair competition law.[322] At the least, unfair competition law protection should be excluded if trademark protection does not subsist due to the specific exclusions and limitations[323] of Trademark Act, sections 3(2), 23 and 24.[324] Moreover, the necessary assessment of the question of whether certain conditions or limitations of the existing IPRs are threatened to be undermined by the application of unfair competition law to a particular case should be made in a comprehensive way. Hence, the necessary *e contrario* argument should be developed on the basis of a comprehensive overall assessment of *all* potential analogies of the given case to the objectives of the existing IPRs and their respective limitations and exceptions.

(v) Overlap Between the Rules on Comparative Advertising and Trademark, Copyright and Design Laws

If a trademark is used in the course of an admissible comparative advertisement, under Unfair Competition Act, section 6, following European case law in the field,[325] such use will not in principle constitute infringement of that trademark under German law.[326]

However, such situations might raise an additional overlap issue if a copyright or design protected product or sign of a competitor is used for an admissible comparative advertisement. If such advertisement makes undue use of the reputation of the competitors' products, such unfair use might violate Unfair Competition Act, section 6(2)(no 4).[327] However, if use of the competitor's copyright or design protected product or sign is necessary and proportionate for the comparison, thus fulfilling the (conclusive) requirements for an admissible comparative advertisement, the question arises of whether the rules on the (admissible) comparative advertising can prevail over the alleged infringement of copyright or design protection. There is no case law from Germany on that specific issue. However, in literature it has been suggested that if the requirement of proportionality is met, ie if the use of the copyright or design protected product is necessary and proportionate for the advertisement, the principles of the German Court of Justice's

[320] See Köhler, in Köhler and Bornkamm, *Gesetz gegen den unlauteren Wettbewerb* (n 255) s 4, para 9.9.
[321] See above section VIII.B(iii).
[322] See early in German literature, C Rohnke, 'Schutz für Produktgestaltung durch Formmarken und wettbewerbsrechtlichen Leistungsschutz' in H-J Ahrens *et al* (eds), *Festschrift für Willi Erdmann zum 65. Geburtstag* (Cologne, Heymanns, 2002) 455, 462 *et seq*; see also Ohly, 'Areas of Overlap Between Trade Mark Rights, Copyright and Design Rights in German Law' (n 8) 711.
[323] See on these exclusions and limitations above section III.B(ii).
[324] Ohly, in Piper, Ohly and Sosnitza, *Gesetz gegen den unlauteren Wettbewerb* (n 262) s 4, para 9/19.
[325] See chapter 3, section IV.B above.
[326] See from German case law *Genealogie der Düfte*, Federal Court of Justice (2004) *Gewerblicher Rechtsschutz und Urheberrecht* 607, 612.
[327] See Ohly, in Piper, Ohly and Sosnitza, *Gesetz gegen den unlauteren Wettbewerb* (n 262) s 6, para 20.

Parfumflakon case[328] (and the Court of Justice's *Evora* case[329]) should be applied, justifying such use also in copyright (and possibly design) law.[330]

Finally, Unfair Competition Act, section 6 provides the conditions for admissible comparative advertising, and thus implements the mandatory requirements of Directive 2006/114/EC concerning misleading and comparative advertising in this area.

IX. CONCLUSION: IDENTIFICATION OF PRINCIPLES GOVERNING OVERLAPS IN GERMAN LAW AND REMAINING OPEN QUESTIONS

A No General Normative Principle Governing Overlaps in German Law

Although legal doctrine and an increasing body of case law have dealt with specific overlap situations of late, the principle of *cumulative applicability* of different overlapping IPRs remains the unchanged starting point to assess overlaps in German law. However, more than ever it is true that this basic principle is no more than a starting point for legally balancing the different interests involved in overlap situations.

Beyond the principled starting point of cumulative application, no governing normative principle can hitherto be identified for this flexible case-by-case adjustment process in German law. Neither a principle of genuine independence (ie a principle of genuine and substantively unrestricted cumulative application of overlapping IPRs), inevitably favouring the interests of the right-holder, nor a principle of freedom of competition (or imitation), favouring the interests of the users, seem to be apt to achieve balanced results in all of the very different particular overlap situations. Wherever a principled solution was formulated by the courts, such as in the field of unfair competition protection (where the principle of freedom to imitate is the initial principle to assess cases of product imitation in case law), such principled solutions have invariably been undermined in German court practice. This seems to illustrate that the mere formulation of a general principle governing overlaps cannot reasonably guide the flexible and necessarily case (group) orientated process of concretely adjusting different IPRs in overlap situations. Instead, it is increasingly acknowledged in recent German literature that overlap issues require an appropriate balancing of exclusive IPR protection and the remaining realm of the public domain on a case-by-case basis. This necessary process of balancing of interests is fundamentally underpinned by the framework of fundamental rights and the principle of free competition.[331] The main function of conflict rules is regarded as to provide for problem specific solutions where specific overlap situations lead to an exclusion of effective competition with respect to certain protected subject matter or to unjustified curtailments of fundamental rights, namely the right to freedom of expression. From this perspective, the main problematic issues, as well as some of the flexible mechanisms to achieve reasonable solutions, have been identified in the preceding analysis.

[328] See above n 119.

[329] See chapter 3, section III.B(i) above.

[330] See Ohly, in Piper, Ohly and Sosnitza, *Gesetz gegen den unlauteren Wettbewerb* (n 262) s 6, para 20.

[331] See eg Kur, 'Funktionswandel von Schutzrechten' (n 10) 42 *et seq*; Ohly, 'Von einem Indianerhäuptling, einer Himmelsscheibe, einer Jeans und dem Lächeln der Mona Lisa' (n 14) 203 *et seq*. See gradually more restrictive, Sosnitza, 'Konvergenz und Interferenz der Schutzrechte' (n 8) 896 *et seq*.

B Problematic Overlap Issues

In particular, three overlap issues deserve specific attention.[332] First, problems may arise with regard to different thresholds concerning the essential *conditions of protection* of different IPRs. Wherever two IPRs protect interests with regard to an essentially similar immaterial subject matter, ie a single unitary creative, technical or commercial human effort, more liberal protection criteria for one right may potentially undermine stricter conditions of protection of another right.[333] Undoubtedly, this issue has become more urgent recently, as the continuous broadening of the ambit of different IPRs has led to an undeniable process of convergence concerning the respective conditions of protection of different IPRs, such as in the area of overlapping trademark and design protection.

Secondly, overlapping IPRs will typically provide for different *terms of protection*: therefore, when one of the overlapping rights expires, application of the other IPR at least has the potential to unduly restrict freedom of competition and, more generally, the free use of public domain material by the general public.[334] This problem has typically arisen in German law, where the overlap of different IPRs with trademark and unfair competition law protection is concerned.[335]

Thirdly, in the field of *limitations and exceptions* to IPR protection, differently drafted exceptions to different IPRs might lead to a situation where the provisions on the exceptions to one of the rights can effectively be circumvented by the right-holder on the basis of relying on another overlapping IPR. This is because German law does not usually contain broadly formulated, umbrella clause-style fair use exceptions to IPR protection but rather relies upon specifically drafted catalogues of exceptions.[336] Therefore, a flexible reaction, taking into account the legal evaluation underpinning the exception to only one of the overlapping IPRs, is usually not easy for the courts to achieve in the (rigid) statutory system of the other IPR. The phenomenon has been characterised as a situation of 'asymmetric convergence'; that is, the recent proliferation of IPR protection leads to an increasingly broad application of different IPRs to the same subject matter, and thus to a process of convergence of different protection systems (with regard to the respective conditions of protection). By contrast, this process of convergence has hitherto not been accompanied by a corresponding convergence of the provisions on exceptions.[337]

C Legal Mechanisms to Regulate Overlaps

Undoubtedly, these issues require a balancing of interests in overlap situations, taking all the different normative evaluations underpinning the various different overlapping provisions into account when applying each of them in a particular overlap situation. This balancing process takes place on different levels in German law.

332 See Ohly, 'Areas of Overlap Between Trade Mark Rights, Copyright and Design Rights in German Law' (n 8) 711 *et seq*.

333 See ibid.

334 See ibid.

335 See above section VIII.B(iv).

336 See Ohly, 'Areas of Overlap Between Trade Mark Rights, Copyright and Design Rights in German Law' (n 8) 711 *et seq*.

337 Kur, 'Funktionswandel von Schutzrechten' (n 10) 42 *et seq*.

First, express statutory rules governing specific overlaps and differentiating one IPR from the other with regard to certain specific subject matter are rare in German law, as has been emphasised at the outset. Moreover, the preceding analysis has shown that German courts have applied such explicit delineation rules rather reluctantly, because very often their legal consequence will be the principled exclusion of certain subject matter from the ambit of one of the involved IPRs. To avoid such rigid legal consequences, as a general rule of thumb, German courts have the tendency to give a narrow construction to principled exclusions from protection. Instead, German legal doctrine and case law suggest that the necessary adjustment of different IPRs in a given case should rather take place on the level of the different provisions on conditions and scope of protection, as well as on the level of the rules on limitations and exceptions to protection. These provisions are interpreted in a flexible way in overlap situations, ideally taking into account the evaluations of all the different overlapping IPRs.

Secondly, in some cases, the conditions of protection are interpreted taking into account alternative protection systems. This is the case with regard to the overlap of German copyright and design protection in the field of the 'applied arts' (designs, craftmanship, etc) where German courts have developed the so-called 'two-level theory' of protection of designs (*Stufentheorie*[338]), according to which the 'higher' level of copyright protection is reserved to outstanding designs showing a particular 'level of creativity' (*Schöpfungshöhe*).

Thirdly, in overlap situations in a wider sense, the different objectives (ie the conceptual difference of the specifically protected immaterial subject matter or effort) of overlapping IPRs will often allow the reasonable balancing of the involved interests by constructing the scope of protection in infringement cases corresponding to the separate and specific objectives of protection. Indeed, the flexible consideration of the overlap in the framework of constructing the scope of protection of the different overlapping IPRs will typically allow the achievement of more balanced solutions than any attempt to exclude certain subject matter from the ambit of one of the overlapping IPRs by way of hard and fast conflict rules. Thus, the overlap issues which arise from the potential availability of additional trademark protection for work titles, product designs, and so forth (in particular with regard to the limited term of protection of copyright and design law) are typically solved in German infringement cases by applying strict criteria to the trademark law condition of the use of the protected elements of the sign by the infringer as a trademark in the course of trade, and to the establishment of the element of likelihood of confusion. In these cases, the flexible interplay of the substantive conditions of protection and the resulting scope of protection in infringement cases will often allow the courts to achieve reasonably balanced results, taking into account the interests of the right-holder, the users, and in particular the interests of the general public in freedom of information and competition with regard to work titles and product designs. It is submitted that the full potential of interpreting the scope of protection of different overlapping IPRs flexibly, taking into account the availability of different IP instruments in a given case, has not yet been realised in German law. Thus, as regards the overlap of copyright and patents in the field of computer program protection, patent law's doctrine on equivalents should certainly draw some inspiration from the flexible and proportional relationship between the degree of individuality and the scope of protection in copyright law.[339]

[338] See ibid.

[339] See further above section VI.A(iii).

Fourthly, on the level of exceptions to protection, differently drafted provisions on exceptions to different IPRs pose intricate problems in overlap situations when certain uses are only exempted from protection by one of the overlapping IPRs.[340] However, although the issue has very early been identified as an overlap problem in German literature,[341] in most of these cases the underlying problems are not due to the overlap as such. Instead, the overlap situation rather merely helps to identify a specific imbalance or loophole *within* the system of one of the overlapping IPRs. However, that imbalance will very often be of a general nature, ie will not be specific to the area of overlap. The issue of copyright protection, conflicting with the legitimate marketing and sales of products for which trademark rights are already exhausted, is an example in point. The problem, which has also been dealt with by the Court of Justice, has been solved by the German Federal Court of Justice by extending the exhaustion of the copyright distribution right to certain acts of reproduction, merely accessory to legitimate acts of distribution (ie associated marketing and sales measures).[342] Indeed, this 'copyright internal' solution is perfectly correct from a systematic viewpoint, because the issue as such is not an overlap problem but rather due to a general systematic contradiction *within* the system of German copyright itself. This is because in German copyright, when interpreting the statute strictly, the reproduction right could be relied upon by the copyright holder to undermine the effectiveness of the principle of exhaustion of the right of distribution in certain cases. Thus, the contradiction is within the system of copyright law itself. It is of a general nature and not limited to trademark protected creations. Therefore, to avoid it and to safeguard the effectiveness of the principle of exhaustion in light of its more general objective, the exhaustion principle has to be extended generally to certain necessary accessory acts of reproduction.[343] The overlap with (exhausted) trademark protection is not characteristic of the problem, but merely highlights the contradiction within the system of copyright law.

However, cases where different provisions on exceptions concerning different IPRs do indeed conflict with each other (and not just within one of the systems), and where the exceptions to one right are threatened to be undermined by the application of another IPR certainly do exist, as the issue of trademark parody clearly shows.[344] In these cases, while German copyright's doctrine of free transformative use allows a flexible assessment of parody cases, German trademark law does not provide for an applicable exception to protection. The crucial question in this and similar cases is whether the interests of the right-holder should always prevail, ie indeed applying both IPRs entirely independently from each other, or whether the interests of the users and the general public should prevail in certain cases, ie (partly) extending certain exceptions from one of the involved IPRs to the other overlapping IPRs. Yet again, it is submitted that the issue is not really an issue of overlap, and cannot be solved by focusing on the overlap as such. Instead, in such situations the basic values underpinning the exception to only one of the involved rights have to be the focal point of the legal assessment. Where these basic values justify the (independent) construction of an exception to the other involved IPR, the

[340] See Ohly, 'Areas of Overlap Between Trade Mark Rights, Copyright and Design Rights in German Law' (n 8) 712.

[341] Kur, 'Funktionswandel von Schutzrechten' (n 10) 47 *et seq*.

[342] See above section III.A(iv).

[343] See further above section III.A(iv).

[344] See further above section III.A(iv).

overlap effectively identifies a gap in the system of exceptions to that other right with respect to the basic values in question. Hence, instead of focusing on the overlap issue as such by attempting to strictly delineate both areas of law, from the perspective of German doctrine, the overlap ideally helps to identify and possibly correct certain (sector-specific) imbalances or gaps within the system of one of the involved IPRs by changing that system itself. Particularly in cases of exceptions underpinned by certain fundamental rights, like the right to freedom of expression, such gaps should be closed by recourse to a construction of the law in conformity with the fundamental right concerned, or even by direct reliance upon the fundamental right in question. Indeed, German courts have done so in cases of trademark parody on the basis of German Constitution, article 5(1).[345] Undoubtedly, another basic value which *might* justify the factual extension of certain provisions on exceptions in overlap cases is the principle of freedom of competition. Thus, the extension of exceptions, which are specifically intended to limit an IPR in order to avoid specific and unjustified restrictions on competition, from one IPR to another IPR should be considered in certain overlap cases.[346] However, the legal methodology required in practice to achieve such extension of the general objective underpinning an exception to one IPR to the realm of an overlapping IPR is far from clear. In that area, the fact that German intellectual property law does not generally provide for broad and flexible fair use exceptions is particularly problematic. In German literature, it has even been suggested that the phenomenon of converging IPRs constitutes an additional political argument in favour of a more flexible system of exceptions to several IPRs.[347] Taking everything into account, no conclusive solution as regards the issue of exceptions to IPR protection in overlap situations has yet emerged in German law.

Finally, the relationship between German unfair competition law protection against product imitations and the system of genuine, exclusive IPRs is particularly difficult and uncertain. Although German courts have not adhered to this principle consistently, it is submitted that with respect to this specific overlap issue in German law, a principle of normative pre-emption should apply.[348] That is, besides the realm of the particular provisions on passing off practices in German law, which are mainly intended to protect consumers against confusing trade practices, the traditional German tort of unfair competition protection against product imitation should only be granted in two cases. Firstly, the tort remains applicable to entirely new subject matter, which is beyond even the potential reach of the existing IPR system (subject matter test). Secondly, the tort remains applicable in cases where a genuine extra element of unfair competition, such as a danger of confusion, an illicit obtaining of the necessary source material, or a systematic and repeated free-riding concerning particularly time-sensitive products or services, is involved (extra element test).

Summarising the different mechanims and strands of thought outlined above, it seems that from the perspective of German law, most of the situations which are characterised as overlap problems should be solved by a flexible construction of the provisions on conditions of protection, scope of protection, and limitations to protection of the different

[345] See above section III.A(iv).

[346] See above section VI.A(v) where it has been remarked that such adaptation, however, is typically a task for the legislator reacting to certain inconsistencies identified within the system of one IPR because of an overlap with another IPR.

[347] Kur, 'Funktionswandel von Schutzrechten' (n 10) 47 *et seq*.

[348] Similarly Ohly, in Piper, Ohly and Sosnitza, *Gesetz gegen den unlauteren Wettbewerb* (n 262) s 4, para 9/15.

involved IPRs. Where such flexible solutions cannot be achieved within the given (and often rigid) framework of German intellectual property statutes, an interpretation in conformity with fundamental rights, underpinning certain limitations and exceptions, or even the direct reliance upon certain fundamental rights, such as freedom of expression in particular, might help to achieve reasonable solutions on a case-by-case basis. However, in most cases the overlap can be taken into account *within* the respective systems of the overlapping IPRs by interpreting these rights in a way which respects the value judgements of the legislator underpinning the provisions of the other IPRs involved in a given case. In particular, in many cases a narrow construction of the scope of the different involved IPRs, strictly taking into account their specific essential objectives of protection, will be sufficient to give a reasonable solution to the conflict between the overlapping rights. By contrast, principled solutions, or the application of hard and fast conflict rules on the delineation of different conflicting IPRs with regard to the protection of certain subject matter, have tended to fail in German practice.

7

Comparative Analysis, Conclusion and Outlook

THROUGHOUT THIS BOOK, we have examined the overlaps horizontally: one by one, level by level, ie at international, regional and national levels. It is now time to compare them vertically, in other words, examine the rules established by the legislatures and courts on each specific overlap at each level to discover their similarities and differences (section I). The reasons behind these rules will also be scrutinised as they help in developing general principles applicable to all overlaps (section II). Section III recapitulates, vertically, the literature's proposals to solve problems caused by each overlap and criticises their respective merit. The adequacy of the legal rules discussed in section I to solve overlaps is also analysed at that point. This analysis enables us to formulate which criteria or principles best solve the different overlap problems. Section IV uses these criteria to propose solutions *de lege lata* and *de lege ferenda* to the twin problems caused by cumulation of rights, namely regime clashes and overprotection. Finally, section V sets out our preferred solutions *de lege lata* and *de lege ferenda*.

I. SIMILARITIES AND DIFFERENCES BETWEEN THE LEGAL SYSTEMS IN THE RULES REGULATING THE OVERLAPS

A Generally

As to similarities, the main and most striking one is that at every level the overwhelming majority of overlaps are allowed, either explicitly or implicitly. There are only two overlaps explicitly prohibited at European and national levels, namely that prohibiting the cumulation of national and Community plant variety rights and that prohibiting a patent on a plant variety as such. In addition, one overlap is prohibited at international level and therefore also at European and national level, namely between plant variety right denomination and trademark. The other striking resemblance at all levels is that although the overlaps are allowed, there are virtually no explicit rules regulating any problems that may arise from them, namely overprotection or regime clashes. There are however, scattered here and there, a few specific rules within particular IPRs which regulate some aspects of each overlap in question. For instance, the European and national legislators have ensured a maximum of convergence between patents and plant variety rights to avoid regime clashes. But otherwise, the overall picture is that the various legislators have not explicitly addressed the problem, or have left it to contracting parties to sort out where possible.

Another similarity between the European and national legal systems is the basic importance of the notion of free, unhindered and undistorted competition. It is either an overarching/governing principle underlying the entire IPR legal framework (France), or a firmly embedded judge-made rule (United Kingdom, Germany). Moreover, it is explicitly laid down as a constitutional principle in EU law. In the European Union, it is also clearly expressed in the Green Paper on the Legal Protection of Industrial Design and the Explanatory Memorandum to the Trademark Directive and Regulation, and is repeated over and over in Directives and Regulations. As a principle of primary law, the notion of free and undistorted competition underlies any European harmonisation measure. More specifically, in France, courts have prohibited the *a posteriori* overlap between trademarks and patents because they find it contrary to the principle of freedom of commerce and its corollary, the freedom to compete. The German Federal Court of Justice, at least in theory, has repeatedly emphasised the principle of freedom of competition, encompassing freedom to compete by imitation outside the boundaries of the system of existing IPRs. In the United Kingdom, most clearly, free competition is a fundamental tenet of common law: 'imitation is the lifeblood of competition'.[1] Free market principles are strictly adhered to so that in the absence of an IPR, copying is a right rather than a wrong.[2] The British have frowned upon the creation of monopolies since the very beginning of the twentieth century and this has not changed.[3] In short, in both civil and common law jurisdictions, freedom of competition is the common starting point for adjudicating unfair competition law cases.[4] The principle of free competition also underlies many of the specific rules enshrined in the various IPR legislation (eg Trademark Directive 2008/95/EC, article 3(1)(e), Design Directive 98/71/EC, article 7, etc).

Another EU constitutional principle, more precisely one of the internal market objectives, but which has no equivalent at international level, is the principle of the free movement of goods and services. Again both the Green Paper on the Legal Protection of Industrial Design and the Explanatory Memorandum to the Trademark Directive and Regulation refer to it as a regulator of conflicts or overprotection. Finally, the principle of priority governs, at EU and thus also national level, the clash between trademarks, designs and copyright in the case of trademark and design registrations (Community Design Regulation (EC) 6/2002, article 25(1)(f), Design Directive, article 11(2)(b), Trademark Directive, article 4(4)(c) and Community Trademark Regulation (EC) 207/2009 (CTMR), article 53(2)).

As to differences, the main one is that the principles of the freedom of movement of goods and services and free competition are not found in all international instruments. The WTO's aims, as per the first recital of the Preamble to the WTO Agreement, are to raise standards of living, ensure full employment and a large and steadily growing volume

[1] R de Vrey, *Towards a European Unfair Competition Law: A Clash Between Legal Families* (Leiden, Martinus Nijhoff, 2006) 25, citing Kaufmann, 'Passing Off and Misappropriation: An Economic and Legal Analysis of the Law of Unfair Competition in the United States and Continental Europe' (Dissertation, Weinheim, VCH Verlag, 1986) 5. See also de Vrey (above) 279.

[2] de Vrey, *Towards a European Unfair Competition Law* (n 1) 205, adding that 'the UK formally subscribes to strict free market principles', in accordance with which citing J Reichman, 'Legal Hybrids Between the Patent and Copyright Paradigms' (1994) 94(8) *Columbia Law Review* 2432, 2465 and J Lahore, 'Products Simulation and Copying the Get-Up of Goods' (1979) *European Intellectual Property Review* 146.

[3] As the recent *Roho* case demonstrates: *RoHo/Hodgkinson & Corby v Wards Mobility Services* [1995] FSR 169.

[4] De Vrey, *Towards a European Unfair Competition Law* (n 1) 281.

of real income and effective demand, and expand trade in and production of goods and services. The pursuit of free trade is only a means to achieve this end and not an end in itself.[5] It is highly likely, however, that, also under WTO rules, free competition is the principle underlying free trade. However, the exhaustion principle is not regulated at international level (TRIPs Agreement, Article 6). Other international instruments only refer to a 'balance of rights and obligations' in their Preambles (eg WCT, WPPT) or in actual provisions of treaties (TRIPs Articles 7 and 8). Finally, the fundamental rights to freedom of expression and freedom of the arts regulate the parody exception in both copyright and trademark laws in Germany. The same cannot be said as strongly for France but decisions seem to use the right to freedom of speech as a tool to regulate the overlap. In the United Kingdom, freedom of speech, along with other human rights, has only been formally enshrined by the Human Rights Act 1998, so that it has not yet been extensively used in intellectual property cases.[6] In any case, as all Member States are states parties to the European Convention of Human Rights (ECHR) and must respect the fundamental right to freedom of expression as part of the principles included in the EU legal order, the principle is bound to become important in the regulation of overlaps in future.

B Copyright and Designs

As to similarities, at both the international and EU level, the overlap between copyright and designs is explicitly allowed. Moreover, at EU level, in principle it is even mandatory, although the regulation of scope and conditions of the overlap are left to the Member States.[7] Since the overlap is heavily regulated at EU level, the same rules appear in the Member States. Therefore, the following three rules as regards the overlap are also found in German, British and French laws. First, computer programs cannot be protected by national or Community registered design right.[8] Secondly, an overlap between the Community unregistered design right (CUDR) and a newly created national unregistered design right (UDR) is expressly prohibited by the Green Paper. The third rule is provided by Design Regulation, article 96(2) and Design Directive, article 17. This is in fact an option left to Member States. Thus, in effect, those Member States which choose to exercise it can (partially) prevent the cumulation. The United Kingdom and Germany are good examples of this, as they both require a higher level of creativity for works of applied art in copyright law.[9] Otherwise, there are not really any rules at EU level regulating the overlap. The rule in Design Directive, article 7 (excluding purely functional shapes from design law) helps to separate the subject matter of designs and of patents, but can also be said to reflect the idea/expression dichotomy in copyright law. The only real rule

[5] J Wouters and B De Meester, *The World Trade Organisation: A Legal and Institutional Analysis* (Antwerp, Intersentia, 2007) 19.

[6] See, however, *Hyde Park Residence Ltd v Yelland and others* [2000] EMLR 363 (CA) and *Ashdown v Telegraph Group* [2001] 4 All ER 666 (CA).

[7] See European Commission, Green Paper on the Legal Protection of Industrial Design, Working Doc 111/F/5131/91–EN (June 1991) recital 8 and Design Directive, art 17, and Design Regulation, recital 32 and art 96(2). This mandatory character already existed in France prior to the Design Directive and Design Regulation through the (still applicable) theory of the unity of art.

[8] They are expressly excluded in Design Directive, art 1(b) and the corresponding article of the Design Regulation.

[9] In the United Kingdom the works concerned are less numerous than in Germany, however, as the higher level of creativity only applies to works of artistic craftsmanship.

is article 95 of the Design Regulation, which aims to avoid clashing judicial decisions between national registered design right (RDR) and Community design rights. In addition, both the Design Regulation and Design Directive prohibit the registration of a copyright work as a design without authorisation of the owner of the copyright work. Germany does not have statutory rules either, and France's only additional rule is in fact a consequence of the theory of the unity of art. Because of this principle, it is not possible to transfer the design right without the copyright. This rule helps to avoid conflicts in case of overlap to keep the rights in the hands of only one person. This rule does not seem to apply to Community designs, however.

The differences are found only in UK law by way of additional rules. For historical reasons, the British legislature has enacted a number of rules organising the overlap between copyright and both its designs rights, namely UDR and RDR. It has no less than six rules which either prevent an overlap or regulate a regime clash. First, UDR does not protect surface decoration; therefore most two-dimensional products and three-dimensional decoration can only obtain the protection of copyright and RDR (Copyright, Designs and Patents Act (CDPA) 1988, section 213(3)(c)). CDPA 1988, section 224 and Registered Designs Act (RDA) 1949, section 19(3B) provide for the automatic transfer of both RDR and UDR when both rights are owned by the same person and the latter only transfers one of them. CDPA 1988, section 51 provides that it is not an infringement of the copyright in a two-dimensional depiction of a three-dimensional object, which is not an artistic work too, to manufacture this three-dimensional object. This greatly restricts the overlap between copyright and UDR. In the same vein, if an article is protected both by copyright and UDR, copyright prevails at the stage of infringement and UDR is therefore not infringed (CDPA 1988, section 236). Section 53 similarly regulates the interface between copyright and RDR. If someone does an act restricted by copyright in pursuance of an assignment or licence under registration of a corresponding design, it does not infringe any copyright in that design. Finally, CDPA 1988, section 52 shortens the copyright life of many artistic works which are commercially exploited, matching it almost perfectly[10] with the maximum life of an RDR, namely 25 years.

C Copyright and Trademarks

There are two main similarities as regards the overlap between copyright and trademarks. First, again, the rules set out in EU law will apply in the Member States where no option was left to them. There are three such rules. First, Trademark Directive, article 3(1)(e) and the corresponding CTMR, article 7(1)(e), which prohibit the trademark protection of shapes which give substantial value to the goods, also apply in the Member States. Secondly, like the Design Regulation, the CTMR also organises the potential conflicts that would result from different decisions involving the same mark registered both at national and EU level (article 105). Thirdly, both the CTMR and Trademark Directive have rules against the registration as a trademark of a copyright work or an

[10] Not perfectly because the 25 years start from the moment of commercialisation which can happen at any time during the term of the copyright, whereas the 25 years in RDR are fixed and start from registration. However, in practice, the terms will match as the copyright owner will only recoup its investment through commercialisation. The additional previous years of protection granted through copyright will not really have any impact on this recoupment.

industrial property right (CTMR, article 53(2)(c) and (d) and Trademark Directive, article 4(4)(c)).

The second similarity is that rules comparable to that set by the *Dior v Evora* ruling also apply in the United Kingdom, France and Germany. In *Dior v Evora,*[11] the Court of Justice held that when copyright forbids the reproduction of a work 'attached' to a trademarked good or service (ie commercialised as such by the trademark owner) but there is no trademark infringement, copyright law cannot trump the free movement of goods or services which would have prevailed if trademark law had been exclusively applicable. Accordingly, the freedom of movement of goods and services includes the freedom to resell goods but also to bring to the public's attention the further commercialisation of those goods unless such use of the trademark (or goods) for this purpose seriously damages the reputation of the trademark (or goods).[12] The *Dior v Evora* decision set out a rule that in this situation, copyright law must yield before the EU principle of freedom of movement of goods and services. This freedom is thus not intrinsic to any of the IPR regimes but is a higher rule stemming from the Treaty on the Functioning of the European Union (TFEU). Therefore, it is thought that it could apply in analogous situations involving other IPRs and not just copyright and trademarks.

CDPA 1988, section 63(1) is close to the *Dior* ruling but is slightly less broad. It provides that 'it is not an infringement of copyright in an artistic work to copy it or to issue copies to the public, for the purpose of advertising the sale of the work'. This provision differs in two ways from *Dior*: it does not imply that if the copyright work is also a trademark, the trademark would not be infringed. In addition, *Dior* covers any copyright work, not just artistic works. Thanks to *Dior*, these situations are also covered. In a similar vein, French Intellectual Property Code (IPC), article L122-5(3)(d) provides that it is not an infringement to copy, partly or entirely, artistic works where the purpose of the copy is to be displayed in the catalogue of a judicial sale carried out in France for the sole aim of describing the works for sale. In addition, the name of the author and source must be indicated. It is somewhat stricter than the British provision as it applies only to judicial sales carried out in France. In Germany, the *Dior* ruling has a parallel in the Federal Court of Justice's *Parfumflakon* case. The Federal Court of Justice held that the copyright principle of exhaustion of the distribution right generally (ie also in purely national cases) prevails over attempts to undermine the objective of free movement of goods by using another overlapping economic right to prohibit 'usual advertisement measures'.

The remainder are differences and additional rules. The first, striking, difference is that, contrary to EU and national law, the international instruments are silent on the overlap so that it is implicitly allowed but no rules organising it exist. Secondly, France has a rule which impacts to some extent on the *a posteriori* overlap. IPC, article L 22-4 provides that, even if the copyright in the title of a work has expired, if the use by another person of the title for a work of the same kind creates confusion with the once copyright protected work to which it relates, this will be an infringement. This rule prevents the *a posteriori* overlap by another person than the copyright holder but allows the overlap by the copyright holder. The moral right of integrity, which in France is perpetual, could be used to the same effect, but for all kinds of works, and even if there is no similarity as

[11] Case C-337/95 *Dior v Evora* [1997] ECR I-6013.
[12] Ibid paras 48 and 59.

to the kind of work for which the title is used. The right could be invoked to prevent the trademark registration of any work by persons other than its author. Article L122-4 therefore partially prevents the overlap *a posteriori*. Finally, German courts have developed rules which help to reduce the copyright/trademark overlap. According to the Federal Court of Justice, as a general rule, the scope of protection of work titles should be extremely narrow because of the typically low level of distinctiveness represented by such titles. Also, for most courts a rule of thumb applies in the sense that the more famous a piece of art is (eg 'Mona Lisa') the less likely it is to be distinctive.

D Trademarks and Designs

Again the difference is that the international instruments are silent on the overlap while EU law, and national law as a result, explicitly allow it and have a number of rules organising it. So what are these rules? First, there is CTMR, article 53(2)(d), which lists in its relative grounds for invalidity the case where the mark conflicts with an earlier industrial property right. A similar rule exists in the Design Regulation, whose article 25(1)(e) states that a design may be declared invalid 'if a distinctive sign is used in a subsequent design'. Identical rules exist in the Trademark Directive and Design Directive. Then there are Trademark Directive, article 3(1)(e)(ii) and (iii) (CTMR, article 7(1)(e)(ii) and (iii)), which prohibit the protection by trademark law of shapes of goods which are necessary to obtain a technical result or give substantial value to the goods. None of the three Member States examined have additional rules on the overlap. Therefore, EU and national laws are similar. However, in the United Kingdom, as regards the *a posteriori* overlap, Aldous LJ in *Philips v Remington* went further than the Court of Justice and held that Trademark Act (TMA) 1994, section 3(2)(b) and (c) (which correspond to Trademark Directive, article 3(1)(e)(ii) and (iii)) appeared to seek 'to exclude from registration certain shapes which are protectable under *patents, registered designs, copyright and other such intellectual property rights*'.[13] As a result, the UK courts seem to be even more broadly against this *a posteriori* overlap than the EU courts.

E Trademarks and Patents

Again, the difference is that the international instruments are silent about the trademark/patent overlap whereas it is explicitly allowed in EU law. However, the overlap will rarely occur in any event as EU courts case law[14] expressly excludes trademark registration of concepts and this comes in addition to the exclusion of functional shapes by the Trademark Directive and Trademark Regulation. Because this overlap is heavily harmonised at EU level, the rules are the same at national level. The three Member States have no additional specific rules organising this overlap.

[13] Emphasis added. *Philips Electronics v Remington Consumer Products* [1999] RPC 809, 816.

[14] See EU cases: Case C-299/99 *Koninklijke Philips Electronics v Remington Consumer Products* [2002] ECR I-05475, Case C-321/03 *Dyson v Registrar of Trademarks* [2007] ECR I-687 and Case C-48/09 P *Lego Juris v Mega Brands* (14 September 2010, nyr), available at www.curia.europa.eu.

F Patents and Copyright

Internationally, the overlap is implicitly allowed whereas it is explicitly allowed in the European Union.[15] However, a common characteristic is that neither the international instruments nor European or German law have specific rules organising the overlap between patents and copyright. In France and the United Kingdom, however, two courts have held that patent applications (the text in France and the drawings in the United Kingdom) cannot be protected by copyright, at least once they are published by the patent office. These precedents have not been questioned so far. In Germany, the same result is reached under German Copyright Act, section 5(2) on the non-protectability of 'official works'.

G Patents and Designs

Again the difference is that the international instruments are silent on the overlap while in the European Union, the overlap is specifically allowed.[16] The overlap is regulated by Design Directive, article 7 (designs dictated by their technical function and designs of interconnections). Neither of the three Member States has additional rules.

H Patents and Plant Variety Rights

The main similarity is that the international, European and national laws explicitly allow the overlap in principle.[17] Another similarity between all levels is by definition dictated by international law: there cannot be an overlap between the trademark and the denomination that must be given to a plant variety because the UPOV Convention specifically forbids it (Article 20).

The main difference is that international texts do not lay down rules to regulate the overlap while EU and national law do to some extent. European Patent Convention (EPC), Article 53(b) implies that plant varieties are not patentable as such. National plant variety rights can subsist but cannot be cumulated with the Community right (Community Plant Variety Right (CPVR) Regulation (EC) 2100/94, article 92) so that level overlap can never occur. The Biotech Directive 98/44/EC further specifies that plants are patentable as long as the application of the invention is not confined to a single plant variety. Because of the degree of convergence at EU level between many aspects of the two rights, the three Member States' laws also reflect this convergence, albeit to different degrees. None of the legal systems has additional rules to organise the remaining few areas where the overlap can pose a problem.

15 Software Directive, art 9(1).

16 Design Directive, art 16 and Design Regulation, art 96(1).

17 The 1991 act of the UPOV Convention only implicitly allows it while the TRIPs Agreement does so explicitly.

I IPRs and Unfair Competition

Yet again, international texts only implicitly allow an overlap between IPRs and unfair competition whereas EU law explicitly allows it in principle. While explicit cumulation is generally the rule, none of the EU texts regulates this specific overlap. The only exception is where a Member State provides that confidential information can be protected by contract, then it cannot trump copyrighted computer programs in relation to decompilation. Under Software Directive 2009/24/EC, articles 6 and 9(1), decompilation is permitted under certain conditions. A contract cannot take this users' privilege away. As these provisions are mandatory for the Member States, the same applies in France, Germany and the United Kingdom.[18] In addition in the United Kingdom, France and Germany, the 'observe, study and test' exception is also imperative.[19]

Because they are civil law countries, German and French laws are not surprisingly rather similar in the rules relating to this overlap. Many of these rules are case-law based. In short, both French and German unfair competition laws are based on the principle of freedom of competition and its corollary, the freedom to copy. Therefore, they both provide that the copied achievement must not be banal, nor be a necessary and functional form, and an element in addition to copying, namely (a risk of) confusion, damage to reputation or breach of confidentiality, is necessary to trigger an unfair act. Therefore, simple imitation is not reprehensible. In Germany, the courts apply the so-called 'theory of interdependency', according to which the degree of originality and the intensity of one of the additional elements of unfairness, embodied in a particular case, are interdependent. This means that a lower degree of one of the additional elements of unfairness can be compensated by a higher degree of competitive originality of the copied product, and vice versa. France does not have such a principle but in effect the decisions often reflect it. This all seems neat in theory but the picture is far patchier in practice. In effect, both in Germany and France, courts sometimes punish simple imitation for all three types of overlaps. This is even more frequent in France than in Germany, as German courts tend to construct these cases very narrowly.[20]

As to trademarks, the two countries' case law also converges in principle but the overlap is less marked in France. In France, there needs to be an element in addition to (likelihood of) confusion (if the sign and/or goods/services are not identical) or damage to goodwill (if the trademark has reputation) in order for the unfair competition action to succeed. The act implementing the Unfair Commercial Practices Directive 2005/29/EC (UCPD) does not give a separate action to private parties. Only a criminal action is possible on its basis.[21] In Germany, since the implementation of the UCPD, the specific unfair competition action based on misleading advertising applies independently from trade mark law when an element of consumer confusion is present in a case (Unfair Competition Act, section 5(2)). Thus, the overlap is accepted. As for the unfair competition action based on misappropriation (Unfair Competition Act, section 4(no 9)), a doctrine of

[18] See CDPA 1988, s 50B(4); IPC, art L122-6(1) *in fine*; and German Copyright Act, s 69e.

[19] See CDPA 1988, s 50BA(2); IPC, art L122-6(1)(V);and German Copyright Act, ss 69d(3) and 69g(2).

[20] As regards copyright, this seems now excluded as recent case law requires a genuine extra element, ie an element of unfairness in competition, which is not encompassed in the usual copyright law action (see the *Michel Nummern* judgment of the Federal Court of Justice, discussed in chapter 6, section VIII.B(ii)(a)).

[21] Law of 4 August 2008, no 2008-776 (*de modernisation de l'économie*) modifying, among others, the Code de la Consommation which deals with unfair commercial practices (see in particular art L121-1 *et seq*).

'priority of trade mark law' arguably still applies, although it is also criticised in literature against the background of the different objectives of the laws. As for three-dimensional product shapes, in Germany, the Federal Court of Justice has held that the existence of trademark protection for them (with its strict requirements concerning distinctiveness or the acquirement of distinctive character through use) does not in principle exclude the parallel application of unfair competition law with regard to three-dimensional product shapes which do not (yet) fulfil the strict requirements of trademark protection.

Perhaps surprisingly, where in the United Kingdom unfair competition law does not exist as a comprehensive concept, the courts have nonetheless developed a few rules which exist in neither France nor Germany. Although there is not strictly a rule, as a consequence of the case law,[22] if the patented computer-implemented invention is sold on the market, it seems that the source code is in the public domain as it can be reverse-engineered through legitimate access to the object code. The court in *IPC Media v News Group Newspapers*[23] interpreted the Misleading and Comparative Advertising Directive 2005/29/EC (MCAD) strictly so that apparently, comparative advertising does not trump copyright law at least when the reproduction of the copyright work was not strictly necessary for the purpose of the comparative advertising. However, unlike France and Germany, the UK courts have long allowed the cumulation of the passing off and trademark infringement actions.

In conclusion, not too surprisingly, overlaps are more and more regulated once one descends the levels. At international level, they are barely talked about, and most of them are simply implicitly allowed. At EU level, they are generally explicitly allowed in principle and some rules exist to regulate most of them but they do not cover all potential problems. Finally, at national level, rules exist in addition to European ones, and even more so in the United Kingdom than in France and Germany, but again no overlap is systematically organised in all its aspects to avoid potential regime clashes or overprotection. A common feature of all three levels, however, is the general lack of systematic organisation of the overlaps.

II. REASONS FOR THE PROHIBITION OR AUTHORISATION OF OVERLAPS

As we have seen in section I, there are a number of legal rules which organise the overlaps. This section summarises the reasons behind these rules. It can already be said that their rationales derive from the higher principles that we saw in section IA and which underlie at least the European and national legal frameworks.

A. International Level

TRIPs Articles 7 and 8, fittingly named 'objectives' and 'principles', may be said to embody the reasons which implicitly should regulate any problems that may arise from the overlaps which the Agreement, implicitly or explicitly, allows. Article 8 allows Member

[22] *Mars UK Ltd v Teknowledge Ltd* [2000] FSR 138.
[23] [2005] FSR 35.

States to take measures if IPRs 'unreasonably restrain trade'. This is an implicit reference to the importance of competition. Article 7 insists that IPRs should contribute to a balance of rights and obligations. According to the literature, this balance should be established using well-established principles of intellectual property law. Thus, this means that while IPRs must exist, as they are necessary to recoup investment, they cannot 'stifle competition for an unduly long period of time'.[24]

The WIPO Copyright Treaty (WCT) and WIPO Performances and Phonograms Treaty (WPPT) strike the same chord as the TRIPs Agreement. However, the idea of competition is not intrinsically inherent to the balance of rights and obligations. Perhaps this is so because copyright has traditionally been seen as less likely than patents to lead to monopolies, and also because the Berne Convention and the Internet Treaties only envisage copyright and neighbouring rights and not any other IPR.

B EU Level

The explicit rules set out in EU law mainly amount to prohibitions of certain kinds of overlap and they are all underpinned by either one of the two principles identified above in section IA, namely the principle of unhindered competition and the freedom of movement of goods and services.

Trademark Directive, article 3(1)(e) (and its identical twin CTMR, article 7(1)(e)) is arguably the most sweeping rule on overlaps of the IPR legal system at EU level as it is relevant to three overlaps, namely those between (on the one hand) trademarks and (on the other) copyright, designs and patents. The reason for the rule is found in the Explanatory Memorandum to the Proposal for a Trademark Directive and Trademark Regulation. It says that 'the shape of goods will not be refused registration unless the fact of registration would make it possible for an undertaking to monopolise that shape to the detriment of its competitors and of consumers'.[25] The EU courts have repeatedly used the same rationale to construe Trademark Directive, article 3(1). In *Philips v Remington*, the Court of Justice held that article 3(1)'s aim is 'to prevent trademark protection from granting its proprietor a monopoly on technical solutions or functional characteristics of a product which a user is likely to seek in the products of competitors'.[26] The Advocate-General in *Lego* recently added that trademark protection and the protection conferred by other forms of intellectual property must be kept separate.[27] For the Advocate-General, the purpose of Trademark Regulation, article 7(1)(e)(ii) is 'overwhelmingly to protect competition'. The Advocate-General in *Dyson* also repeated the same *leitmotiv* (allowing registration in this case would harm competition) and added

[24] D Gervais, *The TRIPs Agreement, Drafting History and Analysis,* 2nd edn (London, Sweet and Maxwell 2003) 117, para 2.76.

[25] COM(80)635 final (19 November 1980) 57.

[26] Case C-299/99 *Koninklijke Philips Electronics v Remington Consumer Products* [2002] ECR I-05475, para 78. See also para 82: indent (ii) 'reflects the *legitimate aim* of not allowing individuals to use registration of a mark in order to *acquire or perpetuate* exclusive rights relating to technical solutions' (emphasis added). The same was repeated in Advocate-General Mengozzi's Opinion, 26 January 2010, in Case C-48/09 *Lego Juris v OHIM*, para 55, available at www.curia.europa.eu.

[27] Advocate-General Opinion in *Lego Juris v OHIM*, para 55. The Court of Justice followed the Advocate-General, Case C-48/09 P, 14 September 2010, nyr, available at www.curia.europa.eu.

that it would also be against TRIPs Article 7.[28] This additional comment confirms the importance of TRIPs Article 7 for the resolution of overlap problems. The Advocate-General was even more explicit: allowing the trademark registration of concepts would give an exclusive right to inventions whereas this is not the purpose of trademark law.[29] It would allow the circumvention of patent law's stringent requirements in addition to giving the right-holder a protection (potentially) unlimited in time.[30] The Advocate-General in *Lego* further specified: 'the exclusion of functional shapes from the possible benefit conferred by that article 7(3) caters for the legislature's wish to prevent an object which has enjoyed patent or design protection from benefiting from that possibility'.[31]

The EU courts have constantly held that the various grounds for refusing registration set out in Trademark Directive, article 3(1)(b)–(e) must be interpreted in the light of the public interest underlying each of them.[32] This interest is that it would be wrong to grant exclusive (trademark) rights to a single operator as it could hinder competition on the market for the goods or services concerned.[33] The same goes for two-dimensional trademarks: the public interest lies 'in not unduly restricting the availability of colours for other traders who market goods or services of the same type as those in respect of which registration is sought'.[34] As the literature has rightly further explained, this public interest transcends trademark law[35] and is based on market freedom or effective competition, not simply the objectionable character of the overlap per se.[36]

Virtually the same reasons, namely free competition and preventing the circumvention of the stricter patent requirements, underlie Design Directive, article 7 which regulates much of the design/patent overlap. The MCAD also sees comparative advertising as a stimulator of competition.[37]

Part of the copyright/trademark overlap is also regulated by the *Dior v Evora* ruling, which is underpinned by the freedom of movement of goods and services. Arguably, as we have seen, the ruling should apply in analogous cases involving any IPR overlap.

Finally, only one 'rule' specifically authorises an overlap, that between IPRs and unfair competition. The reason behind it is that in that case, cumulation is natural because the intellectual property and unfair competition rules have a different nature. Unfair competition laws are based on liability rules and punish the unfairness in the behaviour of

[28] Advocate-General in Case C-321/03 *Dyson v Registrar of Trademarks* [2007] ECR I-687, para 94. Therefore, the Advocate-General considered TRIPs Art 7 as an important tool to interpret not only international law but EU law, which is similar to what we advocated in chapter one.

[29] Advocate-General in *Dyson*, ibid paras 95–97.

[30] Ibid paras 95–96. See also Advocate-General's Opinion in Case C-299/99 *Philips v Remington* (n 26) para 38.

[31] Advocate General's Opinion in *Lego Juris v OHIM*, paras 75–76. See also Case C-48/09 P, *Lego Juris v Mega Brands,* 14 September 2010, nyr, paras 45–46, available at www.curia.europa.eu.

[32] See Joined Cases C-108/97 and C-109/97 *Windsurfing Chiemsee* [1999] ECR I-2779, paras 25–27; Case C-299/99 *Koninklijke Philips Electronics v Remington Consumer Products* [2002] ECR I-05475, para 77; Joined Cases C-53/01–C-55/01 *Linde, Winward Industries and Rado Uhren* [2003] ECR I-3161, para 71.

[33] Joined Cases C-108/97 and C-109/97 *Windsurfing Chiemsee* [1999] ECR I-2779, para 25; Joined Cases C-468/01 P–C-472/01 P *Procter and Gamble v OHIM* [2004] ECR I-5141, para 73 (tablets for washing machines or dishwashers not distinctive).

[34] Case C-49/02 *Heidelberger Bauchemie* [2004] ECR I-6129, paras 41 and 42, citing Case C-104/01 *Libertel Groep BV v Benelux-Merkenbureau* [2003] ECR I-3793, paras 52–56.

[35] A Quaedvlieg, 'Concurrence and Convergence in Industrial Design: Three-Dimensional Shapes excluded by Trade Mark Law' in W Grosheide and J Brinkhof (eds), *Intellectual Property Law, Articles on Crossing Borders between Traditional and Actual* (Antwerpen, Intersentia, 2004) 23, 33.

[36] U Suthersanen, 'The European Court of Justice in *Philips v Remington*: Trade Marks and Market Freedom' (2003) *Intellectual Property Quarterly* 257, 282–83.

[37] See MCAD, recital 6.

competitors, while IPRs are property rights and protect certain subject matter as such against use by third parties.

C National Level

Member States, of course, have to follow the EU courts' case law so that what was said in section II.B above applies. It is interesting to note that French courts, before the EU courts, condemned the trademark/patent overlap for its inconsistency with the principle of freedom of commerce. The reason in France for not allowing the text of a patent application to be protected by copyright is the destination or aim of the work. In the United Kingdom, the first judge in *Catnic* based the abandonment of copyright in drawings of a patent application on the election of patent protection by the patentee.[38]

III. DETERMINATION OF CRITERIA TO ORGANISE THE OVERLAPS

As we identified in the introduction, overlaps can pose two problems: regime clashes and overprotection. In order to discover whether any of the overlaps create such problems, we need one criterion, or probably several criteria, as they may differ per overlap. These criteria can be found in the specific reasons identified above for authorising or preventing overlaps (section II), in the aims of the several laws (section IIIA), in the literature's proposals (section IIIB) and our assessment of these proposals and own reflections (section IIIC).

A Rationales, Aims and Justifications of the Intellectual Property and Unfair Competition Laws

In order to find criteria to organise overlaps, especially in respect of the overprotection problem, a good starting point is to examine the specific objectives of each of the intellectual property laws and of the unfair competition laws. First, this inquiry will establish whether the provisions in the law relating to each IPR and the provisions of unfair competition law in themselves respect these objectives. This is because very often overlap problems will be caused by an internal imbalance *within* the system of *one* of the overlapping IPRs which is thus just revealed or highlighted but not genuinely caused by the overlap as such. Secondly, where the provisions reveal no overprotection in each right itself, ie when the cumulation of several protections as such leads to overprotection, the analysis will help establish whether one of the rights should prevail on the basis of the overriding interests underlying them. Thus, in the first case, we are not confronted with a genuine overlap issue, but an internal malfunctioning of one right, and the solution is to fix that right, mainly by trimming it back to normal. To expand on the metaphor used in the introduction, the idea is to cut the leaves or branches of the plant or bush that go beyond its (initial) boundaries. If this does not work or, as in the second case, we are confronted with a genuine overlap problem, as we shall see in section III.B below, the

[38] '[A] patentee necessarily makes an election accepting that, in return for a potential monopoly, upon publication, the material disclosed by him in the specification must be deemed to be open to be used by the public': [1982] RPC 183, 206.

assessment criterion will often have to be *external*. This first section is not meant to be a comprehensive review of all justifications and their merit. There is no space and it is not the place in a book like this one to do so. The idea is really to bring out what comes through in terms of justifications at EU level.

(i) Copyright Law

Contrary to trademarks, designs, patents and plant variety rights, copyright is not entirely harmonised at EU level so that its justifications can be found not only in the relevant EU Directives (the Software Directive and Infosoc Directive 2001/29/EC[39]), but also in the national laws. Copyright is generally justified by the following rationales.[40] As with patents, a first justification which is proposed is straightforwardly based on fairness.[41] It seems just that an author should benefit, through property or another mechanism, from the fruits of his or her mind. This is also called the reward argument.[42] This argument has been further developed, secondly, on the basis of the labour theory, according to which everyone should have the property in results of their own labour. It is based on a natural rights argument.[43] A related justification is based on the protection of the personality of the author. Copyright preserves the author's name and honour by protecting the work's integrity. Thirdly, there is the utilitarian rationale or incentive theory from which derives the economic justification, which is based on economic theory. Its foundation is the public goods character of IPRs, which involves non-excludability and non-rivalry, and which has to be counter-balanced by granting protection, for example, a property right, in order to prevent underinvestment in creative expression.[44] When correctly applied, this justification 'serves to limit actual inefficiencies [in the several IPRs underpinned by it] by emphasising the public interest in free competition'.[45] This justification seems to be the prevalent one since copyright has come to protect technological endeavours such as computer programs.[46] Finally, the more recent justification is that copyright is a human right because it is a property right or at least because, under article 27 of the Universal Declaration of Human Rights and article 17(2) of the Charter of Fundamental Rights of the European Union, both the moral and material interests of authors must be protected.

German and French laws were, and for a great part still are, based on the personality rights theory, although with time this has evolved. The more recent German literature emphasises the dual character and basis of copyright law, based at least on both the

[39] As a reminder, only those two Directives in the field of copyright are relevant to the issue of overlaps.

[40] J Sterling, *World Copyright Law* (London, Sweet and Maxwell, 1998) 55–62, paras 2.27–2.42, provides a good list and summary of the justifications, some of which are not mentioned here as they have been criticised or not adopted (eg social contract argument). For an overview of the copyright justifications, see also eg L Bently and B Sherman, *Intellectual Property Law*, 3rd edn (Oxford, Oxford University Press 2009) 34–39.

[41] Sterling, *World Copyright Law* (n 40) 56–57, para 2.32, referring to some English decisions.

[42] Bently and Sherman, *Intellectual Property Law* (n 42) 36.

[43] Ibid 35–36.

[44] See eg K Arrow, 'Economic Welfare and the Allocation of Resources for Inventions' in R Nelson (ed), *The Rate and Direction of Economic Activity: Economic and Social Factors* (Princeton, Princeton University Press, 1962) 609; N Mankiw, *Principles of Economics*, 3rd edn (Ohio, Thomson/South-Western, 2002) 224.

[45] J Reichman, 'Charting the Collapse of the Patent–Copyright Dichotomy: Premises for a Restructured International Intellectual Property System' (1995) 13(2) *Cardozo Arts and Entertainment Law Journal* 475, 495.

[46] P Torremans, *Holyoak and Torremans Intellectual Property Law*, 5th edn (Oxford, Oxford University Press 2008) 22.

incentive and personality rights theories. In France, the right is not entirely justified by the protection of moral aspects as economic interests are also of prime importance. However, current French copyright law is based on the labour or property (natural rights) theories rather than on the incentive theory.[47] While the public interest has a place in French copyright law, it is less important than in the British and American traditions as the hierarchy of interests favours the author.[48] On the other hand, even if the United Kingdom has since 1988 properly integrated moral rights, the incentive theory predominates.

What do the Software and Infosoc Directives provide as justifications? Both Directives predominantly refer to the economic rationale.[49] This is not surprising as the European Union has so far not harmonised moral rights and this area is still regulated solely by national law. However, Software Directive, recital 17 also states that the rules of the Directive are without prejudice to competition rules. And interestingly, the Infosoc Directive insists several times on the interests of users of copyright works,[50] of society in general,[51] freedom of expression[52] and culture,[53] in addition to the interests of authors, performers and producers. Recital 31 also adds that '[a] fair balance of rights and interests between the different categories of right-holders, as well as between the different categories of right-holders and users of protected subject matter must be safeguarded'. In addition, all Member States also have to give free speech proper consideration in the interpretation of their copyright laws. In addition, the EU courts' case law now makes very clear that although the aim of high protection of the Infosoc Directive must be respected, as per the recitals of the Directive, the freedom of movement of goods and services also governs copyright law, as the *Peek and Cloppenburg v Cassina* ruling demonstrates.[54] The decision also confirms that there is no principle according to which an ambiguity in the Directive must by definition be interpreted in favour of right-holders simply because of the Directive's goal of a high level of protection.[55]

(ii) Design Law

As Bently and Sherman point out, very few commentators have discussed the justification for granting design protection.[56] This is because commentators assume that 'the general arguments which justify the protection of works by copyright or inventions by patents, whether based on instrumental philosophies or ethical beliefs, are equally applicable to designs'.[57] The basic argument is the economic rationale and this is also reflected in the Green Paper on the Legal Protection of Industrial Design (at 2) and the Design

[47] See PY Gautier, *Propriété Littéraire et Artistique*, 4th edn (Paris, Presses Universitaires de France, 2001) 22–25, para 9-11, 35, para 20; A Lucas and HJ Lucas, *Traité de la Propriété Littéraire et Artistique*, 2nd edn (Paris, Litec, 2001) 34, para 28.

[48] Lucas and Lucas, *Traité de la Propriété Littéraire et Artistique* (n 47) 36, para 28.

[49] Software Directive, recital 2 and Infosoc Directive, recitals 4, 9, 10, 11.

[50] Infosoc Directive, recital 9.

[51] Ibid recitals 3 ('the public interest') and 9 ('the public at large').

[52] Ibid recital 3.

[53] Ibid recitals 9 and 12.

[54] Case C-456/06 *Peek and Cloppenburg v Cassina* [2008] ECR I-2731, and the Advocate-General's Opinion, discussed by M Leistner, 'Copyright Law in the EC: Status Quo, Recent Case Law and Policy Perspectives' (2009) 46 *Common Market Law Review* 847, 860–65.

[55] Leistner, 'Copyright Law in the EC: Status Quo, Recent Case Law and Policy Perspectives' (n 54) 865.

[56] Bently and Sherman, *Intellectual Property Law* (n 40) 608.

[57] Ibid.

Regulation, recital 7.[58] The Green Paper on the legal protection of industrial design adds the notion of competitiveness of the European industry.[59] Very rarely has design protection been justified by 'the natural rights of individual designers in their creations. This reflects a commonly held assumption that designs are less creative than artistic works because designing is subject to a number of inevitable constraints'.[60] Like the Software Directive, the Design Directive also adds that its provisions are without prejudice to the application of the competition rules (recital 18).

(iii) Trademark Law

With design rights, the justification for trademark law is the one that has been the least considered in comparison to other IPRs.[61] As we shall see, it is also the one which has changed the most in recent years. The first, original and still the main function of trademarks is to serve as an indication of the origin of goods or services.[62] This is also what the EU courts have continued to repeat over the years.[63] The seeds of an extension of the justifications for trademark law were already reflected, however, in the Trademark Directive, recital 11 of which states: 'The protection afforded by the registered trademark, the function of which is *in particular* to guarantee the trademark as an indication of origin' (emphasis added). This is repeated in CTMR, recital 8. And even before that, the Memomandum on the creation of EEC Trademark stated even more clearly:

> By virtue of their role as an indicator of origin and quality and as a means of advertising, trademarks are indeed an indispensable means of promoting trade and in doing so assist the further interpenetration of national markets. They help manufacturers to acquire new markets and thus help to promote the expansion of economic activity beyond national borders.[64]

This added, therefore, two justifications, which are also repeated in the literature.[65] In the words of the authors of *Kerlys' Law of Trademarks and Trade Names*:

> the quality function of a trademark is that the trademark offers a guarantee to the consumer that the quality of the goods or services will be that to which the consumer has become accustomed. The 'advertising' function relates to the 'cachet' or 'aura' which the consumer associates with the mark and its goods or services.[66]

[58] Ibid; I Govaere, *The Use and Abuse of Intellectual Property Rights in European Community Law* (London, Sweet and Maxwell, 1996) 26–27.

[59] Green Paper on the Legal Protection of Industrial Design (n 7) 2.

[60] Bently and Sherman, *Intellectual Property Law* (n 40) 608–9.

[61] Ibid 717.

[62] Ibid 717; Torremans, *Holyoak and Torremans Intellectual Property Law* (n 46) 368.

[63] See Case C-349/95 *Loendersloot (Frits) (t/a Loendersloot Internationale Expeditie) v George Ballantine & Son* [1997] ECR I-6627, paras 22 and 24; Case C-39/97 *Canon Kabushiki Kaisha v Metro-Goldwyn-Mayer Inc* [1998] ECR I-5507, para 28; and Case C-299/99 *Koninklijke Philips Electronics v Remington Consumer Products* [2002] ECR I-5475, para 30, all cited in case C-273/00 *Sieckmann (Ralf) v Deutches Patent- and Markenamt* [2002] ECR I-11737. The courts have used the term 'guaranteeing the identity of the origin' but there is arguably no difference between guaranteeing the identity of the origin and guaranteeing the origin. J Phillips, *Trade Mark Law: A Practical Anatomy* (Oxford, Oxford University Press, 2003) 25.

[64] Bulletin of the European Communities, Supplement 8/76, adopted by the Commission on 6 July 1976, para 21.

[65] Bently and Sherman, *Intellectual Property Law* (n 40) 717–19; D Kitchin, D Llewelyn, J Mellor, R Meade, T Moody-Stuart and D Keeling, *Kerly's Law of Trade Marks and Trade Names,* 14th edn (London, Sweet and Maxwell, 2005) 9.

[66] Kitchin *et al*, *Kerly's Law of Trade Marks and Trade Names* (n 65) 9.

For some commentators, some trademarks even have a descriptive function: 'some of the most powerful trademarks are those which indicate origin but also contain an allusion to some characteristic of the goods or services'.[67] For others, trademark law seeks to protect undistorted competition.[68] From the standpoint of information economics, the main argument to justify trademark law is that marks 'increase the supply of information to consumers and thereby increase the efficiency of the market'.[69]

Other more dubious justifications have been proposed in the literature. Some have tried to justify trademarks on the same basis as copyright, ie on the basis that they are creations.[70] However, this argument is probably weak 'in part because while the associations between the mark and a source of goodwill may be instigated and nurtured by the trader, they are as much created by the customers and the public'.[71] Probably, it is best to say, if one wishes to justify trademarks along those lines, that trademarks are also justified by the incentive theory. They serve as a reward for the investment: the mark helps to ensure that the trademark owner, and not an imitating competitor, reaps the 'financial, reputation-related rewards associated with a desirable product'.[72] Finally, ethical justifications have also been proposed. One is the idea that it is wrong to lie.[73] However, this would only support a very narrow conception of trademarks as it would not cover those who use the trademark innocently. The other is the idea of fairness or justice. One should not reap what one has not sown,[74] which translates, in trademark terms, into the idea that no one should take advantage of the goodwill generated by the trademark owner. This justification is close to those justifying unfair competition and unjust enrichment and has been used to justify extended protection to trademarks with reputation.[75] However, the law does not punish 'every case of reaping without sowing (eg copying an unpatented business idea)'.[76] Therefore, the current extension of the protection conferred by trademark law is more difficult to justify soundly on those additional bases.[77]

Nevertheless, the attitude towards the functions of trademarks has certainly changed in recent years. Although, undoubtedly, for the EU courts, the 'essential function' of the trademark is still the indication of origin function, the Court of Justice has now also confirmed the quality and advertising functions of trademarks.[78] The Court of Justice has even explicitly held that trademark's functions also include that of communication and investment.[79]

[67] Ibid.
[68] Phillips, *Trade Mark Law: A Practical Anatomy* (n 63) 25.
[69] Bently and Sherman, *Intellectual Property Law* (n 40) 718.
[70] Ibid 717.
[71] Ibid 718.
[72] Ibid, citing Breyer J of the US Supreme Court in *Qualitex v Jacobson Products* (1995) 115 S Ct 1300.
[73] Bently and Sherman, *Intellectual Property Law* (n 40) 720.
[74] Ibid 719.
[75] Ibid 719–20.
[76] Ibid 720.
[77] Along the same lines, see ibid 717.
[78] See Case C-487/07 *L'Oréal SA, Lancôme Parfums et Beauté & Cie SNC and Laboratoire Garnier & Cie v Bellure NV, Malaika Investments Ltd and Starion International Ltd* [2009] ECR I-5185, para 58. See also para 63.
[79] Ibid.

(iv) Patent Law

As regards the justifications of patent law, nothing can be found in the EPC as such but the following justifications are nevertheless applicable at least to France, the United Kingdom and Germany. As in copyright law, a first simple justification for patents is that it seems just that the inventor be granted exclusive property rights on his or her invention. In other words, it is fair that inventors should be rewarded for their innovations.[80] A second reason, which can be said to be a subcategory of this 'fairness argument', is the labour or natural rights theory. A third justification for patents is to give inventors an incentive to innovate (utilitarian or economic rationale). Fourthly, patent laws can also be based on a social contract. According to this theory, the patentee obtains an exclusive right in his or her invention but in return s/he must disclose it to the public in such a way that it can be understood and reproduced by persons skilled in the art.[81] According to this theory, patent law's function is mainly an informative one. The fifth patent theory is based, as in copyright law, on the personality of the inventor but as patent law protects the expression of the personality of the inventor to a lesser degree than copyright law, the justification is less important in the field of patents.

It has been claimed that each of these theories can on its own justify the introduction of patent laws and that the theories are therefore independent of each other.[82] However, to the contrary, the development of modern patent law has shown that these theories are not independent and that it is rather a combination of them which underlies modern patent laws.[83] In any case, the different theories are not (necessarily) conflicting. Clearly, the incentive theory provides the single most important justification at the basis of current patent laws in Europe.[84] This is also reflected in Biotech Directive, recital 2.[85] The Biotech Directive, however, also reiterates that the European Union must respect the fundamental rights guaranteed in the European Convention on Human Rights (ECHR), recital 43.

(v) Plant Variety Rights

Plant variety rights focus not only on the breeder's interests in giving an incentive to breed new plant varieties but also on other interests. This is why their name shifted over the years from 'breeder's rights' to 'plant variety rights'.[86] While the plant variety right is

[80] Such was the first justification for patents in France (1791 Act). See H Gaumont-Prat, *Droit de la propriété industrielle* (Paris, Litec, 2009) 2.

[81] This was gradually adopted as the main justification in France. See Gaumont-Prat, *Droit de la propriété industrielle* (n 80) 2, citing Roubier; J Azéma and JC Galloux, *Droit de la propriété industrielle*, 6th edn (Paris, Dalloz, 2006) 89.

[82] F Machlup and E Penrose, 'The Patent Controversy in the Nineteenth Century' (1950) 10(1) *Journal of Economic History* 10, 11; V Denicolo and L Franzoni, 'The Contract Theory of Patents' (2003) 23 *International Review of Law and Economics* 365; M Fisher, 'Classical Economics and Philosophy of the Patent System' (2005) *Intellectual Property Quarterly* 1, 5, 21; J Phillips and A Firth, *Introduction to Intellectual Property Law*, 4th edn (London, Butterworth, 2001) 24.

[83] W Cornish and D Llewelyn, *Intellectual Property: Patents, Copyright, Trade Marks and Allied Rights*, 6th edn (London, Sweet and Maxwell 2007) 141–42: 'The experience with biotechnology underscores how the justifications for the patent system are not independent. Rather they are cumulative, and each imposes its limitations'.

[84] For instance, German literature agrees that modern patent law is justified by a modern and thus balanced incentive theory.

[85] 'Whereas, in particular in the field of genetic engineering, research and development require a considerable amount of high-risk investment and therefore only adequate legal protection can make them profitable.'

[86] M Llewelyn and M Adcock, *European Plant Intellectual Property* (Oxford, Hart Publishing, 2006) 21–29.

based on the economic rationale[87] (which is represented here by the *time* invested in producing a new variety[88]), it is also strongly based on the notion of public interest.[89] Patent law is also justified by the public interest, but the Community Plant Variety Right (CPVR) Regulation (EC) 2100/94 is more strongly influenced by it than patent law, which is in contrast more focused on the patentee's rights.[90]

The fact that the CPVR is seen as an industrial property right, that the European Union is a party to the TRIPs Agreement and that plant variety rights have been 'patentised' has led some to think that the public interest is now less important in plant variety rights and that it will be more difficult to curb monopolisation of plant material on the basis of the public interest.[91] We respectfully disagree because of TRIPs Articles 7 and 8, which require a balance of rights and obligations, as we have seen in the international chapter. Moreover, the differences in aims between the two rights are still clearly reflected in their provisions. The conditions to obtain a patent are tough to meet and this is why they justify comparatively strong rights. In plant variety rights, inventiveness is not required and plant variety rights can be given to discoveries. Consequently, the right is less strong than a patent.[92]

(vi) Unfair Competition Law

At the outset, unfair competition law aimed at protecting individual competitors from unfair behaviours of other competitors[93] and therefore ensured that 'all market participants . . . compete in a fair and decent manner and in accordance with the rules of the "game" in the field of competition'.[94] As most unfair trading practices were equivalent to the acts prohibited by industrial property law, protection against unfair competition was recognised as forming part of industrial property protection.[95] Paris Convention Article 1(2) states that the proscription of unfair competition is part of industrial property. In other words, unfair competition encompasses all aspects of industrial[96] or even intellectual[97] property law. Unfair competition law also aims to 'secure the freedom of competition structures, thus maintaining undistorted competition as the foundation of the free-enterprise system'.[98] The main principle underlying Paris Article 10*bis* is thus the enforcement and guarantee of free competition.[99]

[87] Bently and Sherman, *Intellectual Property Law* (n 40) 592.

[88] Llewelyn and Adcock, *European Plant Intellectual Property* (Oxford, Hart Publishing, 2006) 32.

[89] The UPOV Convention's mission statement states that the right is granted for 'the benefit of society'. See also the objectives of the CPVR Regulation summarised by Llewelyn and Adcock, *European Plant Intellectual Property* (n 86) 204–5, as being among the relevant ones for our discussion: to stimulate the breeding and development of new varieties and be available for all botanical genera and species and recognise that certain restrictions should be placed on the rights for reasons of public interest. See also CPVR Regulation, recitals 17–20.

[90] Llewelyn and Adcock, *European Plant Intellectual Property* (n 86) 235.

[91] Ibid 235–36.

[92] Ibid 31–32.

[93] A Kamperman Sanders, *Unfair Competition Law, the Protection of Intellectual and Industrial Creativity* (Oxford, Clarendon Press, 1997) 22; de Vrey, *Towards a European Unfair Competition Law* (n 1) 12.

[94] de Vrey, *Towards a European Unfair Competition Law* (n 1) 11.

[95] Ibid 12.

[96] Kamperman Sanders, *Unfair Competition Law, the Protection of Intellectual and Industrial Creativity* (n 93) 23.

[97] de Vrey, *Towards a European Unfair Competition Law* (n 1) 12.

[98] Kamperman Sanders, *Unfair Competition Law, the Protection of Intellectual and Industrial Creativity* (n 93) 23.

[99] Ibid 86.

Despite their close relationship, intellectual property law and unfair competition law have different goals, which can justify cumulative protection. As the German Federal Court of Justice recently held, cumulative application of design protection and the unfair competition action can be justified because of the different objectives of both laws. This has also been often stressed by the Green Paper on the Legal Protection of Industrial Design[100] and in the literature.[101] For instance, as trademark law and unfair competition pursue different goals, the concept of likelihood of confusion need not be the same in both laws.[102] Indeed, IPRs are property rights while unfair competition law is based on civil liability.[103] While IPRs sanction a property right which prevents simply making or copying an achievement, unfair competition law usually only applies to competitors, and requires an extra element which makes the action of the defendant unfair, such as misleading consumers or breaching an obligation of confidentiality. Not much can be inferred from the MCAD and UCPD, but similarly to the Biotech and InfoSoc Directives, UCPD, recital 25 states that the Directive respects human rights.

In conclusion, at EU and national level, all IPRs, partly even trademarks now, are in essence based on the economic rationale.[104] The economic rationale or incentive theory is based on a balancing of the IPR holder's rights and those of the public. This is specifically stressed in the Infosoc Directive. Therefore, as well put by Kur, each IPR is the result of 'a conscious and thorough balancing of specific protection interests on one hand and interests in free competition on the other, with free competition prevailing – in theory – where such rights do not apply'.[105] In other words, 'the objective pursued by each right can . . . serve as a tool to distribute the protections, by refusing that one right be instrumentalised, outside its normal sphere of operation to protect a market share'.[106] Therefore, this balance must be maintained, in other words, no right must be curtailed nor extended. So when an overlap occurs, the main question is whether this balance is maintained.[107] The respect for human rights is also specifically mentioned in the Infosoc, Biotech and Unfair Commercial Practices Directives. This reinforces the accent the EU legislature puts on the preservation of the balance between IPRs and other rights or interests. The goals of undistorted competition and freedom of movement of goods and services, which are also paramount at EU level, reinforce this idea yet again. Finally, unfair competition law is also driven by the guarantee of free competition. In sum, the

[100] Green Paper on the Legal Protection of Industrial Design (n 7) para 11.6 refers to the different nature of the unfair competition rules, which tend to deal with fairness of behaviour of operators in trade and which require, in addition to the objective facts of misbehaviour, the existence of a subjective element of fault or negligence on the part of the offender.

[101] C Gielen, 'Design Protection and Unfair Competition' in J Kabel and G Mom, *Intellectual Property and Information Law: Essays in Honour of Herman Cohen Jeroham* (The Hague, Kluwer Law International, 1998) 261, 263–64 (cumulation between design and unfair competition laws is possible as their aims are different. Under unfair competition law, emphasis is put on the avoidance of confusion in the market place').

[102] F Henning Bodewig, *Unfair Competition Law: European Union and Member States* (The Hague, Kluwer Law International, 2006) 5.

[103] See eg ibid.

[104] This is now (since June 2009) the case even for trademark law, although its main, essential, function is still indication of origin. In fact, over the years, there seems to have been a convergence between the rationale for IPRs. They all now seem to be driven, for better or for worse, simply by the need to recoup an investment.

[105] A Kur, 'Cumulation of IP Rights Pertaining to Product Shapes: An "Illegitimate Offspring" of IP Law?' in G Ghidini and M Genovesi (eds), *Intellectual Property and Market Power, ATRIP Papers 2006–2007* (Buenos Aires, Eudeba, 2008) 613, 614.

[106] S Dusollier, 'Introduction' in S Dusollier and A Cruquenaire (eds), *Le cumul des droits intellectuels* (Brussels, Larcier, 2009) 5, 8.

[107] Kur, 'Cumulation of IP Rights Pertaining to Product Shapes' (n 105) 613, 614.

aims and justifications for IPRs and unfair competition law do play a vital part in the resolution of the overlap problem.

B Criteria Proposed by the Literature

In this section, we examine the criteria proposed by commentators which can apply to every content and type (simultaneous, negative and a posteriori) of overlap. Of course, many of the rules identified at the several levels in section I could also be used as criteria or solutions to overlaps and they will be evaluated along with the literature's proposals in section IIIC. The literature's proposals for each separate overlap at each level have been presented in each preceding chapter and will not be repeated here. However, we evaluate their merit in section IIIC as well.

The examination of the literature brings out no less than ten possible 'overarching' rules or principles which could regulate the interplay between IPRs and between IPRs and unfair competition.

First, the literature reiterates that in most legal systems, including the European Union, no general rule exists which prohibits overlaps.[108] More than that, 'it seems a universally acknowledged rule that several IP rights can concur in one and the same product'.[109] This rule seems natural as, if several interests are involved at the same time, several rights may be granted to protect each of these interests.[110] In other words, overlapping protection is inevitable as there are many different IPRs and ideally, this is not pathological, 'it only highlights the complexity of the material'.[111] Therefore Kur starts from the premise that overlaps do not pose a problem per se:

> Neither competition nor the general structure of intellectual property rights will be negatively affected as long as:
>
> - the requirements for protection under the different legal regimes are formulated and applied so as to fully justify the protection granted, and
> - each one of the rights applied is adequately balanced in itself, in particular as regards the relationship between the requirements, the general scope of protection and limitations.[112]

This statement links to the second idea, stressed by many commentators, that the aims of the different intellectual property laws are important and need to be respected in order to have a 'healthy overlap situation'. A general tenet of most IPRs is that the laws also aim at balancing IPRs with society's interests. This is why IPRs are not unlimited property rights but exclude subject matter from protection and/or allow certain uses of the material.[113] The public interest, which includes the preservation and enhancement of

[108] Ibid 615; V Moffatt, 'Mutant Copyrights and Backdoor Patents: The Problem of Overlapping Intellectual Property Protection' (2004) *Berkeley Technology Law Journal* 1473, 1531 (discussing the United States).

[109] Quaedvlieg, 'Concurrence and Convergence in Industrial Design' (n 35) 23.

[110] A Quaedvlieg, 'Overlap/Relationships Between Copyright and Other Intellectual Property Rights' in E Derclaye (ed), *Research Handbook on the Future of EU Copyright* (Cheltenham, Edward Elgar Publishing 2009) 479, 480.

[111] JC Galloux, *Des possibles cumuls de protection par les droits de propriété intellectuelle* (Paris, Litec, Coll IRPI, 2003) vol 23, 92.

[112] A Kur, 'Cumulation of Rights with Regard to Three-Dimensional Shapes: Two Exemplary Case Studies' in S Dusollier and A Cruquenaire (eds), *Le cumul des droits intellectuels* (Brussels, Larcier, 2009) 155, 159.

[113] Suthersanen, 'The European Court of Justice in *Philips v Remington*' (n 36) 270; A Quaedvlieg, 'Protection of Three-Dimensional Models as a Trade Mark, in Adjuncts and Alternatives to Copyright' in

the public domain and also the maintenance of a competitive marketplace, is in fact the centre of the utilitarian rationale,[114] which, as we have seen in section IIIA, is nowadays the most important general justification for all IPRs. Even more so, the goal of the utilitarian theory of intellectual property is, at least in theory, 'to provide the minimum amount of incentive (that is, the fewest rights to spur an appropriate level of creation) at the lowest cost to society'.[115] Against that general background, nonetheless, in theory the different branches of IPRs follow different specific objectives. As a consequence of these different specific objectives (at least of patents, designs and trademarks), normally 'the object of their protection cannot coincide'.[116] In other words, the several IPRs exist independently of each other because they have different purposes.[117] Therefore, since the rights have different purposes, they should not normally clash. However, other authors have warned that we should also not create a general rule which allows all types of overlaps across the board.[118] If the aims of IPRs change or are not respected by the actual rules in the laws, then overlaps can become problematic, at least from a utilitarian perspective. In some cases, instead of allowing the overlap, it might be better to eliminate one right and increase or strengthen the scope and/or rights of the remaining IPRs.[119]

Another consequence of these premises is that we should not adopt one general rule or principle prohibiting all overlaps in the field of IPRs.[120] This is because most of the time the problems created by the overlaps between different IPRs in general do not arise from the occurrence of the overlaps themselves but from an undue extension of one or more IPRs (eg trademarks) over the last few years. These extensions are detrimental to the general tenet we saw above, namely that all IPRs are based on a 'conscious and thorough balancing of protection versus competition interests'.[121] As we have seen throughout the book, many exclusions in intellectual property laws are explicitly based on this principle (eg the exclusion of certain shapes in trademark law, the must-fit exclusion in design law,

J Ginsburg and J Besek (eds), *Adjuncts and Alternatives to Copyright, Proceedings of the ALAI Congress, June 13–17, 2001, New York USA* (New York, Columbia University School of Law, 2002) 576, 577, suggests that 'the object of copyright is not only to determine what is protected but also to safeguard from monopolisation subject matter which intentionally has been reserved to the free domain'.

[114] Moffatt, 'Mutant Copyrights and Backdoor Patents' (n 108) 1481, 1488, 1508.

[115] Ibid 1517.

[116] A Folliard-Monguiral and D Rogers, 'The Protection of Shapes by the Community Trademark' (2003) *European Intellectual Property Review* 169, 178. See also Dusollier, 'Introduction' (n 106) 8.

[117] G Dinwoodie, 'Copyright, Trade Marks and Trade Dress: The Overlap (and Conflict?) in Intellectual Property Regimes Concerning Designs and Visual Images, General Report' in J Ginsburg and J Besek (eds), *Adjuncts and Alternatives to Copyright, Proceedings of the ALAI Congress, June 13–17, 2001, New York USA* (New York, Columbia University School of Law, 2002) 497, 511. See also J Carpenter 'Intellectual Property: The Overlap Between Utility Patents, Plant Patents, the PVPA and Trade Secrets and the Limitations on that Overlap (2005) *North Dakota Law Review* 171, 197: 'Based on the complementary nature of the intellectual property rights, and the boundaries inherently created in each, external limitations are often not required'. As we shall see in more detail below, some overlap problems are caused by an internal imbalance so that external remedies are not necessary.

[118] Dinwoodie, 'Copyright, Trade Marks and Trade Dress' (n 117) 497, 519.

[119] Moffatt, 'Mutant Copyrights and Backdoor Patents' (n 108) 1515.

[120] Dinwoodie, 'Copyright, Trade Marks and Trade Dress' (n 117) 497, 519–21. *Contra*: Moffatt, 'Mutant Copyrights and Backdoor Patents' (n 108) 1530, who thinks that all overlaps should be prohibited and new ones avoided but proposes freedom of competition as a rule in the meantime to curb overprotection caused by overlaps.

[121] A Kur, 'Exceptions to Protection where Copyright and Trade Mark Overlap: Parody, News Reporting and Other "Speech" Use of Trade Marks, General Report' in J Ginsburg and J Besek (eds), *Adjuncts and Alternatives to Copyright, Proceedings of the ALAI Congress, June 13–17, 2001, New York USA* (New York, Columbia University School of Law, 2002) 593, 596.

etc). In addition and as part of this concern for leaving a certain amount of competition unencumbered, these exclusions also serve to trace the borders of the four main IPRs, copyright, patent, trademark and design right, as the Green Paper on the Legal Protection of Industrial Design and the Explanatory Memorandum to the Trademark Directive and Regulation explicitly or implicitly state.[122] In many cases, these rules accordingly ensure that there are no overlaps between these rights.

Accordingly, the literature also stresses the importance of freedom of competition for developing detailed solutions to overlap problems.[123] Therefore, the concern for free competition should be (part of) the solution to problems caused by overlaps. As a side effect, the principle of free competition also serves to 'effect intra-intellectual property harmonisation'.[124] A first solution based on this principle or a concrete application of this principle is to trim the IPRs in overlap situations rather than to adopt a general non-cumulation rule applying to all IPRs.[125] For instance, trademark law should in many cases be trimmed as it is the main culprit as far as creation of overlaps is concerned.[126] So, freedom of competition is the first 'rule' or principle proposed by the literature to deal with overlaps in general.

These initial ideas are well summarised by Kur under the form of a thesis:

> Although overlaps do not pose a problem per se, they tend to enhance the visibility of imbalances which might otherwise remain undetected. If conduct is permitted under one right which is prohibited under the other, this begs the question whether the different results are in fact justified in light of the specific character[[127]] of each of the two rights or whether they are indicative of the fact that there is something wrong with at least one of them.[128]

The proposal, made by Feer Verkade in relation to the overlap between trademark and copyright,[129] that 'one law should not be able to cut across the object of another' or 'across the result another law evidently intended to produce' is a more precise way of expressing the idea that a right needs to be trimmed if the balance of interests underlying that specific right is extended beyond its initial borders and therefore contradicts the result another law intended to reach. It is an interim solution to legislative trimming. It

[122] Green Paper on the Legal Protection of Industrial Design (n 7); COM(80)635 final (19 November 1980) 57.

[123] For some authors, IPRs are exceptions to the principle of freedom of commerce and industry (C Caron, *Droit d'auteur et droits voisins* (Paris, Litec, 2006) 19; Dusollier, 'Introduction' (n 106) 19, which would entail that the principle *singularia non sunt extendenda*, which has a long tradition and was applied in Roman law (see eg R Moufang, 'Protection for Plant Breeding and Plant Varieties: A Frontier of Patent Law' (1992) 3 *International Review of Intellectual Property and Competition Law* 328, 345) would apply.

[124] Dinwoodie, 'Copyright, Trade Marks and Trade Dress' (n 117) 497, 521.

[125] Quaedvlieg, 'Protection of Three-Dimensional Models as a Trade Mark' (n 113) 583, 591; Kur, 'Exceptions to Protection where Copyright and Trade Mark Overlap' (n 121) 599; Dinwoodie, 'Copyright, Trade Marks and Trade Dress' (n 118) 519.

[126] Quaedvlieg, 'Protection of Three-Dimensional Models as a Trade Mark' (n 113) 583, 591; Dinwoodie, 'Copyright, Trade Marks and Trade Dress' (n 118) 520–21.

[127] One might even say the aim/rationale of the IPR.

[128] Kur, 'Cumulation of IP Rights Pertaining to Product Shapes' (n 105) 616.

[129] D Feer Verkade, 'The Cumulative Effect of Copyright Law and Trademark Law: Which Takes Precedence?' in J Kabel and G Mom, *Intellectual Property and Information Law: Essays in Honour of Herman Cohen Jeroham* (The Hague, Kluwer Law International, 1998) 69, 70. See also Reichman, 'Charting the Collapse of the Patent–Copyright Dichotomy' (n 45) 495 (copyright law should not encroach on patent law if it would disrupt competition); and Dinwoodie, 'Copyright, Trade Marks and Trade Dress' (n 118) 497, 511 (if the IPR holder were allowed to pick and choose between copyright and trademark law, it would 'negate legislative intent because the construction of a one regime has often implied rejection of application of the other to the particular subject matter in question').

asks, on the basis of the aims of the laws, which IPR should take precedence in a particular overlap situation where two different specific and comprehensive balances of interests with regard to different IPRs contradict each other.[130] Feer Verkade then lists a number of reasons which should help to specifically implement this principle in a particular case:

> abuse of a right; exercise incompatible with the principles of reasonableness and fairness; exercise incompatible with freedom of information under article 10 of the ECHR; nullity of a relevant legal relationship under article 85 of the EC treaty [now TFEU Article 101]; precedence for the free movement of goods (including advertising the goods offered) under article 30–36[sic] of the EC treaty [now TFEU Articles 34–36].[131]

Arguably they are some further reasons, as we shall see below. This principle could be called the principle of prevalence, as opposed to hierarchy (where one IPR is by definition superior to other IPR[132]) or priority (where one IPR was created before a second IPR[133]).

A second principle, which is addressed less by commentators[134] but arose out of the Court of Justice decision in *Dior v Evora* and was already firmly grounded in the preparatory materials for the EU trademark and design rights, is that of the free movement of goods and services. This principle works well for regulating the simultaneous overlap which involves exhaustion of rights. If an overlap (be it simultaneous, negative or *a posteriori*) also runs counter to the freedom of movement of goods and services principle, it is clear that in the European Union, this principle will have to take precedence as it is a fundamental rule of the TFEU, which is above any secondary legislation such as intellectual property Directives and Regulations.

However, as Quaedvlieg warns, it is probably right to say that one should not forget that general principles, such as the general principle of freedom of trade and enterprise and the freedom of movement of goods and services, often 'offer no clear guidance in concrete cases' because they lack precision.[135] For instance, they cannot be said to decidedly prohibit the prolongation of protection by a trademark right of a copyright work fallen into the public domain.[136] Hence, these two principles will just serve as rules of thumb or interpretative tools for courts which will have to decide on a case-by-case basis. Courts will have to scrutinise the particular provision at stake to determine its underlying policy and decide how far the provision should extend.[137]

Another potent principle, which is arguably based on the principle that some competition should be available, is that in certain cases, through his or her conduct (ie choosing

[130] See for an example Quaedvlieg, 'Overlap/Relationships Between Copyright and Other Intellectual Property Rights' (n 110) 479, 512 ('as copyright contains many detailed exceptions, each supported by its own individual cocktail of public and private interests, the subject of exceptions typically is one where certain copyright rules or interests might take precedence over other IP rights').

[131] Feer Verkade, 'The Cumulative Effect of Copyright Law and Trademark Law' (n 129) 71 n 16.

[132] This rule has been proposed by some French commentators for certain overlaps. See chapter IV.

[133] Priority rules exist in EU law and because of harmonisation, also in national laws. EU law prevents a person from registering (without authorisation) a copyright work or protected design as a trademark or a copyright work or trademark as a design. See chapter 3, sections II and III.

[134] See nonetheless Quaedvlieg, 'Concurrence and Convergence in Industrial Design' (n 35) 29–30 (freedom of movement of goods and services is an example of negative convergence); E Derclaye, *The Legal Protection of Databases: A Comparative Analysis* (Cheltenham, Edward Elgar Publishing, 2008) 185–87 (in respect of the overlap between contracts and the database *sui generis* right).

[135] Quaedvlieg, 'Concurrence and Convergence in Industrial Design' (n 35) 35.

[136] Ibid.

[137] Ibid.

a certain IPR), the right-holder has elected to receive (or has received if the exploitation of the right has been fruitful) the benefits of a specific IPR.[138] Therefore, s/he has been appropriately rewarded, or rather s/he has benefited from the incentive given in that (chosen) law and should not be granted an additional (and unnecessary) incentive.[139] Otherwise, there is arguably overprotection of the subject matter in question. There are specific rules in certain countries reflecting this principle, for instance those which limit the protection of subject matter by unfair competition law after the IPR's expiry, and that of UK Copyright Act, section 52, limiting to 25 years the protection of certain works exploited on an industrial scale.[140]

A fourth rule can be based on fundamental rights, especially freedom of expression, as it is the most relevant human right in the intellectual property law field.[141] In the framework of the Charter of Fundamental Rights of the European Union, freedom of expression has to be balanced with the duty of the Member States to protect intellectual property. If an overlap breaches a human right, this human right has to prevail. Or if, less radically, an overlap encroaches too much on a human right, a solution must be found so that the balance is restored in accordance with the principle of proportionality. As many German commentators have said, both this principle and that of free competition should be combined to resolve overlap problems.

Another principle, proposed mainly for the copyright/trademark *a posteriori* overlap, is to ask what the function of the subject matter, the character of the achievement or the mode of exploitation of the achievement is. This rule can also be formulated as the rule of the most significant relationship (*principe de proximité*), whose wording, at least, is borrowed from the private international law field.[142] The question to ask is: does the subject matter function (primarily) as a trademark or as a copyright work? If its primary function is to be a trademark (eg a logo specifically created to distinguish the goods of an undertaking), then only trademark law should apply, and vice versa.[143] If an artistic work was first created as a cartoon character or an illustration in a children's book and only that, it cannot thereafter be 'transformed' into a trademark for goods or services. However, it may not always be possible to determine the nature of the subject matter in each particular situation. This may even be the more so precisely because the intellectual property categories have become increasingly blurred.[144] Hence, 'the determination of what is the *dominant aspect* of the work could entail arbitrary and subjective decisions'.[145] Finally, it is to be noted that a rule based on the intention of the creator rather than the function of the work is even more dangerous as it is more easily by-passed or manipulated if the creator is intellectual property-aware.

[138] Along the same lines, see Moffatt, 'Mutant Copyrights and Backdoor Patents' (n 108) *Berkeley Technology Law Journal* 1532.

[139] Along the same lines, see Dinwoodie, 'Copyright, Trade Marks and Trade Dress' (n 118) 510.

[140] Dinwoodie, 'Copyright, Trade Marks and Trade Dress' (n 117) 510.

[141] Feer Verkade, 'The Cumulative Effect of Copyright Law and Trademark Law' (n 129) 71 n 16; and German literature, see chapter VI.

[142] Quaedvlieg, 'Overlap/Relationships Between Copyright and Other Intellectual Property Rights' (n 110) 489; N Binctin, 'Le cumul d'appropriation: du parfum au logiciel' (2006) 12 *Communication Commerce Electronique* (December) no 36, para 13, claiming it is possible to establish relationships between private international law not on the substance, but concerning the technique to resolve conflicts.

[143] Quaedvlieg, 'Concurrence and Convergence in Industrial Design' (n 35) 54.

[144] Ibid 39.

[145] Ibid. See also Quaedvlieg, 'Overlap/Relationships Between Copyright and Other Intellectual Property Rights' (n 110) 489–91.

Some solutions proposed by the literature are not really directly applicable *de lege lata* but would require legislative changes. We summarise them here.

Azéma and Galloux, propose, on the basis of the dependency established between patents and plant variety rights through the compulsory cross-licences, that this new approach of dependency could apply by analogy to all situations where several intellectual property rights exist on the same object, have different right-holders and it is not possible to divide the object.[146] This is very close to the convergence solution.

In French law, some rules regarding the infringement tests are different in the several IPRs for no reason. JPassa thus proposes to harmonise them;[147] one obvious advantage of this proposal is that they do not clash in case of overlaps when two or three rights are infringed on the same object at the same time. Some differences include the punishment, or absence of punishment, for providing means to infringe an IPR,[148] and the requirement, or absence of requirement, of *mens rea* for civil infringement.[149] Some of these differences also exist in UK law and German law. However, Passa is aware that 'the diversity of the functions of different intellectual property rights renders delicate and perhaps illusory any attempt to unify the definition of the material element of infringement'.[150]

Procedural rules can also help resolve overlaps. A solution would be to extend a rule which exists in French law, at least as regards trademarks and designs. In France, when an action is based on a trademark and another action is based on a design, the same court (the TGI) is competent for both even if the two parties are merchants. The multiplication of such consolidation rules for the different overlap situations would be welcome.[151] While it does not solve the overlap as such, it is a simple way of at least avoiding possible diverging decisions simply because two judges rather than one decide on the same object/product, albeit protected by two different rights.

Another procedural rule with an effect on substance is, if the overlap is unavoidable, to prevent the addition of damages. As Galloux rightly points out, while it is logical that 'an indemnity be granted for each right breached by the infringement acts, this does not take account of the often unique character of the damageable fact: because of multiple qualifications, its effects are multiplied'.[152] The judge can take this into account when deciding upon the indemnity. For him, this situation is similar to that of the '*cumul idéal d'infractions*' and '*cumul réel d'infractions*' in criminal law. The solution cannot be a simple addition of damages and penalties.[153]

The last proposal is also the most radical, namely to 'create' a new intellectual property paradigm. This new paradigm would also need to be adopted by the legislature and

[146] Azéma and Galloux, *Droit de la propriété industrielle* (n 81) 324.

[147] J Passa, 'Les divergences dans la définition de l'acte de contrefaçon dans les différentes branches du droit de la propriété intellectuelle. Plaidoyer pour une clarification' (2004) 10 *Propriétés Intellectuelles* 513.

[148] Ibid 517.

[149] Passa ibid proposes that the intentional element be also required for civil, not only criminal infringement, in all IPRs (at 520–22). Likewise, the reseller should not be treated differently according to the nature of the rights in the products he resells, especially if more than one right applies to one single product. 'If the solution in patent law is justified by the idea that the seller (who does not make) can have ignored the infringing character of the product because of the technical complexity of the area and the importance of the claims, why not extend the solution to other areas where the scope of protection is not always easy to determine?'. Ibid 522.

[150] Ibid 517.

[151] Galloux, *Des possibles cumuls de protection par les droits de propriété intellectuelle* (n 111) 91.

[152] Ibid 90. See also Moffatt, 'Mutant Copyrights and Backdoor Patents' (n 108) 1532, who, in a similar vein, advocates the election of remedies.

[153] Galloux, *Des possibles cumuls de protection par les droits de propriété intellectuelle* (n 111) 90.

cannot really be applied as such as a solution *de lege lata* to overlaps. For Reichman, the hybrid regimes (ie registered and unregistered design rights, plant variety rights, database *sui generis* right and the *sui generis* right protecting topographies of semi-conductor chips[154]) have disturbed 'the historical balance between free competition and legal incentives to create'.[155] This historical balance has changed over the years and these new hybrids have reduced competition and contributed to create a new intellectual paradigm.[156] However, according to Reichman, we do not need to do away with the hybrids; instead we need to curtail them to avoid overprotection. He proposes to determine the 'common denominator that underlies these regimes, and devis[e] a unified response to the challenge'.[157] Accordingly, the new paradigm for these hybrids (ie unpatentable, non-copyrightable innovations) would be based on liability rules, ie what he calls a 'default liability regime for applied know-how'.[158]

Suthersanen suggests that intellectual property laws are based on two factors, namely creativity and market constraints.[159] She explains:

> The common denominator of the entire intellectual property spectrum is the act of creation . . . Inherent in all creative activity is the freedom and latitude available to the creator in respect of the consumer and market. Thus, intellectual property rights are, in some areas, delineated by the subject matter of protection and, to varying degrees, by the imposition of external constraints from the market.

Her idea works well to situate design on the intellectual property spectrum. She suggests that it may also be a 'starting point for our analysis of any existing and future intellectual property right'[160] but does not develop it further, ie by applying it to all IPRs. The principle's use is limited to the idea that the lesser the creativity and the higher the market constraints, the more cautious the courts and legislatures should be in granting protection.[161] In fact, British and German law already reflect this by denying copyright law to works of applied art (Germany) or to works of craftsmanship which are not artistic (United Kingdom). It is also reflected in Design Directive, article 7. The idea also goes back to the balance between protection and competition. The more choice there is, or in other words, the fewer constraints there are, the more creation is possible and thus the more protection can be granted because it does not hamper competition (as there is space). Therefore, it really seems to boil down to the first principle we have discussed above: freedom of competition.

[154] Reichman, 'Charting the Collapse of the Patent–Copyright Dichotomy' (n 45) 449–503.

[155] Ibid 479.

[156] Ibid 508, 514–15.

[157] Ibid 511.

[158] Ibid 519.

[159] U Suthersanen, 'Breaking Down the Intellectual Property Barriers' (1998) *Intellectual Property Quarterly* 267, 278–83. Her proposal is based and expands on a paper by M Franzosi, 'Patentable Inventions: Technical and Social Phases – Industrial Character and Utility (1997) *European Intellectual Property Review* 251.

[160] Suthersanen, 'Breaking Down the Intellectual Property Barriers' (n 159) 294.

[161] However, Suthersanen adds (at 290) that 'it is not suggested that protection should be automatically curtailed in instances where a work has high (C), and equally high (M); merely, that in such situations, the courts should tread cautiously in delineating the scope of protection'. For ideas along the same lines, see Quaedvlieg, 'Three Times a Hybrid Between Copyright and Industrial Property' in J Kabel and G Mom, *Intellectual Property and Information Law: Essays in Honour of Herman Cohen Jerobam* (The Hague, Kluwer Law International, 1998) 47, 49 ('Those aspects of the work which have exclusively been determined by functional considerations cannot have been inspired by "personal expression", and therefore should not enjoy copyright protection').

In the same vein, some commentators have recently proposed to redesign intellectual property laws, inter alia, because of the fear of overprotection caused by cumulation of rights. The idea would be to reorganise intellectual property on a uniform basis, ie by not letting the rights develop autonomously, or even regrouping all rights around a single right, declined according to the categories of subject matter to be protected against copying.[162] Again, freedom of competition should drive such a model if it comes to fruition.[163]

Finally, as a methodological instrument to systematise the implementation of the outlined general principles to specific instances of overlap, a 'three step method' could be based largely on proposals by Kur. This method is at least applicable to the copyright/design/trademark overlap. In fact, it is based on some of the principles discussed above and helps to systematically apply them.[164] Kur has pointed out that, because of its general character, the method might even be applicable beyond the realm of the copyright/design/trademark overlap, in cases of unjustified imbalance due to overlapping IPRs. The first step would be to identify whether the problem is caused by an undue extension of one of the IPRs in question so that it unduly encroaches on the domain of the other IPR. Looking at the aims of the two IPRs will help to answer this question. If this is so, then the culprit should be trimmed. Normally, if the rights 'are applied in a sensible, somewhat cautious manner, and . . . are adequately balanced in themselves', then the overlap is 'not necessarily detrimental'.[165] The first step thus focuses on the internal problem, ie the problem which lies within a single IPR, which is not caused by the overlap. If this is not sufficient to fully resolve the cumulation problem, or if it is not relevant, ie if we encounter a genuine overlap problem, the second step consists in the application of one or of all the other, *external*, above-mentioned principles. If this is still insufficient, as a third step, then the legislature should act.

In conclusion, leaving aside the other, of course worthy, proposals for harmonisation by convergence, we can now see emerging five possible overarching principles or rules potentially able to map the overlaps, namely:

(1) freedom of competition and its corollary: one law should not be able to cut across the object of another or across the result the other intended to produce, which means that one right will prevail over another (principle of prevalence);
(2) freedom of movement of goods and services;
(3) principle of election;[166]
(4) fundamental rights;
(5) function of the subject matter, character of the achievement or mode of exploitation involved (most significant relationship).

To these can be added Kur's two step method (the third step being what we have left aside for the moment, namely legislative modification) and the general principles of fairness and

[162] Dusollier, 'Introduction' (n 106) 19, although not referring to any literature.

[163] Ibid 19.

[164] See Kur, 'Cumulation of IP Rights Pertaining to Product Shapes' (n 105) 613 *et seq* and Kur, 'Cumulation of Rights with Regard to Three-Dimensional Shapes' (n 112) 174.

[165] Kur, 'Cumulation of Rights with Regard to Three-Dimensional Shapes' (n 112) 174, discussing the overlap in relation to shapes.

[166] This principle when applied will by definition be conducive to the application of a single remedy, which is also another procedural proposal that was made, and is implicitly based on the fact that the reward has already been reaped (the basis of the principle of election) because the damageable fact is the same.

reasonableness, as well as the prohibition of abuse of right proposed by Feer Verkade and also proposed in Kur's second step. In that context, it is to be noted that the German principle of good faith also encompasses the general prohibition of abuse or misuse of a right.

As we can now see more clearly, many of these proposals (namely, free competition, prevalence of one law over the other on that basis, freedom of movement of goods and services) are similar or identical to the EU rules or the rationales underlying the EU rules already applicable for many overlaps (such as the idea/expression dichotomy,[167] Trademark Directive, article 3, Design Directive, article 7) and the principles which govern international intellectual property law as well (balance of rights and obligations, IPRs cannot stifle competition for an unduly long time). The two questions now are: what is the merit of these principles and do one or instead several of them work to resolve overprotection and/or regime clashes? We shall answer the first question in the next section and the second in section IV.

C Evaluation

Let us first evaluate the merit of the general proposals reviewed in section IIIB and then return to the specific ones developed by commentators, which we discussed in each chapter, adding finally a word on the merit of the remaining existing legal rules we reviewed in section I.

We can only agree with the two premises we discussed at the start of section IIIB: overlaps are not per se problematic and thus should not all be prohibited per se, and the law's justifications are most influential for further assessing the different overlaps. In fact, some cumulation problems arise from an undue, internal, expansion of certain IPRs (such as trademarks).

Likewise, the principles of freedom of competition and freedom of movement of goods and services and the respect of human rights are incontestably principles which must guide the solution to problematic overlaps. They are already reflected in the existing legal or judicial rules regulating the overlaps (section I). Furthermore, they are guaranteed both at the EU constitutional and at international level (TRIPs Articles 7 and 8 and the ECHR). As to the freedom of movement of goods and services, it is an overarching principle in two ways. First, it may apply to overlaps concerning all IPRs but will generally not apply to all problems caused by overlaps (it seems mainly to apply to those caused by overlaps in the area of exhaustion of rights). Secondly, the freedom of movement of goods and services is also an important rule for achieving harmonisation in the absence of any other rule to do so. A good example is the current freedom to cumulate IPRs with unfair competition, which leads to divergent situations in Member States (some allow the cumulation with slavish imitation when others do not) and thus creates obstacles to the freedom of movement of goods and services.[168] There is, however, one problem with the freedom of movement of goods and services. It is not, *de lege lata*, an overarching principle at international level because a principle of international exhaus-

[167] This principle in our view not only applies for delimiting the patent/copyright spheres but also the trademark/patent sphere as it seems to be implied in the *Dyson* case (Case C-321/03 *Dyson v Registrar of Trademarks* [2007] ECR I-687). The term 'expression' can also be used here because the sign needs to be graphically represented, so in a way 'expressed'. Thus as was said in *Dyson*, an abstract concept cannot be a trademark.

[168] Gielen, 'Design Protection and Unfair Competition' (n 101) 269.

tion does not exist. Its applicability at present is therefore only European or regional if other customs unions have adopted it. Finally, despite their utmost importance, it is true that those two principles are rather vague and must be complemented by others.

The principle of prevalence, derived from one or more of these principles, depending on the specific overlap issue, is also one that is commendable for its logic. Probably, the main situation where the rule makes obvious sense is the relationship between IPRs and unfair competition. The reason is that, in this case, courts can indeed undermine decisions made by the legislator in a specific field.

The principles of election and function may be much more difficult to apply depending on the situation.

As to election, how can one say *de lege lata* that if the creator of a computer program has decided to patent it s/he cannot benefit from copyright law? What if the rights are owned by two different persons? That would be plainly contrary not only to national and European law but also to international law. It boils down to the same proposal as stating that there is hierarchy of rights and patent 'wins' over copyright.

As to function or character of the achievement, as pointed out by Quaedvlieg who himself proposed it, it may not be possible or easy to apply, for instance because some works may be created with two functions from the start. The reason is that, in this case, courts can undermine decisions made by the legislator in a specific field. Perhaps a better principle, as Quaedvlieg has also suggested, is to look at the overriding interest behind a/the specific provisions for each specific overlap and see which interest should prevail. If there is no overriding interest or underlying justification for the rule, then overlap must exist unless it would be contrary to the fundamental principles (free competition, freedom of movement of goods and services, human rights, etc).

The procedural fixes proposed mainly by French commentators seem also to make good sense and while one needs legislative amendment (same court for different IPRs on same subject matter), the other (non-cumulation of damages) can already be applied by the courts.

As to the new intellectual property paradigm which is burgeoning, while we welcome research in this respect, it is premature to try and use this paradigm in the context of this book, as scholarship is barely emerging.

Finally, the three step method is an excellent tool to start to solve any overlap problem. In essence, it is a method which can combine the several reasonable proposals and principles examined above, and is at the same time precise and flexible enough. We think that it can be used as a start and tailored to the particular overlap, using what seem to be the most relevant principle(s) for the specific situation (such as human rights, abuse of right, prevalence). It is this method that we shall use in section IV to resolve the problems caused by the overlaps.

When analysing the proposals for each overlap examined in preceding chapters, certain common suggestions emerge across the overlaps. Most (except as we shall see in the following paragraphs the second and probably also the fifth one) are for legislative reform and therefore cannot be readily applied before such reforms are undertaken.

A first important suggestion is modifying the law to make several IPRs increasingly converge at the level of exceptions. This has been proposed for the overlaps copyright/design, copyright/trademark, design/trademark, copyright/patent and patent/plant variety right. As we have said above, this is certainly a commendable solution to many regime clashes from a long-term, legislative perspective.

A second recurrent proposal is to prohibit outright some *a posteriori* overlaps, namely the copyright/trademark, patent/copyright and trademark/patent ones. The reason is because these overlaps are against public policy or because one right should prevail (applying a hierarchy principle or the function/core competence principle we saw above in section III.B). The suggestion that one right is hierarchically superior to another (eg patent to copyright, patent to trademark) presents two problems. However, it is arguably against international law when the rights belong to two different owners. If the copyright in a computer program is owned by X and the patent by Y, how can it be said that X's right should be curtailed because of Y's patent right? This solution diminishes the (internationally guaranteed) right of another person. Public policy or public interest might be a better justification for legislative proposals in that field. In fact this rule already exists for some overlaps at EU level (eg the patent/trademark overlap). In this case, often the reference to public policy boils down to the first governing principle we identified above, namely free competition.

Thirdly, the principle of 'the accessory follows the principal' or 'the major part attracts the minor part' has been proposed to avoid regime clashes for the copyright/patent overlap. But, like the general proposal based on the function/character of an achievement, it will often be difficult to apply in practice. Moreover, it also threatens to violate international law, at least clearly when the rights belong to two different persons.

A fourth proposal is to require the publication of the source code in patent applications for computer program related inventions. This would radically solve the overlap between patents and trade secrets which in the field of computer programs is highly problematic, as the overlap patent/trade secret should by definition not occur at all.[169] It would also be more in line with the essential disclosure element of the patent system and one of its aims. Therefore, we agree with this proposal.

A fifth proposal is that trademark law takes precedence over arguably all IPRs in the case of lawful comparative advertising. We cannot see a reason why this should not be the case, at least for copyright and designs (which at first sight seem to be the only other relevant IPRs in such situations). Indeed, otherwise, in many cases it would be very simple to evade the application of comparative advertising law by arguing that one's trademark is also protected by copyright or design. And the MCAD clearly states in its recital 6 that '[c]omparative advertising can also stimulate competition between suppliers of goods and services to the consumer's advantage'. This goal would be frustrated if copyright or design right could be used to prevent comparative advertising. However, it is another thing to use a competitor's copyright work or a design as such in addition to the competitor's trademark (such as in situations similar to that in the *IPC Media* case). In each case, the courts will have to decide whether the use was necessary for the advertising or whether it was a disguised copyright or design infringement.

Finally, the most radical proposal to deal with some overlaps is to abolish certain rights, namely some or all design rights and copyright for computer programs. While abolishing design right would not violate international law (as TRIPs Articles 25–26 do not prescribe the creation of design rights), it would simply not be possible in some

[169] We acknowledge the fact that patent applications do not have to reveal additional information which may help improve the making of the invention (which corresponds to some extent to the best mode in US law) but often reverse engineering the product once on the market can help discover the trade secrets not disclosed in a patent application. Reverse engineering software is quasi-impossible, or else so time-consuming that it is very rarely worth embarking on.

Member States, such as Germany and the United Kingdom, without ensuring that copyright can cover works of applied art. As we discuss further in section V, less drastic and equally efficient solutions would be to enact rules comparable to the British provisions regulating the interface between design and copyright in order to eliminate regime clashes and overprotection; or alternatively inscribe the election principle in the law, as this leaves the choice to the IPR holder of the protection which is best suited for his or her particular achievement. As to computer programs, abolishing copyright protection would clearly violate international law. In addition, it would do away with a cheap and efficient anti-piracy tool. It would also greatly disadvantage the open source movement which relies upon copyright for its licences. Open source software would also be damaged by the replacement protection, namely patents, and arguably already is by the current European patent law concerning software patents. So we do not think this is the best way to solve the problems caused by the overlap.

As to the proposal to abolish the tort of parasitism, where it is in practice identical to an IPR infringement action, we have already discussed elsewhere that this is indeed the solution *par excellence* to the overprotection caused by the overlap IPR/unfair competition.[170] Application of the tort of parasitism in such cases breaches two of the fundamental principles identified in section III.B, namely, the principle of freedom to compete and the election principle, as well as in many cases freedom of speech. Therefore, from our point of view, an extra element should strictly be required to trigger unfair competition actions with regard to subject matter potentially protectable by IPRs. In many cases, risk of confusion will be such an extra element (except for trademarks, of course).[171] Indeed, benefiting from the reputation of the creator or inventor is not an extra element or fact distinct from infringement. The concept of infringement already includes this and therefore the damages granted for infringement already adequately compensate the IPR holder. Another, procedural, rule can have an effect on the substantive law and avoid overprotection. It is the rule that bans a choice between the infringement action and the action for unfair competition. Normally, the principle of pre-emption should apply and there should be no choice. If there is an infringement of the IPR, the IPR holder must act on that basis. Having a choice can lead to overprotection because the conditions of the unfair competition action for parasitism are less stringent than those of IPRs. Such a rule exists in France but the courts do not always abide by it.[172] Such a rule should be enacted in all Member States, and if at all possible at EU level.

Finally, this leaves us with a handful of legal rules to comment on. Indeed, as we have seen in the preceding paragraphs, many of the rules identified at the several levels in section I can also be used as criteria or solutions to overlaps. The rule of priority is obviously

[170] Derclaye, *The Legal Protection of Databases: A Comparative Analysis* (n 134) 289; M Leistner, 'The Protection of Databases' in E Derclaye (ed), *Research Handbook on the Future of EU Copyright* (Cheltenham, Edward Elgar Publishing, 2009) 427, 453.

[171] As an exception, systematic and repeated free-riding of time-sensitive information could still be unfair competition. These products are not protected by an IPR and there would be no overprotection. Indeed, perhaps we may still witness, as for the database *sui generis* right and performers' rights, the creation of a property right on this basis, which would lead to the demise of the unfair competition action on this basis. Likewise, now that the Court of Justice has created a tort of parasitism for marks with a reputation in *L'Oréal*, it should replace Member States' laws on parasitism for such marks. There may well be other cases emerging in the future as well where unfair competition can fill a gap (ie where an IPR has not (yet) been recognised in respect of an achievement but may well be worthwhile). However, the remaining area is most probably rather small as there has been a proliferation of IPRs recently.

[172] Derclaye, *The Legal Protection of Databases: A Comparative Analysis* (n 134) 164–67.

one we agree with, as it is based on a basic long-used property law principle. As we have already hinted, we believe that the UK rules regulating the copyright/design interface in principle represent a commendable model, although they need further honing here and there to be flawless. The rule prohibiting the possibility for the same sign to be at the same time the trademark and the plant variety's denomination avoids a perpetual monopoly after the expiry of the plant variety right and could also be extended to the patent/trademark overlap, as will be further discussed in section IV. Finally, IPC, article L122-4 only very partially solves the *a posteriori* overlap between copyright and trademarks as it allows it for the copyright owner but not for other persons. Therefore, it is of little use and other proposals will be made in section IV in relation to this overlap.

In conclusion, as will be seen in section IV, we think that there is no one overarching rule which can solve all overlap issues.[173] There are the principles above which will serve as a rule of thumb or starting point to each enquiry but, depending on the specific overlap at issue, different principles or rules may have to be applied.[174] Furthermore, we believe that there are some genuine overlap situations (patent and copyright for computer programs) and some 'false' ones (eg asymmetric convergence in the overlap copyright/trademark).[175] In the latter case, the problem is internal (there is an inner imbalance in one of the IPRs) and ideally, it should be remedied internally (eg by adopting a more flexible fair use system of exceptions instead of the rigid and conclusive system of exceptions). In the first case (genuine overlaps), where restrictions of competition occur because of the combination of the several intrinsically balanced rights, the application of external rules to limit the exercise of one of the rights may be more appropriate in many cases. To reflect this therefore necessarily gradual approach to remedying the problems caused by different kinds of overlaps, we will use the three step method which encompasses such gradual application of both types of rules in section IV to resolve the two main concerns posed by overlaps.

IV. SOLUTIONS TO PROBLEMS CAUSED BY THE OVERLAPS ACCORDING TO CRITERIA DEVELOPED IN SECTION III

As we have seen, cumulation of rights presents two problems: regime clashes and overprotection. The problem of regime clashes is very straightforward; it results from different rules applying to the same subject matter or same object and can lead to an impossibility to apply the two rules together as they result in conflicting outcomes. Therefore, regime clashes will only occur in cases of simultaneous overlaps. Regime clashes also often produce overprotection. On the other hand, overprotection can result from any of the three types of overlaps (simultaneous, negative and *a posteriori*). Let us

[173] In the same vein, Dinwoodie, 'Copyright, Trade Marks and Trade Dress' (n 117) 521, thinks that for the copyright/trademark overlap, no grand rule applies *en bloc*.

[174] This is what G Zimmerman, 'Extending the Monopoly? The Risks and Benefits of Multiple Forms of Intellectual Property Protection' (2001) 17 *Canadian Intellectual Property Review* 345, 365, seems to think as well ('whether overlapping protection between different forms of intellectual property is desirable or permitted depends on the particular combination in question').

[175] Along the same lines, see Dinwoodie, 'Copyright, Trade Marks and Trade Dress' (n 117) 510, who says that if a grand rule is to be elaborated for the copyright/trademark overlap, its formulation should be found 'within the broader copyright debates concerning the appropriate role for exceptions and limitations in copyright law and the development of unified ("converged") copyright rules'.

apply the three step method to regime clashes (section IV.A) and overprotection (section IV.B).

A Regime Clashes

Generally, conflicts will arise only at the level of ownership, rights and exceptions, not at the level of requirements or (excluded) subject matter as the latter simply cumulate. In addition, in most cases, conflicts occur at national level because in many of the rights, the ownership rules and the exceptions are not (fully) harmonised at EU level. Similar problems recur in most simultaneous overlap situations in relation to ownership and dealings, rights, the infringement test and exceptions.

(i) Ownership and Dealings

As regards ownership and dealings, provisions do not always initially give the rights to the same persons (eg in case of employment or commissioned achievements) and rules regarding transfers also often differ within the several IPRs. Several legislative solutions are conceivable. The first is convergence when there are no reasons justifying differences between the systems (eg different provisions currently exist for the Community trademark and Community design).[176] Often, if the law does not provide that the employer owns the respective IPR of the employee *ab initio*, contracts will achieve the same result. However, this does not always happen and thus renders the legal situation uncertain. For industrial property rights, such convergence is welcome whereas when copyright is involved, contracts would be better, as at least the law respects the continental principle that the author should be the first owner.

In some cases, consistent delineation at the level of subject matter and conditions of protection will reduce or eliminate clashes at the level of ownership and dealings. This can be done for the overlap between copyright and designs by requiring a higher level of creativity for all works of applied art, as in Germany. If clashes occur and contractual convergence has not been foreseen, the principle of abuse of right can be used. The problem is not really internal, in the sense that the issue of ownership does not concern the inner balance between the interests of right-holders and users. It is the overlap which might create the problem.

Note that the special rules applying to employee inventions in patent laws, providing special remuneration for employees, do not per se create a clash. What creates the clash is when a patent in an invention is owned by, say, the employee and the copyright in the same invention (say a computer program) is owned by the employer.

(ii) Rights and Infringement

Similar clashes between different IPRs also occur at the level of rights. Three problems typically arise. The first is when one right is an anti-copying right and the other a monopoly

[176] By contrast, in some situations, convergence will not be possible, eg between plant variety rights and patents, as the plant variety right owner can be the person who discovered the plant variety. In this case, therefore, the patent and plant variety right owners will always be different persons.

right (such as copyright/trademark or copyright/patent). The second problem is when rights have different infringement tests. A third problem arises when copyright's moral rights block an exploitation which is lawful under another IPR. The first two problems simply lead to the fact that one right may be infringed when the other is not. In this case, we do not really witness a clash but possible overprotection. If the rights are balanced in themselves, then the aims are respected and the clash does not really create an overprotection problem. There will also probably be no abuse by the IPR owner(s). Therefore, one right will simply prevail over the other. The problem is relegated to the next level, namely that of exceptions. However, in some cases, the cumulation of rights will pose problem even if the rights are separately well balanced. This may arguably be the case between copyright and designs and copyright and patents for computer programs. *De lege ferenda*, the British rules regulating the interface between copyright and designs could be used as a model to avoid overprotection. *De lege lata*, courts could use the rule that suits the facts of the case best, namely freedom of movement of goods and services or the prohibition of abuse of a right, where this is justified. As regards the third problem, if the moral rights block imports (such as when the copyright work's context is changed, which can in certain countries breach the right of integrity), we face a genuine overlap. As part of the specific subject matter of copyright law, the moral rights of the copyright holder will typically prevail over the principle of the free movement of goods and services in these (rare) cases where they are genuinely concerned. Only the application of the abusive exercise of rights, as well as a very narrow construction of the moral rights with regard to specifically technical subject matter, such as computer programs, on the basis of the principle of the (rather technical) nature of the subject matter and mode of exploitation in question, can arguably help in such cases where moral rights are involved.

(iii) Exceptions

As regards the exceptions, regime clashes also typically create overprotection. Therefore, this problem is examined here and not repeated in the next section. Again, an increasing degree of convergence is the ultimate, legislative, solution when it makes sense, as we shall conclude in the next paragraph. Indeed, in all overlaps, the problem is essentially internal and should accordingly be solved by trimming the respective rights and adding (more flexible) provisions on exceptions where necessary.

In the meantime, for the copyright/trademark overlap, where parodies are allowed in copyright law but not trademark law, courts can refer to the fundamental right of free speech when the parody is genuine and yet infringes the trademark because it concerns a mark with reputation and (likelihood of) confusion is not necessary (ie if the parody is not a mere pretext to take advantage of the trademark's reputation). The motive of the parodist will thus be an additional factor in the assessment of such cases. The same human right can be used to allow news reporting as well as criticism, review and use for scientific, pedagogic or other information aims (which are allowed under copyright law but not trademark law, although often such uses will not affect the trademark function or will not be uses as a trademark in the course of trade).

As for the design/copyright overlap, it can be argued that the scientific research exception in copyright law matches that of experimental purposes in design law.[177] Likewise,

[177] This can be argued because the design exception was modelled on the similar patent exception. At least in the United Kingdom, this patent exception is limited to experiments carried out for scientific purposes only.

freedom of expression can be used when the patent regime trumps the design exception for citation and teaching purposes. As to decompilation, it is underpinned by freedom of competition so this principle can be used to make the exception apply also in patent law. To this effect, the exception in favour of experimental use in patent law should be teleologically extended to cover this. The making of a back-up copy of one's lawful copy of a computer program, applicable in copyright law, is reflecting the balance that must exist under any utilitarian justification between the IPR owner's and user's respective interests. The rights of the patent and copyright owners are not unduly prejudiced if the user can make one back-up copy.

When there is a cumulation between trademark and design and copyright and design, as regards the design exception, which exempts uses for purposes of facilitating temporary transit and does not exist in trademark or copyright law, the freedom of movement of goods and services seems to be the appropriate rule in most situations, otherwise abuse of right may be applicable. In fact, one use covered by this exception, repair, is already exempted through Court of Justice trademark case law.[178] Finally, when convergence is not total in cases where a patent and plant variety right subsist in the same subject matter, the aims of the laws or abuse of right could be used.

As all these exceptions are underpinned by a human right, which reflects a public interest which the incentive theory would also require to be safeguarded, or are required by the utilitarian rationale, consideration should be given to making the relevant IPRs converge on these points. Trademark law here must be trimmed, as protection of marks with a reputation currently goes too far when it prevents free speech. Likewise, patent and copyright exceptions should be made to converge in respect of computer programs. The decompilation and back-up copy exceptions should be equally applicable in patent law for computer programs and the 'transit' exception should also apply in copyright and trademark laws.

Finally, it should be noted that there are areas where the laws differ but this does not nevertheless create a regime clash. This is the case when a right-holder wishes to benefit from a registered right in addition to an unregistered one; for instance, s/he has to register his or her trademark or patent and pay initial and renewal fees. While these requirements do not exist in copyright and unregistered design law, they are only additional and do not prevent the unregistered right subsisting. Another example: if a trademark owner forgets to renew his or her trademark right, copyright will not be affected even if the trademark right lapses. Likewise, where both parties must sign a written document for a right to be validly transferred, the non-compliance with this formality does not affect the validity of the assignment of the other right for which such a formality is not required.

B Overprotection

We can now identify the similarities and differences between content and level overlaps in situations of potential overprotection. These overprotection issues are examined by type of overlap, namely, simultaneous, negative and *a posteriori*.

[178] Case C-63/97 *BMW v Deenik* [1999] ECR I-905.

(i) Simultaneous Overlap

Since EU law leaves it to the Member States to determine the level of originality (provided *Infopaq* has not changed this), it in fact acts like Pontius Pilate and washes its hands of the problem of whether there is overprotection between designs and copyright at national level. This is a genuine overlap, except perhaps in the realm of exceptions, as we have seen in section IV.A. Solutions *de lege ferenda* include abolishing design law insofar as design law and copyright cumulate, as the cumulation arguably rewards the same effort twice. Such a radical solution could be based on the principle of freedom of competition. However, it would need a corresponding extension of copyright protection in national systems which do not grant it to works of applied art or require a very high level of creativity or artistic merit. Alternatively, an election rule could be enacted to the effect that if a creator decides to rely on copyright, s/he cannot rely on any design right, and vice versa. In fact, one could justify such solutions by the specific comment in the Green Paper on the Legal Protection of Industrial Design that the cumulation between designs and copyright 'should be reconsidered in the context of the further harmonisation of the laws of copyright of the Member States'.[179] *De lege lata*, if both rights are infringed, the French procedural rule which prevents the cumulation of damages should also be applied by courts in other jurisdictions, on the basis that the overlap clashes with the aim of both copyright and design laws which is to provide an incentive, but at the same time preserve users' interests. Granting double compensation does not safeguard those interests and must be excluded. In Germany, overprotection cannot occur for works of applied art because very few will reach the level of creativity required and therefore the majority of average works of applied art will only be able to benefit from design protection. In the United Kingdom, there is no danger of overprotection where both UDR and copyright are infringed, because CDPA 1988, section 236 prevents it. However, such rule does not exist when UDR and RDR, or when RDR and copyright, both subsist in the same subject matter. There is no reason why a rule similar to section 236 could not be adopted. Similar overlap problems can occur when both the patent and copyright in a computer program are infringed, and sometimes[180] when a plant variety right and a patent are infringed. The same principles can be used as the overlaps are genuine, except again at the level of exceptions.

Overprotection can occur when subject matter which should normally not be protectable either by trademark or copyright nevertheless is. The problem is generally caused by an extensive interpretation of one right by the courts. The problem here is therefore not caused by the overlap itself. The problem is instead caused respectively by copyright law or by trademark law, or at least their interpretation, being overgenerous, namely in the case of protection of titles and fictitious characters. The problems are therefore mainly internal. In France, titles are given far too generous protection by copyright. So courts should apply the requirements of originality more strictly and the overlap should not occur. In Germany, the area of overlap should be reduced by a restrictive practice with regard to the registration of work titles or fictitious characters as trademarks. In the other cases, simultaneous overprotection does not occur, as most shapes are excluded from trademark law and/or copyright law and protected either by design or patent law. As to two-dimensional achievements, when a simultaneous overlap occurs between copy-

[179] Green Paper on the Legal Protection of Industrial Design (n 7) 142.

[180] We are cautious here because there may not be an exact overlap as to the subject matter in all situations. Therefore, in this case, the same effort is not rewarded twice and the overlap is not overprotective.

right or design laws and trademark law, since the aims of the laws and their provisions are different, overprotection does not occur except, as we saw, in the area of exceptions.

Another main simultaneous overlap problem is caused by the possibility of cumulating an action for IPR infringement and for unfair competition. A first problem is the deficiency of the MCAD so that comparative advertising trumps neither copyright nor design laws. *De lege lata*, courts could interpret the Directive by analogy, using the principles of freedom of competition and/or abuse of right, where appropriate. MCAD, recital 6 could be used as a hook to support the application of the free competition principle in order to trump all IPRs. *De lege ferenda*, this could easily be fixed by adding copyright and design, and even all relevant IPRs along with trademarks.

A second problem is the possibility of cumulating the tort of parasitism with an IPR (France and Germany) and the tort of passing off with trademark law (United Kingdom, Germany and the European Union). The first is an internal problem whereby unfair competition law must be forced to respect its aims. The other is a genuine overlap, at least in UK law. Passing off should arguably have been abolished for registered marks when the first Trademark Act was passed. As to the first problem, as parasitism is case-law based, courts could simply reject the tort on the basis of the principles of election, prevalence and freedom of competition. The second problem is trickier as the UCPD explicitly allows the overlap between trademark law and passing off, or else unfair competition, for risk of confusion at national level (UCPD, article 6(2)(a)). This rule has also been implemented in German law. Arguably, unlike in UK law, this is an internal problem and European law must imperatively be changed. Should courts in the meantime apply the same principles of free competition and election, and accordingly limit the overlap of unfair competition law and trademark law by giving trademark law precedence, their rulings would directly violate EU legislation in that field. In the United Kingdom, overprotection is less acute as cumulation between trademark and passing off is quasi-impossible for titles and three-dimensional aspects (mainly get-up and packaging), as passing off rarely succeeds for these types of subject matter. But overprotection will, however, be more frequent for two-dimensional aspects and also because of the overlap between the author's right of attribution (CDPA 1988, ss 77–79) and every person's right against false attribution (CDPA 1988, s 84) and passing off. As we have seen in chapter three on the European Union, the *L'Oréal* ruling created a tort of parasitism for marks with a reputation. It should therefore replace Member States' tort of parasitism or passing off[181] for such marks so that no simultaneous overlap is possible. National courts should be expressly (made) aware of this so that they do not wrongly cumulate the two and repair the same damage twice. Finally, as regards the overlap between trade secrets and IPRs, in the case of a design, trademark or copyright work, if the work or design is not yet published, the overlap is broader because confidential information will protect not only the form but also the very information, the ideas behind the work, trademark or design. Once the trademark, design or copyright work is published, confidential information ceases to have effect. Therefore, the simultaneous overlap does not create overprotection as both the IPR in question and confidential information play their own role and do not go outside their boundaries.

[181] Note that it is not yet clear that passing off also includes dilution, but as some courts have extended the protection beyond likelihood of confusion for well-known goodwill, passing off must be cited in this scenario too.

One last common issue relates to exhaustion. A typically French problem exists. The copyright right of destination prevents the application of the exhaustion principle and arguably leads to overprotection. The literature has called for its abolition as it does not comply with EU law. As it is case-law based, it is up to the courts to erase it. But as litigation can be slow and in the meantime the law is uncertain, legislative action to that effect would be welcome.

(ii) Level Overlap

Level overlaps can create overprotection in addition to regime clashes. Level overlaps occur when a national right (eg copyright, trademark, design, patent) can be cumulated with a Community right, namely a Community trademark or a Community registered or unregistered design. If, say, a national design can be cumulated with a Community design or copyright and a Community design, that unnecessarily multiplies the legal basis for infringement actions, which might lead to forum shopping and other attempts at cherry-picking, including double compensation. The Green Paper on the Legal Protection of Industrial Design suggested solutions in this respect. It proposed to prohibit the creation of new national unregistered designs, specifically mentioning that 'it could even be counter-productive as regards the functioning of the internal market if such rights were to be introduced'.[182] Likewise, the Green Paper expressly forbade a cumulation between the Community registered design right (CRDR) and national registered designs. The reason was that '[t]he legal force in the state concerned of a registered national design and of any registered Community design would be the same. There is therefore no reason for multiplying the number of identical protections in the hand of the same right-holder in the same territory'.[183] The Green Paper also specifically referred to the principle of free competition and the internal market objectives, in particular free movement of goods and services, as regulators of conflicts or overprotection. Nonetheless, the second rule was not adopted, so *de lege lata*, national RDR and CRDR can be cumulated. Because this can cause overprotection and increase costs, the Green Paper recommended that the law should be changed to reinstate the non-cumulation rule. *De lege lata*, to solve this genuine overlap, courts could use in isolation or combination, depending on the facts of the case, the principles of freedom of competition, freedom of movement of goods and services, election and the objectives of the law.

By contrast, the chord struck in the Green Paper on the Legal Protection of Industrial Design is not repeated in the CTMR. Its recital 6 expressly states:

> The Community law relating to trade marks nevertheless does not replace the laws of the Member States on trademarks. It would not in fact appear to be justified to require undertakings to apply for registration of their trademarks as Community trademarks. National trade marks continue to be necessary for those undertakings which do not want protection of their trade marks at Community level.

Therefore, Community trademarks (CTMs) can be cumulated with national trademarks according to European law. If this rule is to be limited in the future, it would require legislative change.

[182] Green Paper on the Legal Protection of Industrial Design (n 7) 137.
[183] Ibid 138.

(iii) Negative Overlap

The negative overlap in fact offers the creator or inventor a choice. The question is whether the choice is legitimate. In many cases it is. Therefore, no overprotection occurs with most negative overlaps; they are just natural. It is normal that if one IPR is not available, the other should be, because in many cases the other IPR exists because the first one cannot be obtained and the two rights protect a different effort or subject matter. The product or object is the same but what is protected in it is different. The negative overlaps also show that there is a more or less perfect delineation between IPRs, which in turn confirms, to take the metaphor of the book's introduction, that the fences around the plants in the garden are still in rather good condition.

A good example is the negative overlap between trademarks and designs. Single letters or numbers and simple combinations of colours which would not be protected by design right because they would not be designs or, if they were, they would not be novel or have individual character, can be protected by a trademark right. But otherwise, trademark protection is not possible because of Trademark Directive, article 3. The only possible negative overlap will be for some two- or three-dimensional designs which are neither novel nor have individual character but which can be distinctive. For them, trademark protection is the natural right. Conversely, if trademark protection is unavailable, there could still be signs which could be novel and have individual character despite their absence of distinctive character. It is not a problem if a shape cannot be registered as a trademark because it gives substantial value to the good as it can be protected under design or copyright law. In fact, this is the purpose of design and copyright law and the exclusion in trademark law has been included to reflect this.

An even better example is the negative overlap between trademarks and patents. If a sign is an idea or is a shape which is necessary to obtain a technical result, then trademark protection will not be available, but patent law might be if the protection requirements can be fulfilled. On the other hand, a two-dimensional aspect may attract trademark protection but cannot be patented as it will not be technical.

Sometimes, however, the neat demarcation between the garden's beds has eroded and overprotection occurs. This is the case in France with the overlap between copyright and trademarks. Many French courts have granted protection for short titles which cannot be trademarked for lack of distinctiveness. For instance, 'Soie et moi' (Silk and me)[184] was an invalid trademark for clothing but the court considered the terms original and thus granted them copyright protection. Here we witness an undue extension of copyright law which encroaches on the trademark domain. As has been noted, the negative overlap here is even perverse: slogans are more strongly protected by copyright law than by trademark law, because unlike copyright, trademark law is not an absolute right due to its principle of specialty.[185] The overlap is not genuine, instead the problem is internal: copyright has to be pruned back to its boundaries. A stricter interpretation of the requirement of originality should in itself solve this problem.

In sum, in the main, negative overlaps do not cause overprotection. Some negative overlaps nevertheless cause two other problems, however: the existence of one IPR or type of protection makes the second one redundant (copyright/design in French law and most

[184] TGI Paris, 10 April 1986. For a discussion, see chapter 4, section III.B.

[185] J Passa, 'Titres et slogans: entre marque et droit d'auteur' (2005) 14 *Propriétés Intellectuelles* 31, 44.

flagrantly certain cases with regard to the overlap between IPRs and unfair competition) or encourage innovators to artificially modify their innovation so that it can fit an IPR, whereas its natural protection should have been another IPR (patent/plant variety rights).

The first problem of redundancy can also often lead to overprotection. In France and other Member States, but much less in Germany and the United Kingdom (because of the higher level of originality required for many works), copyright generally fills the gap when design right is not available, and even when it is.[186] Design right can fill the gap when copyright is not available but since requirements are higher (novelty and individual character), it may occur less often. The problem is most pressing in France, where copyright law in fact absorbs in large part design law. The only two advantages of design law over copyright are the monopoly right it gives (no need to prove copying in an infringement action) and the lesser and narrower exceptions. Therefore, arguably design law is not totally redundant, but in many cases it is, mainly because of copyright law's advantage of immediate protection and generally more generous infringement test. Unregistered design is even more redundant because it has this same advantage of immediate protection as copyright. Likewise, when patent protection is unavailable for a computer program, often copyright will fill the gap, as a program generally will be original even if it is not new or inventive. Nevertheless, copyright protection will not be available for patentable functions so that the gap, even if largely, is not entirely filled by copyright. Solutions *de lege lata* are rarely applicable. The solution lies *de lege ferenda*, either by making both rights converge so that the choice becomes less interesting, by applying the principle of election or more radically by abolishing one right.

The most problematic negative overlap is that between IPRs and unfair competition. EU law explicitly allows the negative overlap between IPRs and unfair competition, as when the several Directives and Regulations are read together, they in fact state that practically all IPRs are without prejudice to national unfair competition laws. In France, this overlap exists in effect for virtually all IPRs, whereas in Germany it exists for fewer IPRs (namely, it is comparatively limited for patents). In the United Kingdom, the passing off action is much more limited than the tort of parasitism as it requires misrepresentation, so that the negative overlap is much less frequent than in France and Germany. Nevertheless, passing off can definitely replace trademark law because of its greater flexibility. In addition, passing off can protect images and themes which cannot be graphically represented because they cannot be expressed through the means of a specific word or logo. Passing off can thus protect advertising campaigns and advertisements, whilst trademark law will often be unable to. Passing off even cuts across trademark law when it protects descriptive or generic names.

Of course, if protection against simple copying by unfair competition law is justified, then as in the past (as for eg photographers, phonogram producers, broadcasting organisations or database makers), such subject matter can begin to be protected by the courts in case law, and later on that unfair competition case law can be replaced by specific IPR legislation. This could potentially happen for advertising campaigns and smells, for instance. It is doubtful that trademark law or another new IPR should protect descriptive and generic names (apart from geographical indications and appellations of origin, of

[186] A good example is the Benelux, see A Strowel and CH Massa, 'Le cumul du dessin ou modèle et du droit d'auteur: orbites parallèles et forces d'attraction entre deux planètes indépendantes mais jumelles' in S Dusollier and A Cruquenaire (eds), *Le cumul des droits intellectuels* (Brussels, Larcier, 2009) 21, 74–77 and 83–84 (statistics for the Benelux countries).

course) as it is in total contradiction with its aim (indication of origin) and freedom of competition, which is not only the basis of IPRs but also unfair competition law. Smells may have a brighter future: they are often already de facto protected by unfair competition law through trade secrets but legislators could decide to protect them by copyright or a new *sui generis* right, although we would not recommend this.

What can be done when the negative overlap creates overprotection (namely, when it circumvents an existing IPR and its limits)? Here the problem is internal to unfair competition law. If unfair competition were applied correctly taking into account the principles of freedom of competition, of election, and of prevalence, generally simple copying should not be reprehensible with regard to subject matter potentially in the realm of any of the existing IPRs. Thus, courts should simply reject the tort of parasitism or passing off when it replaces the IPR (for passing off thus only the trademark right) in question. The rule of freedom of competition and its corollary 'one law should not be able to cut across the object of another or across the result the other intended to produce' are perfectly applicable here. Ideally, of course, the EU legislature should modify the relevant provisions of its secondary law to ensure that parasitism and passing off cannot undercut intellectual property laws. A further reason is that with regard to unified or harmonised rights, the additional application of unfair competition law also undermines effective harmonisation in certain cases.

The second problem is caused by the negative overlap between patent/plant variety right. If plant variety right protection is unavailable, ie the plant variety does not have one of the required characteristics (eg it is not uniform or stable), then the breeder can try and use the patent system if s/he can meet the requirements. Indeed, the EPO does not consider a plant variety to be one if it fits the definition of plant variety but does not meet the requirements for a plant variety right.[187] This encourages breeders who prefer patent protection to 'create in the plant a genetic characteristic to ensure the unavailability of PVR protection (for example, insufficient uniformity), so as to avoid the application of the exclusionary provision'.[188] However, as the two systems already converge to a considerable extent, the cost of making the plant unstable, etc often outweighs the benefit of acquiring a patent and the problem will not occur often.

Finally, there is a rare case of underprotection which reflects a problem internal to UK copyright law. In the British Isles, make-up and works involving scenes with *objets trouvés*, such as in the *Creations Records* case, are not protectable by copyright nor UDR and probably also not by RDR (make-up is not as it is not a design for a *product* and static scenes involving objects are hardly designs for a *product* either). The solution here lies again *de lege ferenda* (ideally by abolishing the conclusive character of the categories of work), although judges could very well fill the gap: the scene with *objets trouvés* in *Creation Records* could arguably be a database and there is no reason why, on the face of the relevant law, make-up could not be a painting.

(iv) A Posteriori *Overlap*

When the aims of the rights are essentially similar or identical and they cover similar or identical subject matter, then again overprotection can occur if one right lasts longer

[187] *Ciba-Geigy* [1984] 3 OJ EPO 112, 114; Case T 320/87 *Lubrizol/Hybrid Plants* [1990] EPOR 173.
[188] A Christie, 'Patents for Plant Innovation' (1989) *European Intellectual Property Review* 394, 397.

than another. Because of the double protection during the lifetime of both rights through the simultaneous overlap, the *a posteriori* overlap makes this overprotection last even longer. Arguably, because the reward has or could already (have) been reaped during the life of the first IPR, the second should not be allowed to prolong this exclusivity as this can amount to rent-seeking. In addition, some *a posteriori* overlaps stifle competition for an unduly long time, therefore not respecting the balance between right-holders' and users' interests, as well as with the public interest. One could say the problem is internal and that one right's duration, namely copyright, should be reduced at least for technical subject matter (such as works of applied art[189] and computer programs). But, of course, this cannot be done *de lege lata*. However, when trademarks are involved, the overlap problem is genuine.

In the case of the copyright/design *a posteriori* overlap, at least in France, the legislative solution would be to abolish design right, reduce the copyright term or prevent copyright protection for subject matter registered as designs through the principle of election. The British delineation rules in this respect would be a good starting point if the legislature favoured this solution. Overprotection can also occur in some cases if copyright or design right is prolonged via a trademark right, passing off or unfair competition caused by (risk of) confusion. This will be the case for famous works. It is true that they will often not be distinctive because of their very famous character. However, distinctiveness can be acquired through use. In such a case (eg 'Mickey Mouse' for clothes), as the protection granted by current trademark laws has become much stronger, in many cases, because the trademark is famous, it may not be used commercially at all. This is because the concepts of 'use as a trademark' and 'in the course of trade' are now rather broad concepts.[190] Furthermore, the exact coverage of the 'due cause' exemption is not yet clear. Therefore, it is not entirely clear whether for instance, it may be lawful to use 'Mickey Mouse' in a Powerpoint presentation to illustrate a point if the presentation is to a commercial entity. It is even more uncertain whether trademarks can be lawfully used in artistic works (such as the depiction of the 'Campbell' trademark on products by Warhol). Therefore, this can clearly restrict free speech and create a perpetual monopoly. *De lege lata*, all the principles we have identified in section III.B can be used to combat this overlap, alone or in combination depending on the factual situation at hand. There could be one exception, however; it is that of logos and shapes which have been created to be trademarks and are still used to distinguish the goods and services they have been created for. If they are also copyright works or designs, as their main function has always been and still is to distinguish goods, the trademark right should not end at the same time as

[189] Note that, as we saw in chapter five, this is the case for some copyright works in the United Kingdom when they are industrially produced (CDPA 1988, s 52).

[190] Already in Case C-48/05 *Adam Opel v Autec* [2007] ECR I-1017, the Court of Justice 'implied that *any use* that achieved one of the effects mentioned in article 5(2) (ie conferred an unjustified advantage on Autec or tarnished or blurred the distinctiveness of Opel's mark) would infringe' (emphasis in original). See Bently and Sherman, *Intellectual Property Law* (n 40) 929. As a result of the *L'Oréal* ruling, the functions of the mark include guarantee of quality, communication and advertising. Therefore, use of a mark arguably also includes simply communicating the mark, at least in the case of famous marks. Some commentators have even argued that use as a mark is not required under Trademark Directive, art 5(2). See I Simon, 'Embellishment: Trademark Use Triumph or Decorative Disaster?' (2006) *European Intellectual Property Review* 321. In the United Kingdom, 'trade' includes 'any business or profession' (TMA 1994, s 103(1)). In addition, the Court of Justice has 'suggested uses which are in the context of commercial activity with a view to economic advantage are "in the course of trade"'. Bently and Sherman, *Intellectual Property Law* (n 40) 923.

the copyright. Their original and continued function is to act as a trademark; copyright attaches to the logo or shape secondarily.[191]

Overprotection through the *a posteriori* overlap between trademark/patent can also occur. A sign can particularly easily develop into a common denomination of the patented product or service, if due to patent protection the product or service as such is not subject to effective competition. Patent protection thus effectively becomes a springboard for establishing the sign as a denomination of the patented product or service. After expiry of patent protection, the question arises whether trademark protection has to end. Two possibilities arise: either the mark becomes generic and therefore protection is lost through the simple application of the law and there is no danger of overprotection, or the trademark retains its distinctive character. Two situations spring to mind in this latter respect. The first can be illustrated by the following two examples. 'Hoover' is still a valid mark although people often use it interchangeably with the term 'vacuum cleaner'. The same can be said of the word mark 'Bic' in French. Often people use the term 'bic' instead of 'biro' but there is another common French word for the term (*stylo à bille*) and the trademark holder ensures that the mark is not becoming generic. Therefore, competition is not stifled since competitors can still market biros and vacuum cleaners under other trademarks because another name is invented or already exists for the product. A second situation can occur when the trademark corresponds to the actual name of the product (such as the compound of a medicine) and stays distinctive. A rule could be enacted, as for plant variety rights, that the denomination of the product cannot be its trademark, and this even if it has obviously acquired distinctive character throughout the life of the patent. The patent owner would thus have to invent a trademark for his or her product and could not use the denomination of the product as the trademark for it too. In the meantime, depending on the facts in question, the rules of free competition, freedom of movement of goods and services, the aims of the laws and the principle of election can be used to curb overprotection where necessary.

Overprotection through the longer term of copyright for computer programs which were also patented is less problematic. Indeed, in many cases, similar programs, expressed in different code, can be developed, as the patent has expired. However, in some cases (big complex programs), it may not be possible to do so because the copyright interoperability exception does not allow reverse engineering to make competing programs. Here the problem is internal to copyright and the law should be modified to open up the exception. The French, British and Canadian decisions[192] can also eliminate overprotection in both the simultaneous and *a posteriori* overlaps in relation to copyrighted material, as well as material protected by design rights in patent applications. Once these applications have been published by the respective patent offices, copyright and designs

[191] Quaedvlieg, 'Concurrence and Convergence in Industrial Design' (n 35) 54 ('A first approach would consist of saying that if, 70 years after the death of the author, the shape is still used by a particular undertaking in order to distinguish those goods as to their origin, and if the relevant public identifies the origin of these goods on the basis of their shape, there is no reason to suddenly terminate trademark protection. The reason for this is that if the sign has in fact acquired distinctiveness and is actively used as a distinctive sign – and would perhaps have been so for generations – it seems rather drastic to change that status quo, unless there would be very strong reasons to the contrary . . . If, however, at any moment after the expiry of the copyright term, such shapes have been without trademark protection, a new registration should not be allowed. Trademark law should respect the status quo of what has been absorbed by the free domain, just as the free domain should respect the status quo of what is still protected, used and perceived as an identification of origin').

[192] See chapter 4, section VII.A and chapter 5, section VII.A.

rights subsisting in patent applications should become unenforceable. These rulings could be applied on the basis of the principle of election in other Member States as well, before the EU legislature enacts such a rule.

On the other hand, the *a posteriori* overlap poses no or a relatively minor overprotection problem for the patent/design and patent/plant variety right overlaps. In the first case, if the registered design right is renewed for up to 25 years, it will 'prolong' the patent protection for five years. But this wording already sounds odd. Indeed, patent and design will not protect the same effort as designs cannot protect exclusively technical designs. So a product may have a patent for its technical aspect and a design right for its appearance. Therefore, there is no overprotection as the two efforts are different. Plant variety rights can slightly prolong a patent (5–10 years maximum depending on the variety) but in practice it is rare, as generally it takes years to develop and then market a plant variety, so that the plant variety right's term in many cases may well in practice coincide with, or be even shorter than, the patent term.

Finally, as for the simultaneous overlap and negative overlap, unfair competition (ie slavish imitation for all IPRs except trademarks where there is unfair competition by causing (risk of) confusion) should not be able to prolong the life of any IPR. This is clearly against the objectives of both intellectual property and unfair competition laws, as well as the principles of prevalence and freedom of competition. The courts can use these principles to curb the overprotection caused by this internal problem before the EU legislature enacts a rule reflecting this.[193] A typical example is the overlap between copyright and/or patents, on the one hand, and trade secrets, on the other. In some cases (big complex programs), it may not be possible to make similar programs as the code is nearly impossible to reverse-engineer so that trade secrets protect the program after the term of any one of these IPRs, even if there is no contract between the IPR holder and the person who wishes to decompile. The problem is internal to patent law and the solution *de lege ferenda* is to require the publication of the source code in the patent applications. *De lege lata*, the aims of the laws and the principles of prevalence and of freedom of competition should be taken into account in such cases. On the other hand, one *a posteriori* overlap does not pose a problem. Confidential information can subsequently be protected by an IPR (it then loses its quality of confidentiality because of the necessary publication that ensues) if it fulfils the IPR's conditions, so that the subject matter can in effect be protected much longer than the duration provided by the IPR. However, here both laws respect their different aims (secrecy and publication) and the protection can never be perpetual.

A final point: regime clashes and overprotection are, of course, even more frequent if the overlap concerns three, four or more, rather than two rights.[194] Such overlap often

[193] As we have seen in chapter two, it is unclear whether the TRIPs Agreement encompasses the whole of unfair competition law or only confidential information and geographical indications. It is problematic if the TRIPs Agreement only applies to those two subsets of unfair competition law because unfair competition law can (re)create an IPR by the back door and TRIPs Arts 7 and 8 cannot apply as the TRIPs Agreement does not govern this part of unfair competition law. The problem does not pose itself at EU level but it does at international level because of this uncertainty in the scope of the TRIPs Agreement. As we said in chapter two, it is to be hoped that if ever the issue comes before a WTO panel, and even before EU and national courts, common sense will dictate a similar approach to that of TRIPs Arts 7 and 8 in these cases so that unfair competition cannot (re)create an IPR, as it would add essential coherence to the framework.

[194] See eg the 'Rubik cube' in which, in France at least, copyright, patent, trademark and design rights coexist(ed). See Caron, *Droit d'auteur et droits voisins* (n 123) 19, para 23, citing CA Paris, 25 June 1987 (1988) 4 *Cahiers de Droit d'Auteur* 23.

occurs, for instance, between copyright, trademarks and designs and between copyright, patents and trade secrets. In this case, a combination of the rules stated for each dual overlap can be applied.

V. CONCLUSION AND OUTLOOK

What comes out of this long reflection on the overlaps? First of all, real, genuine overlaps are not numerous, although in certain cases they create unwanted regime clashes and overprotection which need to be remedied. Secondly, the remaining overlaps are not genuine. They exist because of an extension of an IPR beyond its initial, natural, boundaries. In this case, the right needs to be trimmed back and the problem vanishes. For this to happen, in some cases a teleological (or in other words purposive) construction of the problematic provisions can help, while in other cases statutory law needs modification. Thirdly, three general principles should govern all the overlaps at all levels, namely freedom of competition and commerce, the objectives of the laws (both of which include the balance of rights and obligations referred to in the international instruments), and the freedom of movement of goods and services. The latter, however, can only govern overlaps at EU level as it is not established at international level and does not apply directly to purely national cases. However, in many cases, these principles will be too general and other external principles need to be used as well to eliminate the problematic overlaps. As per the discussion in section IV, before the law is modified, litigants and courts can use the solutions for the problems we have identified, so we shall not repeat them. In some cases, the ideal solution would be for the law to be changed. In short, we think that the following solutions are the most suitable *de lege ferenda*. For all IPRs:

- convergence of the rules on ownership and dealings where there is no reason for the divergence;
- increasing convergence (and possibly flexibilisation) of exceptions underpinned by human rights or by a public interest which the incentive theory requires to be safeguarded.

In addition:

- Modify the MCAD so that the rules on permissible comparative advertising prevail over all IPRs.
- Modify EU law (if necessary all Directives and Regulations on unitary or harmonised IPRs) to ensure that unfair competition cannot be triggered where no additional element (compared to the infringement action with regard to a unified or harmonised IP right) is present in a case, and that passing off cannot be cumulated with trademark law (so in this latter case more precisely modify UCPD, article 6(2)(a)).
- Enact a rule which prevents the registration of at least famous copyright works as trademarks after the copyright term has expired.
- Enact a rule to prevent the denomination of a patented product from being protected as a trademark, and this even if it has acquired distinctive character throughout the life of the patent.
- Require publication of the source code where a computer program related invention is patented.

As to the level overlaps, it is too drastic to abolish national trademarks and designs, as there are reasons for still having national registered rights (mainly where there is only a national market or a market restricted to a handful of countries). Therefore, a rule could be enacted along the lines of that in the CPVR Regulation so that one right cannot coexist with the other; or in short, enact an election principle. The same solution could be adopted for the overlap between copyright and designs. Thus, to take the example of trademarks, if a business opts for a national trademark, it should not be able to obtain a CTM. If however, the business grows and would like a CTM later on, the rule could provide that it could acquire one but should then relinquish its national trademark. Conversely, if the business needed to downsize, it could decide to abandon the CTM and return to a national mark. This is the easiest way to deal with the overlap problem, all the more so for designs (using a higher level of creativity is far more uncertain as essentially left to the fluctuations of case law) and not too much of a burden on creators and their employers. We therefore recommend it. Otherwise, if the EU legislature cannot agree, using the level of creativity as a delineation criterion in combination with the British rules regulating the copyright/design interface at EU level, albeit further honed, would be a partial solution to eliminate this problematic overlap issue (in particular in French law).

As to computer programs, increasing convergence with regard to the exceptions to patent law in the area of computer programs, along with an obligatory publication of the source code executing patented computer-implemented inventions as per the above proposals, would be recommendable legislative improvements. Finally, to reduce *a posteriori* overlaps, a shortening of the copyright term at least in certain fields, such as computer programs and other economically short-lived works, would be a conceivable solution. However, for the moment, this is not only a rather idealistic proposal, but also contrary to international law if the term were to be limited to less than 50 years following the death of the author. The debate over the length of copyright protection is nevertheless maturing fast and we may see movements to reduce the term if more and more empirical evidence is adduced and governments become gradually convinced. However, in the meantime, there is not much that can be done. The main problematic overlap here concerns software, but if the source code of patented programs must be published, the problem caused by the copyright term becomes in practice insignificant. Indeed, technology will advance more quickly and the copyrighted program will often become obsolete long before the expiry of the copyright term.

A final point must be made about the exhaustion principle. It would be appropriate to reinforce it. First, although it is unlikely that the *Dior* ruling will be reversed or modified, it would be stronger if it was embodied in statutory law. Secondly, it would also be better if it was expanded to cover more uses than only advertising purposes, and all relevant IPRs and not only copyright. In addition or alternatively, one could expand the wording of Infosoc Directive, article 5(3)(j) and make the exception mandatory.[195] Finally, the extended exhaustion principle, such as in *Dior*, should be applicable not only at EU level but also to purely national cases. This is the case in Germany through the *Parfumflakon*

[195] Kur, 'Exceptions to Protection where Copyright and Trade Mark Overlap' (n 121) 611. The article provides: 'Member States may provide for exceptions or limitations to the rights provided for in Articles 2 and 3 in the following cases: . . . use for the purpose of advertising the public exhibition or sale of artistic works, to the extent necessary to promote the event, excluding any other commercial use'.

case, but not in French nor UK law.[196] Ideally therefore, national laws should be modified to clearly reflect the national application of the principle.

In conclusion, the main solution to overlap problems is to be a good gardener. A good gardener takes care of his or her plants so that they do not overgrow and cross the boundaries assigned to them. Otherwise, the garden becomes messy. Legislators should simply be good gardeners and keep each IPR properly trimmed. When a right is extended or when new species are added to the garden without proper thought, it is of course much more difficult to eradicate them as their roots are hard to take out and scattered seeds can germinate for a long time. The analogy applies perfectly to the copyright and related rights term extensions, as well as to the introduction of certain new IPRs, such as the premature introduction of the *sui generis* right for substantial investments in databases, which is flawed in some essential aspects. Such errors can be corrected by the legislator (and sometimes, where possible, by courts[197]) but subsequent correction is unlikely, costly and/or takes a long time, if it happens at all. Better still, is to ponder abundantly before creating new rights, extending the scope of a right to a new subject matter, or lengthening one right's duration. We dare to hope that our reflection on the issue of intellectual property overlaps in Europe has been a worthwhile gardening effort for the European Union and its Member States but also more generally for countries beyond our borders and at international level.

[196] In UK law, whether the common law doctrine of implied consent could apply in such situations is far from clear.

[197] See eg Case C-203/02 *British Horseracing Board Ltd v William Hill Organisation Ltd* [2004] ECR I-10425; Case C-444/02 *Fixtures Marketing Ltd v Organismos Prognostikon Agonon Podosfairou (OPAP)* [2004] ECR I-10549; Case C-46/02 *Fixtures Marketing Ltd v Oy Veikkaus AB* [2004] ECR I-10365; Case C-338/02 *Fixtures Marketing Ltd v Svenska Spel AB* [2004] ECR I-10497.

Index

Introductory Note

References such as '178–9' indicate (not necessarily continuous) discussion of a topic across a range of pages. Wherever possible in the case of topics with many references, these have either been divided into sub-topics or only the most significant discussions of the topic are listed. Because the entire work is about 'intellectual property', the use of this term (and certain others which occur constantly throughout the book) as an entry point has been minimised. Information will be found under the corresponding detailed topics.

www.ingramcontent.com/pod-product-compliance
Ingram Content Group UK Ltd.
Pitfield, Milton Keynes, MK11 3LW, UK
UKHW021705230926
475560UK00015B/307

9 781841 139500